Between Rashi and Maimonides:
Themes in Medieval Jewish
Thought, Literature and Exegesis

Between Rashi and Maimonides

Themes in Medieval Jewish Thought, Literature and Exegesis

edited by

Ephraim Kanarfogel and Moshe Sokolow

THE MICHAEL SCHARF PUBLICATION TRUST
OF THE YESHIVA UNIVERSITY PRESS
NEW YORK

Copyright © 2010 Yeshiva University Press

Library of Congress Cataloging-in-Publication Data
Between Rashi and Maimonides: themes in medieval Jewish thought, literature
and exegesis / edited by Ephraim Kanarfogel and Moshe Sokolow.
p.   cm.
The genesis of this volume was an international conference held at Yeshiva
University in late 2004, to mark both the 900th anniversary of the passing of Rashi
(1040-1105) and the 800th anniversary of the passing of Maimonides (d. 1204).
ISBN 978-1-60280-138-7
1. Jewish philosophy—Congresses.   2. Philosophy, Medieval—Congresses.
3. Maimonides, Moses, 1135-1204—Congresses.   4. Rashi, 1040-1105—
Congresses.   I. Kanarfogel, Ephraim.   II. Sokolow, Moshe.
B755.B48   2010
181'.06—dc22
2009052383

Layout: Marzel A.S — Jerusalem

Distributed by
KTAV Publishing House, Inc.
930 Newark Avenue
Jersey City, NJ 07306
orders@ktav.com • www.ktav.com
(201) 963-9524 • Fax (201) 963-0102

Contents

Contributors   431

Preface

The genesis of the studies found in this volume was an international conference held at Yeshiva University in late 2004, to mark both the 900th anniversary of the passing of Rashi (1040–1105) and the 800th anniversary of the passing of Maimonides (d. 1204). The conference was also organized as part of a year-long university-wide celebration to mark the 50th year since the founding of the university's undergraduate women's college, Stern College for Women in 1954, and was sponsored jointly by the Rebecca Ivry Department of Jewish Studies at Stern College, and by the Bea and Leonard Diener Institute of Law at the Benjamin N. Cardozo School of Law. As the reader will note, several of the authors make reference to the fructifying collegial comments and discussions that took place as the papers were presented, yielding insights that are reflected in the published versions of their studies.

As the title of the volume suggests, the studies have been grouped under three larger areas of Judaic scholarship. At the same time, however, they represent a much wider and yet more focused array of methods and interests in addition (as the session titles from the conference suggest): comparative perspectives, methodologies of legal interpretation, dimensions of Maimonidean thought including its relationship with mysticism, and examples of multi-disciplinary approaches. These articles are not intended to exhaustively treat a particular dimension of medieval Jewish studies. Rather, they are meant to provide the reader with cutting-edge treatments of a series of topics and issues that stand at the center of the study of medieval Jewish intellectual history and allied fields in the first decade of the 21st century.

To that end, a brief survey of the contents of this volume

is in order. Daniel Lasker compares the attitudes of Rashi and Maimonides to Christianity, suggesting that Rashi was neither deeply concerned with Christian exegesis nor very conversant with Christian theology, while Maimonides, despite living his entire life in Islamic lands, puts forward a rather well-informed and pronounced reaction to Christianity on a variety of levels. Menahem Kellner analyzes the differences between Rashi and Maimonides in their respective views on the nature of the law taught in the Torah, and the extent to which Abraham and his descendants kept the Torah before it was given at Sinai. Dov Schwartz presents a close textual and philosophical study of the sections in the Guide for the Perplexed in which Maimonides deals with the problem of separate intellects and the structure of the soul and the intellect, and Aviezer Ravitsky uncovers new dimensions within the sharp denigration by Maimonides (and his students) of the uses and conceptions of magic. By focusing on Nahmanides' citations and critiques of Rambam's writings, Moshe Idel is able to more precisely delineate Maimonides' place as a theologian, who had much to offer those who were partial to Jewish mysticism as well.

On the basis of a thorough survey of a variety of commentaries and works, Nahum Rakover contends that the well-known rabbinic dictum that appears to place penitents on a higher level than the completely righteous does so only with respect to certain exceptional types. Robert Chazan demonstrates that the First Crusade narrative composed by the leading German Talmudist, R. Eliezer ben Nathan (Raban), blurs the details provided by other chronicles in order to provide a more useful source for his readership in the mid-twelfth century, as they were confronted with renewed accusations and attacks. J. David Bleich studies and addresses the exceedingly complex issue of locating or defining human identity on the basis of philosophical and talmudic sources, with particular emphasis on the diverse approaches taking by leading medieval halakhists. In looking at the presence of Ashkenazic rabbinic teachings in Spanish talmudic writings, Ephraim Kanarfogel identifies the use of Tosafist materials by

R. Yom Tov b. Abraham ibn Ishvilli (Ritva) as more extensive than that of his Spanish predecessors, Ramban and Rashba, and suggests that the availability of *Tosafot Rabbenu Perez* may hold the key to these developments. Scott Goldberg and Moshe Sokolow compare and contrast the approaches of Rashi, Radak and Maimonides to the role that teachers play in the educational process, showing that elements of constructivism (by which the teacher aids the student in 'uncovering' the material rather than simply imparting conclusions) are decidedly apparent.

Alfred Ivry insightfully delineates the differences between Rashi's and Maimonides' use of midrash, in terms of both method and scope. Similarly, Mordechai Cohen compares the philosophically oriented Sefardic tradition of interpreting and understanding the book of Job (with particular emphasis on Maimonides) to the exegetical methods of the northern French *peshat* school (headed by Rashi), identifying the different foci and interests of each approach. Naomi Grunhaus takes up the important question of the relationship between *peshat* and *halakhah* in the biblical exegesis of R. David Kimhi (Radak), while Michelle Levine highlights Nahmanides' unique literary method, to use and to understand biblical dialogue as a means of substantively portraying and characterizing the often complex figures involved. Eric Lawee brings us to the later middle ages, focusing on the criticism of Rashi's use of midrash found largely in unremarked Spanish super-commentaries from that period.

We are most grateful to Yeshiva University's President Richard M. Joel and Provost Morton Lowengrub for their deep engagement and support; to the Michael Scharf Publication Trust for underwriting the production of this handsome volume, and to Mr. Bernard Scharfstein of KTAV. Dean Karen Bacon of Stern College and the outgoing Dean of the Cardozo Law School, David Rudenstein (and their staffs) were instrumental in making both the conference and this volume a reality. Dr. Jeffrey S. Gurock and Mrs. Cali Orenbuch, who served as the volume's managing editor, provided expert (and much needed) technical assistance. We also wish to recognize the thoughtfulness and generosity of Majorie

Diener Blenden, chairwoman emerita (and continuing member) of the Board of Overseers of Stern College for Women. Finally, *li-badeil bein hayyim le-vein hayyim*, we dedicate this volume, with love and admiration, to the memory of an extraordinary woman of great charm and wisdom, and an unforgettable benefactor of Yeshiva University and its schools, E. Billi Ivry a"h. *Yehe zikhrah barukh.*

EK and MS
Erev Rosh ha-Shanah, 5750

PART 1

1.

Rashi and Maimonides on Christianity

Daniel J. Lasker

The common wisdom holds that Christianity was a major concern of Rashi, whose Biblical commentaries are replete with anti-Christian comments and whose attempt to find the contextual interpretation of the text (the *peshat*) is a reaction to Christian allegory. For instance, Rashi's commentaries on Genesis, Isaiah, and Psalms, favorite books among the Christians, have been described as full of explicit and acerbic anti-Christian polemic. Rashi was particularly interested in refuting Christianity both because of Christian conversionary propaganda and also as a result of the First Crusade of 1096, which caused so much death and destruction to North European Jewry.[1] Furthermore, it

---

1. The literature is extensive; see the discussion in Avraham Grossman, "Pulmus Dati u-Megamah Hinukhit be-Ferush Rashi la-Torah," in Mosheh Ahrend, *et al.*, eds., *Pirkei Nechama. Prof. Nechama Leibowitz Memorial Volume*, Jerusalem, 2001, pp. 187–205. Examples of authors who have detected a polemical motive in Rashi's exegetical work are Yitzhak Baer, "Rashi and the Historical Reality of his Time," *Tarbiz*, 20 (1949): 320–332 (in Hebrew); Avraham Grossman, "Perush Rashi li-Tehilim ve-ha-Pulmus ha-Yehudi-ha-Nozri," in Dov Rappel, ed., *Mehqarim ba-Miqra uve-Hinukh Mugashim li-Prof. Mosheh Ahrend*, Jerusalem, 1996, pp. 59–74; Esra Shereshevsky, "Rashi and Christian Interpretations," *Jewish Quarterly Review*, 61 (1970): 76–86; Erwin I.J. Rosenthal, "Anti-Christian Polemics in Medieval Bible Commentaries," *Journal of Jewish Studies*, 11 (1960): 115–135; Sarah Kamin, "Rashi's Commentary on the Song of Songs and Jewish-Christian Polemic," *Shenaton la-Miqra u-le-heqer ha-Mizrah ha-Qadmon* 7–8 (1983–1984): 218–48 (in Hebrew; reprinted in *Idem, Jews and Christians Interpret the Bible*, Jerusalem, 1991, pp. 31–61); Eleazar Touitou, "Rashi's Commentary on Genesis 1–6 in the Context of Judeo-Christian Controversy," *Hebrew Union College Annual*, 61 (1990): 159–183; and Judah Rosenthal, "Anti-Christian Polemics in the Biblical Commentaries of Rashi," in Simon Federbush, ed., *Rashi: Torato re-Ishiyyuto* (Rashi, His Teachings and Personality), New York, 1958, pp. 45–59 (in Hebrew; reprinted in Rosenthal,

is believed, Maimonides, in contrast to Rashi, had little interest in Christianity. Although it is well known that Maimonides considered Christianity, unlike Islam, to be idolatry, the assumption is usually made that if Maimonides had lived in a Christian country, where Jews had economic reasons for absolving Christianity of the charge of idolatry, he would have seen things differently.[2] In short, Christianity was peripheral to Maimonides' worldview, but it was central to Rashi's.

This common wisdom makes a lot of sense, since Maimonides was born and worked in Islamic countries his entire life, and was greatly influenced by Islamic thought, whereas Rashi lived among Christians who were antagonistic to Jews and Judaism. Although Maimonides obviously had more contact with Christians, who were a significant minority in Egypt,[3] than Rashi had with Muslims, who were non-existent in northern Europe, his frame of reference was Islamic and Rashi's was Christian. Nevertheless, I believe that this common wisdom is misleading, since Rashi was much less interested in, not to say knowledgeable of, Christianity as such, whereas Maimonides, who referred to Christianity throughout his literary oeuvre (despite Moses Mendelssohn's assertion to the contrary, based on censored editions of Maimonides' works),[4] understood Christian theology very well and responded to it on quite a number of occasions. In fact, Maimonides stated that he

---

Studies and Texts, Jerusalem, 1967, vol. 1., pp. 101–116).

2. Maimonides' comments on the status of Muslims and Christians can be found, e.g., in R. Moses b. Maimon, *Responsa*, ed. by Jehoshua Blau, Jerusalem 1958–1961, vol. 2, pp. 515–516, 725–728; Hilkhot Ma'akhalot Asurot, 11:7; 13:11. Most discussions of Maimonides' attitude towards Christianity have been in the context of his relation to both Christianity and Islam; see, e.g., David Novak, "Maimonides on Judaism and Other Religions," The Samuel H. Goldenson Lecture, February 23, 1997, HUC-JIR, Cincinnati, Ohio; Howard T. Kreisel, "Maimonides on Christianity and Islam," in Ronald A. Brauner, ed., *Jewish Civilization: Essays and Studies* 3, Philadelphia, 1985, pp. 153–162. I have discussed the topic in my "Tradition and Innovation in Maimonides' Attitude toward Other Religions," in Jay M. Harris, ed., *Maimonides after 800 Years: Essays on Maimonides and His Influence*, Cambridge, Mass./London, 2007, pp. 167–182.
3. A number of Maimonides' responsa deal with actual questions concerning Christians; see *Responsa*, vol. 3, p. 215, s.v. "Nozri."
4. See Alexander Altmann, *Moses Mendelssohn. A Biographical Study*, Philadelphia, 1973, p. 792, n. 21.

could bring a thousand scriptural proof texts, or close to a thousand, to prove that Jesus was not the Messiah.[5] If one were to ask, which of these two great luminaries had a more accurate picture of Christianity, and which one polemicized against this religion more directly, I would say it was actually Maimonides and not Rashi.

❦ ❦ ❦

Let us begin with Rashi who died before Maimonides was born. In evaluating the extent to which Rashi was responding to Christian exegesis in his biblical commentaries, it might be useful to outline three methodological points. First, according to such scholars as Yitzhaq Baer, Judah Rosenthal, Avraham Grossman, Elazar Touitou, and others, Rashi's commentaries responded to the historical events of his time, for instance, the Crusades and the Christian mission to the Jews.[6] There is an assumption that the events of 1096, which occurred less than ten years before Rashi's death, had a great impact upon him, even though most of his literary work must have been completed before that date. Furthermore, based on the conjecture that Jews of Rashi's time, in the words of another author, "were being bombarded with Christian propaganda,"[7] Rashi must have been aware of Christian exegesis. Yet, when Rashi died in 1105, the Christian twelfth-century renaissance[8] was just beginning (Anselm of Canterbury, a major inspiration of the renaissance, was Rashi's contemporary and died four years after him in 1109). Although by the end of the twelfth century there are signs of a newly developed mission to the Jews with renewed vigor and energy, at the beginning of that century, namely in Rashi's last years, there was almost no mission to the Jews (as we recall, the Crusaders who massacred Rhineland

---

5. In his *Epistle to Yemen*; see *Epistles of Maimonides. Crisis and Leadership*, Translations and notes by Abraham Halkin and discussions by David Hartman, Philadelphia, 1985, p. 126.

6. See above, n. 1.

7. Mayer Gruber, *Rashi's Commentary on Psalms*, Leiden/Boston, 2004, pp. 88–89.

8. This term was coined by Charles Homer Haskins, *The Renaissance of the Twelfth Century*, Cambridge, Mass., 1928.

Jewry did not attempt to convert Jews by means of arguments based upon Christian biblical exegesis). Two generations after Rashi, exegetes such as Rashbam and Joseph Bekhor Shor had much more contact with Christian scholars and were well aware of Christian biblical interpretation.[9] That is not the case with Rashi.

A second point to consider when evaluating the extent to which Rashi polemicized against Christianity is the difference between Christianity and Christians; between polemics against Christianity as a religion and unflattering references to the Christian majority or expectations that Christianity and Christians would disappear in the messianic future. Avraham Grossman, for instance, deals with a number of passages in which Rashi refers to Esau or Edom, namely Christianity, in his commentary on Psalms,[10] and he shows that Rashi was not an especially committed ecumenist. Rashi, like other Ashkenazic Jews, expected what Yisrael Yuval has called the "avenging redemption",[11] and he thought that King David had already anticipated that redemption in the Book of Psalms. Grossman believes that for Rashi, the avenging redemption will be followed by a "conversionary redemption," in which those Gentiles, who survive God's vengeance, will convert to Judaism, and that Rashi expressed this belief in his commentary on Psalms. Nonetheless, even if we take every passage in Rashi's commentary that mentions Esau, Edom, Amalek, or "the nations of the world" as referring specifically to contemporary Christians, despite the midrashic background of many of the comments, it would still be difficult to read these passages as polemic against the Christian religion. Rashi did not refer to Christian beliefs, but only to the fate of Christians, and all other idolaters, at the end of days. When evaluating Rashi's knowledge of, and reaction to, Christianity, it is not enough to

---

9. See Martin I. Lockshin, *Rashbam's Commentary on Deuteronomy: An Annotated Translation*, Providence, 2004, pp. 18–24.
10. See above, n. 1.
11. "Vengeance and Damnation, Blood and Defamation: From Jewish Martyrdom to Blood Libel Accusations," *Zion*, 58:1 (1993): 33–90 (in Hebrew).

analyze the extent of Rashi's religious tolerance in general, or his love and hatred of Christians in particular.

A third point. Most readers who have argued for the influence of the Jewish-Christian debate on Rashi's commentaries have looked at verses which were used by Christians as testimonia for the truth of their religion, have seen that Rashi's interpretations of those verses is different than the Christian ones, and have concluded that Rashi was responding to Christianity. On this reading, Rashi's commentary on these verses was a forced or unnatural response to the Christian position. David Berger[12] has suggested that this methodology is flawed, since it assumes that when Rashi's interpretation was different than the Christian one, it was a forced one. Berger argues that oftentimes Rashi's explanation of so-called Christological verses is consistent with his exegetical methodology, and, thus, not necessarily a response to Christianity. With Berger's standards of identifying anti-Christian interpretations, only clearly unnatural interpretations, or comments in which Rashi mentions Christians explicitly, would indicate a response to Christianity. In this manner, the number of anti-Christian comments in Rashi's commentaries is greatly reduced. The problem remains, however, when to evaluate a comment as forced and when to see it as consistent with Rashi's other comments.[13]

In light of these caveats, I propose a different methodology for determining the extent of Rashi's response to Christianity, namely comparing his comments on specific verses in the Bible with the use of the same, and additional, verses in the polemical literature. In light of Mayer Gruber's recent excellent edition, translation and notes of Rashi's commentary on Psalms,[14] and in light of the claim that Psalms is Rashi's most anti-Christian commentary, I would like to focus on that book as a case study of my methodology. I believe that a comparison between Rashi's commentary on Psalms and the polemical literature will show

---

12. In lectures and private conversations.
13. Grossman is aware of this problem; see his "Pulmus Dati."
14. Gruber, *op cit.*

that Rashi was neither deeply concerned with Christian exegesis nor very conversant with Christian theology.[15]

❧ ❧ ❧

To illustrate the central contention here, reference should be made to the appended table. It schematizes the use of Psalms in the New Testament, in Jewish anti-Christian polemical treatises, and in Rashi's Commentary to Psalms. We can see that twice in his commentary to Psalms, Rashi reacted to Christianity explicitly (marked by x) by writing that a particular comment was a "teshuvah la-minim." Without entering into the debate as to whether "teshuvah" means a response to Christian questions or exegesis,[16] or a direct attack;[17] and whether minim means apostate Jews,[18] or any Christians,[19] only twice in all of his commentary to Psalms did Rashi refer directly to Christians. In both cases, Psalms 2 and 21, Rashi distinguished between the rabbinic midrash which understood these psalms as referring to the Messiah, and the need to answer the "minim," because of whom it is good to give another

15. Shaye J.D. Cohen, "Does Rashi's Torah Commentary Respond to Christianity? A Comparison of Rashi with Rashbam and Bekhor Shor," in Hindy Najman and Judith H. Newman, eds., *The Idea of Biblical Interpretation. Essays In Honor of James L. Kugel*, Leiden/Boston, 2004, pp. 449–472, shares some of the concerns expressed in the present discussion. By comparing Rashi's commentary on the first chapters of Genesis with the commentaries of his grandson Rashbam, and Rashbam's contemporary, Joseph Bekhor Shor, he argues that Rashi's commentary on Genesis was not motivated by polemical concerns. He repeats, however, the generally accepted notion that the "anti-Christian polemic in the Psalms Commentary is unmistakable and unambiguous" (p. 459). See also Robert A. Harris, "Rashi and the 'Messianic' Psalms," in Chaim Cohen, et al., eds., *Birkat Shalom: Studies in the Bible, Ancient Near Eastern Literature, and Postbiblical Judaism Presented to Shalom M. Paul on the Occasion of His Seventieth Birthday*, Winona Lake, Indiana, 2008, pp. 845–862, which appeared after I had written the present article.
16. This was the opinion of my uncle, Herman Hailperin, in his *Rashi and the Christian Scholars*, Pittsburgh, 1963, p. 60.
17. Gruber, *Psalms*, pp. 179–180; and Touitou, "Le-Mashma'ut ha-Musag 'Teshuvat ha-Minim' be-Khitvei Raboteinu ha-Zarfatim," *Sinai* 99:3–4 (1986): 144–148.
18. Hailperin, (above, n. 16). Although Hailperin's view is most likely a result of his own apologetic motives, the medieval Christian Nicholas de Lyra (c. 1270–1349) also understood Rashi as referring to apostates; *ibid.*, p. 178.
19. Gruber and Touitou (above, n. 17).

interpretation. Mayer Gruber identifies five more comments (on Psalms 9, 22, 72, 84, and 105, identified as x(G) in the table), in which he believed that Rashi gave an alternate interpretation to the Christian interpretation, including transferring the psalm from the messianic realm to a description of the Jewish people. Esra Shereshevsky (x(S) in the table) has found eight more psalms in which, he claims, Rashi responded to Jerome's exegesis,[20] and Judah Rosenthal (x(R) in the table) added a few more verses.[21] Nevertheless, in none of these places did Rashi use the key words "teshuvat ha-minim" or relate specifically to Christians. Most of the other readers, who have identified responses to Christianity in additional psalms, have pointed to descriptions of the suffering of the Jews at the hands of Esau or the revolutionary change that will occur in the relations between idolaters and Jews in the end of days, but again without a specific reference to Christians or Christianity.

We may now compare these references in Rashi's commentary with the other columns in the table. The first column includes chapters in Psalms, direct quotes of which appear in the New Testament, and we see there are many such verses, even without taking into account indirect references. The second column records those psalms discussed in the most important Ashkenazi polemic work, *Sefer Nizzahon Yashan*, from the end of the thirteenth century.[22] The other columns include references to Psalms in other early polemical books: *Sefer Yosef ha-Meqanneh* of Joseph ben Nathan Official (mid-thirteenth century France);[23] *Sefer ha-Berit* of Joseph Kimhi (Spain-Provence, 1170);[24] the Psalm

---

20. See above, n. 1.
21. See above, n. 1. It should be noted that since most of the verses mentioned by Shereshevsky and Rosenthal were not important verses in the Jewish-Christian debate, as the table indicates, it is unlikely that Rashi had an anti-Christian motive in his commentary on them.
22. The Hebrew text and an English translation are provided by David Berger, *The Jewish-Christian Debate in the High Middle Ages*, Philadelphia, 1979.
23. *Sepher Joseph Hamekane*, ed. by Judah Rosenthal, Jerusalem, 1970.
24. The Hebrew edition was edited by Frank Talmage, Jerusalem, 1974; Talmage provided an English translation in Joseph Kimhi, *The Book of the Covenant*, Toronto, 1972.

commentary of David Kimhi (Radak, Joseph Kimhi's son),[25] and *Sefer Milhamot ha-Shem* of Jacob ben Reuben (also of the Spanish school from the end of the twelfth century).[26] From this chart we see that Jewish polemicists were familiar with many more Christological interpretations of Psalms than Rashi, and their polemical discussions of this book are much more inclusive than those of Rashi. In addition, one can see that the central psalms in the Jewish-Christian debate were 2, in which Rashi has a "teshuvah la-minim"; 22, where Rashi did not refer to Christian exegesis but simply stated that the psalm refers to Israel in exile; 72, where both Gruber and Grossman write that Rashi's comment on verse 16 is a response to Christianity, but I am not convinced, and there is clearly no direct answer to Christianity in his commentary here; 87, with no comment by Rashi, and 110, where again there is no direct comment about Christianity despite the efforts of Shereshevsky, Rosenthal and others to find an anti-Christian angle. In sum, Rashi did not have many interpretations in his Commentary on Psalms which included explicit answers to Christian exegesis.

This conclusion is not only quantitative. If we compare Rashi's anti-Christian comments with those of true polemicists, we see qualitative differences. Even when we know that Rashi is responding to Christianity, it is often difficult to know from Rashi's words which Christian doctrine he was rejecting. Let us look, for instance at Rashi on Psalm 2, in Mayer Gruber's translation.[27]

> Verse 1: "Why do the nations assemble? Our rabbis interpreted the subject of the chapter as a reference to the King Messiah. However, according to its basic mean-

---

25. R' David Kimhi, *Ha-Perush ha-Shalem al Tehillim*, ed. by Avraham Darom, Jerusalem, 1967. Radak's anti-Christian comments, which have been censored from many editions of his commentary, have been collected in a book entitled *Teshuvot Radak la-Nozrim*, published with *Hesronot ha-Shas*, Tel-Aviv, 1966; see also Bernard H. Mehlman and Daniel F. Polish, "The Response to the Christian Exegesis of Psalms in the Teshuvot La-Noẓrim of Rabbi David Qimḥi," in Brauner, *Jewish Civilization*, pp. 181–208.

26. Ed. by Judah Rosenthal, Jerusalem, 1963.

27. Pp. 177–178.

ing and for a refutation of the Christians it is correct to interpret it as a reference to David himself." Verse 7: "You are my son. I.e., the head of Israel who are called Sons [of God]... and they will be sustained [by you], for all of them depend on you. I, by making you king over them, Have fathered you this day so that [you] are called My son and are dear to Me, thereby for their sake... We have found also that those among the kings of Israel who are dear to Him He called 'sons' as it is stated in the Bible concerning Solomon."

Rashi here rejects the Christian views that the messiah, as the anointed king of Israel, has any special status as son of God.

Let us compare these comments with the treatment of this psalm by a real polemicist. A good example is *Sefer Nizzahon Yashan* written by an Ashkenazi author almost two hundred years after Rashi. The author wrote (in David Berger's translation):[28]

"The Lord has said unto me, You are my son; this day have I begotten you. They defiantly say that this verse refers to the hanged one. The answer is: In the account of creation it says: "Let us make man," and they interpret it as meaning that the father told the son, "Let the two of us make man." Now, if he existed then and was born today, it follows that he was born twice. In addition, tell him: If they are merely three names, but all is really one, then when the son was born, so was the father; they were both born at the same time, since they are inseparable. If so, which of them calls the other my son and which is called father? After all, one did not precede the other by so much as a hairbreadth. You are therefore forced to the conclusion that the father preceded the son by many days during which the father was childless and alone with no son... I shall now ask a further question to which I should appreciate an answer: You say that the son was

---

28. Berger, *Debate*, p. 137.

formed in Mary's womb. Inform me as to whether the
father and impure spirit[29] were in the stomach with the
son or whether the son was there alone. If you will say
the son alone, then your words are self-contradictory, for
you say that they are never separated from each other.
On the other hand, if you will say that the three of them
were in the stomach and grew there, then all three were
also on earth among people and all three were hanged.
Who, then, was in heaven all the time, inasmuch as they
are inseparable? Furthermore, who ran the world during
the three days when they were buried and none of them
was either in heaven or on earth? Consequently, any wise
man can understand that their words have no substance."

This is certainly anti-Christian polemic, especially when compared to Rashi's approach. Similar polemical treatments of this psalm can be found as well in the works of other polemicists, such as the Jacob ben Reuben,[30] David Kimhi,[31] and Joseph Official.[32]

Putting it all together, we can discern that the Christian exegesis of Psalm 2 provided the polemicists an opportunity to raise questions concerning the trinity, and not just to deny that the psalm made references to the Messiah in general or Jesus in particular. It is also of interest that the questions about the trinity found in these polemical compositions were originally asked by the anonymous author of the Judaeo-Arabic polemic, *Qissat Mujadalat al-Usquf,* "The Account of the Disputation of the Priest," translated into Hebrew as the *Book of Nestor the Priest.*[33] It would appear that the author of *The Account,* who lived in an Islamic country, was much more interested in Christian theology than Rashi, who lived in a Christian country and who, if some

---

29. The author's term for the third person of the trinity.
30. *Milhamot Ha-Shem,* pp. 63–65.
31. *Perush al Sefer Tehillim,* pp. 14–15.
32. *Sepher Joseph Hamekane,* pp. 99–101.
33. See Daniel J. Lasker and Sarah Stroumsa, *The Polemic of Nestor the Priest,* Jerusalem, 1996, vol. 1, pp. 56–58; 102–105.

of the scholars are to be believed, so much wanted to answer the claims of his Christian neighbors.

It is clear, therefore, that it is hard to distinguish an unambiguous polemical motive against Christianity in Rashi's Commentary on Psalms, and his explicit comments about that religion are few and far between. Rashi was somewhat aware of Christian scriptural exegesis, but we see no signs of comprehensive familiarity or a polemical fixation: a concern with polemics was not at the top of Rashi's priorities in his Commentary on Psalms.

In light of this conclusion, it might be useful to inquire further as to the picture of Christianity, which can be drawn from Rashi's Commentary on Psalms. What did Rashi really know about Christianity? I think the answer is: not very much. He knew that the Christians believed that Jesus was the son of God, in some form or other, and that he was King Messiah. This conclusion is drawn from the two places in the Commentary in which Rashi recorded his "answer to the heretics," namely Ps. 2 and 21. In his commentary on these two psalms, Rashi stated that interpreting them as messianic played into the hands of the Christians, and, therefore, one should find an alternate interpretation. In contrast to the polemicists who have been mentioned, Rashi did not exploit the opportunity to respond to the Christian doctrine of trinity or to wonder how God could be born and still be the son of God. Trinity and incarnation are concepts that were foreign to Rashi.

It is true that if we wished to make a full evaluation of Rashi's knowledge of Christianity, it is not enough to rely solely on a comparison of his commentary on Psalms.[34] Indeed, if we were to read the rest of Rashi's commentaries to the Bible, as well as those to the Talmud and his other oeuvre, we are sure to be able to add other details of Rashi's knowledge of Christianity. For instance, he apparently knew that the Christians believe that the Messiah

---

34. Presumably a full comparison of his commentaries with the Jewish anti-Christian polemical literature would provide similar results as did the comparison with the Psalms commentary.

is meant to suffer and that the verses of the Servant of the Lord in Isaiah refer to Jesus.[35] It is unclear how well he understood the trinity of father, son and spirit, or what this doctrine actually entails (after all, most Christians of his time and place did not have a clear notion of this doctrine, and Rashi did not have the philosophical background concerning divine attributes which the later polemicists had). There is no clear sign of original sin, for instance in Rashi's commentary on Psalm 51:7 ("I was conceived in sin"), even though there may be a hint of this belief in Rashi's statement that Adam and Eve had sexual relations in the Garden of Eden.[36] In short, from the doctrinal aspect as well as the exegetical, it is hard to see Rashi as someone who understood Christianity and perceived an overwhelming need to refute it.

❧ ❧ ❧

Let us now consider Maimonides. As stated previously, Maimonides ruled that Christianity is idolatry, a ruling with practical applications, for instance, in the case of possibly deriving benefit from Christian wine.[37] Although Ashkenazic Jews generally found ways of absolving Christians of the charge of idolatry, for the economic benefits which this entailed,[38] it would be difficult to say that Maimonides had an economic motive in his halakhic decision making. Maimonides was well aware of the differences between Islam, with its strict monotheism, and Christianity, with its trinitarian unity. This can be seen clearly in Maimonides' discussion of divine attributes.

As a number of scholars have shown,[39] Islamic theology developed in response to Christian challenges to the nascent religion. When the first Muslims emerged from the Arabian peninsula,

---

35. Cf. Hailperin, *Rashi*, pp. 56–59.
36. See Cohen, "Rashi," pp. 467–468.
37. See above, n. 2.
38. Jacob Katz, *Exclusiveness and Tolerance*, London, 1961.
39. See, e.g., Harry A. Wolfson, *The Philosophy of the Kalam*, Cambridge, Mass., 1977, pp. 112–143; 205–234; 304–354.

armed intellectually only with the Quran, they met a philosophically sophisticated Christian community which was more than
ready to engage the Muslims in religious debate. The chief issue
of contention was the Christian trinity, denied explicitly in the
Quran. Christians attempted to convince Muslims that certain of
God's attributes, notably His wisdom and life, could be hyposta-
sized into divine Persons, namely Son and Holy Spirit. Muslims
were forced to respond to such argumentation by developing
their own theories of attributes. Even those Muslims, who did
believe that God's essence could be described by positive terms,
denied that those terms are the same as the persons of the trinity.
Many other Muslims, the anti-attributists, denied the existence
of real, essential attributes all together, specifically to combat the
Christian doctrine. A number of Jewish thinkers of the Muʿtazilite
Kalam school, such as Dawud al-Muqammmis[40] and Rav Saadia
Gaon,[41] followed the Muslim lead in this respect and included
anti-trinitarian polemics in their discussions of divine attributes.

Maimonides acted in like manner, although he rejected
Kalam-type theories of attributes. His *Guide of the Perplexed* mentioned Christianity three times, each one in the context of God's
unity. In Part 1, chapter 50, Maimonides stated that those who
maintain a belief in positive essential attributes, while at the same
time saying that God is one, are similar to the Christians who say
that "[God] is one, but He is three and the three are one."[42] In Part
I, chapter 71, Maimonides stated that the Kalam, whose views on
divine unity were adopted by the Geonim and the Karaites, is
traced back to Christian apologetics, which tried to refute philosophy for theological purposes.[43] In his detailed discussion of
the Kalam proofs of divine unity, Part I, chapter 75, Maimonides
rejected one of their proofs because methodologically, it might

40. Sarah Stroumsa, *Dāwūd ibn Marwān al-Muqammiṣ's* Twenty Chapters (ʿIshrūn
    Maqala), Leiden, 1989, pp. 164–225.
41. Saadia Gaon, *The Book of Beliefs and Opinions*, trans. by Samuel Rosenblatt, New
    Haven, 1948, pp. 103–110.
42. Moses Maimonides, *The Guide of the Perplexed*, trans. by Shlomo Pines, Chicago,
    1963, p. 111.
43. *Ibid.*, pp. 177–178.

have the same failing as Christianity, namely: "Perhaps just as the Christians think that [God] is three, and He is not, so, too, we think that he is one, and He is not?"[44] Thus, Maimonides' discussion of divine unity took into account Christian trinitarianism, and like his Muslim neighbors, Maimonides rejected it as intellectually incoherent.

Maimonides mentioned the Christian trinity as well in the *Epistle on Resurrection*, one of his last compositions. While defending his own orthodoxy against his detractors, Maimonides allowed himself to express great frustration with his critics. Thus, Maimonides began by saying that he is not really surprised that his words were misunderstood; after all, when God Himself tried to teach the lesson of divine unity, he was quite explicit: Hear O Israel, the Lord our God, the Lord is one. Nevertheless, Christians understood that to mean that there is a trinity and not true unity.[45] We see here that not only was Maimonides familiar with Christian doctrine, he also knew at least one proof text employed by their theologians to justify it. The use of Deut. 6:4 as an indication of the trinity can be found, for instance, in the *Dialogue of the Patiarch John I with 'Amr al-'As*,[46] the *Disputation between the Christian Patriarch Timothy and Mahdi, the Third Abbasid Caliph*,[47] and in the *Apology of al-Kindi*.[48] In short, based on his familiarity with Christian theology, Maimonides well understood the philosophical issues involved in the doctrine of the trinity, and he was able to reject it accordingly. It is undoubtedly that awareness of Christian doctrine which was one factor that led Maimonides to rule that it is an idolatrous religion. An additional consideration apparently was his knowledge that Christians used statues and icons, since he attributed to them the verse in Deut. 4:28: "And there you will serve gods of wood and stone (*etz va-even*), the work of men."[49]

---

44. *Ibid.*, p. 225.
45. *Crisis and Leadership*, p. 211.
46. See N.A. Newman, *The Early Christian-Muslim Dialogue*, Hatfield, Pennsylvania, 1993, p. 25.
47. *Ibid.*, p. 225.
48. *Ibid.*, p. 423.
49. Commentary on the Mishnah, Avodah Zarah 1:4. Cf. Judah Halevi's use of this verse

A corollary of the doctrine of the trinity is the belief that one of the three persons of the Godhead was incarnated in the person of Jesus of Nazareth, the messiah, whose mother bore him without sexual relations. Maimonides rejected the possibility that Jesus was God incarnate in his *Epistle to Yemen*, where he wrote that Jesus was the son of a Jewish woman and a non-Jewish father, and even though many Jews referred to him in an exaggerated manner as a *mamzer*, he was not actually one (since the engaged Mary's adulterous partner was a non-Jew rather than a Jew).[50] Furthermore, Maimonides most likely had the doctrine of incarnation in mind when he declared in *Guide*, 3:15, that there are impossible things, which are not subject to divine power. Thus, he stated: "Likewise that God should bring into existence someone like Himself, or should annihilate Himself, or should become a body, or should change — all of these things belong to the class of the impossible; and power to do any of these things cannot be attributed to God." [51] While it is difficult to determine with certainty that the intention here is to incarnation, nevertheless, on the basis of the literature, which preceded Maimonides, one can suppose that the aforementioned impossibilities are connected to the Christian belief.

Maimonides knew more about Christianity than the trinity and incarnation. He understood Christian history including, for instance, the fact that Jesus was not the founder of Christianity as it developed; Paul of Tarsus was responsible for that. Maimonides did not mention Paul explicitly, but he did make apparent reference to him in his *Epistle to Yemen*, where Maimonides distinguished between Jesus, who wished to abolish the law by calling himself the Messiah and pretending to do miracles, with a later personality, presumably Paul, who started the new religion.[52]

---

in *Kuzari* 4:23, referring to both Christianity and Islam.
50. *Crisis and Leadership.*, p. 98. A *mamzer*, who cannot marry most other Jews, is the product of an incestuous or adulterous relationship, but if the father is not Jewish, the child does not have this status.
51. *Guide*, p. 460.
52. *Crisis and Leadership.*, p. 99.

Maimonides implicitly denied Jesus' messianic pretensions as well by declaring in the *Commentary on the Mishnah*,[53] the *Book of Commandments*,[54] and the *Epistle to Yemen*,[55] that the messiah will be a descendant of King David through his son Solomon. In Luke 3:31, the genealogy of Joseph, the husband of Jesus' mother, is traced back to Nathan the son of David.

Maimonides was aware as well that Judaism and Christianity shared a common divine Scripture. It is for this reason, that he allowed Jews to teach Christians Torah, something which is forbidden to do for Muslims. Christians, according to Maimonides, could possibly be persuaded to understand the Torah correctly and thus become Jews, whereas in light of the Islamic denial of the validity of the Torah, there was no reason to try to persuade Muslims that Jewish interpretations of it are correct.[56] It might be added that Maimonides, with no first hand experience of life under Christianity, wrote that exile under Islam was worse than under any other nation in Jewish history.[57] Here, Rashi would probably have disagreed.

Maimonides differed from Rashi in his relationship to Christianity in another important aspect. Unlike Rashi, who expected the idolaters to be destroyed with the advent of the Messiah, Maimonides understood that Christianity, and Islam, actually contributed to the messianic future. By spreading knowledge of the messianic idea throughout the world, these two religions were preparing humanity for the true Messiah's arrival.[58] The Ashkenazic "revenging redemption" is not mentioned.

❦   ❦   ❦

53. Introduction to Chapter Heleq; see *Mishnah im Perush Rabbeinu Moshe ben Maimon*, ed. by Yosef Kafih, Vol. 4, Jerusalem, 1964, p. 216.
54. *Sefer Ha-Mizvot*, Negative Commandment 362, ed. by Yosef Kafih, Jerusalem, 1971, pp. 345–346.
55. *Crisis and Leadership.*, p. 121.
56. *Responsa*, vol. 1, pp. 284–285.
57. *Crisis and Leadership.*, p. 126.
58. *Mishneh Torah*, Laws of Kings, 11:4 (in uncensored versions).

The comparison here between anti-Christian polemics in the works of Rashi and those of Maimonides is intended to correct the erroneous notion that Rashi was obsessed with Christianity. In truth, Maimonides had no such obsession either, but he understood well Christian doctrines and responded to those doctrines much more than is generally thought. In Ashkenaz, it was not until after Rashi's lifetime that Jews were fully exposed to both Christian interpretations and doctrines. The Christian mission to the Jews was launched, the Talmud was burned and Jewish thinkers turned more and more to a refutation of Christianity, in both their exegetical works as well as in specifically polemical treatises.[59] To see this development already in the works of Rashi is anachronistic. He was undoubtedly aware of Christianity, but it did not play a central role in his thought or provide an important stimulus to his understanding of the Bible. In contrast, to ignore Maimonides' reaction to Christianity is shortsighted. Like many other Jewish thinkers in Islamic countries, Maimonides found Christianity offensive and responded to it.[60] Each of these two greats responded in his own way to the challenges of the time, forming a model for later generations.

Prof. Daniel J. Lasker is the Norbert Blechner Professor of Jewish Values in the Goldstein-Goren Department of Jewish Thought, Ben-Gurion University of the Negev, Beer Sheva

---

59. These developments are described well by Robert Chazan, *Daggers of Faith*, Berkeley, 1989.
60. See my "The Jewish Critique of Christianity Under Islam in the Middle Ages," *Proceedings of the American Academy for Jewish Research*, 57 (1991): 121–153.

References to Christianity in Rashi's Commentary on Psalms – Comparative Table

Chapter	NT	Nizzahon Yashan	Yosef Ha-Meqanneh	Sefer Ha-Berit	Radaq	Milhamot Ha-Shem	Rashi
1		x	x				
2	x	x	x		x	x	x
3		x					
4		x	x				
5	x	x					
6		x					
7		x			x		
8	x	x		x			x (G)
9		x					
10	x	x					
11		x					
12		x					
13		x					
14	x	x	x				
15		x	x	x			
16	x	x	x				x (S)
17		x					
18	x	x					
19	x	x			x		
21		x	x		x		x
22	x	x	x	x	x	x	x (G)
24		x					
28		x					
31	x	x					
32	x		x				
34	x						
35	x						
36	x						
40	x						x (S)
41	x						
44	x						
45	x		x		x	x	
47						x	
50			x			x	

Chapter	NT	Nizzahon Yashan	Yosef Ha-Meqanneh	Sefer Ha-Berit	Radaq	Milhamot Ha-Shem	Rashi
51	x		x				
53	x						
62	x						
68	x		x			x	
69	x		x			x	
72		x	x	x	x	x	x(G)
75			x				
78	x						
80							x(S)
82	x						
84							x(G)
85			x	x		x	
86		x					
87			x	x	x	x	
88							x(S)
89	x		x				
91	x						
94	x						
95	x						
96							x(S)
98							x(S)
99							x(S)
102	x						
104	x						
105							x(G)
109	x						
110	x	x	x	x	x	x	x(S)(R)
116	x						
117	x						
118	x						
132							x(R)
135	x						
140	x						
146		x					

Source of New Testament:
http://www.ccel.org/bible/phillips/CN711NTinOT.htm

2

Rashi and Maimonides on the Relationship Between Torah and the Cosmos[1]

Menachem Kellner

R ashi and Maimonides are good examples of the fact that while individuals may live similar lives (in this case, lives governed by halakhah, love of Torah and love for the Jewish people), share similar religious views (in this case, many of the theological presuppositions which make possible unreserved halakhic observance), and even be revered by the same people, they may live in remarkably different spiritual universes. Comments by Rashi and Maimonides on the creation of the cosmos exemplify this.

Rashi opens his commentary on the Torah by paraphrasing from Midrash Tanhuma (parashat bereshit, xi) as follows:

> Rabbi Isaac said: It was not necessary to begin the Torah [the main object of which is to teach commandments] with this verse, but from *This month shall be unto you [the first of the months]* (Exodus 12:2) since this was the first commandment that Israel was commanded to observe. But what is the reason that the Torah begins with *In the*

---

1. My thanks to James Diamond, Raphael Jospe, Avram Montag, and Kenneth Seeskin for helpful comments on an earlier draft of this essay. Earlier versions of portions of this essay appeared in M. Kellner, *Maimonides' Confrontation with Mysticism* (Oxford: Littman Library of Jewish Civilization, 2006). This essay was originally supposed to have appeared before the publication of that book. For other studies comparing Rashi and Maimonides, see the notes to Eric Lawee, "Maimonides in the Eastern Mediterranean: The Case of Rashi's Resisting Readers," in Jay M. Harris (ed.), *Maimonides after 800 Years: Essays on Maimonides and His Influence* (Cambridge: Harvard University Press, 2007): 183–206.

beginning? Because of the verse, *The power of His works He hath declared to His people in giving them the heritage of the nations* (Psalms 111:6), for if the nations of the world should say to Israel: "You are robbers, because you have seized by force the lands of the seven nations [of Canaan], Israel could reply to them: "The entire world belongs to the Holy One, Blessed be He; He created it, and gave it to whomever it was right in His eyes. Of His own will He gave it to them [the seven Canaanite nations] and of His own will He took it from them and gave it to us.

Rashi here expands on the Tanhuma text, but, so far as I can judge, in no way distorts it. Emphasizing what I take to be a central focus of his gloss here, Rashi continues, this time paraphrasing Gen. R. I.1:

In the beginning He created: This passage calls for a midrashic interpretation, as our Rabbis have interpreted it: "[God created the world] for the sake of the Torah since it is called *the beginning of His way* (Proverbs 8:22) and for the sake of Israel, since they are called *the beginning of His crops* (Jeremiah 2:3).

In the previous gloss, the Cosmos is created so that the Land of Israel can be given to the Jews; here we find the Cosmos being created, in effect, so that the Torah could be given to the Jews.

How does Maimonides handle the opening passage of the Torah? Here is one of his comments on the subject, from the Introduction to the *Guide of the Perplexed*:

Do you not see the following fact? God, may His mention be exalted, wished us to be perfected and the state of our societies to be improved by His laws regarding actions. Now this can come about only after the adoption of intellectual beliefs, the first of which being His apprehension, may He be exalted, according to our capacity. This, in its turn, cannot come about except through divine science and this divine science cannot become actual except after a study of natural science [al-'ilm al-tiba'i]. This is so since natural science borders on divine science [al-'ilm al-ilahi], and its study precedes that of divine science in time as has been made clear to whoever has engaged in speculation on these matters. Hence God, may He be exalted, caused His book to open with the "Account of the Beginning," which, as we have made clear, is natural science. And because of the greatness and importance of the subject and because our capacity falls short of apprehending the greatest of subjects as it really is, — which divine wisdom has deemed necessary to convey to us — we are told about these profound matters in parables and riddles and very obscure words.[2]

In this text, I understand Maimonides to be making the following claims:

1. God revealed laws concerning behavior in order to improve society in general and to bring individuals to the highest perfection they could attain.
2. But in order that the laws which improve society may also bring individuals to their perfection, these individuals must learn certain truths, the most important of which concern God.
3. In order to learn truths about God, one must study metaphysics.
4. But one can not study metaphysics unless one has already studied physics.
5. Thus, the Torah opens with a discussion of matters of physics, but, since the subject is not one which all can grasp, it does so using what we today would call mythic language.[3]

---

2. I quote here and below from the translation of Shlomo Pines (Chicago: University of Chicago Press, 1963); our text is on p. 9.
3. To be very precise, the Torah *opens* with a metaphysical claim (that the cosmos as a whole is created) but immediately continues with a parabolic exposition of issues in physics.

Maimonides does *not* claim here to know why the world was created. In this he differs mightily from Rashi. Indeed, in *Guide of the Perplexed* III.13 Maimonides rejects the validity of asking the question which Rashi answers in his gloss to the first verse of the Torah.[4] There Maimonides writes (pp. 454–455):

> Thus we are obliged to believe that all that exists was intended by Him, may He be exalted, according to His volition. And we shall seek for it no cause or other final end whatever. Just as we do not seek for the end of His existence, may He be exalted, so do we not seek for the end of His volition, according to which all that has been and will be produced in time comes into being as it is.

And again (p. 456):

> This is what one ought to believe. For when man knows his own soul, makes no mistakes with regard to it, and understands every being according to what it is, he becomes calm and his thoughts are not troubled by seeking a final end for what has not that final end; or by seeking any final end for what has no final end except its own existence, which depends on the divine will — if you prefer, you can also say: on the divine wisdom.

For Maimonides, Rashi's very project in his gloss to Gen. 1:1 is misconceived; it is both a philosophical mistake, and I am confident he would have said, an act of unparalleled hutzpah.

But what about the claims Maimonides does make about the account of creation (in the passage quoted just above from the introduction to the *Guide of the Perplexed*)? Chapter III.27 (p. 510) of the *Guide* illuminates the first of these claims. There Maimonides writes:

> The Law as a whole aims at two things: the welfare of the

---

4. For a discussion of the religious and philosophical issues behind this debate, see M. Kellner, "Gersonides and His Cultured Despisers: Arama and Abravanel," *Journal of Medieval and Renaissance Studies* 6 (1976): 269–296.

soul and welfare of the body... As for the welfare of the body, it comes about by the improvement of their ways of living one with another. This is achieved through two things. One of them is the abolition of their wronging each other. This is tantamount to every individual among the people not being permitted to act according to his will and up to the limits of his power, but being forced to do that which is useful to the whole. The second thing consists in the acquisition by every human individual or moral qualities that are useful for life in society so that the affairs of the city may be ordered.

Many of the laws of the Torah which regulate behavior (as opposed to those which regulate thought[5]) aim at making us into better human beings so that our societies be well-ordered.[6] Moreover, Maimonides was convinced that in order to attain intellectual achievement to the greatest extent possible to us, we must first attain (and preserve) a high level of moral perfection.[7] While obedience to the Torah was not the only route available for achieving such perfection, it was certainly the best, and, for Jews, obligatory.

Maimonides' second claim above reflects his abhorrence of what today would be called "orthopraxy."[8] Admirable behavior must aim at some end; there is no more admirable end than know-

---

5. Maimonides may have been the first Jewish thinker to claim that the Torah included laws governing thought. For discussion, see M. Kellner, *Must a Jew Believe Anything?* 2nd ed. (London: Littman Library of Jewish Civilization, 2006), pp. 44–51.

6. Maimonides' attitude towards the status of moral laws is hotly debated in the scholarly literature on him. For a recent salvo, with references to much of the earlier literature, see Daniel Rynhold, "Good and Evil, Truth and Falsity: Maimonides and Moral Cognitivism," *Trumah* 12 (2002): 163–82.

7. For sources, see Guide of the Perplexed I.34 (pp. 76–77), I. 62 (p. 152), III.27 (p. 510), III.54 (p. 635); Commenatary on Mishnah Hagigah II.1; for discussion, see Howard Kreisel, *Maimonides' Political Thought* (Albany: SUNY Press, 1999), pp. 160, 238, 317 and M. Kellner, *Maimonides on Human Perfection* (Atlanta: Scholars Press, 1990), pp. 26–28.

8. Two very clear expressions of this abhorrence are Maimonides' insistence on placing Judaism on a firm dogmatic footing in his 'Thirteen Principles' and the fact that he opens his *Mishneh Torah* with four chapters dealing with philosophical and theological issues.

ing what can be known about God. Indeed, for Maimonides, the highest human end is to learn what can be learned about God.[9]

The third and fourth claims above need considerable unpacking. A convenient way of doing so is to use another text of Maimonides, his commentary on Mishnah Hagigah II.1. There he writes:[10]

> Listen to what has become clear to me according to my understanding on the basis of which I have studied in the words of the Sages; it is that they call *maʿaseh bereshit* the natural science [*al-'ilm al-tiba'i*] and inquiry into the beginning of creation.[11] By *maʿaseh merkavah* they mean the divine science [*al-ilm al-ilahi*], it being speech on the generality of existence[12] and on the existence of the Creator,[13] His knowledge,[14] His attributes,[15] that all created things must necessarily have come from Him, the

9. For discussions of this issue see the following studies by W. Z. Harvey: "R. Hasdai Crescas and His Critique of Philosophic Happiness," *Proceedings of the Sixth World Congress of Jewish Studies* 3 (1977): 143–49; "Averroes and Maimonides on the Obligation of Philosophical Contemplation (I'tibar)," *Tarbiz* 58 (1989): 75–83; and "Maimonides' First Commandment, Physics, and Doubt," in Yaakov Elman and Jeffrey S. Gurock (eds.), *Hazon Nahum: Studies ... Presented to Dr. Norman Lamm* (New York: Yeshiva University Press, 1997): 149–62.

10. For the full text, see M. Kellner, "Maimonides' Commentary on *Mishnah Hagigah* II.1: Translation and Commentary," in Marc D. Angel (ed.), *From Strength to Strength: Lectures from Shearith Israel* (New York: Sepher-Hermon Press, 1998): 101–111.

11. *Maʿaseh bereshit* thus includes two topics: the science of physics (as exposited in the opening chapters of "Laws of the Foundations of the Torah") and analysis of the question of creation. This latter is the dangerous part of the subject. A person who studies the question of creation and who (mistakenly) becomes convinced that the world is uncreated will reject the Torah, as Maimonides explains in *Guide of the Perplexed* II.25.

12. By this I take Maimonides to mean "existence as such." This is the subject matter of metaphysics as classically defined by Aristotle: the study of being *qua* being.

13. I.e., proofs for the existence of God. Maimonides discusses these in *Guide of the Perplexed* I.71–II.1.

14. I.e., the analysis of the nature of God's knowledge. See *Guide of the Perplexed* III.13–24.

15. I.e., the question of which attributes may be predicated of God. See *Guide of the Perplexed* I.51–60.

angels,[16] the soul, the intellect which links with humans,[17] and existence after death.[18] Because of the importance of these two sciences, the natural and the divine[19] — and they were justly considered important[20] — they[21] warned against teaching them as the mathematical sciences are taught.[22] It is known that each person by nature desires all the sciences,[23] whether he be an ignoramus or a sage. [It is further known] that it is impossible for a person to begin the study of these sciences, and direct his thought towards them, without the appropriate premises, and without entering the stages of science; they therefore forbade this and warned against it.

Maimonides here explains that the rabbinic Sages use the Hebrew expression, *ma'aseh bereshit* to mean what the ancient Greeks and contemporary Muslim philosophers called physics. They used the Hebrew expression *ma'aseh merkavah* to mean what the ancient

---

16. Which for Maimonides are the "separate intellects" of the neoplatonized Aristotelianism which Maimonides adopted. See "Laws of the Foundations of the Torah," chapter 2 and the seventh of Maimonides' 'Thirteen principles', in conjunction with "Logical Terms," chapter 14. The equivalence: angel = separate intellect is made explicitly in the *Guide of the Perplexed*. See I.49 (pp. 108–10), II.4 (p. 258), II.6 (p. 262), II.7 (p. 266), II.10 (p. 273), and II.12 (p. 280). Further on Maimonides on angels, see chapter eight in *Maimonides' Confrontation with Mysticism* (above, note 1).

17. The Active Intellect, the last of the separate intellects, and the immediate source of prophecy. See *Guide of the Perplexed* II.4, and II.36 (p. 369).

18. I.e., the question of human immortality, life after death. This is not the place for an extended discussion of Maimonides' extremely intellectualist account of human immortality. Suffice it to say that for Maimonides the *sole* criterion for achieving a share in the world to come is intellectual perfection (after moral perfection, which is achieved by Jews through obedience to the commandments). For details, see Kellner, *Maimonides on Human Perfection*, pp. 1–5 and Kellner, *Maimonides on Judaism and the Jewish People* (Albany: SUNY Press, 1991), pp. 29–32. In this passage here, Maimonides has just listed the main topics of metaphysics.

19. I.e., physics and metaphysics.

20. Note well: the Sages considered physics and metaphysics important.

21. I.e., the Tannaim whose views are cited in *Hagigah* II:1.

22. I.e., discursively, and to anyone who wishes to learn.

23. An obvious reference to the opening sentence of Aristotle's *Metaphysics*: "All humans by nature desire to know." Humans, after all, are rational animals; knowing is the activity unique to them. It is no surprise that truly human beings have a great desire for knowledge.

Greek and contemporary Muslim philosophers called metaphysics. One of the main subjects of physics is the question of the creation or eternity of the world; one of the main subjects of metaphysics is the proof of God's existence.

Connecting all this to the passage quoted above from the Introduction to the *Guide of the Perplexed*, we see that Maimonides indeed maintains that the Torah opens with the creation account since that account teaches physics; physics must be studied before one attempts the study of metaphysics; the study of metaphysics must be undertaken if one is to actualize one's potential as a human being.

On the face of things, Rashi and Maimonides seem worlds apart. But are they? Rashi opens his commentary on the Torah by wondering why it does not begin with the first law addressed to the Jews as such. In other words, Rashi sees the Torah as essentially a book of laws; the presence in it of anything but laws must be explained.[24] But remember, Maimonides opened the passage about creation quoted above as follows: "God, may His mention be exalted, wished us to be perfected and the state of our societies to be improved by His laws regarding actions." Thus for Maimonides, too, the Torah appears to be nothing but a book of laws. But what sort of laws? In the body of this essay I shall show that while both Rashi and Maimonides agree that the Torah is a book of laws, they disagree mightily on the nature of those laws and the reasons for which they were commanded. But first, I want briefly to allude to other ways in which they disagree, disagree-

---

24. Compare Elazar Touitou, "Between Exegesis and Ethics: The World-View of the Torah According to Rashi's Commentary," in Sarah Yafet (ed.), *Ha-Mikra Be-Re'i Meforshav: Sefer Zikkaron Le-Sarah Kamin* (Jerusalem: Magnes, 1994), 312–34, p. 312 (Hebrew). Abraham Grossman is the author of a series of important studies on what might be called Rashi's *weltanschaung*. See his Hebrew book, *Rashi* (Jerusalem: Merkaz Zalman Shazar, 2006) and, most recently, "Studying Rashi's 'Jewish Worldview'," in Shmuel Glick (ed.), *Zekhor Davar Le-Avdekha: Asufat Ma'amarim Le-Zekher Dov Raffel* (Jerusalem: Churgin School of Education, 2007): 283–298 (Hebrew). Other studies by Grossman on Rashi as thinker include: "Martyrdom in the Eleventh and Twelfth Centuries: Ashkenaz vs. The Lands of Islam," *Pe'amim* 75–76 (1998): 27–46 (Hebrew); and, "Exile and Redemption in Rashi's Thought," in Yossi Barukhi (ed.), *Me-Shi'abud Le-Ge'ulah, Me-Pesah Ad Shavu'ot* (Merkaz Shapira: Or Etzion, 1996): 230–266 (Hebrew).

ments expressed in the two passages with which we began this study.

It is obvious that Rashi reads the Torah particularistically, Maimonides universalistically.[25] For Rashi the message of Genesis 1 is that God created the cosmos so that the Torah could be given to the Jews. For Maimonides the message of Genesis 1 consists in the laws of physics, laws which are universal, understandable to all, and applicable to all.[26] But there are other differences to be found here as well. As Moshe Idel perceptively noted in his presentation at the conference which generated this volume, for Rashi, creation vs. eternity is not a Jewish question. For Maimonides, on the other hand, it is a question of cardinal importance. He thus writes (*Guide of the Perplexed* II.25, p. 329):

> Know that with a belief in the creation of the world in time, all the miracles become possible and the Law becomes possible, and all questions that may be asked on this subject, vanish. Thus it might be said: Why did God give prophetic to this one and not to that? Why did God give this Law to this particular nation, and why did He not legislate to the others. Why did He legislate at this particular time, and why did He not legislate before it or after? Why did He impose these commandments and these prohibitions? Why did He privilege the prophet with the miracles mentioned in relation to him and not with some others? What was God's aim in giving this Law? Why did He not, if such was His purpose, put the accomplishment of the commandments and the non transgression of the prohibitions into our nature? If this

---

25. Compare: "Rashi answers his own question [apropos Gen 1:1] with the most narrowly nationalistic answer possible…" See p. 184 in Gordon Lafer, "Universalism and Particularism in Jewish Law: Making Sense of Political Loyalties," in David Theo Goldberg and Michael Krausz (eds.), *Jewish Identity* (Philadelphia: Temple University Press, 1993), pp. 177–211. On Maimonides' universalism, see *Maimonides' Confrontation with Mysticism* (above, note 1), *passim* and especially pp. 250–264.

26. I develop this point in "Overcoming Chosenness," in Raphael Jospe, Truman Madsen, Seth Ward (eds.), *Covenant and Chosenness in Judaism and Mormonism,* (Fairlawn: Associated University Presses, 2001): 147–172.

were said, the answer to all these questions would be that it would be said: He wanted it this way; or His wisdom required it this way.

Creation is thus not *a* Jewish question, it is *the* Jewish question. With creation, the Torah (as an expression of God's will) becomes possible; without creation, we find ourselves in an uncreated Aristotelian cosmos, one in which there is no room for God's will.

Perhaps a good way of accessing this point is to note that Rashi and Maimonides both agree that we need revelation in order to know God's law, not in order to know philosophical truths.[27] Since Rashi thinks that knowing philosophical truths is unimportant Jewishly,[28] he wonders why the Torah begins with a philosophical topic, creation. Since Maimonides thinks that philosophical truth is the essence of Judaism, his Torah must begin with a discussion of the physics of creation (expressed in poetic, mythic language).[29]

---

27. For Maimonides there is an important exception to this generalization, namely, creation; but the basic point here is unaffected by this.

28. Compare Touitou, "Between Exegesis and Ethics..." p. 333.

29. Another obvious point of contention between Rashi and Maimonides concerns God's corporeality. For Maimonides, as is well-known, attributing corporeality to God is tantamount to idolatry (for one example of many, see *Guide of the Perplexed* I.36). I have no idea whether Rashi's God was corporeal or incorporeal, and, if the latter, in a sense acceptable to Maimonides. But it is fairly clear that the whole matter was not an issue of concern for him. Otherwise, he would not have allowed himself to say that the hand of God mentioned in Ex 7:5 means *yad mamash le-hakot bahem* ("an actual hand with which to smite them"). Rashi's intention here is made clear in his gloss to Ex. 14:31, discussed by Richard Steiner in "Saadia vs. Rashi: On the Shift from Meaning-Maximalism to Meaning-Minimalism in Medieval Biblical Lexicology," *Jewish Quarterly Review* 88 (1998): 213–58, at pp. 240–241. Steiner explains that "Rashi felt that words have only one basic meaning from which all of the contextual meanings are derived, and that the task of the lexicographer is to find that meaning" (p. 213). In other words, Rashi appears to be making a linguistic point, that the essential meaning of the word *yad* is "physical hand" (as opposed to "monument," for example) — this is a comment about how to understand the word *yad* in context, not a comment about God's corporeality, an issue which was not on Rashi's radar at all. For other examples of Rashi's equanimity in the face of attributions of corporeality to God, see his glosses to Gen. 1:27, Ex. 12:2, Ex. 15:2, and Ex. 33:23 and his comment to Eruvin 21a (s.v., *esrim be-amah*). Rashi's casual anthropomorphism shows that the issue was of no interest to him, even though his close study of Onkelos makes it unlikely that he was wholly unaware of the issue. On the medieval and modern debates over Onkelos' alleged opposition to anthropomorphism, see *Maimonides' Confrontation with Myticism* (above, note 1), pp. 177 and 193–197. While Rashi was apparently uninterested in whether or not

Having made these introductory points, we may now actually compare Rashi and Maimonides on the nature of the law taught in the Torah. A convenient point of access to this discussion is Rashi's gloss to Genesis 26:5.[30] Because of a famine in the land of Israel, Isaac considers going to Egypt. God tells him not to, in the following words:

> *Do not go down to Egypt; stay in the land which I point out to you. Reside in this land, and I will be with you and bless you; I will assign all these lands to you and your offspring, fulfilling the oath that I swore to your father Abraham. I will make your descendants as numerous as the stars of the heaven, and give to your descendants all these lands, so that all the nations of the earth shall bless themselves by thy offspring — inasmuch as Abraham obeyed Me and kept my charge: My commandments, my statutes, and My teachings.*

God was corporeal or incorporeal, he was very much aware of other theological issues, especially some of those relating to Christian attacks on Judaism. See the fascinating discussion in Elazar Touitou, "Rashi's Commentary on Genesis 1–6 in the Context of Judeo-Christian Controversy," *Hebrew Union College Annual* 61 (1990): 159–83. Other studies on Rashi as anti-Christian polemicist include the following essays by Avraham Grossman: "Rashi's Commentary to Psalms and Jewish-Christian Polemic," in Dov Rappel (ed.), *Mehkarim Bi-Mikra U-Ve-Hinnukh Mugashim Le-Prof. Moshe Arend* (Jerusalem: Touro College, 1996): 59–74; "Religious Polemics and Educational Trends in Rashi's Commentary to the Torah," in Moshe Arend et al (eds.), *Pirkei Nechama: Prof. Nechama Leibowitz Memorial Volume* (Jerusalem: Eliner, 2001): 187–205 (Hebrew); and, "The Text of Rashi's Commentary to Nakh and the Jewish-Christian Debate," *Sinai* 137 (2006): 32–66 (Hebrew). Earlier studies on the subject include Ephraim E. Urbach, "Rabbinic Homilies, Origen's Commentaries on Song of Songs, and the Jewish-Christian Debate," *Tarbiz* 30 (1961): 148–170 (Hebrew) and Sara Kamin, *Rashi — Peshuto Shel Mikra u-Midrasho shel Mikra* (Jerusalem: Magnes, 1986), pp. 247–262. Shaye J. D. Cohen, on the other hand, argues that in his Torah commentary Rashi ignores Christianity. See his "Does Rashi's Torah Commentary Respond to Christianity? A Comparison of Rashi with Rashbam and Behor Shor," in Judith H. Newman and Hindy Najman (eds.), *The Idea of Biblical Interpretation: Essays in Honor of James L. Kugel* (Leiden: Brill, 2004): 449–472. Cohen does find an engagement with Christianity in Rashi's commentary on Psalms, but not in his commentary on the Pentateuch.

30. It was while listening to a d'var Torah by David Novak in Nashville's Congregation Sherith Israel that I was struck by the depth of the difference between Rashi and Maimonides on these matters. My thanks to David for an excellent d'var Torah and to Lenn Goodman for bringing us both to Nashville that Shabbat.

On the last verse, Rashi comments as follows:

> *Abraham obeyed me* — "when I tested him."
>
> *and kept My charge* — these are the precautionary decrees instituted by the Sages, which are intended to make us avoid the violation of Biblical laws, such as second degrees of forbidden marriages and certain prohibited acts on the Sabbath."
>
> *My commandments* — "these are precepts which, had they had not been written in the Torah, were requisite to have been written, such as robbery and murder."
>
> *My statutes* — these are matters against which the evil inclination and the nations of the world argue, such as the prohibition of eating the swine and the wearing of garments woven of wool and linen, there being no apparent rationale for them except that they are decrees of the King imposed on His subjects."
>
> *and my teachings* — "the plural is intended to include, [besides the Written Law], the Oral Law as well as those rules given to Moses from Sinai."[31]

While there is obviously much to be said about these glosses, here I want to restrict myself to one point: it is clear that Rashi subscribed to the rabbinic teaching that the patriarchs obeyed the commandments of the Torah, and the later prohibitions of the Rabbinic sages.[32] I will argue below that Maimonides did not subscribe to that teaching and will further argue that this disagreement between Rashi and Maimonides has some far-reaching implications.

A staple of rabbinic literature is the idea that the Patriarchs

---

31. I cite Rashi as translated by Charles B. Chavel in his translation of Ramban on Genesis (who quotes Rashi) (New York: Shilo, 1971), p. 329. It is worth noting that Rashi's grandson, Rashbam, in his commentary on our verse, seems to go out his way to deny the claim that Abraham observed the commandments of the Torah. My thanks to Martin Lockshin for drawing my attention to this.

32. See also Rashi's gloss to Gen. 7:2, in which he affirms that Noah studied Torah.

observed all the 613 commandments of the Torah.[33] This idea is expressed in a variety of places, including Mishnah Kiddushin IV.14,[34] Yoma 28b, Nedarim 32a, and J Ber 2.3/4c. This view has become very popular in traditionalist Judaism today, and was held by some important early authorities (e.g., Nahmanides on Gen. 26:5).[35]

So far as I (and many kind friends) was able to discover, Maimonides makes no explicit reference to this idea anywhere in his writings.[36] There are plenty of good reasons for him to have rejected the notion. As we shall see, it is incompatible with "Laws

---

33. For discussion, see Arthur Green, *Devotion and Commandment: The Faith of Abraham in the Hasidic Imagination* (Cincinnati, Hebrew Union College Press, 1989), pp. 9–10, 25 and 30–41; see also pp. 181*-187* in Uriel Simon, "Peshat Exegesis of Biblical Historiography: Historicism, Dogmatism, and Medievalism," in Barry Eichler, Mordechai Cogan, and Jeffrey Tigay (eds), *Tehillah le-Moshe: Biblical and Judaic studies in Honor of Moshe Greenberg* (Winona Lake IN: Eisenbrauns, 1997): 171*-203* (Hebrew); and Jon D. Levenson, "The Conversion of Abraham to Judaism, Christianity, and Islam," in Judith H. Newman and Hindy Najman (eds.), *The Idea of Biblical Interpretation: Essays in Honor of James L. Kugel* (Leiden: Brill, 2004), pp. 3–40, esp. 23 and 25.

34. The relevant part of the mishnaic text is missing in Maimonides' edition; he obviously did not comment on it. On the textual issues, see J. N. Epstein, *Mavo le-Nusah ha-Mishnah* (Jerusalem: Magnes, 2000), Vol. 2, pp. 976–977 and Saul Lieberman, *Tosefta ke-Feshutah* (New York: Jewish Theological Seminary of America, 1973), Part 8 (Seder Nashim), p. 986. Lieberman there cites a lengthy list of texts in which the idea of patriarchal obedience to the commandments is mention. My thanks to Hillel Newman for sending me to these sources.

35. I discuss this subject further in "Did the Torah Precede the Cosmos? — A Maimonidean Study," *Da'at* 61 (2007) [=Yohanan Silman Festschrift]: 83–96 (Hebrew).

36. Although, as Raphael Jospe reminded me, there is an explicit denial that the Patriarchs observed the commandments in a letter purported to have been written by Maimonides to one Hasdai ha-Levi. The text is translated in Twersky, *A Maimonides Reader* (New York: Behrman House, 1972), p. 478. Unfortunately (indeed! there are other ideas in this text for which I would love to have clear Maimonidean textual warrant) the two scholars who have closely examined this text both agree (on independent grounds) that it cannot be properly attributed to Maimonides. See Ya'akov Levinger, *Ha-Rambam ke-Philosoph u-ke-Posek* (Jerusalem: Mossad Bialik, 1989), pp. 167–171 and Y. Sheilat's edition of *Iggerot ha-Rambam* (Jerusalem: Ma'aliyot, 1988), vol. 2, pp. 683–687. Furthermore, in his introduction to the Mishnah Maimonides says that "there was no halakhah in the time of Shem and Ever." See Y. Sheilat, *Hakdamot ha-Rambam le-Mishnah* (Jerusalem: Ma'aliyot, 1992), p. 55. In Rabbi Kafih's dual language edition, *Mishnah im Perush Rabbenu Mosheh ben Maimon*, 6 vols. (Jerusalem: Mossad ha-Rav Kook, 1963–1967), vol. 1, it is on p. 39 and in Fred Rosner's English translation, *Moses Maimonides' Commentary on the Mishnah* (New York: Feldheim, 1975) it is on p. 119.

of Idolatry," I, according to which Abraham taught philosophical monotheism, which, it turns out, could not hold its own against the pressure of idolatry, and had to be later supplemented with the 613 commandments of the Torah. "Laws of Kings," IX.1 also militates against the possibility that Maimonides accepted the notion under discussion. In that text, Maimonides lists the single commandment given to each of the Patriarchs (circumcision, in the case of Abraham; tithes, in the case of Isaac; and the prohibition of eating the sinew of the thigh, in the case of Jacob). I have also found a passage in the *Guide of the Perplexed* relevant to the issue (III.49, pp. 603–604):

> From the story of *Judah* a noble moral habit and equity in conduct may be learnt; this appears from [Judah's] words: *Let her take it, lest we be put to shame; behold, I sent this kid* (Gen. 38:23). Before the *giving of the Torah* sexual intercourse with a *harlot* was regarded in the same way as sexual intercourse with one's wife is regarded after the *giving of the Torah*. I mean to say that it was a permitted act that did not by any means arouse repugnance.

Judah's behavior is here explained by the fact that before giving the Torah, sex with a prostitute was not forbidden. Maimonides' point is not that the patriarch Judah flouted the prohibition against having sexual intercourse with a prostitute; rather, he explicitly says that for the Patriarch Judah (and by implication the other Patriarchs) sex with a prostitute in his day was permitted in the same way as sexual intercourse with one's wife was permitted after the giving of the Torah. Just as sexual intercourse within marriage after the giving of the Torah arouses no repugnance, so sexual intercourse with a prostitute before the giving of the Torah aroused no repugnance. I do not know if Maimonides was consciously trying to signal his rejection of the idea that the Patriarchs observed the commandments, but that certainly appears to be the upshot of this passage.

Indirect proof that Maimonides rejected the idea that the Patriarchs observed all the commandments of the Torah may be found in an examination of his attitude towards the idea of ante-mundane Torah. While there is no logical connection between the belief that the Patriarchs observed the commandments and the belief that the Torah pre-exists the Cosmos, it will surely come as no surprise that the two views go hand in hand. Rashi certainly held that the Torah pre-exists the Cosmos since, as we saw in his commentary on Genesis 1:1, he maintains that the entire Cosmos was brought into existence so that the Torah could be given to the people of Israel. Technically, all one can infer from this is that Rashi held that the *idea* of the Torah pre-exists the Cosmos, but I think no reader will quibble with me over this, especially in light of the wide acceptance of the idea of an ante-mundane Torah in medieval and post-medieval Judaism. Despite this wide acceptance, there are actually only a small number of rabbinic texts which teach that the Torah pre-exists the Cosmos.[37] Thus, for example, Mishnah Avot III.14 states that the Torah is a "desirable instrument" (*kli hemdah*) through which the world was created. In some early midrashim, God is depicted as, in effect, using the Torah as a template or blueprint for creation.[38] According to the eighth century midrash, *Chapters of Rabbi Eliezer* (*Pirkei de-Rabbi Eliezer*) (chapter 3), seven things were created before the world: "The Torah, Gehenna, the Garden of Eden, the Throne of Glory, the Temple, Repentance, and the name of the Messiah."[39] We shall

---

37. There are biblical antecedents for this. In Proverbs 3:19 and 8:22–36 wisdom is described as ante-mundane. On this, see Naomi G. Cohen, "Context and Connotation: Greek Words for Jewish Concepts in Philo," in James L. Kugel (ed.), *Shem in the Tents of Japhet: Essays on the Encounter of Judaism and Hellenism* (Leiden: Brill, 2002): 31–61, p. 46.

38. Genesis Rabbah I.1, I.4, and VIII.2. For other texts along the same lines, see Ephraim Urbach, "Seridei Tanhuma-Yelamdenu," *Kovetz al-Yad* 14 (NS, no.6), pt 1 (1966), pp., 1–54, at page 20.

39. In this, *Chapters of Rabbi Eliezer* apparently reflects Pesahim 54a, which presents the list in the following order: "The Torah, repentance, the Garden of Eden, Gehenna, the Throne of Glory, the Temple, and the name of the Messiah." Compare Midrash on Psalms, 90:12; in 93:3 God is represented as having *thought* of the Torah (and other things) before creation, not that the Torah was already in existence before creation. Passages from *Chapters of Rabbi Eliezer* will be cited from Gerald Friedlander (ed. and trans.) *Pirke de Rabbi Eliezer* (New York: Hermon Press, 1965), with emendations (to bring it line with Pines' translation of the *Guide*). *Chapters of Rabbi Eliezer*, it is interesting (and, given Maimonides' problems with it, not surprising)

return to this particular text below. Another expression of this idea is found in Shabbat 88b:

> R. Joshua b. Levi also said: When Moses ascended on high, the ministering angels spake before the Holy One, blessed be He:
>
> "Sovereign of the Universe! What business has one born of woman amongst us?"
>
> "He has come to receive the Torah," answered He to them.
>
> Said they to Him: "That secret treasure, which has been hidden by Thee for nine hundred and seventy-four generations before the world was created, Thou desirest to give to flesh and blood! *What is man, that thou art mindful of him, And the son of man, that thou visitest him?* (Ps. 8:5) *O Lord our God, How excellent is thy name in all the earth! Who hast set thy splendor[40] upon the Heavens!* (Ps. 8:2)[41]

The Torah, God's "secret treasure," is presented here as pre-existing the world by 974 generations.[42]

There are perhaps a dozen places in rabbinic literature in which this idea finds clear expression.[43] It has had quite an

---

to note, is one of the principal "rabbinic" sources of the Zohar. See Pinchas Giller, *Reading the Zohar: The Sacred Text of the Kabbalah* (New York: Oxford University Press, 2001), p. 11. For an interesting side-light on the text from Pesahim cited here see the discussion of Isaac Abravanel's use of it in Alfredo Fabio Borodowski, *Isaac Abravanel on Miracles, Creation, Prophecy, and Evil: The Tension Between Medieval Jewish Philosophy and Biblical Commentary* (New York: Peter Lang, 2003), pp. 114–116.

40. Here understood as signifying the Torah.

41. I cite the Soncino translation.

42. I.e, a thousand generations before Sinai. See Rashi *ad loc.*

43. For discussion, see Ephraim Urbach, *The Sages* (Jerusalem: Magnes, 1975), pp. 180–182. See also Gen R 49:2 in which God is presented as giving a new interpretation of the Torah every day, and the description of the "academy on high" in BM 86a. Both stories reflect a view of Torah as in some sense existing independently of God. See further p. 921 in Marc Hirshman, "Torah in Rabbinic Thought: The Theology of Learning," in Steven Katz (ed.), *The Cambridge History of Judaism* Vol. 4 (Cambridge: Cambridge University Press, 2006): 899–924.

impressive afterlife, however.[44] One example of that, as already noted, is found in the commentary of Rashi to Gen. 1:1, in which it is implied that the cosmos was created so that the Torah could be given to the Jews.[45] The idea was also to become very important in kabbalistic texts.[46]

That most enigmatic of ancient Jewish texts, *Sefer Yezirah*, has a role to play in this discussion. If the book is as ancient as some scholars think, and if it indeed teaches that the cosmos was created out of the letters of the Hebrew alphabet, then it may at the very least hint at the notion of the ante-mundane Torah, which is, after all, the quintessential Hebrew document.[47]

---

44. It was a popular motif in piyyutim, ancient synagogue poetry. See Leon J Weinberger, *Jewish Hymnography: A Literary History* (London: Littman Library of Jewish Civilization, 1998), pp. 54 and 69; and Michael D Swartz, "Ritual About Myth About Ritual: Towards an Understanding of the Avodah in the Rabbinic Period," *Journal of Jewish Thought and Philosophy* 6 (1997): 135–155. Compare also Yizhak Baer, *Mehkarim u-Masot be-Toldot Yisrael* (Jerusalem: Israel Historical Society, 1987), Vol, 1, pp. 111–112.

45. See Chaim Pearl, *Rashi* (New York: Grove Press, 1988), p. 49. Rashi's comment, of course, could be interpreted as teaching that God *planned* to create the Torah and give it to the Jews *after* the creation of the cosmos, but that, to my mind, is a useless quibble since, even on this interpretation, the idea of the Torah pre-exists creation.

46. See most recently, and in great detail, Moshe Idel's absorbing book, *Absorbing Perfections: Kabbalah and Interpretation* (New Haven: Yale University Press), 2002. The entire book is relevant, but see pp. 31–53, and pp. 358–389 in particular. For an earlier study, which connects the idea of the ante-mundane Torah to magic, see Gershom Scholem, *On the Kabbalah and its Symbolism* (New York: Schocken, 1969), pp. 38–40. See also, Moshe Idel, "Midrashic versus Other Forms of Jewish Hermeneutics: Some Comparative Reflections," in Michael Fishbane (ed.), *The Midrashic Imagination: Jewish Exegesis, Thought, and History* (Albany: SUNY Press, 1993), pp. 45–58.

47. See Ithamar Gruenwald, "Ha-Ketav, ha-Mikhtav, and the Articulated Name — Magic, Spirituality and Mysticism," in Michal Oron and Amos Goldreich (eds.), *Masu'ot: Mehkarim ... le-Zikhro shel Prof. Ephraim Gotlieb* (Jerusalem: Mossad Bialik, 1994), pp. 75–98, and Milka Rubin, "The Language of Creation or the Primordial Language: A Case of Cultural Polemics in Antiquity," *Journal of Jewish Studies* 49 (1998): 306–333. Gershom Scholem summarizes the attitude of many generations of Jewish mystics to the notion of an ante-mundane Torah in the following passage: ...all Jewish mystics, from the Therapeutae, whose doctrine was described by Philo of Alexandria, to the latest Hasid, are at one in giving a mystical interpretation to the Torah; the Torah is to them a living organism animated by a secret life which streams and pulsates below the crust of its literal meaning: every one of the innumerable strata of this hidden region corresponds to a new and profound meaning of the Torah. The Torah, in other words, does not consist merely of chapters, phrases and words; rather it is to be regarded as the living incarnation of the divine wisdom which eternally sends out new rays of light. It is not merely the

Was Maimonides familiar with this notion of a pre-existent Torah?[48] Undoubtedly — he certainly knew the texts just cited and quotes one of them himself, as we shall see immediately. Did he accept it as literally true? There is very little reason to think so. Harry Austryn Wolfson analyzed the notion of what he calls a "primordial" Torah in post-rabbinic texts and showed that a long line of thinkers was familiar with the idea, but refused to take it literally.[49] In particular, Sa'adia did not feel bound by the literal meaning of the idea.[50] Even Judah Halevi, in *Kuzari* III.73, refuses to take the idea literally, understanding it as an expression God's ante-mundane intention to give the Torah to Israel.[51] Maimonides, I want to show here, was aware of the idea and consciously rejected it. This rejection is important, not just for what it teaches concerning the issue at hand, but for what it indicates about Maimonides' notion of Torah generally.

Let us first quote and analyze the relevant passage from *Chapters of Rabbi Eliezer*:

> R. Eliezer ben Hyrcanos opened and said: ... seven things
> were created before the creation of the world: the Torah,

---

historical law of the Chosen People, although it is that too; it is rather, the cosmic law of the Universe, as God's wisdom conceived it. Each configuration of letters in it, whether it makes sense in human speech or not, symbolizes some aspect of God's creative power which is active in the universe.

See his *Major Trends in Jewish Mysticism* (New York: Schocken, 1954), pp. 13–14.

48. Not every doctrine taken as "orthodox" today was even known to Maimonides, let alone accepted by him. For an important example of this, see M. Kellner, *Maimonides on the 'Decline of the Generations' and the Nature of Rabbinic Authority* (Albany: SUNY Press, 1996).

49. Harry A. Wolfson, *Repercussions of the Kalam in Jewish Philosophy* (Cambridge: Harvard University Press, 1979), pp. 85–113. Wolfson's discussion also focuses on the Islamic idea of a pre-existent Koran. It may be that part of Maimonides' motivation in denying the pre-existence of the Torah is to polemicize against this Islamic doctrine. Similarly, the connection between Torah and logos (as implied in John 1:1 and many other places) may have played a role in bringing Maimonides quietly to take issue with the notion of a pre-existent Torah.

50. See Wolfson, pp. 92–93 and Alexander Altmann, "Saadya's Theory of Revelation: Its Origin and Background," in E.I.J. Rosenthal (ed.), *Saadya Studies* (Manchester: Manchester University Press, 1943), pp. 4–25.

51. See p. 141 in Salo Wittmayer Baron, "Yehudah Halevi: An Answer to an Historical Challenge," *Ancient and Medieval Jewish History: Essays by Salo Wittmayer Baron*, ed. Leon A. Feldman (New Brunswick: Rutgers University Press, 1972): 128–148.

Gehenna, the Garden of Eden, the Throne of Glory, the Temple, Repentance, and the name of the Messiah… Forthwith, the Holy One, Blessed be He, took council with the Torah, whose name is *Tushiyah*,[52] with reference to creation of the world. … Wherefrom were the heavens created? From the light of His garment.[53] He took some of it, stretched it like a cloth, and thus they were extending continually, as it said: Who coverest Thyself with light as with a garment. *Who stretchest out the heavens like a curtain* (Ps. 104:2). Wherefrom was the earth created? From the snow under the throne of His glory. He took some of it and threw it, as it is said: *For he saith to the snow, Be thou earth* (Job 37:6).

This text may be understood as teaching that reward and punishment (Gehenna and the Garden of Eden) precede creation; in other words, right and wrong are not socially determined,[54] but part of the very fabric of the Universe. In this context, the inclusion of the Temple, the site at which Jews brought the sacrifices which atoned for their sins, makes excellent sense: God knows that people will sin, and graciously created the tools for overcoming sin (sacrificial cult and repentance) even before creating the world. By including Messiah in this list, the authors of this text make clear that in their eyes the destruction of the Temple is part of a much larger historical plan, and that exile will ultimately eventuate in redemption. To teach that God "consulted" the Torah in order to create the cosmos implies that nature is not value-neutral. But it can be taken to imply much more; it can and

---

52. I.e., "resourcefulness."
53. For the use of similar expressions in Hekhalot literature see Gershom Scholem, *Jewish Gnosticism, Merkabah Mysticism, and Talmudic Tradition* (New York: Jewish Theological Seminary, 1960), pp. 58–64; Scholem, *On the Mystical Shape of the Godhead: Basic Concepts in the Kabbalah* (New York: Schocken, 1991), p. 29; and Raphael Loewe, "The Divine Garment and Shi'ur Komah," *Harvard Theological Review* 58 (1965): 153–160. Might Maimonides' discussion of this text, analyzed below, be, among other things, a silent polemic against the use of this expression in Hekhalot texts?
54. Maimonides *appears* to have held that right and wrong are socially determined (*Guide of the Perplexed* I.2); see above, note 6.

was taken to imply that the cosmos reflects the Torah and that the Torah, in a real sense, is therefore linked to the nature of the universe at the deepest possible levels. A thinker who takes this view seriously will be led to believe that the ceremonial laws of the Torah are not simply historically conditioned institutions, many or perhaps all of which could be other than they are. No, such ceremonials reflect an antecedent reality, itself conditioned by the ante-mundane Torah. A person who takes this view is likely to arrive (as did Nahmanides) at the view that Torah and nature are one and the same thing; there is no objective nature which follows its own immanent and essential character[55] — it is all Torah.[56] Such a person would have to be convinced (as were figures like Halevi and Nahmanides) that obedience to these laws was directly beneficial to the Jew who obeyed them, and that disobedience to them was directly harmful to the Jew who disobeyed them.[57]

Maimonides' treatment of the idea of an ante-mundane Torah is thus more important than the question of how he understood a particular midrashic motif — it goes to the very heart of his view of Torah and cosmos. Maimonides discusses our passage from the *Chapters of Rabbi Eliezer* in several places in the *Guide for the Perplexed*. Let us look at two of them.

Discussing God's names in *Guide of the Perplexed* I. 61 (148–149) Maimonides writes:

> …Hence Scripture promises that an apprehension that will put an end to this delusion [that God has many attributes] will come to men. Thus it says: *In that day shall the Lord be one, and His name one* (Zech. 14:9); which means that in the same way as He is one, He will be invoked at that time by one name only, by that which is indicative

---

55. In our language: which follows its own immanent laws.
56. I owe the ideas in this paragraph to discussions with Jolene S. Kellner.
57. This helps us to understand the particularism of Halevi and Nahmanides: the Torah reflects reality; the Jews have the Torah, all other people live at a lower level of reality (and I dare add, of goodness) than do the Jews; what they do, what becomes of them, these matters are much less important than what Jews do and what becomes of them.

only of His essence and which is not derivative. In the *Chapters of Rabbi Eliezer* they have said: *Before the world was created there were only the Holy One, blessed be He, and His name.* Consider how this dictum states clearly that all the derivative names have come into being after the world has come into being.

What is at stake here is God's unity (which, for Maimonides, also means God's uniqueness). Had anything existed with God before creation, God's uniqueness would be put in doubt. Maimonides uses a text from *Chapters of Rabbi Eliezer* to prove that such was not the case: before creation *nothing* whatsoever existed but God and God's name.[58] Maimonides' use of this text in our context is particularly suggestive, since the passage quoted by Maimonides is followed almost immediately by the text cited above, concerning the seven things which were created (and thus already existed) before the creation of the cosmos. In itself, then, Maimonides' source does not really teach what Maimonides wants it to teach, that nothing existed with God (even "temporarily") before creation. His use of selective quotation here may very well be meant to hint to his reader that the sequel in *Chapters of Rabbi Eliezer* should be read in light of the message of the earlier text; namely that nothing coexisted with God before creation.[59] This interpretation is supported by an earlier passage (which may be construed as hinting at our text in *Chapters of Rabbi Eliezer*).

Guide of the Perplexed I.9 (pp. 34–35) is devoted to the term "throne" (*kisse*). Maimonides explains that the term indicates

---

58. In his introduction to his commentary on the Torah, Nahmanides famously maintained that the Torah was indeed the name of God. I doubt that he made this claim in order to avoid the conclusion that I think ought to be derived from Maimonides' comment here (that the Torah did not pre-exist the cosmos); rather, this is one more reflection, as if one were needed, of the vast gulf between Maimonides and Nahmanides.

59. Another relevant text: Avot V.5 teaches that ten things were created at twilight (of the sixth day of creation); among these are the *ketav* and the *mikhtav*. In his commentary to this text Maimonides explains that the former refers to the written Torah and the latter to the tablets of the decalogue. That being so, not only did the Torah not pre-exist the world, it was one of the last things created. My thanks to James Diamond for pointing these texts out to me.

grandeur, high rank, and dignity. Thus, the heavens are called "throne" since they bear witness (to those who study them properly) to God's greatness, grandeur, and power. He goes on to explain:

> The matter is just as we have pointed out: namely, every place such as the *Sanctuary* or the heaven, distinguished by God to receive His light and splendor, is called a *throne*. The term is given a wider meaning in the Hebrew language when it says: *For my hand upon the throne of the Lord* (Ex. 17:16). What is meant is the attribute of His greatness and sublimity; this ought not to be imagined as a thing outside His essence or as a created being from among the beings created by Him, so that He, may He be exalted should appear to exist both without a *throne* and with a *throne*. That would be infidelity beyond any doubt. For it states explicitly: *Thou, O Lord, sittest for all eternity, Thy throne is from generation to generation* (Lam. 5:19); whereby it indicates that the throne is a thing inseparable from Him. Hence the term *throne* signifies, in this passage and in all those similar to it, His sublimity and greatness and do not constitute a thing existing outside His essence, as will be explained in some of the chapters of this Treatise. (p. 35)

To say that something exists alongside God before creation is "infidelity [i.e., heresy] beyond any doubt."[60] Maimonides talks of the throne here but there is no doubt that the same reservation applies any other entity thought to exist, along with God, before creation. It is likely that his strong language reflects his abhorrence of the idea that anything might be co-eternal with God. As he notes elsewhere: "For the purpose of every follower of the Law

---

60. Indeed, "Laws of Repentance," III.7 states the same point in a halakhic context, calling a person who holds that anything exits along with God before creation a sectarian (*min*) and excluding that person from the world to come. One wonders how Maimonides squared this with his claim in *Guide of the Perplexed* II.25 to the effect that Plato's doctrine of creation was Jewishly acceptable.

of Moses and Abraham our Father or of those who go the way of these two is to believe that there is nothing eternal in any way at all existing simultaneously with God..." (*Guide* II.13, p. 285). In *Guide* I. 68 he calls this belief a "foundation of the Torah," writing: "We have mentioned this likewise in our great compilation, since this, as we have made clear there, is one of the foundations of our Law; I mean the fact that He is one only and that no other thing can be added to Him, I mean to say that there is no eternal thing other than He" (p. 163). But could not one say that God created the Torah, throne, etc., and then created the "rest" of the cosmos? I think that Maimonides would respond as follows: there was no "before" before creation (time, as I will note below, being one of the created things). Anything which exists with God "before" creation is by definition eternal and God is no longer one. It is for this reason that denial of any ante-mundane entities but God is a foundation of Judaism, and affirming such existents is "infidelity beyond any doubt."[61]

Maimonides' second explicit citation from the *Chapters of Rabbi Eliezer* is found in II.26 (330–332). This is a long passage, but worth quoting at length:

> I have seen a statement of *Rabbi Eliezer the Great*, figuring in the celebrated *Chapters* known as *Chapters of Rabbi Eliezer*, which is the strangest statement I have seen by one who follows the Law of *Moses our Master*. Here the text of the statement he made. He says: *Wherefrom were the heavens created? From the light of His garment. He took some of it, stretched it like a cloth, and thus they were*

---

61. Moshe Idel (*Absorbing Perfections*, p. 45) expresses the point made here as follows: "Ancient Jewish monotheism was generally uncomfortable with the idea of the preexistence of any entity to the creation of the world, a premise that would imperil the uniqueness of God as the single creator. The coexistence of an additional entity would produce a theological dynamics that would question the most singular religious achievement of ancient Judaism. Implicitly, allowing any role to such a founding and formative entity would reintroduce a type of myth that could recall the pagan mythology, where once again the relationship between the preexistent deities as a crucial condition for the cosmogonic process would be thrown into relief."

extending continually, as it said: Who coverest Thyself with light as with a garment. Who stretchest out the heavens like a curtain (Ps. 104:2). *Wherefrom was the earth created? From the snow under the throne of His glory. He took some of it and threw it, as it is said: For he saith to the snow, Be thou earth* (Job 37:6). This is the text of the statement he made there. Would that I knew what that *Sage* believed. Did he believe that it is impossible that something should come into being out of nothing and that there must necessarily be matter out of which that which is generated is produced? Did he for this reason seek to find *wherefrom were created* the heavens and the earth? However, whatever results from this answer, he ought to be asked: *Wherefrom was the light of His garment created? Wherefrom was the snow under the throne of glory itself created?* If, however, he wished to signify by *the light of His garment* an uncreated thing and similarly by the *throne of glory* something uncreated, this would be a great incongruity. For he would have admitted thereby the eternity of the world, if only as it is conceived according to Plato's opinion. As for the *throne of glory* belonging to the created things, the *Sages* state this expressly, but in a strange manner. For they say that it was created before the creation of the world. But the scriptural texts, in connection with it, do not refer in any way to creation, with the exception of David's statement: *The Lord hath established His throne in the heavens* (Ps. 103:19), which statement admits very well of figurative interpretation. ... Now, if *Rabbi Eliezer* believed in the eternity a parte ante of the *throne*, the latter must have been an attribute of God, and not a created body. But how is it possible for a thing to be generated from an attribute?[62]

Implying that "the light of God's garment" or "the throne of glory"

---

62. *Chapters of Rabbi Eliezer* 3 is also cited in II.30, p. 349; but the issue discussed there (temporal creation) is not directly related to our question.

were uncreated entities, existing alongside God before the creation of the Universe "would be a great incongruity."[63] Maimonides' continues and lays out the incongruities, along the way pointing out that the Scriptural basis for believing in ante-mundane existence is nearly nonexistent; the one verse which might be taken to teach this idea is easily interpreted metaphorically.

The throne of glory is one of the seven things which *Chapters of Rabbi Eliezer* teaches existed before creation; it beggars imagination to think that Maimonides would be any happier with any of the other six.[64] Believing that the Torah existed before creation, I submit, is, in Maimonides' eyes, "infidelity beyond any doubt" and leads to great incongruities.[65]

In an important sense, however, this whole discussion is "academic": for Maimonides it makes no sense whatsoever to speak of anything pre-existing the world, since time itself was created along with the cosmos. To speak of an ante-mundane Torah in any but the most allegorical sense is not only to commit a religious error, but it is also to make a logical blunder.[66]

---

63. For an interesting discussion of this passage, see pp. 212–213 in Y. Tzvi Langermann, "Cosmology and Cosmogony in *Doresh Reshumoth*, a Thirteenth-Century Commentary on the Torah," *Harvard Theological Review* 97 (2004): 199–227.

64. One might further note that, given his understandings of gehenna and the garden of Eden, Maimonides could not possibly take in any literal sense that they are ante-mundane. For gehenna and the garden of Eden, see his "Introduction to Perek Helek." A translation may be conveniently found in I. Twersky, *A Maimonides Reader* (New York: Behrman House, 1972), pp. 402–423; see pp. 423–424 in particular. It may be that Maimonides discusses the throne explicitly because of its centrality in ancient Jewish mysticism. For details, see Gershom Scholem, *Major Trends in Medieval Jewish Mysticism*, 3rd ed. (New York: Schocken, 1954), pp. 43–46, Meir Bar-Ilan, "The Throne of God: What is Under it. What is Opposite it. What is Near it," *Da'at* 15 (1985): 21–36 (Hebrew), and most recently, Nathaniel Deutsch, *The Gnostic Imagination: Gnosticism, Mandaeism, and Merkabah Mysticism* (Leiden: Brill, 1995), pp. 68–79.

65. Possibly relevant is the following from I.65 (p. 158): "I do not consider that … you require that the denial of the attribute of speech with reference to Him be explained to you. This is the case particularly in view of the general consensus of our community on the Torah being created. This is meant to signify that His speech that is ascribed to Him is created." Implied here is the claim that the Torah does not pre-exist the Cosmos, but that is not definite since it could be argued that God created the Cosmos and then immediately created the Torah.

66. On time as created, see *Guide of the Perplexed* II.13. Kenneth Seeskin has recently subjected Maimonides' discussion of creation to careful analysis. See his *Searching*

Maimonides does not accept the idea of an ante-mundane Torah.[67] That should be clear. We can further illuminate the issue if we take up what will turn out to be two points related to this one: why was the Torah given to Israel, and what is the nature of its laws?

According to Maimonides, God's choice of the Jews as the chosen people was actually a consequence of Abraham's discovery of God and not a historically necessary event. The founder of the Jewish people is the Patriarch Abraham. It is worth paying close attention to Maimonides' description of Abraham's career, as presented in the first chapter of "Laws Concerning Idolatry."[68] In this chapter, Maimonides presents what might be called a natural history of religion. The Bible presents its readers with an implicit problem: Given that Noah and his immediate descendants knew God, how did the world become entirely idolatrous by the time of Abraham, ten generations after Noah? Here is Maimonides' explanation:[69]

In the days of Enosh [Gen. 4:26; 5:7–11] mankind fell into

---

for a Distant God: The Legacy of Maimonides (New York: Oxford University Press, 2000), pp. 66–90 and "Maimonides, Spinoza, and the Problem of Creation," Jewish Themes in Spinoza's Philosophy, ed. Heidi M. Ravven and Lenn E. Goodman (Albany: SUNY Press, 2002) 115–130.

67. A further note might be added here. If Maimonides believed that the Torah actually pre-existed creation, he could hardly have interpreted the story of the Garden of Eden as he does in Guide of the Perplexed I.2 and II.30. On the basis of his (admittedly) allegorical account, humans were not in the first instance meant to observe commandments. The giving of the Torah is concession to human weakness, not part of the eternal divine plan, as it were. For a traditionalist reader who admits that Maimonides sees the story of Adam and Eve as an allegory, see R. Joseph Kafih's commentary to "Laws of the Sabbath;," V.3 in his monumental edition of the Mishneh Torah.

68. For a helpful discussion of this text, which supports the reading I am about to give it, see Lawrence Kaplan, "Maimonides on the Singularity of the Jewish People," Da'at 15 (1985): v–xxvii. For an interesting literary analysis, see Jonathan A. Cohen, "Maimonides as Literary Artist: The Philosopher Tells a Story," in Felice Ziskind (ed.), The Pardes Reader: Celebrating Twenty-Five Years of Learning (Jerusalem: Pardes Institute, 1997): 13–19.

69. I cite the translation of Bernard Septimus from his forthcoming translation of the Book of Knowledge for the Yale Judaica Series. I have eliminated almost all of Professor Septimus' extremely learned notes. It is my pleasant duty to thank him here for his kindness in furnishing me with an advance copy of his translation.

grave error; the wise of that generation turned brutish in counsel; and Enosh himself was among the errant. Their fallacy was to say as follows: "Since God created the stars and spheres to govern the world, set them on high, and granted them honor, and [since] they are ministers who serve Him, they deserve to be praised, extolled and honored. Indeed, it is the will of God (blessed be He) that [we] magnify and honor those whom He has magnified and honored, just as a king wants his servants and attendants to be honored — for this redounds to the honor of the king." Once this notion got into their heads, they began to build temples to the stars, offer them sacrifices, praise and extol them verbally, and bow down toward them, in order to win divine favor, by their corrupt lights. That was the root of alien worship.

Having explained the origin of idolatry,[70] Maimonides turns to describe Abraham's rebellion against it:

After much time had passed, false prophets arose among the human race, claiming that God had commanded them: "Worship such and such a star (or all the stars): offer it these sacrifices and libations; build it a temple; and fashion its image ... Thus it was that they began to make images in temples, under trees, atop mountains and on hills. They would come together, bow down to them, and tell the whole populace: "This image can help or harm, and ought to be worshiped and feared." The priests would then tell them: "Through this worship you will multiply and prosper: do such and such; don't do such and such." ... It thus became the universal practice to worship the [various] images with distinct rites, and to sacrifice and bow down to them. With the passage of time, the Honored and Revered Name sank [into oblivion, fading] from the mouths and minds of all beings: they

---

70. *Avodah Zarah*; Septimus translates this more literally as "alien worship."

recognized it not. So all the commoners, women, and children, knew nothing but the wood or stone image and fabricated temple that they were brought up from childhood to bow down to, worship, and swear by. The wise among them — priests and the like — imagined there was no deity save the stars and spheres, for which those images had been made as [symbolic] representations. But as to the Eternal Source, none recognized or knew Him save singular individuals like Enoch, Methuselah, Noah, Shem, and Eber. Thus was the world was declining by degrees, till the World's Pillar, Our Father Abraham, was born. No sooner was this hero was weaned than he began to ponder, though but a child, and to meditate day and night, wondering: "How can the Sphere forever follow its course with none to conduct it? Who causes it to rotate? For it cannot possibly cause *itself* to rotate?" He had no one to teach or instruct him in anything, but was immersed in [the culture of] Ur of the Chaldees among the foolish adherents of alien worship. His father, mother and the entire populace worshiped alien deities, and he worshiped along with them, while his mind was searching and seeking to understand — till he grasped the true way and understood the right course of his own sound reason: He realized that: there is a single God, He conducts the Sphere, He created the universe, and, in all that exists, there is no god but He. And he realized that all the people were in error, and [that] what had caused them to err was worshiping the stars and images for so long that the truth [of God's existence] was lost to their minds. It was at age forty[71] that Abraham recognized his Creator.

Maimonides goes on to describe how Abraham then refuted the inhabitants of Ur, argued with them, broke their images, and began instructing them in the truth. After convincing his

---

71. When he had reached intellectual maturity, and not at age three, as a midrash has it. See R. Abraham ben David's gloss here.

fellow-countrymen (and thus apparently upsetting the traditional order), the King sought to kill him. He was miraculously saved, whereupon he emigrated and "began to call out loudly to all the people, teaching them that the world has [but] one God, who [alone] ought to be worshiped." He traveled from city to city and from kingdom to kingdom, teaching this truth which he had discovered. Arriving in the land of Canaan, he proclaimed his message, instructed the inhabitants, implanted truth in their hearts, composed books on it, and taught it to his son Isaac.[72]

Prominent in these texts is the noteworthy emphasis on the activity of Abraham. God is entirely absent from this account, as anything but the object of philosophical speculation. On this account, God does not even issue the command which opens the Abraham story in the Torah (Gen. 12:1), "Get thee hence..." Even the (midrashically based) miracle by which Abraham was saved from the King of Ur is presented without directly and clearly involving God — the text literally says: "a miracle was performed for him" (na'asah lo nes).[73] Throughout these passages

---

72. Compare Maimonides' account in Guide of the Perplexed III.29: "However, when the pillar of the world grew up and it became clear to him that there is a separate deity that is neither a body nor a force in a body and that all the starts and the spheres were made by Him, and he understood that the fables upon which he was brought up were absurd, he began to refute their doctrine and show up their opinions as false; he publicly manifested his disagreement with them and called in the name of the Lord, God of the world (Gen. 21:33) — both the existence of the deity and the creation of the world in time by that deity being comprised in that call" (p. 516). For other parallels in the Guide, see II.39 (p. 379) and III.24 (p. 502). See also Book of Commandments, positive commandment 3. The issue also comes up in Maimonides' famous responsum to R. Ovadiah the Proselyte. The slight variations in the next as cited by Blau (#293, p. 549) and by Sheilat (Iggerot ha-Rambam [Jerusalem: Ma'aliyot, 1987], pp. 232–233) are of great interest. Sheilat, true to his vision of Maimonides, chooses readings which subtly but clearly diminish the universalist impact of the passage; or, Blau chooses readings which subtly but clearly augment the universalist impact of the passage (the former seems more likely an explanation than the latter, given what I know of Rabbi Sheilat's other writings). I examine this matter in"'Farteitsht un Farbessert': Comments on Tendentious 'Corrections' to Maimonidean Texts," B. Ish-Shalom (ed.), Be-Darkei Shalom: Iyyunim be-Hagut Yehudit Mugashim li-Shalom Rosenberg (Jerusalem: Bet Morashah, 2006): 255–263 (Hebrew), English translation in Me'orot [= Edah Journal] 6.2 (2007). (http://www.yctorah.org/content/view/211/64/).

73. Pesahim 118a. The Talmud here has God insisting on saving Abraham Himself (the angel Gabriel had sought the assignment); Maimonides clearly presents the story

it is Abraham, and not God, who is the subject of active verbs: Abraham meditated, pondered, wondered, searched, grasped, understood, realized, recognized, refuted, argued, broke images, convinced, emigrated, proclaimed, travelled, taught, instructed, implanted, and composed.[74] God is cognized on this account, but does not act.[75]

The upshot of all this is that Abraham discovered God on his own, so to speak.[76] God did not choose Abraham, God did not

---

in an entirely different light. See also Gen. Rabbah 39.3.

74. My thanks to Zev Harvey for drawing my attention to this point.

75. The God described here is the "God of the philosophers." Compare Howard Kreisel, *Maimonides' Political Thought: Studies in Ethics, Law, and the Human Ideal* (Albany: SUNY Press, 1999), p. 43: "What is crucial to stress in this context is that Abraham is depicted by Maimonides as an Aristotelian philosopher. His deduction that God 'created' everything as depicted in "Laws of Idolatry," I.3, is in reality the Aristotelian view that God is the First Cause of all existence." Agreeing as I do with Kreisel's interpretation, I think it apposite to quote Judah Halevi's parallel account of Abraham in Kuzari IV.17: "The Sage said: Well, then, by that standard, it was right for Abraham to have undergone all that he did in Ur of the Chaldees, and then in departing from his homeland, and also in accepting circumcision, and again in expelling Ishamel, and even further in his anxiety about slaughtering Isaac, since all that he experienced with respect to the divine order (*al-amr al-ilahi*), he experienced by savoring [*dhawq*], not by reasoning." This passage is found in the context of Halevi's distinction between the philosophic God of Aristotle (and of Abraham, according to Maimonides!), known in the tradition as Elohim, and the experienced God of the Patriarchs, known in the tradition by the tetragrammaton. Halevi's Abraham goes beyond the God of the philosophers to the God of experience. Halevi makes this clear in the sequel: "God ordered him to abstain from his scientific studies based on reasoning ... and to take upon himself the duty of obeying the One he had experienced by savoring, just as it says: *Savor and see how good the Lord is* (Ps. 34:9)." On this passage, see the discussion in Diana Lobel, *Between Mysticism and Philosophy: Sufi Language of Religious Experience in Judah Ha-Levi's Kuzari* (Albany: SUNY Press, 2000), pp. 89–93. Compare also Hasdai Crescas' comment (*Or Ha-Shem*, I.iii.6, p. 122 in the edition of Shlomo Fisher [Jerusalem: Ramot, 1990]) to the effect that while it was Abraham's philosophical reasoning which *prepared* him for prophecy, this reasoning did not bring him to certain knowledge of God, which is the province of prophets, not philosophers: "...even though he desired the truth, he did not escape all doubt until God caused His light to emanate upon him, it [i.e., God's light] being prophecy." This passage is discussed by Warren Zev Harvey, *Physics and Metaphysics in Hasdai Crescas* (Amsterdam: Gieben, 1998), pp. 47–48 and 60–65. Note well Harvey's comment (p. 48) about the Maimonides whom Crescas criticized: "His Abraham is an Aristotelian philosopher, or, if you prefer, his Aristotle was an Abrahamic philosopher." It is noteworthy also that a rabbinic text (Sab. 156a, Ned. 32a), "abandon your astrology [=philosophical-scientific research]..." used by both Halevi and Crescas in the present context, is nowhere cited by Maimonides.

76. In other words, Abraham discovered God through *hekhre'a ha-da'at*, reasoned

seek him out, God did not make Himself known to Abraham. God waited till someone discovered the truth about Him; that someone happened to be Abraham, progenitor of the Jews. It did not have to be Abraham. Had the first human being to discover the truth about God been, say, a Navajo, and had that Navajo philosopher the courage and effectiveness of Abraham, then the Navajos would be the chosen people, the Torah would have been composed in the Navajo language, its narratives would reflect their history, and many of its commandments would reflect that history and the nature of Navajo society at the time of the giving of the Torah to them. The inner meaning of the Torah, its philosophical content and spiritual message would all be equivalent to the inner meaning, philosophical content and spiritual message of the Torah is it was indeed revealed to Moses at Sinai, but its outer garment would be dramatically different.

Here in its starkest fashion is the profound gulf which separates Maimonides from Halevi and thinkers like him.[77] For Halevi, God chose the Jews because of their antecedent special character, the only people on earth in whom the *inyan elohi* was permanently lodged.[78] For Maimonides, it is Abraham's choice of

---

conviction. He also brought his contemporaries (Noachides in the most literal sense of the term) to acceptance of monotheism through *hekhre'a ha-da'at*. It is a safe assumption that, on Maimonides' view, Abraham himself and those whom he brought near to God achieved shares in the world to come; that being the case, the standard reading of "Laws of Kings," VIII.11 (*ve-lo me-hakhmeihem*) cannot be correct — on this issue, see the discussion in *Maimonides' Confrontation with Mysticism* (abote, note 1), pp. 81 and 241–250.

77. I do not mean to imply that Rashi would have accepted Halevi's views. I do not know. I cite Halevi (and Nahmanides) for the purpose of sharpening my presentation of Maimonides. It is likely that Rashi stood closer to Halevi and Nahmanides than to Maimonides on many issues; but the route that brought him to these positions was probably significantly different from the route followed by Halevi and Nahmanides. Further on the comparison of Maimonides and Halevi vis-à-vis Abraham, See Aviezer Ravitzky, "On the Image of the Leader in Jewish Thought," *Pirsumei Hug Bet ha-Nasi le-Tanakh u-le-Mekorot Yisrael* 1 (1998): 33–46 (Hebrew) and Ravitzky, "Introduction — the Binding of Isaac and the Covenant: Abraham and His Descendants in Jewish Thought," in Hannah Kasher, Moshe Hallamish, and Yohanan Silman (eds.), *Avraham, Avi Ha-Ma'aminim: Demuto Be-Re'i He-Hagut Le-Doroteha* (Ramat-Gan: Bar-Ilan University Press, 2003), pp. 11–38, esp. p. 15–19 (Hebrew).

78. For two statements of many, see *Kuzari*, I.48 and 95.

God which makes his descendents special, so long as they remain loyal to that choice.[79]

Our point finds further expression in the continuation of Maimonides' account:

> Our Father Jacob taught all his children; but he singled out Levi, appointing him "head" and installing him in an academy to teach "the way of the Lord" (Gen. 18:19) and keep Abraham's charge. He directed his children that there be an uninterrupted succession of Levite appointees, so that the teaching not be forgotten. This enterprise was gathering strength among Jacob's children and those who joined them, a God-knowing nation was coming into being — till Israel's stay in Egypt became prolonged and they retrogressed, learning [the Egyptians'] deeds and worshiping alien deities like them (the sole exception being the tribe of Levi, which remained steadfast to the Patriarchal charge: never did the tribe of Levi worship alien deities).   The root planted by Abraham was on the verge of being uprooted and Jacob's descendents, of reverting to the error and aberrance of the nations.[80]

---

79. I was once discussing conversion to Judaism in a class in the United States. Two of my students, both daughters of Baptist ministers, asked me, in amazement: "The Jews are God's chosen people; how can one choose to be chosen?" This question goes to the heart of the debate between the Judaism of Judah Halevi, *Zohar*, Nahmanides, etc., and the Judaism of Maimonides. In a very real sense, for the former, one cannot choose to be chosen. For Halevi, converts remain unequal to born Jews; for the *Zohar* there really is no such thing as conversion — true proselytes are persons born to gentile parents into whose bodies Jewish souls have been placed. For Maimonides, on the other hand, in a very real sense, true Jews are not chosen by God, but, rather, are individuals (whoever their parents might be) who choose God. For Maimonides, as I argued in *Maimonides on Judaism and the Jewish People* (see the next note) all Jews are converts to Judaism.

80. This last point deserves expansion, since it is important for the thesis being developed here. Maimonides, following midrashic tradition (Mekhilta, Bo, paragraph 5; ed. Lauterbach, vol. 2, p. 36) maintains that the Jews in Egypt had assimilated to the idolatrous norms of the Egyptian culture around them ("Laws of Idolatry," I.3; compare the opposed picture drawn by Halevi in *Kuzari* I.95). Those of Abraham's descendents who stood at Sinai quite literally converted to Judaism (the new religion expressed in the Torah of Moses). This may be seen from the way in which Maimonides opens his discussion of the laws of conversion in "Laws of Forbidden Intercourse," XIII: "With three things did Israel enter the covenant: circumcision,

But because God loved us and stood by [his] oath to Our Father, Abraham, he elected Moses — Our Master and the Master of all the Prophets — and charged him with his [prophetic] mission. When Moses our Master attained to prophecy and God chose Israel as His own, He crowned them with commandments, and taught them: how to worship Him and what rules should govern alien worship and all who stray after it.

Israel thus becomes God's chosen people because of Abraham's antecedent choice of God.[81]

Maimonides is not shy about adopting the implications of this position. The specific laws of the Torah reflect historical circumstances which could have been different.[82] The clearest example of this is Maimonides' notorious explanation for the reason that God

---

immersion, and sacrifice....." So, Maimonides continues, must converts today undergo circumcision and immersion (sacrifice being no longer possible). See the fuller development of this point in M. Kellner, *Maimonides on Judaism and the Jewish People* pp. 85–87.

81. Compare III. 51 (p 623): "This was also the rank of the *Patriarchs*, the result of whose nearness to Him, may He be exalted, was that His name became known to the world through them: *The God of Abraham, the God of Isaac, and the God of Jacob ...; this is my name forever* (Ex. 3:15). Because of the union of their intellects through apprehension of Him, it came about that He made a lasting *covenant* with each of them...Also the providence of God watching over them and over their posterity was great." This idea even finds expression in Maimonides' Epistle to Yemen, a text in which he must have been greatly tempted to use a stronger notion of the choice of Israel than the one expressed here. Towards the beginning of the Epistle, he emphasizes the importance of the following teaching: "...ours is the true and divine religion, revealed to us through Moses, chief of the former as well as of the later prophets. By means of it God has distinguished us from the rest of mankind, as He declares: *Yet it was to your fathers that Lord was drawn in His love for them, so that He chose you, their lineal descendants, from among all the peoples* (Dt. 10:15). This choice was not made thanks to our merits, but was rather an act of grace, on account of our ancestors who were cognizant of God and obedient to Him, as He states: It is not because you are the most numerous of peoples, that the Lord set His heart on you and chose you — indeed, you are the smallest of peoples [but it was because the Lord loved you and kept the oath He made to your fathers] (Dt. 7:7)." I cite from the translation of Abraham S. Halkin in Halkin and David Hartman, *Crisis and Leadership: Epistles of Maimonides* (Philadelphia: Jewish Publication Society, 1985), p. 96–97. This text reads as if it were written in direct opposition to the views of Judah Halevi on the election of Israel.

82. Were this not the case, human freedom, which Maimonides calls "the great root [*ikkar*] which is the pillar of the Torah and commandments," ("Laws of Repentance," V.4) would be destroyed.

commanded the sacrificial cult.[83] Maimonides presents the entire
sacrificial cult as a concession to the primitive character of the
Jews in Egypt. Considering how many biblical commandments
relate directly to the sacrificial cult (including all the commandments concerning the tabernacle and all the commandments
concerning ritual purity and impurity) this is quite a remarkable
claim. But not just the sacrifices, Maimonides interprets all the
laws known to the tradition as *hukkim* (statutes) in this manner.
The prohibition against *sha'atnez* (wearing a garment of linen and
wool), reflects, Maimonides teaches (*Guide* III.37, p. 544), the
historically contingent fact that idolatrous priests in the ancient
world wore such garments. We saw above that Rashi held that
Abraham indeed fulfilled all the *hukkim*.

We may now finally address the implications of the different
views of Rashi and Rambam concerning the nature of the laws
of the Torah. If the Torah pre-exists creation, if in some sense or
other it serves as blue-print of the universe, then quite obviously,
the laws of the Torah bear some sort of constitutive relationship
to the cosmos and fulfilling those laws can (or must) have some
sort of impact on that cosmos. From here, full-blown theurgy
is but a short step.[84] It is quite obvious also that the laws of the

---

83. For Maimonides' historical explanation of the sacrificial cult see *Guide of the Perplexed* III.32 (p. 526). For a recent and thorough discussion, see Josef Stern, *Problems and Parables of Law*, pp. 23–35 and 140–150. Stern examines Nahmanides' outraged rejection of Maimonides' position. For the wider context, see Stephen D. Benin, *The Footprints of God: Divine Accommodation in Jewish and Christian Thought* (Albany: SUNY Press, 1993).

84. See Morris Faierstein, "'God's Need for the Commandments' in Medieval Kabbalah," *Conservative Judaism* 36 (1982): 45–59; for context and background, see Moshe Idel, *Kabbalah: New Perspectives* (New Haven: Yale University Press, 1988), chapter 7. Further relevant studies include Daniel Matt, "The Mystic and the *Mizwot*," in Arthur Green (ed.), *Jewish Spirituality: From the Bible through the Middle Ages* (New York: Crossroads, 1986), pp. 367–404, and Dov Schwartz, "From Theurgy to Magic: The Evolution of the Magical-Talismanic Justification of Sacrifice in the Circle of Nahmanides and His Interpreters," *Aleph* 1 (2001): 165–213. The notion that in some sense the fulfillment of the commandments on the part of Israel is crucial for God's own "well-being," as it were, is a reflection of the ancient idea of theurgy. See, E. R Dodds, *The Greeks and the Irrational* (Berkeley: University of California Press, 1964), pp. 283–311 and, Görg Luck, "Theurgy and Forms of Worship in Neoplatonism," in E. Frerichs, Jacob Neusner, and P. Flesher (eds.), *Religion, Science, and Magic: In Concert and in Conflict* (New York: Oxford University Press, 1989), 185–225.

Torah could not be other than they are; else nature would have to be different than it is. There are further implications. If the Torah is given to Israel alone, then Israel alone holds the true key to the true nature of the universe, and Israel's obedience to the laws of the Torah can be construed as the key to the continued proper functioning of that universe. Getting Jews to fulfill the commandments becomes a matter of cosmic concern. For a person holding such views (and Rashi certainly appears to have held them), it is literally inconceivable that Abraham, Isaac, and Jacob, the pre-ordained progenitors of Israel from before creation, did not obey all the commandments of the Torah, both Sinaitic and rabbinic. Note a further implication of the notion of a pre-existent Torah: those who fulfill the commandments are superior to those who do not. This is true on every level: Jews, who were given the commandments, are superior to Gentiles, who were not given the commandments; Jews who fulfill the commandments are superior to those who do not fulfill them.[85] On this view, if the Patriarchs did not observe the commandments then they turn out to have lived spiritually impoverished lives, and were, Jewishly, inferior to their descendants. This, of course, contradicts the widely-accepted notion of the "decline of the generations."[86]

From Maimonides account it appears that Abraham, the self-taught philosopher *par excellence*, had no need of Sinai. Sinai is a concession to the sad fact that the root planted by Abraham was on the verge of being uprooted. In order to preserve the philosophical core of the Torah, it had to be hedged about by laws and ceremonials, which do not accomplish anything in themselves, but were instituted in order to serve moral, social, or

---

85. One wonders if this explains part of the attraction of "humrot" (halakhic stringencies) among Jews who accept this account of the nature of the commandments. In another context I tried to show that the different attitudes described here might be useful in understanding debates over the notion of "da'at Torah" in contemporary Orthodoxy. See Kellner, "Rabbis in Politics: A Study in Medieval and Modern Jewish Political Theory," *State and Society* [=*Medinah ve-Hevrah*] 3 (2003): 673–698 (Hebrew).

86. A notion with which Maimonides was apparently unaware; had he been aware of it, he certainly would not have accepted it. See Kellner, *Maimonides on the "Decline of the Generations"* (above, note 47).

philosophical ends. For a person holding these views, it is literally inconceivable that Abraham, Isaac, and Jacob observed laws and ceremonials later given at Sinai in response to the degeneration of the Jews in Egypt.

I have no doubt that Rashi and Maimonides both accepted the idea that the Torah was revealed to Israel at Sinai; we know very well that each lived his life in accordance with that idea. The spiritual context of those lives, however, appears to have been worlds apart; they both accepted Sinaitic revelation, but meant dramatically different things by it.

Professor Menachem Kellner is a Professor of Jewish Thought at the University of Haifa

3

The Separate Intellects and Maimonides' Argumentation
(An Inquiry into *The Guide of the Perplexed* II, 2-12)

Dov Schwartz

The nature of Maimonides' argumentation in general and in *The Guide of the Perplexed* in particular has been discussed in a variety of scholarly forums.[1] The common view is that Maimonides prefers the syllogism to other modes of logical argument, and his attitude to dialectical reasoning has also been considered. I believe, however, that Maimonides' explicit declaration in the Introduction to the *Guide*, as to the principles of argumentation in physics and metaphysics, as well his metaphor of lightning, have been disregarded in this context. It will be shown in this article that analogical reasoning plays a major role in the arguments of the *Guide*, making for a new understanding of his esoteric style. In order to clarify the meaning of the analogical argument in Maimonides' thought, I intend to focus attention on one typically metaphysical issue — that of the separate intellects.

Chapters 2–12 in Part II of *The Guide of the Perplexed* constitute a single unit dealing with the problem of the separate intellects[2] and the structure of the spheres (soul and intellect). Maimonides

---

1. See A. Hyman's important article: A. Hyman, "Demonstrative, Dialectical and Sophistic Arguments in the Philosophy of Moses Maimonides," in E. L. Ormsby (ed.), *Moses Maimonides and his Time* (Washington, D.C., 1989), pp. 35–51.
2. For the origin of the term "separate" see, e.g., H. J. Blumenthal, "Neoplatonic Elements in the *de Anima* Commentaries," in R. Sorabji (ed.), *Aristotle Transformed: The Ancient Commentators and Their Influence* (Ithaca, NY, 1990), p. 318. For the whole issue see also H. Davidson, *Alfarabi, Avicenna and Averroes on Intellect* (New York & Oxford, 1992).

adopts the peripatetic system: The intellects are construed first and foremost as the movers of the spheres; the movement of the spheres is caused by the apprehension of the intellect of the sphere, which strives to resemble the separate intellect, and by the movement of the soul as the source of the permanent desire to perform regular, eternal, movement, which is imitation. The Active Intellect is not included in this framework, since it does not move a sphere, but functions as the formal principle of material objects in the world and as the source of the human intellect. The issue of the separate intellects in the *Guide*, which brings together *Maʿaseh Bereshit* (literally: "The Account of the Beginning") and *Maʿaseh Merkavah* (lit.: "The Account of the Chariot"), has been discussed from various points of view.[3] In the first part of this article, I shall deal with the literary aspects of the unit formed by the initial chapters of Part II in the *Guide*. It will be shown that the stamp of Maimonides' unique style, fraught with tension and contradictions, is clearly evident in these chapters, and the nature of that style will be analyzed. In the second part of the article, I shall deal with medieval interpretations of this literary unit.

(I) Exoteric and Esoteric Elements in Maimonides

This part of the article will present three theses in relation to Maimonidean esotericism as exemplified by *Guide* II, 2–12:

(i) **The purpose of *The Guide of the Perplexed*.** Maimonides declares that his purpose in writing the work was religious, that is to say, an attempt to understand the texts of revelation, rather than philosophical. The chapters of the Bible and the Talmudic sources concerned with esoteric matters require interpretation and clarification. This declaration, which opens a discussion concerned specifically with metaphysics (spheres, separate intellects), merits some examination. In the spirit of the esoteric commentaries written in the Middle

---

3. See Z. [H.] Blumberg, "The Separate Intelligences in Maimonides' Philosophy" (Heb.), *Tarbiz* 40 (1971), pp. 216–225.

Ages, I shall show that Maimonides' intention in writing the work was dual: Science for its own sake (esoteric), and science as a theological tool for religious purposes (exoteric).

(ii) **Order.** A clarification of this question may help to solve another problem. As intimated above, the position of this group of chapters (2–12) just before the chapters of the *Guide* that discuss Creation needs explanation. It will be argued here that Maimonides placed these chapters here for methodological rather than substantial reasons.

(iii) **Authority.** Maimonides considers rabbinical authority in regard to the sciences, concluding that scientific truth is not subject to non-scientific authority. His discussions of the separate intellects contain even more radical allusions, distinguishing between the teachings of the prophets, which express careful, accurate scientific views, and those of the Sages, which are not scientifically sound. Between the lines, Maimonides tries to find a historical-apologetic explanation for this apparently puzzling situation. The question of the Sages' position in this context arises from the fact that the discussion is concerned with mystical tradition (*Ma'aseh Bereshit* and *Ma'aseh Merkavah*).

This part of the article will end with a comment on the implications of these chapters on Maimonides' conception of creation *ex nihilo*. I intend to show that an understanding of Maimonides' argumentation, in particular, of his analogical reasoning, is the key to understanding the style and content of this literary unit in particular and of the *Guide* in general.

Metaphysics and Creation (1): Questions

Why does Maimonides discuss separate intellects *before* he concerns himself with Creation? Scholarly discussions of the order of the chapters in the *Guide* have emphasized the contextual association of chapters 2–12 with the later account of Creation.[4]

---

4. See S. Rawidowicz, "The Structure of 'The Guide of the Perplexed,'" in *Iyyunim*

Maimonides seems to have sought to clarify the question of emanation as the source of the spheres and the terrestrial world before his polemical treatment of the proofs for Creation. In other words, simple logic demands that the meaning and nature of Creation be clarified before its actual existence is proved. However, that is not the implication of Maimonides' own declaration:

> Now I think it fit that I should complete the exposition of the opinions of the philosophers, that I should explain their proofs concerning the existence of separate intellects, and that I should explain the concordance of this opinion with the foundations of our Law — I refer to what the Law teaches concerning the existence of angels. I accordingly shall complete this purpose. After that I shall go back, as I have promised, to arguing with a view to proving that the world has come into existence in time. For our strongest proofs for this are valid[5] and can be made clear only after one knows that the separate intellects exist and after one knows how proofs for the existence may be adduced.[6]

Maimonides states that the meaning of the separate intellects must be explained before one can formulate and understand the proofs for Creation. In other words, the fact of Creation cannot be proved without consideration of the issue of separate intellects. Now, all the proofs that Maimonides cites are rooted in physics and astronomy, and it is well known that he was dubious about

---

bemahashevet Yisrael: Hebrew Studies in Jewish Thought, ed. B. C. I. Ravid (Heb.; Jerusalem, 1969), I, pp. 271–273; H. Kreisel, "Moses Maimonides," in D. H. Frank & O. Leaman (eds.), *History of Jewish Philosophy* (London & New York, 1997), pp. 254–256. Studies dealing with the possibility of conjunction with the Active Intellect and metaphysical knowledge, which also rely largely on the theory of intellects, will not be cited here.

5. See Maimonides, *The Guide of the Perplexed*, Hebrew translation... by Michael Schwarz (Tel Aviv, 2002), p. 268 n. 9.

6. Moses Maimonides, *The Guide of the Perplexed*, translated... by Shlomo Pines (Chicago & London, 1963), pp. 252–253; all subsequent quotations in English are from this edition [with very slight changes]. I have compared the translation with M. Schwarz's Hebrew rendition (see previous note). The original Arabic text was published by S. Munk and I. Joel (eds.), *Dalālat al-Hā'irīn* (Jerusalem, 1931).

the consistency of astronomical theories with physics;[7] none of his proofs appeals to metaphysics (in the sense of a theory of Separate Intellects).[8] There is no need of a theory of intellects to consider proofs of Creation; on the contrary, Maimonides already took care to detach the theory from the issue of Creation when he based his argument concerning the different motions of the spheres and their velocities (II, 19) on the matter of the spheres, not on their movers: the separate intellects. He writes near the end of chapter 19 [Pines ed., p. 311]:

> But who is the one who particularized the differences that are found in the spheres and the stars unless it be God, may He be exalted? If, however, someone says that the separate intellects did it, he gains nothing by saying this. The explanation of this is as follows: The intellects are not bodies, which they would have to be in order to have a local position in relation to the sphere...

This statement is made not in the course of Maimonides' discussion of the diversity of celestial motion, but at its conclusion. Since the separate intellects are not subject to the laws of motion, they have no place in a detailed discussion of Creation, and so the issue of the intellects is not essential for an understanding of the argument. They have two functions: they move the spheres, as already made clear by Aristotle, and they play an important role in the question of existence, a function which Neoplatonic literature associated with emanation. Thus, not only does Maimonides make no use of the separate intellects in his arguments for Creation; he almost completely ignores their role as movers. It might be suggested that the argument from the diversity of celestial movement relies on the theory of the separate intellects, for without the homogeneity of the intellects the argument would fail. The

---

7. See Y. Z. Langerman, "The True Perplexity: The Guide of the Perplexed, Part II, Chapter 24," in J. L. Kraemer (ed.), *Perspectives on Maimonides* (Oxford, 1991), pp. 159–174.
8. See H. A. Wolfson, "The Classification of Science in Medieval Jewish Philosophy," in *HUC Jubilee Volume* (Cincinnati, 1925), pp. 291–292.

intellects cannot be the source of different movements. This is a negative argument: diversity of movement cannot be inferred from the intellects — and one should note that Maimonides, in the chapters dealing with the attributes, declares that negative knowledge is also knowledge (I, 59). Nevertheless, it hardly seems probable that Maimonides would have devoted so many chapters to this particular argument.[9]

Moreover, in II, 3, Maimonides argues, citing Alexander of Aphrodisias, that the theory of the separate intellects is based on "simple assertions for which no demonstration has been made, yet they are, of all the opinions put forward on this subject, those that are exposed to the smallest number of doubts and those that are the most suitable for being put into a coherent order..." [Pines ed., p. 254].[10] In chapter 22, Maimonides even challenges the validity of the theories of the separate intellects and of emanation as formulated by the peripatetic philosophers. Could a merely plausible theory, whose absolute validity still remains in doubt, be essential for proofs of Creation?! Nevertheless, Maimonides insists that the issue of the intellects is important for the *procedure* of proving the truth of Creation. While the proofs adduced for Creation are not apodictic, as Maimonides himself admits, they are at least partly based on sciences that are based on apodictic proofs, such as physics. Hence the festive declaration in chapter 2 of the necessity of separate intellects for an understanding and proof of Creation is puzzling. These perplexities prepare the reader for the tension awaiting him in the "Preface" that Maimonides included in that chapter. We shall now see how this tension helps to understand

---

9. It might equally well be argued that a knowledge of the separate intellects is needed to understand the refutation of the inference from existence to coming into being (II, 17). The movement of the spheres is the origin of the processes that take place in the material of the terrestrial world, and the object of this movement is the separate intellects. See G. Freudenthal, "Maimonides' Stance on Astrology in Context: Cosmology, Physics, Medicine and Providence," in F. Rosner & S. S. Kottek (eds.), *Moses Maimonides: Physician, Scientist, and Philosopher* (Northvale, NJ, & London, 1993), p. 78. Once again, it hardly seems possible that Maimonides would devote a whole literary unit to this question, which relies indirectly on the intellects.

10. See Sh. Pines, "Translator's Introduction: The Philosophic Sources of The Guide of the Perplexed," in his edition, p. lxviii.

the allusions in the context of the link between the separate intellects and the problem of Creation.

The Purpose of *The Guide of the Perplexed*

Maimonides explains in the Preface included in chapter 2 that his purpose in writing the *Guide* was not science for science's sake. He had no intention of treating topics in physics and metaphysics in themselves. "Know that my purpose in this Treatise of mine was not to compose something on natural science, or to make an epitome of notions pertaining to the divine science..." [Pines ed., p. 253]. His purpose was theological, that is, to elucidate the meaning of the Bible and the Prophets. Strauss argued that the *Guide* was a work of *Kalām*, and his thesis has been repeatedly debated.[11] His statement is questionable: Both in his commentary to the Mishnah and in the *Guide*, Maimonides reiterates that, according to the Bible, perfection is bound up with a knowledge of the sciences. In his view, the prophets themselves advocate "perfection of the soul" (III, 27), that is, a knowledge of existents, and that is the meaning of their teachings. Since the prophets' message is a call to acquire a knowledge of science for its own sake, it may be inferred that such is the object of the *Guide* — science for its own sake.[12] But rather than consider Maimonides' general purpose, which has been hotly debated and concerning which opinions differ widely, let us concentrate the ambiguous,

---

11. Since we are dealing with the Preface to the Creation chapters, mention should be made of one place in those chapters where there is an allusion to the nature of the book. Maimonides notes in II, 16 [p. 293]: "I have already set forth for your benefit the methods of the Mutakallim(n in establishing the newness of the world, and I have drawn your attention to the points with regard to which they may be attacked." Now the proofs adduced by the Mutakallim(n were indeed described in I, 74, but nowhere does Maimonides refute them. Moreover, in II, 16 he promises to show that the doctrine of eternity of the world, as a polemical goal, is more dubious than the doctrine of Creation, which also lacks apodictic evidence. This propensity to expose the opponents' weaknesses, even when they also point to difficulties in one's own arguments, is typical of the *Kalām*. Perhaps Maimonides was hinting, as suggested by Strauss, that he too was using *Kalām* techniques.
12. See also S. Harvey, "Maimonides in the Sultan's Palace," *Perspectives on Maimonides*, pp. 56–57.

convoluted exposition in chapter 2 (in the Preface to part II [Pines ed., pp. 253–254]):

> No you know already from the introduction of this my Treatise that it hinges on the explanation of what can be understood in the *Account of the Beginning* and the *Account of the Chariot* and the clearing-up of the difficulties attaching to prophecy and to the knowledge of the deity. Accordingly in whatever chapter you find me discoursing with a view to explaining a matter already demonstrated in natural science, or a matter demonstrated in divine science, or an opinion that has been shown to be the one fittest to be believed in,[13] or a matter attaching to what has been explained in the mathematical sciences[14] — know that that particular matter necessarily must be a key to the understanding of something to be found in the books of prophecy, I mean to say of some of their parables and secrets. The reason why I mentioned, explained, and elucidated that matter would be found in the knowledge it procures us of the *Account of the Chariot* or of the *Account of the Beginning* or would be found in an explanation that it furnishes of some root regarding the notion of prophecy or would be found in the explanation of some root regarding the belief in a true opinion belonging to the beliefs of Law.

In this passage, Maimonides twice lists four issues that form the subject-matter of the *Guide*. However, a comparison of the beginning of the passage with its concluding lines reveals a discrepancy between the two lists, in their third and fourth items:

(i)   The Account of the Beginning (*Ma'aseh Bereshit*)

---

13. Probably meaning knowledge cannot be demonstrated by an apodictic proof.
14. Arabic: *fi al-ta'ālīm*. The hierarchy is thus: metaphysics, physics, plausible beliefs, and other sciences (say biology and psychology). Pines and M. Schwarz translate here "mathematics," perhaps under the influence of Ibn Tibbon's rendition, *limmudim*, on the assumption that this was essentially a translation of the term *al-riyāḍī*.

(ii)   The Account of the Chariot (*Ma'aseh Merkavah*)

| (iii1) "difficulties attaching to prophecy" | (iii2) "some root regarding the notion of prophecy" |
| (iv1) "knowledge of the deity" | (iv2) "a true opinion belonging to the beliefs of Law" |

What is the reason for this difference? In the works of Al-Fārābī, Avicenna and Ibn Rushd, for example, the question of divine attributes ("knowledge of the deity"), is a philosophical one, dealt with using the tools of philosophy. Ibn Rushd considers it at length in his commentary on the *Metaphysica*.[15] Perhaps, one might suggest, Maimonides was hinting that the *Guide* had also been written to elucidate philosophical matters in themselves, like divine attributes, and that he was obscuring this fact by exchanging "knowledge of the deity" in the first list (iv1) for "a true... beliefs of the Law" in the second (iv2). This would also explain the difference between (iii1) and (iii2): the *Guide* was written not only to resolve doubts, that is, to interpret the words of the prophets and revelation, but also to discuss in themselves principles that the prophets had mentioned.

Maimonides makes it plausible that the *Guide* was designed (among other things) to explain *Ma'aseh Bereshit* and *Ma'aseh Merkavah*, which he identifies, as is evident from the Introduction to the work, with physics and metaphysics.[16] The disjunctive formulation (...or... or...) at the end of the quoted passage also indicates that the purpose of the *Guide* included physics and metaphysics as independent areas. Maimonides seems to

---

15. M. E. Marmura, "Some Aspects of Avicenna's Theory of God's Knowledge of Particulars," *Journal of the American Oriental Society* 82 (1962), pp. 299–312; D. Schwartz, "Divine Immanence in Medieval Jewish Philosophy," *Journal of Jewish Thought and Philosophy* 3 (1994), pp. 249–278.

16. One might infer from Maimonides' text that the terms *Ma'aseh Bereshit* and *Ma'aseh Merkavah* are not pure philosophy — physics and metaphysics as presented in the works of the philosophers — but the contents of the prophetic books (S. Klein-Braslavy, *King Solomon and Philosophical Esotericism in the Thought of Maimonides* [Heb.; Jerusalem, 1997], pp. 41–42). I believe one could argue that Maimonides did not distinguish between the meaning of prophecy and the physics of the philosophers, e.g., in his insistence that physics is wholly true (II, 22).

be stating that the first two, scientific, matters were intended to explain the last two, theological issues. But that statement itself is problematic: Prophetic matters include "mysteries of the Torah," which, as stated, are identified with *Ma'aseh Bereshit* and *Ma'aseh Merkavah*. Hence the exposition of physics and metaphysics is an end in itself, not only an aid to understanding prophecy as claimed in the above passage.

Thus, the purpose of the *Guide* is a challenge to any reader seeking the inner substance of the text.

Metaphysics and Creation (2): Answers

The solution to this problem lies in the importance of scientific methodology. As early on as the Introduction to the work, Maimonides explains that method is an essential factor in questions of physics and metaphysics. This includes intuitive and analogical approaches to many matters. The parable of the lightning also contributes to the unsystematic nature of these sciences. The terms *Ma'aseh Bereshit* and *Ma'aseh Merkavah* thus have two dimensions: one of substance (the theory of the separate intellects, the spheres and the laws of physics) and a methodological one (analogy). Maimonides is implying that the mysteries of the prophets include not only matters of substance but modes of thought. In fact, that is the nature of physics and metaphysics:

> Know that with regard to natural matters as well, it is impossible to give a clear exposition when teaching some of their principles as they are. For you know the saying of [the Sages],...: "*Ma'aseh Bereshit* ought not to be taught in the presence of two men" [bHagigah 11b]. Now if someone explained all those matters in a book, he in effect would be *teaching* them to thousands of men. Hence these matters too occur in parables in the books of prophecy. The Sages..., following the trail of these books, likewise have spoken of them in riddles and parables, for there is a close connection between these matters and

> the divine science, and they too are secrets of that divine
> science (*Guide* I, 1 [Pines, p. 7]).

The study of metaphysics is important in itself, one the one hand; but on the other, its methodology helps to understand the teachings and thought of the prophets ("parables and riddles" as defined by Maimonides in the Introduction), and also to solve problems attaching to their thought, for the prophets spoke in analogies and parables. Hence, Maimonides is speaking here both of science for its own sake and of science as an aid to understanding the message of the prophets. This explains the difference between the two lists of issues to which the *Guide* is devoted. Maimonides' account of metaphysics and physics possesses a philosophical, content-oriented dimension, as expressed in the theoretical account of divine knowledge (iv1), and a methodological dimension of analogical thought, which dictates the formulation of the beliefs of the Torah (iv2).

Given the analogical dimension of the sciences, we can answer the question posed at the very beginning of this article. In order to understand the object of the unit chapters 2–12 — the separate intellects as a tool for comprehension of the account of Creation and the relevant proofs — one must realize that the theory of the separate intellects is based on analogical reasoning. To my mind, the key to Maimonides' systematic, up-to-date ("the opinion of the later philosophers"), presentation of the theory of the intellects is the following rather obscure passage (II, 4 [Pines ed., p. 258]):

> In this way the giver of a form is indubitably a separate
> form, and that which brings intellect into existence is an
> intellect, namely, the Active Intellect. Thus the relation
> of the Active Intellect to the elements and that which is
> composed of them is similar to the relation obtaining
> between every separate intellect particularly related to
> a sphere and that sphere. Furthermore, the relation of
> the intellect *in actu* existing in us, which derives from an
> emanation of the Active Intellect and through which we

apprehend the Active Intellect,[17] is similar to that of the intellect of every sphere that exists in the latter, deriving its being in it from the emanation of a separate intellect — an intellect through which the sphere apprehends the separate intellect, makes a mental representation of the latter, desires to become like it, and in consequence moves.[18]

This passage is quite mystifying: The Active Intellect does not move any sphere, and it has nothing to do with the topics discussed in these chapters. Why, then, did Maimonides bring it into play? According to Strauss's rules for the identification of esoteric elements, this is an indication that the issue at hand is significant for the meaning of the entire literary unit. In this passage Maimonides was alluding to two systems of proportional relationships:

$$\text{(I)} \quad \frac{\text{separate intellect}}{\text{sphere}} = \frac{\text{Active Intellect}}{\text{elements and objects in the material world}}$$

$$\text{(II)} \quad \frac{\text{Active Intellect}}{\text{intellect } in\ actu} = \frac{\text{separate intellect}}{\text{intellect of the sphere}}$$

Hence, it is clearly possible to understand the activity of the Active Intellect through understanding that of the separate intellects, by way of analogy. This is a clear-cut example of the mutual analogical relationship between physics (in this case the theory of the intellect, with its affinity to the laws of physics and the emergence of those laws) and metaphysics. The analogical-proportional dimension of metaphysics is also reflected in the discussion of the theory of attributes.[19] It will be remembered that Maimonides, in his discussion of divine knowledge (III, 19–21), uses the parable of

---

17. M. Schwarz adds in brackets: "to the Active Intellect."
18. M. Schwarz adds in brackets: "to the same separate intellect." For various scholarly discussions of this particular passage see M. Schwarz's note to his translation, p. 273 n. 30.
19. See *Guide* I, 58; D. Schwartz, *Contradiction and Concealment in Medieval Jewish Thought* (Heb.; Ramat-Gan, 2002), p. 71.

the artisan as an expression of the analogical method; the discussion exemplifies the existence of the dimensions of substance and methodology and the need to combine them.

The activity of the Active Intellect is important for arguments concerning Creation, as is evident, for example, from *Guide* II, 18 (first method). The question of matter's desire to assume a form also occupies a significant place in the argument from the diversity of spherical motions (II, 19). Since physics and metaphysics are interdependent, from a methodological point of view at least, the theory of intellects must be a prerequisite of any discussion of the laws governing the material world. Hence the theory of the intellects is important for an understanding of arguments and modes of argument concerning Creation.

Let us return now to the purpose of the *Guide*. Maimonides' declaration that the purpose of his work was theological concerned the methodological aspect of *Ma'aseh Bereshit* and *Ma'aseh Merkavah*, that is, it referred to the analogy. The analogical method applied in the sciences is an important tool for the interpretation of prophecies. Maimonides was not referring to the sciences, with whose substance the *Guide* would indeed deal, as he himself indicates in the immediate sequel. As far as that substance is concerned, the study of physics and metaphysics is a central part of the work's purpose. On the other hand, analogy plays a role not only in science but also in exegesis. The substance of physics and metaphysics constitutes an end in itself; the methods are designed to uncover these truths in the prophetic teachings. Analogies and metaphors already play an important part in the Biblical exegesis of chapters 5–6. In chapter 5, for example, Maimonides considers the verse, "The heavens declare the glory of God" (Ps. 19:2) and asserts that just as on a human plane speaking and telling are indications of intellectual perception (*taṣawwur* = concept), the Biblical account of the spheres speaking and telling must be understood as implying that they possess some intellectual perception. Thus analogy is a major tool both in scientific thinking in physics and metaphysics and in understanding what the prophets said about such matters.

The Prophets and the Sages

Maimonides was aware of scientific developments and of the mutual relationship between the Jewish world and those developments. One might, therefore, expect to find some linear development in scientific outlook, from the prophets to the Sages. However, it would appear that Maimonides implicitly alluded in *Guide* II, 2–12 to the superiority of the prophets' scientific knowledge to that of the Sages.[20]

As already stated, chapters 5–6 were intended to reveal the scientific conceptions reflected in prophetic and Talmudic literature. However, the relevant Biblical and Midrashic sources are not presented in a balanced manner. Chapter 5 cites sources of both types for the view that the spheres are "living and rational." The Biblical verse already mentioned from Psalms 19 indicates that the spheres are rational; it is as if the prophets passed over the animative qualities of the spheres and referred immediately to their intellectual capacities, their ability to apprehend. The Midrashim, however, begin with the statement that "those above are alive"[21] and are not "dead [bodies] like the elements"; for the Sages, it would seem, the fact that the spheres possess a living soul was something new.

In chapter 6, Maimonides cites scriptural proofs for the existence of the separate intellects; but he cites only one Midrash, which he openly criticizes: "Marvel at their saying 'contemplating [the host above],' for Plato uses literally the same expression, saying that God looks at the world of the intellects and that in consequence that which exists emanates from Him" [Pines ed., p. 263]. In other words, the Sages picked up the theory of separate intellects from Plato's theory of ideas, which Maimonides considers in error. Shem Tov Falaquera superimposed a further allusion on Maimonides' own hint: "That is his wont in all Midrashim, to

---

20. Maimonides' attitude to the Sages has been frequently discussed; my object here is confined to the context of separate intellects and spheres. See, e.g., M. Kellner, *Maimonides on the "Decline of the Generations" and the Nature of Rabbinic Authority* (Albany, 1996).
21. *Genesis Rabba* 2:1 (ed. Theodor-Albeck, p. 15).

interpret them in a near-rational manner."[22] The other Midrashim referred to in chapter 6 are concerned solely with psychology and biology, that is, with the meaning of the term "angel" as a natural force. Once again, Maimonides hints that the Sages possessed considerable knowledge of the terrestrial but not of the celestial world.

Chapters 8–9 describe the scientific error of the Sages as against the prophets' accurate knowledge. Chapter 8 presents the Sages as supporting the Pythagorean doctrine that the spheres emit sounds as they move. Maimonides comments that it is not wrong to expose the Sages' error in a scientific matter, and buttresses this comment with the Sages' own admission that they were mistaken in certain astronomical beliefs (bPesaḥim 94b). Chapter 9, for its part, may be construed as a song of praise for the prophets' scientific stature. The chapter is concerned mainly with "saving" the theory of four spheres in which there are stars or planets. The ancients believed that the spheres of Mercury and Venus were above the sun, but Ptolemy rejected this belief. Maimonides claims that Andalusian astronomers who were "very proficient in the mathematical sciences" had reestablished the ancients' model. Moreover, this model had not been entirely refuted. It made it possible to count four spheres with stars [or planets] — a number which Maimonides considers "a very important basis for a notion that has occurred to me." Classical commentators and modern scholars agree that Maimonides was alluding to the four beasts in the *Ma'aseh Merkavah* (*Guide* III, 2).[23] The chapter opens with the Sages' assertion that there are "two firmaments" (bḤagigah 12b), which are interpreted as a general division of the spheres into two: the all-encompassing sphere and the spheres in which there are stars. Thus, the prophet Ezekiel, in his vision of the *Merkavah* (Chariot), had alluded to the precise number of spheres, whereas the Sages were content with a mere general statement. Moreover,

---

22. Shem Tov ibn Falaquera, *Moreh ha-Moreh*, ed. Y. Shiffman (Jerusalem, 2001), p. 245 l. 91.
23. This is the view of the commentators Moses Narboni, Ephodi, and Shem Tov. For the scholarly aspect see ed. M. Schwarz, p. 285 n. 12.

while the Sages held faulty views in the areas of metaphysics (the ideas) and astronomy (the sounds of the spheres), the prophets' views were true. The principle enunciated by R. Moses Narboni in his commentary to the *Guide*, according to which Maimonides believed that the prophets and the Sages had simply formulated the scientific views that were held in their respective periods, archaic as they may seem to us, is not violated by my suggestion. My thesis is that the prophets' knowledge had led them to metaphysical and scientific views that would survive the test of time, whereas the Sages had lacked such knowledge.

In the tenth chapter, Maimonides leaves the independent discussion of intellects and spheres to consider their influence on the laws of nature. Discussing the terrestrial meaning of "angel," that is, the four elements, he cites a Midrash [Pines ed., pp. 272–273]:

> They said in *Midrash Rabbi Tanhuma*: "How many steps were in the ladder? Four" — which refers to the dictum: "And behold a ladder set up on the earth" (Genesis 28:12). And in all the Midrashim it is mentioned and repeated that there are four camps of angels. However, in some manuscripts I have seen the text: "How many steps were in the ladder? Seven." But all the manuscripts and all the Midrashim agree that the angels of God whom [Jacob] saw ascending and descending were only four and not any other number — two ascending and two descending — and that the four gathered together upon one step of the ladder, all four being in one row — namely, the two who ascend and the two who descend. They even learned from this that the breadth of the ladder seen in the vision of prophecy was equal to the dimension of the world plus one third. For the breadth of one angel in the vision of prophecy is equal to the dimension of one third of the world according to the dictum: "And his body was like *tarshish*" (Daniel 10:6). Accordingly the breadth of the four is equal to that of the world plus one third. In his parables, Zechariah — when describing

that "there come four chariots... these are the four airs of the heavens which go forth after presenting themselves before the Lord of all earth... You shall hear an indication regarding this.

As for their dictum that an angel is equal in breadth to a third of the world — namely, their dictum in *Bereshit Rabbah* which reads textually: "That the angel is the third part of the world" — it is very clear. And we have explained it in our great compilation on the legalistic study of the Law. For all created things are divided into three parts: the separate intellects, which are the angels; the second, the bodies of the spheres; the third, first matter — I mean the bodies subject to constant change, which are beneath the sphere.

In this way will he who wants to understand the prophetic riddles understand them. And he will awaken from the sleep of negligence, be saved from the sea of ignorance, and rise up toward the high ones...

Maimonides is alluding here to the four elements, two of which are light, their natural motion being upwards ("ascending"), while the other two are heavy and their natural motion is downwards ("descending").[24] The attribution of this knowledge of natural laws to the Sages is also not absolute, for Maimonides is aware of the existence of a few other formulations ("seven"). Nevertheless, it is generally clear from this passage that, in his view, the Sages knew the laws of the physical world. However, his use of the metaphor of "one third," "one third of the world," requires clarification.

At first, the Midrash states that the breadth of the ladder was "the world plus one third." The word "third," Hebrew *shelish*, reflects the size of the sphere of the each element relative to the spheres of the sublunary elements.[25] Maimonides probably means

---

24. For other associations of the number four with the regularity of the material world see S. Klein-Braslavy, "Maimonides' Commentary on Jacob's Dream of the Ladder" (Heb.), in M. Hallamish (ed.), *Moshe Schwarcz Memorial Volume* [= *Bar-Ilan Annual* 22–23] (Ramat-Gan, 1987), p. 336.

25. See *Hilkhot Yesodei ha-Torah* 3:10. The expressions "sphere of fire," "sphere of air,"

that the three spheres of the sublunary elements (earth, water and air) are in the visible world, whereas the elemental fire, tangent to the lunar sphere, is neither seen nor sensed; it is therefore construed as "one third" outside the world. Later, Maimonides returns to the "third" measure, now as one of the three parts of the created world — separate intellects, spheres and the world of matter. The resulting scheme might be illustrated schematically as follows:

Out of the ⎧ separate intellect
discussion ⎩ spheres

fire air water earth
↓ ⎵⎵⎵⎵⎵
third world

This is the Midrashic interpretation, i.e., that given by the Sages. The prophets ("In his parables, Zechariah... Lord of all earth"), however, explained the matter differently, placing only God outside the world:

God
separate intellects
spheres
the elements

Maimonides clearly separates the two Midrashic interpretations (*Tanḥuma*'s and *Rabbah*'s) by interposing the words of Prophecy ("Zechariah's parables"). It might be suggested that he is intimating — for the understanding reader — that the two interpretations of "angel" and the "third" are equivalent. The implication is that the Sages, in their exegesis of the dream of the ladder, apprehended only the physical world. After all, Maimonides has already declared that "even the elements are in their turn called 'angels'" (*Guide* II, 6 [Pines, p. 262]). It follows that the Sages' comprehension did not go beyond the processes of the terrestrial world. They did not consider the spheres in themselves, and *a*

---

etc., are common in medieval literature even before Maimonides. See, e.g., *Sefer ha-Kuzari* 5:2; Ibn Ezra's commentary on Daniel 7:14; etc.

fortiori the separate intellects, which constitute the remaining "third." This contrasts with the prophetic vision, which contemplated the spheres in themselves, as Maimonides explained in the preceding chapter, and as he will further elucidate at length at the beginning of part III of the *Guide* (the "living creatures" in the vision of the Chariot). The Sages confined their attention to one third of the world only, that is, to the world of generation and corruption, which is also called "angel." In general, it should be noted that Maimonides' identification of the "third" with a material element ("a body formed of burning fire") did not satisfy him, for in chapter 6 he attributes that opinion to "those who deem themselves the Sages of Israel."[26] Whenever the Sages discussed the Active Intellect or the sphere, it was in the context of the physical-lower world.

It seems quite clear that Maimonides intended consistently to inform the understanding reader that the prophets and the Sages differed in their scientific apprehension of the separate intellects and the spheres. There are no errors in the prophets' visions, because they knew how to differentiate between dubious scientific concepts, which would ultimately evolve and change, and scientific concepts that would remain constant over time. Now the prophets were also acquainted exclusively with the scientific perceptions of their own times, and their ability to predict the future did not endow them with a knowledge of more progressive scientific theories.[27] In this respect, there was no difference between prophets and Sages. Moreover, there is some gradation among the prophets themselves; some of them, such as Ezekiel, did fall into scientific error.[28] What set the prophets above the Sages, however, was their intellectual caution. Hence the prophets' scientific views were lucid and enduring, in contrast to those of

---

26. Cf. Klein-Braslavy, "Maimonides' Interpretations," pp. 335–336 n. 14.
27. This may be alluded to at the beginning of chapter 11, where Maimonides enunciates the principle of economy in scientific theory ("it is preferable for us to rely on the arrangement postulating the lesser number of motions"). However, the Biblical verse he cites implies the opposite: "'Is there any number of His armies?' [Job 23:5] — he means because of their multiplicity."
28. See Kellner, *Maimonides*, p. 59.

the Sages, who at times tended to adopt scientific ideas that later proved wrong. The Sages' errors were particularly evident when they had already stated their opinions in the areas of metaphysics (platonic ideas) and astronomy (the sounds of the spheres). The reason for their adoption of erroneous views is given in chapter 11 [Pines ed., p. 276]:

> We have already explained that all these views do not contradict anything said by our prophets and the sustainers of our Law. For our community is a community that is full of knowledge and is perfect, as He, may He be exalted, has made clear through the intermediary of the Master who made us perfect, saying, "Surely, this great community is a wise and understanding people" (Deuteronomy 4:6). However, when the ignorant from among the ignorant communities ruined our good qualities, destroyed our words of wisdom and our compilations, and caused our men of knowledge to perish, so that we again became ignorant (*jāhiliyya*)....

Maimonides surely does not mean to say that there is no contradiction between the true "views" and "anything said by... the sustainers of our Law," for he has already pointed out at least two mistaken views of the Sages. The Biblical verse cited in the name of Moses also refers to the prophets alone. The subsequent explanation clarifies the distinction between the prophets and the Sages: the Sages lived in troubled times, plagued by persecutions, so that their wisdom was adversely affected and a disparity formed between them and the earlier generations of the prophets. Hence, the prophets possessed the true, correct philosophy, which was appropriated by the Gentile nations of the world when they conquered the Land of Israel. This passage is not only a legitimation of the pursuit of philosophy, but also a historical-apologetic explanation of the fact that Aristotle, not the Sages, held the correct view of various metaphysical and astronomical issues.

However, the systematic reason for Maimonides' distinction between the prophets and the Sages in these chapters is the prophets' reliance on analogical reasoning. Their approach to metaphysical secrets was in keeping with the criteria that Maimonides laid down in the Introduction. Neoplatonic hermeneutics posits a division into three stages: (a) Image (*eikon*) and likeness (*homoia*), where we are concerned with direct reflection, as in the case of a picture and its subject; (b) symbol (*symbolon*) — expression of the object through a part or characterization of itself, e.g., Jerusalem represented by the Old City; (c) analogy, that is, juxtaposition of the plain or outward meaning of the text with its inner, profound meaning.[29] A correct analogy is thus the result of the use of images and symbols. The prophets, through their employment of analogical thought, successfully created images, symbols, and analogies that led them to real achievements in the metaphysical field. The Sages, whose main activity was exegetical, frequently misunderstood the prophets' intention. Analogical reasoning is thus the key to understanding the chapters on the separate intellects from the standpoint of prophetic and Rabbinic authority as well.

Again: Emanation and Creation

Chapter 11 formulates the thesis that the world of existents is based on emanation (*fayḍ*), and in the course of the chapter Maimonides explains the order of emanation from God to the material world.[30] The last chapter of the literary unit we are considering elucidates the action of emanation, which depends neither on distance nor on time, but only on disposition.[31] Such action is hard to reconcile with the concept of creation *ex nihilo*, since emanation cannot

---

29. See J. Dillon, "Image, Symbol and Analogy: Three Basic Concepts of Neoplatonic Allegorical Exegesis," in R. Baine Harris (ed.), *The Significance of Neoplatonism* (Norfolk, VA, 1976), pp. 247–262.

30. There has been much debate over the relationship between emanation and Creation — see M. Schwarz's notes in his edition of the *Guide*, II, 12. I am only interested here in the unit II, 2–12 and its implications. See also D. B. Burrell, "Creation or Emanation: Two Paradigms of Reason," in D. B. Burrell & B. McGinn (eds.), *God and Creation* (Notre Dame, Indiana, 1990), pp. 27–37.

31. See Y. T. Langerman, "Maimonides' Repudiation of Astrology," *Maimonidean Studies* 2 (1991), pp. 132–133.

take effect unless the matter in question is suitably receptive. The concept of creation *ex nihilo* ("after having been nonexistent") appears in chapters 2–13 in chapter 2 as an alternative to the concept of the eternity of the world. But from then on it disappears,[32] to reappear at the beginning of the group of chapters concerning Creation (II, 13), where Maimonides explains the three opinions with regard to the world as having been created in time or as being eternal. The Torah holds that "the world as a whole… was brought into existence by God after having been purely and absolutely nonexistent." In chapter 12, however, Maimonides uses the term *ʿadam*, "nonexistence," in the sense of the lack of disposition in existing matter. Hence the discussion of the action of the separate intellects and the spheres is based on the concept of eternity, that is, of given, pre-existent matter, and only later, in the chapters devoted to Creation, does Maimonides formulate the concept of Creation *ex nihilo*.

Up to this point, I have explained the position of the unit chapters 2–12 in the second part of the *Guide*, as clarifying the methodology necessary to understand natural and intellectual activity. An understanding of the action of the Active Intellect, which is essential for Maimonidean natural science, relies on analogy; conversely, the activity of the separate intellects and the spheres becomes comprehensible as a result of analogy — and this is only one example of the importance of the analogical method. This brings out another aspect of the location of these chapters. The first unit in part II of the *Guide* is devoted to the issue of Creation, and it is there that Maimonides expresses his support for the doctrine of Creation *ex nihilo*, as he declares in the opening chapter of the unit. Nevertheless, the explanation of the action of the intellects and the spheres relies on the concept of eternity, which is the target of Maimonides' polemics. The position of these chapters may therefore be explained in a negative sense as well: Maimonides expounds at length on the concept of eternity in

---

32. This approach is mentioned only at the ends of chapters (6, 11), as a reference to the discussion to come in chapter 13 and later.

order to acquaint the reader with the elements of the view that he wishes to confront. The peripatetics were persuaded to adopt the doctrine of eternity because of not only the laws of motion but also metaphysics, that is, the nature of the emanating action of the separate intellects and the spheres.[33] Maimonides saw fit to tackle the question of the laws of physics in a direct manner, while expressing doubt as to the functional structure of the intellects and the spheres (II, 22). Hence the position of these chapters is explicated not only by methodological reasons, but also by reasons of substance. The special nature of this literary unit attests, therefore, to Maimonides' esoteric style and the unique structure of *The Guide of the Perplexed*.

(II) Medieval Exegesis of *The Guide of the Perplexed*

This part of the article investigates how medieval commentators on *The Guide of the Perplexed* dealt with the problems raised in the preceding analysis and other issues connected with chapters 2–12 in part II. Particular consideration will be given to the writings and commentaries of Moses Narboni and Mordekhai Comtino. Moses Narboni has received considerable attention in the scholarly literature on medieval Jewish thought. Comtino was a figure of exceptional stature in the Byzantine-Jewish thought of the Middle Ages: His style is frequently precise and economical; he wrote several genuinely scientific works in such areas as logic and astronomy.[34] Comtino wrote a running commentary on the *Guide*, in the course of which he pondered the location of the chapters we have been considering. We now consider some issues in his commentary, as well as works of Provençal and Spanish commentators who might influence him.

---

33. See R. Sorabji, *Time, Creation and the Continuum* (Ithaca, NY, 1983). For the combination of these arguments see, e.g., R. C. Dales, *Medieval Discussions of the Eternity of the World* (Leiden, 1990), p. 58.
34. See J.-C. Attias, *Le commentaire biblique: Mordekhai Komtino ou l'herméneutique du dialogue* (Paris, 1991); D. Schwartz, "Rationalism and Astral Magic in Jewish Thought in Late Medieval Byzantium," *Aleph* 3 (2003), pp. 165–211.

The Location of Chapters 2–12 in Part II

Maimonides explains the location of these chapters in chapter 2 [Pines ed., pp. 252–253]: "Now I think it fit that I should complete the exposition of the opinions of the philosophers, that I should explain their proofs concerning the existence of separate intellects... After that I shall go back, as I have promised, to arguing with a view to proving that the world has come into existence in time." He himself considered chapters 2–12 an independent literary unit, a digression from the general discussion of Creation. For that reason, both Profiat Duran and Shem Tov b. Joseph ibn Shem Tov stated that the unit was concerned with *Maʿaseh Merkavah*[35] and that was essentially "prolegomena to *Maʿaseh Merkavah*, which deals with emanation."[36] That is, before dealing with the issue of Creation, namely, the process of emanation that gave rise to the material world, Maimonides described the separate intellects and the spheres as the source of the emanation. Mordekhai Comtino, however, thought differently, as he writes in regard to chapter 3:

> After the preceding chapters, from which he extracted the three supreme prerequisites[37] in relation to the belief in the eternity [of the world], he introduced this chapter, an exposition from which he will proceed to explain the production [of the world] in time, that is the dispute between us and the philosophers, as he mentioned previously. And this is also a supreme prerequisite for religious people, for the belief in the eternity [of the world] would demolish the entire Torah.[38]

That is to say, in Comtino's view, the discussion of Creation begins

35. *Sefer Moreh Nevukhim* with four commentaries: Ephodi, Shem Tov, Ibn Crescas and Abravanel (Jerusalem, 1960), II, p. 17b.
36. Shem Tov, *ibid.*, p. 29b.
37. The existence, uniqueness and non-corporeality of God.
38. Comtino's commentary on *Guide of the Perplexed*, Ms. Cambridge, Trinity College 126, f. 71v. See also D. Schwartz, "Creation in Late Medieval Byzantine Jewry: A Few Aspects" (Heb.), *Peʿamim* 97 (Autumn, 2003), pp. 63–80.

in chapter 3, not chapter 13, where Maimonides lists the opinions relating to "the eternity of the world or its production in time." Comtino's view is interesting both in light of Maimonides' explicit affirmation that he was placing the issue of the intellects and the spheres before that of Creation, and in view of the fact, mentioned above, that Creation *ex nihilo* is not mentioned until chapter 13. Clearly, Comtino thought that the proofs of God's existence, uniqueness and non-corporeality, as well as His movement of the spheres, were concentrated in the two opening chapters of part II of the *Guide*, and that from then on Maimonides was dealing directly with the issue of Creation.

Analogy

Attention was drawn in the preceding analysis to the significant role of analogy in the *Guide*, and to the use of the Active Intellect as an auxiliary tool in understanding the position of the separate intellects. Some commentators, such as Shem Tov b. Joseph ibn Shem Tov, simply explain Maimonides' text as it is, while others take a more critical stance. One of the critical commentators is Moses Narboni, who comments at length on Maimonides' discussion of the proportions in *Guide* II, 4, in his own commentary on Ibn Rushd's *Epistle on the Possibility of Conjunction*, chapter 14.[39] Narboni compares Maimonides' views with those of Ibn Rushd on the topic. Ibn Rushd would have agreed to the first proportion (the separate intellect is to the sphere as the Active Intellect is to the elements). Maimonides and Ibn Rushd differ, however, with regard to the second proportion. Maimonides argues that the soul of the sphere, the intellect of the sphere and the separate intellect that moves the sphere are three distinct entities. Ibn Rushd, however, followed by Narboni, rejects the very existence of the intellect of the sphere as "the form of the celestial body,"[40]

---

39. See above at note 13.
40. K. P. Bland (ed.), *The Epistle on the Possibility of Conjunction with the Active Intellect by Ibn Rushd with the Commentary of Moses Narboni* (New York, 1982), Hebrew Section, p. 126 l. 229 [English translation: p. 96].

that is, as the form of the sphere. In his view, "The soul and the intellect [of the sphere] and the separate intellect are substantially one but conceptually three, contrary to what the late Master believed, that it is a composite."[41] The distinction between the three animative and intellectual agents moving the sphere is functional but not ontological. Narboni therefore concludes in regard to Maimonides' second proportion, which distinguishes between the intellect of the sphere and the separate intellect, that "the relation [posited by Maimonides] is not true in existence, for they are things which have absolutely no existence. And nature does not act in vain."[42] Hence Narboni's approach (following Ibn Rushd) makes it possible to combine Maimonides' two proportions into one:[43]

$$\frac{\text{Active Intellect}}{\text{human intellect (2nd preparation)}^{44}} =$$

$$= \frac{\text{Active Intellect}}{\text{elements and composites in the material world}} =$$

$$= \frac{\text{separate intellect}}{\text{sphere}}$$

Nevertheless, this is not a perfect proportion. Narboni comments that, while the separate intellect is the only form of the sphere,

---

41. *Commentary on The Guide of the Perplexed*, ed. J. Goldenthal (Wien, 1832), p. 27b.
42. See, e.g., *De Caelo* 271a33; *Epistle on the Possibility of Conjunction*, ed. Bland, p. 127 ll. 239–240 [English: p. 96].
43. *Ibid.*, p. 130 ll. 275–277 [p. 96].
44. Narboni states that "the relation of the Active Intellect insofar as it conjoins with us — it being a form in us — is the relation of the Separate [Intellect] with the sphere in one respect, I mean, in certain ways, but different in certain ways, as is clear from what has already preceded" (*ibid.*, ll. 240–242 [p. 98]). According to the *Espistle on the Possibility of Conjunction*, the Active Intellect conjoins with man after the material disposition of the intellect has disintegrated in the highest stage of intellection and is replaced by a second disposition, which makes conjunction possible. See on this question H. Davidson, "Averroes and the Material Intellect," *AJS Review* 9 (1984), pp. 174–184; D. Schwartz, *Old in New Vessels: The Philosophy of a Fourteenth-Century Jewish Neoplatonic Circle* (Heb.; Jerusalem, 1997), p. 179; G. Holtzman, "The Theory of the Intellect and Soul and the Thought of R. Moshe Narboni, Based on His Commentaries on the Writings of Ibn Rushd, Ibn Tufayil, Ibn Bajja and Al-Ghazali" (Heb.), Ph.D. dissertation, The Hebrew University (Jerusalem, 1997), pp. 86–87 and *passim*.

elements and composites have a material form, on the one hand, and on the other, a form "in the sense of absolute existence,"[45] that is, the Active Intellect. Thus, Narboni discusses Maimonides' proportions and criticizes them in light of Ibn Rushd's theory of the intellect. His discussion, however, is philosophical-technical, not literary-methodological. Neither in his commentary on the *Guide* nor in his commentary on Ibn Rushd's *Epistle of the Possibility of Conjunction* does Narboni consider the proportions as reflecting Maimonides' general system.

God as Mover of the Sphere

There has been much deliberation over Maimonides' self-contradiction both in the *Guide* and in the legal code *Mishneh Torah* (in *Hilkhot Yesodei ha-Torah*) on the question of whether God is the mover of the highest sphere.[46] In some passages, Maimonides asserts that God moves the sphere. In *Guide* II, 4, however, he states that "it cannot be true that the intellect that moves the highest sphere should be necessary with the necessary of existence" [Pines ed., p. 258–259]. Comtino clearly believes that God does move the sphere:

> What is clear from Aristotle's principles is that the mover of the first sphere is the Creator, blessed be He, and moreover the Master explained this in chapter 70 of the first part,[47] and that is the truth, for there is no separate [intellect] that is not a mover, for nature does not act in vain. But Master's argument rejecting this view, saying that if that were the case it would have something in common with the other movers, that is the opinion of the commentators on Aristotle's books. Now this doubt may be resolved, for the movement of the Prime Mover is universal and voluntary, while the movement of the

---

45. Bland ed., l. 277.
46. See M. Schwarz's translation, p. 274 n. 34.
47. "Similarly, the deity... is the mover of the highest heaven, by whose motion everything that is in motion with this heaven is moved" (I, 70 [Pines ed., p. 172]).

other movers is partial and necessary, and they can have nothing at all in common.[48]

Even if God moves the sphere, he is still clearly distinct from the intellects, for (1) the intellects move only part of the system of spheres, whereas the movement of the highest sphere causes that of the entire system; (2) the intellects move necessarily, while God moves voluntarily. Comtino thus rejects the Neoplatonic approach taken by Maimonides in these chapters.

"The World plus One Third"

Commentators on the more esoteric aspects of Maimonides' thought have been at a loss to understand his ambiguous explanation of the puzzling Midrash. I have tried to propose a solution that combines his two interpretations of the "third," on the assumption that he masked his opinion of the Sages' approach to scientific matters. R. Joseph Kaspi explains "that sometimes these four angels will meet in one line across the ladder; so it seems to [Jacob] that the width was one world and a third."[49] He means to say that the steps along the length of the ladder are three: the world of the intellects, the world of the spheres, and the sublunar world. Jacob saw in his vision the lower step — that of the sublunar world — divided into four; that is to say, the width of the lower step is divided into four, namely, the four elements or four sides of the world (the four directions). Since "the size of the one angel is one third of the world, as will be explained below," Jacob believed that the width of the lower world is "one world and a third." The second step, that of the spheres, Kaspi adds, also divides into four, that is, the four spheres described in chapter 9. To my mind, Kaspi is intimating that, according to the Midrash, Jacob believed that the width of the lower world exceeds its length by one third, something that is not scientifically true.

What seems to have been clear to Kaspi, as he indicates, was

---

48. Commentary on *The Guide of the Perplexed*, Ms. Cambridge, f. 72r-v.
49. *Ammudei kesef u-maskiyyot kesef*, ed. S. Werbluner (Frankfurt a/M, 1848), p. 96.

not so for Moses Narboni. "Now these four that came together on one step [of the ladder] were the four directions, and the four directions of the heavens are precisely the four angels come together on one step, and those constitute only a third part, that is one third of the world; so how could that be one world and a third?!" Narboni indirectly rejects the interpretation of Jacob's vision as referring to the excessive width occupied by the elements, for the width of the sublunar world cannot exceed that of the world of the spheres. Narboni explains simply that since each element is called an "angel," and the Midrash added that "an angel is one third of the world," it follows at first sight that the width of the lower world is indeed one world and a third. However, further examination reveals that the width of the four elements is only one third of the world ("the four of them are but that angel, who is one third of the world, he is the third, lowest, part, of the parts of the created beings").

When Comtino wrote his own commentary, Narboni's commentary was at his disposal. Referring to the passage in the *Guide*, he quotes Narboni and expresses his dissatisfaction:

> This is the explanation offered by superior commentators, but I say that such an explanation is consistent neither with the Midrash nor with the context if explained thus. I shall explain now what I have been able to understand after much study. Know that caused existence is divided into three parts, namely, the parts of existence mentioned everywhere [= matter and form], and existence corresponding to privation. But you will find a further, fourth part, and that is what is alluded to in the Midrash stating that there are four camps of angels.[50] And it is not wrong to include everything under the noun "angels," seeing that the noun "angel" is an equivocal word, and the formulation of [the Midrash] was guided by the majority usage [of the noun "angel"]. By "ladder" [the Midrash]

---

50. See M. Schwarz's edition, p. 288 n. 28.

is alluding to the totality of existence corresponding to privation, and since the three parts constitute existence, and the fourth part is above it, [the Midrash] sets it apart [from them] after including it, saying "[God was] standing over him." The Midrash also understands the *bet* of *ba-sullam* [= "on the ladder"] as extending the meaning or again follows the majority usage. The angels of God ascending and descending are four in number: The two <descending ones>[51] are man and the rest, and the two ascending ones are the celestial bodies, both the eternal and the corrupted, and all of caused existence, that is, the world whose parts are three in number. And when you contemplate the linkage of the totality of existence with the [First] Cause which fashions it and does everything, you will find that everything [measures] one world and a third, and that is the width of the ladder. And the Master did not have to bring this because of the steps of the ladder, of which there were four, for he had already stated in some versions "seven"; but it was only because of those ascending and descending.[52]

Comtino has found a simple solution: The noun "angel" has several meanings, among them "privation." Thus Jacob's ladder symbolizes not only the levels of being, but also modes of being: existence (intellects, spheres, and the lower world) and privation. An "angel" in the sense of intellects, spheres and the material world is "one third of the world," and an "angel" in the sense of privation is the third in "one world and a third." Of course, Comtino has to postulate a correspondence between existence and privation for "privation" to be possess, as it were, absolute existence, as is required by his interpretation. However, given Maimonides' basic philosophical and scientific assumption, that "nonexistence" is not a species or mode of existence, the interpretation seems highly problematic, to say the least, despite Comtino's efforts.

---

51. The manuscript reads here "who speaks with" (*ha-medabber ʿim*) (?).
52. Commentary on *The Guide of the Perplexed*, Ms. Cambridge, f. 74v-75r.

Conclusion

The interpretations of Jacob's dream and the discussion of "one world and a third" reflect the difference between modern scholarship and various trends in the medieval exegesis of *The Guide of the Perplexed*. Medieval commentators explained ancient Midrash on the basis of a knowledge of the four spheres, considering the Rabbinic interpretation of the theory of separate intellects as part of the three parts of existence.[53] Modern esoteric research, on the other hand, points to the difference between prophecy and Rabbinic Midrash. In the modern view, the dominant motive for the concealment of esoteric lore was agnostic; for the medieval commentators, however, it was the sciences that had to be concealed, because of their abstruseness and high level of sophistication.[54] We have tried to emphasize the methodological aspect, that is, the use of analogy, as part of the motive for concealment. Analogical thought did not enjoy high regard in Aristotelian scientific circles, being considered an inferior method of proof. Maimonides, however, acknowledging his use of analogical methodology, declared that certain truths were inherently unprovable. Nevertheless, he concealed the level of his use of analogy. The unit of *Guide* II, 2–12 thus reflects the general nature of *The Guide of the Perplexed*.

Appendix: On Analogy and the Attributes

Analogical arguments are very common in the *Guide*. The chapters dealt with above present only one example of Maimonidean methodology. I would like to present another example of an analogical argument of key importance for understanding Maimonides' thought in the *Guide*. It is concerned with the discussion of the theory of divine attributes.

---

53. See e.g. the commentary of Shem Tov b. Joseph (f. 26r). Shem Tov himself adopts an esoteric approach in his interpretation of the chapters of the *Guide*. See Schwartz, *Contradiction and Concealment*, pp. 196–217.
54. See A. Ravitzky, "The Secrets of the Guide to the Perplexed: Between the Thirteenth and the Twentieth Centuries," in I. Twersky (ed.), *Studies in Maimonides* (Cambridge, MA, & London, 1990), pp. 159–207.

In the relevant chapters of the book, Maimonides raises the problematic issue of how to distinguish between knowledgeable people, once the theory of divine attributes has been rejected. To be precise: if no positive attribute can be associated with the deity, how can a distinction be made between the wisest of the wise (e.g., "Moses our Master and Solomon") and an ordinary individual? In the two chapters most relevant to this issue, Chapters 59 and 60 in Part I, Maimonides answers that, for the wise man, negation of the attributes is based on a demonstrative argument.[55] These two chapters follow immediately on a series of almost desperate attempts to distinguish between God and those existents which can be described in positive terms. The difficulty is obvious: One cannot make a distinction between *a* (God) and *b* if *a* is indescribable and indefinable. Since the attributes, first and foremost that of existence, are associated with God and the objects in a "purely equivocal" manner (II, 56), there is no real way to describe the difference between God and the objects, and the discussion is pointless. To overcome the difficulty, Maimonides proposes two conceptual schemes that provide insight into the distinction between God and the other existents:

(i) *Distinction between essence and existence*, postulating that God's essence and existence are identical, but that is not so in the other existents (I, 57). If we accept Rahman's interpretation of the accidentality of existence in Avicenna and Altmann's interpretation of the same issue in Maimonides, we cannot, it seems, assume a world of essences, some or all of which become existent. In their view, the distinction is between an object that has a cause for its existence and one that does not.[56] In that case, this approach is not particularly

---

55. See Hyman, "Demonstrative, Dialectical and Sophistic Arguments" (above, note 1). For demonstration in relation to the theory of attributes see *ibid.*, p. 43.

56. F. Rahman, "Essence and Existence in Avicenna," *Medieval and Renaissance Studies* 4 (1958), pp. 1–16; A. Altmann, "Essence and Existence in Maimonides," *Studies in Religious Philosophy and Mysticism* (London, 1969), pp. 108–127. But see A. L. Ivry, "Maimonides and Neoplatonism: Challenge and Response," in L. E. Goodman (ed.), *Neoplatonism and Jewish Thought* (Albany, 1992), pp. 146ff.

helpful in enabling one to differentiate the deity from other existents.

(ii) *Analogy*. A partial description, e.g., of man as an animal (since man is defined as an intelligent animal; hence "animal" is part of the definition of a person), is in some degree analogous to negative attributes. Maimonides is probably alluding to the following analogy:

$$\frac{\text{animal}}{\text{man}^{57}} = \frac{\text{negative attributes}}{\text{God}}$$

In Maimonides' view, this analogy implies "some particularization" (I, 58, p. 134), but he admits the deficiency of such an analogy between attributes of affirmation and attributes of negation. The analogy becomes more accurate to the degree that its members are more narrowly defined or closer together (e.g., in an inference from primates to human beings). Thus, negative attributes constitute "guidance"[58] toward the greatest possible apprehension.

Having suggested two ways to overcome the total non-apprehension of God, so as to distinguish between Him and the attributes of the existents, Maimonides then tries to distinguish between the knowledge of perfect, wise persons and superficial or deficient knowledge. The distinction between essence and existence and the analogy seem to imply a gradation of apprehension, even when the object of apprehension cannot be conceived of in positive terms. Briefly: The wise man understands the profound meaning of the term "existence" and is acquainted with the elements of the analogy, and in that respect he differs from the ignorant person. Hence Chapters 57 and 58 constitute an introduction to Chapter 59, where Maimonides proposes the

---

57. "For instance, if you would see a man at some distance and if you would ask: What is this thing that is seen? and were told: This is a living being — this affirmation would indubitably be an attribute predicated of the thing seen, though it does not particularize the latter, distinguishing it from everything else. However, a certain particularization is achieved through it; namely, it may be learnt from it that the thing seen is not a body belonging to the species of plants or to that of the minerals" (I, 58 [p. 134]).

58. Arabic *irshād* (Munk and Joel, p. 92 line 11).

distinction between the apprehension of the wise and that of the ignorant. Thus, analogy plays a major role in Maimonides' theory of attributes.

4.

"The Ravings of Amulet Writers": Maimonides and His Disciples on Language, Nature and Magic[1]

Aviezer Ravitzky

> "Its trace was not effaced though the Law has opposed it for thousands of years."
>
> (*Guide* III:37)[2]

Amorite Ways

Maimonides was the greatest Jewish critic of what is described today as "popular religion;" as he saw it, its practices and beliefs constituted "Amorite ways." He declared bitter war against widespread beliefs and universal practices that monotheism (as he understood it) firmly opposed but that remained prevalent even among his fellow Jews. Accordingly, Maimonides extended as far as possible the reach of the biblical admonitions against acts of soothsaying and divination, sorcery and magic, necromancy and casting spells. He applied these prohibitions to all aspects of these activities and everything associated with them, from astrology and astral magic to sleight-of-hand and use of verbal spells for

---

1. Translated from the Hebrew by Joel Linsider.
2. Pines trans., p. 546. (Except as otherwise noted or indicated by brackets, quotations from the *Guide* are presented in the Pines translation: Moses Maimonides, *The Guide of the Perplexed*, Shlomo Pines, trans. [Chicago and London, 1963]). Maimonides makes this comment in the specific context of the magical act of passing a child through smoke from a fire in order to ensure his wellbeing (the vestige of a symbolic idolatrous practice of ancient fire worshippers; cf. Deut. 18:2). The broader context treats all "those that set up these false opinions, which have no root or any utility, in order to fortify belief in them [among human beings]." (*Guide* III:37 [Pines trans. pp. 545–546].)

medicinal purposes to "establishing signs [of blessing] for oneself, [saying] 'if thus and such happens to me, I will take a particular action [and succeed] but if it does not happen, I will not take that action.'"[3] Maimonides' mighty hand placed such activities far beyond the bounds of Jewish religion and made them, and others like them, accessories of idolatry and incitements to worshipping false gods.

But in attacking magic in all its manifestations, Maimonides did not focus exclusively on halakhic or normative considerations, on questions of good and evil or of proscribed and permitted conduct. He denied the validity of magic from a cognitive, intellectual point of view as well, as a matter of truth or falsity, of rational activity versus mere imaginings:

> All these things are false and deceitful... anyone who believes in these things and others like them, regarding them to be matters of truth and wisdom that the Torah has nevertheless forbidden, is nothing but a fool lacking intelligence.[4]
>
> I know that most people, perhaps all, are greatly fooled by them... and even good and pious people of our Torah think they are correct and only forbidden by the Torah, failing to recognize that they are idle and false, and the Torah admonished [us] about them just as it admonished [us] about falsehood.[5]

Every act of sorcery or divination expresses a mistaken understanding of reality. It reflects a misguided human pretension to break out of the natural order and intervene in the workings of the

---

3. Maimonides, *Mishneh Torah, Hilkhot Avodat Kokhavim* 11:4. See the comment of *Kesef Mishneh ad loc.*: "The divination forbidden by the Torah refers to one who makes his actions depend on a sign that reason suggests has no effect, positive or negative, such as his bread falling on the ground or a deer stopping near him on the road, for these and similar things are Amorite ways. But one who relies on signs that reason suggests have positive or negative effects is not engaged in divination, for all worldly activities proceed in that manner."
4. Maimonides, *Mishneh Torah, Hilkhot Avodat Kokhavim* 11:16.
5. Maimonides, *Commentary on the Mishnah, Avodah Zarah* 4:7. Maimonides is referring to the making of talismans to draw spiritual bounty from the astral array.

world through the use of some other, imaginary, causal system, following "supernatural" or "sub-natural" rules. All that stands in opposition to the divine wisdom that is embodied precisely in nature's rational laws and in demonstrated physical causality.

Magic is thus based on error, both scientific and theological. On the scientific plane, each magical technique expresses a cognitive distortion in some area, for it is grounded in a vain belief regarding some definite aspect of the natural order (such as belief in the stars' spiritual influence, belief in the wondrous capabilities of substances, or belief in the energy embodied in holy names). On the theological plane, however, the magical technique can be caught up in the overall, ultimate falsehood of idolatry. If it is not rooted in idolatry, it leads toward it via its inherent inner logic. The magician attributes independent metaphysical powers to physical substances, thereby challenging divine sovereignty; he imagines the existence of supernal beings that mediate between God and the world, thereby impairing God's transcendence; and he will eventually entice his believers into straightforward idolatry, as he directs their desire and their esteem toward the stars (supernal substances) and the spiritual bounty (metaphysical forces) they imagine can be drawn from them:

> These are called by [the Sages], may their memory be blessed, Amorite usages, for they are branches of magical practices, inasmuch as they are things not required by reasoning concerning nature and lead to magical practices that of necessity seek support in astrological notions. Accordingly the matter is turned into a glorification and worship of the stars.[6]

The campaign against magic, accordingly, is nothing less than the campaign to purify and refine monotheistic belief. Maimonides ventures forth on its behalf in both his halakhic rulings and his philosophical teachings, and he does so at the cost of disregard-

---

6. *Guide* III:37 (Pines trans. p. 543). Cf. *Hilkhot Avodat Kokhavim* 1:1.

ing, and, on occasion, knowingly setting aside, magical elements to be found in rabbinic literature.

Written Amulets

Contemporary scholars have already dealt with various aspects of Maimonides' view of magic[7] and have comprehensively considered his view of astrology.[8] The situation differs, however, with respect to Maimonides' merciless critique of the belief in written amulets and, more broadly, of the belief in the magical force of the holy tongue (Hebrew) and the holy names (of God). That critique has not yet undergone the independent examination it merits; on the contrary, it has been portrayed in the literature as simply one branch, perhaps a marginal one, of the broader

---

7. I. Twersky, "*Halakhah and Science: Aspects of Maimonides' Epistemology*" (Hebrew), *Jewish Law Annual* 14–15 (1988–1989), pp. 136–147; id. *Introduction to the Code of Maimonides* (New Haven and London, 1980), pp. 479–484; D. Schwartz, "Magic, Experimental Science and Scientific Method in Maimonides' Teachings" (Hebrew), in A. Ravitzky, ed., *From Rome to Jerusalem: Memorial Volume for Joseph Barukh Sermonita (Jerusalem Studies in Jewish Thought*, vol. 14) (Jerusalem, 1998), pp.26–45; id., *Astrology and Magic in Medieval Jewish Thought* (Hebrew) (Ramat-Gan,1999), pp. 92–121), M. Halbertal, *Between Torah and Wisdom* (Hebrew), pp. 41–49, 162–170; S. Lewis, "Maimonides on Superstition," *JQR*, 17 (1905), pp. 475–488; B. Safran, "Maimonides' Attitude to Magic and Related Types of Thinking," B. Safran and E. Safran, eds., in *Porat Yosef: Studies Presented to Rabbi Dr. Joseph Safran* (Hoboken, NJ 1992), pp. 93–110; J. D. Bleich, "Maimonides on the Distinction between Science and Pseudoscience, "in F. Rosner and S.S. Kottek, eds., *Moses Maimonides: Physician, Scientist, and Philosopher* (Northvale, NJ and London, 1993), pp.105–115; J. Stern, *Problems and Parables of Law* (New York, 1998), pp. 117–133.

8. Maimonides' attitude toward astrology has been studied more comprehensively than his view of any other aspect of popular religion or pseudo-science. Scholars disagree over whether he considered astrology primarily a religious hazard, primarily a scientific fraud, or equally objectionable on both counts. See R. Barkay, *Science, Magic and Mythology in the Middle Ages* (Hebrew) (Jerusalem, 1987, pp.12–16; H. Kreisel, "Maimonides' Approach to Astrology" (Hebrew), *Proceedings of the Eleventh World Congress of Jewish Studies* (Jerusalem, 1994), section 3, vol. 2, pp. 25–32; Y. T. Langerman, "Astronomical Issues in Maimonides' Thought" (Hebrew), *Daʿat* 37 (1996), pp.111–113; R. Lerner, "Maimonides' Letter on Astrology," *History of Religion* 8 (1968), pp.143–158; J. Helborn, *Le Monde Juif et Astrologie* (Milano, 1985); Y. T. Langerman, "Maimonides' Repudiation of Astrology," *Maimonidean Studies*, 2 (1991), pp. 123–158; G. Freudental, "Maimonides' Stance on Astrology in Context: Cosmology, Physics, Medicine and Providence," in F. Rosner and S.S. Kottek, eds., *Moses Maimonides: Physician, Scientist and Philosopher* (Northvale, NJ and London, 1993), pp. 77–90.

critique of astral magic and has been subsumed within it. In what follows, therefore, I will try to consider the significance and distinctiveness of the Maimonidean polemic against language-based magic. It is true that Maimonides' naturalistic deliberations led him to reject uniformly all magical phenomena. But, as we shall see, the rejection of linguistic magic was marked by its own definite considerations, beginning with Maimonides' reliance on a specific theory of language and encompassing a sharp theological warning against turning the sacred into an instrument for profane purposes. No wonder, then, that Maimonides' disciples and early interpreters showed special interest in this aspect of Jewish magic. They probed the significance of the difficulties raised by the Master's words, and they cleared new paths for his teachings.

A written amulet is intended to affect reality by means of letters and words, in order to derive some benefit in a supernatural manner. It thus constitutes a magical act making use of language, and it comes as no surprise that Maimonides interpreted the phenomenon in the context of considering the names of God. As early as in his *Commentary on the Mishnah*, in discussing the Ineffable Name of God, he protested against the use of amulets and rejected it outright as foolishness: "Do not burden your mind with the ravings of amulet writers and stupid people [who invent holy names themselves]."[9] He later reiterated this position in the *Guide*, this time adding a warning to the reader:

> Do not let occur to your mind the ravings of the writers of [amulets] or what names you may hear from them or may find in their stupid books, names that they have invented, which are not indicative of any notion whatsoever, but which they call the *names* [of God] and of which they think that they necessitate *holiness and purity* and work miracles. All these are stories that are unfit for a perfected man to listen to, much less believe in.[10]

---

9. Maimonides, *Commentary on the Mishnah*, Sotah 7:4.
10. *Guide* I:61 (Pines trans. p. 149. Pines uses "charm" for the term here translated as "amulet." — *translator's note*)

These two works — the *Commentary on the Mishnah* and the *Guide of the Perplexed* — were written a generation apart in time, but the interval in no way dulled the polemical sting; as we shall see, the opposition to amulets and linguistic magic reflects a series of basic principles in Maimonides' thought. One later commentator on the *Guide*, R. David Messer Leon, went so far as to regard that opposition as they keystone of the *Guide* in its entirety. As might be expected of a Jewish thinker in Renaissance Italy, David Messer Leon conflated linguistic magic with the wisdom of (practical?) Kabbalah,[11] and, in his view, Maimonides made the rejection of amulets the focus of his declared war against such phenomena. Messer Leon writes as follows in *'Ein ha-Qore*, his commentary on the *Guide* (the work is only extant in ms.):[12]

> The Master [Maimonides] denies Kabbalah, for you know what he wrote about the names of 42 letters and 12 letters; he considered the entire matter in accordance with reason and denied the effectiveness of amulets, and that is the basis of his book... He revealed the fraud of amulets, dedicating a chapter to it,[13] which is the opposite of what is written in the Kabbalah and its operations, as is well known from that wisdom, its names, and its actions.[14]

Messer Leon certainly goes far afield here; the denial of linguistic magic is not "the basis of [Maimonides'] book." Still, it is necessar-

---

11. M. Idel, "The Magical and Neo-Platonist Interpretation of the Kabbalah During the Renaissance" (Hebrew), *Jerusalem Studies in Jewish Thought* 4 (1982), pp. 60–111.
12. Hava Tirosh-Rothschild, *Between Worlds-The Life and Thought of Rabbi David ben Yehudah Messer Leon* (Albany, 1991).
13. *Guide* I:62.
14. David Messer Leon, *'Ein ha-Qore* (on the *Guide of the Perplexed*), ms. Oxford-Bodleian Reggio 41 (Neubauer 1263) (film no. 22077 of the Hebrew Institute for Microfilmed Manuscripts at the Jewish National Library, f.n. 53, n.79), p. 155. Cf. id. p. 125: "For he undermined this wisdom — the Kabbalah — all the way to its basic principles, and he treats as foolishness the dealing with such amulets" (id. p.21). Messer Leon himself did not share the views he attributed to Maimonides; he sought to harmonize philosophy with Kabbalah and the mystery of the names: "What the philosophers attribute to natural matters and causes, the Kabbalists regard as being alluded to and received in the names and writings and letters and names, but it is all a unity to one who understands the basic principles." (id., p.125).

ily implied by the book's religious and philosophical roots. What, then, is the fulcrum of this forceful argument against amulet writers and believers? What disturbed Maimonides and on what analytical foundations did he construct his critique? I attempt below to clarify these foundations in accordance with their place in Maimonides' teachings and as they evolved in his disciples' writings.

The Theory of Language

To begin, the phenomenon of written amulets is based on a dangerous error regarding the essence of language in general and religious language in particular. Amulet writers attribute to the Hebrew language an intrinsic, sacral value. For them, language serves not only as an instrument for transmitting content; rather, it itself *is* content. A word does not merely represent something external; it also has its own inherent significance. Moreover, believers in amulets attribute an efficient power to words and letter-combinations. Not only do Hebrew words acquire independent; imminent standing, no longer constituting simply an array of signs that represent reality; beyond that, language is understood as an activating mechanism, as an agency that shapes and creates reality. It necessarily embodies a unique energy and effectuating force that enable it to operate externally. In that sense, the array of signifiers precedes the array of the signified; the word determines existence; and from the word, the owner of the amulet draws the magical power to change reality to his benefit.

Maimonides disagreed entirely with this metaphysical conception of language, and even more with its magical usage. From his viewpoint, language is a semantic phenomenon, not an ontological reality; it is based on human convention rather than objective truth.[15] Accordingly, one should neither attribute inherent

---

15. *Guide* II:30. See A.S. Halkin, "The Medieval Jewish Attitude Toward Hebrew," in A. Altmann, ed., *Biblical and Other Studies* (Cambridge, MA, 1963), pp. 233–248; B. Septimus, "Maimonides on Language," in Aviva Doron, ed., *The Heritage of the Jews of Spain* (Tel Aviv, 1994), pp. 35–54.

value to words nor look for substantive intrinsic correspondence between signifier and signified. Words are useful signs, means of expression and communication, and they are peculiarly suited for their purpose precisely because they are a human phenomenon, the result of convention, the fruit of mankind's collective creative spirit. This applies no less to the Hebrew language, which, though selected by God to be the language of revelation, was not directly invented or formed by Him. In stating that "the man gave names [Gen. 2:20]," Maimonides explained, the Torah "inform[s]... us that languages are conventional and not natural."[16] His commentator Moses Narboni added: "And there is nothing natural there, in certain words leading us to certain matters, but all is conventional, whether on the part of one person or many."[17] Accordingly, the sanctity of the holy language should not be conceived of as essential, metaphysical sanctity: no human phenomenon and no human creation, including the Hebrew language, could possibly attain such heights. Hebrew, to be sure, is singled out from other languages and is superior to them, but that conclusion rests on ethical and aesthetic criteria, not transcendent ones.[18]

---

16. *Guide* II:30 (Pines trans., pp.357–358). Cf. *Pirqei Mosheh bi-Refu'ah*, ed. Z. Montener (Jerusalem, 1959), p.361.
17. Moses Narboni, Commentary on the *Guide* (Y. Goldenthal edition, Vienna, 1832; reprinted in *Three Early Commentaries on the Guide* [Hebrew], Jerusalem 1961), II:30, p. 42a. Of particular interest, Narboni contrasted conventional language not to divine language but to the inferior language of animals, "who have naturally distinct sounds for asking, calling, and pushing aside; for animals can only comprehend the particular, and therefore their concern is with natural indication, but we comprehend the general, and are therefore concerned with conventional indication." Human linguistic convention flows from the powers of abstraction and conceptualization that distinguish humans from other animals. For more complex views, see M. Idel, *Abraham Abolafia: Language, Torah and Hermeneutics* (Hebrew) (Jerusalem and Tel-Aviv, 1994), pp.23–43. H.A. Wolfson sought to interpret Maimonides' remarks against their plain sense and reconcile them with the metaphysical conception of language. I find his effort unpersuasive, and, in any case, I know of no medieval thinker, whether disciple or critic of Maimonides, who read him as Wolfson would. See H.A. Wolfson, *Religious Philosophy* (New York, 1965), pp. 235–236.
18. *Guide* III:8 (Pines trans., p. 435) — "I can also give the reason why this our language is called *the Holy Language*... for in this holy language no word at all has been laid down in order to designate the organ of copulation... neither the urine nor the excrements... they being signified by terms used in a figurative sense and by allusions. It was intended thereby to indicate that these things ought not to be mentioned and consequently that no terms designating them should be coined."

Maimonides' fundamental view here comes close to the Aristotelian concept (as distinguished from the Platonic or Stoic concept) of language, its source, and its essence. For Maimonides, however, this was more than an abstract, philosophical outlook; the conceptual doctrine had direct parallels in the normative, halakhic field. For example, Maimonides rules that "all blessings may be recited in any language," not necessarily in Hebrew.[19] Similarly, Maimonides did not require a Jew to pray in the holy tongue; in the *Commentary on the Mishnah* he heartily recommended doing so but did not demand it, and in the *Mishneh Torah* he omitted even the recommendation.[20] In both situations, the content, not the wording, is of primary importance.[21] How vast the distance between this approach on the part of a man of *halakah* and the various mystical or magical conceptions of prayer and its wording! Moreover, Maimonides unreservedly preferred Arabic songs "in praise of courage or gravitas" to Hebrew poems of indecent or questionable content, "for whether speech is forbidden or permitted, desirable or revolting, or worthy of being uttered, follows not from the language in which it is said but from its subject."[22] He thereby cast down the gauntlet to "great and pious men of our nation," who, he said, tended to prefer Hebrew poetry almost unconditionally. Again, from Maimonides' consistent perspective, not the language but the content it conveys is of primary importance.

Joseph ibn Kaspi, Maimonides' radical disciple, went even further toward aesthetic criteria, asserting that Hebrew is called the holy language because "none is like it in precision and detail" (*Kappot Kesef*, in *Asarah Kelei Kesef* [Pressburg, 1903], 2, p. 17). In contrast, many other sages expressed surprise at Maimonides' assertions. See, for example, Nahmanides, *Commentary on the Torah* on Ex. 30:13; Ritva, *Sefer ha-Zikkaron* (ed. K. Kahana, Jerusalem, 1983), p. 72: "May God grant him atonement for [this], for he attributed so great and awesome a matter [as the sanctity of Hebrew] to something so insignificant… and it is an unintended error on the part of the master."

19. *Mishneh Torah, Hilkhot Berakhot* 1:6.
20. G. Blidstein, *Prayer in Maimonides' Halakhic Teaching* (Hebrew) (Jerusalem, 1994), p. 39.
21. J.Levinger, *Maimonides as Philosopher and as Decisor* (Hebrew) (Jerusalem, 1992), pp. 94–98.
22. Maimonides, *Commentary on the Mishneh*, Avot 1:16, p. 419. See I. Twersky, *Introduction to the Code of Maimonides*, p. 324, n. 1.

Traces of this outlook likely can be seen as well in Maimonides' fundamental concept of the nature of prayer. Maimonides rules that prayer without attention to meaning does not constitute prayer. Not only does a person who merely articulates the words fail to discharge his obligation of a statutory prayer, he is not considered to have prayed at all. In other words, concentration on meaning is not merely an element of prayer or a condition of prayer; it is, rather, what truly constitutes prayer! Prayer depends not on the word but on the state of mind. Language is not considered here to be a communication tool as much as an expression of divine worship, but it is precisely on that account that any ascription of independent value to the words is even more emphatically negated.

Interestingly, a fourteenth-century Maimonidean sage, Judah Romano, told in one of his books how he had stayed away from the synagogue for an extended period to avoid taking part in rote repetition of the forms of prayer in a manner void of content. "For they opened their mouths, paying no attention to any of the words they uttered," he said of his community, "and when I heard the sound of the people as they shouted, I said 'it is the noise of them that sing that I hear' [cf. Ex. 32:17–18], sounding and blasting... for no one understood the sound of any syllable."[23] R. Judah resumed worshipping with the congregation only after he was able to compose an exegetical tract in which he assigned philosophical meanings to key passages of congregational prayer ("*Be'ur ha-Qaddish ve-ha-Qedushah*"). Although his practical ruling would have differed, Maimonides would have understood R. Judah's sensitivity nonetheless.

If that is the case regarding prayer, how much more so with respect to belief, which involves not oral declaration but inner

---

23. Caterina Rigo, *The Be'urim on the Bible of R. Yehudah Romano* (Hebrew), doctoral dissertation, Hebrew University, Jerusalem 1996, p. 137; Y. B. Sermoneta, "Judah and Immanuel of Rome — Rationalism Culminating in Mystical Faith" (Hebrew), in M.Halamish and M. Schwarz, eds., *Revelations, Faith, Understanding* (Hebrew) (Ramat-Gan, 1976), pp.60–61; G. Sermoneta, "La dottrina dell'intelleto e la 'fede filosofica' di Jehudah e Immanuel Romano," *Studi Medievali*, III 6, 11 (1965), pp. 3–78.

cognitive conviction. As Maimonides puts it: "Belief is not the notion that is uttered, but the notion that is represented in the soul when it has been averred of it that it is in fact just as it has been represented."[24] It is not hard to imagine Maimonides' reaction to his teachings and principles of faith having evolved, over the ages, into poetic formulations and rote declarations. R. Joseph Kapah, the modern translator of Maimonides' writings into Hebrew, commented ironically: "It is interesting that they have made the thirteen principles of religion compiled by our teacher into a literal 'credo.'" (Kapah hastened to add: "It is not to be found in the Yemenite prayer book.")[25]

Maimonides' theory of language thus comprised philosophical, theological and halakhic perspectives. The philosophical assessment leaned toward the Aristotelian concept regarding the nature of language and its human source. The theological determination sought to maintain the divide between man and God and deny human language any metaphysical or transcendent importance. Finally, the halakhic decisions strongly emphasized content rather than Hebrew language and denied an inherent value to bare, rote utterance.[26]

It need scarcely be said that these viewpoints foreclosed *ab initio* any effort to invest words with some inherent energy or active force. They left room neither for theurgic presence to influence the divinity of force of language nor for magical pretense to thereby influence the universe; they precluded such manipulation whether by means of written amulets or by means of spoken words. Maimonides' theory simply rules out all such possibilities.[27]

---

24. *Guide* I:50 (Pines trans, p. 111). See S. Rosenberg, "The Concept of '*Emunah*' in Post-Maimonidean Jewish Philosophy" (Hebrew),Bar-Ilan University Annual (Ramat-Gan,1988),pp.355–365; A. Ravitzky, *Crescas' Sermon on the Passover and Studies in His Philosophy* (Hebrew) (Jerusalem, 1989), pp.49–56.

25. Y.Kapah, a note in his Hebrew translation of the *Guide of the Perplexed* (Hebrew) (Jerusalem, 1972), part 1, p. 113, n. 4.

26. A. Elkayyam, "Between Referentialism and Effectuation: Two Approaches to Understanding the Kabbalistic Symbolism in *Sefer Ma'arekhet ha-Elohut*" (Hebrew), *Da'at* 24 (1990): 37–40.

27. In other words, language operates solely on consciousness. It affects intellectual and emotional life but not the natural, cosmic or divine world.

Language is intended to describe and articulate, not to create or effectuate.[28] Religious language is no exception: the holy names attributed to God (in the Talmud and *midrash*) are not God's implements; on the contrary, they are soubriquets assigned to God in the wake of His actions. They have no *a priori* standing in advance of the created world; they are *a posteriori* only, derived from the created world. In Maimonides' words: "All the derivative names have come into being after the world has come into being. This is correct, for all these names have been laid down so as to correspond to the actions existing in the world."[29]

This concept of the divine names is rooted in Maimonides' "negative theology." God Himself has no names, for no words can describe Him. Language falls short of being able to definitively represent divine content. The holy names, accordingly, were formulated — "[came] into being," in Pines'translation — at the time of creation, and they represent functions, actions, or natural laws embodied in the world. Only one name, the Ineffable Name, has independent, ontological standing. It alone refers to the divine essence itself and is not derived from the created world. For that very reason, it refers to the divine existence as existence ("I am what I am"), not to any attribute or characteristic whatsoever.[30] None of the other names have any original, essential standing; their very differences and their very number mean that they refer not to God but His creations. "All of them are names set down in accordance with the acts to be found in the world."

---

28. For an examination of the conflicting premises that underline Hebrew linguistic magic, see Y. Dan, *On Holiness* (Hebrew) (Jerusalem, 1997), pp. 127–130; Y. Harari, "How to Perform with Words: Philosophical *Halakah* and Magical Acts" (Hebrew), *Jerusalem Studies in Jewish Folklore* 19–20 (2000), pp. 363–392. These works include comprehensive bibliographies on linguistic magic in general.
29. *Guide* I:61 (Pines trans. p. 149).
30. "All the names of God, may He be exalted, that are to be found in any of the books derive from actions. There is nothing secret in this matter. The only exception is one name: namely, *Yod, He, Vav, He*. This is the name of God, may He be exalted, that has been originated without any derivation, and for this reason it is called the *articulated name*. This means that this name gives a clear unequivocal indication of His essence, may He be exalted"(*Guide* I:61 [Pines trans., p. 147]). See A. Hyman, "Maimonides on Religious Language," in J.L. Kraemer, ed., *Perspectives on Maimonides* (Oxford, 1991), pp. 175–191.

Were it otherwise — were we to attribute the holy names to the essence of God Himself and infuse them with independent metaphysical standing — we would thereby create a multiplicity within God and impair the monotheistic belief. Indeed, practitioners of linguistic magic are likely to rely on just such heretical premises. As Jacob Anatoli (Naples, thirteenth century) wrote, "these sciences [physics and metaphysics] brought about their great disgrace, causing them to err and term the vain names that they devised in their own mindless minds 'the Account of the Chariot,'[31] may God grant them atonement."[32]

It is no wonder, therefore, that when Maimonides mentions the Talmudic tradition about the concealment of the primeval holy names, he turns the mystics' and magicians' premises on their head. In his account, the names were indeed kept secret and transmitted only orally, to exceptional individuals; but that was not because they conveyed some non-rational content or some mysterious active force. On the contrary, they were secreted away because of the opposite concern, that people might make them the bases for faulty beliefs (such as these or others), beliefs foreign to "the comprehension of the Active Intellect" and to "divine science," that is, the truth of physics and metaphysics. When "blameworthy people started learning *the name having twelve letters,* and through this corrupted beliefs... the Sages made a secret of this *name* likewise."[33]

Deceit and Fantasy

The writing of amulets thus rests on faulty beliefs and reflects both scientific and religious error. But that does not end the matter: the practice needs to be condemned not only for theoretical reasons

---

31. The Account of the Chariot (*ma'aseh merkavah*), referring to Ezekiel's vision in chapter 1 of his book, has a variety of connotations for mystics. Maimonides, however, associated it with the science of metaphysics. — *translator's note.*
32. Jacob Anatoli, *Malmad ha-Talmidim,* Lik 1866 (Israel, 1968), Introduction, p. 11. Anatoli attributes this to "the view of most of our sages, the rabbis."
33. *Guide* I:62 (Pines trans., pp. 150–151).

but for normative ones as well. Regardless of whether amulets are constructed of made-up "names," as Maimonides thought, or of authentic holy names, which Maimonides denied, they must be invalidated for reasons of good and evil. If the amulet comprises fictitious letter combinations, newly devised, it constitutes willful deceit. If, on the other hand, it comprises authentic letter combinations — the original, primeval holy names — its use demeans the sancta, making them into mere secular instrumentalities.

Let me first consider the former possibility. On this premise, which Maimonides favored, we now possess no authentic holy names. The ancient names have been hidden and lost to us, and we have no others to replace them. Accordingly, the existing phenomenon of linguistic magic necessarily entails deceit. It uses imaginary names not derived from divine actions: "they indicate nothing whatsoever." What is the source of the belief in amulets and how did it spread among the masses? Maimonides sketched out an interesting paradigm for the development of that fraudulent esoteric tradition. Its originators formed a willful conspiracy, inventing holy names and deceiving people with them. Eventually, their disciples reduced their teachings to writing, thereby giving them the aura of an ancient, authoritative tradition. At the next stage, these writings were hidden from the masses, adding to their aura of mystery and profundity. And now, the tradition has become widespread, a part of the popular culture. In other words, nothing can win people's hearts and become a widely held popular belief like an "underground," occult literature that has been uncovered. As Maimonides writes:

> When wicked and ignorant people found these texts [the Talmudic terminology regarding the names of God], they had great scope for lying statements in that they would put together any letters they liked and would say: this is a *name* that has efficiency and power to operate if it is written down or uttered in a particular way. Thereupon these lies invented by the first wicked and ignorant man were written down, and these writings transmitted to good,

pious and foolish men who lack the scales by means of which they could know the true from the false. These people accordingly made a secret of these writings, and the latter were found in the belongings left behind them, so that they were thought to be correct. To sum it up: "*A fool believes everything*" [Prov. 14:15].

We have gone beyond our noble subject and our subtle speculation, turning to speculation designed to invalidate vain imaginings the lack of which is manifest to every beginner in speculation. However the necessity that made us mention the *names* and their meaning and the opinion concerning them that is generally accepted by the vulgar has led us to do so.[34]

This, then, is the story of the secret tradition of Hebrew linguistic magic: it begins with the evil willfulness of individuals and concludes with the innocence and folly of the masses.[35] To sharpen our understanding of Maimonides' approach in portraying that history, we may compare it to the alternative account appearing in *Tiqqun ha-Deʿot* by Isaac Albalag, a thirteenth-century Jewish Aristotelian rationalist who wholeheartedly joined in Maimonides' negative assessment of amulet writers. Albalag, like Maimonides, rejected linguistic magic and presented it as "a vain idea," but Albalag offered a different view of the phenomenon's development: he saw it, first and last, as growing out of speculative deviation rather than willful planning. The story of the phenomenon is one of gradual philosophical corruption, beginning with early Neo-Platonic through and extending to "the Ishmaelite philosophizers," to "the would-be wise ones of our nation" (in the Middle Ages), and on to "the amulet writers" and "some naïfs among the kabbalists."

The philosophical error began with the Neo-Platonic thinkers. They depicted reality according to an ontological hierarchy, on

---

34. *Guide* I:62 (Pines trans., p. 152).
35. See below for Maimonides' concept regarding the development and spread of idolatry.

which each upper substance emanates one (and only one) entity below it: "for only one can come of one." Later, Muslim thinkers (apparently a reference to Avicenna and his circle) and Jewish thinkers translated the erroneous philosophical system to the language of religious belief. They taught that each upper entity ("angel") performs one (and only one) action in the reality below it: "for a single agent can produce only a single act." Accordingly, they said, the fact that many actions go on in our world means that the upper world is correspondingly populated with many active substances. Still later, naïve kabbalists and "amulet writers" translated this into their own language of mysticism and magic: they presumed to reveal the secret of the hidden "name" of each supernal agent and, thereby, to uncover as well the mystery of the one-to-one correspondence between each hidden name and its potential action in the world. When they attained that understanding, they imagined, they would possess the keys to the workings of the universe, at which point they would be able to accomplish anything they wished. As Albalag wrote in *Tiqqun ha-De'ot*:

> The [Neo-Platonist] philosophizers' belief that only one could come of one is simply an error... and because the Ishmaelite philosophizers[36] were not careful in their speculation... they thought that a single agent could produce only a single act... and our nations' would-be wise ones erred in the same respect... and thought that a single angel does not perform two missions, to the point that they required each and every act that takes place in the world to have its own angel in charge of it, and they therefore called each one by the name of the act unique to him... and these are the names that reached the amulet writers, and some naïfs among the kabbalists were misled by them and counted them among the holy names because of the similarity in their structure and

---

36. Apparently a reference to Avicenna and his circle.

the combinations of letters, and they believed them to be part of tradition. But in fact, according to the opinion of the [Aristotelian] philosopher, this is nothing but a fraud and vain idea issuing from the kabbalist.[37]

This is an original depiction of the evolution of ideas over time: from philosophy to theology, from theology to mysticism, and from mysticism to the magic of amulets and names. In truth, Albalag, the Aristotelian (Averroist?) *par excellence*, portrayed his rivals here in his own image: a purely intellectual one. In contrast to Maimonides (and despite the latter's influence on him),[38] he did not conceive of linguistic magic as the product of the creative imagination or of an evil will; rather, he saw it as the outgrowth of a speculative error having its own inner logic. In other words, the dispute with the amulet writers was simply one more link in the long-standing dispute that spread throughout the Middle Ages[39] between followers of Averroes and followers of Avicenna.[40]

In any event, Maimonides and Albalag were in agreement in their assessment of the extant phenomenon of linguistic magic and of the letter combinations it employs: "according to the

---

37. Isaac Albalag, *Sefer Tiqqun Ha-Deʾot*, ed. Y.A. Vajda (Jerusalem,1973), p. 60. See G. Vajda, *Isaac Albalag — Averroiste juif traducteur et commentateur de ʾAl-Ghazali* (1960), pp. 205–206.
38. In addition to the above, compare, for example, the following remarks by Maimonides: "And when the names deriving from the actions pertaining to Him, may He be exalted, were multiplied, they produced in the fantasy of some men the thought that He has many attributes, just as there is a multiplicity of actions from which these names derive" (*Guide* I:61 [Pines trans., p. 148]).
39. See Avicenna, *Al-Shifa*, ed. Yusef Musa and Saʾid Ziʾad (Cairo, 1960), part 2, pp. 405 et seq; Averroes, *Tahafut al-Tahafut*, ed. M Bouyges (Cairo, 1930), pp. 216 et seq. And see A. Ravitzky, *Al Daʾat ha-Maqom* (Jerusalem, 1991), pp. 200–201; H. A.Wolfson, "The Plurality of Immovable Movers in Aristotle, Averroes, and St. Thomas," in I. Twersky and G.H. Williams, eds., *Studies in the History of Philosophy and Religion* (Cambridge MA 1973), pp. 1–11.
40. According to Albalag, Maimonides, too, can be counted in many respects on Avicenna's side, in that he failed to adhere consistently to Aristotelianism: "And this happened to R. Moses in his book called *Guide of the Perplexed*, in the concepts of science that he cited. In truth, his error in the realm of science was no greater than his error in the realm of belief... for both drew on the same spring and taught a common system, and that is the system of Al-Farabi and Avicenna" (*Tiqqun ha-Deʾot*, p. 5). See K. Sirat, *Philosophical Thought in the Middle Ages* (Hebrew) (Jerusalem, 1975), p. 315.

opinion of the philosopher, this is nothing but a fraud and a vain idea."

Holiness and Desecration

A certain paradox now emerges. It is only on the premise that amulets are constructed of made-up "names" that Maimonides could rest content with merely disparaging their writers and mocking their believers, stopping short of excluding them from the community and denouncing them as absolute deniers of the Torah.[41] Had the amulets relied on authentic and reliable holy names, he would have had to judge them far more stringently, as he did in other instances where sancta were made into secular instrumentalities and magical devices for material benefit to humans.

For example, Maimonides strictly forbade the use of biblical verses as medicinal incantations, as well as the magical use of sancta such as Torah scrolls or phylacteries. But he went far beyond the halakhic prohibition itself in condemning such practices: "It is not enough for them to engage in divination and spells; they also deny the Torah, in that they make words of Torah into physical cures, when they are exclusively spiritual cures."[42] Maimonides took special pains to sharply deplore the magical use of the *mezuzah*, given its dangerous (imagined) resemblance to an amulet. In his view, a *mezuzah* and an amulet are in no way variations on the same theme; indeed, they are polar opposites:[43]

Those who write the names of angels or holy names or a

---

41. In this section, I focus only on the use of sancta for secular purposes, disregarding for now the risk of "Amorite ways."
42. *Hilkhot Avodat Kokhavim* 11:12. See M.Halbertal, *Between Torah and Wisdom*, pp. 41–42. Maimonides distinguishes carefully between one who recites verses for magical purposes and one who recites them "so that the merit of reciting them will protect him." The magical use is invalid and disgraceful, but reading verses to gain merit is permitted.
43. Maimonides emphasizes an analogous distinction between astrology as fraud and astronomy as science. See *Maimonides' Epistles*, ed. Y. Shilat (Hebrew) (Jerusalem, 1988), part 1, pp. 481–482.

verse or insignia inside [a *mezuzah*] are within the category of those who have no place in the world-to-come. For these stupid people are not satisfied with [merely] annulling the commandment; worse, they take a great commandment — [acknowledging] the unity of the name of the Holy One Blessed Be He and loving and serving Him — and treat it as an amulet for their own pleasure, like one who foolishly imagines that this is a source of pleasure amid the vanities of the world.[44]

In the case of the *mezuzah*, to be sure, we are dealing not only with the risk of inverting values, of theological corruption; in addition, the *mezuzah* itself may be impaired halakhically. But it is clear that the former consideration is the decisive one for Maimonides; as he puts it, "they are not satisfied with [merely] annulling the commandment." We can illustrate this by comparing Maimonides' ruling to the contrary rulings of more or less contemporary Ashkenazi sages. For example, R. Eliezer of Metz (Re'em) ruled as follows on the very same subject: "People have become accustomed, for enhanced protection of the home, to write, at the end of the lines [in the *mezuzah*], insignia and names of angels. These are not required nor part of the commandment, put they provide additional protection."[45] R. Simhah b. Samuel (author of *Mahzor Vitry*) went even further: "One should take care that the twenty-four names and twelve angels and their twenty-four insignia be prominent on the sheet [of the *mezuzah*] at the end of the lines."[46] R. Eliezer permitted what Maimonides forbade and R. Simhah actually required it, and it is obvious that this disagreement involved more than a formal halakhic dispute.

---

44. *Hilkhot Mexuzah* 5:4. See the limiting interpretation in *Kesef Mishneh* ad loc.: "For the *mezuzah* protects the home when it is properly written, but not so the [names of] angels written within it. The purpose in making it is not to protect the home; rather, one should intend to fulfill the commandment of the Holy One Blessed Be He, and it follows of itself that it will protect the home." The need for such a position demonstrates the radicalism of Maimonides' position.
45. Re'em of Metz, *Sefer Yerei'im ha-Shalem*, sec. 400.
46. Simhah b. R. Samuel of Vitry, *Mahzor Vitry* (Berlin, 1893), p. 648. See E.E. Urbach, *The Tosafists* (Hebrew) (Jerusalem, 1968), p. 138.

It represented as well a gap between different cultures and different religious conceptions.

In sum, according to Maimonides, those who make the *mezuzah* into "an amulet for their own benefit" thereby forfeit their place in the world to come. On the other hand, those who invoke made-up "names" and combine letters into amulets certainly perform acts of "raving" and "folly" that "are unfit for a perfected man to listen to, much less believe in," but they do not give up their share in the world to come; their acts desecrate not God's name but only the fruits of their false imaginings.[47]

And what if we had authentic holy names? How far would the Maimonidean protest against linguistic magic reach? Interestingly enough, it is kabbalistic literature that may provide a vivid illustration of that sort of forceful protest. I am referring to the writings of certain kabbalists who, on the one hand, firmly believed in the authenticity of the holy names, but, at the same time, internalized Maimonides' teachings and his profound horror of using sancta for secular purposes. It is those writers who can be expected to man the ramparts against the magical use of names, and a surprising example appears in the book *Sha'arei Orah* by R. Joseph Giqatilla, one of the greatest kabbalists in thirteenth-century Spain:

> How can one born of woman utilize His holy names, making of them an axe with which to slice? And who is the one so presumptuous as to appropriate the sovereign crown and make use of it?...If the angels on high are admonished with regard to uttering the Name of God, may He be blessed, how much more so [is one destined to become] maggots and worms, and still more so one who misleads himself into using the crown of his Creator? A fortiori, since there is no one nowadays who

---

47. See above, n. 9. It thus appears that what is decisive here is not only the amulet writer's intention or state of mind (for he intended, after all, to use sancta for his own benefit), but also — indeed, primarily — the objective truth regarding the actual status of the holy names. The subject warrants examination in relation to Maimonides' teachings overall.

has expertise in uttering the Name of God and actively using it. Given that, one who does utter it will achieve only the loss of his share in the world to come; and of this the Rabbis of blessed memory said: "One who does not care for the honor of his Creator would be better off not having come into this world." And now, my son, heed my voice and let your ears attend to my counsel. "My son, if sinners try to lead you astray, do not yield to them." If they say, "Come with us, and we will deliver to you names and utterances that you can use," "my son, do not set out with them and keep your feet away from their path," for those names and usages are all types of nets and snares for hunting souls and going to oblivion.[48]

In all of Jewish literature, it would be difficult to find another so forceful and florid an admonition against the magical use of holy names. But we should not be misled by Giqatilla's comments, for it would not even have occurred to him to question the importance of contemplating the names of God. In fact, Giqatilla made that inquiry the focus of his treatise and the pinnacle of his religious consciousness: he argued against the drive to act in the world through the list of names, but not against spiritual inquiry and study of the names' mysteries. He trumpeted against religious magic,[49] not against the mysticism of language.[50] But

---

48. Joseph Giqatilla, Sha'arei Orah, Introduction (ed. Y. Ben-Shelomo, Jerusalem, 1971, part 1, pp. 46–47).
49. As Moshe Idel has noted, a different tendency can be identified in Giqatilla, according to which "when a person knows the meaning of certain utterances regarding the distinctive Name he utters... the force of that utterance compels doing his will." (Joseph Giqatilla, Ginat Egoz [Hanova, 1615], p. 46.) Our concern here is restricted to the critique of linguistic magic. See M. Idel, The Writings and Teaching of R. Abraham Abolafia, doctoral dissertation, Hebrew University (Jerusalem, 1976), part 1, pp. 129–130; id., "Judaism, Jewish Mysticism, and Magic" (Hebrew), Mada'ei ha-Yahadut 36 (1997), p. 37. Idel there also cites R. Abraham Abolafia, who came out against the use of made-up names and understood the names of God as mechanisms for changing consciousness, not for action.
50. On the relationship between mysticism and magic in the kabbalists' conception of language, see G. Scholem, Basic Understanding of the Kabbalah and Its Symbolism (Hebrew) (Jerusalem, 1976), pp. 41–47; Y. Dan, On Holiness (Hebrew), pp. 108–130; A. Greenwald, "Spelling, Writing, and the Ineffable Name" (Hebrew), Masu'ot,

Maimonides, writing before him, had rejected both equally, for reasons of both religious faith and philosophical outlook.

The Cosmic Path and the Linguistic Path

How does the specific critique of linguistic magic with its amulets fit into Maimonides' overall battle against the phenomenon of magic in all its manifestations? And what is the relationship between this battle and Maimonides' underlying and comprehensive religious naturalism? On its face, the answer seems self-evident: the critique of amulets is one specific instance of fundamental religious naturalism; and the specific case entails nothing not encompassed by the general rule. Indeed, most contemporary studies suggest that neat pattern. As I see it, however, the writings of Maimonides and his disciples paint a more complicated picture, inviting finer distinctions; and not in vain did it grip the attention of followers and opponents alike during the Middle Ages.

Without doubt, Maimonides in many respects understood linguistic magic as a derivative of magic in general. When a magician aspires to act on reality by means of the energy embodied in words, he does not differ in essence from his colleague who aspires to do the same thing by means of wondrous qualities attributed to substances (the magic of charms) or a spiritual effluence attributed to the stars (astral magic). All of them rest on the same false basis: they pretend to draw their power from an independent cosmic metaphysics, from strange and exalted forces that flow through the universe, neither subservient to natural law nor derived directly from the divine Source. In that sense, the opposition to the magic of names is simply one expression among many of the religious philosopher's fundamental recoiling from any belief in immanent supernatural powers that operate in lower worlds (according to the magician) and would thereby diminish

---

pp. 90–93; G. Scholem, "The Name of God and the Linguistics of the Kabbalah," *Diogenes*, 79 (1972), pp. 59–30, 80 (1973), pp. 164–194.

Heaven's exclusive sovereignty. According to Maimonides, we encounter divine wisdom precisely through its being instilled in the natural, causal order; it is embodied not in suspensions of that order but in the world operating in its normal course. (Not for nothing did Nahmanides note with surprise that Maimonides "diminishes miracles and empowers nature."[51]) Accordingly, any human manipulation intended to annul the natural systems or to impose on them some other form of causality sets itself willy-nilly in opposition to the heavenly conduct of the universe. In other words, such manipulation contradicts Maimonides' religious naturalism; and that is so even in the case of a linguistic magician who presumes to overcome nature by means of holy names attributed to God Himself.

Samuel of Lunel, a radical commentator on Maimonides in the late fourteenth century (whose treatise remains preserved only in manuscript[52]) expressed the idea as follows: the manipulators of names "think they are honoring God," but they are in error, "for it demeans Him, may He be blessed, to do things contrary to the nature of reality." R. Samuel forcefully protested against the magical use of the Ineffable Name and its theoretical roots in kabbalistic wisdom:

> Many have erred in thinking that the mystery of the Ineffable Name is a profound matter whose truth is not known, and that its profundity lies in the wonders and marvels performed by uttering it. These are the kabbalists and the writers of amulets, who the Master [Maimonides] fiercely detested....We should not believe what many of the kabbalists believe, who use it to perform many acts contrary to nature and attribute them to the Ineffable Name. God forbid that should be the case, for they intend

---

51. Nahmanides, *Torat ha-Shem Temimah*, in *The Writings of Nah*manides (Hebrew), ed. C.Chavel (Jerusalem, 1963), p. 154.
52. I am now preparing the treatise for publication in a critical, annotated edition.

to honor Him, but it demeans Him, may He be blessed, to do things contrary to the nature of reality.[53]

In this decisive sense, Maimonidean religious naturalism drew no distinctions among the various branches of magic, denying them all. But did Maimonides regard them as parallel in all respects? That indeed appears to be the case with respect to astral magic and the magic of charms; he portrays them equally as slippery slopes leading their practitioners directly to idolatry: "They…lead to magical practices that of necessity seek support in astrological notions. Accordingly the matter is turned into a glorification and a worship of the stars."[54] But did he encompass linguistic magic within the same rubric? Did Maimonides regard written amulets as direct incitements to idolatry? I have found no textual proof for that proposition. On the contrary, it is reasonable to distinguish clearly between an (invented) supernatural *cosmic* path that ultimately depends on the pinnacle of the physical universe, i.e., *heavenly forces*, and an (imagined) supernatural *linguistic* path that ultimately depends on the pinnacle of metaphysical existence, i.e., *God Himself*. Both paths are invalid and disgraceful, and both represent analytical snares and religious ruin; but only the first leads straightforwardly to idolatry.[55] The second, to be sure, constitutes "ravings" and "deception," but it is not to be judged in terms of idolatry and absolute heresy.

This distinction may also help explain a familiar *halakhah*

---

53. Samuel of Lunel, Commentary on the *Guide*, ms. Vatican Neophyti 17 (film no. 625 in the IMHM of the Jewish National Library, cf. n. 14), I:61, pp. 33b–34a. See also id., 1, 62, p. 33b: "The mystery of the Ineffable Name depends on demonstrated truths… but this can only be conceived in the mind of a perfect sage."

54. *Guide* III:37 (Pines trans. p. 543).

55. Logically, it seems that Maimonides' approach requires a distinction between holy names attributed to God Himself and holy names attributed to angels or other supernal beings; it is not at all inconceivable that the latter could lead to idolatry. One can easily envision, for example, Maimonides' reaction to a comment such as the following, found in a geonic responsum: "There are some areas in which angels act as they see fit, needing no authorization from on high, and amulets accordingly are written, and names are uttered, in order to assist the angels in that respect"! (*Teshuvot ha-Ge'onim*, ed. A. Harkavy [Berlin, 1887], p. 373.) Still, Maimonides never formulated such a distinction between the two classes of names.

in the *Mishneh Torah* that many have noted with surprise. "One may go out [to the public domain on the Sabbath] with a tested amulet,"[56] writes Maimonides; that is, it is permissible on the Sabbath to carry such an amulet, which is considered a personal ornament or article of clothing.[57] The ruling is not innovative or original; Maimonides simply paraphrased the *Mishnah* and subjected himself to the authority of the Sages.[58] Moreover, Maimonides was dealing with a formal point of law rather than a theological question; he allowed a particular, commonly found item to be carried on the Sabbath, without thereby intending to validate its use or magical effectiveness. Indeed, Jacob Levinger has noted that "the *Mishneh Torah* is striking in its inclusion of laws whose underlying premises Maimonides certainly did not accept. For example, Maimonides cites the law that one may go out on the Sabbath with a tested amulet… 'What is a tested amulet? One that has cured three people'… But it cannot be assumed that Maimonides believed that there ever in the world existed an amulet that cured anyone."[59] All that being true, I nevertheless doubt Maimonides would have treated an actual instrumentality of idolatry — or an object able to lead directly to idolatry — in the same way. More likely, he would have found a way to circumvent or omit the authoritative source (as he did in other contexts[60]). On the other hand, if we assume that the Maimonidean *halakhah* dealt only with an amulet using holy names but not with an astral amulet (that is, merely with foolishness but not with idolatry), its problematic aspect is immeasurably eased.[61]

---

56. *Mishneh Torah, Hilkhot Shabbat* 19:14.
57. Moses Narboni, Commentary on the *Guide*, I:61, p. 11a.
58. *Mishnah, Shabbat* 6:4.
59. J.Levinger, *Maimonides' Halakhic Thought* (Hebrew) (Jerusalem, 1965), p. 129.
60. Maimonides omitted or circumvented the original law when he believed it rested on erroneous scientific principles. See Levinger, *Maimonides' Halakhic Thought* (Hebrew), pp. 118–140; Twersky, *Introduction to the Code*, pp. 235, 479. A different overall approach is presented in B.Z. Benedict, *Maimonides In Line With the Talmud* (Jerusalem, 1985).
61. For a different approach to the subject, see J.D. Bleich, "Maimonides on the Distinction Between Science and Pseudoscience," pp. 111–115, (F. Rosner & S. Kottek, eds., *Moses Maimonides: Physician, Scientist* (Northvale, 1993)).

Speculation and Nature

Thus far, I have proposed drawing a distinction between the two branches of magic — the cosmic and linguistic — and treating the latter more leniently (from Maimonides' viewpoint) with regard to the risk of idolatry. Let me now turn to other consequences of that distinction, primarily from the perspective of Maimonidean naturalism.

As noted above, Maimonides greatly expanded the category of "Amorite ways." He subsumed within it any act undertaken for medical or other supposedly beneficial purposes in the absence of a natural explanation or empirical verification of its effectiveness. A legitimate action, therefore, must satisfy at least one of two conditions: theoretical foundation or experiential verification. On the one hand, "all that is required by speculation concerning nature is permitted, where other practices are forbidden;" on the other, "it is allowed to use all remedies similar to those that experience has shown to be valid, even if reasoning does not require them."[62] These conditions — natural speculation and empirical verification are derived from it. "Amorite ways" are intended to diverge from the physical order (that is, from the divine plan), while "the ways of Torah" are yoked to and act within it:

> The commandments may be violated [where necessary in a health emergency] only for medical treatment, that is, measures that heal by natural means, as shown by speculation and experience. But it is forbidden [to violate a commandment] to [attempt to effect a] cure through the use of charms, for their power is weak, they are not based on theory or experience; it involves a weak, erroneous claim. Know and remember that principle, for it is great.[63]

---

62. *Guide* III:37 (Pines trans., pp. 543–544). See Y. Kremer, "On Aristotle and the Scientific Method According to Maimonides" (Hebrew), in M. Idel, Z. Harvey, and A. Schweid, eds., *Festschrift for Shlomo Pines* (*Jerusalem Studies in Jewish Thought* 9) (Jerusalem, 1990), pp. 215–216; A. Hyman, "Maimonides on Causality," in S. Pines and Y. Yovel, eds., *Maimonides and Philosophy* (Boston, 1986), pp. 153–158.

63. Maimonides, *Commentary on the Mishnah, Yoma* 8:4. He attributes the point to "Sages," in opposition to the view of R. Matiya b. Harash, who allows a person bitten

Maimonides appears to have delineated clear, sharp criteria for distinguishing sorcery from medicine, magical acts from rational ones. But his followers and his critics alike soon complicated matters, wondering about the status of magic that had achieved empirical success or of an amulet that had been examined and found to be effective time and time again. Would they be forbidden on the basis of theoretical analysis or permitted on the basis of factual results? On the one hand, Maimonides had written that everything experientially verified is permitted. On the other hand, the magician claims that all his actions are tested and effective; and if the decisive criterion is experience rather than principle, the dispute over magic loses its essential force and becomes a superficial debate over results and facts, over the effectiveness of one or another technique. This question was the focus of an intense polemic that broke out in early-fourteenth-century Provence between Rashba and Abba Mari ha-Yarḥi. The issues in that polemic have been thoroughly clarified by modern research.[64]

But the issue continued to trouble later Maimonidean sages. They directed their attention specifically to linguistic magic, which poses distinctive problems. As long as the magician uses a physical object, the philosopher can attribute any empirical successes to the object's previously unknown natural characteristics, to some physical quality that could not be examined before having been experimentally discovered (such as magnetism).[65] He need not deny the facts. But what can the philosopher do when confronted with the experientially confirmed magical use of linguistic tools? Can he assign similar qualities and internal

---

by a mad dog to eat the dog's liver for medicinal purposes even on Yom Kippur.

64. See, recently, Schwartz, *Astrology and Magic in Medieval Jewish Thought* (Hebrew), pp. 111–114; Halbertal, *Between Torah and Wisdom* (Hebrew), pp. 165–168.

65. Maimonides himself in his medical writings spoke of natural qualities such as those concealed in medicines: "and the actions that drug will perform within his body as a result of its form... are what physicians call 'qualities'... such as the laxative qualities of laxative drugs or the emetic qualities; or drugs that are fatal to one who consumes them or that save one bitten by a venomous animal." (Maimonides, *Pirush le-Pirqei Abuqeret*,ibn Tibbon trans., p. 11. See Schwartz, *Magic, Empirical Science, and Scientific Method in Maimonides' Teachings* (Hebrew), p. 35; A.C. Crombie, *Medieval and Early Modern Science* (New York, 1959), vol. 1, pp.120–122.

forces to words and verses? Will he deny the Maimonidean linguistic theory that sees words as nothing more than signs and symbols? Naturally enough, this problem raised eyebrows and led to differences of opinion. Let me therefore briefly trace the principal approaches adopted by Maimonides' interpreters over the ages: they range from an extreme naturalist conception that rules out even some psychological influence of the amulet on its user (lest that be interpreted as empirical verification) to a clearly magical concept that did not balk at attributing to Maimonides himself a belief in the wondrous power of amulets and names.

Let me begin with Moses Narboni, one of the greatest commentators on the *Guide* (his treatise was completed in 1362). Narboni vividly described his personal impressions of contemporary acts of linguistic magic:

> What appears to the eye to be [the effective] operation of amulets and names does not negate the Master's [Maimonides'] comments, for it is chance or the work of the imagination. And in our own time, while we were studying science, one of the great scholars conducted an experiment, writing an amulet in which he included words of derision, scoffing, and ridicule, and he achieved repeated success: women in difficult labor, on whom all other remedies had been ineffective, placed the amulet [on their bodies] and gave birth. One day, the distinguished people of the town, Bourges, were seated before him, talking about the names, and he denied their belief in them. They cited many proofs of its truth, the greatest of which was the verification provided by the amulet that he himself had made. He directed that it be brought to him, and he disclosed what he had done, showing the mockery that was in it, and they were mortified. But he later suffered grievous injury to himself.
>
> We have also seen a weak-minded person who would utter a name and pierce his hip with a needle or an awl, suffering no pain and not even bleeding. But when I tried

to [do the same and] bring it near me, I fled from it, sensing the undoing of the joint. We had heard that name together from some person in our youth. Yet he, because of the strength of his imagination and the weakness of his intellect, was not afraid; but for me, [because] it was [in my consciousness] within the class of impossibilities, it was impossible [in reality as well].[66]

The phenomena described by Narboni are known in various, diverse cultures, and his proposed explanations for the magician's success — chance and autosuggestion — are not at all surprising. Maimonides himself had already made use of the first explanation in his *Commentary on the Mishnah*: "Everything that is regarded as the action of these 'talismans' is something that could happen by chance, and they attribute it [in error] to them [acts of magic]."[67] But while Maimonides had resorted to that explanation only to account for the "efficacy" of astral magic, Narboni extended it to linguistic magic as well. Narboni's second explanation tied magical success to autosuggestion: the hidden "name" operates not on reality but on consciousness.

Interestingly enough, Narboni wrote all this only on the basis of Maimonides' reasoning;[68] he himself declined to rule out the effectiveness of a magical act.[69] Nor did he see any need to distinguish between the linguistic and cosmic branches of

---

66. Moses Narboni, Commentary on the *Guide*, I:61, p. 11a.
67. Maimonides, *Commentary on the Mishnah, Avodah Zarah* 4:7; *Guide* III:37: "Now this [the affliction threatened by the sorcerer] may happen by accident some day to a certain individual" (Pines trans., p. 546). See Schwartz, *Astrology and Magic in Medieval Jewish Thought* (Hebrew), p. 105.
68. Even in this context, one can sense the uncertainty about whether there might be something real to magic: the man who mocked linguistic magic "later suffered grievous injury to himself;" the name used by the Jewish fakir was one "we had heard together from some person in our youth."
69. K. Sir'at, "*Pirqei Mosheh* by Moses Narboni" (Hebrew), *Tarbiz*, 39 (1970), pp.302–306; A. Ravitzky, "The Anthropological Doctrine of Miracles in Medieval Jewish Philosophy," in *History and Faith* (Amsterdam,1996), pp. 177–8; id., *Crescas' Sermon on the Passover*, p. 89; Gatit Holtzman, "The Reasons for the Commandments According to R. Moses Narboni"(Hebrew), *Asufot* 9 (1995), pp. 280–283; id., *The Doctrine of the Soul and the Intellect in the Thought of R. Moses Narboni*, doctoral dissertation, Hebrew University (Jerusalem, 1997),pp. 309–314.

magic. On the contrary; there is a direct link between the magical potential inherent in "names" and that inherent in "minerals and vegetation."[70] In contrast to Maimonides' theory of language, words on this view are not merely symbols; they are beings as well, possessed of their own ontological status. Thus, just as every inanimate object and every piece of vegetation has the capacity to absorb its own specific heavenly influence, so can every written letter and every spoken word absorb that sort of specific bounty from on high and impress its unique mark below. Looking at the matter that way, there is no reason to distinguish in principle between linguistic magic and other magical phenomena; all deal with substances and all deal with forces. Indeed, linguistic magic may be preferable to the other forms, for its words (=its beings) emanate from the human spirit and overpower the spiritual beings in nature (the essences, the "ideas"). Of course, Narboni never meant to attribute any of these concepts to Maimonides, and though he wrote about them in his commentary on the *Guide*, he took pains to distinguish between his own opinions and Maimonides'. In Narboni's view, again, magic is not an impossibility: "I do not regard it as farfetched." But, he concluded, "according to our late Master Moses [Maimonides], peace be upon him, this is in the class of impossible things!"

To sum up: For Narboni the independent thinker, not only is magic confirmed by empirical trials; natural speculation tends to support it as well. For Narboni the Maimonidean commentator, not only does speculation contradict magic, even empirical experience cannot confirm it. Both sages agree (at least in Narboni's opinion), however, that all branches of magic are intertwined and need to be considered as one, for better or worse.

It is no wonder that other interpreters of the *Guide* took issue with Narboni. The most prominent among them was the fifteenth-century Spanish rationalist Shem Tov b. Joseph. Needless to say, he absolutely rejected Narboni's own belief in magic; beyond that, he harshly brushed aside Narboni's stories about instances

---

70. Moses Narboni, *Bi'ur le-Moreh Nevukhim*, I:61, p. 11a-b.

of autosuggestion and imagination. Throughout Shem Tov's writings, one senses a grave concern that these accounts and others might be interpreted as experiential validation of amulets and the use of names. Even the psychological explanation proposed by Narboni poses a risk, for it, too, as a matter of experience, attributes the cure to the amulet, even though it accounts for it by a distinct (psychological) chain of causation.[71] Even here we find a slippery slope that can lead to permitting linguistic magic on the basis of empirical verification.[72] And so we are left with physical nature alone: the woman in difficult labor finally delivered her child not because of the amulet's influence but only because her time had come; the master of the name withstood the pain of the wound not by force of a mysterious "name" but by force of his sense of calm. And never has there been a "tested amulet" outside the natural order: "And in tractate *Shabbat*,[73] consideration is given to whether or not one may go out [on the Sabbath] wearing an amulet, and it is said there that one goes out with a tested amulet. To undo that confusion, the Master [Maimonides] wanted to write at length!"[74] Shem Tov thus consistently reduced

---

71. But see Maimonides, *Mishneh Torah, Hilkhot Avodat Kokhavim* 11:11 — "If one has been bitten by a scorpion or a snake, it is permissible even on the Sabbath to utter incantations over the site of the bite, in order to settle his mind and strengthen his heart, even though doing so is useless; for because this is a situation of danger, it is permitted for him, so he does not become deranged over it. Cf. Mena*h*em ha-Me'iri, *Beit ha-Beh*irah, ed. J.S. Lange, *Shabbat* [67a] (Jerusalem 1965), p. 250: "Inasmuch as the masses at that time were convinced of these matters, they would be strengthened [by using it], and by force of habit it would become a natural aid for them; but something that can in no way be regarded as a natural or distinctive aid partakes of Amorite ways, even if the utterance does not include the name of some star or idol or anything like it."

72. Indeed, we find just that in *Sefer ha-Batim* by R. David b. R. Samuel Kokhavi (writing at the end of the thirteenth century): Something not derivable by natural logic "may be something that functions within the imagination, or matters that made an impression through experience…and so the authorization for amulets with written names…and perhaps they cited experience, as in the condition imposed with regard to charms, and it entails no misgivings about idolatry." *Sefer ha-Batim*, ed. M. Hirschler (Jerusalem, 1983), p. 313.

73. Supra, n. 55.

74. Shem Tov b. Joseph, Commentary on the *Guide*, printed in the standard editions of the *Guide*, I:61, p. 92b.

linguistic magic to part of the natural order.[75] He wrote as follows with respect to Narboni:

> The sage R. Moses of Narbonne said: what appears to the eye to be [the effective] operation of amulets and names does not negate the Master's [Maimonides'] comments, for it is chance or the work of the imagination. Said Shem Tov: What that sage [Narboni] said about "what appears…" does not make sense at all; but if a person was sick or a woman was in hard labor and the amulet was suspended above him or her and he was immediately cured or she delivered her child, it was because the time had come, not otherwise.
>
> Rabbi Narboni also wrote: we have also seen a weak-minded person who would utter a name and pierce his hip with a needle, suffering no pain …Said Shem Tov: This is a false opinion and imagining, for imagining cannot negate feeling; and if the matter were as that sage believed, many people would not be burned when thrown into the fire for proclaiming the unity of God, given the strength of their imagining that God will rescue them.
>
> But with respect to his statement that "we had heard that name together from some person in our youth," it has already been explained that it is not the utterance of

---

75. R. Samuel of Lunel had taken a similar stance: "It demeans Him, May He be blessed, to do things in His name contrary to the nature of reality, for He has made a rule not to do things solely by speech." This writer reduced all "wonders" to one of four phenomena: (1) "what is done through nature;" (2) "what is done by special skill;" (3) "what is done by sleight-of-hand;" and (4) "what is done by a prophet," in accordance with the anthropological theory of miracles (supra, n. 68). See his commentary on the *Guide* (supra, n. 52), p. 34a. As early as the tenth century, the Karaite Jacob Qirqisani had attacked "the matter of sorcery and everything resembling it, which the rabbinite Jews use, such as amulets and similar things," and he ties all magical phenomena to natural forces. (He, like Shem Tov, resorted to the well known example of a woman whose difficult labor was eased by some object, attributing the result to the workings of nature.) See L. Nemoy, "Maimonides and His Opposition to Sorcery in Light of the Writings of Jacob al-Qirqisani," (Hebrew), *The Jewish Physician* 27,2 (1954), pp. 102–109.

the letters that accomplishes the act but that it is done in some other way, for he has to take some substance and smear it over the place to be pierced, so he does not feel the undoing of the joint, or to cause the person to fall asleep and lose sensation, and it is possible for such things to be done. But that the letters would work as a charm in these matters — that is in the category of impossible things, and of them [Maimonides] said: *"A fool believes everything."*[76] For if that were so [that the letters possess magical power], existence would be affected by a speaker's speech, and that is a lie and a deceit, unless [the speech is] in the nature of prayer or petition.[77]

But Isaac b. Shem Tov — another Maimonidean commentator, not far removed in time or place — took an opposing view, turning the words of the *Guide* on their head. R. Isaac sought in general to reconcile philosophy with Kabbalah and harmonize them as much as possible,[78] but he went even further with respect to amulets: he maintained that Maimonides fully believed in the magical powers of authentic names and tested amulets, denying only made-up names and counterfeit amulets. Amulets can be validated by both sources of knowledge — talmudic tradition and empirical testing — thereby offering a superb example of the Maimonidean synthesis of Torah and science! In *Leh̄em ha-Panim*, his treatise on the *Guide* (still preserved only in manuscript), R. Isaac wrote as follows:

> It is certainly true, as the Master [Maimonides] said, that many amulets come from madmen, lacking in mind, who made them up in their own minds and wrote them down, as the Sages of blessed memory said in tractate *Shabbat*,

---

76. *Guide* I:63, supra n. 33.
77. Id, Commentary on the *Guide*, I:62, p. 94a. "Prayer or petition" are addressed to the will of God; magic, in contrast, sets out to impose on created nature a mechanistic process alien to its essence.
78. Julia Schwartzman, "The Commentary of R. Isaac ibn Shem Tov on the *Guide of the Perplexed*" (Hebrew), *Daʿat* 26 (1991), pp. 43–59.

telling us not to rely on all amulets but only on those that have been tested two or three times. But there are many amulets and names that point to wondrous matters, as we see today with our own eyes that many names produce great things in the real world, and the truth is clear. And the Master did not intend to refer to names that are true, for it then would have been impossible to say what the Sages said in tractate *Shabbat*, but he was referring in his statement only to the madmen lacking in mind. Do not think otherwise of the Master's statement; his statement was specific [regarding made-up amulets], not general, for otherwise there would be great heresy and something at odds with the senses, and the Master nowhere disputes the opinion of the Sages, nor does he at all deny what is perceived and sensed.[79]

R. Isaac, the author of these comments, was none other than the uncle of Shem Tov b. Joseph, discussed earlier. The positions taken by the two relatives on this issue were polar opposites, one to Narboni's "left" and the other to his "right." One did not show favor even to the sages ("To undo that confusion [in Tractate Shabbat], the Master [Maimonides] wanted to write at length"); the other passionately clung to them ("otherwise there would be great heresy"). And, in fact, the tension between "natural speculation" and "what experience validates" remained a vital issue among Maimonides' students throughout the ages.

NOTE: This issue of experiential verification can be relevant to halakhic analysis as well: will a substantial change over time in the state of empirical knowledge (or in the state of natural speculation) have consequences for normative *halakhah*? Might it open the door to movement with respect to earlier rulings regarding what was or was not as "Amorite ways"? For example, the Sages permitted going out on the Sabbath wearing "the nail of one who

---

79. Isaac b. Shem Tov, Commentary on the *Guide*, ms. London, British Museum 912 (film no. 5964 in the IMHM of the Jewish National Library, cf. n. 14), p. 177a-b.

has been crucified or a fox's tooth"[80] for medicinal reasons, but Maimonides and his readers knew full well that this lenient ruling lacked any scientific basis. In Maimonides' words, "You must not consider as a difficulty certain things that they have permitted, as for instance *the nail of one who is crucified and a fox's tooth. For in those times these things were considered to derive from experience and accordingly pertained to medicine.*"[81] But does that mean that when ideas change and new information is acquired, the lenient ruling nevertheless stands (in which case the legal situation would be severed from the scientific[82]), or must we draw a practical halakhic conclusion — as Rashba suggested — and "once again forbid the nail of one who has been crucified or a fox's tooth on account of Amorite ways, even after having permitted them"?[83] Conversely, if what was earlier thought to be a superstition suddenly acquires a scientific basis, would the traditional prohibition remain in place? But this is not the place for extended consideration of the matter.[84]

A Cultural and Existential Perspective

In this article, I have concentrated primarily on the theoretical basis for the critique of the belief in amulets. But the critique went beyond theory alone, finding expression as well in the believers' existential world and in the cultural world of their communities.

---

80. *Mishneh Shabbat* 6:10.
81. *Guide* III:37 (Pines trans. p. 544); cf. *Commentary on the Mishneh, Shabbat* 6:10.
82. See *Hilkhot Shehitah*, 10:12–13 — "We do not add to these [enumerated injuries that render an animal] *tereifah* [unfit to eat] ... even if it becomes known to us as a matter of medicine that [an additional sort of injury] would be fatal to the animal. Similarly, those [injuries] that the Sages enumerated as [rendering an animal] *tereifah* [remain so] even if it appears as a matter of medicine that some are not necessarily fatal and it is possible [for the animal suffering from them] to recover, as it is said, "[you shall act] in accord with the instruction they provide you" [Deut 17:11]. Cf. *Hilkhot Nezirut* 2:10–10.
83. Rashba, *Teshuvot ha-Rashba*, ed. H.Z. Dimitrovsky (Jerusalem, 1990), part 1, vol. 1, pp. 287–288.
84. See Twersky, *Halakah and Science: Legal Perspectives in Maimonides' Epistemology* (Hebrew),pp. 143–147; N. Gotel,*Halakhic Treatment of Changes in Nature* (Hebrew) (Jerusalem, 1995), pp. 139–144; S. Sternberg, Introduction, in S. Gandz, *Studies in Hebrew Astronomy and Myth*, ed. S. Sternberg (New York, 1979).

First, the critique of magic directly touched the personal and emotional lives of men and women. It dealt with questions of sickness and cure, anguish and hope; it aggravated open emotional wounds; and it often led to a stringent ruling with respect to halakhic questions arising out of deep concern for the lives of children and the well-being of parents and relatives. The denial of amulets on theological grounds often demanded heroic practical decisions, requiring the believing thinker to overcome, at a time of intense stress, the temptation offered by promise or delusion.

Second, the dispute over magic in general, and the magic of the written word in particular, was rooted in the broader cultural and social context. It signaled the profound gap that had opened between the critical and rationalist positions developed in Spain and Provence and the mystical-magical spirit prevalent in Franco-German culture. In recent years, various documents reflecting that divinde have been collected.

As Y. Schmelzer and Moshe Halbertal have shown, the sages of Narbonne as early as the 1240s had erected a high wall between their religious-philosophical world and the world of the "leading French Jews and their sages," who deal with "the vanity of names assigned to angels and demons, making invocations and writing amulets to mislead fools...and they are mad fools, filled with delusions."[85] As I have shown elsewhere, in the 1270s, Zerahiah b. She'altiel Hen (of Barcelona) attacked Hillel b. Samuel (of Verona) for having made himself "as one of the Ashkenazim who have never seen the light of day," and who therefore never understood that "he [Maimonides] does not deal in mysteries or riddles, not with anything in the category of numerology or letter combinations and not with anything in the category of names and forms and amulets used by masters of the names and amulet writers."[86] And as Dov Schwartz has shown, in the first half of the four-

85. A Letter of the Sages of Narbonne, pub. in Y. Schmelzer, "On the Depiction of the First Maimonidean Dispute" (Hebrew), *Zion* 34 (1969), p. 143. See also Halbertal, *Between Science and Wisdom* (Hebrew), p. 115.

86. Zerahiah b. She'altiel Hen, A Letter to Hillel b. Samuel, *Ozar Nehmad* 2 (1857), p. 133. See Ravitzky, *Al Da'at ha-Maqom*, p. 155.

teenth century, Isaac Pollegar (in Spain) recounted the existence of "certain epistles related to the imagined actions of names of angels or demons, in accord with the opinion of the people of Germany (Ashkenaz) and France and others like them."[87] The dispute thus was portrayed not only as a theoretical debate but also as a cultural and communal breach, and the critique was openly and consciously directed to a particular cultural address. I also discussed earlier the great divide between Maimonides' strict ban on writing "angels' names or holy names" inside the *mezuzah* and the recommendation — or even the requirement — that emerged within the French Ashkenazi halakhic tradition to do just that (Re'em of Metz and the author of *Mahzor Vitry*).[88]

Conclusion

At the end of the eighteenth century, R. Elijah of Vilna mounted a sharp criticism of Maimonides' rationalist stance against magical acts: "Many incantations are presented in the *gemara*, but he was drawn to the accursed philosophy, and he therefore wrote that sorcery and names and incantations and demons and amulets are all lies. But he has already been refuted, for we find many accounts in the *gemara* of names and sorcery."[89] Nevertheless, from the point of view of Maimonides and his disciples, it is the pure belief in God's unity that is joined here with (true) philosophy in denying magic in all its manifestations. They stand together against "Amorite ways," but they have not yet prevailed. As the *Guide* puts it in discussing one Canaanite practice: "Those that set up these false opinions, which have no root or any utility, in order to fortify belief in them use the device of spreading among the people [false information about the consequences of failing to take a particular

---

87. Isaac Pollegar, *Ezer ha-Dat*, ed. J. Levinger (Tel-Aviv, 1984), p. 116. See Schwartz, p. 265.
88. Supra, nn. 44, 45.
89. R. Elijah ha-Ga'on of Vilna, *Be'ur le-Yoreh De'ah, Hilkhot Me'onen u-Mekhashef* 179:13. See J.J. Dienstag, "Did the Ga'on of Vilna Object to Maimonides' Philosophical Teachings?" (Hebrew), *Talpiyyot* 4 (1959),p. 253.

action in accordance with those beliefs]...Know that traces of this action subsist up to now as a consequence of its having been generally accepted in the world...so that its trace was not effaced though the Law has opposed it for thousands of years."[90]

---

90. Supra, n. 2.

5.

On Maimonides in Nahmanides and His School and Some Reflections

Moshe Idel

1. Introduction

Historically speaking, an influential phenomenon is both what it was in its original occurrence or its first emergence, and whatever happened to it ever since. The authentic visions of an author about his intentions, paramount as they may appear to be for scholars interested in theology, in philosophy, in history of ideas, or when dealing with structure of systems, are much less interesting for the historian of culture, or the historian of ideas, who deal more with ongoing processes of reception, interpretation and misinterpretation, and in general with the transformations of the initial intention. This complexity of intension and receptions, between original and its subsequent metamorphoses is much more obvious in the cases of famous authors, whose prestige has been used, and also quite often abused in the process of dissemination of their views. Either *bona fide*, or as part of premeditated manipulations, ideas have been interpreted as pointing in many different directions, some of them quite antagonistic to each other and to the authorial intention.

Maimonides is no exception. Perhaps, he represents an exceptional case for exploring the vicissitudes of understanding remote forms of thought, of their transmission, appropriation, and distortion, as part of a sharp restructuring of a cosmopolitan culture. Scholars who are not theologically inclined, may perceive this giant of knowledge as a renaissance figure who was, among many other things, not only the most important Neo-Aristotelian thinker in Judaism, a head of a school going in this direction, a sharp anti-magical and anti-astrological critic but, spuriously, to be sure, also an operator who resorted to both magic and astrology. Something a little bit less terrible than a magician, he was conceived also as a Kabbalist, a lore he was not acquainted with and thus he did not have the opportunity even to criticize. In short, his prestige was so great, that everyone wanted to have him in his field, either by interpreting him in a biased manner, or even by inventing spurious texts and by attributing them to him. Not a very nice practice, to be sure, but what is culture if not just a vast and complex process of interpretation, misinterpretation, misreading, misprision and abuse, as Harold Bloom put it? Sometimes misinterpretations may be more interesting and even more influential than the original source, adding to it a luster that was not anticipated by the original thinker. To be sure: Any great thinker creates both in a positive manner, and by forcefully doing so, he/she also does so in a negative manner, by stirring reactions of opponents. What is greatness if not the possibility to generate a sharp change, which is at the same time a challenge and thus an inevitable invitation to dispute the religious routine?

The greatness of Maimonides the thinker and the lawyer, have already been dealt with by many great scholars and I certainly do not attempt to add or to detract something from it and its interpretations. Interested in theology and philosophy, Maimonidean studies still have to address some more simple questions like appropriation, distribution, and even more — the misunderstandings of his thought.[1] These questions are simple, though in order to answer them much more complex tools than those needed to understand the original Maimonides. The overwhelming

---

1. For the importance of misunderstandings of the Bible see, for the time being, M. Idel, "On Angels in Biblical Exegesis in Thirteenth-Century Ashkenaz," in D. A. Green and L. S. Lieber (eds.), *Scriptural Exegesis, Shapes of Culture and Religious Imagination, Essays in Honour of Michael Fishbane*, (Oxford University Press, Oxford 2009), pp. 211–212.

anonymity of the agents of distribution, the pseudonym form to which the falsifiers resorted, the lack of the simplest coordinates of time and space of those documents, are only few examples of these complexities. Processes of appropriation and misunderstanding are not only a matter of obscure second rank people who could not penetrate the depth of Maimonides' thought. How many first-rate scholars, we may ask, sharply disagree insofar as what Maimonides thought? Distortions are inherent in the very changing situations in which the *Guide of the Perplexed* was read over generations. This is the reason why an erudite scholar like Moses Narboni — no doubt one of the most learned and influential commentators on the *Guide* — resorts to so many diverse sorts of speculative sources, including magical ones, some of which are rather dissenting from Maimonides' own thought. We may also mention in this context the manner in which Isaac Abravanel, and several centuries later on, Solomon Maimon, have interpreted the *Guide of the Perplexed*. Each generation has its sorts of Maimonides, which reflects not only the original thinker but also the mindset of the recipients. Even in one generation there are more than one Maimonides, as we shall see below. Though polarizing Jewish thought in quite a dramatic manner, Maimonides' thought also polenized its different ramifications. The vast polemical literature that emerged in the wake of the dissemination of Maimonides' books is only the most evident, though not the most profound, expression of the galvanizing effect of Maimonides' thought.

However, I would like to turn here to the understanding of Maimonides by a giant figure of Jewish thought, Nahmanides, and that of some of his followers. To be sure: I am not the first scholar to deal with Maimonides's image in Nahmanides' thought: Joseph Stern has dedicated an entire book to one specific aspect of this issue.[2] Many observations as to the affinities between the two

---

2. See his *Problems and Parables of Law: Maimonides and Nahmanides on Reasons for the Commandments (Ta'amei Ha-Mitzvot)* (SUNY Press, Albany 1998).

masters are spread in the scholarly literature.[3] Nevertheless, it seems that a certain aspect of Nahmanides' resort to Maimonides has been neglected in scholarship and deserves to be highlighted.

2. A Passage of Maimonides in Nahmanides's Sha'ar ha-Gemul.

Unlike other opponents of Maimonides, whose stature was less prominent than that of Nahmanides', the Catalan master was not only an outstanding figure but also the head of a school that developed in two main directions: the Kabbalistic followers on the one hand, and the halakhic school on the other. His first writings emerged toward the end of the first controversy over Maimonides' books, and they constitute part and parcel of books that become classics in Judaism. Let me underline the importance of this observation: while most of the anti-Maimonidean rich literature remained at the margin of Jewish culture and some of its documents have been lost, some being retrieved recently by modern scholarship from forgotten manuscripts, Nahmanides' critique of the great eagle was an integral part of a much more coherent, influential, and I would say incisive sort of critique. Nahmanides' critique outweighed by its impact for generations the entire anti-Maimonidean corpus generated during the first controversy. Or, to put it in other words, Nahmanides' few statements in his *Commentary on the Torah*, and in his other writings, together with the emergence of a literature of super-commentaries on his *Commentary*, represent the one single most effective critique and at the same time they were an integral part of a speculative alternative to the Maimonidean edifice. It is even more efficient because of Nahmanides' special status as a Halakhic figure, who

---

3. See, e.g., Samuel Krauss, *Ha-Yahas ha-Mada'y bein ha-Ramban ve-ha-Ramban*, (Sheftel, Berdichov, 1906) and the numerous references to Nahmanides in Isadore Twersky, *Introduction to the Code of Maimonides (Mishneh Torah)* (Yale University Press, New Haven, 1980). For the juxtaposition between the divergent views of the two figures see David Hartman, *A Living Covenant* (The Free Press, New York, London, 1985).

took issue with specific stands of Maimonides, both Halakhic and speculative. When compared even with the Rabad's *Hasagot*, it is clear that the impact of Nahmanides' critical views were more widespread.

This is the basic framework of our discussion below. This basic conceptual antagonism was, however, not translated in a sharp negative language, which tries to systematically deconstruct Maimonides. A respect for the greatness of the great eagle is transpiring from Nahmanides' writings. Moreover, I would like to draw attention to a neglected discussion of Maimonides' eschatology as found in his *Commentary on the Mishnah*, and quoted in Nahmanides's *Sha'ar ha-Gemul*. There is no need to be a great scholar in order to understand that the last part of *Torat ha-'Adam* constitutes a sustained effort to offer, inter alia, also an alternative to Maimonides' mentalistic approach to eschatology. There is hardly one single specific idea Maimonides articulated about this topic that has been actually accepted by Nahmanides. However, I am less concerned here with a systemic comparison of the basic divergences between the two masters, which are indeed numerous, but to deal with the implications of an authentic quote from the early Maimonides, as found in Nahmanides' book, and its positive reception.

Toward the end of this treatise Nahmanides refers to Maimonides in more explicit terms, quoting in Hebrew from the Arabic *Commentary on the Mishnah, Pereq Heleq*.[4] In the quoted passage Maimonides offers a noetic interpretation of some of the rabbinic locutions describing the *post-mortem* situation of the soul in the Paradise. Nahmanides is very interested in those discussions of the young Maimonides, since they interpret some anthropomorphic expressions in cognitive terms. This means that a great part of the rabbinic discourse, which was not afraid, as Maimonides and his followers were, of the anthropomorphic

---

4. On the various translations of this commentary see Efrayim Kupfer, "An Early Translation of Maimonides' *Commentary to Mishnah*, chapter Heleq, from the Tract Sanhedrin," *'Alei Sefer*, I (1975), pp. 59–80 (Hebrew).

expressions, is spiritualized. Let me quote Maimonides's passage as cited in a Hebrew version, presumably translated by Nahmanides:

"In the world-to-come our souls intelligize some secrets of the Creator, just as they intelligize in this world some secrets of the stars and spheres, or more. And thus did the sages said: "In the world-to-come there is no eating or drinking, but the righteous are sitting and their diadems are on their head, and they enjoy the splendor of the *Shekhinah*."[5] And the meaning of [the locution] "their diadems are on their heads" is the existence of the soul by [the dint of] the existence of the thing she knows, and its being identical with that thing [*Hi' ve-hu' davar 'ehad*][6] as those among the philosophers who understand, said on this issue, and it takes long to explain it. And what they [the sages] say "they enjoy the splendor of the Shekhinah" their intention is that those souls delight what they intelligize from the secret of God, blessed be He, as the holy living creatures [*hayyot ha-qodesh*] and the other groups of angels [delight] what they intelligize and they know something of the secret of the Creator. Therefore, the good retribution [*ha-gemul ha-tov*] and the aim of the intention is that man should comprehend the supernal retribution [*ha-gemul ha-'elyon*][7], and will enter in that category. And the existence of the soul will be endless like the existence of the Creator, Blessed be He, since He is the cause of her existence and her comprehension of Him."[8]

---

5. *BT, Berakhot*, fol. 17a.
6. On this specific phrase see the remarks of Georges Vajda, *Recherches sur la philosophie et la Kabbale dans la penséee juive du Moyen Age* (Mouton, Paris, 1962), p. 26 note; idem, "An Analysis of the *Ma'amar Yiqawwu ha-Mayim* by Samuel ibn Tibbon," *JJS*, vol. X (1959), 147 note 28 and M. Idel, *Studies in Ecstatic Kabbalah*, (SUNY Press, Albany, 1989), p. 5. Neither I nor Vajda, has been aware of Maimonides' passage under consideration here and the discussions referred in this note should be modified accordingly.
7. On the mistake related to the translation that generated this phrase see more below.
8. Cf. Yehudah Eisenberg's edition *of Sha'ar ha-Gemul*, entitled *Torat ha-Gemul*,

Maimonides' passage has been introduced in an extremely lauda-
tory manner: "the words of the great Rabbi that are dear" and
at the end Nahmanides says: "these are pure words." Later on
in this context he even says that Maimonides' words are "correct and we should accept them and praise their virtue belonging to their author."[9] Those are very powerful formulations of
agreement, especially if we remember that in the above passage
Maimonides resorted explicitly to philosophical stands which,
for Nahmanides, were quite problematic.[10] These praises differ
dramatically from the critiques addressed by Nahmanides immediately afterwards to views found in other books of Maimonides
dealing with eschatological issues.

In Maimonides' worldview as formulated already in his youth
before he arrived to Egypt, the meaning of spiritualization is not
adding one more layer to the original rabbinic one, but an implicit
dislocation of the earlier, archaic terminology, and the instaura-
tion of a 'pure' cognitive theory that negates any morphic expression.[11] However, this move is not explicit in the above passage.
The situation changes in the second major book of Maimonides,
Mishneh Torah, where he straightforwardly distinguishes between
the world-to-come and the Paradise, and negates forcefully the
existence of anything corporeal in the world-to-come, though the

(Haskel, Jerusalem, 1982), p. 64. There are several differences between Nahmanides'
translation of Maimonides' Arabic source, and all the other extant translations, but
we shall be concerned only with a major discrepancy to be dealt with below. All
the quotes from *Sha'ar ha-Gemul* below will refer to this edition. On Nahmanides'
acquaintance with Arabic see Raphael Jospe, "Ramban (Nahmanides) and Arabic,"
Tarbiz, vol. 57 (1988), pp. 67–93, and on our passage see ibidem, p. 80 (Hebrew).

9. Ibidem, p. 65.

10. See M. Idel, "*Nishmat 'Eloha*: On the Divinity of the Soul in Nahmanides and His
Schools," in *Life as a Midrash, Perspectives in Jewish Psychology*, eds. S. Arzy, M.
Fachler, B. Kahana, (Yediy'ot Aharonot, Tel Aviv, 2004), pp. 343–345 (Hebrew).

11. Warren Zeev Harvey, "On Maimonides' Allegorical Reading of Scriptures," in
ed. Jon Whitman, *Interpretation and Allegory*, (Brill, Leiden, 2002), pp. 181–188,
James Diamond, *Maimonides and the Hermeneutics of Concealment: Deciphering
Scripture and Midrash in the Guide of the Perplexed* (SUNY Press, Albany, 2002), and
Moshe Halbertal, *Concealment and Revelation, Esotericism in Jewish Thought and
its Philosophical Implications*, (Princeton University Press, Princeton and Oxford,
2007).

Paradise is described in a terrestrial manner.[12] Indeed there is a difference in rhetoric between the two stages of Maimonides' creativity: the earlier one is interpretive, the later is more systematic and apodictic. Nahmanides quotes those passages immediately after the above passage, and this time he is much less positive. He implies that Maimonides changes the agree time of the world-to-come[13], — *meshanneh 'aleinu* — and even resorts to a much strong expression that can be translated as "it is a wonder" or "a surprise" or even better "it is astonishing".[14] He assumes that the eschatological issues cannot be understood but by God alone, implying that Maimonides' quite explicit views do not represent the secret of eschatology as it is.[15]

Nahmanides' own hermeneutics is found somewhere in the middle between anthropomorphic and the noetic. He does not subscribe to the extremes but attempts to find a middle path, which adopts elements from the two modes of thought and discourse. He chooses a third stand, that can be called a theory of a spiritual body[16], that is close to Maimonides — as Nahmanides understood it — without however renouncing to the morphic Rabbinic elements. To be sure: I believe that both Maimonides and Nahmanides do not represent rabbinic thought, since both medieval masters spiritualize, and adopt one of many more rabbinic stands as the only representative one. However, Nahmanides, unlike Maimonides, does not attempt to dislocate an earlier, traditional mode of discourse. On the contrary, he attempts to strengthen it by adducing what he believed was a rabbinic reliable source, and we shall return to it in a moment.

Why was Nahmanides so enthusiastic about Maimonides' early views? His answer is quite simple: because, as he put it, "all

---

12. *Commentary on the Mishnah*, on Sanhedrin, ch. X.
13. *Sha'ar ha-Gemul*, p. 65.
14. Ibidem, p. 66.
15. P. 66. See also ibidem, p. 62.
16. See Moshe Idel, "*Nishmat 'Eloha*: On the Divinity of the Soul in Nahmanides and His Schools," in *Life as a Midrash, Perspectives in Jewish Psychology*, eds. S. Arzy, M. Fachler, B. Kahana, (Yediy'ot Aharonot, Tel Aviv, 2004), p. 352 (Hebrew).

are found in the words of the sages."[17] I am concerned here only with the claim that the view that the soul of the righteous is found with "the group of the holy creatures and the angels". Nahmanides asserts that the rabbinic stand for this statement is "with them under the seat of glory, and they engraved its place within wisdom [*haqequ meqomo ba-hokhmah*] and this is the very comprehension and the perfect retribution."[18] That the soul of the righteous is found under the seat of Glory is indeed a rabbinic view found in *BT, Shabbat*, fol. 152b, or in *Avot de-Rabbi Nathan*, ch. 12. However, the second part of the statement "He engraved its place within wisdom" is not found in the classical rabbinic literature. It stems from the book of *Bahir*, where we read that

> "the seat of Glory is adorned and embellished and praised and deemed happy [*me'ushar*], and it is the house of the world-to-come and its place is engraved within wisdom [*meqomo haquq be-hokhmah*]."[19]

Nahmanides, who did not read modern scholarship on Kabbalah about the Gnostic or Christian sources of this book, considered the *Bahir* an ancient Rabbinic authoritative book, and he understood the cognitive potential of the term *Hokhmah* as parallel to the world-to-come and thus cogent to compare with Maimonides's cognitive eschatology. That Nahmanides indeed envisioned the book of *Bahir* as the pertinent parallel, or perhaps even the source for Maimonides's passage, is obvious since he quotes verbatim this very passage from the *Bahir* immediately before quoting Maimonides's *Commentary on the Mishnah*.[20] Thus Nahmanides has framed Maimonides's passage on the supernal

---

17. *Sha'ar ha-Gemul*, p. 64.
18. P. 64.
19. Ed. Daniel Abrams, *The Book Bahir*, (Cherub, Los Angeles, 1994), par. 96, p. 183. See also ibidem, p. 43. For the nexus between *Male'* and *Hokhmah* see *Bahir*, par. 3, ed. Abrams, p. 19. On the concept of Wisdom in the book of *Bahir* see Elliot R. Wolfson, "Hebraic and Hellenic conceptions of Wisdom in "Sefer ha-Bahir"," *Poetics Today* 19,1 (1998), pp. 147–176.
20. Nahmanides, *Sha'ar ha-Gemul*, pp. 63–64.

pleroma, between two quotes from the *Bahir*, the book where the term *male'* occurs.[21]

Let me turn to the content of this passage. The distinction between the this-world type of cognition and that of the angels and the souls of the righteous in the World-to-Come, seems to reflect the difference between the knowledge of physics and metaphysics. Stars and spheres belong to the realm of physics while the secrets of God to that of metaphysics. According to such a distinction, in this world it is hard to know anything precise about metaphysics.[22] However, when intelligizing, presumably only post-mortem, the soul, (I assume that in fact only the intellect) joins the company of the groups of angels, and of the holy beasts mentioned in Ezekiel. This event is described in the above translation of Maimonides' Arabic original as attaining "the supernal retribution" *ha-gemul ha-'elyon* is a mistake. In lieu, the form *he-melo' ha-'elyon* should be preferred, as it appears in some variants of Nahmanides' book[23], and indeed in R. Shlomo ben Yoseph ibn Ya'aqov of Saragossa's translation the phrase is *ha-ḥevrah ha-'elyonah.*[24] Both Hebrew forms translate the Quranic *al-mala' al-'a'la* an expression that reverberated also in medieval philo-

---

21. On the various explanations for the *male'* in the book of *Bahir* see Gershom G. Scholem, *Origins of the Kabbalah,* tr. A. Arkush, ed. R.Y.Zwi Werblowsky, (Princeton University Press, JPS, Philadelphia, 1987), pp. 68–71, Yehuda Liebes, "Berekhah u-male' be-*Sefer ha-Bahir,*" in *Kabbalah,* vol. 21 (2009), pp. 121–142, and Michael Schneider, "The Myth of the *Satan* in the Book *Bahir,*" *Kabbalah,* vol. 20 (2009), pp. 339–343 (Hebrew).

22. See Shlomo Pines, "The Limitations of Human Knowledge according to Al-Farabi, Ibn Bajja, and Maimonides," in his *Studies in the History of Jewish Thought,* eds. W.E. Harvey — M. Idel (The Magnes Press, Jerusalem, 1997) = *The Collected Works of Shlomo Pines,* vol. V, pp. 404–431.

23. See, e.g., the quote from Nahmanides' *Sha'ar ha-Gemul,* in R. Moshe Alashqar, *Hasagot 'al mah she-katav Rabbi Shem Tov* (Ferrara, 1556), fol. 2a.

24. May be another vocalization would be *ha-Ḥavurah ha-'Elyonah.* It should be mentioned that in the three major books of Maimonides, he resorts to the biblical phrase *Tzeror ha-Ḥayyim* the bundle of Life" in order to describe the manner in which the soul survives in the afterlife. However, it is only in the *Commentary on the Mishnah* that the supernal assembly occurs. See *Commentary on the Mishnah,* Sanhedrin X, *Mishneh Torah,* in several places, e.g., Hilkhot Melakhim VII:15, and in the *Guide of the Perplexed,* I:41, III:52. See however, the discussion of the term *Male'* in the *Guide* I:8, in a totally different context.

sophical literature in Arabic and Hebrew.[25] This phrase occurs also in the above-cited passage from Maimonides' *Commentary on the Mishnah*, and should be understood in Maimonides's passage as a parallel to the group of angels that occur in connection to the descriptions of Paradise in several sources in both Arabic and Jewish medieval thought. Some of those occurrences, though not Maimonides' passage, have been already pointed out in two important and learned footnotes of David Kaufmann[26]. In one of those discussions he mentions the occurrence of this phrase in R. Yehudah ha-Levi's *Kuzari*, IV:3[27], in the context of the revelation of the angelic world, but he also adduces a passage by Al-Ghazzali's *The Incoherence of the Philosophers*, parallel to ha-Levi's passage from some points of view, though constituting an even better parallel to Maimonides' passage adduces above:

"And at the moment of death, when he will detach himself from the body and the obstacle was removed, then the delight[28] will be complete and the veil will be revealed and the happiness will last forever, and he will adhere to the supernal pleroma[29] and will become a companion

---

25. See *Qur'an* 37:8, 38:69.
26. See his "R. Shlomo ibn Gabirol's Allegorical-Philosophical Interpretation," printed in the collection of his articles, *Studies in Hebrew Literature in the Middle Ages*, tr. Israel Eldad, (Mossad ha-Rav Kook, Jerusalem, 1965), p. 129 note 12, and in his earlier *Geschichte der Attributenlehre in der Judischen Religionsphilosophie*, (Perthes, Gotha, 1877), pp. 211 note 191, 506. According to Adolph Jellinek, the impact of the passage of ibn Gabirol can be found already in R. Asher ben David's *Commentary on Thirteenth-Attributes*, though the term *melo' 'elyon* does not occur in the Kabbalist's passage. See his treatise printed in *Kerem Ḥemed*, ed. S. Sacks, vol. VIII (1854), pp. 159–160 (Hebrew).
27. *Geschichte*, ibidem, p. 211 note 191. For Al-Ghazzali's impact on ha-Levi see Diana Lobel, *Between Mysticism and Philosophy, Sufi Language of Religious Experience in Judah Ha-Levi's Kuzari*, (SUNY Press, Albany, 2000), passim, and also Moshe Idel, "The World of Angels in Human Shape," *Jerusalem Studies in Jewish Thought* = eds. J. Dan — J. Hacker, *Studies in Jewish Mysticism, Philosophy and Ethical Literature Presented to Isaiah Tishby* (Jerusalem, 1986), pp. 15–16 (Hebrew).
28. On the issue of delight in the context of Avicenna's and Maimonides' noetics see Dov Schwartz, "Avicenna and Maimonides on Immortality; a Comparative Study," *Medieval and Modern Perspectives on Muslim-Jewish Relations*, ed. Ronald L. Nettler, (Harwood Academic Publishers, in cooperation with the Oxford Centre for Postgraduate Hebrew Studies 1995), pp. 185–197 and Warren Z. Harvey, !.
29. The Hebrew translation is *ha-melo' ha-'elyon*.

to the angels insofar as the nearness to the true One, a nearness that is not of place but of rank."[30]

It stands, therefore, for reason that the philosophers mentioned by Maimonides are no other than Al-Ghazzali or Avicenna, as scholars have pointed out.[31] Also pertinent is the discussion found in *Ma'amar ha-Yiḥud*, a short spurious tract attributed to Maimonides:

> "the soul that was perfected by this form is passing and comprehending the existence of its Creator in accordance to its capacity, and comprehends the holy forms[32], and there is doubt that it comprehended the supernal pleroma[33], and will live an infinite life."[34]

Therefore, the supernal pleroma, a phrase found in the Qur'an, has been interpreted in a series of 12th century Jewish texts and in some more other medieval texts, as related to the world of the angels, which can be either contemplated as part of a revelation while some is alive, according to Yehudah ha-Levi, or as an entity joined post-mortem by the intelligizing soul. In both cases, the term 'supernal pleroma' stands for a complex structure constituted by angels, conceived to be spiritual, and as being close to God. Understood in such a manner, the term *'al-mala'* as an inclusive spiritual realm, into which the soul can enter, is reminiscent of the inclusive theosophy of the book of *Bahir*. Both in Maimonides's passage and in the *Bahir*, the images used are those

---

30. III,3,11, printed by Kaufmann, *Attributelehren*, p. 211. A similar stand is found also in Avicenna's *The Intentions of the Philosophers*, which Al-Ghazzali criticized.
31. For the impact of Al-Ghazzali on Maimonides see Shlomo Pines's Introduction to *The Guide of the Perplexed*, (The University of Chicago Press, Chicago — London, 1963), pp. CXXVI-CXXXI. For the impact of Avicenna's view of immortality on Maimonides see Schwartz, "Avicenna and Maimonides on Immortality; a Comparative Study," Sara Stroumsa, "True felicity": Paradise in the Thought of Avicenna and Maimonides," *Medieval Encounters* 4,1 (1998), pp. 51–77, and Amira Eran, "Al-Ghazali and Maimonides on the World to Come and Spiritual Pleasures," *Jewish Studies Quarterly*, vol. 8 (2001), pp. 137–166.
32. *Tzurot qedoshot*.
33. *Ha-melo' ha-'elyon*.
34. Ed. Moritz Steinschneider, (Berlin, 1846), p. 36. See also ibidem, p. 27.

of a spiritual space in which the soul enters. In the *Bahir* it is identical with the sixth *sefirah, Tiferet,* which itself is part of a more complex theosophical system. In Maimonides the expression "groups of angels" constitutes a parallel inclusive stand. It should be also pointed out that both the *Bahir* and Maimonides — as well as in the pseudo-Maimonides *Maʾamar ha-Yiḥud,* — there is also a common resort to the term *tzurah* and *tzurot,* as pointing to angels.[35] This point is important since in Arabic sources dealing with the pleroma and angels that possibly influenced Maimonides, the term 'forms' as a term for angels does not occur to my best knowledge.

I do not assume that the two passages: Maimonides' *Commentary on the Mishnah,* and the *Bahir,* both dealing with the world-to-come are related historically directly. In my opinion, they draw on common sources. They may be found in both the rabbinic and Jewish esoteric sources composed before Islam. In *Sefer Shiʿur Qomah*[36], in *Sefer ha-Razim*[37], and in *ʾAvot de-Rabbi Nathan*[38] the term *maleʾ* is found as a technical term, and these texts might serve as sources for the book of *Bahir,* though on his side, most plausibly Maimonides has being influenced by some Arabic sources. What are the sources of the eschatology of the Arabic books, including the *Qurʾan,* is a complex story since it

---

35. Moshe Idel, "On the Problem of the Study of the Source of the Book of Bahir," *The Beginning of Jewish Mysticism,* ed. J. Dan, (Jerusalem, 1987), pp. 67–70 (Hebrew).

36. See Idel, ibidem. It should be mentioned that the young Maimonides was more open to the possibility to interpret *Shiʿur Qomah* in a meaningful manner, than the stringent rejection of the book in one of his responsa written latter in his life. On this development see M. Idel, "*Sitre ʿArayiot* in Maimonides' Thought," in *Maimonides and Philosophy,* eds. S. Pines and Y. Yovel, (Kluwer Academic Publishers, Dordrecht, 1986), pp. 84–86. For another understanding of Maimonides' early view of the book *Shiʿur Qomah* see Raphael Jospe, "Maimonides and *Shiʿur Qomah,*" in eds., M. Idel, D. Dimant, S. Rosenberg, *Tribute to Sara: Studies in Jewish Philosophy and Kabbalah Presented to Professor Sara O. Heller Wilensky* (Magnes Press, Jerusalem, 1994), pp. 195–209 (Hebrew). For Maimonides's other important shift see now Yair Lorberbaum, "Changes in Maimonides' Approach to Aggadah," *Tarbiz,* vol. 78 (2009), pp. 81–122 (Hebrew).

37. See Abrams, in his introduction to his edition of the book of *Bahir,* pp. 5–6.

38. See Abrams, ibidem and Yair Lorberbaum, *Imago Dei: Rabbinic Literature, Maimonides and Nahmanides,* (Ph.D. Thesis, Hebrew University, Jerusalem, 1997), pp. 208–218 (Hebrew).

is not only the Hebrew sources resorted to the term *male'* but also the recurrence of the term *pleroma* in Gnosticism should, at least in principle, be seriously taken in consideration as a possible sources for the Qur'anic expression. I would say, following a scheme that I have attempted to develop earlier as to the history of themes that surface in medieval Kabbalah, that earlier Jewish mythologoumena have been circulated in the Near East, and multiple sources, Jewish or not, should be taken in consideration for understanding medieval material.[39] Multiple contexts, not just one, are a better way to understand complex processes of transmission and systematization of sources written in multicultural areas. Thus, Nahmanides' passage discussed above may be read in more than one type of history of ideas. Thus, framing Maimonides' passage between two expositions based on the book of *Bahir,* and attempting to find an affinity between them is not only a matter of Nahmanides' literary ingenuity. It points to the historical status of Maimonides as coming after the Heikhalot literature on the one hand, and as preceding the emerging Kabbalistic literature, on the other hand.

An examination of the Hebrew translations of the *Commentary on the Mishnah* demonstrates that it is only in Nahmanides' case that the Arabic original has been translated literally 'the supernal pleroma'. Ibn Ya'aqov translated this phrase by the Hebrew *ha-ḥevrah ha-'elyonah,* namely the supernal assembly, anonymous translator resorted to the phrase *ha-sheleymut ha-'elyon,* the supernal perfection[40], while Joseph Kappiḥ translated it as *ha-ma'amad ha-'elyon,* the supernal rank.[41] It turns, therefore, that it is the Kabbalist Nahmanides who translated and understood Maimonides' passage substantially better than three specialists in philosophy. This example is quite an interesting lesson for any attempt to draw too simple distinct lines between Kabbalists and philosophers. Let me clarify that I do not assume that Kabbalists

---

39. See Idel, "On the Problem," pp. 69–70, 72.
40. See Kupfer, "An Early Translation of Maimonides' Commentary to Mishnah," p. 70.
41. *Mishnah 'im Perush Rabbinu Moshe ben Maimon* (Mossad ha-Rav Kook, Jerusalem, 1965), *Seder Neziqin,* p. 205.

understand better Maimonides as a rule but, on the other hand, philosophers may misunderstand their own tradition. Or, to put it in more explicit terms: a Kabbalist or a philosopher is not someone possessing a given distinct mindset.

Maimonides had many occasions to deal with eschatology elsewhere in his later writings, but he never reverted to the term *'al-mala' 'al-a'la'*. The absence of the phrase is interesting since it represents part of a certain restructuring of Maimonides' thought, found also — for example — in the case of *sitrei 'arayyot*.[42] However, the disappearance of this terminology for angelic pleroma was related also the disappearance of the epistemological assumption that angels, and to a certain extent also the intellects of the departed righteous, may become one with God. Indeed, also the expression "He and he is one" an interesting formulation of a main Aristotelian noetic principle, claiming that the intellect becomes one with the intelligibilia during the act of intellection, when it has been applied to God as it is the case in the above passage, disappeared both terminologically and conceptually in the later writings of the Great Eagle, though it reverberated in some Kabbalistic sources by the mediation of Nahmanides's influential *Sha'ar ha-Gemul*.[43] Thus, a formula that will be adopted by Abraham Abulafia in order to express the concept of union on the one hand, and the term *melo'*, that expresses a sort of supernal pleroma that is so characteristic of the theosophical Kabbalah occurred in the same passage of Maimonides quoted above. These occurrences demonstrate that the affinities between the thought of the Great Eagle and that of the different schools of Kabbalah is quite a complex one, and still need detailed investigations.[44]

---

42. Idel, "*Sitre 'Arayiot* in Maimonides' Thought," pp. 79–91.

43. See, e.g.,, Isaiah Tishby, *Commentarius in Aggadot, auctores R. Azriel Geronensi* (Mekize Nirdamim, Jerusalem, 1945), p. 20 and the editor's note 11 (Hebrew), where the possibility that Nahmanides' rendering of Maimonides' passage is suggested as the possible source of R. Azriel; and the highly influential anonymous *Holy Letter*, ed., Seymour J. Cohen, (Jason Aronson, Northvale, 1993), pp. 154–155.

44. For a pioneering study on Maimonides and his reception in Jewish mysticism see Alexander Altmann, "Maimonides' Attitude toward Jewish Mysticism," *Studies in Jewish Thought*, ed., A. Jospe (Detroit, 1981), pp. 200–219. See also M. Idel, "Abulafia's Secrets of the *Guide*: A Linguistic Turn," in eds., A. Ivri, E.R. Wolfson,

One last remark in our context: Maimonides, the main founder of Jewish Neoaristotelian philosophy, and the book of *Bahir*, one of the main founders of the theosophical Kabbalah, agree, presumably independently, on the existence of the supernal pleroma. Both use a word derived from the same Hebrew word *ML'*. Interestingly enough both Maimonides' followers, the Tibbonides for example, and the theosophical-theurgical Kabbalists, renounced to this word as an important technical term in their respective theological systems. This is especially evident in Nahmanides and his school, since he seems to be the only thinker who had access to the two sources, which used the *Bahir*. Therefore, views found in the young Maimonides, were conceived of by Kabbalists, both theosophical and ecstatic ones, as closer to their views — either because they were influenced by Maimonides' sources or by Maimonides himself — than the older Maimonides. In other words, scholars of Maimonides should be much more open to a developmental understanding of the thought of the great eagle, in addition to the problem of the exoteric/esoteric problematic characteristic of the Straussian understanding of his thought. I would like not to commit myself to an explanation that derives the Bahiric *Male'* from one single source. What I wanted to show is that it cannot be denied that one of the early Kabbalists, Nahmanides, was aware of the philosophical meaning of the *Male'* as found in Maimonides' rendition of Arabic philosophical sources, in a passage that he praised and compared it to the *Bahir*. Whether indeed the book *Bahir* itself

---

A. Arkush, *Perspectives on Jewish Thought and Mysticism*, (Harwood academic publishers, Amsterdam, 1998), pp. 289–329; idem, "Maimonides' "Guide of the Perplexed" and the Kabbalah," *Jewish History* vol. 18,2–3 (2004), pp. 197–226, idem, *"Deus sive Natura*, The Metamorphosis of a Dictum from Maimonides to Spinoza," *Maimonides and the Sciences*, eds. S. Cohen and H. Levine, (Kluwer Academic Publishers, Dordrecht, 2000), pp. 87–110; idem, *"Sitre 'Arayiot*," Charles Mopsik, "Maimonide et la cabale. Deux types de rencontre du judaisme avec la philosophie," *Chemins de la cabale*, (Editions de l'eclat, Paris, Tel Aviv, 2004), pp. 48–54; and Elliot R. Wolfson,"The Impact of Maimonides' *Via Negativa* on Late Thirteenth Century Kabbalah," *Maimonidean Studies* vol. 5 (2008), pp. 393–442. For the relations between the proto-Kabbalistic Jewish myths and magic and Maimonides see Menachem Kellner, *Maimonides' Confrontation with Jewish Mysticism* (The Littman Library, 2006).

was influenced by the passage of the great eagle is quite another issue.

3. Maimonides and Nahmanides in a Pseudepigraphic Letter

Nahmanides has brought together different sources, which may help understanding both the unique stand of Maimonides, and the divergence between him and Nahmanides himself. Let me turn now to a text in which the stand of Nahmanides has been compared with that of an apocryphal Maimonides, whose views were presented as close to or identical with some forms of magic.[45]

R. Shem Tov ben Abraham ibn Gaon, a late 13th and early 14th century Kabbalist, a student of R. Shlomo ibn Adret, mentions, for the first time, a Kabbalistic vision of Maimonides. He states that he has seen in Spain an epistle of 'Maimonides', where the great eagle was depicted in terms strongly reminiscent of the Heikhalot literature. In his *Migdal 'Oz*, a commentary on Maimonides' *Hilekhot Yesodei Torah*, he writes that he has seen in *Sefarad*, on a very old parchment, *qelaf yashan me'ushan*, an epistle that starts with the following sentence:

"[a] I, Moses, the son of Maimon, when I had descended to the chambers of the *Merkavah*, have understood the issue of the end etc., [b] and his words were similar to the words of the true Kabbalists, which were alluded by our great Rabbi, *Ramban*, blessed be his memory, at the beginning of the commentary on the Torah."[46]

The book from which this passage has been quoted had been written around 1320 in the Galillee, probably in Safed but it refers to something R. Shem Tov has seen already in *Sefarad*, a term which

---

45. See now Yossef Schwartz, "Magic, Philosophy and Kabbalah: The Mystical and Magical Interpretation of Maimonides in the Later Middle Ages," in eds, A. Elqayam — D. Schwartz, *Maimonides and Mysticism, Presented to Moshe Hallamish*, (Bar Ilan University, Ramat Gan, 2009), pp. 99–131 (Hebrew).
46. See his commentary on *Hilekhot Yesodei Torah*, ch. I.

is quite ambiguous from the geographical point of view. We may assume, though this is not quite sure, that this term may point to Castile, where this author was in his youth for a while, to study Kabbalah with R. Moshe of Burgos.[47] This would mean that the fabrication of the document, described as written upon an old parchment, must have been done not later than the early eighties of the 13th century. If so, I wonder whether Scholem's assumption regarding the nexus between the second controvercy around the *Guide of the Perplexed*, which has presumably have inspired the composition of this forgery.[48] However, the truncated form of the quote, short as it is, may nevertheless help us understand better the background of the forgeries. When mentioning the similarity between the content of the epistle and the words of Nahmanides at the beginning of his commentary on the Torah, R. Shem Tov apparently refers to Nahmanides' preface to his commentary. There he mentions only once words of Kabbalists, namely the statement about the Torah as the continuum of Divine Names. I suppose, following Scholem's suggestion to this effect, that Shem Tov ibn Gaon has compared this particular view of Nahmanides' to the content of the lost spurious epistle.[49] Moreover, as Scholem has suggested, the phrase "I have descended to the chambers of the Merkavah" may reflect a reverberation of an expression he found only in R. Ezra *Commentary on the Talmudic Aggadot*.[50] Moreover, as R. Shem Tov ibn Gaon put it elsewhere in his commentary on Maimonides' *Mishneh Torah*, Maimonides has offered rationales for the commandments from his own reason, an approach that astonished the Kabbalist, who claims that something like that should not be done, especially by someone "who has received the secrets, orally from a person to another."[51] This

---

47. See *Badde Ha-Aron u-Migdal Hanan'el*, ed. David Samuel Levinger, (Orient and Occident, Jerusalem, 1977), p. 33.
48. "Mi-Hoqer li-Mequbbal, Aggadat ha-Mequbbalim 'al ha-Rambam," *Tarbiz*, vol. 6 (1935), pp. 92–93; "Maimonides dans l'ouevre des Kabbalistes" *Cahiers juifs* vol. 3, (1935), pp. 104–105.
49. ibid., p. 93; Idel, "Maimonides and Kabbalah," p. 74 note 158.
50. Scholem, ibid., p. 93.
51. See *Hilkhot Tefillin*, III:5.

conception of transmission of secret may also reflect the view of Nahmanides regarding initiation in secrets of the Torah, which again, has been projected onto Maimonides.[52]

The time of the forgery of the epistle quoted by R. Shem Tov would be not earlier than the beginning of the seventies of the 13th century, when Nahmanides' commentary on the Bible was already circulating. Thus, it would be safer to conjecture that the Kabbalistic interpretation of Maimonides was undertaken early in the seventies of the 13th century Catalunia, a presupposition that coincides with the time Abraham Abulafia started his Kabbalistic career in Barcelona. Both Abulafia and the anonymous forger of the epistle have combined Maimonides with Nahmanides' type of discussions.[53] It should be emphasized that like Abulafia's claim that he was revealed the time of the end also the anonymous forger has attributed to Maimonides knowledge of the time of the end. The preoccupation with eschatological topics fits perfectly one of Abulafia's sentences where he declared, in a letter sent to Barcelona at the end of the eighties that God has announced to him "the time of the end of the exile and the beginning of the redemption."[54] If Scholem's two conjectures that related the epistle to Geronese material are correct, as well as my two suggestions related to another Geronese linkage and one related to Abulafia, then the locale for the fabrication would be rather Catalunia than Castile, though the possibility of a Castilian locale for the fabrication may be strengthened by a series of pseudepigraphic writings that emerged from this region, including the most famous Kabbalistic book, the *Zohar*. However, also the circle of writings designated in scholarship as the 'Contemplation Circle', produced pseudepigraphies attributed to late antiquity Jewish figures.

However, it should be emphasized that in our case, the

---

52. See M. Idel, "We Have No Kabbalistic Tradition on This," in ed., I. Twersky, *Rabbi Moses Nahmanides (Ramban): Explorations in His Religious and Literary Virtuosity* (Cambridge, Mass. 1983), pp. 51–73.

53. See idem, *Absorbing Perfections: Kabbalah and Interpretation*, (Yale University Press, New Haven, 2002), pp. 321–335.

54. *Ve-Zo't li-Yhudah*, ed., Adolph Jellinek, *Auswahl Kabbalistischer Mystik*, Erstes Helf (Leipzig, 1853), p. 18.

attribution to Maimonides is not a regular case of projecting one's ideas on an ancient figure, whose views are rather vague and fragmentary, in search for authorizing own Kabbalistic innovations, but on the contrary, the conversion of a famous and strong opponent to some views into their advocate. An additional observation regarding forgery in the Castile region is however, related to the early 13th century Kabbalist R. Yehudah ben Yaqar and also to Nahmanides, as we may learn from some statements of R. Moshe ben Shimeon of Burgos, also he was an acquaintance with Abulafia.[55] Interestingly enough, this Moses of Burgos was one of the earliest teachers of R. Shem Tov ibn Gaon in matters of Kabbalah. However, even if the Castilian circles of Kabbalists would be among the possible candidates to forge the epistle quoted by Shem Tov, I doubt whether this may be the case with the epistle that portrays Maimonides as a magician. Again, the time of the forgery of the epistle quoted by R. Shem Tov would be not earlier than the beginning of the seventies, when Nahmanides' commentary on the Bible was already circulating. Thus, it would be safer to conjecture that the Kabbalistic interpretation of Maimonides was undertaken early in the seventies of the 13th century Catalunia, a presupposition that coincides with the time Abraham Abulafia started his Kabbalistic career in the same region. Both Abulafia and the anonymous forger of the epistle combined Maimonides with Nahmanides' type of discussions.

4. Magical Interpretations of Maimonides

As pointed out the emergence of the *Bahir* created the possibility that Maimonides will be compared with a passage from this early Kabbalistic book. Nahmanides, who accepted the authority of this book, immediately did so. Then the emergence of Nahmanides's writings created the possibility to compare "Maimonides" apocryphal lost epistle with Nahmanides. Naturally, those interested

---

55. M. Idel, "Maimonides and Kabbalah," ed. Isadore Twersky, *Studies in Maimonides* (Harvard University Press, Cambridge, 1990), p. 61.

in this affinity are part of Nahmanides' school, and I assume that the epistle itself has been forged in the vicinity of the towns in which Nahmanides' school flourished.

Another development that left its impact also in Nahmanides' and his school, generated another comparison to the great eagle, which is even farther from Maimonides' thought. Since the sixties of the 13th century in addition to Jewish earlier forms of linguistic magic, a new wave of Hermetic or talismanic magic is evident in several centers of Jewish learning: Castile, Catalunia, Sicily and perhaps also in Rome.[56] The Hermetic renascence constitutes, to a certain extent, a renewal of the interest in Hermes mid-12the century Spain in the writings of R. Abraham ibn Ezra and R. Yehudah ha-Levi on the one hand, and a reaction to Maimonides' intellectual crusade against talismanic magic in principle, and his contemptuous remark concerning Hermes' books,[57] on the other hand.

One of the first testimonies that confirm the linguistic-magical interpretation of Maimonides, which has been discussed above, adding also new elements, is found in a passage of R. Zeraḥia ben She'altiel Ḥen, a radical Maimonidean thinker original from Barcelona but active in his mature years in Rome.[58] He claims that in Maimonides' book

"[a] there are no secrets or enigmas [ḥiddot] from the category of the gematriah or of the combination of letters, neither from the category of the names, of the talismans [tzurot] and of the amulets, used by the masters of the names[59], writers of the amulets, nor of the multiplicity of

---

56. See M. Idel, "Hermeticism and Kabbalah," in eds. P. Lucentini, I. Parri, V.P. Compagni, *Hermeticism from Late Antiquity to Humanism*, (Brespols, 2004), pp. 389–408.
57. Ibidem.
58. On this figure see the numerous discussions of Aviezer Ravitzky, *History and Faith, Studies in Jewish Philosophy*, (Amsterdam Studies in Jewish Thought, 2, Gieben, Amsterdam, 1996), passim.
59. *Ba'alei ha-Shemot*. Abulafia mentions this phrase in an explicit negative context: see his *Sheva' Netivot ha-Torah*, printed by Adolf Jellinek in his *Philosophie und Kabbala*, (Leipzig, 1854), p. 22. See also Maimonides' own negative attitude to the

angels or anything mentioned in *Sefer Yetzirah* or *Sefer Raziel* or *Sefer Sh'ur Qomah*. [b] Everything the Gaon, our Rabbi, blessed be the memory of this righteous, has mentioned from the words of the sages, blessed be their memory, small and great, concerning an issue related to prophecy, or dealing with the *Merkavah* or on the account of Creation, [which are] written in the Torah, all are from the category I have mentioned[60] or related to their intention. And if someone has some secrets or enigmas or allusions or parables, which are not from the category I have mentioned to you, they are all vain and worthless things."[61]

Two books which represent Hebrew material based mainly on linguistic type of speculations: *Sefer Yetzirah* and *Sefer Raziel*, have been interpreted in a talismanic-magical manner at the beginning of the second half of the 13th century. *Sefer Yetzirah* has been interpreted in such a manner by R. Yehudah ben Nissim ibn Malka[62], while *Sefer Raziel* has been translated at the court of Alfonso Sabio as including images, which presumably point to talismanic magic.[63] R. Yehudah ibn Malka has also mentioned this book[64] as well as twice by Abraham Abulafia.[65]

---

issue of amulets in the *Guide of the Perplexed* I:61.

60. Namely things related to natural topics.

61. Printed by Raphael Kircheim, *'Otzar Neḥmad* vol. 2 (Wien, 1857), p. 133. On this passage see Moshe Idel, *R. Abraham Abulafia's Writings and Doctrine* (Ph. D. Thesis, Hebrew University, Jerusalem, 1976), p. 40 note 28 and in Ravitzky, *History and Faith*, pp. 265–266 where a different translation of this text has been offered.

62. See Georges Vajda, *Juda ben Nissim ibn Malka, philosophe juif Marocaine* (Larose, Paris, 1954), pp. 171–172.

63. Alejandro Garcia Aviles, "Alfonso X y el Liber Raziel: imagenes de la magia astral judia en el scriptorium alfonsi," *Bulletin of Hispanic Studies*, vol. LXXIV (1997), pp. 21–39.

64. See Vajda, *Juda ben Nissim ibn Malka, philosophe juif Marocaine* pp. 7–9, 97, 170–171; Nicolas Sed, "*Le Sefer ha-Razim* et la methode de 'Combination de Lettres," *REJ* vol. 130 (1971), pp. 295–304.

65. See *Sheva' Netivot ha-Torah*, p. 21 as part of a list of older magical-mystical texts, and again, p. 2, where he quotes a gematria from this book, as part of a tradition. I did not find this gematria in the various extant versions of this book. The second time he refers to divine names he learned from this book. It should however be mentioned that a book with this name had been quoted already by R. Abraham ibn

Maimonides, never mentioned *Sefer Yetzirah,* in my opinion deliberately, because he opposed the linguistic magic and mysticism that play such an important role in its cosmology. Therefore, the juxtaposition between Maimonides and *Sefer Yetzirah* constitutes a sharp misinterpretation of Maimonides' thought, which is shared by the anonymous author.

Let me turn to another extant letter attributed, spuriously to Maimonides. It represents an approach that is quite consonant, though not identical to the material to which R. Zeraḥia reacted:

> "In the verse[66] 'And there I will meet with thee, and I will speak with thee from above the covering, from between the two Cherubs which are upon the ark of the Testimony, of all things which I will give thee in commandment to the children of Israel'. You may find in it twenty-two words, hinted at in *Sefer Yetzirah* when it was said: "Twenty-two letters, He engraved them and He extracted them and weighted them and permuted them and combined them, and He created by them 'the soul of all the formation', and 'the soul of all the speech, which will be formed in the future'[67] and these are twenty-two simple letters, and the intention was that all that was created, beginning with the spiritual forces of the angels to the human souls[68] have been engraved by the twenty-two words and man will have knowledge of the hidden[69] and will remember from what he has forgotten insofar as pos-

---

Ezra in the 12th century and, in the 13th century, by R. Jacob ben Jacob ha-Kohen in Castile. See M. Idel, *Language, Torah and Hermeneutics in Abraham Abulafia,* tr. M. Kallus, (SUNY Press, Albany, 1989), p. 152; and, apparently also in this milieu, in a Kabbalistic text attributed to R. Meshullam Tzarfati, Meshullam the Frenchman: Ms.Oxford 123, fols. 70b-71a; See Idel, *The Mystical Experience* p. 105 and Mark Verman, *The Book of the Contemplation, Medieval Jewish Mystical Sources,* (SUNY Press, Albany, 1992), p. 205.

66. Exodus 25:22.

67. *Sefer Yetzirah,* II: 2.

68. *Nefashot 'Enoshiyot.* In print *Nefashot ḥitzoniyot,* apparently, impure souls or demons.

69. *ba-ne'elam.* So in Ms. London and *Liderosh 'Elohim.* In *Ḥemdah Genuzah* the version is *Ba-'Olam* which is a copyist's error.

sible things. Know that Moses our master, blessed be his memory, all his comprehensions were the announcement of the divine nomos [*ha-nimus ha-'Elohi*] as arranged out of all the names of the angels, when he was meeting with them always[70] this being the reason of [the description of Moses][71] 'for he is the trusted one in My house'. And from this verse seven names emerge, which correspond to seven angels of the firmaments that are Saturn, Jupiter, Mars, Sun, Venus, Mercury, Moon, and they correspond to seven [types of] sacrifices of oxen, and corresponding to them the holidays are arranged according to sevens, and seven units of seven are the year of the Jubilee, and out of seven years is the *Shemittah*, and [at the end of the of seven months, the New Year, and after seven weeks the reception of the Torah, and out of the seven days Sabbath, and corresponding to them the seven altars built by Balaam[72]...And you already know, from what you have read with me concerning the science of astronomy[73] that the Moon will turn into an opposite configuration in the seventh day, this is why her emanation onto the lower world will change. All this is a hint at and an observation as to what will be emanated here from the movers of these seven planets.[74] Behold, this is the order of the seven names [emerging out of] the abovementioned verse, and the first line consists of the first letters of the words, the second from the last letters and their vocalization is that of the Bible, forward and backward. These are the names: *WLSh W'M HMSh HMSh H" "H' "BY YKM YKL TNY MRL NTT LRT KLYL*. And this is the way of [magical] use of this matter: Let

---

70. *Tamid*, namely 'in a constant manner'.
71. Num. 12:7.
72. Num. 23:14.
73. *Ḥokhmat ha-tekhunah*. The anonymous forger is often insinuating a common study of Maimonides and his student, of Kabbalah and astronomy or astrology.
74. This view represents an Avicennian approach.

him fast Wednesday, which is the day of Mercury, which
is appointed upon wisdom and the knowledge of the
hidden things and he should behave in an extremely pure
manner and with a feeling of shame toward people. And
when he will go to bed, he should wash all his flesh with
water in the first hour of the night and cloth himself in
a pure and clean robe and trousers and he should sleep
alone and pronounce those verses, one time with an
intense concentration[75] and pure heart and low spirit and
afterwards he should pronounce the abovementioned
names and his heart is directed to heaven always. And
you should do it so seven times namely you should read
the seven the abovementioned verse and the seven names
of the angels[76] and he should arrange in his mouth the
doubt that he has, whatever it may be, after the perfect
imagination and the evacuated thought[77] And he should
sleep afterwards on the left side[78] and you will find, in
the midst of your sleep, that the spirit of the holy God
will dwell upon you and the hair of your flesh will bristle
up,[79] when the sleep of *tremendum* will come upon you
and fear on your thought. During the dream of night you
will see the visions of a man who will awake you from
your sleep and will dispute with you and will tell you
the secrets of wisdom, and twice as much understanding. Then he will appear as if he has a controversy with
you showing to you the place that you were in doubt.
Stronger your concentration[80] will be and your compli-
ance to the wondrous deed [greater] the doubt that you
had will be explained in a more true and correct manner

---

75. *be-kavvanah 'atzumah.*
76. *Min ha-mal'akhim*, literally 'from the angels'.
77. *Maḥashavah penuyah.*
78. This is a recurrent recommendation for obtaining a divinatory dream, found in many recipes, already in ancient texts.
79. Cf. Job 4:25.
80. *hitbodedutkha.* On this meaning of the term *hitbodedut* see Idel, *Studies in Ecstatic Kabbalah*, pp. 103–169.

and the firmament of your intellect will be purified from all the great doubts, by a strong catharsis, so that no room for a doubt related to your question will remain [at all]."[81]

As I attempted to show elsewhere the hermetic aspects of this text are quite conspicuous.[82] Here I am concerned with the sacrifice as practice within the astro-magical worldview. The assumption that indeed sacrifices are addressed to celestial bodies is widespread in the Hermetic literature. Some impact of this stand can be discerned in 12th century Jewish philosophical stands, but for our purpose it is important to refer to Nahmanides' interpretation of this issue.[83] This Catalan leader drew his concept of magic from eminently Arabic sources, which he was acquainted with in Spain, rather than from Ashkenazi kinds of linguistic magic. Thus, we may speak about the trends in Islamicate Spanish traditions, the mental-Neoaristotelian one, versus the Hermetical one, represented by an Andalusian, versus a Catalan Jewish thinker, respectively.[84]

Projecting into the spurious letter the hermetic understanding of sacrifice, may have therefore, something to do with Nahmanides' and his circles' understanding of sacrifice. However, some elements in this passage are strongly related to ideas found in the same period in Abraham Abulafia's ecstatic Kabbalah, especially the emphasis on the mystical technique in which divine names and combinations of letters played an important role.[85]

---

81. Ms. London, British Library Or. 19788, fols. 4b-5a; R. Abraham Hamoi, *Liderosh 'Elohim*, [Livorno, 1870], fols. 19b-20a; Z. Edelman, ed., *Ḥemdah Genuzah*, (Koenigsberg, 1856), fols. 43b–44a.
82. See also M. Idel, "Astral Dreams in Judaism: Twelfth to Fourteenth Centuries," *Dream Cultures, Explorations in the Comparative History of Dreaming*, eds. David Shulman and Guy G. Stroumsa, (Oxford University Press, New York, 1999), pp. 235–250.
83. See Dov Schwartz, "From Theurgy to Magic: The Evolution of the Magical-Talismanic Justification of Sacrifice in the Circle of Nahmanides and his Interpreters," *Aleph*, vol. 1 (2000), pp. 165–213.
84. Compare, however, Jose Faur's claim of an Ashkenazi extraction for Nahmanides's theory of *ruḥaniyyut*. Cf. his "Anti-Maimonidean Demons," *Review of Rabbinic Judaism*, vol. 6,1 (2003), pp. 3–52.
85. See M. Idel, *The Mystical Experience in Abraham Abulafia*, tr. J. Chipman, (SUNY Press, Albany, 1987), pp. 13–54.

5. The Dispute over the Nature of Prophecy

Few are the issues that drew more the attention of various thinkers than Maimonides' innovative interpretation of the nature of the prophetic process. Like in many other instances, Maimonides was inclined to substitute, or displace, the plain, concrete understanding of the Bible, and of Rabbinic literature, when describing prophetic events, by resorting to intellectual concepts like intellectual influx, Agent Intellect, human intellect, and imagination. All are linguistic innovations in medieval Hebrew, reflecting conceptual innovations in Jewish thought, depending mainly upon Al-Farabi's theory of prophecy, and to a certain extent on Avicenna, which both depend upon some forms of Neoaristotelianism. The spiritual novelty of this approach aside, its religious implications were understood as far-reaching and disputes about the allegorical understanding proposed by Maimonides are well known in the 13th century.[86]

Nahmanides was one of the most important critiques of Maimonides' intellectual reform of Judaism, and his deconstruction of Maimonides is based upon the inadequacy of the hermeneutical claims of the great eagle, when compared to the textual reality of the Bible. New forms of interpretations, especially when they consist in strong readings based upon what I call intercorporal situations,[87] constitute violent approaches. Caught between the systemic logic that is characteristic of the alien corpus, in our case Neoaristotelianism, and the totally different textual reality of the Jewish sources that have been interpreted, they have sacrifice elements from at least one of them. This decisive choice has been well articulated by the most important of Maimonides' followers: R. Shmuel ibn Tibbon, when he said: "It is better to force language [namely text] rather than reality."[88] 'Reality' is, to be sure, what he

---

86. See Moshe Halbertal, *Between Torah and Wisdom, Rabbi Menachem ha-Meiri and the Maimonidean Halakhists in Provence*, (Magnes Press, Jerusalem, 2000), passim (Hebrew).
87. See Idel, *Absorbing Perfections*, pp. 251–252, 340–342, 415–416.
88. *Maʾamar Yiqawwu ha-Mayyim*, ed. M. L. Bisseliches (Anton Edlen u. Schmidt, Pressburg, 1837), p. 17.

learned from Aristotle's books dealing with physics, a scholastic reception of some type of knowledge that has nothing related to an experimental type of knowledge. Thus, between the claims of Aristotelianism, understood, scholastically, as 'reality' and that of the canonical text, it is the later that should be sacrificed or interpreted in a forced manner. Ibn Tibbon's revealing and quite courageous formulation epitomizes Maimonides' propensity, and it was conceived of as being in a flagrant conflict with the deepest convictions of commentators on the Bible, like Nahmanides and his followers.

Let me return to ibn Tibbon's statement: it has been reverberated in R. Yom Tov Ashvili's *Sefer ha-Zikkaron*, after a lengthy discussion of Nahmanides' critique of Maimonides' interpretation of prophecy.[89] He uses this language in order to characterize Maimonides' approach. Unlike many other cases in the book, in which he attempted to rescue some of the views of the great eagle from the nails of the revered Nahmanides, on this particular point he writes:

> "The path of Nahmanides on the issue of Abraham's vision is accepted and paved[90], and no one should diverge from it right or left. But I have pity of the Rabbi *the Guide*,[91] blessed be his memory, of all his labor, since all his words were for the sake of heaven and in great wisdom. And I, and those like me, should not deride him, as many do. And if it is appropriate to our Rabbi, blessed be his memory, to speak and do as he likes, for those coming after him it is an iniquity and a guilt [to do so]."[92]

Written during the second debate on Maimonides's books, this statement reflects to a great extent, also the stand of his teacher

---

89. *Sefer ha-Zikkaron*, ed. Calman Kahana, (Mossad ha-Rav Kook, Jerusalem, 1982), p. 61.
90. *Derekh...selulah.*
91. *Ḥemlati 'al ha-rav ha-Moreh.*
92. *Sefer ha-Zikkaron*, p. 62.

the R. Shlomo ben Abraham ibn Adret during the second controversy: Recognition of Maimonides' greatness while nevertheless, bowing, to the critique addressed by Nahmanides.[93] It is an
attempt to close the account by recognizing both the correct-
ness and the superiority of Nahmanides' stand, without keeping
deriding Maimonides' shortcomings in the way Maimonides'
opponents did. In a way, R. Yom Tov Ashvili has defended
Maimonides' logic as an independent way of thinking, but the
latter's views have also been explicitly subordinated to the higher
secrets of Kabbalah, and to Nahmanides' views.

6. Some Conclusions: On Maimonides and Maimonideanism

In the above analyses of medieval texts, there are better and
worse readings of Maimonides. This is self-evident and I make
no attempt to marginalize the seminal differences between the
thinker and his receptions. I have rather focused on the sharp and
deliberate misinterpretations, which are part and parcel of history, as much as the views of Maimonides himself are, though he
veiled his theological views quite often. However, it is important
to be aware of both since both counted, at least from an historical point of view. If someone does not prescribe to a theological
project, the original Maimonides, (and I doubt if indeed there
was one such figure, though a historical Maimonides no doubt
existed) is one of the many images of Maimonides that recurred
in history and of Maimonideanism. I am confident that the original one is the most important one, since its greatness created the
occasion and the content for the other pictures of Maimonides
and thus of the emergence of the variety of Maimonideanism.
It can be reconstructed, due to the great and laudable efforts of

---

93. Gregg Stern, "Philosophical Allegory in Medieval Jewish Culture: The Crisis in
Languedoc (1304–1306)," in ed. Jon Whitman, *Interpretation and Allegory*, (Brill,
Leiden, 2002), pp. 189–209; Charles Touati, "Les deux conflits autour de Maimonide,"
Juifs et Judaisme de Languedoque, eds. M. Vicaire and B. Blumenkranz, (Toulouse,
1977), pp. 173–184.

so many scholars who, not so surprisingly, reach quite different conclusions. Some of those pictures of the original are sometimes closer to the pseudepigraphical pictures of Maimonides than to the other scholars' picture of the original Maimonides. So, for example, Jose Faur's book on Maimonides, *Homo Mysticus*, is somehow closer to Abraham Abulafia's picture of Maimonides as a mystic, and perhaps also to that of Maimonides's son, Abraham Maimon,[94] than to Leo Strauss's understanding of the great eagle. From other points of views however, the political esotericism, Strauss's Maimonides is closer to Abulafia's image of Maimonides than to Isadore Twersky's understanding of Maimonides. I would like not to multiply my examples, and I resorted only to instances related to scholars who hopefully are found now in Maimonides' world-to-come. I could easily bring some more contemporary examples too. Though all eminent scholars, their Maimonides is as much a projection of their intellectual biography, as of their immersion in studying his writings. This is the reason for the existence of so many images of the thinker in the writings of the modern scholars.

This is not an imaginary game, let me emphasize: however, the various types of *imaginaire* of Maimonides's figure made a greater impact on the way in which he was conceived than the real historical being. Someone should only have a look in two books on the hagiography regarding Maimonides printed recently by Yitzhak Avishur[95] and Tamar Alexander[96], in order to see the dense cloud of unknowing that surrounds the thought and personality of the real Maimonides in vast parts of Jewish population. Likewise, for many Christian Renaissance intellectuals too, Maimonides was a mystic.[97]

---

94. It seems that they are reading the young Maimonides as representative. This is the reason why they use the formula "She is she". Compare what I wrote in *Studies in Ecstatic Kabbalah*, p. 5 and note 5 above.

95. *In the Praise of Maimonides, Folktales in Judaeo-Arabic and Hebrew from the Near East and North Africa* (Magnes Press, Jerusalem, 1998).

96. Tamar Alexander and Elena Romero, eds., *Once Upon a Time... Maimonides. [The Philosopher in Legendary Tales]*, (Labyrinthos, Lancaster, CA, 2002).

97. See Chaim Wirzubski, "*Liber Redemptionis* — the Early Version of R. Abraham

Why may such a game of interpretations, restricted to small circles, count for the "serious" scholars of Maimonides? May the interest in this relativization wound serious types of scholarship? The answer is, first, a sad one. No doubt the answer is yes. Maimonides' own thought is obscured by introducing interpretations that are alien of the gist of his approach. However, this is certainly not the final answer: another would assume a certain sense of liberation created by relativization. Let me just mention the names of David Blumenthal[98], Jose Faur[99], and Yair Lorberbaum.[100] None of them started with any Kabbalistic assumption, and at least one of them, Jose Faur, has demonstrated his consistent opposition to Kabbalah as a religious phenomenon in many of his recent writings. Nevertheless, the picture of the Great Eagle emanating from their studies is much less that of a stringent rationalist, but as somewhat closer to what may be designated as a more mystical thinker. In a way, our emphasis here and in the studies on Abulafia on the mystical possibilities inherent in some developments of Aristotle's noetics is reminiscent of the way in which Philip Merlan described some developments in medieval Neoaristotelianism.[101]

Is the presentation above corresponding to something deeper in Maimonides than a rationalistic thought that is strictly mono-

---

Abulafia's Kabbalistic *Commentary on the Guide of the Perplexed* in the Latin Translation of Flavius Mithridates," *Divrei ha-Akademia ha-Le'umit ha-Israelit le-Mada 'im* III (Jerusalem 1970), pp. 139–149; idem, *Pico della Mirandola's Encounter with Jewish Mysticism* (Harvard University Press, Cambridge, 1988), pp. 84–99.

98. David Blumenthal, "Maimonides' Intellectualist Mysticism and the Superiority of the Prophecy of Moses," *Studies in Medieval Culture* vol. X (1981), pp. 51–67 and idem, "Maimonides' Philosophic Mysticism," in eds, A. Elqayam — D. Schwartz, *Maimonides and Mysticism, Presented to Moshe Hallamish*, (Bar Ilan University, Ramat Gan, 2009), pp. V-XXV.

99. *Homo Mysticus, A Guide to Maimonides's Guide for the Perplexed*, (Syracuse University Press, Syracuse, 1999).

100. See his "'The Men of Knowledge and the Sages are Drawn, as it were, Toward this Purpose by the Divine Will (*The Guide of the Perplexed*, Introduction): Maimonides' Conception of Parables," *Tarbiz*, vol. 71 (2002), pp. 87–132 (Hebrew), idem, "On Contradictions, Rationality, Dialectics, and Esotericism in Maimonides' *Guide of the Perplexed*," *Review of Metaphysics*, vol. 55 (2002), pp. 95–134.

101. See his *Monopsychism, Mysticism, Metaconsciouness* (The Hague, 1963). More on Neoaristotelian intellectual mystical see Alan Brill, *Thinking God: The Mysticism of Rabbi Zadok of Lublin*, (Yeshivah University, New York, 2002), pp. 391–415.

theistic and become in some tiny forms of Judaism — Isaiah Leibowitz's one for example — orthodoxy? Or, to put it differently: is there something vital in Maimonides' thought that is lost in his transformation into an icon of orthodoxy, at least in some small circles? Are the multiple interpretations, traditional and scholarly, just historical accidents. The answer is, in my opinion, negative. First and foremost, Maimonides started a new game of esotericism in Judaism in the most elaborated, sophisticated, and exclusive manner. Games with secrets that someone does not ultimately reveal, or even contradicts himself, invite different fillings, and we may say that Maimonides is, at least to a certain extent, directly responsible for the misunderstandings his thought had suffered. The play with religious exclusiveness invites animosities and provokes conservative reactions that attempt to defend earlier traditional stands, whom Maimonides attempted to deride, to replace or at least to correct. Rejecting Hermes Trismegistus in such a dramatic manner that has no parallel before or after him, intellectually speaking, Maimonides has been transformed into one of the most hermetic writers in the history of Judaism.

Are we now-a-day in a better position than the earlier commentators on the *Guide*? From some points of view the answer is yes: our access to Maimonides' sources is greater today than ever; terminological studies, which are done by resorting to computers, help immensely in having a better understanding of the way in which he used crucial terms. The wider philosophical context of Maimonides' activity is much better known today like, for example, the problems related to esotericism or allegory in Arabic philosophy available to the great eagle.[102] This privileged situation notwithstanding, Maimonides is still understood by scholars, at least in some cases, too ideologically, or if you like an even stronger word, too theologically. It is his quite revolutionary and inno-

---

102. See, e.g., Alfred Ivry, "Maimonides and Neoplatonism: Challenge and Response," in ed., Lenn E. Goodman, *Neoplatonism and Jewish Thought*, (SUNY Press, Albany, 1992), pp. 137–155; idem, "Isma'ili Theology and Maimonides' Philosophy," *The Jewish of the Medieval Islam, Community, Society, and Identity*, ed. Daniel Frank, (Brill, Leiden, 1995), pp. 271–299, and Halbertal, *Concealment and Revelation*.

vative theology that has nothing parallel in the early history of Judaism — with the exception of Philo of Alexandria's original and influential literary corpus in early Christianity — that gives him a special, I would even say, an unparalleled status of the established theologian of Orthodox Judaism *par excellence*. Maimonides succeeded brilliantly where another distinguished Egyptian Jew, Philo of Alexandria, had totally failed: to reform Judaism without however confessing he is doing so. The iconodoric approach to this figure in modern thought — while he was in my opinion a classical form of iconoclastic thinker — significantly reduces his historical achievement, to that of the best formulator of a perennial religious truth of Judaism. His great victory as a theologian in some circles, and the attacks from the directions of others, costed him the historical status of one of the greatest revolutionary in Jewish thought in the last millennium. Changing some of the beliefs of traditional Judaism so that they will resonate with the Neoaristotelian theories, he created the illusion — historically speaking — that he recovered a lost Jewish theory or secret. Some form of Aristotelianism were, he claimed, dormant secretly for centuries in the canonical Jewish writings and it is he who has recovered and expressed them in an enigmatic manner. He was capable to convince some few of the greatest Jewish minds that indeed he was right. Is not this the greatest of the magical achievement ever performed in the history of Judaism? To be sure, like in many works of magic, much depends upon the prior beliefs of the participants. The Andalusian *internationale* in the early 13th century[103], the Berlinese 'enlightened' Jewish elite in the late 18th and early 19th century, and even thinkers like Hermann Cohen and Isaiah Leibowitz and their followers in the 20th century, all very learned audiences, turned to Maimonides as a major source of inspiration, and for helping them to graft a variety of contem-

---

103. For the importance of the Andalusian connections that are an important background from the dissemination of Maimonides' thought see Idel, "Maimonides' 'Guide of the Perplexed' and the Kabbalah," pp. 197–199.

poraneous philosophical stands as the only 'true', or 'authentic' Judaism.[104]

I am confident that between the two achievements, of an accepted leading theologian, or of being recognized as an original religious revolutionary, Maimonides would prefer the first, namely to be remembered as a theologian who was able to convince so many Jews about the 'true' nature of God and religion. The famous 13th century dictum to the effect that from Moses to Moses there was no one like Moses, can be read, theologically, that Maimonides was unparalleled by anyone after the ancient founder of Judaism. Though the main intention of this statement is to praise Maimonides's greatness, I would emphasize the possibility that no other thinker has revolutionized Judaism since the Biblical period, more than Maimonides did.

---

104. See Waren Zeev Harvey, "The Return of Maimonideanism," *JSS*, vol. 42, 3/4 (1980), pp. 249–268.

PART 2

6.

Where Penitents Stand, Even the Wholly Righteous Cannot Stand

Nahum Rakover

Everyone is familiar with the saying, "Where penitents stand, even the wholly righteous cannot stand." Fewer people remember, however, that this is the opinion of one Talmudic sage, R. Abbahu; it is contested by R. Yohanan, who expresses greater appreciation for the wholly righteous. Early thinkers were divided in their interpretation of R. Abbahu's view; some limited its application in various ways, while others proposed interpretations that turned the saying, as it were, on its head.

The passage in the Talmud (BT Ber. 34b) is as follows:

> R. Hiyya b. Abba also said in the name of R. Yohanan: All the prophets prophesied only on behalf of penitents; but as for the wholly righteous, "No eye has seen them, O God, but You" [Isa. 64:3]. He differs in this from R. Abbahu. For R. Abbahu said: In the place where penitents stand, the wholly righteous do not [or: cannot; see below] stand, as Scripture says: "Peace, peace to the far and the near" [Isa. 57:19] — to him that was far first, and then to him that is near. R. Yohanan, however, said: What is meant by "far"? One who from the start was far from transgression. And what is meant by "near"? One who was once near transgression and has now gone far from it.

The gist of the passage would seem to be that in R. Yohanan's view, the wholly righteous are superior to penitents; while R. Abbahu

167

holds that, on the contrary, penitents stand on a higher plane than the wholly righteous.

Two questions come to mind here. First, what does the text mean by "where penitents stand"? Second, which of the two views should be accepted. The two questions are interconnected, since while some authorities do indeed accept R. Abbahu's dictum, they do so subject to their own particular interpretation of his declaration.

One of the earliest discussions of R. Abbahu's view is by Rav Nissim Gaon, one of the greatest Torah scholars in North Africa (d. 1050, Qairouan). In his work *Hibbur yafeh meha-yeshuᶜah*[1], he cites R. Abbahu in a discussion of the penitent's merit:

> It is inconceivable that the penitent's rank in the World to Come should not be high. It will surely be higher and loftier than that of the upright, as the Sages… said: "In the place where penitents stand, the wholly righteous do not stand." For indeed a wholly righteous person has never become habituated to forbidden deeds; that person acquired righteousness and integrity naturally, and knows nothing else. The penitent, however, enjoyed forbidden deeds and became habituated to them; so that by leaving and renouncing them that person is worthy of a large reward.

Rav Nissim Gaon thus places emphasis on the "rank," or religious merit, of the penitent who, unlike the righteous person, whose good qualities are natural, was accustomed to sinning and its pleasures; so that the penitent, by setting the sinful past aside, surely earns a *reward*.

There are two points to consider here. First, Rav Nissim associates the greater merit of the penitent with *recompense* — the penitent will receive a greater reward than the righteous. He may be saying that the penitent is superior only in respect of his reward. Moreover, he is referring to the penitent's reward *in the*

---

1. Ed. H. Z. Hirschberg, p. 84.

World to Come, as he clearly states in the opening sentence of the passage quoted; and the same idea is repeated farther on in his discussion (ibid., p. 85): "Moreover the rank of the penitents in the World to Come exceeds that of the upright."

Maimonides, in his *Mishneh Torah* (Laws of Repentance 7:4), also agrees with R. Abbahu, regarding the penitent as more worthy than a person who has never sinned:

> Let not the penitent think that he is far removed from the merit of the righteous on account of the iniquities and sins that he has committed. That is not so. For he is loved and desired by the Creator as if he had never sinned, and furthermore his reward is great, for he has indeed tasted sin and renounced it and controlled his desires. The Sages said, "In the place where penitents stand, even the wholly righteous cannot stand." That is to say, their merit is greater than the merit of those who have never sinned, because they control their desires more than the latter.

Maimonides, like his predecessor Rav Nissim, is thus also concerned with the issue of the reward due a penitent. His statement "his reward is great" echoes Rav Nissim's "that person is worthy of a large reward" (though he does not say that the penitent's reward *exceeds* that of a righteous person). As to the question of "merit" (Heb. *ma'alah* = rank, level), while Rav Nissim was concerned with recompense in the World to Come, Maimonides makes no such reference, saying only that "their merit is greater than the merit of those who have never sinned." Does this imply that in Maimonides' view the phrase "in the place where penitents stand" refers to their merit, beyond the question of reward? A passage in Maimonides' *Guide of the Perplexed* (III:36) would seem to confirm that such is indeed the case: "If, however, he believes in repentance, he can correct himself and return to a better and more perfect state than the one he was in before he sinned."

However, Maimonides' statement in *Mishneh Torah* that penitents' merit is greater "because they control their desires more than they [= the righteous]" seems to contradict what he writes in *Shemonah Perakim* (the introduction to his commentary to Tractate Avot of the Mishnah). The question is discussed in the sixth chapter, whose title is "The difference between the pious person and the one who controls his desires" (but he does not concern himself there with an actual sinner who has repented, in contrast to a person who has never sinned). First he outlines the view of the philosophers, that "the pious person is more meritorious and perfect than one who controls his desires." The Sages, however, argue that "one who strives for transgressions and desires them is more meritorious and perfect than one who does not strive for them."

> The philosophers have said that a person who controls his desires, even though he does noble things, does good while at the same time desiring to do evil things and yearning for them…. But the pious person will be guided in his deeds by what his desire and character inspire him to do. That person does good deeds and desires them and yearns for them. The philosophers all agree that the pious person is more meritorious and perfect than one who controls his desires….
>
> When we examined the words of the Sages, however, we found that in their view a person who desires sins and yearns for them is more noble and perfect than one who does not desire them and feels no pain upon renouncing them. Indeed, they said that the greater and more perfect a person, the greater his desire for sins and the more intense his pain upon renouncing them. To illustrate this, they cited various tales, and said, "The greater the person, the greater his Evil Inclination" [BT Sukkah 52a]. But that is not all, for they said that the reward of one who controlled his desires is greater, in keeping with the pain suffered in controlling his desires. And they said, "According to the suffering so is the reward" [Mishnah Avot 5:23]….

Maimonides now notes that there seems to be a contradiction between the view of the philosophers and that of the Sages, and tries to resolve it:

> At first glance, according to the plain meaning of the two statements, they seem to contradict one another. But that is not so, for they are both true and there is no conflict at all between them. When the philosophers spoke of evil things, saying that whoever did not desire such things was on a higher level than one who did desire them but controlled himself, [they were speaking of] those generally accepted evils, such as murder, robbery, theft, fraud, harming of someone who never did evil, ungratefulness, ill-treatment of one's parents, and the like. These are the commandments of which the Sages... say, "had they not been written [in Scripture], they should rightly have been written" [bYoma 67b]. And some of our recent scholars, upon whom the *Kalam* sickness has fallen, call these "rational commandments." There is no doubt that any soul that desires and yearns to [transgress] any one of them is a deficient soul. The meritorious soul would not desire to transgress any of these evil things at all and would in no way be troubled by avoiding them. But those things of which the Sages said that a person who controls his desires is greater and will receive a greater reward are those [prohibited by] the "revealed commandments." And the truth is that, were it not for the Torah, they would not be considered evil at all...
>
> It has now been clarified by everything we have said, which transgressions are those that whoever does not yearn for them is greater than the person who yearns for them but exercises self-control, and which are those for which the reverse is true.

Maimonides' conclusion is that both approaches are true, that there is no contradiction at all. The philosophers were concerned with people who long to commit universally condemned offenses, such as murder, theft, and the like — the commandments that the contemporary *mutakallimun*, and consequently Rav Sa'adiah Gaon, called "rational commandments." Such peoples' souls, says Maimonides, are surely deficient. The Sages, for their part, were speaking of offenders against the so-called "revealed commandments," i.e., offenses which, if not explicitly prohibited in the Torah, would not be considered offenses at all. The soul of a person wishing to commit such offenses is not inferior to one who has no such desires.

The apparent difficulty is, however, that while in *Shemonah Perakim* Maimonides proposes a kind of compromise, in *Mishneh Torah*, where he is dealing with a person who has actually committed some transgression and subsequently repented, he makes no such distinction between "rational" and "revealed" commandments. However, in the context of the laws of repentance he is not dealing with a person who has no desires at all, but with one who has never actually sinned; such a person, Maimonides declares, is superior to a penitent.

R. Abraham bar Hiyya (Barcelona, Spain, early 12th century) also cites both approaches to the relative merit of a person with no desire to sin and one who has such desires but controls them. But he goes on to propose a third approach, according to which the two categories are equal:[2]

> There is a difference of opinion among the scholars in regard to these two persons, which of them is more praiseworthy, and which of them is worthy before God to be considered more meritorious.
>
> The multitude of scholars have said that one who desires the pleasures of this world and yearns to indulge in them, but controls his passions and quashes his desires, is greater than another who neither desires nor yearns for them. For the former toils and suffers, while the latter is calm and content. Surely one who toils and

---

2. *Hegyon ha-nefesh ha-azuvah*, ed. G. Wigoder, p. 63.

labors should be considered more meritorious in accordance with his toil and his labor…. These are the words of the multitude who praise the oppressed person who controls his desires.

But those who are more accurate in this matter say the contrary, and give praise and greatness to the person whose desires are from the start subdued, who is humble and subdues his nature; such a person is called lowly in spirit. And they say that one who yearns and desires but then controls his passions has not been spared [sinful] thought, while the other does not think [of sin] at all. This may be compared to the case of the wholly righteous person and the penitent. Each of them is praiseworthy and meritorious, but the merit of the wholly righteous person, who has never sinned, is greater and more praiseworthy, for he is meritorious on every count; but the other is meritorious [only] after forgiveness of the sin. But there are some who think to prove from Scripture that they are of equal merit.

While Abraham b. Hiyya attributes the view giving preference to a person who longs to sin and controls himself to "the multitude of scholars," he refers to the proponents of the contrary view as "those who are more accurate in this matter." Hence he himself is inclined to the view that a person who has never experienced desire has the greater merit, compared with a person who would like to sin but exercises self-control. (In addition, the comparison this author makes with the wholly righteous person, who has never sinned, implies that the latter's merit is superior and more praiseworthy.)

R. Isaac Arama (d. 1494, Spanish rabbi, philosopher, and preacher, lived in Naples after the expulsion from Spain) also discusses the philosophers' preference for the wholly righteous rather than a person who controls his passions. He believes, however, that the view of the Torah is otherwise. He first cites the "compromise" proposed by Maimonides (in the *Shemonah*

Perakim), that is, the distinction between rational and revealed commandments:[3]

> In truth, this theory [which considers the person who controls his desires superior to one who has no desires at all] is inconsistent with what we find in the words of the philosopher [= Aristotle], Chapters 1 and 12 of Book VII in the *Book of Ethics* [= *Nicomachean Ethics*], where he said that the upright [Heb. *yashar*] person, [that is,] one who has no evil desires, is superior to the worthy [Heb. *kasher*] person, who has [such desires] but controls them. [...] Now [Maimonides], in Chapter 6 of the Introduction to Avot, mentioned this theory and confirmed it, on the basis of what is written, "The desire of the wicked is set upon evil" (Prov. 21:10); and it is further said, "Justice done is a joy to the righteous; to evildoers, ruination" (ibid., v. 15). And he pointed out a contradiction with what the Sages said, "According to the suffering so is the reward" [mAvot 5:22], and with what they said, "The greater the person, the greater his Evil Inclination" [BT*Sukkah* 52a; and further with what the Sages said, "Let not a person say, I do not desire to eat pork or to wear *kil'ayim*; rather [one should say,] I do desire them, but what shall I do for my Father in heaven has forbidden them to me" [*Torat Kohanim, Kedoshim*, 9]. But lo, he resolved the contradiction, saying that the Sages were speaking only of things that are forbidden by dint of the revealed commandments, which are not forbidden by the rational mind, for the perfect person should shun such things and avoid them only because of religious prohibition and fear of God; and with regard to these things, the greater the desire for them, the greater is the reward. This is proved by [the Sages'] reference to pork, meat in milk, and *kil'ayim*, while they did not refer to murder,

---

3. *Akedat Yizḥak, Niẓavim, Sha'ar* 100, p. 113b.

theft, adultery, or the like. Now it is quite clear that once he [= Maimonides] had agreed with their view regarding those things affected by physical desires, that are reprehensible according to the human mind, saying that the upright person, free of those desires, is superior to the worthy person who has them but controls them — how much more so, then, shall he reject for that reason the statement that those persons who have been vanquished by human sins, doing evil, reprehensible, and shameful things, would be superior in rank to the wholly righteous, who have never tasted sin. And while he did not mention that saying [in *Shemonah Perakim*] and did not point out the contradiction, he did mention it and agree with it in Chapter 7 of the Laws of Repentance [*Hilkhot Teshuvah*].

He goes on to contrast the approach of the Torah and that of the philosophers, arguing that they are contradictory:

Indeed, it seems to me best in the resolution of these matters that the words of the Torah are one thing and the words of philosophy another. For in truth, the philosophers do not believe that there is any merit in a person implanted by God, that a person may possess merit by virtue of deeds that he performs of his own volition upon [God's] command, nor that [God] should set a reward for [that merit] in any way. But they say that every person may achieve perfection by nature, as he perfects himself in virtues and knowledge, not paying any attention to the will of God, may He be exalted. They therefore necessarily hold that natural impediments undoubtedly detract from a person's degree of perfection, and at any rate they are of no benefit. For what avails the worthy person his effort to control his desires? Better is the person who had no need of that, but his desires were controlled from the start. This may be likened to a vessel which is always pure by its own nature, or needs to be purified with much labor; it is obvious that one that is perfect by nature is more stable and superior. Thus in their [= the philosophers'] view a person who has always been upright is superior to one who controls [his desires]. For one who controls [his desires] becomes good by dint of effort, while the upright person is so by nature.

Now the Sages of the Torah do not deny the perfection of a person who is upright by virtue of his own nature. But they believe that, from the standpoint of the aims of the Divine Torah and the reward for the performance of its commandments, it was necessary to set a volitional reward for every single person, according to his labor and burden and pain in the performance of that commandment. For bethink yourself, that a person had an opportunity to perform a commandment and he did so, while another expended upon it much labor and riches, is it conceivable that they should be rewarded equally by the Commander and true Rewarder? In truth, it was in this sense that it was said, "According to the suffering so is the reward."

In other words, Arama stresses the question of the reward due those who fulfill the Divine command, and it is in this respect that the approach of the Torah differs from that of the philosophers. The former, while not denying the importance of a person who is "upright" by his very nature, holds that the aims of the Torah require every person to be rewarded in accordance with the trouble taken or effort expended; and the effort and pain of a repentant sinner are greater than those of a person who has never sinned.

Arama further proposes an interpretation of the statements of R. Yohanan and R. Abbahu: They were not disagreeing, but speaking from "different aspects;" that is, each one was speaking from a different standpoint: R. Yohanan from the standpoint of the person himself, R. Abbahu from that of the Torah's goals:

It would seem that in these aspects lies the disagreement between R. Hiyya [quoting the view of R. Yohanan] and

R. Abbahu. For R. Hiyya gives a person who is far from sin precedence over a person who is close to it, from his own point of view, and he therefore said, "But the righteous themselves, 'No eye has seen them, O God, but You,'" and [Maimonides] followed him in what he wrote of these matters, as we have said. R. Abbahu, on the other hand, spoke from the standpoint of the goals of the Torah and its commandments, which indeed should be judged according to labor and pain. That is the reason for his disagreement with R. Abbahu, that is, they spoke in this matter from different aspects, and that is what [Maimonides] maintained in the Laws of Repentance as mentioned....

🍂 🍂 🍂

As we shall now see, the conflicting views of R. Yohanan and R. Abbahu regarding the difference between the righteous and the penitent receive a variety of interesting interpretations. Some, unlike Maimonides, state explicitly that a righteous person is superior to a penitent.

Thus, for example, R. Abraham B. Hiyya, already quoted above in regard to the difference between a person who desires to sin and controls that desire, on the one hand, and a person who has no desire at all to sin, on the other, suggests that one should not apply the term "penitent" to a person "whose soul and good virtue dominate his Evil Inclination from the day of his birth till the day of his death," because such a person is, as it were, too holy for the term[4]:

> Those persons who walk the straight path and those who leave it may be divided into five categories. Two of these are wholly righteous. The first is the one called "lowly of spirit," and that is one whose soul and good virtue domi-

---

4. *Hegyon ha-nefesh ha-aẓuvah*, ed. Wigoder, p. 92.

nate his Evil Inclination from the day of his birth till the
day of his death. The term "repentance" is not applicable
to such a person, because he is holier than it. The second
is one who is called "contrite of heart," who controls his
desiring inclination and his heart, which desires and
leans toward this world, but he suppresses his inclination
and represses it and weakens it from infancy to old age.

Other authors try in various ways to harmonize their own views
with that of R. Abbahu, by somehow limiting the scope of his
statement to a specific category of penitents, or by rejecting what
seems to be the plain meaning of his statement in the context of
the Talmudic debate.

The Spanish thinker R. Jonah of Gerona, in his commentary
to *Ethics of the Fathers* (Mishnah Avot 3:16, s.v. *"veha-pinkas
patuah"*), states that "One who does not [commit a sin] is superior
to one who does and is forgiven." As to R. Abbahu's dictum, he
explains it as follows: "He means that they should avoid even what
is permitted in the matter in which they sinned. For example,
if a person committed a sexual offense, he should deny himself
even to his wife. In regard to the subject of his sin, he should
deny himself even what is permitted, more than even the wholly
righteous should do." R. Abbahu's statement, therefore, does not
imply that penitents are superior to the righteous, but that their
behavior should be different, avoiding even modes of behavior
permitted the righteous.

Another view favoring the righteous person over the penitent
is that of the [anonymous] author of *Sefer ha-Yashar*[5]. In his
view, a penitent cannot reach the level of a righteous person. A
righteous person has merits. A penitent, however, while having
cleansed himself of sin, has no merits: "Know that full repentance cleanses an evil person of all his sins, so that he resembles
a newborn babe. Just as the newborn babe is clean of sin, but has
no merit, so is the evil person who has fully repented cleansed of

---

5. Chapter on Repentance, p. 147.

all his sins and exempt from any Divine punishment, but he has no merits, and he cannot aspire to the level of the pure righteous who have never their lives committed an offense."

The meaning is illustrated by a parable: "One cannot compare two servants of the king, one loyal from his very birth, who has never been found guilty, and another, who conspired against [the king], angered him, and rebelled against him, but afterwards surrendered to him and recognized his sin, like Shimei son of Gera, who flung himself before King David, of blessed memory [2Sam. 19:19] — it is clear that, even though the king forgave him, he did not value him as highly as he did his loyal servant." And the author continues: "Our logic tells us that Manasseh son of Hezekiah repented as no man had ever repented, and afflicted his soul in Divine worship all his life — he surely never attained the rank of Moses our Master, may he rest in peace, or the rank of David King of Israel, who feared God from his youth."

He now makes an attempt to harmonize his view with that of R. Abbahu by reinterpreting the latter: "As to what our Sages said, 'In the place where penitents stand, the wholly righteous do not stand,' they spoke the truth. For it is known that righteous and average people each have their own rank in the eyes of the Creator, blessed be He, one above the other, and therefore our Sages of blessed memory said that the righteous do not stand on the rank of the penitents, for it is not their place, and they are not included in the category of penitents but elsewhere."

What does he mean? He seems to be implying that the wholly righteous do not stand where the penitents stand ("in their place"), because their merit ("rank," Heb. *ma'alah*) is higher than that of the penitent. However, this interpretation is rather problematic, in light of the context of R. Abbahu's dictum in the Talmud — where it is cited in opposition to the view of R. Yohanan, who indeed considered the righteous as more meritorious than the penitent!

So the anonymous author goes on to offer an alternative interpretation, according to which R. Abbahu is not speaking of the merit of penitents at all, but of God's special love for penitents, which exceeds the love He shows the righteous. Because of this love He even performs miracles for them more than He does for the righteous, in order to keep them near Him, lest they resume their sinful ways. This interpretation, too, severely limits R. Abbahu's meaning.

Finally, *Sefer ha-Yashar* offers yet another interpretation, a kind of compromise between the two others, calling it "the correct one." Namely, the text claims that there are ways in which penitents possess greater merit than the righteous person. A distinction must be made between two categories of offenders who have repented. Some offenders were originally upright, good people, and committed an offense either because of a mistake or because an opportunity offered itself and they could not control their desires; later, however, they returned to their original, pure state. Of such penitents the author says that "their righteousness is doubled," and their merit indeed exceeds that of the righteous. Only of such penitents was R. Abbahu speaking in his dictum.

A different distinction, not between types of sinners but between types of sins, is made by R. Baḥya ibn Paquda, in his *Duties of the Heart*. He defines different categories of penitents according to the type of sin or offense that they had committed: (i) Violation of a positive commandment which does not involve the punishment of *karet* (excision); (ii) a minor offense, violating a negative commandment that does not involve *karet*; (iii) a major sin, violating a negative commandment punishable by *karet* or capital punishment by a human court. While these three categories are in ascending order of gravity, the merit of a repentant sinner of any one category is not measured on the same scale. A penitent whose offense was of the first category is equal in merit to a righteous person who has never sinned. One whose offense was of the second category is considered superior to a person who has never sinned; but in the case of the third category, the penitent is inferior in merit. The relevant passage reads as follows:[6]

---

6. *Duties of the Heart* 7:8; English translation by M. Hyamson, II [New York, 1970], pp. 160 ff., slightly modified.

Is the penitent to be considered the equal of the righteous man (who has not sinned)? To this I would reply, that one kind of penitent is equal to a righteous man; another may be his superior; while to a third penitent, notwithstanding his repentance, the righteous man is superior.

To elucidate: The first kind of penitent is a sinner who has failed to fulfill a positive commandment, the neglect of which does not involve *karet*, such as the wearing of *zizit* [Num. 15:37–41], the *lulav* and the *sukkah* [Lev. 23:40–43], and the like. When one who has neglected these observances repents inwardly and outwardly, endeavors to fulfill them, and does not again neglect them, the Creator will forgive him, and he will be equal to the righteous man who has not been negligent. Of such a penitent it has been said, "Whoever repents of a sin is like one who has not committed the sin," and our Sages declare, "If one transgresses a positive commandment, the neglect of which does not involve *karet*, and repents, he is forthwith forgiven, as it is said, "Turn back to me, and I will turn back to you" [Mal. 3:7].

Belonging to the second class, in which the penitent is superior to one who has not sinned, is a penitent who has committed a minor sin, such as the violation of a prohibition that does not involve *karet*, and then fully repents with all the requisite conditions of repentance, is constantly mindful of his sin, beseeches forgiveness for its commission, is ashamed and abashed before the Creator — his heart seized by fear of punishment, his soul contrite, always humble and abashed before God — his sin having occasioned his humility and caused him to endeavor to fulfill his duties to the Creator, while he is not in the least proud of anything in his good deeds, which do not seem great to him, he does not glory in them, and he is ever watchful throughout the rest of his life not to stumble again — such a sinner enjoys superiority over the righteous person who has not committed that sin or its like. For there is no assurance that the righteous man will not become haughty, that his heart will not be uplifted, that he will not feel exalted in his activity. It is an old saying that a sin may be more useful to the penitent than all the righteous deeds of the righteous person, and there is a righteousness which is more injurious to the righteous person than all his sins are to the penitent. That is so, if the righteous person empties his heart of humility and contracts pride, hypocrisy, and love of praise. As a righteous man once said to his disciples, "If you were completely without iniquity, I would be apprehensive of something in you worse than iniquity." "What is worse than iniquity?" they asked him. He answered, "Pride and hypocrisy." Of such a penitent our Sages said, "In the place where penitents stand, the wholly righteous cannot stand."

In the third class is the penitent who has committed grave transgressions, violating prohibitions for which the punishment is death inflicted by human authority or *karet* by Divine will, such as blasphemy [other reading: profanation of the Sabbath], perjury, and similar grave offenses. The offender then turned away from his evil path, and fulfilled all the conditions and requirements of repentance. Forgiveness will not be granted to such a person till he has been tested in this world by suffering that he can endure and so be cleansed of his iniquities. Concerning such a person our Sages said, "If one has violated a prohibition for which the penalty is excision or capital punishment by judicial sentence, and repents of the same, sufferings cleanse him and death atones for his offense, as it is said, 'I will punish their transgression with the rod, their iniquity with plagues' [Ps. 89:33]; furthermore it is written: 'This iniquity shall never be forgiven you until you die' [Isa. 22:14]". The righteous man who has not committed such offenses is undoubtedly superior to one who repents of them.

Thus, R. Bahya's explanation, distinguishing between different categories of sin, does not invoke the gravity of the offense but rather the nature of the sinner's penitence, remorse, and atonement.

A person who has offended by failing to observe a positive commandment, but then repents, is forgiven immediately upon resolving to observe the commandment from that time on. His remorse is relatively minor, and therefore he is considered on an equal level to that of the righteous person, but not more.

However, someone who has committed a serious offense, violating a prohibition not punishable by *karet*, will not be forgiven by merely undertaking to refrain from such action in the future. He must "fully repent with all the requisite conditions," constantly recalling his sin, feeling deep shame and entreating God for forgiveness; he will therefore never be overly proud of his good behavior — and there lies his superiority over the wholly righteous person, who may feel proud of his exceptional piety. In other words, the penitent, by his own behavior, may raise himself to an ethical level higher than that of the righteous person. It was of this kind of penitent that R. Abbahu was speaking.

On the other hand, a person who has committed a more serious offense, punishable by death or *karet*, will not be forgiven — even if he repents — until he has experienced suffering. Only his death will completely atone for his sin, and he therefore does not achieve the level of a righteous person who has never committed such violations.

An interpretation that gives a completely new meaning to the saying under discussion here was offered by the author of *Mikdash Me'at* and by R. Joshua ibn Shu'eib in his homilies, writing in the name of R. Jonah, as cited by R. Isaac Arama[7]. According to this interpretation, R. Abbahu's intent is as follows: Wholly righteous people are not entitled to place themselves in a position that might cause them to sin. That is not so with regard to penitents, "who have not acquired that designation [= penitent] truly unless they have been placed in such dangerous positions, such as being

---

7. *Akedat Yizhak, Ki teze, sha'ar* 97, p. 83b.

alone with a forbidden woman in a place and at a time conducive to sinning with her as is customary, where they have controlled their desires." The words "unless... placed in such dangerous positions" are alluding to the Talmud (BT *Yoma* 86b): "How is one proved a repentant sinner? — Rav Judah said: If the object which caused his original transgression comes before him on two occasions, and he keeps away from it. Rav Judah indicated: With the same woman, at the same time, in the same place." In other words, a person is not called a "penitent" unless he re-experiences the position in which he originally committed the violation, that is, in a position in which he is liable to sin, and nevertheless controls himself and avoids sinning. A righteous person, however, should take care never to be in such a situation.

Yet another interpretation cited by Arama states that the value of an action should be measured in accordance with the person performing the action: "A penitent will be called 'good' and be desirable to the Lord... [when he performs] some actions in relation to which a righteous man would be called 'evil." Accordingly, R. Abbahu is not speaking of the merit of the person himself, the penitent or the righteous person, but of the relationship between the person and the action: the weight of the same action may be greater when performed by a penitent.

R. Israel Al-Nakawa, in his book *Menorat ha-Maʾor*, stressing the penitent's merit, does not consider the penitent as superior to the righteous person, but only as not far removed from the latter's merit. Relying on R. Abbahu's dictum, he states that for that reason the penitent's reward is great:[8]

> The penitent should not think that he is far removed from the level of the righteous and the pious in the World to Come because of sins and offenses committed before he repented; and he should not imagine that his former sins will be mentioned after he has repented and abandoned them and is ashamed of them. That is not so: he

---

8. *Menorat ha-maʾor*, ed. H.G. Enelow, III, Repentance, p. 69.

is beloved, and favored, and considered a friend, and his former sins are forgotten, as Scripture says, "Never again shall they be the trust of the House of Israel, recalling its guilt in having turned to them" (Ezek. 29:16); and further, "He will take us back in love; He will cover up our iniquities, You will hurl all our sins into the depths of the sea" (Micah 7:19). And the penitent's penitence is highly praiseworthy and his merit is great, and his penitence is desirable to the Lord, blessed be He, for once he had tasted sin, he suppressed his desire and abandoned his sin, wholly repenting before the Lord.... in all his heart and all his soul, and destroyed his lust and left his evil deeds. That is what the Sages said, "In the place where penitents stand, even the wholly righteous do not stand." That is to say, the wholly righteous have never sinned and never tasted the taste of sin, and if they were to taste it perhaps they would not be able to renounce it. But the penitents who have sinned and become accustomed to sin and it has become their nature, but they suppressed their desire and changed their nature and reached the very opposite extreme from their nature, having repented — their reward is therefore great.

A similar idea was proposed by R. Isaac Arama, except that in his view the penitent's reward should exceed that of the righteous person — recalling the idea already cited in the name of R. Nissim and Maimonides. Moreover, he holds that the penitent's merit also exceeds that of the righteous person. The penitent, he argues, has made greater efforts than a person who has never sinned, because he was forced to contend with his previous habits:[9]

> See, now, that in accordance with all these truths, R. Abbahu was very correct in saying, as already mentioned, that "in the place where penitents stand, even the wholly righteous cannot stand, as Scripture says: "Peace, peace

9. *Akedat Yizḥak, Niẓavim, shaʾar* 100, p. 113a.

to the far..." — a saying that many have pondered over,
and most of the commentators say that their reward is
greater and their merit higher than those of the righteous
because they have suppressed their accustomed desire for
sin, and [the penitent] fights the Lord's war every day...
That is for him a constant test of himself, and he should
receive a reward for it in accordance with its seriousness,
as the Sages said, "According to the suffering so is the
reward."

R. Isaac Arama does not say merely that the penitents' reward
exceeds that of the righteous, but also that their merit is greater.
Perhaps, then, his interpretation should be understood in the
broadest possible sense: he is not saying that R. Abbahu considers the penitent superior only in the reward he receives compared
with the righteous person.

In addition, he goes on to distinguish between a person who
repents out of fear [of punishment, or God] and one who repents
out of love; that is, a person who repents out of fear stands on a
level below that of the righteous person, but one who repents out
of love is superior:

Now, since he has repented, he must necessarily have
repented either out of fear or out of love. The former is
inferior to a righteous person, while the latter is superior.
Hence we do not find any dictum of our Sages comparing
him with a righteous person, but they considered his sins
as errors or as merits, and we have already explained the
sayings mentioned previously in relation to our intentions in the matter of repentance and its secret.

Arama himself does not agree with the interpretations that
impose limitations on the penitent's merit. Those interpretations,
he holds, ignore the context of the Talmudic debate in which R.
Abbahu's dictum was cited: R. Abbahu's prooftext was "Peace,
peace to the far and the near," giving preference to "the far"
over "the near." "And if so, that is not the way, but surely he was

speaking of the merit of those brave persons who control their desires"; in other words, R. Abbahu was not speaking of where the righteous should (or should not) stand because of danger.

Further restrictions on the meaning of R. Abbahu's statement, in different senses, may also be found in the thought of later scholars. Maharsha,[10] in his *Hiddushei Aggadot* on the Babylonian Talmud (Ber. 34b, s.v. '*she-baʿalei teshuvah*), first comments, "It seems rather implausible that penitents should be viewed as superior to wholly righteous people." Noting that various commentators had tried to resolve the difficulty, he offers his own interpretation: R. Yohanan, he says, is speaking of a "penitent" who has mended his ways after having been "near transgression," that is, on the point of sinning, without having actually sinned. Surely R. Yohanan would not have described an "active" sinner as only "near transgression"; he was referring to a person who was near in his thought or intent to committing some sin, but then overcome his desire. The "repentance," therefore, was not from sin itself, but from the thought of sin. R. Abbahu, too, was referring to such a person only, when he said that "in the place where penitents stand, even the wholly righteous do not stand." He would never have suggested that a person who had actually sinned, even after repenting, should be considered superior to a wholly righteous person.

Conclusion

In the Babylonian Talmud's comparison of the status of penitents in comparison with that of the righteous, opinions are divided. R. Yohanan holds that the prophets prophesied only on behalf of penitents, but that the wholly righteous were beyond the prophets' apprehension. R. Abbahu disagrees, saying that "in the place where penitents stand, even the wholly righteous do not stand." This aphorism is one of the cornerstones of the concept of

---

10. R. Samuel Eliezer Idels, Craców, 1555 — 1631, one of the greatest commentators on the Talmud.

repentance. However, our survey of comments on it has revealed that they considerably restricted its scope.

In the *Mishneh Torah*, Maimonides takes R. Abbahu at face value, explaining that penitents stand on a higher level of merit than those who have never sinned, because they control their desires more than the latter. This explanation, however, seems to contradict what Maimonides himself wrote in *Shemonah Perakim*, where he compares the view of the philosophers with that of the Sages. While the philosophers hold that a pious person is superior to one who controls his desires, the Sages state that one who has a desire to sin but suppresses it is superior to one who has no such desire. According to Maimonides, the two views are not in conflict: the philosophers are speaking of a person who wants to violate a "rational commandment," that is, to do things that are considered evil by all reasonable people, such as murder or theft. The Sages, however, were referring to violation of the so-called "revealed commandments." In the former, which any rational person accepts, such as the prohibition of theft or murder, a person who controls his desires is less meritorious than one who is righteous by nature. In regard to "revealed commandments," however, which we observe only because we were instructed to do so at Sinai and which we would readily violate otherwise, a person who willingly avoids such prohibitions is more praiseworthy than one who is naturally righteous. Thus, in *Shemonah Perakim* Maimonides achieves a kind of compromise, while in *Mishneh Torah* he makes no distinction between "rational" and "revealed" commandments.

But it would seem that there is no real contradiction in Maimonides' treatment, since he was speaking of two different categories of people. In *Shemonah Perakim*, Maimonides is speaking of a person who does not desire to sin at all, while in the Laws of Repentance in *Mishneh Torah* he is speaking not of such a person, but of one who has never actually sinned. He may well be referring to a person who does wish to commit sins but has not done so; Maimonides says that such a penitent stands on a higher level.

While Maimonides agrees with R. Abbahu, other scholars hold the view that the dictum cannot be understood in its plain sense, which is highly implausible. They therefore tend to seek restrictive interpretations, either by defining the "place" of which R. Abbahu is speaking, or by proposing that his dictum is true only under certain conditions. In some cases their interpretations are inconsistent with the plain meaning of the Talmudic text.

The first interpretation is that, while R. Abbahu indeed says that "in the place where penitents stand, even the wholly righteous do not stand," nowhere does he imply that "where the penitents stand" is higher than where the righteous stand; it is even consistent to say that their place is lower! (*Sefer ha-Yashar*). Others interpret R. Abbahu's dictum as a kind of guideline for penitents' behavior, proposing a new meaning for the penitents' "place." Namely, the penitent should avoid even permissible things that might cause him to repeat his offense, whereas the righteous need not do so (R. Jonah of Gerona). Or, on the contrary, the penitent becomes a penitent only after he has taken the risk of committing the same sin and controlled himself; not so the righteous person, who should not endanger himself in the same way (*Sefer ha-Akedah*, citing R. Jonah). Yet another interpretation of the penitent's "place" suggests that God shows his love for penitents more than for the righteous (and therefore performs more miracles for their sake), drawing penitents near Him lest they repeat their offenses (*Sefer ha-Yashar*).

Other commentators lay emphasis on the penitent's behavior, pointing out that the same behavior on the part of a penitent is viewed favorably, whereas a righteous person behaving in that fashion would be considered in a negative light (R. Isaac Arama). The penitent's reward is also greater than that of the righteous (R. Isaac Al-Nakawa).

Another approach to restricting the scope of R. Abbahu's dictum suggests that R. Abbahu is not speaking of an absolutely evil person who has repented, but of a person who sinned under special circumstances. His "penitent" is an originally honest person who unintentionally violated a prohibition, or who was presented with an opportunity and could not control himself; later, that person repented and in fact became doubly righteous (*Sefer ha-Yashar*, saying that this interpretation is "the correct one").

Another limitation on R. Abbahu's view is the assumption that he is speaking of a sin on a certain level: neither a particularly minor offense (for then the penitent would have been forgiven immediately and would have been considered the equal of the righteous person), nor a particularly grave one, carrying a sentence of death (in which case only his death could atone for his sin); rather, he violated a negative commandment. Such a person, having repented, constantly recalls his sin and is ashamed, begs Divine forgiveness, and is thus in no danger of excessive pride over his repentance and will always guard against falling into the same offense. In other words, the penitent's merit is not his actual act of remorse for having sinned; it is his later humility and contrite behavior that raise him above the level of a person who has never acquired such merit (R. Baḥya ibn Paquda).

Another way to restrict the validity of R. Abbahu's view is to confine it to persons who repent out of love, in contrast to those who repent only out of fear (Radbaz).

Another explanation is that R. Abbahu's dictum does not refer to a person who has actually sinned, but to one who was thinking of sinning but controlled himself and did not (Maharsha).

❧ ❧ ❧

In sum, most of the commentators and scholars whose views we have considered believe that R. Abbahu's dictum is concerned not with the rule, but with the exception to the rule. The rule, however — paraphrasing R. Abbahu's formulation — is that "where the wholly righteous stand, penitents do not stand"!

7

The First Crusade Narrative of R. Eliezer bar Nathan

Robert Chazan

The scholarly publication in 1892 of five medieval Hebrew narratives, devoted to persecutions that took place across northern Europe, primarily in Germany, during the eleventh and twelfth centuries and all related to the first three crusades, opened up a rich lode for subsequent Jewish historical research — a fount of data that has not yet been exhausted and that continues to attract scholarly attention, for both the reconstruction of Jewish history and insight into medieval Jewish historical thinking and writing.[1]

The first three narratives in the 1892 publication — arguably the most important of the five — portray the crusader-burgher assaults of 1096, largely upon the great early Jewish communities of the Rhineland. The three 1096 narratives were presented in the following order: the lengthy narrative ascribed to an unknown Solomon bar Simson, viewed by the 1892 editors as the earliest, fullest, and most useful of the three accounts; the briefer narrative written by Eliezer bar Nathan, assumed to be the well-known halakhist of the second half of the twelfth century; and the fairly brief and truncated account designated the *Mainz Anonymous*,

---

1. Adolf Neubauer and Moritz Stern (ed. and trans.), *Hebraische Berichte uber die Judenverfolgungen wahrend der kreuzzuge* (Berlin: Leonhard Stein, 1892). This edition has now been superceded by the new critical edition with German translation by Eva Haverkamp, *Hebraische Berichte uber die Judenverfolgungen wahrend des Ersten Kreuzzugs* (Hannover: Hahnsche Buchhandlung, 2005). The Haverkamp edition presents the Hebrew text in two formats, first comparatively with the three texts lined up side by side and then in a straightforward presentation. I shall generally cite the latter.

perceived as the latest and least useful of the three.[2] Subsequent research has altered these initial conclusions as to time of composition and relative importance of the three 1096 narratives. Increasingly, the *Mainz Anonymous* has been acknowledged as the oldest and, in many ways, the most valuable of the three compositions, for the light it sheds on the events of 1096 and the understanding it provides of Christian and Jewish views of those bloody events.[3] The Solomon bar Simson account is a composite work, organized by a skilled editor on the eve of the Second Crusade, when repetition of crusader hatred and violence threatened the Rhineland communities.[4] The Eliezer bar Nathan narrative, generally recognized as a derivative of the Solomon bar Simson composition, thus is now seen as the latest of the three.

In my work on the events of the 1096, I accorded almost no attention to the Eliezer bar Nathan account, since it provided no new data on the event themselves.[5] In my subsequent work on the three narratives and the historiographic perspectives they present, I discussed the Eliezer bar Nathan narrative briefly. My analysis focused largely on the organization of the narrative and the ways in which the author reworked his source, the lengthier Solomon bar Simson record. I noted briefly the poetic inserts, which constitute a major — perhaps the major — innovation introduced by Eliezer bar Nathan.[6] In the present paper, I would

---

2. Precisely the same order is followed in the re-publication of these texts by Abraham Habermann, *Sefer Gezerot Ashkenaz ve-Zarfat* (Jerusalem: Tarshish, 1945) and in the English translations of Shlomo Eidelberg, *The Jews and the Crusaders* (Madison: University of Wisconsin Press, 1977). Haverkamp — in deference to the Neubauer and Stern edition — maintains the same order, but indicates clearly that in her view the order of composition was *Mainz Anonymous*, Solomon bar Simson narrative, Eliezer ben Nathan narrative.

3. See Anna Sapir Abulafia, "The Interrelationship between the Hebrew Chronicles on the First Crusade," *Journal of Semitic Studies* 27 (1982):221–239, and Robert Chazan, *God, Humanity, and History: The Hebrew First Crusade Narratives* (Berkeley: University of California Press, 2000), chap. 2.

4. Ibid., chaps. 3–5.

5. Idem, *European Jewry and the First Crusade* (Berkeley: University of California Press, 1987).

6. Idem, *God, Humanity, and History*, chap. 6.

like to extend my examination of the Eliezer bar Nathan account in a number of directions.

The starting point for this examination lies in the fact that the modern preference for the *Mainz Anonymous* and the Solomon bar Simson narrative over the Eliezer bar Nathan account has run counter to the preferences of medieval Jews. While the former two records have survived in one manuscript only and are not cited in subsequent medieval sources, the Eliezer bar Nathan account has survived in multiple manuscripts and was available to medieval Jews through lengthy citations in Joseph *ha-Kohen*'s '*Emek ha-Bakha* and David Gans's *Zemah David*. The reason for this relative popularity may well lie in the impact of the name Eliezer bar Nathan and the assumption — correct or incorrect — that the author was the famed halakhist.[7] Nonetheless, we would do well to explore the possibility that there is something in the narrative itself that was appealing to medieval readers. Put differently, the relative popularity of the latest of the three 1096 accounts should move us to inquire as to the author's intentions and successes in fashioning a narrative meaningful to his medieval Jewish readers.

Prior to addressing the intentions and successes of Eliezer bar Nathan, let us buttress briefly the contention that his narrative is grounded in that of Solomon bar Simson. I have treated this issue elsewhere and will here only point to conclusions.[8] Two factors necessitate some kind of relationship: first, the absolute parallels in sequencing and, second, the striking verbatim repetitions. Three possibilities have been advanced: Solomon bar Simson is the source for Eliezer bar Nathan; vice versa, Eliezer is the source for Solomon; both are derived from communal letters. The third of these possibilities is belied by explicit reference in the Solomon bar Simson narrative to oral sources and by the verbatim repetition of sections that can only be attributed to the later author/editors. The second of these possibilities is refuted by comments in the Solomon bar Simson narrative that show it to be an origi-

---

7. For reflections on this vexing question, see below.
8. Chazan, *God, Humanity, and History*, chap. 6.

nal composition and by clarifications offered in the Eliezer bar Nathan narrative that show it to be derivative. We are thus left with only the first possibility as viable. The Eliezer bar Nathan narrative is based on that of Solomon bar Simson.

This leads to one last preliminary observation, and that has to do with the identity of the author of this last of the three narratives. There is broad agreement that the Eliezer bar Nathan who penned the last of the 1096 narratives was none other than the well-known halakhist. This conclusion is based on the evidence for the well-known halakhist's interest in liturgical poetry, the evidence of his own poetic compositions, and the parallel use of acrostics spelling out his own name by both the well-known Eliezer bar Nathan and the author of the 1096 narrative.[9] I have noted one jarring item in this case, and that is the overwhelming place of the Jewish community of Cologne in the Eliezer bar Nathan 1096 narrative. The prose Cologne segment in this narrative far exceeds the prior three segments devoted to Speyer, Worms, and Mainz, in contradistinction to the space allocation in the Solomon bar Simson source. In addition, the poetic lament over Cologne Jewry likewise far exceeds in length the prior three. Both these factors strongly suggest an author focused on the Cologne community and thus — in all likelihood — a member of the late-twelfth-century Jewish community of Cologne.[10] So far as is known, the halakhist Eliezer bar Nathan was in fact a member of the Jewish community of Mainz, which would lead in one of two directions: Either the 1096 narrative suggests a new piece of evidence on the life of Eliezer bar Nathan or, alternatively, the author of the 1096 was not the well-known figure.

Whoever the author of our narrative might have been, the dating or at least the *terminus a quo* is clear. Based on the prior Solomon bar Simson account, the narrative of Eliezer bar Nathan was surely written after the Second Crusade, that is to say during the second half of the twelfth century at the earliest. In the course

---

9. Ibid.
10. Recall that the focus on Mainz was the basis for the naming of the *Mainz Anonymous*.

of the Second Crusade, the Jews of Germany rightly feared repetition of the radical 1096 violence, but in fact this radical violence did not materialize. The radical violence of 1096 was perpetrated by bands of militant crusaders abetted by similarly exhilarated burghers; these groups were motivated by intense millenarian views as to the cosmic nature of the confrontation to which they had committed themselves; as a result, they were determined to wipe out the Jewish communities they encountered in their entirety either through conversion or through slaughter.[11]

On occasion, this sense of the 1096 massacres has been challenged.[12] These challenges have been met with two reinforcements of the prior sense of a millenarian anti-Jewish ideology at the core of the radical 1096 Rhineland assaults. The first reinforcement has involved a closer look at the narratives — particularly the *Mainz Anonymous*, a growing sense that this narrative was written close to the events of 1096, and burgeoning awareness of the extent to which the *Mainz Anonymous* parallels available Christian sources in its depiction of key aspects of the First Crusade. The Mainz Anonymous has emerged as a reliable source for the events of 1096.[13] The second reinforcement of the prior view of a millenarian commitment to destruction of the Jews has come from Haym Soloveitchik's careful analysis of the subsequent halakhic literature on martyrdom. Soloveitchik has argued convincingly that the subsequent halakhic treatment of martyrdom shows marked deviation from prior rabbinic tradition. In Soloveitchik's view, this deviation can only be explained as the result of an intervening event that skewed the thinking of the

11. Robert Chazan, "'Let Not a Remnant or a Residue Escape:' Millenarian Enthusiasm in the First Crusade," *Speculum* 84 (2009); 289–313.
12. Outright rejection of the Hebrew First Crusade narratives is no longer proposed. Some mitigations of their message have recently been advanced. Note, e.g., David Malkiel, "Destruction or Conversion: Intention and Reactions, Crusaders and Jews, in 1096," *Jewish History* 15 (2001):257–280, who suggests that conversion of the Jews was not an initial goal of the popular crusaders, and Kenneth Stow, "Conversion, Apostasy, and Apprehensiveness: Emicho of Flonheim and the Fear of Jews in the Twelfth Century, *Speculum* 76 (2001):911–933, who suggests that the impression of near-total martyrdom in the major Rhineland communities is exaggerated.
13. See again Chazan, *God, Humanity, and History*, chap. 2.

halakhic authorities. For Soloveitchik, this intervening event was the massive Jewish martyrdom of 1096 — especially the activist martyrdoms that involved Jews taking the lives of their kin, which demanded rabbinic approbation, despite its problematic aspects. He further suggests that the massive Jewish martyrdom only makes sense against the backdrop of a unique kind of assault, and I have urged that this uniqueness lies in the radical millenarian thinking associated with some participants in the First Crusade.[14]

The Jews living on the cusp of the Second Crusade had every reason to fear a repetition of the unique kind of violence that had been spawned in 1096. In fact, however, such assaults are nowhere in evidence. While Ephraim ben Jacob of Bonn uses many of the rhetorical flourishes of the 1096 narratives, in fact the story he tells is totally different. Jews are occasionally attacked and occasionally killed. Nowhere, however, does Ephraim of Bonn describe assaults remotely parallel to those that took place in 1096.[15] Why this was so need not detain us. Suffice it to note the following factors: Crusading had matured and its more limited objectives were increasingly clear; more specifically, the spiritual leader of the Second Crusade, Bernard of Clairvaux, went to great lengths to delegitimize the religious grounding for the millenarian anti-Jewish sentiments of 1096 and the violence they spawned. To be sure, protective moves by the temporal authorities and by the Jews themselves played a role as well, but the ideological base for the extreme 1096 massacres was decisively undermined by the general maturation of crusading and by Bernard of Clairvaux.

Thus, I would suggest that the first element in Eliezer bar Nathan's refashioning of the earlier 1096 narratives resulted from the failure of the radical `violence that took place in conjunction with the First Crusade to reemerge during the course of the

---

14. Haym Soloveitchik, "Halakhah, Hermeneutics, and Martydom in Medieval Ashkenaz," *Jewish Quarterly Review* 94 (2004):77–108 and 278–299; Chazan, "'Let Not a Remnant or a Residue Escape.'"
15. See Neubauer and Stern, *Hebraische Berichte*, 58–66, and Habermann, *Sefer Gezerot*, 115–123. Note that Ephraim of Bonn, like Eliezer bar Nathan, added poetry to his prose composition. A comparison of the two bodies of poetry might well be illuminating.

twelfth century. As I have argued elsewhere, the author of the *Mainz Anonymous*, writing in the immediate aftermath of 1096, set as one of his major objectives detailing the circumstances of the tragedy. He was interested in depicting the onset of the crusade and of crusade-related anti-Jewish sloganeering; he was concerned that his readers know of the various stances adopted by the Rhineland burghers and by the Rhineland authorities. Jewish readers had to be well informed as to the dynamics of crusading and of the massacres of 1096, since the attacks seemed highly likely to be repeated. Four and a half decades later, on the eve of the Second Crusade, this intense need was not felt by Solomon bar Simson, as he organized his composite account of 1096. To be sure, danger was high, and Jewish willingness for martyrdom had to be buttressed. But Solomon bar Simson did not sense the obligation to clarify for his readers diverse stances within the Christian majority and the Jewish minority, and in fact he did not provide such clarification. Instead of careful delineation of a variety of crusaders and a variety of burghers, Solomon bar Simson spoke in terms of generic enemies of the Jews. Eliezer bar Nathan took this process yet further, blurring the lines clarified by the *Mainz Anonymous*, especially through his considerable shortening of the more extensive earlier reports.

Yet more significant was the blurring by Eliezer bar Nathan of the Jewish behaviors of 1096. A number of researchers have linked the precise nature of the First Crusade assaults to the radical Jewish martyrdoms of 1096. The author of the *Mainz Anonymous*, for whom the radical Jewish martyrdoms were crucial from many perspectives, highlighted these extreme behaviors in two ways. The first was by setting them in a context of variegated Jewish responses to the assaults. Jews prayed; Jews negotiated; Jews fought; Jews let themselves be killed; Jews killed themselves; Jews killed their wives and children. The very diversity of behaviors serves to highlight the most extreme among them. Moreover, the author of the *Mainz Anonymous* further highlights the radical martyrdoms through a series of vignettes that are utterly unforgettable. No reader of the *Mainz Anonymous* can fail to recall

Meshullam ben Isaac of Worms, the Jewess Minna of Worms, and — surely most strikingly — the Jewess Rachel of Mainz. These figures are indelibly etched in memory, and through them the radical Jewish behaviors are stunningly foregrounded.

All this is lost in the narrative of Eliezer bar Nathan. The diverse styles of Jewish martyrdom are noted, but in simple declarative terms. Regarding Worms, for example, there is the following description: "Those who were killed sanctified the Divine Name before all and sundry and stretched forth their necks so that they might be cut off in the name of their Creator. They likewise slaughtered themselves, one Jew killing another and one Jew killing his relative, his wife, and children, his sons-in-law and his daughters-in-law."[16] The differentiated information is provided. Some Jews submitted to death at the hands of their enemies; others killed themselves; yet others took the lives of their dear ones. Similar sequencing is presented in Eliezer's Mainz account as well. He asserts the cruelty of the crusaders in their relentless killing; he describes Jews waiting patiently to be massacred by their attackers; he speaks of women and men killing their loved ones.[17] Once again, however, the blandness of this string of descriptions serves to blur the remarkable differences among these alternative Jewish behaviors. The *Mainz Anonymous* highlighted these differences through its powerful and detailed narration of individual incidents; Eliezer bar Nathan diminished these differences by the flat enumeration of diverse styles of martyrdom.

The blurring of the unusual Jewish behaviors of 1096 must, of course, be understood once more against the backdrop of post-1096 realities. Just as the millenarian crusading ideology was not reprised during the second and subsequent crusades, so too the unique Jewish reactions were not repeated as well. The Christian militancy of 1096 engendered the radical Jewish counter-crusade

---

16. Neubauer and Stern, *Hebraische Berichte*, 38; Habermann, *Sefer Gezerot*, 73; Haverkamp, *Hebraische Berichte*, 557.
17. Neubauer and Stern, *Hebraische Berichte*, 39; Habermann, *Sefer Gezerot*, 75; Haverkamp, *Hebraische Berichte*, 553.

militancy. With the disappearance of the former, the latter disappeared as well. To be sure, Jewish life continued to be endangered. The nature of the danger, however, shifted, and thus the Jewish responses shifted as well.

The first danger during the twelfth century involved sporadic anti-Jewish violence during periods of crusading exhilaration. The fourth and fifth of the records published in 1892 — the *Sefer ha-Zekhirah* of Ephraim of Bonn on the Second Crusade and the brief and striking memoir of Elazar ben Judah of Mainz on the Third Crusade — provide illustrations of this kind of violence. The key differentiation between this later violence and that of 1096 lies in the organized and ideological aspect of the former and the sporadic nature of the latter. None of the twelfth-century crusade-related violence involved military units or organized coalitions intent on total destruction of the Jews. The sporadic violence of these later crusades could hardly engender the kind of radical Jewish martyrdom that was triggered by the assaults of 1096. When an organized coalition did threaten the Jews of York in 1191, the earlier Jewish propensity for radical martyrdom briefly reemerged. To be sure, the aftermath of the York massacre — that is to say, the assault on the cathedral and the burning of documentation of Jewish lending — indicates how different the York assault was from the attacks of 1096.

A second kind of sporadic anti-Jewish violence emerged during the twelfth century as well. From the middle decades of the century, anti-Jewish allegations grounded in the notion of gratuitous Jewish murder of Christian neighbors began to circulate.[18] These new stereotypes endangered Jews and, on occasion, cost Jewish lives. Such instances, however, likewise did not engender a sense of militant and cosmic confrontation between Christianity and Judaism and did not necessitate on the part of Jewish victims the radical declaration of Jewish truth and superiority that the martyrdoms of 1096 represented. The sporadic violence of the

---

18. On these allegations, see Robert Chazan, *Medieval Stereotypes and Modern Antisemitism* (Berkeley: University of California Press, 1997), chaps. 3–4.

twelfth century required, rather, resigned constancy. For example, the Jewish victims of an 1171 judicial murder by the authorities of the French principality of Blois were lauded by their Jewish contemporaries for precisely this kind of constancy. In the face of death, they were unwavering, recapitulating the stance of the Jewish martyrs of antiquity, rather than the innovative stance of the martyrs of 1096.

I would thus argue that the circumstances of twelfth-century persecution and concomitant Jewish reaction required a refashioning of the 1096 story, with at least some significant adjustments. The kind of heroism portrayed glowingly and movingly in the *Mainz Anonymous* and to a lesser but significant extent by Solomon bar Simson had to seem somewhat inappropriate to the new and more pedestrian circumstances of the later twelfth century. Christian-Jewish tensions still ran high, but they no longer involved the militant and millenarian elements of the confrontation between Christian soldiers of God and Jewish defenders of their deity and faith spawned out of the exhilaration of the first call to religious battle in 1095. Adapting the story of 1096 heroism to the new circumstances of the latter half of the twelfth century is what we see in the Eliezer bar Nathan narrative. The first step in this process was a flattening of the remarkable Jewish behaviors of 1096. That is not to say that the radical Jewish martyrdoms were denied or even overlooked; rather, in the prose sections of the Eliezer bar Nathan narrative they were assimilated into the broader story of crusader murderousness and Jewish death. More important, through the failure to tell these stories in all their graphic detail the unusual behaviors of 1096 were not allowed to achieve the centrality they did, for example, in the *Mainz Anonymous.*

To be sure, there is a second and distinctive feature of the Eliezer bar Nathan narrative, and that is its addition of poetic dirges to the brief prose depictions of events in Speyer, Worms, Mainz, and Cologne. The other two Hebrew 1096 narratives and medieval narratives both Jewish and Christian regularly include petitions of one kind or another, often placed at the close of episodes or entire narratives. The truncated ending of the *Mainz Anonymous*, for example, shows the beginning of such a petition. More fully, the closing section of the Solomon bar Simson narrative ends with passionate petition, calling upon God to deliver just punishment upon the Christian murderers and to provide a just reward to the suffering but steadfast Jewish victims.[19] Eliezer bar Nathan's addition of four full-fledged dirges, however, goes far beyond the normal addition of such closing petitions, and the tenor and role of these dirges merits consideration.

Liturgical poetry comes in a number of shadings, ranging from the relatively specific to the highly abstracted.[20] At the specific end of the spectrum is the dirge *Adaberah be-Zar Ruhi*. While the author of the poem is an unknown Abraham, there can be no mistaking the location, which is clearly Mainz, or the date, which is surely 1096. The poem is full of detailed information, noting for example the central figure of Kalonymous the *parnas*. Beyond that, there is reference to the attraction of attackers from the surrounding countryside, to the intention of destroying totally the Jews, to the siege of the courtyard, and to the varied forms of Jewish martyrdom, including the most radical. While the level of detail in *Adaberah be-Zar Ruhi* cannot match that of the *Mainz Anonymous*, the circumstances the poet laments are nonetheless obvious.[21]

The poetic dirges composed by Eliezer bar Nathan fall very much toward the abstract end of the spectrum I have proposed. Were these four dirges not embedded in Eliezer's 1096 narrative, it would be impossible to identify their circumstances. Nothing in them reflects the specifics of 1096. I would suggest that this abstraction is not at all accidental. In fact, what Eliezer bar Nathan set out to do is to adapt his more detailed source, the Solomon

---

19. Neubauer and Stern, *Hebraische Berichte*, 30; Habermann, *Sefer Gezerot*, 59; Haverkamp, *Hebraische Berichte*, 489.
20. See the valuable observations on Jewish poetry in medieval France of Susan L. Einbinder, *Beautiful Death: Jewish Poetry and Martyrdom in Medieval France* (Princeton: Princeton University Press, 2002).
21. Habermann, *Sefer Gezerot*, 61–62.

bar Simson narrative, to the circumstances of passing time and altered realities. The attacks of 1096 were not repeated, and the radical Jewish martyrdoms were not reprised. What was required with the passage of time and the change of circumstances was a blurring of some of the uniqueness of 1096 and an assimilation of those unique attacks and responses to the historic paradigms of Jewish persecution and suffering. This was achieved by Eliezer bar Nathan by foreshortening the prose materials at his disposal and — yet more important — integrating into his prose narrative liturgical poetry, with its innate tendency toward projection of the here-and-now onto the plane of the metahistoric. Put differently, Eliezer bar Nathan was writing for the needs of a later twelfth-century audience. The accuracy of his perceptions of these needs is reflected in the ongoing popularity of his narrative, a popularity that far exceeded that of the more highly specified of the 1096 accounts.

This analysis of the Eliezer bar Nathan narrative highlights the striking differences between medieval and modern historical sensibilities. As moderns, we are very much oriented toward the specific, the innovative, and the different. As a modern historian of 1096, I personally have been most interested in the innovative aspects of the crusading assaults and the Jewish martyrological responses. My interest has thus been very much attracted to the *Mainz Anonymous* and its focus on the new and the different. It should be emphasized of course that the medieval Jewish author of the *Mainz Anonymous* very much shared my valorizing of the new and different. As I have suggested, he shared this interest in order to achieve his time-bound objective of forewarning his Jewish contemporaries of dangers he correctly perceived as unprecedented. He also concluded — in a yet more striking way — that the theological dilemma posed by the assaults of 1096 could best be solved by highlighting the unprecedented quality of the crusading assaults and the equally unprecedented quality of the Jewish martyrdoms these assaults triggered. The *Mainz Anonymous*'s theological message was itself innovative and radical: The massacres of 1096 did not reflect — as Christians claimed

— God's abandonment of the Jewish people; rather, they reflected God's testing of the Jewish people, a test that the Rhineland Jews decisively passed. The Christian realities were new; the Jewish reactions were new; the theological explanation was new.

Yet newness, recognized and accepted by the author of the *Mainz Anonymous*, was not a dominant value during the Middle Ages (whether it is a dominant value in our own times is open to debate). During the Middle Ages, the precedented was preferred to the unprecedented, the traditional to the innovative. While the author of the Mainz Anonymous appreciated the newness of 1096, Eliezer bar Nathan appreciated the medieval preference for the traditional. His narrative cum poetry represented an assimilation of 1096 into the mainstream of Jewish history, thinking, and literary expression. His sense of audience was acute, and his narrative is the one that resonated among medieval Jewish readers.[22]

22. Note the important general observations on the medieval preference for the traditional over the innovative by Yosef Hayim Yerushalmi, *Zakhor: Jewish History and Jewish Memory* (Seattle: University of Washington Press), chap. 2.

8

The Problem of Identity in Rashi, Rambam and the Tosafists

J. David Bleich

I. The Problem

Persons as well as things endure over time. People are born as infants, grow into adolescence, mature into adults and decline in senescence. An acorn takes root, a sapling emerges, a tree develops verdant foliage and eventually enters into a decline. Change is an ongoing and omnipresent phenomenon. Yet change is devoid of meaning unless understood as an accident, in the Aristotelian sense of the term, of some underlying substratum or of a Kantian *Ding-an-sich* that remains constant. The problem of identity has long been the bane of philosophers. Common sense tells us that, despite the flow of time and the assumption of different characteristics, there exists a constant element in every person or thing. What is the essence of continuity that exists despite change? Certainly, it is that elusive quintessential element that is captured in the notion of identity.

Long before becoming aware of the fact that, from antiquity until the present, the problem of identity had engaged the intellects of foremost philosophers, I was gripped by the enormity of the problem as a result of its reflection in a seemingly frivolous legal maneuver.

Most people are familiar with the horrendous acts committed by Nathan Leopold and Richard Loeb, two Chicago play-boys who abducted a child and subsequently murdered him. It was a purposeless, senseless crime. Both because of its frivolous nature and because of the fact that it was committed by wealthy, privileged young men, the incident was surrounded with notoriety. Leopold and Loeb were both sentenced to life in prison. They were extremely bright, well-educated young men. In prison they became jailhouse lawyers and continuously peppered the courts with writs and motions, petitions for retrial etc., etc.

By chance, I came upon a report of a particular petition filed by one of those young men. He applied for a writ of *habeas corpus* on very, very ingenious grounds. As are most of us, he was also aware that, with perhaps the exception of the brain and the central nervous system, in the process of time every single cell of the human body is destroyed and then regenerated. To be sure, destruction and regeneration does not occur to every cell simultaneously but together they constitute a constant, ongoing process affecting the entire body. Thus, for example, every time a person claps his hands he destroys perhaps many hundreds of cells but, fortunately, others are continuously created to take their place. Cells simply outlive their usefulness and disintegrate, only to be replaced by others. It is reported that, within a period of seven years, all cells are destroyed and replaced. Apparently, it is a virtual certainty that no single cell that is present in the body at the beginning of any given seven-year period will still be present in the body at the expiration of that seven-year period. That phenomenon, he claimed, provided ample grounds for *habeas corpus* — quite literally. More than seven years had elapsed since the time of the crime. Accordingly, they argued, "Give us the body". The imprisoned convicts are not the perpetrators. Leopold and Leob alleged that they did not share the identity of the persons who had committed the crime and therefore they were being unjustly incarcerated.

Needless to say, the petition was dismissed. In rejecting the petition for *habeas corpus*, the judge, in effect, asserted that the legal system embraces the common sense notion of personal identity. The law will not allow itself to be confused by scientific facts because, at least with regard to this matter, it regards them as totally irrelevant. The notion of personhood and the notion of individual identity have nothing to do with the permanence versus the transience of the cells of a body. Identity is a reflection of some other concept — a concept that a jurist may not be responsible for apprehending, much less explicating — but one with which a philosopher, and certainly a legal philosopher, must grapple.

As stated by one contemporary writer, "People age, some trees regularly shed their leaves, ice melts with the coming of spring, and wood, when burned, gives way to fire and ash."[1] The question is whether the toddler in the pictures that a mother displays is the same individual as the grown, mature adult. If so, in what sense? By the same token, one can ask whether, when ice melts and becomes water, is there a preservation of identity? When wood is burned, and gives way to charcoal and then to ash, is there any continuum of identity between the wood that formed the tree and the ash which is the residue subsequent to combustion? The problem, for philosophical as well as legal reasons, is of course most acute with regard to the personal identity of human beings, but essentially the same problem exists with regard to the identity of members of the animal kingdom and even of inanimate objects.

II. Philosphical Resolutions

Philosophers have dealt with this issue in a variety of different ways. David Hume, in his *Treatise of Human Nature*, concedes that the problem admits of no resolution. According to Hume, the very notion of identity is specious because human consciousness is naught but a collection, or bundle, of perceptions. The notion of identity is nothing more than a construct of the mind which it imposes upon an uninterrupted series of perceptions. Hence, Hume categorizes the notion of identity as a fiction and the notion of an intuitively apprehended self as not genuine. Thus, in effect, he dismisses the problem as specious and hence as not

---

1. Avrum Stroll, "Identity," *Encyclopedia of Philosophy*, ed. Paul Edwards (New York, 1972), IV, 121.

requiring a solution: there is no need to explicate the nature of personal identity because there is no personal identity.[2]

Putting aside the question of identity with regard to inorganic entities, John Locke, in *An Essay Concerning Human Understanding*, proposes a solution to the problem of personal identity by attempting to make identity contingent upon memory. Each individual possesses a unique set of memories and it is those memories that constitute his or her unique identity. In effect, it is the series of memories that constitutes the person. For Locke, the identity of person is the identity of consciousness.[3]

That categorization of personal identity has been challenged for cause. Imagine that a prince went to sleep in a royal palace. In the morning the prince awakens and utters the memory claims of a cobbler. He looks at himself and does not really believe that he is a prince since he has no memory of his royal station. The same evening, a cobbler living in his miserable abode hundreds of miles away went to sleep and wakes up believing that he is the prince. He proceeds to demand that he be taken to the royal palace and treated in a manner appropriate to his station. We are confronted with two different people — at least *we* would call them different people — and each one claims the retained memories of the other. If identity is nothing more than a chain of memories there are no grounds to distinguish between veridical memories and hallucinatory memories. And indeed Locke seems to be prepared to say that the prince and the cobbler are the same person.[4] In an attempt to obviate that problem, some philosophers, such as Thomas Reid, in his *Essays on the Intellectual Power of Man*,[5] and Joseph Butler, in an essay entitled "Of Personal Identity," published as an addendum to the first volume of *The Theology of Religion*, ed., W.E. Gladstone (Oxford, 1897), retain the notion of identity defined in terms of memory but couple it with

---

2. See *Treatise of Human Nature*, Book I, Part IV, sec. 6 and Appendix. See also A. J. Ayer, *Language, Truth and Logic* (New York, 1946), p. 127.
3. See *An Essay Concerning Human Understanding*, Book 2, chap. 27.
4. *Ibid.*, point 15.
5. Essay III, chap. 4.

the postulation of a mind or spiritual substance in which memories adhere. In the introduction to his *Critique of Pure Reason*, Immanuel Kant develops the thesis that empirical experiences are imposed upon an *a priori* faculty of cognition which seemingly requires a persisting subject or owner.

In more recent times, A. J. Ayer, in his *Philosophical Essays*, develops a notion that had at least been suggested in earlier philosophical writings, particularly in Locke's discussion of the identity of inanimate entities, and seeks to define identity in terms of spatio-temporal continuity.[6] I prefer the term spatio-temporal contiguity rather than spatio-temporal continuity for reasons that may become a bit more obvious later. Basically, according to Ayer's thesis, a person preserves his identity as an individual because he has succeeded in time and place to the same individual who occupied the same or contiguous space a nanosecond earlier. Identity is thus dependent upon both spatial and temporal contiguity. A person who passes out of existence and reappears at some future time would not be the same person, no matter how brief the interval between his disappearance and his reappearance. Nor, according to Ayer, would a person who disappears only to appear instantaneously in some other place be the same person.

Later, in *The Problem of Knowledge*, Ayer modifies that definition somewhat, and insists that, although spatio-temporal contiguity is essential to the definition of personal identity, it must, however, be modified by incorporating the notion of physical characteristics. When spatio-temporal contiguity exists and is also accompanied by appropriate persistent physical characteristics, Ayer is willing to recognize that the two in tandem are what we mean when we speak of personal identity.[7]

It seems to me that there is a much older solution to the problem, although it was not formulated as a solution to this particular problem. In discussing the nature of causality, Aristotle enumerates four separate notions of causality, the last of which

---

6. *Philosophical Essays* (New York, 1963), p. 15.
7. See *The Problem of Knowledge*, chap. 5.

he calls the final cause. The final cause is the *telos* or purpose of the act. Although the final cause is chronologically subsequent to the other causes in that it cannot be achieved without them, it is nevertheless logically prior. Accordingly, Aristotle informs us that the effect is really present in its cause from the very beginning.[8]

Aristotle also presents the notion of *entelechies* as an explanation of how it is, for example, that an acorn develops into an oak tree.[9] *Entelechies* are those things which have their end in themselves. If one thinks of the *enteleche* as some kind of metaphysical entity it is that entity that transforms potentiality into actuality. If the *enteleche* is identified as the mediator responsible for the actualization of the final cause, those two notions taken together represent a highly sophisticated theory of causality. Causation is the process of actualization of the potential by means of the *enteleche*. In contradistinction to Hume, who denies the reality of causality, Aristotle may be understood as formulating a very clear notion of causality.

It seems to me that Aristotle's unique notion of causality gives us not only a definition of causality but provides us with a notion of identity as well. Cause and effect are intrinsically related. As mediator of the final cause, the *enteleche* establishes an identity between the causal entity and the effect that is already present in that cause. The presence of the effect in the cause creates a nexus between them; it is that nexus of which we speak when we speak of the continuum of identity.

---

8. It is this understanding of the nature of causality that led both Rambam and Crescas to reject the possibility of the emergence of matter directly from God in the form of emanation. Rambam, *Guide of the Perplexed*, Part II, chap. 22, states, "Aristotle and the philosophers assume as an axiom that a simple element can only produce one simple thing." Crescas, *Or ha-Shem*, II, *klal* 3, chap. 4 (p. 68a) comments, "Inasmuch as this matter is extremely imperfect, it could not have come by necessity from God who is infinitely perfect." That argument is based upon the presumption that an effect is, in some sense, already present in the cause and hence cannot be dissimilar to the cause.

9. *Metaphysics*, Book Theta.

III. Personal Identity in Talmudic Sources

The issue of identity, both individual identity as well as identity as a member of a species, was certainly a matter of concern to rabbinic scholars. Identity as a member of a species was perhaps the focal point of their attention because of its relevance in determining the status of a particular animal as a member of a kosher or of a non-kosher species. Nevertheless, personal identity was also a matter of concern and an analysis of rulings formulated by the Gemara reveals that the talmudic notion of identity is even more far-reaching than its common sense counterpart.

The Gemara, *Bava Batra* 159a, states as follows:

> If a son sold property of his father during his father's lifetime and then died, his son may recover [the property] from the purchasers. And it is this that is difficult among the laws of jurisprudence for [the purchasers] ought to be able to say to him, "Your father sold and you are recovering?" But what is the difficulty? Perhaps [the grandson] might say, "I come with the rights of the father of my father as it is written, 'In place of your fathers shall be your sons [whom] you shall make princes in all the land' (Psalms 45:17)."

It is virtually axiomatic that a person cannot transfer or devise property interests that are not vested in him. If so, the son could not possibly bequest to the grandson property that he has already alienated.[10] Yet the Gemara declares that the grandson's claim to recover the alienated property presents no doctrinal difficulty because property passes directly from the grandfather to the grandson by operation of the law of inheritance thereby obviating any property interest that might have been asserted in the name of the son.

The Gemara then proceeds to formulate the difficulty in another manner:

---

10. The obvious question of the invalidity in Jewish law of a transfer of a future interest is addressed by *Tosafot, ad locum.*

If a first born-son sold [his] primogeniture share during his father's lifetime and then died during his father's lifetime, his son may recover [the property] from the purchasers. And it is this that is difficult among the laws of jurisprudence: His father sold and he recovers?

If you say that in this case as well the grandson might say, "I come with the rights of the father of my father," nevertheless, what is his connection to the share of primogeniture?

But what is the difficulty? Perhaps [the grandson] might say, "I come with the right of the father of my father but I stand in the place of my father."

In this retort the Gemara establishes not simply that the transfer of property is directly from grandfather to grandson but that the grandson literally stands in the place of the father, i.e., he has acquired the legal persona of the father with all the rights and prerogatives consequent thereto.

The Gemara herein presents a theory akin to the notion of inheritance by representation found in Roman law. In Roman law the heir succeeds not only to the estate of his progenitor but becomes liable for his debts as well. That rule follows from the notion that, juridically speaking, the two individuals are regarded as a single person. However, in Jewish law a son bears no personal responsibility for discharging a debt incurred by his father; liability of heirs is limited to recovery from the inherited assets.[11]

Nevertheless, the only cogent theory that allows for a grandson to succeed to the son's right of primogeniture without title first passing through the son is the notion that, for the limited purpose of inheritance, they are deemed to be one person. Thus, the grandson, as a sort of alter ego of the son, enjoys the positive benefit of inheritance but is not responsible for personal debts of his forebears and is also not bound by his progenitor's attempt to

---

11. For a detailed discussion of the liability of heirs see *Encyclopedia Talmudit*, XXIII, 516–550. For some authorities such an obligation does exist but is not jurisprudential in nature; rather, it is rooted in the son's duty to honor his father. See *ibid.*, p. 521.

alienate property. That thesis flows from a literal reading of the verse "In place of your fathers shall be your sons."

This theory is unique to the case of inheritance by a son but does not pertain to inheritance by other relatives. It is not the case that this doctrine has a practical effect solely with regard to the right of primogeniture which, by definition, is limited to a son; the doctrine of filial inheritance by representation is reflected in the rule codified by Rambam, *Hilkhot Melakhim* 1:7, providing for the inheritance of the monarchy and other communal appointments by lineal descendants. Collateral heirs enjoy no such rights. That distinction is readily understood if it is recognized that direct descendants — and only direct descendants — are not really heirs at all but are the extension of the same persona.[12] Similarly, filial inheritance of property — but only filial inheritance — is based upon a notion of representation.

This talmudic discussion of inheritance certainly reflects a doctrine of identity and, moreover, establishes that the notion of identity is not at all predicated upon the phenomenon of memory. It may be shown that early-day authorities understood identity as predicated upon spatio-temporal contiguity or in terms of a causal nexus akin to the Aristotelian notion of an *enteleche*.

---

12. See R. Elchanan Wasserman, *Kovez Shi'urim*, II, no. 12, who invokes this theory in explaining why the posthumous issue of a proselyte succeeds to his father's property even though it has already been seized as ownerless property by another. *Kovez Shi'urim* compares the situation of a posthumously born child to the phenomenon of a person dying only to reappear and lay claim to his property. *Kovez Shi'urim* also invokes this theory in explaining why a son may collect certain fines due his mother even though fines cannot be inherited.

Although self-endangerment is permitted, and, according to some authorities, even mandatory in order to rescue another person from certain death, sacrifice of one's life in order to preserve the life of another is forbidden. See R. Jacob Emden, *Migdal Oz, Even ha-Bohen* 1:85, who states that the matter is self-evident; R. Jacob Ettlinger, *Teshuvot Binyan Zion*, no. 165; R. Yitzchak Ya'akov Weisz, *Teshuvot Minhat Yizhak*, V, no. 8, addendum; and R. Moshe Feinstein, *Iggerot Mosheh, Yoreh De'ah*, II, no. 174, *anaf* 4. Nevertheless, R. Jacob Emden, *loc. cit.*, suggests that a parent may sacrifice his life in order to preserve a child from certain death. Although *Migdal Oz* does not advance this consideration, if parent and child constitute a single person, such an exception is readily fathomed. Cf. also, R. Shlomoh Kluger, *Imrei Shefer, Parashat Kedoshim*, sec. 14, who expresses a similar concept in a different context.

IV. Species Identity in Jewish Law

1. The Principle of Yozei

Quite apart from the concept of the personal identity of a human being, identity is a significant halakhic notion with regard to animals. With regard to the dietary code and similar matters the issue is primarily that of identity as a member of a particular species. But, as will be shown, species identity is a direct consequence of intergenerational personal identity.

The quest for a halakhic theory or theories of identity begins with an analysis of a talmudic statement presented in *Hullin* 62b and *Niddah* 50b:

> Rav Papa said: The *tarnegola de-agma* is forbidden; the *tarnegolta de-agma* is permitted. Your sign [to remember which is forbidden and which permitted is] "An Ammonite but not an Ammonitess." Meremar expounded: The *tranegolta de-agma* is forbidden: We see that it stomps [its prey] and eats it; it is the [forbidden] *giruta*.[13]

Despite the attempts of translators and scholars to identify the species that are the subject of this talmudic discussion there is no halakhically acceptable manner of determining the species to which reference is made. The fact that the classic talmudic commentators disagree with regard to the meaning of Rav Papa's statement only underscores our inability to identify any ornithological species named in the Pentateuch or in rabbinic literature other than on the basis of received tradition.

A literal reading of the text would seem to indicate that there is some species of *tarnegol* indigenous to the *agma*[14] and that

---

13. The Soncino translation renders "*giruta*" as "parrot." Jastrow more cautiously defines the term as "moor-hen" or "hen of the marshes."
14. The term "*agma*" or "*agamma*" is ambiguous and may denote either an uncleared field, a meadow, a marsh, stagnant water or a lake. Thus, the Soncino translation renders "*tranegol de-agma*" as "moor-cock" and "*tarnegolta de-agma*" as "moor-hen" while Jastrow translates the latter term as "moor-hen" and as "hen of the marshes."

the male of that species is forbidden while the female is permitted. That is certainly the impression conveyed by the use of the masculine "*tarnegol*" in juxtaposition with the feminine form "*tarnegolta*" as well as by the mnemonic supplied. *Tosafot, Hullin* 62b, regard such a literal reading to be halakhically absurd since all members of every kosher species, male as well as female, are permitted. Or, as declared in the talmudic principle quoted by *Tosafot*: "*Kol ha-yozei min ha-tahor tahor* — All that emerges from the pure is pure." Accordingly, *Tosafot* hasten to explain that the two terms do not denote the male and female of a single species but are the names of two distinct species, one of which is kosher and the other non-kosher. *Tosafot, Hullin* 62b, peremptorily dismiss any other possible interpretation of the text. It follows, of course, that, according to this analysis, in each of those species both the male and female are either kosher or non-kosher.

However, both Rashi and one opinion cited by *Tosafot* in their commentary on *Niddah* 50b understand the Gemara's distinction quite literally: the male of the species to which reference is made is forbidden whereas the female is permitted. The male is forbidden because it lacks the criteria of a kosher bird. In resolving the obvious problem posed by the dictum "All that emerges from the pure is pure," which would render the bird permissible regardless of its physical criteria, *Tosafot, Hullim* 62b, state that birds do not give birth to young directly; rather, they lay eggs and the gestating embryos are nurtured by putrid matter within the eggs. That putrid matter is categorized by the Gemara as having the status of "dust." Thus, since the hatchling is produced by "dust" rather than from a living creature, there is no continuity of identity between the bird and its young.

The principle cited by *Tosafot* is formulated by the Mishnah, *Bekhorot* 5b:

> ... a clean animal that gives birth to an unclean animal [the offspring] is permitted to be eaten; an unclean animal that gives birth to a clean animal [the offspring] may not be eaten, for that which emerges from the

impure is impure and that which emerges from the pure
is pure.

Tosafot's statement asserting that the principle of *yozei* does not
apply to birds hatched from eggs is an application of the principle formulated by the Gemara, *Temurah* 31a, in explaining that
a bird born of an egg laid by a *terefah* is permitted because the
fledgling develops only when the egg becomes putrid "and upon
its becoming putrid it is mere dust." The notion "*me-afra ka-gadil*
— it grows from dust" is employed by *Tosafot* to explain why the
female fledgling is permitted even though its male progenitor is
non-kosher. *Me-afra ka-gadil* serves to establish that the principle
of *yozei* is rendered inapplicable by virtue of the destruction of the
non-kosher source and its replacement by innocuous "dust." But,
then, if it is "dust" that generates the new bird, why should that
bird be non-kosher even if it is endowed with the characteristics
of a non-kosher species? Since it is generated by "dust" which is
"pure" its status should be that of a creature that "emerges from the
pure" and hence it should be kosher as well. Indeed, the concept
"*me-afra ka-gadil*" should be applied to all birds, including the
perfectly usual cases in which both parent birds are non-kosher,
and should yield the result that all their progeny are kosher since
they are the product of putrid dust that is halakhically "clean":
It is precisely for that reason that a bird born of an egg laid by
a *terefah* is permitted. The Gemara, it should be remembered,
justifies that ruling by declaring that the embryo does not begin
to develop until the egg has already become putrid and hence
the embryo must be regarded as having developed from "mere
dust."

Rambam, *Hilkhot Ma'akhalot Asurot* 3:11, seems to be aware
of this difficulty. Rambam ignores the rationale advanced by the
Gemara and rules that a fledgling born of the egg of a *terefah* is
permitted, not because it is generated by "dust," but because "there
is no unclean [bird] in its species." Ra'avad, in a gloss to Rambam's
ruling, takes Rambam to task for substituting his rationale for that
of the Gemara but fails to address the underlying difficulty, *viz.*,

that the same rationale should logically render all the young of unclean species permissible.

Rashi's position is further complicated by a view expressed in his comments on *Hullin* 9a, s.v. *alma*. The Gemara cites the statement of the Mishnah, *Nazir* 49b, declaring that a Nazarite becomes defiled through contact with "a corpse and with an olive-size [piece] of a corpse." The Gemara objects that if a Nazarite is defiled by an olive-size portion of a corpse, *a fortiori*, the Nazarite must be defiled through contact with an entire corpse and hence the initial mention of "a corpse" is superfluous. The Gemara responds by pointing to the reality of the existence of a corpse whose size in its entirety is less than the size of an olive, *viz.*, "an abortus whose limbs were not yet bound together by sinews." Having established that a human embryo can have the status of a corpse even before sinews have developed, the Gemara then deduces that, with regard to animals, the prohibition attendant upon eating the meat of consecrated animals may devolve upon the embryo before the advent of a an independent prohibition against eating the sciatic sinew. In context, the Gemara is struggling with the issue of whether a second prohibition can attach itself to an already prohibited entity. *Tosafot* explain the Gemara's deduction as based upon the presumption that the sciatic sinew develops as a unique structure from already existing undifferentiated tissue. Thus, the tissue that becomes the sciatic sinew was already prohibited as sanctified meat. Rashi, however, comments that the embryo "is sanctified from the moment of creation [when] the sinew was not yet created."

Quite cogently, *Tosafot* apparently assume that the principle of *yozei* assures that tissue "emerging" from already existing tissue has the halakhic status of the tissue from which it is produced. Rashi, in emphasizing that the sinew "was not yet created," seemingly assumes that the principle of *yozei* is applicable even with regard to tissue that is generated *de novo* and compounds that difficulty by assuming that the chronologically prior prohibited status of the original tissue is also somehow immanent in as yet non-existent tissue as well.[15]

There is a yet more perplexing issue with regard to the notion of *yozei*. As noted earlier, the young of unclean species are non-kosher even if they are born with the physical characteristics of a kosher animal. Rambam, *Hilkhot Ma'akhalot Assurot* 1:5, records the prohibition against eating such an animal with the simple statement that such an animal is "forbidden with regard to eating." The implication is that the prohibition attendant upon the progeny is identical to that associated with the mother and carries the identical punishment of forty lashes.[16] The milk of

---

15. Immortality of the soul does not pose a serious problem for most theories of identity. Assuming that the soul has memories of terrestrial events experienced while incarnate it is readily understandable that the continuum of identity survives death. If the notion of spatio-temporal contiguity is crucial to an understanding of personal identity it must be amended to include a notion of meta-spatial and meta-temporal continuity.

Bodily resurrection presents a more formidable problem. In what sense can the physically restored body be deemed identical to the body earlier reduced to the dust? This problem has been raised by at least one philosopher, Terence Penelhum in his essay "Personal Identity, Memory, and Survival," *Journal of Philosophy*, vol. 56, no. 22, pp. 899–903.

From the vantage point of Jewish tradition, one might dismiss the issue as lacking in theological import. Personal identity in bodily resurrection must, in any event, be understood as identity of the soul. Whether the body is the "same" or different is hardly crucial. It should be sufficient to say that the bodies in both existencies are the physical habitat of the same soul.

Yet, the question does have halakhic ramifications that are at least theoretical in nature. Laws predicated upon man's corporeal nature, e.g., matrimonial provisions and property rights, presume personal identity. The issue then is, if the resurrected body enjoys the same identity as its precursor, are earlier marital bonds reestablished and may the resurrected person reclaim property owned in a previous existence?

Such a result should not follow from either of the theories herein advanced in the explanation of the notion of personal identity. According to Rashi, retention of a single identity depends upon a causal nexus manifest in generation and regeneration of the cells of the body. That chain of causal phenomena terminates with death. Accordingly, the resurrected body does not enjoy the same halakhic persona as its predecessor. According to *Tosafot* and Rambam, personal identity is contingent upon a spatio-temporal continuum. It is quite understandable that rules and regulations governing this-worldly institutions are determined by physical, rather than metaphysical, contiguity.

Of course, since the problem is entirely halakhic rather than philosophical, it might be resolved by means of a simple halakhic concept, viz., Halakhah posits death as an event that terminates marriage and extinguishes property rights.

16. See *Pri Megadim, Mishbezot Zahav* 81:1, who questions why this is so but remarks that "not a single one among the decisors can be found" who rules otherwise. R.

a non-kosher animal and the eggs of a non-kosher species are similarly forbidden as recorded by the Gemara, *Bekhorot* 6b, with regard to milk and, *Hullin* 69b, with regard to eggs. The principle underlying those prohibitions is the notion of *yozei*. However, as explicitly codified by Rambam, *Hilkhot Maakhalot Assurot* 3:6, although the prohibition is biblical in nature, the punishment of lashes is not administered for partaking of either the milk or the eggs of unclean species. Clearly, then, the status of a *yozei*, or the emerging entity, is not entirely identical to that from which it arises. Nevertheless, the young of the species have precisely the same status as their progenitors. Also, an adult pig, for example, possesses far greater mass than a newly-born piglet. The additional meat was not present at birth but was produced from tissue existent at birth. Logically, such additional tissue should be in the category of *yozei*. Yet, it is abundantly clear that, unlike consumption of meat or eggs, partaking of an olive-size piece of meat derived from any portion of the animal engenders the statutory punishment of forty stripes.

Although they are closely related, the concept of *yozei* clearly has two different facets: 1) a literal notion of *yozei* predicated upon a causal nexus between the source and the effect, e.g., milk or eggs produced by a prohibited animal; and 2) *yozei* in the descriptive sense which serves to transpose identity and halakhic status as a member of a particular species. The notion of identification as a member of a species is best summed up in a pithy comment attributed to R. Chaim Soloveitchik. It is reported that R. Chaim queried: Why is a horse a horse? Is it a horse because it is a horse or is it a horse because its mother was a horse? To rephrase the question: Is a horse a horse because it manifests the characteristics

---

Chaim ha-Levi Soloveitchik, *Hiddushei ha-Grah al ha-Rambam*, *Hilkhot Maakhalot Assurot* 3:11, *Me-Ginzei ha-Grah* (Johannesburg, 5749), no. 117 and *Kuntres Maatikei Shemuah* (Jerusalem, 5756), p. 24 assumes this to be true as a matter of course. See also the numerous sources cited in *Encyclopedia Talmudit*, XXIII (Jerusalem, 5757), 325, notes 591 and 593. Cf., however, *Teshuvot Yad Eliyahu*, no. 2, cited by *Pithei Teshuvah*, *Yoreh Deah* 79:2, who expresses doubt with regard to the matter. Cf., the somewhat unclear comments of the *yesh min ha-mefarshim* cited by *Maggid Mishneh*, *Hilkhot Maakhalot Assurot* 3:6.

that are the necessary conditions for identification as a member of the equine species or is a horse a horse because its mother was a horse? R. Chaim proceeded to declare that a horse is a horse solely because its mother was a horse and explained that ancestral identity is the sole factor that determines membership in a particular species. Thus, as spelled out by the Mishnah, *Bekhorot* 5b, identity as a member of a clean or unclean species is determined by birth and not by distinguishing physical characteristics. Accordingly, a colt is a horse because its mother's persona is transposed to her young. Of course, the mother is the proximate cause of the existence of her offspring; however, the identity of the young is not rooted simply in the causative factor but in the accompanying transfer of identity. R. Chaim, *Hiddushei ha-Grah al ha-Rambam, Hilkhot Ma'akhlot Assurot* 3:11, as well as *Me-Ginzei ha-Grah* (Johannesburg, 5749), no. 117 and *Kuntres Ma'atikei Shemu'ah* (Jerusalem, 5756), p. 24, describes that form of *yozei* as giving rise to the halakhic status of that which "emerges" as a status *mi-zad azmo*, i.e., a status intrinsic to its identity.[17] Quite obviously, then, since the offspring shares the identity of its progenitors, whatever prohibition is attendant upon partaking of the flesh of the mother is also attendant upon partaking of the flesh of the young.[18] The same principle applies with regard to added weight put on by an animal as it grows into adulthood. The young have the status and identity of the progenitors; *a fortiori*, naturally added tissue also has the status and identity of the entity to which it adheres.

R. Elchanan Wasserman remarks several times in his writings that, although the concept of *yozei* is usually formulated with regard to the status of food products, it does not constitute a novel rule limited to determining the permitted or prohibited nature of a foodstuff for purposes of the dietary code. Rather, asserts R. Elchanan, *any* thing that is emitted by, or proceeds from, a particular entity has the status of the entity that produced it.

---

17. Cf., however, R. Yitzchak Ze'ev Soloveitchik, *Ma'atikei Shemu'ah*, II (Bnei Brak, 5753), p. 106.
18. See endnote.

In his *Kovez Shi'urim, Pesahim*, sec. 120, R. Elchanan demonstrates the operation of the principle of *yozei* with regard to the progeny of animals with whom humans have engaged in acts of bestiality. Any animal, male or female, that has participated in an act of that nature may not be offered as a sacrifice. R. Elchanan demonstrates that, at least in the case of the young born of two animals each of which has engaged in an act of that nature, their progeny may also not be utilized for sacrificial purposes. To be sure, offspring conceived subsequent to such acts has not been employed for immoral purposes; nevertheless, the status of such a newborn animal is that of an animal that has engaged in an act of that nature because it has "emerged" from an animal having that status.

In a separate discussion in his *Kovez Inyanim, Hullin* 17a, R. Elchanan examines the status of milk. The Gemara, *Bekhorot* 6a, finds it necessary to adduce a biblical verse in demonstrating that the milk of a kosher species is permissible. Absent specific license, the milk produced by a living animal would have the status of an entity that "emerges" from an organ of a living animal. A limb or organ torn from a living animal is prohibited and hence the *yozei* of such an organ is also forbidden. However, at least according to one opinion recorded in the Gemara, *Hullin* 103a, a living animal is not viewed as a mere aggregate of limbs and organs (*behemah be-hayyehah lav le-evarim omedet*). Hence the milk it yields is not the *yozei* of "a limb [severed] from a living animal." Why, then, should specific dispensation be required to permit the drinking of milk? R. Elchanan explains that, although no prohibition is attendant upon a non-dismembered living animal, any thing that emerges from the animal is endowed with the status of that animal. R. Elchanan explains, in effect, that the "torn" status of a limb is an "accident" that is imposed upon a limb that is integral to a living animal. Milk yielded by a cow has the same essential status as the cow but is different with regard to one crucial accident, *viz.*, it is "torn" or separated from the cow; upon milking, it becomes separated from the cow. Since the milk "emerges" from the cow it, too, has the status of a separated, and hence ostensibly forbidden, organ of the cow. Accordingly, biblical dispensation is required to render the milk permissible.

The concept of *yozei* as reflected in these halakhic provisions is rooted in the notion that a cause remains present, either physically or metaphysically, in its effect. The notion is also reflected in the principle "*Yesh shevah ezim be-pat* — The enhancement of firewood is [present] in the bread." No benefit may be derived from artifacts that have been used as objects of idolatry. Thus, for example, a deified piece of wood may not be utilized as firewood. The rule forbidding benefiting from objects of idolatry extends to bread baked by use of such firewood as fuel despite the fact that the wood has been destroyed in the process of burning and is no longer in existence. The prohibited status of the bread reflects the notion that the wood, although destroyed, remains in existence in the bread which is enhanced by its presence. Put somewhat differently, the wood is the cause and remains in existence in its effect, *viz.*, the bread.

Consequently, it is quite understandable that when multiple causes contribute to a single effect the rule does not apply. On the contrary, the applicable principle is that *zeh va- zeh gorem*, i.e., when two causes combine to yield a particular effect, the resultant entity is untainted by prohibition. Thus, for example, if forbidden wood is combined with permissible wood to provide fuel for baking bread, the bread is permitted. Rabbenu Nissim, *Avodah Zarah* 48b, goes so far as to describe this rule as an application of the notion of *bittul* or nullification, i.e., the prohibited cause is not present in the effect because it has been submerged in, or overwhelmed by, the parallel innocuous cause. In any event, whether or not the principle relies upon *bittul* it is clear that, where there are multiple causes, Halakhah does not recognize any single cause as identifiably present in the result.

2. Identity as a Member of a Species

The notion of identity as a member of a species, however, is not simply an application of the causal notion of *yozei*. As noted earlier, the milk and eggs of non-kosher species are prohibited but the attendant prohibition is less severe than the prohibition attendant upon consumption of the meat of those species. Partaking of the meat of a colt or a piglet entails precisely the same prohibition and punishment as consuming the flesh of the mare or the sow. The prohibition upon the young of the species flows, not from its nature as a derivative or effect of a prohibited cause, but from a concept of identify transfer: The young is not simply the product of its progenitor but the continuum of the same persona. The young succeeds to the identity of its progenitor in the same manner as an adult animal of massive weight retains in every ounce of its body the identity it acquired at birth or earlier.

The notion of identity as a member of a species certainly applies only to a living entity in contradistinction to physical byproducts such as milk or eggs. But physical characteristics, even those regarded as species-distinctive such as split hooves or ruminant stomachs, are regarded as accidents — in the philosophical sense of the term — having no bearing upon determination of species identity. Accordingly, if a cow gives birth to progeny having all phenomenological characteristics of a pig such an animal is endowed with the halakhic status of a cow in every sense.

The most obvious explanation of this halakhic principle is that it reflects a spatio-temporal notion of an individual identity that is extended to identity as a member of a species. Individual identity is retained from the neonatal state through senescence and beyond by reason of spatio-temporal contiguity. That identity is also transmitted to progeny as is the literal meaning of "In place of your fathers shall be your sons." Thus, identity as a member of a species is simply a concomitant of personal identity. Species identity is one aspect of personal identity and hence is a factor of personal identity passed on by means of a generational continuum.

The phenomenon of spatio-temporal contiguity is most obvious in the maternal-filial relationship since it is clearly manifest in the process of gestational development. The fetus is readily perceived as quite literally developing as part of the mother's body until physically separated in parturition. Transmission of paternal identity is a bit more complex. Identity as a member of a specific tribe and, as noted, the concept of representation in the operation of certain types of inheritance is predicated upon paternal identity and presumably reflects the spatial-temporal contiguity effected through seminal emission and fusion of the sperm with the ovum.[19]

Nevertheless, a fundamental controversy is recorded in the Gemara, *Hullin* 79a, with regard to whether or not paternal identity is transmitted to progeny in the animal kingdom. Consumption of *helev*, i.e., certain fatty tissue located primarily, but not exclusively, in the hind- quarters of an animal classified as a *behemah*, is prohibited; consumption of the same tissue of an animal classified as a *hayyah* is permitted. The commandment requiring covering with earth of a portion of the blood flowing from the slaughterer's incision is limited to the blood of birds and of any species categorized as a *hayyah*; the blood of an animal categorized as a *behemah* need not be covered by earth. Regardless of the status of the sire of the progeny, the status of a mother is transmitted to her young with regard to both the prohibition against consumption of *helev* and the requirement for covering the blood of the slaughtered animal. The status of the offspring of a male *hayyah* and a female *behemah* or of a male *behemah* and a female

---

19. Nevertheless, the identity and status of a non-Jewish male who consorts with a Jewess is not passed on to the offspring of that union. The talmudic formulation of the concept underlying that principle is expressed by the Gemara, *Yevamot* 98a, as "*afkereih Rahamana le-zareih* — God rendered his semen *res nullius.*" That concept should be understood as expressing the notion that identity can be destroyed by "confiscation" of the semen thereby depriving the conceptus of paternal identity. Lacking the identity of the progenitor, the semen cannot transmit that identity to resultant offspring. Similarly, the identity of a child born to a non-Jewish woman and a Jewish father does not share in the identity or status of the father. The Gemara, *Kiddushin* 68b, bases that rule upon Deuteronomy 7:4 which is understood as declaring that "your son born of a gentile woman is not your son but her son."

There are, however, authorities who conflate the two types of *yozei* and others who for various reasons do not regard the young of an animal to be encompassed within the category of *yozei*. See *Encyclopedia Talmudit*, XXIII, 286–87 and 323–27. See also endnote.

hayyah both with regard to the prohibition against partaking of *helev* and with regard to the requirement for covering the blood is that of the mother. For these purposes transmission of maternal identity, in and of itself, is sufficient. The controversy in *Hullin* 79a is with regard to whether or not "one must [also] take account of the seed of the father," i.e., is transferral of identity limited to transferal of maternal identity or is paternal identity transferred as well. If paternal identity is also transferred, the *helev* of the progeny of a male *behemah* is also prohibited and the blood of a male *hayyah* must also be covered.

If the issue is that of spatial-temporal contiguity, the identical issue should arise not only with regard to identity as a member of a species but with regard to personal identity as well. And indeed it does. According to biblical law, a foal delivered after the mother has been slaughtered need not itself be slaughtered. Although slaughter of such an animal is rabbinically required, biblical law regards the act of slaughter performed upon the mother to be efficacious for its fetus as well. Moreover, if two animals delivered post-slaughter mate, their progeny are similarly exempt from slaughter. In effect, the "slaughtered" status of the progenitor is transmitted to the offspring.

Problematic, however, is the case of a foal delivered post-mortem that mates with a conventionally born animal. If the offspring shares only the persona of the mother it must be deemed to be "slaughtered." But if it also shares the persona of the father then part of its persona is "unslaughtered." If so, the animal is partially "slaughtered" and partially "unslaughtered." The rule is that an act of slaughter that is interrupted cannot be completed at a subsequent time.[20] Hence, the foal delivered post mortem to a slaughtered mother that mates with a conventional animal, if regarded as partially unslaughtered, can never be rendered kosher.

---

20. *Shehiyah* or "interruption" is one of the five enumerated impediments to valid slaughter as transmitted orally to Moses at Sinai. See *Hullin* 28a.

3. Rambam and Tosafot: Identity as a Product of Spatio-Temporal Contiguity

Although the principle of *yozei* is accepted by all, the principle of *hosheshin le-zera ha-av* is the subject of talmudic controversy. Clearly, then, the principle of *yozei* is not sufficient to achieve transfer of identity. The consequence of the principle of *yozei* with regard to the product of a causal nexus is that the cause is deemed to be present in the effect in some manner but that principle does not establish an identity of persona. The latter is the product of a much more circumscribed notion of spatio-temporal contiguity.

The distinction is most evident in Rambam's formulation of the distinction between the status of a bird hatched from the egg of a mother of a non-kosher species and a bird hatched from an egg laid by a *terefah*. The Gemara declares the latter to be kosher because the embryo is developed from "mere dust." Ra'avad criticizes Rambam for ignoring that rationale and substituting his own explanation in stating with regard to the *terefah* "for there is no unclean [bird] in its species."

R. Chaim ha-Levi Soloveitchick, *Hiddushei ha-Grah al ha-Rambam, Hilkhot Ma'akhalot Assurot* 3:11, astutely observes that Rambam seeks to underscore the distinction between the factor of *yozei* in establishing halakhic status contingent upon "accidents" and status derived from transmission of identity. *Terefut* is an accident rather than an attribute of essence. Accidents are not integral to identity and, hence, were a single person to be divided, the accident might remain present in one of the divisions but not in the other. Since *terefut* is not an element of identity and since neither the egg laid by a *terefah* nor the hatchling born of the egg is itself a *terefah*, the bird hatched from such an egg cannot have intrinsic status as a *terefah*. Nevertheless, the egg is not kosher, but it is not kosher solely because it is the product, or *yozei*, of a *terefah*.

However, the egg's status as a *yozei* of a *terefah* is not passed on to the hatchling because the hatchling is not the product of the egg but the product of the "dust" produced as the egg becomes rancid. The principle of *yozei* reflects the ongoing presence of a cause in its effect and results in a forbidden entity only if there is constancy in the prohibited nature of its cause. Putrefaction of the egg destroys its nature as a foodstuff and transforms it into a halakhically innocuous substance. Thus the hatchling develops from halakhically innocuous "dust." The cause present in the young bird is not the prohibited egg but the resultant "dust." Accordingly, the hatched bird is not regarded as the stigmatized effect of a prohibited *yozei*.

Rambam assumes that, unlike *yozei*, species identity, and individual identity upon which species identity is predicated, is not rooted in the existence of a causal nexus. Rather, identity is predicated upon spatio-temporal contiguity. Spatio-temporal contiguity does exist between a female bird that lays an egg and the hatchling that emerges from that egg. It is the "dust," rather than the egg, that is the proximate cause of the hatchling but there is a clear uninterrupted continuum connecting the bird, the egg, the dust and the hatchling. It is that continuum of spatio-temporal contiguity that establishes the identity of the hatched bird.

Rambam's statement declaring that "there is no unclean [bird] in its species" is designed to indicate that *terefut* is a mere accident and hence to explain why the hatchling does not succeed to the status of the mother as an intrinsic *terefah*. The Gemara's statement that the hatchling is the product of "dust" rather than of an edible egg explains only why the lesser prohibition of *yozei* of a *terefah* is not attendant upon the bird born of an egg laid by a *terefah*.[21]

As noted earlier, *Tosafot, Hullin* 62b, posit the *tarnegola de-agma* and the *tarnegolta de-agma* as two separate and distinct species. In doing so *Tosafot* declare that were they a single species, the male would be permissible despite the lack of the physical criteria of a kosher species since it is perforce the progeny of a kosher mother and "the *yozei* of the pure is pure." In that state-

---

21. See the comment of R. Shlomoh Zalman Auerbach, cited by Abraham S. Abraham, *Nishmat Avraham, III* (Jerusalem, 5751), 217.

ment *Tosafot* invoke the notion of *yozei* as the principle applicable to establishing species identity and clearly assume that transmission of species identity in birds is no different from transmission of species identity in animals despite the fact that birds develop from putrid eggs. Thus *Tosafot*, as well as Rambam, regard identity as a product of spatio-temporal contiguity rather than of a causal nexus.

4. Rashi: Identity as the Result of Causality

Rashi, *Niddah* 50b, does identify the two birds as members of the same species and understands the Gemara as declaring the male to be permitted. To the challenge that "the *yozei* of the pure is pure," *Tosafot, ad locum*, respond on behalf of Rashi that birds do not give birth to their young; their young are born of eggs in which the embryo develops from "dust." *Tosafot* clearly imply that, for Rashi, putrefaction of the egg is an impediment to transmission of species identity. In the absence of identity derived from a progenitor, identity is established *sui generis* on the basis of physical criteria and hence the distinction between the male which possesses the characteristics of a non-kosher bird and the female which possesses those of a kosher bird.[22]

Although, as R. Chaim so eloquently phrased it, a horse is a horse because its mother was a horse, the primordial horse did not have a mother. If so, how could any horse be forbidden? Assuredly, the answer is that the prohibition against partaking of equine flesh is predicated upon a prohibition devolving upon a specific horse or group of horses at the time of its promulgation. The Torah refers to a specific horse or class of horses and declares them prohibited. Once prohibited, their progeny are also prohibited by virtue of generational transmission of identity as templates of the original horses. The animals originally banned are identified by means of physical criteria, *viz.*, non-rumination and absence of split hoofs. One may, of course,

---

22. Cf. the comments of R. Elchanan Wasserman, *Kovez Shemu'ot, Hullin*, sec. 27.

argue that the horses denoted in this manner are not the animals contemporaneously extant at the time of Revelation at Sinai but the primordial horse that came into existence on the fifth day of creation.

More than a semantic quibble lies in this speculation. Consider the hypothetical phenomenon of a mutation or a series of mutations that occurred some time after creation but before Revelation and yielded a cud-chewing split-hooved colt. Is this animal, and hence also its progeny, kosher or non-kosher?[23] If only non-ruminants possessing cloven hooves alive at the time of Sinaitic Revelation were proscribed the pre-existing mutation would be kosher. However, if God declared at Sinai that the descendants of primordial non-ruminant, cloven-hooved animals are forbidden then the ruminant split-hoof mutation in existence at the time of Revelation was also forbidden.

Noteworthy in this context is Rashi's remark in his commentary on Genesis 7:2. Rashi is puzzled by Noah's distinction between "clean" and "unclean" animals in an epoch in which no animal was, as yet, forbidden. Rashi explains that the appellations "clean" and "unclean" were assigned to animals that were destined to be declared clean and unclean at a future time. A simple, but by no means certain, reading of that comment would indicate that the import of Rashi's remark is that the very animals then depicted as "unclean" were retroactively declared to be members of an unclean species.

The foregoing serves to illuminate *Tosafot's* analysis of Rashi's position. Identity as a member of a particular species is transmitted on the basis of a cause and effect relationship. But when there is no ancestral cause, e.g., when a bird develops from mere "dust," the bird is regarded as *sui generis* insofar as species identity is concerned. The halakhic status of the bird is similar to the primordial bird or the bird extant at the time of Sinai; in effect, the bird

---

23. Were the barbarusa a pig that mutated into a ruminant after Sinai it would be a kosher animal. See this writer's *Contemporary Halakhic Problems*, III (New York, 1989), 66–77.

becomes the founder and sole member of a species whose species identity is established on the basis of its own physical criteria.

Thus, for Rashi, identity must be defined as a causal concept rather than as a spatio-temporal continuum.[24] In the case of a bird, even though the "dust" is the material successor of the mother, the mother is not present in the "dust" in an essential sense since the mother's essential nature has been destroyed.[25] In explaining Rashi's position, *Tosafot* regard the concept of *yozei* governing the permissibility or impermissibility of "emitted" products such as milk and eggs and the concept of *yozei* governing transmission of species identity as one and the same. The sole difference is that, although the principle of *yozei* applies to any "emission," the identity of a living organism can be transmitted only to another living organism which then is, in effect, a template of the first.[26]

Aristotle has been paraphrased as declaring "Metaphysics is

---

24. The notion of identity as a reflection of a causal nexus is perhaps taken to an extreme by R. Zevi Ashkenazi, *Teshuvot Hakham Zevi*, no. 93, who suggests that a *golem* created by a Jew is to be regarded not only as a human being but as having the status of a Jew as well by virtue of the fact that it was created by a Jew for "the works of the righteous are their progeny." Such a conclusion certainly cannot be entertained if identity is the result of a spatio-temporal continuum. If personal and species identity is understood on the basis of a causal nexus in which the cause is transposed and becomes immanent in its effect, a *golem*, which is a living entity, might well be considered as being endowed with the identity of its human — and Jewish — creator.

It is not necessary to dwell upon the point that *Hakham Zevi's* line of reasoning provides insight into the concept of the immanence of the divine nature within man as simply one aspect of the notion that every cause is present in its effect.

25. For Rashi it is no accident that the aggadic report recorded in *Yalkut Shim'oni*, Job 29:18, regarding a bird that is periodically consumed in a conflagration only to be rejuvenated subsequently differs from the Phoenix myth in one salient detail: the Midrash describes the bird as restored from one remaining egg-sized bit of tissue; the Phoenix arises entirely from ashes. Cf., Amos Hakham, *Da'at Mikra*, Job 28:18, note 21. According to Rashi, the bird's identity would be lost were it to arise from ashes; its identity is preserved by virtue of the residual glob of tissue from which it is revivified.

26. Indeed, *Tosafot, ad locum*, contrast the two aspects of *yozei* by questioning why it is, according to the opinion that *zeh va-zeh gorem* is forbidden, that the female (despite possession of kosher characteristics) is not forbidden by virtue of the fact that the father was non-kosher. In posing the question, *Tosafot* are asking simply why the father's status as a cause is ignored. *Tosafot* respond by noting that the male's contribution is also rendered nugatory by virtue of the putrefaction of the egg, i.e., putrefaction negates the prohibited nature of any and all causes.

the most divine of all sciences because it is the least practical."[27] And, indeed, for students of philosophy, adjudication between diverse theories of identity is of scant practical consequence. For students of Halakhah, however, that investigation is divine in the most literal sense of the term: It contributes to a deeper understanding of divine mysteries encoded and revealed in Halakhah.

Endnote

The principle that species identity is determined on the basis of parentage is contradicted by a literal reading of several midrashic sources declaring that the pig will one day be a permitted animal because it will become a ruminant. The published version of *Va-Yikra Rabbah* 13:5 reads:

> The swine is an allusion to Edom [Rome]; "Which does not do *gerah*," i.e., which will not bring in its train (*garar*) another empire to follow it. And why is the last-named called "*hazir*" [i.e., swine or boar] — Because it will yet restore (*hazar*) the crown to its [rightful] owner. This is indicated by what is written, "And saviours shall come up on Mount Zion to judge the mount of Esau; and the kingdom shall be the Lord's" (Obadiah 1:21).

A variant version of that text reads: "Why is it called '*hazir*?' Because it will be restored to Israel in the eschatological era." Various versions of the text are cited by Ritva, *Kiddushin* 49b; R. David ibn Zimra, *Teshuvot Radvaz*, II, no. 828; Recanti, Leviticus 23:2 on the basis of *Midrash Tanhuma* [see *Midrash Tanhuma*, ed. R. Chanoch Zundel (Jerusalem, 5720), *Parashat Shemini*, sec. 7 and *Midrash Tanhuma*, ed. Solomon Buber, *Parashat Shemini*, sec. 12, note 75]; R. Isaac Abarbanel, *Rosh Amanah* chap. 3; R. Jacob Emden, commentary on *Perek Shirah*, chap 4; and R. Moses Sofer, *Torat Mosheh, Parashat Re'eh*.

A similar statement appears in *Midrash Shohar Tov*. no. 146:4:

---

27. Cf., *Metaphysics*, 973a.

"God loosest the bound (*matir assurim*)' 'What is the meaning of '*matir assurim*?' Some say that every animal that is unclean in the present era the Holy One, blessed be He, will purify in the world-to-come." For an entirely different midrashic statement with an even broader connotation regarding abrogation of halakhic prohibitions see *Va-Yikra Rabbah* 13:3 and its reconciliation with halakhic norms by R. Moses Sofer, *Teshuvot Hatam Sofer, Yoreh De'ah*, no. 19.

The obvious halakhic implication of these statements is drawn by Rema of Panu, *Ma'amar Hakor Din*, II, chap. 17, and R. Chaim ben Attar, *Or ha-Hayyim*, Leviticus 11:7. In his comment on the phrase "*ve-hu gerah lo yigar*" — and it does not chew its cud," *Or ha-Hayyim* states: "This constitutes a condition — so long as it does not chew [it is forbidden] but in the eschatolgical era it will chew its cud and return to a permitted state; not that it will remain without a cud, for the Torah does not change."

These versions of the midrashic text are dismissed by R. Isaac Abarbanel, *Yeshu'ot Malko, ha-iyyun ha-revi'i*, chap. 3, as unauthorative and possibly an intentional forgery on the part of a Christian polemicist. See also *Midrash Shohar Tov*, ed. Solomon Buber, no. 146, note 4. Earlier, Rabbenu Bahya, *Commentary of the Bible*, Leviticus 11:7, reported that "the multitude" understand the Midrash as declaring that the pig will one day become a permitted animal. Rabbenu Babya himself, however, rigorously dismissed that contention.

The problem posed by the popular reading of the Midrash is that even if the swine, either miraculously or by means of genetic evolution, were to become a ruminant it would nevertheless retain the status of a pig and remain forbidden on the basis of the principle of *yozei*. That problem is raised by R. Joseph Patzanovsky, *Pardes Yosef*, Leviticus 11:7. *Pardes Yosef* notes that, as recorded by Rambam, *Hilkhot Ma'akhalot Assurot* 2:3, and *Shakh, Yoreh De'ah* 79:4, the prohibited status of *yozei*, e.g., milk of a forbidden animal, is not identical to the prohibited status concerning the forbidden animal that is its source. Prohibited species are expressly forbidden by Scripture; the prohibition against *yozei*

is derived exegetically and its violation carries a less severe punishment than violation of the commandment against eating the
flesh of the animal itself. Accordingly, *Pardes Yosef* suggests that,
although the *yozei* of a proscribed animal is indeed forbidden,
the *yozei* of a *yozei* may be entirely permissible. If so, he argues,
although an animal born to a non-kosher mother that manifests
the physical criteria indicative of a kosher species is forbidden as
yozei, the next generation, i.e., the progeny of the animal prohibited only as a *yozei*, are entirely permissible. Nevertheless, *Pardes
Yosef* cites *Pri Megadim, Yoreh De'ah, Mishbezot Zahav* 81:1 and
Yavin Da'at, Yoreh De'ah 81:1, who rule that the *yozei* of *yozei*, i.e.,
that which is the product of a forbidden entity, is also forbidden.
Thus, declares *Pri Megadim*, the "milk of a cow born of a camel"
is forbidden.

According to the herein formulated distinction between *yozei*
as categorization of the status of the product of a forbidden entity
and *yozei* in the sense of identification as a member of a species,
progeny of an animal must be regarded as entirely identical to
their progenitors with regard to species identification regardless of differences in phenotype. According to that thesis *Pardes
Yosef*'s distinction between *yozei* and *yozei* of a *yozei* could not
be accepted.

Various interpretations of the popular version of this
midrashic statement regarding future permissibility of the animal
have been advanced in an endeavor to reconcile its import with
the principle that commandments will not be abrogated in the
messianic era. The most intriguing is that of *Pardes Yosef, loc. cit.*
The Gemara, *Hullin* 109b, records that, although the swine is forbidden, there exists a counterpart having an identical taste that is
permitted, *viz.*, a fish known as the "*shibuta*." In another reference
to the *shibuta* that occurs in the introduction to *Eikhah Rabbah*,
the Midrash declares that fish were exiled from the Promised
Land together with the people of Israel and upon culmination of
the Babylonian exile returned to the Land of Israel together with
them. The sole exception was the *shibuta* which did not return
from exile but will eventually be restored to its proper habitat

in the messianic era. *Pardes Yosef* suggests that the reference to future permissibility of the *hazir* is actually not a reference to the swine but to the permitted fish having an identical taste, i.e., the *shibuta*.

Radvaz understands the midrashic statement in a figurative manner as referring to foods that are "fat" and delectable as is the pig. Accordingly, Radvaz interprets the Midrash as declaring that during the messianic era those foods will be available in abundance and will be enjoyed "as if" the pig were rendered permissible. Abarbanel, in his *Rosh Amanah*, chap. 13, suggests that the pig may be permitted during the period of reconquest of the Land of Israel just as non-kosher foods, including "sides of swine" were permitted in the days of Joshua during the original war of conquest. See *Hullin* 17a. Recanti interprets the statement as a kabbalisitc reference to the accusing angel *Hazriel* who, in the eschatological era, will no longer denounce Israel but become its defender. A rather similar interpretation is advanced by Rabbenu Bahya. For a fuller discussion of the various interpretations of the popular version of these midrashic statements see R. Abraham Israel Rosenthal, *Ke-Mozei Shalal Rav* (Jerusalem, 5760), *Va-Yikra*, pp. 118–120 and R. Matis Blum, *Torah la-Daʾat*, VIII(Kew Garden Hills, N.Y., 5769), 44–45.

In contradistinction to the reading cited by these scholars, the published versions of these midrashic statements contain no allusion to the effect that the pig will actually become a permitted animal. Those texts declare only that the word "*hazir*" is an allusion to Edom and explain that the term "*hazir*" connotes "return." The import of use of that term in conjunction with Edom is that Edom "will return the crown to its rightful owners." Commentators on Leviticus 23:2 as early as Rabbenu Bahya and as late as *Torah Temimah* as well as a host of other scholars have understood the Midrash as declaring that, although the first two Temples were build by Israel, the Third Temple will be built by Edom; Edom who was responsible for the destruction of the Temple will facilitate its "return," i.e., its restoration.

Dr. Gerold Borodach has drawn my attention to the fact that

images of Neptune, a bull, a ship, and a boar were represented on the standard of the Legio X Fretensis, the Tenth Legion of the Roman Empire. The Tenth Legion, under the command of Vespasian and later of his son Titus, was responsible for the siege of Jerusalem and the destruction of the Second Temple. This observation, although it is is not found in any rabbinic source, serves to illuminate the midrashic identification of Edom, i.e., Rome, with the *hazir*. It should be noted that there is no hint of derision in this linkage of Edom and the swine. If the association is rooted in Roman self-identification the neutral tone of the reference is entirely understandable.

In conclusion, it may be stated that the authenticity of the aphorism that the pig will one day be permitted is without meaningful support in the halakhic tradition. See the comprehensive discussion of R. Chaim Karlinsky, "Ha-Hazir ve-Hetero le-Atid Lavo," *Shanah ba-Shanah*, 5732, pp. 243–254.

9.

Between Ashkenaz and Sefarad: Tosafist Teachings in the Talmudic Commentaries of Ritva

Ephraim Kanarfogel

The extent to which leading rabbinic scholars of northern Europe (Ashkenaz) during the high middle ages were familiar with the writings of their counterparts in Spain (Sefarad) and points further east within the Moslem world remains an interesting area of scholarly research and conjecture. The popular (albeit fanciful) legend that describes a meeting between Rashi and Rambam notwithstanding,[1] Shamma Friedman has recently provided pieces of evidence which suggest that Maimonides (in a revised version of his *Mishneh Torah*) was familiar with talmudic comments made by Rashi (who died thirty years or so before the birth of Maimonides).[2] On the other hand, only if we presume that the ethical will attributed to Maimonides (in which he recommends the Torah commentary of Ibn Ezra for careful study) is authentic,[3] do we have possible evidence for Rambam's familiarity

---

1. See the sources and discussion in Avraham Grossman, *Hakhmei Zarefat ha-Rishonim* (Jerusalem, 1995), 180, n. 201.
2. See Shamma Friedman, "Maimonides' Use of Rashi's Commentaries: A Reevaluation," [Hebrew], *Rashi: The Man and His Works*, ed. A. Grossman and S. Japhet (Jerusalem, 2008), 403–38. Cf. Grossman, 179, n. 198, and E. Kanarfogel and M. Sokolow, "Rashi ve-Rambam Nifgashim ba-Genizah ha-Qahirit: Hafnayah 'el Sefer 'Mishneh Torah' be-Mikhtav me-Et Ehad mi-Ba'alei ha-Tosafot," *Tarbiz* 67 (1998), 411–16.
3. See Isadore Twersky, "Ha-Hishpia' R. Avraham ben Ezra 'al ha-Rambam?" *Rabbi Abraham Ibn Ezra: Studies in the Writings of a Twelfth-Century Jewish Polymath*, ed. Twersky and J. Harris (Cambridge, Mass., 1993), 21–24; and Yitzhak Sheilat, *Igrot ha-Rambam*, (Jerusalem, 2008), 2:697–99.

with the Torah commentary of Rashi (which is cited by Ibn Ezra on occasion).[4]

Ephraim Urbach has demonstrated that the so-called *Hassagot she-hisig ha-Ra'avad 'al Perush R. Shelomoh Zarefati (Rashi) 'al ha-Torah* have been incorrectly attributed to the leading twelfth-century Provencal talmudist and critic of Maimonides' *Mishneh Torah*, R. Abraham b. David of Posquieres.[5] Rabad, however, was quite familiar with Rashi's commentary to the Talmud, as was Rabad's Provencal colleague and contemporary R. Zerahyah *ha-Levi* (Razah), author of the *Sefer ha-Ma'or*. Both Rabad and Razah were aware of at least some of the work of Rashi's Tosafist grandson Rabbenu Jacob Tam as well.[6] But southern France and Spain are not the same in this regard.

R. Yosef *ha-Levi* ibn Migash, who died in southern Spain in 1141 (and was the teacher of Maimonides' father), turned to the scholars of Provence sometime during the early twelfth century seeking a copy of Rashi's commentary to *Zevahim*.[7] Indeed, Rashi's talmudic commentaries were not cited with any frequency in the writings of major Spanish talmudists prior to the commentaries of R. Meir *ha-Levi* Abulafia (Ramah), the most prominent Spanish talmudist (and anti-Maimunist) in the early years of the thirteenth century (who also cites Rashbam and two other

4. On Ibn Ezra's citation and use of Rashi, see A. Mondschein, "Ve-Ein bi-Sefarav Peshat Raq Ehad Minei Elef — Le-Derekh Hityahasut shel R. Avraham Ibn Ezra le-Perush Rashi la-Torah," *'Iyyunei Miqra u-Parshanut* 5 (2000), 221–48. Cf. Uriel Simon, "R. Avraham Ibn Ezra — Bein ha-Mefaresh le-Qor'av," *Proceedings of the Ninth World Congress of Jewish Studies* (Jerusalem, 1988), 23–42.

5. E. E. Urbach, "Hasagot ha-Rabad 'al Perush Rashi la-Torah?" *Qiryat Sefer* 34 (1959), 101–03 [=Urbach, *Mehqarim be-Madda'ei ha-Yahadut*, ed. M. D. Herr and Y. Fraenkel (Jerusalem, 1998), vol. 1, 377–79.]

6. See, e.g., I. Twersky, *Rabad of Posquieres* (Philadelphia, 1980), 232–36; and Israel Ta-Shma, *R. Zerahyah ha-Levi Ba'al ha-Ma'or u-Bnei Hugo* (Jerusalem, 1992), 20–21, 26–27, 34–38, 41–45, 96–112. Interestingly, however, neither Rabad nor Razah are cited by Ashkenazic rabbinic figures until the middle of the thirteenth century. See Ya'akov Sussmann, "Perush ha-Rabad le-Massekhet Sheqalim? Hidah Bibliografit — Be'ayah Historit," *Me'ah Shea'rim*, ed. E. Fleischer et. al (Jerusalem, 2000), 164–65.

7. See my "What Do They Study in Your Yeshivah? The Scope of Talmudic Commentary in Europe During the High Middle Ages," *Printing the Talmud*, ed. S. L. Mintz and G. M. Goldstein (New York, 2005), 49–50. Cf. Bernard Septimus, *Hispano-Jewish Culture in Transition* (Cambridge, Mass., 1982), 25–27; and *Sefer ha-Maspia le-'Ordei ha-Shem*, ed. N. Dana, Ramat Gan (1989), 177–78.

early Tosafists, Rabbenu Tam of Ramerupt and Riva *ha-Levi* of Speyer).[8] By the same token, predecessors and contemporaries of Rashi in northern France, such as R. Yosef Tov Elem and R. Eliyyahu *ha-Zaqen*, were familiar with the writings of liturgical poets from Moslem Spain, just as Rashi and his students were familiar with various Spanish exegetical and grammatical works.[9]

Although Rashbam composed glosses to R. Isaac Alfasi's *Halakhot*,[10] and R. Judah of Barcelona's halakhic writings were also known in northern France by the mid-twelfth century,[11] *Hilkhot ha-Rif* were not cited with any frequency in Ashkenaz until the days of Rabiah (d. c. 1225) and his student, R. Isaac *Or Zarua*. Indeed, the only consistent use of Sefardic talmudic commentary in Ashkenaz during the twelfth century can be seen in the frequent citations from Rabbenu Hanan'el of Kairwan's commentaries by various Tosafists, beginning with Rashbam in northern France and R. Eliezer b. Nathan (Raban) in Germany. And it may well be that R. Hanan'el's Italian origins, which constituted a meaningful pedigree within medieval Ashkenaz, facilitated that usage.[12]

In short, it is not before the end of the twelfth century or the beginning of the thirteenth century that Spanish talmudists begin to systematically utilize the talmudic commentaries of Rashi and the Tosafists, and concomitantly, that the Tosafists begin to pay

---

8. See Septimus, *ibid.*, 134, nn. 36–37, and Ta-Shma, *Ha-Sifrut ha-Parshanit la-Talmud*, vol. 2 (Jerusalem, 2000), 15–16.
9. See, e.g., A. Grossman, "Ha-Qesharim Bein Yahadut Sefarad le-Yahadut Ashkenaz Bimei ha-Benayim," *Moreshet Sefarad*, ed. Haim Beinart (Jerusalem, 1992), 176–77, and idem., *Hakhmei Zarefat ha-Rishonim*, 46–47, 76–77, 102, 247–48.
10. See E. E. Urbach, *Ba'alei ha-Tosafot* (Jerusalem, 1980), 1:56–57.
11. See I. Ta-Shma, *Knesset Mehqarim*, vol. 1 (Jerusalem, 2004), 78, 145. Cf. Elliot Wolfson, "The Mystical Significance of Torah Study in German Pietism," *Jewish Quarterly Review* 84 (1993–94), 65–69, regarding the German Pietsts' use of Judah of Barcelona's speculative commentary on *Sefer Yezirah*.
12. See I. Ta-Shma, *Knesset Mehqarim*, 1:43–61. Cf. A. Grossman, "Me-Andalusia le-Eiropah: Yahasam shel Hakhmei Ashkenaz ve-Zarefat ba-Me'ot ha-12 — ha-13 'el Sifrei ha-Halakhah shel ha Rif veha-Rambam," *Pe'amim* 80 (1999), 16–24. On Rashi's possible awareness of the talmudic commentaries of Rabbenu Hanan'el, see Shamma Friedman, "Perush Rashi la-Talmud — Haggahot u-Mahadurot," *Rashi, 'Iyyunim be-Yezirato*, ed. Z. A. Steinfeld (Ramat Gan, 1993), 173–74, n. 141, and Yonah Fraenkel, *Darko shel Rashi be-Perusho la-Talmud ha-Bavli* (Jerusalem, 1975), 2, n. 5.

sustained attention to Sefardic materials. Maimonides' *Mishneh Torah* is cited by Tosafists in northern France only from the early years of the thirteenth century, leading up to its decisive role in Moses of Coucy's *Sefer Mizvot Gadol* (which was composed around 1240), and its fairly extensive use by a group of rabbinic figures associated with the German Tosafist R. Simhah of Speyer (d. c. 1230).[13] As the thirteenth century unfolds, the most important Spanish talmudic commentaries, composed by Nahmanides and his student, R. Shelomoh ibn Adret (Rashba), consistently refer to Ashkenazic talmudic scholarship, and especially to the comments and methodologies of *Hakhmei* or *Rabboteinu Ba'alei ha-Tosafot ha-Zarefatim*, or *rabbanei/talmidei (ha)-Zarefat(im)*.[14]

The role of various Provencal intermediaries in this process, on both sides of the divide, should not be under-estimated. Two of Nahmanides' major teachers were Provencal talmudists who had significant contact with northern French Tosafists, especially R. Isaac b. Abraham (Rizba) of Dampierre.[15] At the same time,

---

13. See Kanarfogel and Sokolow, "Rashi ve-Rambam Nifgashim," (above, n. 2); Jacob Dienstag, "Yahasam shel Ba'alei ha-Tosafot leha-Rambam," *Sefer Yovel le-Shmu'el Kalman Mirsky*, ed. S. Bernstein and G. Churgin (New York, 1958), 350–79; A. Grossman, *ibid.*, 24–29; Judah Galinsky, "'Ve-Lihyot Lefanekha 'Eved Ne'eman kol ha-Yamim': Pereq be-Haguto ha-Datit shel R. Mosheh mi-Coucy; Jeffrey Woolf, "Maimonides Revised: The Case of Sefer Miswot Gadol," *Harvard Theological Review* 90 (1997), 175–205; idem., "Admiration and Apathy: Maimonides' Mishneh Torah in High and Late Medieval Europe," *Be'erot Yizhak*, ed. J. Harris (Cambridge, Mass., 2005), 427–47; and I. Ta-Shma, *Creativity and Tradition* (Cambridge, Mass., 2006), 175–83. A problem that remains, however, is that *Mishneh Torah* is cited less than a handful of times in the *Tosafot* published in the standard editions of the Talmud. While it is cited in Abraham b. Ephraim, *Qizzur Sefer Mizvot ha-Gadol*, ed. Y. Horowitz (Jerusalem, 2005), it is barely mentioned in the contemporary (and much more widely circulated) *Sefer Mizvot Qatan* by R. Isaac of Corbeil (d. 1280). Moreover, its use in the circle of R. Simhah of Speyer is uneven. I hope to return to these issues in a separate study.

14. See I. Ta-Shma, *Ha-Sifrut ha-Parshanit la-Talmud*, 2:39–55, 59, 64–65; my "On the Assessment of Nahmanides and His Literary Oeuvre," *Jewish Book Annual* 54 (1996–97), 66–80; and Hillel Novetzky, "The Influence of R. Joseph Bekhor Shor and Radak on Ramban's Commentary on the Torah," (M.A. thesis, Yeshiva University, 1992). Cf. B. Septimus, "'Open Rebuke and Concealed Love': Nahmanides and the Andalusian Tradition," *R. Moses b. Nahman: Explorations in His Religious and Literary Virtuosity*, ed. I. Twersky (Cambridge, Mass. 1982), 1–34, and Moshe Halbertal, *'Al Derekh ha-'Emet* (Jerusalem, 2006), 83–85, 102–16, 344–52.

15. See Shalem Yahalom, "R. Nathan b. Meir, Moro shel ha-Ramban — Haspa'atah shel Torat Provence bi-Gerona," *Pe'amim* 91 (2001), 5–25; idem., "R. Yehudah b. Yaqar

R. Abraham b. Nathan of Lunel travelled to study in northern France (and was familiar with the teachings of several German rabbinic figures as well), before returning to Provence and finally settling in Toledo in 1204. His *Sefer ha-Manhig* flits between the customs and decisions of Provence, Spain and northern France, suggesting that he maintained his northern connections and circulated halakhic material to that region even after he had settled in Christian Spain.[16]

We have now arrived at the focal point of our study, the use of Tosafist materials by leading Spanish talmudists in the late thirteenth and early fourteenth centuries with special attention to the *hiddushim* of Ritva, but one final larger observation is in order. The course of major Sefardic halakhic or talmudic writings in the twelfth and thirteenth centuries begins with the forms of codes and responsa, represented by the writings of Alfasi and Maimonides. As the thirteenth century arrives, the preferred genre in Spain shifts to talmudic novellae or *hiddushim* that become dominant, as represented by Ramban, Rashba and the main figure under discussion in this study, Ritva (although these scholars continued to compose responsa which, in Rashba's case, were rather extensive).[17]

In Ashkenazic rabbinic circles, the twelfth century was dominated by the commentaries and comments of Rashi and the Tosafists. As the thirteenth century unfolds, significant halakhic codes composed by successive generations of the students of northern French Tosafists begin to appear, from *Sefer ha-Terumah* to *Sefer Mizvot Gadol* to *Sefer Or Zarua'* (whose author, R. Isaac b. Moses of Vienna, studied with both northern

— Toledotav u-Meqomo be-Mishnat ha-Ramban," *Sidra* 17 (2001–02), 79–107; and cf. idem., "Meqorot 'Alumim be-Perush ha-Ramban la-Torah," *Shenaton le-Heqer ha-Miqra veha-Mizrah ha-Qadum* 15 (2005), 266–93.

16. See, I. Ta-Shma, *Knesset Mehqarim*, 2:118–121; B. Septimus, *Hispano Jewish Culture in Transition*, 32–35; and my *'Peering through the Lattices': Mystical, Magical and Pietistic Dimensions in the Tosafist Period* (Detroit, 2000), 51–58, 193–94.

17. See, e.g., Ta-Shma, *Ha-Sifrut ha-Parshanut la-Talmud*, 2:35, 56–57, 69; A. Grossman, "Yeziratam ha-Hilkhatit shel Hakhmei Sefarad," *Moreshet Sefarad*, 158–62; and below, n 33.

French and German Tosafists) to *Sefer Mizvot Qatan,* among others.[18] Moreover, responsa, which had not been preserved by their authors to a significant degree during the twelfth century, are collected more efficiently especially in the halakhic writings and compendia of thirteenth-century German Tosafists, leading up to the large-scale responsa collection initiated by R. Meir of Rothenburg (that included his own responsa as well as many responsa of his predecessors) in the late thirteenth century.[19]

When the progress of these genres is charted, it appears that Sefardic rabbinic scholarship becomes, in effect, Ashkenazic-like, while the Ashkenazim, in turn, start to follow Sefardic literary patterns. Although there are likely some larger literary tendencies at work here as well,[20] it may be suggested that this role-reversal (or genre-reversal) is one of the (few) positive by-products of the tumultuous Maimonidean controversy. That controversy, which begins to percolate in earnest during the early years of the thirteenth century, brought the rabbinic cultures of Ashkenaz and Sefarad into close contact, more than any other single event or issue. The shift in genres that has been outlined may have resulted, in no small measure, from these contacts.[21]

Having sketched the broader literary background in historical context, let us now look more closely at the place of the teachings of the Tosafists in the leading Spanish talmudic commentaries of the thirteenth century. Although modern scholarship has differed about how to characterize Nahmanides' reliance on the writings of the Tosafists of northern France, no one doubts his extensive use

---

18. See Ta-Shma, *Knesset Mehqarim,* 1:317–44. See also Simcha Emanuel, *Shivrei Luhot: Sefarim Avudim shel Ba'alei ha-Tosafot* (Jerusalem, 2007), which focuses primarily on halakhic works that were produced by German Tosafists and rabbinic figures.

19. Cf. Ta-Shma, 2:173–75; Emanuel, 270–78, 319–28; and my "Religious Leadership During the Tosafist Period: Between the Academy and the Rabbinic Court," *Jewish Religious Leadership, Image and Reality,* ed. J. Wertheimer (New York, 2004), 265–305.

20. See, e.g., I. Twersky, *An Introduction to the Code of Maimonides* (New Haven, 1980), 72, for the notion that a period of literary creativity is often followed by a period of organization or collection.

21. Cf. e.g., B. Septimus, *Hispano-Jewish Culture in Transition;* 48–51, Grossman (above, n. 17); and Ta-Shma (above, n. 16).

and citation of Tosafist literature.[22] It becomes apparent, however, that Nahmanides utilized a somewhat selective, if highly effective, group of Ashkenazic texts from among those that were available to him. Specifically, Nahmanides cites *Tosafot Shanz*, the Tosafist comments authored or collected by R. Samson b. Abraham of Sens (d. 1214), the leading student of R. Isaac of Dampierre (Ri, d. 1189) who was, in turn, the leading student of his uncle, Rabbenu Tam (d. 1171). Israel Ta-Shma has stressed that unlike many subsequent *Tosafot* collections, in which students recorded and edited the *Tosafot* that were developed and presented by their teachers, the *Tosafot* attributed to R. Samson, which are replete with the teachings of Ri and Rabbenu Tam, were actually formulated and composed by R. Samson himself, rather than by his students. This more direct composition process (which included full citations from Ri in their original form, that are not always found in later *Tosafot* collections), and the leading Tosafist teachers who were at its core, account at least in part for the great regard in which these *Tosafot* were held, throughout the medieval period and beyond.[23]

Ramban's selectivity was undoubtedly predicated in part on the quality factor just described — he clearly held that *Tosafot Shanz* contain the most authoritative *Tosafot* texts and positions that were available — but there is a chronological dimension that should be also considered. Ramban, who died in 1270 in Israel after leaving Spain three years or so before, makes scant reference, either by name or by citation, to any French *Tosafot* texts or Tosafist rulings produced after the beginning of the thirteenth century. Ramban was undoubtedly aware of subsequent Tosafist developments and rabbinic figures in northern France from his cousin Rabbenu Yonah (who studied in Evreux during the first quarter of the thirteenth century, and also had access to R. Yehi'el

---

22. See above, n. 14, and see also *Hiddushei ha-Ramban le-Massekhet Ketubot*, ed. E. Schwat (Jerusalem, 1993), editor's introduction, 31–34.
23. See I. Ta-Shma, *Ha-Sifrut ha-Parshanit la-Talmud*, 2:103–07. Ta-Shma also notes that R. Samson's *Tosafot* were composed as a coordinated, referenced work, which would further facilitate their use. See also the references to *Tosafot Shanz* in E. E. Urbach's chapter on '*Tosafot shelanu*'(*Ba'alei ha-Tosafot*, 2:600–76).

of Paris) and from others.[24] Indeed, Nahmanides cites these figures by name in his *derashah* for *Rosh ha-Shanah*.[25]

Nonetheless, references in Ramban's talmudic *hiddushim* to materials from any northern French Tosafist after R. Samson b. Abraham of Sens and his brother R. Isaac b. Avraham (Rizba) of Dampierre are simply hard to come by. Indeed, even the *Tosafot* edited by R. Judah Sirleon (d. 1224), which are also fundamentally the *Tosafot* of Ri, were not utilized by Ramban. This state of affairs is supported by the indication that Ramban (who was born in 1194) composed his talmudic novellae very early in his career, well before he was forty years old.[26] Thus, it is Ri and Rabbenu Tam, the greatest of the twelfth century Tosafists, and their leading students (including Samson of Sens and his brother Rizba with whom both of his Provencal teachers studied) whom Ramban engages, to the exclusion of almost all others.

The selectivity which caused Ramban to limit himself to the quasi-canonical *Tosafot Shanz* dovetails with his nature as a conservative kabbalist, who strove to include in his Torah commentary only those kabblistic teachings that had the imprimatur of prior mystical traditions.[27] Moreover, R. Asher b. Yehi'el (Rosh),

---

24. See, e.g., Ta-Shma, *Knesset Mehqarim*, 2: 109–119; Schwat, *Hiddushei ha-Ramban*, 3, 33; my *Jewish Education in Society in the High Middle Ages* (Detroit, 1992), 74–79, 172–80.

25. *Kitvei ha-Ramban*, ed. C. Chavel (Jerusalem, 1968), vol. 1, 228, 239. See also 1:345, and cf. Ta-Shma, *Ha-Sifrut ha-Parshanit la-Talmud*, 2:20. Although this *derashah* was composed in Akko toward the end of his life, Ramban notes that he had (earlier on) sent a halakhic position which he had developed in his youth (*davar zeh hidashti be-yalduti*) with his cousin Rabbenu Yonah, for presentation before R. Moses, his brother R. Samuel and R. Yehi'el of Paris. Interestingly, "while all of them agreed that this interpretation was correct, some responded that R. Samson (of Sens) had already been aware of this." Ramban reports (ed. Chavel, 1:229) that he saw "now in this city" (=in Akko) the 'long *Tosafot*' of Ri's son, R. Elhanan. Cf. Shalem Yahalom, "Ha-Ramban u-Ba'alei ha-Tosafot be-Akko: Ha-Narativ ha-Histori bi-Derashat ha-Ramban le-Rosh ha-Shanah," *Shalem* 8 (2009), 100–25. Ramban also copied or adapted the so-called '*iggeret ha-musar*' that was initially composed by R. Moses of Evreux, but which is popularly known as a letter by Nahmanides. See, e.g., Tuvia Preschel, "Iggeret she-Yuhsah be-Ta'ut la-Ramban," *Talpiot* 8 (1961), 49–53; my *Jewish Education and Society in the High Middle Ages*, 76, and 174–75, n. 169; and Ta-Shma, *Knesset Mehqarim*, 2:118.

26. See Ta-Shma, *Ha-Sifrut ha-Parshanit la-Talmud*, 2:33, 35.

27. See M. Idel, "'We Have No Kabbalistic Tradition on This'," *R. Moses Nahmanides:*

who died in Spain approximately thirty years after Nahmanides, and who had access in his native Germany to a wide range of Tosafist writings, also preserved primarily *Tosafot Shanz* in the collections of *Tosafot* that he brought with him to Toledo in the early years of the fourteenth century. In the final form of *Tosafot ha-Rosh*, R. Asher (or perhaps his students) added the names (and ideas) of his major teacher, R. Meir of Rothenburg, and others (who were, for the most part, teachers of R. Meir), including R. Yehi'el of Paris and the brothers R. Moses and R. Samuel of Evreux.[28] Pieces of Spanish talmudic interpretation (from Ramah, and Ramban, and occasionally even from Rashba) that Rosh encountered in his new homeland were also included.[29]

Explorations in His Religious and Literary Vitrtosity, 51–73; idem, "R. Mosheh b. Nahman — Kabbalah, Halakhah u-Manhigut Ruhanit," *Tarbiz* 64 (1995), 535–80; and cf. Elliot Wolfson, "'By Way of Truth': Aspects of Nahmanides' Kabbalistic Hermeneutic," *AJS Review* 14 (1989), 103–79; and my "On the Assessment of Nahmanides," 69–73. In the same vein, it should be noted that Ramban refers to mystical or kabbalistic concepts on only four occasions in his talmudic commentaries. Talmudic commentaries (and halakhic writings) were apparently considered (at least by Ramban) to be an inappropriate venue for the exposition of mystical teachings. See my *Peering through the Lattices*, 12, n. 5.

28. For references to R. Yehi'el, the brothers of Evreux and Maharam in *Tosafot ha-Rosh*, see, e.g., *Tosafot ha-Rosh 'al Massekhet Pesahim*, ed. A. Shoshana (Jerusalem, 1997), 1031; *Tosafot ha-Rosh 'al Massekhet Ketubot*, ed. A. Lichtenstein (Jerusalem, 1999), editor's introduction, 11–13; *Tosafot ha-Rosh 'al Massekhet Sukkah*, ed. Y. D. Ilan (Jerusalem, 1997), 96 (25b); *Tosafot ha-Rosh 'al Massekhet Nazir*, ed. B. Deblitzky (Jerusalem, 2004), editor's intorduction, 11; Jose Faur "Tosafot ha-Rosh le-Masskhet Berahot," *PAAJR* 32–33 (1968–69), 49; and cf. below, nn. 49, 54, 55, 59.

29. See Urbach, *Ba'alei ha-Tosafot*, 2:587–99; Faur, "Tosafot ha-Rosh le-Massekhet Berakhot," 41–65 and idem., "Tosafot ha-Rosh le-Pereq ha-Madir," *Sinai* 57 (1965), 18–22; Ta-Shma, *Ha-Sifrut ha-Parshanit la-Talmud*, 2:78–82; idem., *Knesset Mehqarim*, 2:180–81 [in which Ta-Shma also maintains, 2:168, n. 9, that Rosh himself studied in Paris with R. Yehi'el as well]; Schwat, *Hiddushei ha-Ramban*, 35–38; Y. Galinsky, "Ha-Rosh ha-Ashkenazi bi-Sefarad: 'Tosafot ha-Rosh', 'Pisqei ha-Rosh', Yeshivat ha-Rosh," *Tarbiz* 74 (2005), 396–401. As Faur in particular demonstrates, Rosh also includes formulations of Ri as found in the *Tosafot* of R. Judah Sirleon. Other students of Rabbenu Tam mentioned by name in *Tosafot ha-Rosh* include R. Eliezer of Metz, R. Hayyim *Kohen*, R. Jacob of Orleans, R. Joseph of Orleans, R. Jacob of Corbeil, and R. Ephraim of Regensburg, as well as Ri's son (and compiler of *Tosafot*), R. Elhanan. See, e.g., *Tosafot ha-Rosh* to *Pesahim* and *Ketubot* in the above note; *Tosafot ha-Rosh 'al Massekhet Qiddushin*, ed. D. Metzger (Jerusalem, 2006), editor's introduction, 15–16. [R. Menahem of Joigny is also mentioned once on this tractate, and cf. Faur, "Tosafot ha-Rosh le-Massekhet Berakhot, 49, s.v. R. Menahem *me-Una*.] For R. Yosef of Clisson, a colleague of R. Samson of Sens (who made 'aliyyah at the same time as R. Samson, c. 1210–1211), see *Tosafot ha-Rosh 'al*

Nonetheless, *Tosafot Shanz* and the leading northern French Tosafists of the twelfth century are dominant within *Tosafot ha-Rosh*. Interestingly, just as Nahmanides hardly refers in his *hiddushim* to the formulations of German Tosafists, with the minor exceptions of those who (like Ri of Dampierre) had been students of Rabbenu Tam, such as Ri *ha-Lavan* of Bohemia, Ephraim of Regensburg (d. c. 1175) and R. Eliezer of Metz (d. 1198),[30] Rosh, with few exceptions, does not include German Tosafists from the late twelfth and thirteenth centuries in his *Tosafot*, aside from his teacher, Maharam of Rothenburg.[31]

Massekhet Gittin, ed. H. B. Ravitz (Jerusalem, 2004), 63 (8a), 94 (37b), and *Tosafot ha-Rosh 'al Massekhet Ketubot*, ed. E. Lichtenstein, 88 (13a), 359 (53a, cited also in *Hiddushei ha-Ritva*, 416 in the name of R. Yosef *Ish Yerushalayim*), 490 (70a).

30. See Schwat, *Hiddushei ha-Ramban*, 31–32. R. Eliezer of Metz' *Sefer Yere'im* is also cited some thirteen times by Ramban; see below, n. 41. In addition to Ri, who is mentioned explicitly, another of Rabbenu Tam's students, R. Ephraim of Regensburg, is perhaps among the Tosafist authorities in the area of *dina de-garmi* who are lauded so lavishly by Ramban (*Hakhmei Zarefatim…hem ha-morim, hem ha-melamdim, hem ha-megalim lanu nitman*) in the introduction to his *Quntrus Dina de-Garmi*. See Chavel, *Kitvei ha-Ramban*, 1:417–17; and *Hiddushei ha-Ramban*, ed. M. Hershler, vol. 1 (Jerusalem, 1970), 106–11. Cf. S. Emanuel, *Shivrei Luhot*, 289–91 (and esp. the literature cited in 290, n. 117), and Rami Reiner, "Rabbenu Tam: Rabbotav (ha-Zarefatim) ve-Talmidav Bnei Ashkenaz," (Master's thesis, Hebrew University, 1997), 82–92, 96–99, 105–13. Reflecting a fairly common practice among Spanish rabbinic figures, R. Ephraim of Regensburg is referred to by Rashba and Ritva as R. Ephraim *ha-Zarefati* (as a means of distinguishing him from R. Ephraim, the student of Alfasi, although R. Ephraim of Regensburg did study for a time in northern France with Rabbenu Tam); see below, n. 34. The reference by Nahmanides to a comment by R. Barukh b. Samuel (see *Hiddushei ha-Ramban*, vol. 4, ed. S. Dickman [*Yevamot*[, 96), is to R. Barukh b. Samuel *ha-Sefaradi/me-Erez Yavan* (see Shraga Abramson, "Rabbenu Barukh b. Shmu'el ha-Sefaradi," *Sefer Bar Ilan*, 26–27 [1995], 68), rather than to the German halakhist (and author of *Sefer ha-Hokhmah*), R. Barukh b. Samuel of Mainz (d. 1221). Cf. *Hiddushei ha-Ritva le-Massekhet Nedarim*, ed. A. Joffen (Jerusalem, 1982), 23 (2a, and the *hiddushim* of Rashba and Ran, loc. cit.); 163 (16b). Ramban has one reference to R. Moses b. Hisdai Taku (d. c. 1235), in which he characterizes R. Moses as 'a great scholar from *Polonyah*' (and wishes him length of days). See *Hiddushei ha-Ramban* to *Gittin* 7b, with reference to the boundaries of the land of Israel. [Ritva also cites R. Moses b. Hisdai in his *hiddushim* to *Gittin*, ed. Lichtenstein (Jerusalem, 1979), 1:52, referring to him as *mi-Zarefat*.] On R. Moses Taku's interest and expertise in *hilkhot ve-'inyanei Erez Yisra'el*, cf. my "The '*Aliyyah* of 'Three Hundred Rabbis' in 1211: Tosafist Attitudes Toward Settling in the Land of Israel," *Jewish Quarterly Review* 76 (1986), 205.

31. R. Eliezer of Metz is cited by *Tosafot ha-Rosh* nearly thirty times. See, e.g., *Tosafot ha-Rosh 'al Massekhet Pesahim*, ed. Shoshana, 390 (24a); *Ketubot*, ed. E. Lichtenstein, 608 (85b) [=*Qiddushin*, ed. D. Metzger, 408 (47b)]; *Hullin*, ed. Lichtenstein (Jerusalem, 2002), 134 (26b), 405 (85b), 443 (92b), 608–09 (114a); and *Nedarim*, ed.

Nahmanides' most important student in Spain, Rashba (d. c. 1310), follows the pattern set by his teacher in his own talmudic *hiddushim*. Not only are thirteenth-century names fundamentally absent, but references to twelfth-century figures other than Rashbam, Rabbenu Tam or the *'Ba'al ha-Tosafot'* (ostensibly Ri, as well as his students, R. Samson of Sens and Rizba) are found only in more general terms (*kakh pershu rabboteinu ha-Zarefatim*, and the like).[32] To be sure, Rashba in his responsa cites and interacts with a much wider and more contemporary range of figures, as might be expected. He cites and corresponds with R. Meir of Rothenburg and with R. Meir's student R. Dan who, like Rosh, emigrated from Germany to Spain following the serious persecutions at the end of the thirteenth century.[33] But Rashba's use and citation of Tosafist materials in his talmudic commentaries followed the conservative, limiting posture of Nahmanides.[34]

B. Deblitzky (Bnei Brak, 2000), editor's introduction (unpaginated), at n. 17, and in the index of names at the end. R. Eliezer is cited more than twenty times in this tractate, since he composed his own *Tosafot* to *Nedarim* (as Deblitzky notes). See also S. Emanuel, *Shivrei Luhot*, 291–97. On the other hand, Ri *ha-Lavan* and Riva *ha-Bahur* of Speyer are each cited only once — see *Qiddushin*, ed. Metzger, 227 (26b), and 33 (4a) — and R. Simhah of Spires is cited four times. See *Qiddushin*, ed. Metzger, 290 (41a= *Bava Qamma* 15a); *Hullin*, ed. Lichtenstein, 609 (114b); and *Shevu'ot*, ed. Lichtenstein (Jerusalem, 2008), 194. *Qiddushin*, ed. Metzger, 648 (78a) reproduces one passage from R. Yo'el *ha-Levi* of Bonn, with regard to the validity of a *get* given by a *goses*. [As noted by the editor, this passage is also cited in the *Sefer ha-Terumah* of R. Barukh b. Isaac (another leading student of Ri), who made *'aliyyah* c. 1210. Cf. Urbach, *Ba'alei ha-Tosafot*, 1:346, and see also *Tosafot ha-Rosh 'al Massekhet Sotah*, ed. Y. Lifschitz (Jerusalem, 2008), 107, n. 118.] R. Yoel's son Rabiah is mentioned once in *Hullin*, 222 (45b). Rabiah's major work, *Avi ha-'Ezri*, is cited in *Hullin*, 206; *Rosh ha-Shanah*, ed. Ravitz (Jerusalem, 1997), 134; and *Ketubot*, ed. Lichtenstein, 323, 381.

32. See Ta-Shma, *Ha-Sifrut ha-Parshanit la-Talmud*, 2:64–65. This is so despite the fact (as noted by Ta-Shma) that there were more Ashkenazic students present in Rashba's study hall (and in his milieu more generally) than there had been with Ramban (and see also the next note). Like his teacher, Rashba also composed his *hiddushim* at a relatively young age (Ta-Shma, 2:57–58). In his commentaries to three tractates in *Seder Nashim*, Rashba has several references to R. Eli'ezer of Metz or to his *Sefer Yerei'm*. See *Hiddushei ha-Rashba 'al Massekhet Yevamot*, ed. S. Dickman (Jerusalem, 1989), 128; *Qiddushin*, ed. E. Lichtenstein (Jerusalem, 1990), 149, 288, 290, 304, 307, 401; and *Nedarim*, ed. Y. S. Solomon (Jerusalem, 1991), 154, 321l; and cf. Urbach, *Ba'alei ha-Tosafot*, 1:163, n. 67.

33. See Ta-Shma, *Knesset Mehqarim*, 2:157–66. See also *She'elot u-Teshuvot ha-Rashba*, 1:527, 529, 545; 3:369–70.

34. Rashba refers by name to R. Elhanan b. ha-Ri on a number of occasions, while

Indeed, the same may be said in large measure for R. Nissim b. Reuven of Gerona (Ran), the most important Spanish talmudic commentator in the mid-fourteenth century.[35]

Ramban does not refer to him at all. See, e.g. *Hiddushei ha-Rashba 'al Massekhet Beizah*, ed. Y. Sklar (Jerusalem, 1986), 116, 154, 317; *Hiddushei ha-Rashba 'al Massekhet Gittin*, ed. D. Bar-Ilan, *Hiddushei ha-Rashba 'al Massekhet Megillah*, ed. H. Z. Dimitrovsky (Jerusalem, 1981), 77, 95–96, 167, 231; *Hiddushei ha-Rashba 'al Massekhet Niddah*, ed. D. Metzger (Jerusalem, 1989), 24 (4b, *'ahar kakh mazati be-Tosafot R. Elhanan be-shem Rashbam*), 323 (47b, R. Samuel b. Elhanan). Rashba refers to Moses of Evreux once in tractate *Yevamot*, (ed. S. Dickman, [Jerusalem, 1989], 88), once in *Hiddushei Rashba 'al Massekhet 'Eruvin*, ed. Y. D. Ilan (Jerusalem, 1989), 171 (25b), and six times in *Nedarim*, (although all of these are toward the end of the tractate; see *Hiddushei ha-Rashba*, ed. Y. Salomon [Jerusalem, 1991], editor's introduction, 10; Ta-Shma, *Knesset Mehqarim*, 2:117). See also *Tosafot Evreux 'al Massekhet Sotah*, ed. Y. Lifshitz (Jerusalem, 1969), editor's introduction, 24. In one instance, Rashba cites an answer to a question that his teacher Rabbenu Yonah cited in the name of his teacher, R. Moses of Evreux. As we shall see, however, Ritva's use of *Hakhmei Evreux* is much more pronounced. Rasbha to '*Eruvin* 31b (ed. Ilan, 203) cites R. Ephraim *ha-Zarefati ha-Zaqen* (=R. Ephraim of Regensburg, found also in Ritva, *Hiddushei ha-Ritva 'al Masskhet 'Eruvin*, ed. M. Goldstein [Jerusaelm, 1974)], 304), and see also *Hiddushei ha-Ritva 'al Massekhet Yoma*, ed. A. Lichtenstein (Jerusalem, 1976), 393, n. 177 (72a). Rashba cites R. Isaac b. Mordekhai (Ribam, another German student of Rabbenu Tam) twice in his commentary to *Qiddushin*, while R. Eliezer of Metz' *Sefer Yere'im* is mentioned six times; see *Hiddushei ha-Rashba*, ed E. Lichtenstein (Jerusalem, 1983), editor's introduction, 13–14 (and above, n. 32). In his *hiddushim* to *Bava Mezia'*, ed. E. Lichtenstein (Jerusalem, 2006), 210 (24b), Rashba refers to R. Samuel b. Hayyim *ha-Zarefati* (as does Ritva, loc. cit.). This is R. Samuel of Verdun, a younger student of Rabbenu Tam and the brother-in-law of R. Samson of Sens. See Urbach, *Ba'alei ha-Tosafot*, 1:153. Although Ritva had much in common with his Spanish precedessors, not only in terms of talmudic studies and methodology but also in the realm of Jewish thought (see, e.g., his *Sefer ha-Zikkaron*, as characterized by Ta-Shma, *Ha-Sifrut ha-Parshanit la-Talmud*, 2:72–73; my "Levels of Literacy and Sefarad as Reflected in the Recitation of Biblical Verses Found in the Liturgy," [Hebrew], *From Sages to Savants: Studies Presented to Avraham Grossman*, ed. J. Hacker et al, (Jerusalem, 2009), 201–04; and below, n. 88) Ritva's position on the building of the Temple during the messianic era essentially followed that of Rashi and the Tosafists while Rashba was closer to the Maimonidean view. See my "Medieval Rabbininc Conceptions of the Messianic Age: The View of the Tosafists," *Me'ah Shea'rim: Studies in Medieval Jewish Spiritual Life in Memory of Isadore Twersky*, ed. E. Fleischer et al. (Jerusalem, 2001), 157, n. 20, and 166, n. 30.

35. See Ta-Shma, *Ha-Sifrut ha-Parshanit la-Talmud*, 85–89. *Hiddushei ha-Ran 'al Massekhet Pesahim*, ed. E. Lichtenstein (Jerusalem, 1991), editor's introduction 9–11, cites R. Jacob of Orleans, R. Elhanan b. ha-Ri and R. Eliezer of Metz. See also the references to R. Eliezer in *Hiddushei ha-Ran 'al Massekhet Shabbat*, ed. Y. Sklar (Jerusalem, 1993), 339. *Hiddushei ha-Ran 'al Massekhet Bava Batra*, ed. Lichtenstein (Jerusalem, 1996), editor's introduction, 14, refers once to R. Elhanan and to R. Hayyim *Kohen*. Ran, however, mostly refers to the broader title, *rabbotenu shebe-Zarefat*. Note the interesting (and unusual) reference to German rabbinic scholars

Israel Ta-Shma has concluded that "like Rashba, Ritva utilized the exegetical and halakhic traditions of the northern French Tosafists only to the extent that these materials preceded Ramban and were available to Ramban for his analysis. [Ritva] used material of this type that came after Ramban only to a very small extent (*be-middah mu-'etet me'od bilvad*)."[36] To my mind, however, Ritva is a noticeable exception to the relatively neat (and more limited) pattern of usage of Tosafist materials that was followed by Ramban and his successors in their talmudic *hiddushim*. Overall, Ritva's less restrictive approach to the citation of Tosafist materials is rather different than the other leading Spanish rabbinic figures whose talmudic commentaries have been surveyed. In order to

---

in *Hiddushei ha-Ran 'al Massekhet Sanhedrin* in *Sanhedrei Qetanah*, vol. 5, ed. Y. Zaks (Jerusalem, 1978), 261 (67b), that the conjuring of demons through the use of certain materials or utensils (as opposed to the recitation of adjurations and Divine names alone) is not considered to be (forbidden) sorcery: "*ve-'al zeh samkhu Hakhmei Allemagne she-hayu mishtamshim be-khol yom be-ma'aseh shedim*." No specific scholars are named, however, and it is clear that Ran is not identifying these practices on the basis of Ashkenazic rabbinic literature. Cf. B. Septumus, *Hispano-Jewish Culture* (Cambridge, Mass., 1982), 85–86, and my *Peering through the Lattices*, 195, 212, 219, 224–25, 239–40, 245.

36. Ta-Shma, *ibid.*, 73–74. He also writes that Ritva cites "Rabbenu Tam, various *Tosafot* (that are mostly *Tosafot Ri* and *Tosafot R. Samson of Sens*), some (*qezat*) Tosafists by name, mainly Riba" (=R. Isaac b. Asher *ha-Levi* of Speyer, the first German Tosafist, who died in 1133), in addition to various Provencal and Spanish predecessors, especially his immediate teachers. With some irony, Ta-Shma notes that Ritva does not mention by name (even once) either the *Tosafot* of Rosh, or his *pesaqim*, and vice versa. See also Ta-Shma, *Knesset Mehqarim*, 2:171, n. 10. Cf. *Hiddushei ha-Ritva 'al Massekhet Qiddushin*, ed. A. Dinin (Jerusalem, 1985), 423 (42a), where the acronym Rosh is mentioned. According to the editor, however (n. 115), this may refer to R. Asher of Lunel, although see below, n. 87. Cf. *Hiddushei ha-Ritva 'al Massekhet Yevamot*, ed. A. Joffen, vol. 2, 1707 (95b), where Rosh is also cited (and that citation is indeed found in *Tosafot ha-Rosh*), and *Teshuvot ha-Ritva*, Y. Kafih (Jerusalem, 1978), no. 51 (p. 57). See also *Hiddushei ha-Ritva 'al Bava Batra*, ed. Ilan, 819 (107a), *ve-khen piresh ha-R. Asher*; *Tosafot, Shevu'ot* 21a, s.v. *qa mashma lan*; *Tosafot ha-Rosh 'al Massekhet Shevu'ot* 20b, s.v. *'ela 'eima*; and *Hiddushei ha-Ritva*, ad loc., 163. See *Tosafot ha-Rosh 'al Massekhet Ketubot*, ed. E. Lichtenstein, editor's introduction, 6–7: "Where the only source for [a passage in *Tosafot ha-Rosh*] is found in *Hiddushei ha-Ritva*, it would appear that Rabbenu [Rosh] and Ritva drew their words from the same source." Ta-Shma (above, n. 33) notes the correspondence between Ritva and R. Dan *Ashkenazi* and R. Eliezer *Zarefati*, referenced in both Ritva's responsa and in his talmudic commentaries. See also idem., *Ha-Sifrut ha-Parshanit*, 2:64, and 73, n. 117; *She'elot u-Teshuvot ha-Ritva*, nos. 40, 43, 97; and *Hiddushei ha-Ritva 'al Massekhet 'Eruvin*, ed. Goldstein, editor's introduction 13, 19.

demonstrate this, we need to carefully review the rabbinic scholars whom Ritva cites, and the nature of these citations.

Ritva (R. Yom Tov b. Abraham al-Ishvilli), who studied with both R. Aaron *ha-Levi* (Ra'ah) and with Ra'ah's slightly older contemporary, Rashba, died somewhere after the year 1320. As the locator Ishvilli or Ashvilli suggests, Ritva probably hailed from Seville, but he studied primarily in the north (the area dominated by Ramban and Rashba), later serving the community of Saragossa.³⁷ After laying out the contours and presenting a number of samples of Ritva's use of Ashkenazic material, I will argue that Ritva became aware of and received these Ashkenazic teachings through particular textual and personal conduits and contacts, in addition to suggesting possible methodological and tutorial considerations that might have helped to shape Ritva's more expansive posture toward the use and citation of Ashkenazic rabbinic scholarship.³⁸

Ritva cites a number of twelfth and early thirteenth-century northern French Tosafists that his Spanish predecessors include on far fewer occasions or do not mention at all.³⁹ Moreover, Ritva

---

37. Yizhak Baer, *A History of the Jews in Christian Spain* (Philadelphia, 1978), vol. 1, 224, adduces a court document which records that the young Rabbi Yom Tov was severely beaten by one of the parties after adjudicating a dispute between two Jews, apparently at the request of the royal court. This is, however, Baer's only reference to Ritva. Cf. Ta-Shma's critique of Baer's work in this regard in *Knesset Mehqarim*, vol. 2, 279–96.

38. Given Ritva's prodigious productivity and the impact that it had on subsequent talmudic studies, in addition to the other areas of his intellectual vituosity and distinction (e.g., his *Sefer ha-Zikkaron*), the scant attention paid by modern scholarship as a whole to Ritva is rather striking, if not somewhat troubling. Cf. Twersky, above, n. 3, 26.

39. R. Elijah (*ha-zaqen*) of Paris (France) is cited by Ritva in *Berakhot* (ed. M. Hershler [Jerusalem, 1990]), 52; *'Eruvin*, 867; *Yoma*, 202; *Ketubot*, 505; 621; *Qiddushin*, 794; *Bava Batra* (ed. Y. D. Ilan [Jerusalem, 2005], 936; *'Avodah Zarah*, 132, 135, 138; *Hullin*, 94. R. Elhanan b. *ha-Ri* is cited a total of twenty times: in *Berakhot*, 20; fifteen times in *'Eruvin* (see the editor's introduction, 7); *Bava Mezi'a*, 478; *Niddah*, 20, 332. R. Hayyim *Kohen* is cited in *Yoma*, 69, 111; *Makkot*, 199; *'Avodah Zarah*, 96. R. Jacob of Orleans is cited in *Shabbat*, 151, 667; *'Eruvin*, 263, 342, 394; *Makkot*, 188. See also the *Tosafot* interpretation that Ritva cites in the name of R. Yosef *Bekhor Shor* (of Orleans), *Bava Batra*, 464. While Rashba refers twice to *Sefer ha-Terumah* in *Shabbat* (254, 575), Ritva to *Shabbat* cites *Sefer ha-Terumah* twenty three times; see the editor's introduction, 23. Rashba refers only once to R. Elijah of Paris (*Gittin* 6b), and once to R. Jacob of Orleans, although he does refer fourteen times to

also cites a series of northern French and German figures from the mid- and late thirteenth centuries. Although these Ashkenazic names appear far less often in *Hiddushei ha-Ritva* than the names of Rabbenu Tam or Ri or Rizba, their presence is both noticeable and suggestive.[40]

Ritva refers to teachings of the leading northern French Tosafist of the mid-thirteenth century, R. Yehi'el of Paris, with some frequency.[41] Indeed, one of the best-known passages in

---

R. Elhanan b. *ha-Ri* (see above, n. 34, which is on the same order of the twenty references by Ritva). R. Eliezer of Metz is mentioned by Ritva in his *hiddushim* to *Shabbat*, 678 (105a); *Yoma*, 237 (38a); *Yevamot*, 2:88 (76a); and *Qiddushin* 357 (32b), while his *Sefer Yere'im* is cited in *Qiddushin* 232, 236, 554. This is comparable to the number of citations found in *Hiddushei ha-Rashba* (above, n. 32), but is a bit fewer than the number of references in *Hiddushei ha-Ramban*, which cites *Sefer Yere'im* a total of thirteen times (three times in *Shabbat*; four in *Yevamot*; three in *Qiddushin*; and once in *Ketubot*, *Hullin* and *Bava Batra*). On the whole, the pattern of Ritva's citations of these Tosafists seems to be closest to that of *Tosafot ha-Rosh*; see above, n. 29. Indeed, a large section of the so-called *Hiddushei ha-Rashba 'al Massekhet 'Avodah Zarah*, ed. Y. L. Zaks (Jerusalem, 1996), which cites extensively from *Tosafot R. Elhanan* to that tractate and from *Sefer ha-Terumah*, and which mentions R. Ephraim of Regensburg four times (and R. Jacob Orleans and R. Isaac b. Mordekhai of Bohemia one time each) has been shown to be a version of *Tosafot ha-Rosh* to that tractate. See *Sarei ha-Elef*, ed. M. M. Kasher and Y. D. Mandelbaum (New York, 1979), 1:303, 2:622. [With respect to tractate 'Avodah Zarah and its focus on various practical aspects of *kashrut*, as well as tractate *Hullin*, Ritva, Ran and Rashba (in his authentic *hiddushim*), all refer with some frequency to the northern French *Sefer ha-Terumah*, a product of the *beit midrash* of Ri.]

40. The study of Ritva's talmudic *hiddushim* has been aided immeasurably by the publication in recent years of these *hiddushim* by *Mosad ha-Rav Kook* on the basis of new manuscripts, with copious footnotes. These volumes contain not only name indexes, but also (in most instances) an introduction on the way that Ritva composed his commentary to a particular tractate (since Ritva typically issued longer and shorter versions of his *hiddushim*). Cf. Ta-Shma, *Ha-Sifrut ha-Parshanit la-Talmud*, 2:69, n. 109.

41. See *Hiddushei ha-Ritva 'al Massekhet Yoma*, ed. E. Lichtenstein (Jerusalem, 1981), 160–61 (28a), where R. Yehi'el questions the position of Ri (that one who is reading the Torah must stand, without leaning at all), and two references in *Hiddushei ha-Ritva 'al Masskehet Shabbat*, ed. M. Goldstein (Jerusalem, 1996), 310 (51b, in which R. Yehi'el is cited as disagreeing with a position of R. Barukh b. Isaac, author of *Sefer ha-Terumah*), 758 (119b, an interpretation by R. Yehi'el of the talmudic assertion that one who recites *Va-yekhulu* at the onset of the Sabbath receives a blessing from the ministering angels that his sins will removed and forgiven). R. Yehi'el explains that one who does not recite this passage is guilty of 'withholding testimony about the (new) creation of the world'. Thus, one who does offer this testimony is spared any penalty. Because this recitation is considered to be akin to (judicial) testimony, it should be done while standing. Cf. 'Arba'ah Turim, Orah Hayyim, sec. 268, and *Sefer ha-Manhig le-R. Avraham b. Natan ha-Yarhi*, ed. Y. Raphael (Jerusalem, 1978), 1:138.

Ritva's *hiddushim* (to *'Eruvin* 13a, where the halakhic disputes of *Beit Hillel* and *Beit Shammai* are characterized as *'elu ve-'elu divrei Elokim Hayyim*, these and those are words of the Living God), in which Ritva presents the notion (which he attributes to *rabbanei Zarefat*) that there are actually forty-nine pathways of truth (or bona fide interpretation) underlying the teachings of the Torah and Jewish law, is attributed by a variant *Tosafot* text (*Tosafot Rabbenu Perez*) to R. Yehi'el of Paris.

In Ritva's words, "The rabbis of northern France asked how it is possible that both rulings are true, since one prohibits and one permits? They answered that when Moses ascended to heaven to receive the Torah, he was shown for every construct forty-nine ways to prohibit and forty-nine ways to permit. Moses queried the Almighty on this and He indicated that this is given to the scholars of Israel in each generation and the law will be decided according to them." Ritva concludes that this is well-based in *derash* (*nakhon hu lefi ha-derash*), an allusion to a passage in *Midrash Tehillim*, chap. 12), and that according to kabbalistic teachings, there is an esoteric approach to this concept (*uve-derekh ha-'emet yesh ta'am sod ba-davar*). In the variant *Tosafot* text which attributes this interpretation to R. Yehi'el of Paris, the midrashic origin of this approach is explicitly noted (*'itah ba-midrash*, it is found in the midrash), although the mystical dimension is not mentioned. The conclusion, however, is precisely the same. The scholars of each generation were given the prerogative to decide whether to follow the more lenient approach, on the basis of a majority.[42]

Ritva cites R. Yehi'el by name six times in his *hiddushim* to tractate *Ketubot* alone. In one instance, the interpretation presented by Ritva in the name of R. Yehi'el is found in the standard *Tosafot* to *Ketubot* without attribution.[43] A second citation

---

42. See *Hiddushei ha-Ritva 'al Massekhet 'Eruvin*, ed. Goldstein, 107–08, and nn. 8–9. For the place of this passage in its larger historical and intellectual contexts, see my "Torah Study and Truth in Medieval Ashkenazic Rabbinic Literature and Thought," *Study and Knowledge in Jewish Thought*, ed. H. Kreisel (Beer Sheva, 2006), vol. 1, 101–19.

43. *Hiddushei ha-Ritva 'al Massekhet Ketubot*, ed. M. Goldstein, 7, n. 55 (2b). This explanation is also found (unattributed) in *Hiddushei ha-Ra'ah*, ad loc.

by Ritva also appears in R. Yehi'el's name in the late-thirteenth century *Sefer Mordekhai*,[44] while another, which is cited by Ritva as part of a *Tosafot* passage (*ube-Tosafot katvu be-shem R. Yehi'el mi-Paris*) can otherwise be found in R. Yehi'el's name in the glosses of Rabbenu Perez (d. 1298) to R. Isaac of Corbeil's *Sefer Mizvot Qatan* (*mori R. Yehi'el hayah noheg u-manhig she-yivarekh he-hatan le-qadesh ha-'ishah 'al pi ha-Yerushalmi*).[45] Ritva cites a position of R. Yehi'el of Paris concerning the validity of witnesses' signatures that were made in clay or on pottery, which does not appear in any other medieval rabbinic source.[46] Another position of R. Yehi'el cited by Ritva is found in R. Yehi'el's name in the *Maggid Mishneh* commentary to Maimonides' *Mishneh Torah*.[47] The sixth citation is cited as part of a *Tosafot* text, along with an interpretation of Ri, that is not found in any extant *Tosafot* text.[48]

Also in his *hiddushim* to *Ketubot*, Ritva cites R. Yehiel's Tosafist colleague R. Tuvyah of Vienne, that one ought not make the blessing *sheha-simhah bi-me'ono* which reflects deep happiness (and is properly made at a wedding meal) at a meal celebrating the redemption of a first-born son.[49] Later in his commentary, Ritva presents (anonymously) the striking position of R. Tuvyah (which most Spanish authorities rejected; some, like Rashba, do not men-

---

44. *Hiddushei ha-Ritva, ibid.*, 15, n. 56 (3b).

45. *ibid.*, 51, n. 117 (7b). Prior to this (50), Ritva cites the explanation of Rabbenu Yonah of Gerona (*ha-Rav he-Hasid*) in this matter.

46. *ibid.*, 187, n. 9 (21a; the editor notes that this position is not found anywhere else).

47. *ibid.*, 202, n. 33 (22a). See *Maggid Mishneh* to *Hilkhot Gerushin*, 12:1.

48. *ibid.*, 401, n. 25 (50a).

49. *ibid.*, 64 (8a): *uve-shem R. Tuvyah katvu ha-Tosafot she-'ein levarekh*. R. Tuvyah's name is not found in the printed *Tosafot* to *Ketubot*, although it is found in *Tosafot ha-Rosh*. Note that R. Meir of Rothenburg did recite this blessing; see *Haggahot Mordekhai li-Yevamot*, chap. 11, sec. 127. Cf. *Tosafot Mo'ed Qatan* 8b, s.v. *mipnei*, which expresses uncertainty in how to rule in this matter. On the connections between R. Yehi'el and R. Tuvya, see, e.g., Urbach, *Ba'alei ha-Tosafot*, 2:486–88 (in some of the published editions, the first line of this section is missing: *Bi-qesharim 'amizim 'im R. Yehi'el mi-Paris 'amad R. Tuvyah b. Eliyyahu me-Vienne*); *Qizur Sefer Mizvot ha-Gadol le-R. Avraham b. Ephraim*, 80, 88, and the introduction by I. Ta-Shma, 19–20; my "Halakhah and Mezi'ut (Realia) in Medieval Ashkenaz: Surveying the Parameters and Defining the Limits," *Jewish Law Annual* 14 (2003), 222–24; ms. Paris 260, fol. 92v: *ukeshe-bati le-Zarefat, ra'iti bi-Bereshit Rabbah shel mori ha-Rav Yehi'el ve-gam be-B"R shel mori ha-R. Tuvyah, ve-hayah katuv bahen kemo be-sheli*; and the collection of *pesaqim* in ms. Warsaw 258/4, fols. 216r-222v.

tion it at all) concerning the re-marriage of a nursing mother within twenty-four months of the birth of her child, if she had taken an oath that she would continue to nurse the child. Ritva identifies this position as *mi-Ba'alei ha-Tosafot ha-Aharonim*.[50]

Ritva quotes ten formulations from R. Yedidyah b. Yisra'el of Nuremberg. R. Yedidyah studied in northern France with R. Yehi'el of Paris (remaining in Paris after his fellow student R. Meir of Rothenburg returned to Germany, but continuing to send material back to Germany and to consult with R. Meir), and at the academy of Evreux. R. Yedidyah then returned to Nuremberg, and also lived for a time in two locales in the Rhineland.[51] Five citations from R. Yedidyah are found in Ritva's commentary to tractate *Shabbat*,[52] and three citations are found in *Mo'ed Qatan*.[53]

---

50. Ritva to *Ketubot*, 60b, ed. Goldstein, 491: *'aval yesh mi-ba'alei ha-Tosafot ha-aharonim she-katvu she-'im nishbe'ah ha-meneqet harei hi ke-bei resh galuta ve-qala 'it leih u-mutar*. R. Nissim b. Re'uven (Ran) cites this position in his *hiddushim* in the name of R' (without providing the name of the scholar who suggested it). Rashba does not comment on this issue in his *hiddushim*; in his stringent responsum on this matter (1:273), he does not refer to this lenient position at all. Interestingly, a responsum by R. Moses Halawa, a student of Rashba, suggests that R. Yehi'el of Paris concurred with R. Tuvyah's view and may have indeed been its source. On these developments, see Ta-Shma, *Knesset Mehqarim*, 1:232–33, n. 25; my "Halakhah and Mezi'ut," 218, n. 68; and Elisheva Baumgarten, *Mothers and Children* (Princeton, 2004), 150. For Ritva, the term 'later Tosafists' refers perhaps to those who came after Ri and R. Samson of Sens. Regarding the term *Tosafot (ha-) Aharonot* in *Hiddushei ha-Ritva*, cf. below nn. 72, 80, 101, and *Hiddushei ha-Ritva 'al Massekhet 'Eruvin*, 21, 381 (where the references are to R. Judah Sirleon and R. Samson of Coucy).

51. See Urbach, *Ba'alei ha-Tosafot*, 2:566–70; Emanuel, *Shivrei Luhot*, 243–44; *Teshuvot Ba'alei ha-Tosafot*, ed. I. A. Agus (New York, 1954), 231–48; *Tosafot Yeshanim ha-Shalem 'al Massekhet Yevamot*, ed. A. Shoshana (Jerusalem, 1994), editor's introduction, 26; and cf. ms. Bodl. 378, fol. 45v: *ve-hu katav she-shama mi-shemo shel ha-Rav Yedidyah ben ha-Rav Yisra'el, ve-hu 'amar she-shama mi-shemo shel ha-Rav Meir me-Rothenburg*.

52. *Hiddushei ha-Ritva 'al Massekhet Shabbat*, ed. Goldstein, 193 (37b); 218 (40b), where he offers an interpretation different than that of R. Barukh, author of *Sefer ha-Terumah* as well as an unknown R. Yirmiyyah), 342–43 (58a, citing *Tosafot R. Yedidyah*); 425 (70b, an interpretation in response to a question on Rashi that is raised by the standard *Tosafot*), and similarly, 437 (72a). The passages collected in this note as well as in the next, strongly suggest that Ritva received R. Yedidyah's material in literary form. See also below, n. 76.

53. *Hiddushei ha-Ritva 'al Massekhet Mo'ed Qatan*, ed. Z. Hirschman (Jerusalem, 1982), 93 (12a): *ube-Tosafot R. Yedidyah pershuha*. Subsequently Ritva (94) disagrees with an interpretation by R. Yedidyah: *ve-ha R. Yedidyah medamei lah le-hahi ve-lo nehira*. R. Yedidyah appears to have been the compiler of the second part of the *Shitah 'al Massekhet Mo'ed Qatan (le-Talmido shel R. Yehi'el mi-Paris*, ed. M. L.

R. Yedidyah is also cited by name once in tractate *Shevu'ot* (and Ritva agrees with his view, against the standard *Tosafot*) and once in *'Eruvin*.[54]

Another of R. Yedidyah's northern French teachers, R. Moses b. Shne'ur of Evreux, is cited by name six times in Ritva's commentary to tractate *'Eruvin*.[55] In his commentary to *Makkot*, Ritva cites R. Moses ben *ha-Rav* Menahem *ha-Zarefati* in the name of his teachers, the rabbis of Evreux (*be-shem rabbotav rab-banei Evreux*).[56] Ritva cites *Tosafot Evreux* by name twice in his

Zaks (Jerusalem, 1937). On R. Yedidyah's connection to Evreux and especially to R. Samuel b. Shne'ur, and on the references to Rabbenu Yonah in the standard *Tosafot* to *Mo'ed Qatan* (and to *Nedarim*, both of which are also linked to the study hall at Evreux), cf. Ta-Shma, *Knesset Mehqarim*, 2:117. Rashba never mentions R. Yedidyah; as Ta-Shma notes, the so-called *Hiddushei ha-Rashba* to *Menahot* (which do) are, in reality, *Tosafot Evreux*. Nor does Rashba refer to R. Yehi'el of Paris in his *hiddushim*.

54. *Hiddushei ha-Ritva 'al Massekhet Shevu'ot*, ed. E. Lichtenstein (Jerusalem, 1993), 150 (19a); *Hiddushei ha-Ritva 'al Masskehet 'Eruvin*, ed. M. Goldstein, 569 (61a). As noted by the editor (n. 460), this passage from R. Yedidyah is also found in *Tosafot ha-Rosh*.

55. *Hiddushei ha-Ritva 'al Massekhet 'Eruvin*, 321 (33a, with the suggestion of an alternate solution, which Ritva prefers, against the interpretation of Ri); 324 (33b), 354, (36a, explaining a construct of Rashi) 454 (47b, in support of Ri's approach), 458, n. 506 (47b, in explanation of Rashi's approach, which resolves a question raised in *Tosafot Rabbenu Perez*, ad loc.); 638 (69b, in support of a unique interpretation that Ritva favors; see n. 577). R. Moses and his brother R. Samuel were connected with R. Yehi'el of Paris and they collected and edited some of his *pesaqim*. See e.g., Urbach, *Ba'alei ha-Tosafot*, 1:480; S. Emmanuel, *Shivrei Luhot*, 193–97; and C. B. Chavel, *Kitvei ha-Ramban* (Jerusalem, 1968), 1:228. There is an additional citation from *ha-Rav me-Evreux*, 559 (59b, n. 302; this interpretation is not found in the standard *Tosafot*, but it again dovetails [see n. 382] with what is found in *Tosafot Rabbenu Perez*, ad loc.)

56. *Hiddushei ha-Ritva 'al Massekhet Makkot*, ed. I. Ralbag (Jerusalem, 1983), 249 (22b). A R. Menahem is mentioned in *Hiddushei ha-Ritva 'al Massekhet Ketubot*, 313–314 (38a). While Ritva cites a prior comment in the name of R. Moses of Coucy, this passage is cited in *Tosafot ha-Rosh*, 267, in the name of R. Moses of Evreux. Thus, this is possibly R. Menahem b. Samuel, a son of R. Samuel of Evreux and a teacher of Rabbenu Perez; see *Tosafot Rabbenu Perez le-Massekhet Bava Mezia'*, ed. H. Hershler (Jerusalem, 1970), editor's introduction, 10–11. The name R. Menahem is also found in *Hiddushei ha-Ritva 'al Massekhet 'Eruvin*, 626–67 (68a). From the standard *Tosafot* ad loc., however, we learn that this figure is R. Menahem of Joigny. Cf. above, n. 29. Ritva also cites the Tosafist R. Netan'el of Chinon, who is associated with the circle at Evreux, and with R. Yehi'el of Paris. See *Hiddushei ha-Ritva 'al Massekhet Mo'ed Qatan*, ed. Z. Hirschman, 159 (18a, *uba-Tosafot pershu be-shem Rabbenu Netan'el*), and *Hiddushei ha-Ritva 'al Massekhet Bava Batra*, 347–48 (40b, *uba-Tosafot ha-'inyan nakhon be-shem Rabbenu Netan'el*). Cf. my *Peering through the Lattices*, 177–18, n. 104; A. Grossman, "Rabbneu Netan'el me-Qinon: Mi-Gedolei Ba'alei ha-Tosafot ba-Zarefat ba-Me'ah ha-Yod Gimmel," *Mehqerei Talmud* 3 (2005),

commentary to *Bava Batra*: *ube-Tosafot shel Evreux pershu* (which comports with what is found in the standard *Tosafot*),[57] and *ve-khen katvu be-Tosafot Evreux* (with regard to a *get* that was issued on one's deathbed, where Ritva contrasts the view from Evreux with that of the standard *Tosafot*, *'aval ba-Tosafot 'omrim*).[58]

In addition to the cluster of rabbinic scholars linked to Evreux noted above, Ritva's *hiddushim* to *Shabbat* also contain four references to another thirteenth-century northern French Tosafist, R. Jacob of Chinon, that are otherwise unknown. In one instance, Ritva juxtaposes Jacob's description of Rizba's practice (*he-'id R. Ya'aqov 'al Rizba*) to make a blessing on his *tallit* when he arose before dawn in order to study Torah (to which R. Jacob testifies), with the more cautious view of (unnamed Geonim) and R. Samson of Sens.[59]

Also in his *hiddushim* to *Shabbat*, Ritva cites what he heard in the name of R. Meir Ashkenazi (=*mi-Rothenburg*), about where in the home to place the Hanukkah *menorah*.[60] This is one of

---

174–84; Ta-Shma, *Ha-Sifrut ha-Parshanit la-Talmud*, 2:110; *Tosafot Yeshanim ha-Shalem 'al Massekhet Mo'ed Qatan*, ed. A. Shoshana, editor's introduction, 22–24.

57. *Hiddushei ha-Ritva 'al Bava Batra*, ed. Ilan, 512, n. 19 (60b).

58. *Hiddushei ha-Ritva 'al Bava Batra*, 1118 (151a). Regarding the standard *Tosafot* to *Bava Batra*, cf. Ritva, 118 (17b).

59. See *Hiddushei ha-Ritva 'al Massekhet Shabbat*, 142 (25b). See also 250 (44a, *uba-Tosafot 'omrim ki ha-Rav Ya'aqov me-Qinon hayah mattir le-taltel*, which is not found in any extant *Tosafot* texts); 272 (46b, in which Ritva presents a methodological interpretation of R. Jacob — that appears anonymously in the standard *Tosafot*, ad loc. — and characterizes it as 'sweet and sharp', even as he disagrees with it: *perush zeh matoq ve-harif 'ela she-'ein zeh derekh perush ... bi-she'ar dukhteih de-Talmud*); 441 (72b, again citing an unknown *Tosafot* text in the name of R. Jacob). As Urbach notes (*Ba'alei ha-Tosafot*, 2:576, n. 26, and see also 579), R. Jacob is mentioned only twice in standard *Tosafot* texts, although his *Tosafot le-Gittin* are cited by his student R. Perez of Corbeil. See also *Mordekhai le-Massekhet Gittin*, sec. 377, in which R. Jacob cites another ruling of his teacher Rizba. *Tosafot ha-Rosh 'al Masskhet Gittin* mentions R. Jacob three times: 44 (5b, and see also *Perush ha-Rosh le-Gittin*, 1:6), 57 (7b, responding to a question posed by R. Yehi'el of Paris); and 510 (76a, adducing support for an interpretation of Rashi on the basis of Yerushalmi passage). On the seemingly large age discrepancy between R. Jacob and R. Perez, cf. Hershler, *Tosafot Rabbenu Perez*, editor's introduction, 12, and see also *Tosafot Rabbenu le-Massekhet 'Eruvin*, ed. Dickman (editor's introduction, 13–14), in which some twenty citations from R. Jacob of Chinon are found. A number of *pesaqim* from R. Jacob of Chinon can be found in ms. JTS Rab. 645 (*minhagei Zarefat*), 53v–57v.

60. *Hiddushei ha-Ritva 'al Massekhet Shabbat*, 112 (21b, *shama'ati be-shem R. Meir Ashkenazi*). This same view is cited in the name of R. Meir of Rothenburg in

several instances in which Ritva cites something that he heard in the name of Maharam of Rothenburg. The most significant of these citations is perhaps the one recorded in *Shitah Mequbbezet* to tractate *Beizah*:[61] "A leading Ashkenazic rabbi (*rav gadol ba-Ashkenazim*) pointed out in the name of his northern French teachers (*rabbotav ha-Zarefatim*), including Ri and R. Meir of Rothenburg, that the halakhic concept *mutav she-yihyu shogegin* was enunciated only for their generation, meaning the period of the Talmud. But in the present epoch, when the rabbis are lenient in a number of areas, it is appropriate to make a border around the Torah, even in matters that are from the rabbis (*mi-derabbanan*) and to actively restrain and fine people so that they will not transgress, neither accidentally nor willfully. They suggest that this is implied by [a passage in] the *Midrash Yerushalmi*." Ritva concludes, "This appears to me to be the correct approach."[62]

This kind of pattern, in which Ritva hears of Ashkenazic material from a scholar of that area, is found both in Ritva's *hiddushim* and in his responsa. Ritva corresponded with Ashkenazic contemporaries who remained in northern Europe during the mid- and late thirteenth century. In addition, however, other Ashkenazic

---

'Arba'ah Turim, Orah Hayyim, sec. 680. For additional references by Ritva to R. Meir Ashkenazi as a designation for Maharam, see *Hiddushei ha-Ritva 'al Massekhet Makkot*, ed. I. Ralbag, 58 (4b, *ve-ra'iti le-R. Meir ha-Ashkenazi she-katav*); *Hiddushei Ritva 'al Massekhet Yoma*, 174 (30a, *ve-khen katvu be-shem ha-R. Meir Ashkenazi*); and cf. below, n. 67.

61. The *Shitah Mequbbezet* to *Beizah* contains a large number of passages in the name of Ritva that not found in the extant Ritva commentary (which covers only about half of this tractate). See *Hiddushei ha-Ritva 'al Massekhet Beizah*, ed. E. Hurvitz (Jerusalem, 1976), editor's introduction, 7–9, 17–18.

62. *Shitah me-Qubbezet ha-Meyuheset le-R. Bezalel Ashekanzi*, fol. 30a, s.v. *'ela hanah lahem le-Yisra'el (=Qovez Rishonim al Massekeht Beizah*, ed. H. Zimbalist (Tel Aviv, 1988), 465, and cf. below, n. 89. This is another instance in which Ritva uses the terms *Zarefat* and *Ashkenaz* interchangeably (cf. above, n. 30). Although the acronym Ri generally refers to R. Isaac of Dampierre (who died more than a century before Maharam), it can also refer to some other Tosafist who was closer chronologically to Maharam and whose name begins with the letter *yod*. Note that the so-called *Midrash Yerushalmi* is cited by Ritva on one other occasion; see *Hiddushei ha-Ritva 'al Massekhet Bava Mezi'a*, ed. S. Raphael (Jerusalem, 1992), 584, (70b, s.v. *marbeh hono*). The material presented there is close to what is found in *Midrash Tanhuma* (see n. 721), but this identification is still not firm. Cf. *Hiddushei ha-Rashba 'al Massekhet 'Avodah Zarah*, 30a.

talmudic scholars (including R. Asher b. Yehi'el and Rabbenu Dan)[63] left Germany in the late thirteenth or early fourteenth centuries in the face of persecution, as did their counterparts from northern and central France in the period of the expulsion of 1306, and found their way to Spain which was the only thriving, relatively secure center of Jewish learning that remained in western Europe. Ritva was apparently in contact with a number of these scholars as well,

Ritva cites what he heard from *gedolei Zarefat ve-Ashkenaz she-yihyu.*[64] Similarly, Ritva writes, *shamati be-shem gadol mi-gedolei ha-dor 'asher be-Zarefat she-hayah me-hayyev lishon ba-sukkah ba-lailah ha-rishonah shel sukkot va-'afilu yardu geshamim shenat 'ara'i mihat,*[65] and *shamati mi-pi rav Zarefati be-shem rabbotav ha-Zarefatim.*[66] With regard to the blessings for the don-

---

63. See Ta-Shma, *Knesset Mehqarim*, 2:157–60, 170–73; my *Peering through the Lattices*, 247–48; Urbach, 2:587; and above, n. 33.

64. *Hiddushei ha-Ritva 'al Massekhet Yevamot*, ed. Jofen, 2:64, (37b). See also *Hiddushei Ha-Ritva 'al Bava Batra*, ed. Ilan, 22 (18a, *ve-khen shamati be-shem Rabbanei Ashkenaz ve-gam mi-pi mori ha-Rashba ner"u*). Note also *Yevamot* 2:139, n. 476 (39b), *katuv be-Nimmuqqei Rabbotenu ha-Zarefatim*. It is difficult to identify this work in any way based on the context. In *Hiddushei ha-Ritva 'al Massekhet Mo'ed Qatan*, 259 (28a), however, this would seem to be a (late) thirteenth-century work: *ve-khen hiskim 'al yado ba'al Sefer ha-Mizvot [=Sefer Mizvot Gadol le-R. Mosheh mi-Coucy] ve-'ahar kakh mazati ken be-Nimmuqei ha-Zarefatim.* Cf. *Ketubot*, ed. E. Lichtenstein, 56 (7b): *ve-shamati she-yesh maqom be-Ashkenaz ube-Zarefat she-'osim ke-massekhet Soferim* (which intructs that a distinct, second cup of wine be provided over which to recite the *sheva berakhot* that follow the *birkat ha-mazon*). On the presence in Spain of northern French talmudists who had been expelled from their land, see, e.g., see Menahem Ibn Zerah's introduction to his *Zedah la-Derekh* (Warsaw, 1880), and cf. Galinsky, "Ha-Rosh ha-Ashkenazi bi-Sefard," 393–95.

65. See *Hiddushei ha-Ritva 'al Massekhet Sukkah*, ed. A. Lichtenstein (Jerusalem, 1982), 247–48 (27a). Cf. *Tosafot Rabbenu Perez* to *Sukkah*, ad loc. (ed. N. Nussbacher [Jerusalem, 1990], 45). See also *Hiddushei ha-Ritva* to Sukkah 45b (ed. Lichtenstein, 421), *ve-yesh me-rabbotenu hakhmei Zarefat she-katvu de-kevan de-'ikka be-sukkah hiyyuv 'inyanim (me-shunim) [shonim]'akhilah ve-shenah ve-shinun ve-kayoze bahen, she-kol 'et she-qove'a 'azmo la'asot bah 'ehad mi-devarim 'elu havvei ke-hanahah di-tefillin ve-hayyav le-varekh 'af 'al pi she-lo yaza misham*, found similarly in *Tosafot Rabbenu Perez*, ad loc. (ed. Nussbacher, 69).

66. See *Hiddushei ha-Ritva 'al Massekhet 'Avodah Zarah*, ed. M. Goldstein (Jerusalem, 1982), 330 (61b). A non-Jew who is found among sealed wine barrels without authorization, and appears to be a thief, is nonetheless presumed not to have opened the barrels since this would certainly warrant his being caught and prosecuted as a thief. Ra'ah, citing his teachers, relies on this presumption, even when there was not a specific fear of the local constabulary. Ritva then adds, *ve-khen shamati mi-pi*

ning of phylacteries, Ritva writes, "this is the view of my [Spanish] teachers, may they be protected, and I advocated for it before them (*ve-khen danti lifneihem*) and before a great rabbinic scholar of *Zarefat*. He acceded to my words and stated that this was also the view of R. Meir of Rothenburg, may he be protected."[67]

Ritva records an interpretation that he heard directly from (the mouth of) a northern authority (*shamati mi-pi rav Zarefati*), regarding the exchange between Judah and Tamar in Genesis 38, in which Judah asserts that "you are more righteous than I." Judah realized that Tamar never had relations with his sons. As such, she was not required to undergo *yibbum* (*lo zequqah le-yavam*). But what permitted her to have seemingly promiscuous relations with Judah (or with anyone else)? Rather, for a Noachide, the act of sexual relations (with an otherwise permitted husband; marriage between a father-in-law and daughter-in-law is not proscribed for Noachides) establishes a state of matrimony. Although it might be suggested that in the generations prior to the giving of the Torah (*lifnei ha-dibbur*), *yibbum* could be performed by any closely related male (*be-khol qarov*, and that is what allowed the relations between Judah and Tamar), this does not seem to be the essential cause here (*lo mashma hakhi*). Rather, as Ritva had indicated, Tamar was justified because her relations with Judah established a (permitted) state of matrimony.[68] Ritva's own major teacher, R. Aaron *ha-Levi* (Raʾah), had similar contacts with Ashkenazic rab-

---

rav Zarefati be-shem rabbotav ha-Zarefatim. In n. 742, the editor indicates that he is unable to identify this authority.

67. See *Hiddushei ha-Ritva ʿal Massekhet Rosh ha-Shanah*, ed. H. Dimitrovsky (Jerusalem, 1981), 338–39 (34a): *ve-khen daʾat rabbotai nerʾʾu, ve-khen danti lifneihem ve-lifnei hakham gadol me-rabbanei Zarefat ve-hodah li-devarai, ve-ʾamar li she-ken daʾat ha-R. Meir nerʾʾu me-Rothenburg, ve-khen mazati le-Rabbenu Yonah be-Sefer ha-Yirʾah ve-khen nahagu ha-yom kol hakhmei Zarefat.* The last phrase (beginning with *ve-khen nahagu*) comes from R. Zerahyah *ha-Leviʾs Sefer ha-Maʾor*.

68. *Hiddushei ha-Ritva ʿal Masskehet Qiddushin*, ed. Metzger, 100–01 (9b). In his Torah commentary, Nahmanides favors the *yibbum* approach, ostensibly because of the importance and efficacy of this ceremony in kabbalistic thought. Cf. *Tosafot ha-Shalem*, ed. Y. Gellis, vol. 4 (Jerusalem, 1985), 79, where the *yibbum* possibility is raised already in the name of Rashbam and other Tosafist interpretations, and cf. my "On the Assessment of Nahmanides," 70, 79; and my *The Intellectual History of Medieval Ashkenazic Jewry* (Detroit, 2010), chapter four, section two.

binic figures. As Ritva notes, *ve-'omer mori ner"u be-shem ha-Rav ha-Gadol me-Rabbanei Zarefat she-'ein 'omrim be-mamon kasher zamam ve-lo ka'asher 'asah kevan de-'efshar be-hazarah.*[69] Oral transmissions, however, and even written correspondence, do not account for a number of the thirteenth-century Tosafist citations in *hiddushei ha-Ritva* that have been identified. It is instructive in this regard to note the material cited by Ritva from the Italian Tosafist and halakhist, R. Isaiah di Trani (RiD, d. c. 1240). Ritva typically refers to RiD by his surname alone (ר' אושעיא, ר' ישעיא, ר' ישעיה), but he occasionally refers to him as R. Yeshayah or R. Oshaya *Ashkenazi.*[70] This association is an important datum in and of itself. The common supposition is that RiD studied with R. Simhah of Speyer in the Rhineland (where he also came into contact with materials from the German students of Rabbenu Tam) before returning to Italy, but it is has been some-

---

69. *Hiddushei ha-Ritva 'al Massekhet Bava Batra*, ed. Lichtenstein, 478 (56a). *Tosafot Bava Qamma* 4a, s.v. *mamon*, cites this view in the name of R. Isaac b. Asher *ha-Levi* (as well as the conflicting view of Ri).

70. See *Hiddushei ha-Ritva 'al Massekhet Shabbat*, ed. Goldstein, 976 (153b): *ve-khen ha-girsa be-hibbur ha-R. Yeshayah ha-Ashkenazi; Hiddushei ha-Ritva 'al Massekhet 'Eruvin*, 807 (89a), *perush Rashi ke-gon 'ammud shu be-hazer ve-khen piresh ha-Rav R. Oshayah ha-Ashkenazi; Hiddushei ha-Ritva 'al Massekhet Rosh ha-Shanah*, ed. E. Lichtenstein (Jerusalem, 1988), 41 (6a): *ve-khen nimza be-hilkhot ha-R. Yeshayah Ashkenazi*. Ritva appears to have received the text of the citation in this last instance from his teacher Rashba, who refers to R. Isaiah in his *hiddushim* to *Rosh ha-Shanah* (4a), ed. H. Z. Dimitrovsky (Jerusalem, 1981), 28, as *ha-Rav R. Yeshayah ha-Zaqen mi-Trani* (*katav ken bi-pesaqav*). Rashba reports that he heard about R. Isaiah's ruling from R. Moses b. Benjamin of Rome. (R. Moses was a cousin of R. Zedekiah b. Abraham *ha-Rofe*, author of the *Shibbolei ha-Leqet*.) Cf. I. Ta-Shma, *Ha-Sifrut ha-Parshanut la-Talmud*, 2:185, and idem., *Knesset Mehqarim*, vol. 3 (Jerusalem, 2005), 47. Dimitrovsky, *ibid.*, n. 290 (and see also his introduction, 24–25), suggests (implausibly in my view; cf. below, n. 72) that R. Isaiah in this passage is a different figure (possibly a student of Ramban), and that the epithet Ashkenazi given to R. Isaiah by *Hiddushei ha-Ritva* is the copyist's interpolation. It should be noted that there is one place in Ritva's *hiddushim*, *Hiddushei ha-Ritva 'al Massekhet Pesahim*, ed. Y. Lebowitz (Jerusalem, 1983), 126 (42a), in which R. Isaiah is referred to as hailing from Trani. Since, however, the *hiddushei ha-Ritva* to this tractate are not as they flowed from Ritva's pen but rather were preserved by another (see the unpaginated editor's introduction), it is likely in this instance that the designation Trani was added by the redactor/copyist. [The reference to R. Isaiah in the standard *Hiddushei ha-Ritva* to (*'Arvei*) *Pesahim* (Warsaw, 1864; repr. New York, 1950) 104a, *ve-khen katav ha-R. Yeshayah*, occurs in a (section of) commentary that was not composed by Ritva. See, e.g., *Sarei ha-Elef*, ed. Kasher and Mandelbaum, 1:205, and *Hiddushei ha-Ritva 'al Massekhet 'Eruvin*, ed. M. Goldstein, 15–16.]

what difficult to trace RiD's presence in Germany. Ritva's references to him as R. Isaiah *Ashkenazi* help to verify this presence.[71]
More important for our purposes, however, is the fact that Ritva
received R. Isaiah's rulings or *Tosafot* in literary form (only, either
from *Piseqei* or *Tosafot ha-RiD*), and they were available to him
only on particular tractates.[72]

---

71. See Ta-Shma, *Knesset Mehqarim*, 3:24–26, 36–47. R. Mordekhai b. Hillel's *Sefer Mordekhai*, which typically cites rabbinic scholars from northern France and Germany (but not from Italy), mentions R. Isaiah di Trani twice in tractate *Gittin*. In the first instance, however, *Gittin*, sec. 393 [=*Sefer ha-Mordekhai le-Masskehet Gittin*, ed. A. Rabinowitz (Jerusalem, 1990), 580], the words of RiD were transmitted to R. Mordekhai b. Hillel by R. Isaiah Weil; cf. Ta-Shma, *Knesset Mehqarim*, 1:173. In the second passage, found in *Hilkhot Get* (*Mordekhai le-Gittin*, ed. Rabinowitz, 869; cf. *Haggahot Mordekhai*, sec. 456; and S. Cohen in *Sinai* 15 [1944–45], 243), *Sefer Mordekhai* records a responsum from *Ha-R. Yeshayah ha-Gadol mi-Trani* [=*Teshvuot ha-Rid*, ed. A. Wertheimer (Jerusalem, 1975), #55.] R. Isaiah's subsequent literary contacts, with German Tosafists such as R. Simhah of Speyer and R. Isaac *Or Zarua'*, are well-attested. See, e.g., Ta-Shma, *Knesset Mehqarim*, 3:20–23, and S. Emanuel, *Shivrei Luhot*, 155–56, 164–65. Interestingly, no Tosafists from northern France cite RiD, and he is not cited at all in the standard *Tosafot* to the Talmud. See Ta-Shma, *ibid.*, 3:48.
72. In addition to the references discussed above in n. 70, there are some twenty additional citations from *Pisqei* or *Tosafot* R. Yeshayah in *Hiddushei ha-Ritva 'al Massekhet Shabbat*, ed. Goldstein (from the fifteenth chapter, *Ve-Elu Qesharim*, and onward): 721 (114b, *ve-khen mazati be-pisqei R. Yeshaya*), 806 ('*aval ha-Rav R. Yeshayah katav be-shilhei mekhiltin*), 921 (*ve-ahar kakh mazati kakh be-hibbur ha-R. Yeshayah ve-gam be-miqzat Tosafot*; *ve-khen piresh ha-R. Yeshayah*), 925 (*ve-khen piresh ha-R. Yeshayah*), 953 (*ve-khen tirez ha-R. Yeshayah*), 961 (*yafeh piresh ha-R. Yeshayah*), 967 (*veha-R. Oshayah tirez*), 978–79 (*ve-khen katav ha-R. Yeshayah*), 981–982 (*ve-khen gores/piresh ha-R. Yeshayah*), 983 (*ve-khen pershu rabbotai ve-khen katav ha-R. Yeshayah*), 989–990 (*ve-khen piresh/katav ha-R. Yeshayah*), 996 ('*aval ha-R. Yeshayah katav*), 1008 (*ve-zu girsat ha-R. Yeshayah*), 1010 (*veha-R. Yeshayah uba-Tosafot pershu*), 1015 (*veha-R. Yeshayah he-'erikh harbeh be-teruz qushyah zu*). All of these correspond to *Pisqei* (and/or *Tosafot*) *ha-Rid* on this tractate. For addi-tional '*Eruvin* citations, see (ed. Goldstein) 820, 849, 875, 895, 903, 905–09. Note also the remarkable description, apparently of Siamese twins, reported by *Rabbenu ha-Gadol Rabbenu Oshaya* in a manuscript of Ritva's *hiddushim* to *Niddah* 24a (the parallel passage in the published *hiddushim* ed. Metzger, 146–47, nn. 240–42) reads with less elaboration, '*umazati katuv 'al 'ehad meha-gedolim she-he'id 'al 'ishah ba'alat bet gabin u-bet shedrot she-haytah ve-nitqaymah zeman rav*), which Hida locates in a manuscript version of R. Isaiah di Trani's *pesaqim* to tractate *Niddah*): *ve-Rabbenu ha-Gadol Rabbenu Oshaya katav she-hu ra'ah 'ishah she-hayu lah shenei gufin haluqin le-gumrei ve-hozrin lihyot guf 'ehad le-mattah mi-motneha ve-'ein lah 'ela bet raglayim ... vehayu lah daled yadayim ve-daled 'einayim ve-she'okhelet be-rosh 'ehad 'eina 'okhelet be-rosh ha-sheni ve-haytah yoter me-'esrim shanah*. Note also the two references in *Hiddushei ha-Ritva 'al Massekhet Hullin*, ed. S. Raphael (Jerusalem, 1982), 335, 339, to the phrase *ha-Ashkenazim pershu*.

Indeed, like the teachings of R. Isaiah di Trani, much of the material that Ritva cites from northern French Tosafists and their students during the mid- and late thirteenth century described above appears to have reached him in literary form (mainly as *Tosafot*). Thus, for example, I. Ta-Shma assumed that the group of references to R. Moses of Evreux found in Ritva's *hiddushim* to *'Eruvin* (noted above) meant that Ritva had R. Moses' commentary to this tractate in hand.[73] There is, however, a collection of *Tosafot* texts that features virtually all of the Tosafist figures from this period that are found in *Hiddushei ha-Ritva* (and is itself replete with versions or sections of *Tosafot* or *Shitat Hakhmei Evreux* as well), the so-called *Tosafot Rabbenu Perez*. Among R. Perez' teachers and colleagues (as cited in his *Tosafot*) were R. Moses and R. Samuel of Evreux (and Samuel's son, Menahem), R. Yehi'el of Paris, R. Tuvyah of Vienne, R. Yedidyah of Nuremberg, and R. Jacob of Chinon.[74] Rabbenu Perez even studied for a brief period with R. Meir of Rothenburg.[75] These mid- and late-thirteenth century rabbinic figures are precisely those that have been noted above as being cited by Ritva.[76]

R. Perez b. Elijah of Corbeil began to compose his *Tosafot* after 1250 together with his students, with his students complet-

---

73. See Ta-Shma, *Knesset Mehqarim*, 2:116, and cf. above, nn. 34, 55,
74. See *Tosafot Rabbenu Perez le-Massekhet Bava Mezi'a*, ed. H. B. Z. Hershler (Jerusalem, 1970), 9–13; Urbach, *Ba'alei ha-Tosafot*, 2:576; Avigdor Arieli, "'Al ha-Perush ha-Meyuhas la-Rashba le-Massekhet Menahot," *'Alei Sefer* 16 (1990), 149–50; *Tosafot Yeshanim ha-Shalem 'al Massekhet Yevamot*, ed. A. Shoshana, editor's introduction, 24–30; and Ta-Shma, *Ha-Sifrut ha-Parshanit la-Talmud*, 2:110–113.
75. See Urbach, 2:576–77, and my *Peering through the Lattices*, 239–42.
76. At the same time, however, it should be noted that Ritva mentions Rabbenu Perez by name in less than a handful of places. See, e.g., *Hiddushei ha-Ritva 'al Massekhet Ketbuot*, 442 (56b, "*u-mihu shamati be-shem ha-Rabbenu Perez…ve-ra'ui la-hush li-devarav le-khatkhila*", that the groom must be informed if the bride is a *niddah* at the time of the wedding); *Hiddushei ha-Ritva 'al Bava Mezi'a*, 786, n. 69 (95b): *ve-'ahar kakh mazati katuv be-shitat Rabbenu Perez*. This is indeed found in *Tosafot R. Perez* ad loc., ed. Hershler, 167. Similarly, a resolution by R. Samuel of Evreux is found exclusively in *Hiddushei ha-Ritva 'al Masskhet Bava Mezia'*, 70b, and in *Tosafot Rabbenu Perez*, ad loc., ed. Hershler, 143. The standard edition of *Hiddushei ha-Ritva* to Pesahim (whose attribution to Ritva, however, is uncertain; see above, n. 70), fol. 22b (Pesahim 105a), has a citation from *shitat Rabbenu Perez* (that is found in the *Tosafot* to *'Arvei Pesahim* included in the *Sefer Mordekhai* to Pesahim, which are *Tosafot Rabbenu Perez*; on these *Tosafot*, see the next note).

ing several remaining tractates in the early fourteenth century, after R. Perez's death (in 1298). The *Tosafot* of *Rabbenu Perez* have been published to a number of tractates, and several editors have pointed to Ritva's noticeable use of these *Tosafot* texts in his *hiddushim*.[77] Although a complete and detailed survey of these texts is beyond the scope of this study, the presumption that Ritva had certain versions of *Tosafot Rabbenu Perez* available to him can be verified and then utilized productively in clarifying aspects of Ritva's *hiddushim* in a number of different contexts.[78] The standard *Tosafot* to several tractates have been identified as versions of *Tosafot Rabbenu Perez*, and Ritva's use of these standard *Tosafot* may also reflect his familiarity with *Tosafot Rabbenu Perez*.[79]

---

77. A collection of *Tosafot Rabbenu Perez* was published in Jerusalem in 1996, which incorporates a number of previously published tractates as well as several new ones (although some of these cover only portions of the tractates indicated). The contents of volume 1 are *Berakhot*, *'Eruvin* (ed. H. Dickman); vol. 2 contains *Pesahim*, *Yoma*, *Sukkah* (ed. N. Nusbacher), *Beizah*; vol. 3 has *Yevamot* (*Tosafot Maharam ve-Rabbenu Perez*, ed. H. Porush), *Qiddushin* (ed. Dickman); vol. 4 consists of *Nedarim* (ed. N. Y. Weiner); and vol. 5 includes *Bava Mezia'*, ed. H. B. Z. Hershler, and *Sanhedrin*, *Makkot*. Not found in this collection is *Tosafot Talmidei Rabbenu Perez 'al Massekhet Bava Qamma*, ed. B. Z. Pereg (Jerusalem, 1984). In his introduction to *Sukkah*, 7, N. Nusbacher notes that Ritva used *Tosafot Rabbenu Perez* quite a bit in this tractate (and cf. E. Lichtstein's unpaginated introduction to *Hiddushei ha-Ritva* at n. 14, and above, n. 65), as well as in *'Eruvin* (and see Dickman's introduction to his edition of *Tosafot Rabbenu Perez le-Massekhet 'Eruvin*, 8); on *Pesahim* (based on B. Na'eh's introduction to *Gemara Shelemah li-Pesahim*, 3, and see now *Sefer Mordekhai ha-Shalem li-Pesahim*, ed. Y. Horowitz [Jerusalem, 2008], editor's introduction, 14); and in *Bava Mezi'a*, where Hershler observes in his introduction to *Tosafot Rabbenu Perez*, 23, that "Ritva frequently cites *Tosafot*, sometimes by name and somtimes as *yesh 'omrim* or without identification (*bi-setam*). It appears that he did not have the (standard) printed *Tosafot* before him, but only the *Tosafot* of Rabbenu Perez." See also S. Raphael, in his introduction to *Hiddushei ha-Ritva 'al Massekhet Bava Mezi'a*, 13, for a similar assertion. There are indeed close to one hundred parallels, although a number of these may have reached both Rabbenu Perez and Ritva from another *Tosafot* source. Note that on (at least) one occasion (*Hiddushei ha-Ritva*, ed. Raphael, 83, to *Bava Mezi'a* 10b), Rabbenu Perez and Ritva appear to directly disagree.

78. See, e.g., above, n. 49 (regarding *Tosafot Mo'ed Qatan*; see also n. 56, and the next note); n. 55 (regarding Ritva's comment to *'Eruvin* 47b and its resolution of a question raised in *Tosafot Rabbenu Perez*); and see *Hiddushei ha-Ritva 'al Massekhet Yoma*, ed. Lichtenstein, 174, 30a), where Ritva and Rabbenu Perez pose a similar question (and see also the editor's introduction, 5–6, n. 13); and below, n. 87.

79. See Urbach, *Ba'alei ha-Tosafot*, 2:610, n. 54 (*Tosafot le-'Arvei Pesahim*, printed at the end of *Haggahot Mordekhai*, and based on *Tosafot R. Yehi'el* and *Tosafot Hakhmei Evreux*); 612 (*Tosafot Beizah*, based on *Tosafot Shanz* and *Shitat Evreux*); 619, 630–31

In addition, Ritva refers to *Tosafot* throughout his *hiddushim* that are not found in the standard *Tosafot* or in other collections that have been identified.[80] There are a number of texts of *Tosafot Rabbenu Perez* still in manuscript, and others which are cited or referred to by late medieval authorities such as R. Yosef Colon (Mahariq), that may no longer be extant.[81] Rabbenu Perez (and his students) apparently composed *Tosafot* to nearly thirty tractates of the Talmud, although fewer than half of these have been published. Further identification and comparison of these texts will likely yield additional connections between them and *Hiddushei ha-Ritva*. Suffice it to say that the availability of this new *Tosafot* source to Ritva attracted his interest and attention.[82]

The *Tosafot Rabbenu Perez* are, in one crucial respect, the antithesis of *Tosafot Shanz* and the *Tosafot* preserved by R. Perez's younger German contemporary, R. Asher b. Yehi'el; *Tosafot Rabbenu Perez* typically add a great deal of thirteenth-century material to its twelfth-century base or core. These *Tosafot* are more

---

(traces in the *Tosafot* to *Mo'ed Qatan*, and in *Tosafot Qiddushin*, that are essentially *Shitat Evreux*); 635–636 (Rabbenu Perez was the teacher of the editor to *Tosafot Nazir* that are similar to *Tosafot Nedarim* in terms of the use of Evreux material, and see also Ta-Shma, *Knesset Mehqarim*, 2:117); 654–57 (R. Perez was again the teacher of the editor of *Tosafot 'Avodah Zarah*, which contain plenty of material from R. Perez's teachers, R. Jacob of Chinon, and the brothers of Evreux); 658–59 (R. Perez was alive when these *Tosafot* to *Makkot* were prepared, and he is referred to in them as *mashiah= mori she-yihyeh*, and *Shitat Evreux* is found in them as well); 662, 665, 670 (traces of *Tosafot Rabbenu Perez* are included in *Tosafot Zevahim*, and the *Shitah Mequbbezet* uses these *Tosafot* in both *Zevahim* and *Menahot*, as well as *Bekhorot*); 673 (the editor of these *Tosafot* was a student of Rabbenu Perez).

80. See, e.g., *Qiddushin*, ed. Dinin, editor's (unpaginated) introduction, at n. 23; *Ketubot*, ed. Goldstein, 55–57, nn. 153 (*Tosafot Aharonot*), 162, 172, 491); *Rosh ha-Shanah*, ed. Lichtenstein, editor's introduction, 10; *Niddah*, ed. D. Metzger, editor's introduction, 4 (*Tosafot she-'einam lefanenu*); *'Eruvin*, ed. Goldstein, 21–22, and 769 (54b, *Tosafot ha-Aharonot*). See also *Shevu'ot*, ed. Lichtenstein, editor's introduction, 10, and *Sukkah*, ed. Lichtenstein (above, n. 77).

81. See *Tosafot Rabbenu Perez 'al Massekhet Bava Mezi'a*, ed. Hershler, editor's introduction, 19–26, and Urbach, *Ba'alei ha-Tosafot*, 2:580–81.

82. The ready availablity of *Tosafot Rabbenu Perez* in early fourteenth-century Spain is attested by Menahem Ibn Zerah in the introduction to his *Zedah la-Derekh* (*ve-hayinu hozrim tamid yomam va-lailah hu* (= R. Yosef Ibn Shu'ib) *va-'ani me-rosh ha-massekhta be-Tosafot Rabbenu Perez...ve-rov limmudeinu be-shitat Rabbenu Perez*). Ultimately, as Rosh's son R. Ya'akov indicates, Rosh was successful, in his Spanish hometown of Toledo at least, in supplanting the study of *Tosafot Rabbenu Perez* there with the study of 'his' *Tosafot*. See Urbach, 2:579–80, and below, n. 84.

similar in this regard to the so-called *Tosafot Tukh*, redacted by R. Eliezer of Touques (from northern France, or perhaps Turcheim, Germany), that form the basis of many of the standard *Tosafot* published with the Babylonian Talmud.[83] Indeed, Rosh, who favored the approach and format of *Tosafot Shanz* (as we have seen), denigrated both the style (and the substance) of *Tosafot Rabbenu Perez*, in a responsum that he composed in Toledo: "You have written that you have found the view of Ri as cited in *Tosafot Hullin* [according to the version of the *Tosafot* that was compiled by the students of Rabbenu Perez]. Know that these commentaries, which have circulated in this land [=Spain], were composed by unqualified students who wished to claim a high pedigree (*nitlu be-'ilan gadol*). They offered these interpretations before Rav Perez and other *gedolim* but, nonetheless, they should not be relied upon. For I have in my possession the interpretation of [Ri as preserved by] R. Samon [of Sens] and he did not rule thusly."[84]

Rosh criticizes the so-called *Tosafot Talmidei Rabbenu Perez*, which had become popular in Spain among students of the Talmud, because they did not have accurate versions of the views of the earlier Tosafists which was a hallmark of *Tosafot Shanz*. In another responsum, Rosh raises the same kind of concern: "I found in the comments of (*nimmuqei*) R. Perez b. Elijah of Corbeil that he prohibited this. And they [the students who compiled his *Tosafot*] went on at length praising this view, and they cited a case in which Rabbenu Tam ruled similarly." The Rosh continues, "And I was quite amazed (in a negative sense, *ve-tamahti me'od*)."[85]

Although Rosh places the blame for these developments on the student editors, the import of his words is that the *Tosafot*

---

83. On *Tosafot Tukh*, see Urbach, 2:581–85; Ta-Shma, *Ha-Sifrut ha-Parshanit la-Talmud*, 2:111, 119–20; and A.Y. Havazelet, "Zemanam u-Megomam Shel Tosafot Tukh," *Yerushatenu* 2 (2008), 319–23.
84. See *Teshuvot ha-Rosh*, 20:27, ed. Y. Yudlov (Jerusalem, 1994), 105. Cf. Urbach, *Ba'alei ha-Tosafot*, 2:587; *Tosafot ha-Rosh 'al Massekhet Pesahim*, ed. A. Shoshana (Jerusalem, 1997), editor's introduction, 26–28; and Yehuda Galinsky, "Ha-Rosh ha-Ashkenazi bi-Sefarad: 'Tosafot ha-Rosh', 'Pisqei ha-Rosh', Yeshivat ha-Rosh," *Tarbiz* 74 (2005), 396–400.
85. *Teshuvot ha-Rosh*, 2:17, ed. Yudlov, 14.

Rabbenu Perez (which were readily available and quite popular in early fourteenth-century Spain) ought not be considered as fully reliable representatives of Ashkenazic talmudic study and *halakhah*, precisely because they were focused on and derived from the period of the later 'editors and redactors' of the *Tosafot*, rather than the formative period of twelfth-century Tosafist creativity and development.[86] In addition, *Tosafot Talmidei Rabbenu Perez* (like the contemporary *Tosafot Tukh*) tended to shorten, paraphrase or recast the views of Ri and others in his day (in order to more easily include and integrate later *Tosafot* material as well), rather than report their words in verbatim or near verbatim form.

We do not have any response from Ritva to his contemporary, R. Asher b. Yehi'el, on these matters.[87] It is apparent, however, that Ritva felt that the *Tosafot* of *Rabbenu Perez*, at least in the form in which he had them, could and should be cited reliably. Perhaps Ritva extracted from *Tosafot Rabbenu Perez* only the later Tosafist material, and utilized other Tosafist sources or collections for the twelfth-century substrate.

Although Ritva's use of *Tosafot Rabbenu Perez* was the direct result of a felicitous opportunity, namely their availablity in Spain from the late thirteenth century onward, there may have also been other intellectual or halakhic motives that caused Ritva to depart from the approach that Ramban and Rashba had taken regarding the Tosafist corpus. In a word, some of the passages in *Tosafot*

---

86. Rosh cites a resolution of Rabbenu Perez by name (*ve-tirez ha-R. Perez*) once in *Tosafot ha-Rosh 'al Massekhet Ketubot*, ed. Lichtenstein, 490–91 (70). As the editor notes (n. 46), a similar resolution is put forward by Ritva, although he does not mention R. Perez by name; cf. above, n. 78. Rosh also cites and qualified an interpretation or solution of Rabbenu Perez in *Tosafot ha-Rosh le-Gittin*, ed. H. Ravitz (Jerusalem, 2004), 109 (14a), along with one by R. Moses of Evreux. In *Perush ha-Rosh le-Gittin*, 1:19, however, Rosh directly rejects the solution proposed by Rabbenu Perez in favor of his own interpretation (*'aval teruz ha-R. Perez 'eino nakhon*).

87. As indicated above, n. 36, Rosh and Ritva appear to ignore each other's writings, perhaps for this reason, although the *Tosafot ha-Rosh* and the *Hiddushei ha-Ritva* do appear to have been working from the same sources on any number of occasions. Note, e.g., *Qiddushin* 35a-36a, where several passages and interpretations are virtually identical (in *Hiddushei ha-Ritva*, ed. Dinin, 371–82, and *Tosafot ha-Rosh*, ed. Metzger, 287–97). Other examples of overlap in tractate *Qiddushin* are found, e.g., in ed. Dinin, 353, 356, 358, 371, 384, 716, and see also *Hiddushei ha-Ritva 'al Massekhet Bava Mezi'a*, ed. Raphael, *passim*.

Rabbenu Perez spoke to Ritva. The passage on the forty-nine path-ways of the Torah, found in *Tosafot Rabbenu Perez* to *'Eruvin* in the name of R. Yehi'el of Paris (as noted above), appealed to Ritva as both a halakhist and a student of kabbalah. Ritva, not surprisingly, was somewhat less reticent than Ramban about including kabbalistic material within his talmudic *hiddushim*. Although Ramban did this on less than a handful of occasions in his *hiddushim*, *Hiddushei ha-Ritva* contain more than twenty such instances.[88] The legitimacy of multiple halakhic truths that is at the heart of this *Tosafot* passage (and that constitutes a cor-nerstone of Tosafist thought and endeavor) is a fundamentally exoteric concept. Nonetheless, there were Ashkenazic rabbinic figures in both the pre-Crusade period and the Tosafist period for whom this notion had mystical connotations.[89] Ritva understood the importance of this formulation in both exoteric and esoteric ways as well.[90]

Ritva's inclusion of the passage on *mutav she-yihyu shogegin* from R. Meir of Rothenberg and other Ashkenazic predecessors

---

88. See my *Peering through the Lattices*, 12, n. 5, 218, and Ta-Shma, *Ha-Sifrut ha-Parsha-nit la-Talmud*, 2:72–73. Ritva in his *hiddushim* to *Qiddushin*, 404 (40a), interprets the talmudic censure against gazing at a rainbow as a function of the fact that it represents the Divine *Kavod* (as per Ezekiel 1). He then concludes that: "there is a deep *sod* in this that is known to *ba'alei 'emet*, as our teacher (*Rabbenu*= Ramban) alludes to in his Torah commentary (on Genesis 9:12). Needless to say, Ramban makes no such reference in his own talmudic *hiddushim* here, although this may also be an issue of timing; cf. above, n. 26. Interstingly, in the passage immediately prior, 403 (39b) Ritva applauds Rabbenu Tam's questioning and subsequent under-standing of Rashi's comment on the nature of the rewards of the world to come and concludes: "He [Rabbenu Tam] has interpreted well according to the exoteric level of interpretation (*lefi peshatan shel devarim*), but there is a hidden secret contained within them that is known to the masters of esoteric interpretation (*'aval yesh bahem sod nistar le-ba'alei 'emet*)." Cf. my *Peering through the Lattices*, 166–77. On the other hand, earlier in his *hiddushim* to *Qiddushin* (see above, n. 68), Ritva rejects (without referring to him directly) Ramban's partial justification of the relationship between Judah and Tamar, since the performance of *yibbum* by a wider circle of familial males was in vogue prior to the giving of the Torah, on purely exoteric (halakhic) grounds. Ritva also refers to the notion of *shiv'im panim la-Torah* in his *Sefer ha-Zikkaron*. See Hanan'el Mack, "Shiv'im Panim la-Torah — Li-Mehalkho shel Bittui," *Sefer ha-Yovel le-Rav Mordekhai Breuer*, ed. M. Bar Asher (Jerusalem, 1992), 459, and the next note.
89. See my "Torah Study and Truth," (above, n. 42), 113–16.
90. See *ibid.*, 101–02.

is perhaps a reflection of the documented difficulties in religious observance across the board in late thirteenth and early four-teenth century Spain that Ritva, in his role as a communal leader, also encountered.[91] Another significant piece that originated in Ashkenaz (and is found rather expansively in Ritva's commen-tary to *Avodah Zarah*, but was not picked up at all by any other Spanish collection of *hiddushim*), deals with the parameters (and justification) of martyrdom (*kiddush ha-Shem*). Ritva writes, "It is written in the margins (or folios) of *Tosafot* texts [*gilyonei ha-Tosafot*] that Rabbenu Tam asserted that where one is afraid lest he be coerced into violating his religion [through worshipping idolatry], he may harm himself, *mutar la-havol be-'azmo*, that is, he may take his own life." This passage appears in the name of Rabbenu Tam in the standard *Tosafot* to tractate *Avodah Zarah*, although the derivation offered next by Ritva (from the behavior of King Saul) is not the talmudic proof-text that *Tosafot* texts attri-bute to Rabbenu Tam. Ritva then continues his citation: "Under such conditions, taking one's own life is permitted. From this they [also] learned to slaughter their children during the persecutions, lest they [the children] be coerced to violate their religion." Up to this point, Ritva notes, is what he found in the *gilyonei ha-Tosafot*. Ritva then concludes: "These words require great study and inves-tigation but the wise elder (*ha-zaqen*, ostensibly Rabbenu Tam) has already issued his ruling. And we have heard in the name of the great scholars of France (*gedolei Zarefat*) that they actually ruled in this way."[92]

Although the key figure cited is Rabbenu Tam, the (sudden) shift in Ritva's presentation to the killing of others (which Rabbenu Tam does not discuss at all) perhaps reflects the following passage in the glosses of R. Perez (*Haggahot Rabbenu Perez*) to R. Isaac of Corbeil's *Sefer Mizvot Qatan*. Ritva used these glosses elsewhere

---

91. See my "Rabbinic Attitudes Toward Nonobservance in the Medieval Period," *Jewish Tradition and the Nontraditional Jew*, ed. J. J. Schacter (Northvale, 1992), esp. 31–33.
92. See *Hiddushei Ritva 'al Massekhet 'Avodah Zarah*, ed. Goldstein, 81 (18a), and my "Halakhah and Mezi'ut in Medieval Ashkenaz," (above, n. 49), 203–11.

in his talmudic commentaries,[93] and they are also the product, of course, of Rabbenu Perez and his *beit midrash*: "And those holy martyrs (*ve-'otam ha-qedoshim*) who slaughtered themselves and did not want to rely on their being able to withstand the trial [of coercion], they are completely holy (*kedoshim gemurim hem*)."[94] This passage is itself based on a fuller passage from *Avi ha-Ezri*, the halakhic work of the German Tosafist R. Eliezer b. Yo'el ha-Levi (Rabiah, d. c. 1225), who had access to formulations of Rabbenu Tam,[95] although it is not found in the published version of Rabiah's work.[96] It was recently found, however, in the name of *Avi ha-Ezri* in the *Qizur ha-Semaq* or *Sefer Simmanei Taryag Mizvot*, a northern French work composed c. 1265, that is based on Moses of Coucy's *Sefer Mizvat Gadol*. This work was compiled by R. Avraham b. Ephraim, a student of R. Tuvyah of Vienne, and contains other passages from *Sefer Rabiah* not found in the published editions of Rabiah works.[97] We recall that R. Tuvyah was one of the teachers of Rabbenu Perez, whom Ritva had cited.[98] Thus, Ritva, with his unique degree of access to both German and northern French texts of the thirteenth century, may have had available to him a version of this highly suggestive *Avi ha-Ezri* passage as well.[99]

---

93. See, e.g., above, n. 45. See also *Hiddushei ha-Ritva 'al Massekhet Makkot*, ed. Ralbag, 227 (21a), where the position of Rabbenu Tam cited by Ritva is found in *Haggahot R. Perez to Semaq* sec. 70.
94. See *Haggahot Rabbenu Perez* to *Sefer Mizvot Qatan*, sec. 3; my "Halakhah and Mezi'ut," 213; and cf. Haym Soloveitchik, "Halakhah, Hermeneutics and Martyrdom in Medieval Ashkenaz," *JQR* 94 (2004), 286–87.
95. See, e.g., Rami Reiner, "Rabbenu Tam: Rabbotav (ha-Zarefatim) ve-Talmidav Bnei Ashkenaz," (M. A. thesis, Hebrew University, 1997), 124, and S. Emanuel, *Shivrei Luhot*, 29.
96. Indeed, until recently, it was known only from the fourteenth-century *Sefer Semaq mi-Zurich*, which raised the question of its attribution to Rabiah. Cf H. Soloveitchik, "Religious Law and Change: The Medieval Ashkenazic Example," *AJS Review* 12 (1987), 210, n. 8.
97. See, e.g., *Qizzur Sefer Mizvot ha-Gadol*, ed. Y. Horwitz, 32, 94, 129, 179, 194, 106, 225, and cf. above, n. 49.
98. See above, nn. 49–50. R. Perez had a collection of *pisqei R. Tuvyah*. See *Haggahot Rabbenu Perez to Semaq*, sec. 245: 'I found a correction (*mugah*) in the book of R. Tuvyah of Vienne', and cf. Hershler, *Tosafot Rabbenu Perez le-Massekhet Bava Mezia'*, editor's introduction, 13.
99. See my "Halakhah and Mezi'ut," 211–12, 214–16. Note that the standard *Tosafot* to

Contrary to the larger thesis put forward by my distinguished teacher Jacob Katz, I have recently identified a view among Tosafists in northern France and Germany from the late twelfth century onward which held, against Rashi and those Tosafists who followed his approach, that an apostate who wished to return to the Jewish community was required according to rabbinic law to immerse himself for a variety of meta-halakhic (and even some halakhic) reasons. One such formulation is found in Ritva's *hiddushim*, in the name of *Tosafot Aharonot: ve-'af 'al pi khen, hu* [the returning apostate] *tovel mishum ma'alah*. The last phrase does not mean simply 'for the sake of perfection', as some have suggested. Rather, it connotes the elevated status of the returning apostate, similar to the *'eved kena'ani* who must also be immersed (again) when he is set free, because he is moving (in the case of the apostate, returning) from a lower status of religious obligation to a higher one, and this change of status must be recognized and noted. Moreover, manuscript research has uncovered the *Tosafot* text that was the apparent source for Ritva's formulation. It is referred to as *Tosafot Shitah*, and is ostensibly a passage from *Shitat/Tosafot Evreux*. Here again, Ritva's unique awareness of northern French (Evreux) Tosafist teachings put him in a position to retrieve and reproduce highly significant Ashkenazic material that his Spanish predecessors could not. From Ritva's *hiddushim*, this same passages enters the commentary of *Nimmuqei Yosef*.[100]

Finally, the influence or role of R. Aharon *ha-Levi* (Ra'ah) in this matter should be considered further. Rashba studied with both Ramban and Rabbenu Yonah. Ramban was his main teacher in Talmud; from Rabbenu Yonah, Rashba received talmudic interpretations, an approach toward halakhic decision-making, and additional aspects of spirituality. For the most part, Rashba's

---

'Avodah Zarah are *Tosafot Rabbenu Perez*; see Urbach, above, n. 79.

100. See *Hiddushei ha-Ritva li-Yevamot*, ed. Joffen, 330–32 (47b); *Nimmuqei Yosef*, ad loc. (at the top of fol. 16b in the standard pagination of *Hilkhot ha-Rif*); ms. Vercelli (Bishop's Seminary), C 235/4, fol. 291v; and my "Returning to the Jewish Community in Medieval Ashkenaz: History and Halakhah," *Turim: Studies in Jewish History and Thought Presented to Dr. Bernard Lander*, ed. M. Shmidman (New York, 2007), 101–29.

limited use of Ashkenazic sources follows the pattern set by Ramban. As noted above, however, he did receive and include a small number of Evreux interpretations from his teacher (and a student of Evreux), Rabbenu Yonah.[101] Ra'ah was Ritva's major teacher, but Ritva cites Rashba with great frequency as well, since his talmudic interpretations cover the Talmud more fully than those of Ra'ah. However, Ritva's more inclusive attitude toward the use of Ashkenazic sources was perhaps more indebted to Ra'ah than to Rashba.[102]

In his *hiddushim* to (*Hilkhot ha-Rif li-*) *Berakhot*, Ra'ah includes an (anonymous) esoteric interpretation of the *piyyut E-l 'Adon* that has been attributed to R. Yehi'el of Paris (and actually extends back even further to R. Eleazar of Worms and ultimately to R. Judah b. Yaqar, a teacher of Nahmanides who studied in northern France with Rizba).[103] Perhaps following Rabbenu Yonah in his *Sefer ha-Yir'ah*, whose northern French roots and tendencies (especially in this work) are well-documented, Ra'ah (as recorded in a manuscript version of his *hilkhot Rosh ha-Shanah*) subscribes to the decidely Ashkenazic view (which was against the position of Rashba and *Sefer ha-Hinnukh* and virtually every other earlier Spanish halakhist), that the donning of *tefillin* always requires two blessings, whether the wearer has spoken during their placement or not. Ritva agrees with this view as well.[104]

Although Ra'ah's actual citation of *Tosafot* in his own *hiddushim* is sparse at best,[105] Ritva explicitly links the view of his

---

101. See above, n. 34, and cf. Ta-Shma, *Ha-Sifrut ha-Parshanit la-Talmud*, 2:55.

102. In his treatment of Ra'ah's talmudic commentaries, Ta-Shma, *Ha-Sifrut ha-Parshanit*, 2:66–69, portrays Ra'ah as throughly committed to Spanish or Sefardic talmudic interpretation, as was the case for Ra'ah's older brother, R. Pinhas *ha-Levi* (the putative author of *Sefer ha-Hinnukh*) as well. In other venues, however, Ta-Shma does note affinities between Ra'ah's interpretations and those of the Tosafists; see the next two notes. Cf. above, n. 43.

103. See Ta-Shma, "Li-Meqorotav ha-Sifrutiyyim shel Sefer ha-Zohar," *Tarbiz* 60 (1991), 663–65, and idem., *Ha-Nigleh shebe-Nistar*, 30, 66–67.

104. See Ta-Shma, *Ha-Nigleh shebe Nistar*, 75, and *Hiddushei ha-Ritva 'al Massekhet Rosh ha-Shanah* (34a), above, n. 67.

105. For example, Ra'ah quotes (*Ba'alei/Hakhmei ha-*) *Tosafot* only once to in his *hiddushim* to *Sukkah*, ed. Makhon Ahavat Shalom vi-Yerushalyaim, (2001), 195 (35a, n. 202, cited in *Hiddushei ha-Ritva*, ed. Lichtenstein, 334, n. 629, as well), and four

teacher with that of *Tosafot* in a number of instances.[106] There is also an interesting espisode that documents R. Perez of Corbeil's awareness of Ra'ah (as a leading Spanish authority and rabbinic judge in Barcelona), if not the reverse. In a case that originated in Toulouse, a father initially asserted (and confirmed through an oath) that he had betrothed his minor daughter, which would prevent her betrothal to another without a proper bill of divorce. Subsequently, a local rabbinic judge allowed her to marry another man without a *get*, because the father had recanted his claim of

---

times in his *hiddushim* to *Berakhot*, ed. Makhon Ahavat Shalom vi-Yerushalayim (2000), 99, 363, 368, n. 32 (45b, also found in *Hiddushei ha-Rashba* and in *Hiddushei ha-Ritva*, ed. Hershler, 311, in the name of *rabbotenu ha-Zarefatim*), 454–55, n. 84 (59b, cited also in *Hiddushei ha-Ritva*, 404, n. 22), in addition to one citation from *Rabbenu Yizhaq Ba'al ha-Tosafot* (Ri), 260. It should be noted that despite the time that he spent as a student at Evreux, Rabbenu Yonah also fits, for the most part, the Spanish 'Ramban' pattern of Tosafist citation (since Ramban, was, after all, R. Yonah's cousin and almost exact contemporary); see Ta-Shma, *Knesset Mehqarim*, 121–23, and idem., *Ha-Sifrut ha-Prarhsanit la-Talmud*, 22–23. Thus, in his commentary to *Bava Batra*, R. Yonah cites only Rashbam, Rabbenu Tam and *Tosafot Ri ha-Zaqen*, and he mentions his teacher R. Moses of Evreux exactly twice. At the same time, Rabbenu Yonah makes use of unnamed, early *Tosafot* texts much more than R. Meir Abulafia *ha-Levi* (Ramah) did. Ta-Shma notes that Ritva has quite a bit of Rabbenu Yonah's talmudic commentaries before him; see *Ha-Sifrut ha-Parshanit*, 24–25. In addition, Ritva, in his *hiddushim* to *Rosh ha-Shanah*, is the one who confirms unequivocally R. Yonah's authorship of *Sefer Hayyei Olam/ Sefer ha-Yir'ah*; see Ta-Shma, *Knesset Mehqarim*, 2:146–47, n. 67.) Y. N. Epstein, "'Al ha-Kol," Sinai 94 (1984), 123–36, esp. 126 [= J. N. Epstein, *Studies in Talmudic Literature and Semitic Languages*, vol. 2, part two, ed. E. Z. Melammed (Jerusalem, 1988), 776–789, esp. 779; this article was originally published in 1909] has a number of other instances in which R. Yonah cites material from Evreux. Perhaps he is also one of Ritva's conduits for the teachings of Evreux; cf. above, nn. 55–58. Ta-Shma, *Knesset Mehqarim*, 2:116, points to an interpretation in '*Eruvin* 33b which *Tosafot ha-Rosh* cites in the name of Rabbenu Yonah and Ritva cites in the name of R. Moses of Evreux. Cf. *Hiddushei ha-Ritva 'al Massekhet Bava Mezia'*, ed. Raphael, 48 (30a), *be-shem ha-Rav he-hasid* [=Rabbenu Yonah] *shamati*, which *Tosafot ha-Rosh* cites in the name of R. Meir of Rothenburg. Prior to this, Ritva cites an answer by R. Samson (Rash) of Coucy, followed by an answer in the name of Riva (Rizba); these same two answers are found in the reverse order in *Tosafot Rabbenu Perez*, ad loc., ed. Hershler, 68.

106. See, e.g, *Hiddushei ha-Ritva 'al Massekhet 'Avodah Zarah*, 330 (above, n. 66; *Hiddushei ha-Ritva 'al Massekhet Bava Batra*, 478 (above, n. 69); *Hiddushei ha-Ritva 'al Massekhet Sukkah*, 420–21 (45a); *Hiddushei ha-Ritva 'al Massekhet Shabbat*, 817: *ve-tirez mori ve-khen mezatiha be-Tosafot Aharonot*; *Hiddushei ha-Ritva 'al Massekhet Ketubot*, 7 (2b; see above, n. 43); *ibid.*, 202 (22a), n. 31; *Hiddushei ha-Ritva 'al Massekhet Rosh ha-Shanah* 41 (6a): *ve-zeh nir'eh li barur be-shitat rabbotenu ba'alei ha-Tosafot ve-hi shitat mori ha-Ra'ah. 'Aval ha-Rashba makhria' ki-leshon ha-'aher, ve-khen nimza be-hilkhot ha-R. Oshaya ha-Ashkenazi.* Cf. above, n. 70.

betrothal, and had provided an excuse as to why he had made this claim in the first place. A number of leading European rabbinic authorities were asked to render their views in this matter. Rabbenu Perez indicated that he sided with those who prohibited the new marrigage without a prior bill of divorce, as did a certain R. Shemaryah b. Meir of Germany.

Two Provencal rabbinic courts argued, however, that the father could recant his original assertion (apparently because he had not really taken an oath in support of it), without any consequence or need for a *get*. Subsequently, Rabbenu Perez and others removed their objections, in favor of the ruling of the Provencal courts. R. Perez justifies this change, in part, because the case had also been brought to Barcelona, where it was heard by "*morenu ha-Rav R. Shelomoh* [=Rashba] and *Morenu ha-Rav R. Aharon* [=Ra'ah]. If these rabbinic authorities were in agreement with the later ruling, R. Perez was prepared to join them.[107]

Just as we can better assess and understand the nature and scope of Ritva's *hiddushim* in light of his uses of Ashkenazic material, while also considering the stimuli and conduits that brought this about, *Hiddushei ha-Ritva* is a potential source for retrieving or reconstructing unknown or incomplete Ashkenazic Tosafist texts from the thirteenth century. R. Meir of Rothenburg and his students, Rosh, R. Mordekhai b. Hillel and R. Meir *ha-Kohen* (author of the *Haggahot Maimuniyyot*), alligned themselves with the works of Maimonides and Rif as a means of preserving Ashkenazic teachings during and after a period of sharp decline (from the second half of the thirteenth century and beyond).[108] Wittingly or unwittingly, Ritva may have played a significant role in preserving some of this Ashkenazic literature as well. It is fair to say, and it may well be an understatement, that in the case of Ritva, Ashkenaz informed Sefarad, even as Sefarad can continue to inform us about Ashkenaz.

---

107. See *Teshuvot Hakhmei Provence*, ed. A. Sofer (Jerusalem, 1967), 85–95 (and esp. 93).
108. See, e.g., my "Preservation, Creativity and Courage: The Life and Works of R. Meir of Rothenburg," *Jewish Book Annual* 50 (1992–93), 249–59.

10.

Sages on Stages, or Guides on the Side? Rashi, Rambam, Radak and Constructivist Educational Theory

Scott Goldberg and Moshe Sokolow

Section 1: Prologue

The "medievals" were no strangers to questions of educational philosophy and psychology, however obliquely they may have addressed them. Oftentimes, the consanguinity of their opinions with those of contemporary thinkers is striking. It will be our task here to denote some of the observations of Rashi (1040–1105) and Rambam (1135–1204), as well as other rabbinic scholars of that period, on the process of education and relate them to theories of education that are operative today, in general, and to the theory of constructivism in particular.

I. A foreword regarding the Jewish sources

Moreh haNevukhim provides a comprehensive portrait of Rambam's philosophical oeuvre. Even the *Mishneh Torah*, while not intended primarily as a philosophical statement, is replete with sections that deal with the inculcation of ethics and morals no less than with ritual law and practice, including a discreet section expressly on Torah education (i.e., *Hilkhot Talmud Torah*). This section will be supplemented through citations from the *Tibb al-Nufus* (Medicine for the Soul), a comprehensive work of moral philosophy by Rambam's distinguished contemporary, Yosef Ibn Aknin, which contains an extensive chapter on Jewish education including both curricular and instructional advice.

Rashi, no less than Rambam, was surely a systematic thinker; it is difficult, however, to reconstruct a holistic Rashi-styled philosophy because his literary legacy is confined primarily to exegetical compositions, which make poor platforms for systematic presentation. We are fortunate, then, that we can base a significant conclusion regarding Rashi and constructivism upon one of his responsa, which has the normative, operative force absent in the more "academic" commentaries.

II. A Working Definition of Constructivism

According to constructivist theories of learning, the process of learning is an active engagement between learner and information or learner and experience. During this process, the learner literally "constructs" meaning by examining new information in light of his or her current thinking.[1] Thus, learning drives development; learning is not particularly constrained by developmental stages.

Lev Vygotsky's theories of development greatly influenced modern constructivist theories of learning. His emphasis on the social nature of the learning process,[2] in particular, provides the foundation on which cooperative learning methods and the concept of "teacher as facilitator" are built. Indeed, students' interactions with adults or peers provide a window into their thought processes. For instance, it is likely that during a cooperative learning experience, one student will be paired with another who is capable of more complex understanding, thereby allowing

---

1. Tishman, S., Perkins, D. N., Jay, E.: *The Thinking Classroom: learning and teaching in a culture of thinking* (Needham, 1995). Waxman, H.C., Padron, Y.N. & Arnold, K.M., "Effective instructional practices for students placed at risk of academic failure," in G.D.Borman, S.C.Stringfield & R.E.Slavin (Eds.), *Title 1: Compensatory education at the crossroads* (Mahwah, 2001), 137–170. Brown, J. S., Collins, A., & Duguid, P., "Situated cognition and the culture of learning," *Educational Research* 18/1 (1989), 32–42.
2. Salomon, G., & Perkins, D. N.: *Individual and social aspects of learning*, in P.D. Pearson & A. Iran-Nejad (Eds.): *Review of Research in Education*, no. 23, pp. 1–24. (Washington, DC, 1998).

the former to engage in a task that he would otherwise have been unable to perform.

Greeno, Collins, and Resnick[3] discuss how such interaction — within what Vygotsky terms the "zone of proximal development" — provides the learner with "cognitive apprenticeship," whereby the learner gains proficiency through the interaction itself. During this process of mediated learning, the adult, or more capable peer, supplies "scaffolding" for the learner that supports the learner's construction of knowledge and understanding of complex information and processes.[4] Diaz and Berk[5] also discuss the cognitive system of "private speech" as theorized by Vygotsky, i.e., the method by which learners integrate and internalize the speech and knowledge of others and then employ that speech to solve problems. With the guidance of an expert (adult or peer), students are encouraged to make personal discoveries, to construct knowledge and not just receive it. Bruner describes such "discovery learning" as follows:

> We teach a subject not to produce little living libraries on that subject, but rather to get a student to think...for himself, to consider matters as an historian does, to take part in the process of knowledge-getting. Knowing is a process, not a product.[6]

In somewhat greater abstraction:

> In its extreme form, Constructivism claims that there is no objective knowledge about the world, only subjectively constructed knowledge. According to the Constructivists, since knowledge is continuously created

3. Greeno, J., Collins, A., Resnick, L.: "Cognition and Learning," in Berliner, D. & Calfee, R. (Eds.): *Handbook of Educational Psychology* (NY:1996).
4. Kozulin, A., & Presseisen, B. Z.: "Mediated learning experience and psychological tools: Vygotsky's and Feuerstein's perspectives in a study of student learning," *Educational Psychologist* 30/2 (1995), 67–75.
5. Diaz, R. and L. Berk (eds.): Private Speech; From Social Interaction to Self-Regulation (Hillsdale, 1992).
6. Bruner, Jerome. (1966). *Toward a Theory of Instruction* (Cambridge, MA: Harvard University Press), 72.

within societies and cultures, and by definition is tempo-ral and dynamic, it cannot be objective.

The Constructivist approach to education objects to the transmission of knowledge, meaning and inter-pretation from teachers to students, and advocates the creation of optimal conditions for pupils so that they can construct those meanings on their own. Instead of providing students with information and distinct skills, Constructivism prefers to promote an environment in which pupils can acquire knowledge through investiga-tion of relevant questions (often called "authentic ques-tions"), conducted either personally or in small groups.

The Constructivist teacher is presented as one who is able to overcome the traditional authoritative, all-knowing ideal type of a teacher. He or she is presented as a guidance provider, an educator who empowers his or her students and increases their motivation and ability to learn and develop through questioning and objection.

A Constructivist learning environment is presented as one which enables students to work together in a learning community of discovery, a community which is involved in joint thinking, exploration and discussion of significant topics. Communication and information technology, such as computers, the Internet and multi-media devices are often presented as usefully important in such an environment.[7]

III. The Mishnaic and Talmudic Approach to Education:

Pursuant to the previous definition, the Mishnah and Talmud appear to be constructivist in their approach to education.

---

7. Aharon Aviram: "Beyond Constructivism: Autonomy-Oriented Education," *Studies in Philosophy and Education* 19:5–6 (2003), 465–466.

A. Mishnah Avot 5:21 (22)

משנה מסכת אבות פרק ה משנה כא

הוא היה אומר בן חמש שנים למקרא בן עשר למשנה בן שלש עשרה
למצות בן חמש עשרה לתלמוד בן שמונה עשרה לחופה בן עשרים
לרדוף בן שלשים לכח בן ארבעים לבינה בן חמשים לעצה בן ששים
לזקנה בן שבעים לשיבה בן שמונים לגבורה בן תשעים לשוח בן מאה
כאילו מת ועבר ובטל מן העולם:

He [Yehudah ben Teima] would [also] say: At age
5 — Mikra', age 10 — Mishnah, age 13 — Mitzvot, age
15 — Talmud, age 18 — Huppah, age 20 — Lirdof, age
30 — le-Ko'ah, age 40 — Binah, age 50 — 'Eitzah, age
60 — Ziknah, age 70 — Seivah, age 80 — Gevurah, age
90 — la-Su'ah, age 100 — it is as though he had died and
passed, null, from this world.

The commentary of the MAHARAL of Prague (15 25–1609) on
this Mishnah anticipates the three components of a constructivist
view.

1) He cites statement of R. Eliezer (Berakhot 33a, Sanhedrin 92a):

כי משפט אחד להם ובריאה אחת להם... וא"ר אלעזר כל אדם שיש
בו דעה כאילו נבנה בית המקדש בימיו. וביאור זה כי האדם מתדמה
אל בית המקדש...

They are alike in essence and origin... Anyone who has
de'ah (knowledge), it is as though the Temple were built
in his lifetime. This means that Man is comparable to
the Temple...

While the connection is forged via the word *kedushah*, one
cannot help but see that the Gemara connects knowledge with
construction.

2) The Maharal asks why the ages mentioned in the Mishna are
initially up to 5 year increments and then, beginning with age
20, are in 10 year increments. He answers:

ודבר זה מפני כי האדם נולד בלא שכל לגמרי, וכאשר האדם בן חמש
מתחיל השכל באדם, וזה מפני שעברו חצי עשרה שבו האדם משתנה.
וכאן לא אמרינן שצריך עשרה, מפני כי כל השאר השינויים כאן
החדוש בא מעצמו... ולפיכך צריך אל זה עשרה. אבל מקרא משנה
תלמוד שאין הדבר מגיע מעצמו שצריך לו רב אשר ילמד אותו, אין
צריך להמתין עד עשרה רק עד חמש, כי דל פלגא על המלמד ופלגא
על עצמו, שאפשר ללמד אותו כאשר עבר רוב עשרה דהיינו חמשה
שנים ומיד יכול ללמדו מקרא.

This is on account of the fact that Man is born without
any intelligence and [only] when he reaches 5 years of
age does Man's intelligence commence since this is half
of the decade that is required for human change. Here,
however, it doesn't require a full decade because those
other changes are stimulated internally... and therefore
require a full decade. Mikra, Mishnah and Talmud, however, are not qualities that appear automatically. Because
one needs to acquire a teacher to provide instruction,
there is no need to wait a full decade but only to age
5 — because half [the effort] is assumed by the teacher
and [only] half by oneself — therefore one can be taught
after a major part of the decade, namely five years, has
elapsed and one can immediately thereafter be instructed
in Mikra.

According to MAHARAL, the teacher interacts with the
learner in support of the learning process. By mediating the
learning process, the teacher minimizes the time needed for
the student to gain knowledge and understanding.

3) While the Mishnah appears, superficially, to delineate successive cognitive stages according to a Piagetian model (i.e.,
proceeding from concrete to more abstract), the MAHARAL
interprets it as describing a learning process, hierarchical in
nature, wherein learning drives cognitive development.

ועוד, כי כל אלו שלשה – מקרא, משנה,תלמוד – אינם מחולקים
לגמרי כמו שהם השאר; ומקרא עצמו מועיל למשנה, ומשנה מועיל

לתלמוד, ולפיכך אין החלוק ביניהם עשרה לגמרי כמו שהוא בשאר ...
אף כי היה ראוי שיהיה בן ט"ו למשנה, דהיינו עשרה אחר מקרא,
מכל מקום מועיל המקרא עד שאינו צריך רק חמשה שנים, ומועיל
המשנה שאין צריך רק ה' שנים. ועוד כי אלו שלשה – מקרא, משנה,
תלמוד – אף על גב שמתחיל בחכמה, אין זה חכמה גמורה דהא בן
ארבעים לבינה, רק שיוכל לקבל קצת חכמה, ואין הדבר בשלימות
גמור כמו שהוא אצל השאר שהם בשלימות ...

Furthermore, these three — Mikra, Mishnah and Talmud
— are not separated as the others are. Mikra itself assists
in Mishnah, and Mishnah assists in Talmud, therefore
the intervals between them are not a full decade, as in
the rest... Although it ought to have been Mishnah at 15,
a full decade after Mikra, in any event [the presence] of
Mikra makes [the interval] only five years, and Mishnah
requires only five [additional] years [until Talmud]. In
addition, these three — Mikra, Mishnah and Talmud —
although they presuppose intelligence, do not [require]
complete intelligence since comprehension [*binah*] only
comes at age 40. Rather, they presuppose a modicum of
intelligence but not as complete as is presupposed by the
balance of the list...

According to this interpretation, the Mishnah adopts a constructivist view of learning by identifying the ages at which
individuals may be ready for certain learning processes through
which further individual cognitive development will emerge.
These learning processes, as understood by the MAHARAL,
involve interaction with more competent external sources that
support ("scaffold") and contribute to individual development.
Within a specified span of time, the Mishnah focuses on internal mechanisms such as *ko'ah, binah*, and `*eitzah*. Such inter-
nalization of shared knowledge and speech may well represent
the Vygotskian idea of "private" speech.

B. The Talmud

A key Talmudic passage in this regard is Shabbat 63a:

תלמוד בבלי מסכת שבת דף סג עמוד א

אמר רב כהנא כד הוינא בר תמני סרי שנין והוה גמירנא ליה לכוליה
תלמודא, ולא הוה ידענא דאין מקרא יוצא מידי פשוטו עד השתא.
מאי קא משמע לן – דליגמר איניש, והדר ליסבר.

Rav Kahana said: At the age of eighteen, I knew the entire Talmud [by heart], and I still didn't know that a verse cannot be purged of its literal sense until now! [The Talmud asks:] What lesson should we derive from this? That one should study by heart, but subsequently one should study analytically.

In other words, the "transmission of knowledge" via memorization cannot be viewed as the highest or ultimate goal of education; it may be a necessary first step[8], but it must be followed by the experiential (or constructivist) dimension that involves "making sense" out of whatever one has committed to memory.

---

8. In Berakhot 64a (and Horiyot 14a), the Talmud appears to support the opposite contention:

סיני ועוקר הרים איזה מהם קודם? שלחו להו: סיני קודם, שהכל צריכין למרי חטיא.

Who takes precedence — Sinai (i.e., one who commits the Oral Law to memory), or one who uproots mountains (i.e., analyzes the Oral Law)? The answer was sent from there [i.e., the Land of Israel]: Sinai takes precedence, because all need the grain merchant.

The question was posed — in Babylonia — apropos of the need to choose a dean of the yeshiva among two Amoraim: Rav Yosef, who had a prodigious memory, and Rabba bar Nahmani, who had considerable powers of analysis and argumentation (Rashi: *pilpul*). It is significant that while the reply — from Israel — favored R. Yossi, he was reluctant to accept the position and, in fact, they both served; Rabba for 22 years and R. Yossi but two and a half.

It is noteworthy, nevertheless, that the formula employed to confer on a religious judge the right to adjudicate monetary cases independently, combines both elements: [(ונקיטנא רשותא (מבי ריש גלותא] דגמירנא וסבירנא, i.e., "who has committed [the tradition] to memory and analyzed it [and was sanctioned — by the office of the Exilarch] (Sanhedrin 5a).

Roland Barth: *Learning by Heart* (San Francisco: Wiley, 2001), *passim*., refers to this phenomenon as "information rich and experience poor."

Section 2: Rambam's Approach to Education

As we noted in our introduction, a discrete section of the Mishneh Torah is entitled *Hilkhot Talmud Torah*, effectively: "Laws of Torah Education" (literally, of Teaching Torah)[9]. Within the seven chapters that comprise this section, one paragraph in particular exemplifies Rambam's "constructivist" approach.

רמב"ם הלכות תלמוד תורה פרק א הלכה יא

וחייב לשלש את זמן למידתו, שליש בתורה שבכתב, ושליש בתורה שבעל פה, ושליש יבין וישכיל אחרית דבר מראשיתו ויוציא דבר מדבר וידמה דבר לדבר ויבין במדות שהתורה נדרשת בהן עד שידע היאך הוא עיקר המדות והיאך יוציא האסור והמותר וכיוצא בהן מדברים שלמד מפי השמועה, וענין זה הוא הנקרא גמרא. [הלכה יב...] במה דברים אמורים בתחלת תלמודו של אדם אבל כשיגדיל בחכמה ולא יהא צריך לא ללמוד תורה שבכתב ולא לעסוק תמיד בתורה שבעל פה יקרא בעתים מזומנים תורה שבכתב ודברי השמועה כדי שלא ישכח דבר מדברי דיני תורה ויפנה כל ימיו לגמרא בלבד לפי רוחב שיש בלבו ויישוב דעתו.

[11] One is obligated to divide his study time into thirds: One third to the Written Law; one third to the Oral Law; and one third to rational comprehension via deductive reasoning, inference, comparison and Biblical hermeneutics, in order to understand the essence of the hermeneutic principles and how utilize them in ruling on sanction or prohibition or other such matters that are learned via tradition. This [final third] is known as "Gemara."[10] [12] ... This applies to one's elementary education. When he grows intellectually, however, and has no need either to study the Written Law or to continually

---

9. Whereas the standard editions of the Sefer ha-Mitzvot read in Aseh #11: מצות עשה... ללמוד תורה וללמדה, i.e., to study Torah and to teach it, the Kafih editions — exhibiting a greater fidelity to the Arabic original — read: ללמד תורה וללמדה, i.e., to teach Torah and to study it. Furthermore, the proof text cited as the source of the mitzvah is ושננתם לבניך, which clearly mandates tuition in Torah rather than personal study.
10. Other (and more reliable) editions read here (and elsewhere) "Talmud." On the consequences of this variant, cf. n. 11, below.

deal with the Oral Law, let him read the Written Law
and the Tradition periodically — lest he forget matters of
[explicit] Torah law — and devote all of [the balance of]
his time exclusively to "Gemara" according to his breadth
of comprehension and intelligence.

Rambam's source is the Talmudic statement (Kiddushin 30a):

לעולם ישלש אדם שנותיו, שליש במקרא, שליש במשנה, שליש
בתלמוד.

One should perennially divide his years into three parts:
a third to Scripture, a third to Mishnah, and a third to
Talmud.

Isadore Twersky notes that Rambam here has reversed his
usual practice of abbreviating lengthy Talmudic statements, and
declares this "unusually expansive, almost prolix formulation" to
be "highly problematic," particularly "the nonchalant substitution
of what appears to be a genus [Rambam's "Oral Law"] for a species
[the Talmud's "Mishnah"]."[11]

With all due respect to Twersky's conclusion — which equates
Mishnah with "the authoritative corpus of the entire Oral Law"
— it is our contention that by "Mishnah" Rambam did not understand a text, such as the one compiled by R. Yehudah haNasi,
but the cognitive skill of memorization (*lishnot, hashnayah*) by

---

11. *Visions of Jewish Education* (ed. Seymour Fox; Cambridge, 2004), 53.

The identical incredulity is shared by Ralph Lerner: *Maimonides' Empire of Light*
(Chicago, 2000), 30: "It is remarkable that Maimonides identifies the Oral Law
with the Mishnah, pure and simple. By this means, the two Talmuds appear as
complementary and supplementary *to* the Oral Law rather than as strictly speaking
of it" (emphasis in original).

In a note (n. 1, to p.31), Lerner continues in the same vein: "Maimonides' effort
to draw a bright line between the Oral Law and the Talmud is studied, to say the
least. He insists on calling a part of the Oral Law — i.e., the Mishnah — *the* Oral
Law. He insists on calling a part of the Talmud — i.e., the Gemara — *the* Talmud"
(emphasis in the original).

From this, Lerner derives the following textual conclusion: "Those printed editions of the *Mishneh Torah* in which the word 'Gemara' appears in Sefer ha-Madda`
have no warrant in the surviving manuscript tradition... Needless to say, the Oxford
Codex reprinted by Hyamson, and whose accuracy is attested to by Maimonides
himself in a signed statement, never utters the word 'Gemara.'"

which it was originally transmitted. [12] This is borne out, as well, by his otherwise gratuitous notation that the third part of his tripartite curriculum is known as "Gemara" (in other versions, "Talmud"). Given his description of this segment as comprising "deductive reasoning, inference, comparison…," it cannot be a reference to a "genus" at all, nor to the entire "species;" it depicts a "wish-list" of cognitive desiderata, consistent with constructivist theory. Even memorization (as we have noted, above) is only a preliminary stage, as Rambam himself clarifies in the continuation of the halakhah.

At what point does memorization segue into analysis and comprehension? A Maimonidean answer is delivered by Rambam's distinguished contemporary, Yosef [ben Yehudah ben Yosef] Ibn Aknin (115–1220), [13] in his own systematic work of moral philosophy, *Tibb al-Nufus* (Medicine for the Soul). In a chapter (no.

---

12. This understanding of Rambam was also reached by Josef Stern, "Maimonides on Education," in Amelie O. Rorty (ed.): *Philosophers on Education* (London, 1998), 113:

> The highest object of study is what Maimonides here calls "Talmud," which refers not to a text, or even a body of discussions concerning how to act, but to a general activity: reasoning, drawing consequences, and deduction, whose aim is not, or not only, to know *what* is prohibited and permitted, the appropriate act for each circumstance, but *how to derive* the prohibited and permitted, the very exercise of reasoning that is required for justification or understanding. That is, Maimonides' use of the term "Talmud" now refers to dynamic, discursive contemplation and reasoning.

This conclusion appears to be supported by the Tur and Shulhan Arukh, whose paraphrase of Rambam reads (YD 246:4):

שליש במשנה, דהיינו תורה שבעל פה, ופירושי תורה שבכתב בכלל זה.

i.e., One third Mishnah, that is the Oral Law, including the commentaries on the Written Law.

It also appears to be supported by the Maharal who defines these terms as follows:

ואלו שלשה דברים הם השגות חלוקות. מקרא הוא השגה מה ואין ההשגה בשלימות ובבירור. אבל המשנה היא הידיעה בבירור, והתלמוד הוא להבין טעם הדבר שאינו במשנה כלל. ולפיכך אלו שלשה דברים הם מחולקים.

These three items are partial perceptions. Mikra is a perception, but incomplete and unclear. Mishnah constitutes a clear understanding, and Talmud is the comprehension of reasons that are not cited in the Mishnah at all. That is why these three items are partial.

13. Ibn Aknin was born in Barcelona but — on account of the al-Mohade persecutions — lived from an early age in Fez. There he made the acquaintance of Maimonides, on account of which acquaintance he is often confused with the Yosef ben Yehudah [ben Shim'on] on whose behalf Maimonides compiled the *Guide*.

27) devoted entirely to education, he offers a novel interpretation of the aforementioned Mishnah in Avot (5:21) that appears
to associate the basic books of Jewish studies with the students'
ages. Ibn Aknin, however, identifies the books not with their
texts, per se, but — like the MAHARAL, and as per our claim on
behalf of Rambam — with the cognitive skills required for their
study.

> Then they said: "15 is the age for Talmud," i.e., when they
> reach the age of 15, they should be given recitation les-
> sons in Talmud until they know it fluently (סדור על פה).
> Afterwards, when they reach the age of 18, they should
> be taught it comprehensively: cognitively (תפכר) and
> incisively (בחת').
>
> They said: "18 is the age of חופה" — by which they
> meant reading with comprehension and discovery —
> which means drawing inferences from the sources. They
> made this [recommendation] because prior to this age,
> i.e., 18, memorization is best for them and they are stron-
> ger in it and have more leisure for it than for intellectual
> pursuits. [Moreover,] their intellects are not yet mature;
> indeed they possess a great deficiency during this time.
>
> [Learning with] comprehension was euphemistically
> called חופה because [the conjugal meeting] is the desired
> outcome of marriage. Likewise the goal of recitation is
> comprehension.
>
> When they reach this age, their intellects are up to
> the task of comprehension, as well as to discover ques-
> tions not explicit in the Talmud by means of the received
> principles [of hermeneutics]. They will become proficient
> in it and [the teacher] will accustom them to it so that
> throughout their lives they will neither desist nor abstain
> from it. They will reiterate it frequently until it is clear
> to them and until they understand more of it than they
> understood previously.
>
> They said: "You cannot compare one who reviews his

lessons one hundred times [to one who reviews it] one hundred and one times."[14]

Is there a Maimonidean "Taxonomy"?

Rambam's elaboration (above) on the tripartite division of study can also be interpreted as a graduated taxonomy. When viewed according to the following schematic (guided by didactic transcription), Rambam appears to list six stages of what Bloom et. al. call "cognitive objectives." Indeed, the argument could be made that Rambam's is the prototypical educational taxonomy by which modern taxonomies[15] should be measured.[16]

---

14. *Tibb al-Nufus*: Ms. Oxford 1273; Chapter 27, folio 106r, entitled: "On the Conduct of Teachers and Students." The question of age appropriateness in education was addressed — in the classical era — by Aristotle, who stipulates (*Politics* VII:XVII) that there are two periods of life with reference to which education has to be divided, from seven to the age of puberty, and onwards to the age of one and twenty. Prior to age seven, he prescribes: The next period lasts to the age of five; during this no demand should be made upon the child for study or labor, lest its growth be impeded; and there should be sufficient motion to prevent the limbs from being inactive... When the five years have passed away, during the two following years they must look on at the pursuits which they are hereafter to learn. We are unaware of any attempt to relate Aristotle's "curriculum" to that of the Mishnah, although such a connection is entirely plausible. It is clear, nevertheless, that Ibn Aknin's explanation of the Mishnah adumbrates the Vygotskian idea of "scaffolding" by the facilitating teacher or peer. Indeed, earlier in the same chapter (27; folio 102 r ff.), Ibn Aknin stipulates that a teacher must meet seven (pre-) conditions. Note, in particular, the seventh.

   1. he must be perfectly certain of the subject he seeks to teach...
   2. he practices that which his knowledge mandates...
   3. his instruction must be free, without remuneration...
   4. he treats his students like his children...
   5. he directs them to the upright path and the authentic program (מנאהג')...
   6. he should not be hypercritical or impatient [alt., illiberal], rather he should be patient and generous...
   7. he teaches them according to the capacity of their intellects, gradually, one thing after the other, until he promotes them to the highest level, which is the level of perfection...

15. Benjamin Bloom (et. al.): *Taxonomy of Educational Objectives*, The Classification of Educational Goals (NY, 1956); Anderson, Lorin/ Krathwohl, David: *A Taxonomy for Learning, Teaching and Assessing*, A Revision of Bloom's Taxonomy of Educational Objectives (NY, 2001); Robert J. Marzano: *Designing a New Taxonomy of Educational Objectives* (Thousand Oaks, 2001); Lee S. Shulman: "Making Differences, A Table of Learning, *Change* 34:6 (2002), available at: *http://www.carnegiefoundation.org/elibrary/docs/making_differences.htm*

16. Educators must take into account four major critiques of Bloom's taxonomy that

רמב״ם הלכות תלמוד תורה פרק א הלכה יא

וחייב לשלש את זמן למידתו,

שליש

- בתורה שבכתב,

ושליש

- בתורה שבעל פה,

ושליש

- יבין וישכיל אחרית דבר מראשיתו
- ויוציא דבר מדבר
- וידמה דבר לדבר
- ויבין במדות שהתורה נדרשת בהן

עד שידע

היאך הוא עיקר המדות

והיאך יוציא האסור והמותר וכיוצא בהן מדברים שלמד מפי

השמועה,

ועניין זה הוא הנקרא גמרא.

The cognitive stages, then, are as follows:

---

have been voiced based on 50 years of research in cognitive science.

First, the taxonomy was originally developed (at the time that Bloom was director of the Office of Examinations at the University of Chicago) as a tool of assessment, rather than a heuristic for instruction.

Second, taxonomies (including Bloom, the Mishnah, Rambam, and others cited in the previous note) present their respective cognitive stages as hierarchical in nature, whereas contemporary cognitive scientific research has consistently shown that such processes of thinking are parallel in structure and that knowledge and basic understanding need not precede complex understanding. Indeed, such research has demonstrated that what has been termed "higher-order" thinking skills are merely "high-order," not dependent on lower level cognitive functioning, and, as such, are apparent at very early ages — as young as only a few weeks of age.

Third, Bloom based his taxonomy on the notion that learning is domain-general and that cognitive strengths and weaknesses cut across all subject areas, e.g., someone who has strong reasoning skills in mathematics will necessarily have strong linguistic reasoning abilities. Such thinking forms the basis for "homogeneous" tracking across subject areas in most high school programs. Such thinking, however, is flawed; learning is domain-specific and thus a profile of strengths and weaknesses is most often subject specific.

Finally, unlike Bruner's stipulation that knowledge is a process and not a product, Bloom's taxonomy was based on objectives and consequently lacks the emphasis on process that would drive cognitive development, such as the case is with constructivist views.

1. תורה שבכתב (written torah), corresponding to *knowledge* — the acquisition, identification or recollection of data;

2. תורה שבעל פה (oral torah), corresponding to *comprehension* — understanding the meaning of the data and repeating it in one's own words;

3. יבין וישכיל דבר אחרית דבר מראשיתו (drawing conclusions), corresponding to *application* — using the data in a new context;

4. ויוציא דבר מדבר (inference), corresponding to *analysis* — breaking down the data into its components to understand its structure;

5. וידמה דבר לדבר (comparison), corresponding to *synthesis* — putting together old and partial knowledge in new ways, forming new wholes;

6. (hermeneutics), corresponding to *evaluation* — judging the value of methods and materials for a distinct purpose, based upon knowledge.

Rambam's proviso can be construed from a "Paideia" perspective as well:

- תורה שבכתב and תורה שבעל פה would comprise the "acquisition of organized knowledge;"

- יבין וישכיל – ויוציא־וידמה constitute the "development of intellectual skills — skills of learning;" and, finally:

- עיקר המדות and האסור והמותר correspond to the "enlarged understanding of ideas and values."[17]

Section 3: Rashi's Approach to Education

Constuctivism, as opposed to "objectivism," eschews the mere delivery and retrieval of facts and information, advocating in its stead the incremental — and experiential! — formation of

---

17. Mortimer Adler: *The Paideia Proposal; An Educational Manifesto* (NY: Collier, 1982), 23. Also cf. Philip Lewin: "Constructivism and Paideia," in *Radical Constructivism in Action* — Building on the Pioneering Work of Ernst von Glasersfeld, eds. Leslie P. Steffe, Patrick W. Thompson (Taylor & Francis, 2000).

understanding. The following exegetical passage makes Rashi's constructivist approach to education emphatically clear.

רש"י שמות פרק כא פסוק א

אשר תשים לפניהם – אמר לו הקב"ה למשה לא תעלה על דעתך
לומר אשנה להם הפרק וההלכה ב' או ג' פעמים עד שתהא סדורה
בפיהם כמשנתה, ואיני מטריח עצמי להבינם טעמי הדבר ופירושו,
לכך נאמר אשר תשים לפניהם, כשלחן הערוך ומוכן לאכול לפני
האדם:

"[These are the statutes] that you shall place before them:" God said to Moshe: Do not imagine that you can just recite the law to them two or three times until they know it by heart — without troubling yourself to explain it to them!. Therefore does it say, "…that you shall place before them," as a table that is set before a person and is ready for him to eat.

While this passage is not original to Rashi[18], his utilization of it indicates that he subscribed to the principle that comprehensive analysis enjoys priority over rote memorization — a view shared by the Talmud (Shabbat 63a), as noted above. Indeed, just like a host sets a table for the guest to facilitate eating but does not actually eat for the guest, so too a teacher sets forth the tools necessary for learning without learning the material for the student. Even if the teacher wanted to learn the material for the student, it is impossible according to the constructivist view, which requires active engagement and interaction between student and teacher for student learning to occur.

Two additional passages in Rashi's Bible commentary provide significant insight into his view of education.

1. In Genesis 14:14, he explains the word *hanikhav* [OJPS: trained men; NJPS: retainers as follows:

---

18. It appears in the Mekhilta, Mishpatim I; however — it is keyed there to a different verse (Dt. 31:19): "…place it [the song — identified by the Talmud with the corpus of the Torah] in their mouths." Curiously, Rashi offers no commentary there at all.

רש"י בראשית פרק יד פסוק יד

חניכיו – חנכו כתיב זה אליעזר שחנכו למצות והוא לשון התחלת
כניסת האדם או כלי לאומנות שהוא עתיד לעמוד בה, וכן (משלי כב
ו) חנוך לנער, (במדבר ז יא) חנכת המזבח, (תהלים ל א) חנכת הבית
ובלע"ז קורין לו איניציי"ר [לחנוך]:

The [defective, grammatically singular] spelling **hnkw**
refers to Eliezer, who was trained to perform mitzvoth.
[**hnk**] indicates the introduction of a person or a utensil
into a profession in which he/it is expected to persevere.
So **hnk ln'r** (Proverbs 22:6), **hnkt hmzbh** (Numbers
7:11), **hnkt hbyt** (Psalms 30:1). Colloquially, this process
is designated as "**initier**" (to initiate; alt: "**enseigner**," to
instruct).

2. In commenting on the construction of the Mishkan (tabernacle), Rashi explains the figure of speech "to fill the hands"
(Exodus 28:41) as follows:

רש"י שמות פרק כח פסוק מא

ומלאת את ידם – כל מלוי ידים לשון חנוך, כשהוא נכנס לדבר להיות
מוחזק בו מאותו יום והלאה הוא מלוי, ובלשון לעז כשממנין אדם
על פקידת דבר, נותן השליט בידו בית יד של עור שקורין גנ"ט בלעז
[כפפה], ועל ידו הוא מחזיקו בדבר, וקורין לאותו מסירה ריוישטי"ר
בלעז [להסמיך] והוא מלוי ידים:

"You shall fill their hands:" Every instance of "filling the
hands" means training [**hnwk**]. Introducing one into
something in which one is to become well-established
from that day on, is called "filling." When someone is
given an appointment, the sovereign places a leather
glove — called, colloquially, "**gant**" — in his hand as a
sign of his tenure. That presentation is colloquially designated "**revister**" (to invest), and that is "filling the hands."

The "investiture" Rashi describes, wherein the student (or appren-
tice) is provided with the means and opportunity for his advancement and then left to his own devices, captures the essence of
yet another constructivist principle, namely the designation of

the instructor as a "guide on the side," rather than a "sage on the stage."

Rashi's constructivist orientation is also illustrated by the following passage from a responsum he wrote to his son-in-law, R. Meir b. Shmuel.

שו"ת רש"י סימן נט

אני שלמה אהובך מודיעך כי לא חזרתי בי ולא אחזור בי, ולא נתיישבו לי דברי רבותי, ולא השיבו על דברי כי אם מן השפה ולחוץ, ועדיין אני מוסרם לצנועים: ואם לא מפני הצרה הגדולה אשר הורעה בינותנו, הייתי שונה להם אע"פ שלא ישמעו. ואמנם אני נתלה באילן גדול רבי' יעקב בר' יקר. ואף כי לא שמעתי מפיו דבר זה, מ"מ לבי וסברתי והבנתי מפיו יצאו. ואף הם לא מפי השמועה, ואף לא מראיות התלמוד, כי אם מהבנת לבם. ולו ישיבוני דברים הנראים ואשובה לי. אבל קשה לי לאבד ממונם של ישראל על דבר זה הברור והראוי מכמה ראיות להתיר עכ"ל.

I, Shelomo, your beloved, inform you that I have not recanted and will not recant. The words of my teachers are not clear to me; they have responded to my arguments only superficially and still I will reveal them only to those who will respect their privacy. Were it not for the great tragedy that has befallen us, I would repeat myself to them even if they would not listen.

I am relying upon the great sage, R. Yaakov b. Yakar. Despite the fact that I never heard this from him personally, in any case my inclination, my reasoning and my comprehension emanate from him.

They [my opponents] too are not arguing from either tradition or the Talmudic text but from their own understanding. If they would only respond to me appropriately, I might reconsider, but it is difficult for me to cause Jews to suffer monetary loss in a case such as this for which there are several appropriate reasons to issue a sanction.

Had Rashi subscribed to the same educational philosophy as his challengers, he would have been constrained, as they appear to have been, to deciding questions of law entirely on the basis of precedent. By basing himself not on an actual ruling **transmitted** by his teacher, R. Yakov b. Yakar, but on the "inclination, reasoning and comprehension" that he had **constructed** based upon his earlier studies with R. Yaakov, Rashi was able to stake a legitimate claim to a position that was no less authoritative in spite of the fact that it had no explicit precedent.

The purpose of learning is for an individual to construct his or her own meaning, not just memorize the "right" answers and regurgitate someone else's meaning.[19]

Section 4: RADAK and Education

Upon the publication of the conference schedule, it appeared that several of the participants had extended their mandates to include Radak along with Rashi and Rambam. For our purposes, it would be difficult to find a more suitable protagonist than Rabbi David Kimhi (Provence, 1160–1235) who earned his living as an educator.[20]

---

19. Jacqueline and Martin Brooks: *In Search of Understanding; The Case for Constructivist Classrooms* (Alexandria VA, 1999).

While we have seen several examples of Rashi's constructivist views towards education, when it comes to language development, Rashi appears to advocate the position that aspects of human language are innate.

רש״י בראשית פרק ב פסוק ז

לנפש חיה – אף בהמה וחיה נקראו נפש חיה, אך זו של אדם חיה שבכולן, שנתוסף בו דעה ודבור:

Animals and beasts were also designated "living souls," but man the liveliest of them all since he was also granted cognition and speech.

In contrast to this Chomskian and Pinkerian innate language system view, the Rashba in his first comment on the Gemara in Nedarim (כל אומה ולשון...) discusses how each language is a construct of the culture and nation in which it is spoken. Further support for the notion that there is a strong cultural and socially constructed element to language (as in a Vygotskian view) is the Gemara in Sanhedrin 70b (also Berachot 40a) and the Sifre — Devarim 46:19.

20. See his poetic epilogue to Sefer ha-Shorashim (ed. Biesenthal, Lebrecht, Berlin 1847 [Jerusalem, 1967], 420):

ועד הנה עזרני ל'באר כל סתום, לפתח כל חתום, לגלות כל נסתר בתורתנו ובספרי נביאנו וחכמינו, על פי אשר השיגה יד מחשבתי, באשר ה' אתי... ועוד כי כל ימי התעסקי בו, רוב מלאכתי היה בלימוד הנערים בתלמוד...

Cf. Frank Ephraim Talmage: *David Kimhi; the Man and the Commentaries* (Cambridge, 1975), 14 ff.

1. In his Biblical dictionary (Sefer ha-Shorashim), his definition
   of the verb חנ״ך is highly reminiscent of Rashi:

   חנך לנער על פי דרכו, התחיל ללמדהו מקטנותו על דרכו, כלומר:
   מעט מעט, שיוכל לסבול. וכן בדברי רבותינו ז"ל (חגיגה ד ע"א):
   משהגיע לחינוך מצוה, כלומר התחלת חיוב ועו[ו]ל המצוה. וכן אמרו
   (יומא פב ע"א): אבל מחנכין אותן לשעות, כלומר מתחילין להם
   ומרגילין אותן להתענות מעט מעט.

   Instruct a youngster according to his way (Proverbs 22:6),
   begin to teach him from his childhood according to his
   way, i.e., a bit at a time, so that he can bear it. Similarly
   in the words of our Sages: "When he reaches [the age] to
   be educated in mitzvot," i.e., the commencement of his
   obligation to bear the [yoke] of mitzvot. And so: "He is
   educated for hours," i.e., they are initiated and habituated
   to fast a bit at a time.[21]

2. In his commentary on Isaiah 28:29, however, Radak launches
   into an extensive description of the educational process striking, again, a clear constructionist note.

   This also cometh forth from   גַּם־זֹאת, מֵעִם ה׳ צְבָאוֹת יָצָאָה:
   the LORD of hosts:
   Wonderful is His counsel,   הִפְלִיא עֵצָה, הִגְדִּיל תּוּשִׁיָּה.
   and great His wisdom.

   Radak explains the verse within the explicit agricultural context (plowing, sowing, wheat, barley, spelt, cumin, etc.) as a
   parable of education.

---

21. *Op. cit.*, 111. There is a good deal to be said, as well (but not here), about the employ-
    ment of the term "habit" (**hergel**) by all three of the protagonists we have chosen, as
    well as other medieval authors — Muslim as well as Jewish! On the role of habit in
    character education, in particular, see John Dewey: "Human Nature and Conduct,"
    in *The Middle Works of John Dewey*, 1899–1924, vol. 14, ed. Jo Ann Boydston
    (Carbondale: Southern Illinois University Press, 1988).

    All habits are demands for certain kinds of activity; and they constitute the
    self. In any intelligible sense of the word will, they are will. They form our
    effective desires and they furnish us with our working capacities. They rule
    our thoughts, determining which shall appear and be strong and which
    shall pass from light into obscurity (21).

ועתה נפרש המשל: החורש הוא האל יתברך והאדמה הוא ישראל. וכמו שהחורש יתקן האדמה כדי שתהיה נכונה לקבל הזרע, כן האל יתברך תקן ענין ישראל כדי שיהיו נכונים לקבל דבריו...

Now we shall explain the parable. The plowman is God and the earth is [the people of] Israel. Just as the plowman prepares the earth to receive the seed, so did God prepare Israel to receive His words.

The preparation, he explicates, consisted of the exodus from Egypt, the drowning of the Egyptians, the leadership of Moshe [and subsequent prophets] and the manifold miracles that accompanied the crossing of the wilderness and the conquest of their land.

ואחר תקון האדמה, התחיל לזרוע בה והוריד שכינתו לעיניהם בהר סיני בקולות וברקים ולפידים, והשמיע להם דבריו, עד שכולם היו במדרגת נביאים. אבל לא היו כולם שוים.

After the ground was prepared, He commenced to sow it. He manifested His presence before their very eyes on Mount Sinai within thunder, lightning and torches, and broadcast His words to them until they were all on the level of prophets, albeit not equally so.

He next proceeds to compare the different stages of prophetic understanding to the various grains cited in the text, with those that produce a finer flour representing the higher stages and vice versa.

And, finally:

וכמו שהזורע מקוה בזרעו שתוציא לו האדמ' מגרגיר א' כמה גרגירים, כן קוה האל מישראל שיוסיפו על מה שהורם, וישכילו ויבינו דבר מתוך דבר. כי כמו שטבע האדמה להוציא יותר על מה שנזרע בה כן טבע האדם להוציא יותר בכח הנפש המשכלת שנתנה בו, להוסיף על מה שילמדוהו. וכן אמר שלמה, תן לחכם ויחכם עוד, וגומר.

Just as the one who sows anticipates in sowing that one seed will produce several seeds, so God anticipated that Israel would add to that which He instructed them

through inferential reasoning. Just as it is the nature of
the earth to produce more than was actually planted in
it, so it is human nature to produce more — by dint of its
inherent (?) rational faculties — in excess of that which
he was taught. So did Shelomo declare: "Enable the wise
man and he will grow wiser yet."[22]

3. In his commentary on Isaiah 28:10, however, Radak explicitly
   compares education to a builder's use of a plumb-line!

For it is precept by precept, precept	כִּי צַו לָצָו צַו לָצָו,
by precept, line by line, line by line;	קַו לָקָו קַו לָקָו –
here a little, there a little.	זְעֵיר שָׁם, זְעֵיר שָׁם.

כי צו לצו – צו הוא שם, כמו מצוה, ולא נאמרה המצוה בזה הלשון
במקום אחר, ורוצה בו באמרו צו מצוה קטנה. אמר כי הם כמו
הנערים ולנערים יצוה אדם אותם מעט מעט, וילמדם כדי שיקבלו,
כי אין להם לב לקבל אלא דברים מעטי'.

Precept [*tzav*] is a noun, like commandment [*mitzvah*] —
but nowhere else is it so denominated — and it refers to a
minor commandment. The [prophet] compares them to
young men to whom one gives instructions gradually so
they will receive them, because they lack the intelligence
to receive more than a few instructions [at a time?].

וכן פי' קו לקו. והקו הוא קו הבנין והבנאי מטה אותו עד שיעשה
אותו טור אחד, ואח"כ יסלקהו ויטהו לעשות טור אחר. וכן יעשה
מעט מעט עד שישלי' הקיר.

We interpret, similarly, "line by line." The "line" refers
to the builder's [plumb] line, which he stretches out to
draw a row, after which he removes it and uses it to draw
another row, gradually completing the entire wall.

וכן הוא הלמוד וההרגל לנערים. וכן צריך שילמד הנביא לעם הזה, כי

---

22. Radak concludes this passage by comparing the activities of the prophets to those
    of the rain, as it nurtures growth, and to the processes by which the various grains
    and spices are ground or beaten into their final products.

הם מעטי הבינה. ועוד כי הם נלאים לשמוע דבר ה', בעבור שאינם
חפצים בו.

Such is the instruction and habituation [*hergel*] of young
men, and so was the prophet advised to instruct the
people who lacked insight. Moreover, they were unwill-
ing to obey the word of God because they disdained it.

ואחר שאמר צו לצו קו לקו וכפלם לחזק הענין. ואמר זעיר שם זעיר
שם, כלומר יאמר להם מעט בדבר זה ומעט בדבר זה. ואע"פ כן אינם
מקבלים.

After he said: "precept to precept, line to line" — which
he repeated for emphasis — he said: "here a little there
a little," meaning that he spoke to them a bit about this
and a bit about that and they nevertheless declined it.[23]

Addendum

It would be a display of ingratitude towards a particularly atten-
tive and appreciative audience if we were to ignore the helpful
observations they made on our presentation. While we would
have liked to respond to each and every one, we will make due
here with those that referred us to additional citations in Rambam
that bear upon the educational issues we have raised.

1. Rambam, Commentary on the Mishnah: Hagigah 2:1.
    The Mishnah stipulates:

אין דורשין בעריות בשלושה, ולא במעשה בראשית בשניים; ולא
במרכבה ביחיד, אלא אם כן היה חכם ומבין מדעתו.

One may not expound on [laws if] incest in the company
of [only] three, nor of the act of creation in [the company
of] two, nor the [divine] "chariot" with a [solitary] indi-

---

23. In his commentary on Isaiah 28:29 and Proverbs 3:13, Radak launches into an exten-
    sive description of the role of the teacher in the educational process striking, again,
    a clear constructivist tone. Cf. Talmage, *op. cit.*, 15, citing a manuscript source.

vidual — unless he was a scholar and able to comprehend independently.

In his commentary on this Mishnah, Rambam defines חכם ומבין מדעתו as follows:

והוא שיתעורר מעצמו ויבין הכוונה מעצמו, ולא יהיה צריך לפירוש,
אלא שרומזין לו הרמזים, והוא סובר בהן סברתו ושקול דעתו. וזה
עניין אומרם מסרים לו ראשי פרקים, לפי שיש שם עניינים הרבה
יתצירו בנפשות השלמים מבני אדם, ואם פירש אותם אדם בלשונו,
ודמם בדמיונות, יתקשו ויצאו מן הכוונה.

This means that [the solitary scholar] can apperceive the intention independently and autonomously without requiring a commentary, rather he [only] receives hints to which he applies his own critical thinking and rationale. This is what [the Sages] meant when they stipulated (BT Hagigah 13a) that: "one may provide him with a general outline," because there are many things that can be imagined by the perfect souls among men but which if put to words or figures (symbols?) will become complicated and diverge from their [original] intent.

2. Rambam Mishneh Torah, Laws of the Fundaments of Torah 4:13:

וענייני ארבעה פרקים אלו שבחמש מצוות האלו – הם שחכמים
הראשונים קוראין אותן פרדס, כמו שאמרו ארבעה נכנסו לפרדס:
ואף על פי שגדולי ישראל היו וחכמים גדולים היו, לא כולם היה בהן
כוח לידע ולהשיג כל הדברים על בורייין.

The details [described in] these four chapters concerning these five mitzvoth, are what the early Sages called "pardes," as in: "four entered the pardes." In spite of the fact that they were great men of Israel and great scholars, not every one of them had the strength to understand and comprehend everything exactly.

PART 3

11.

The Weight of Midrash on Rashi and Maimonides[1]

Alfred L. Ivry

This paper will survey the use Rashi and Maimonides made of midrashic sources, with which they were fully familiar. I do not mean to imply by the title of my talk that either of them was weighed down by midrashic sources; on the contrary, both made highly creative — and selective — use of them. The midrashim chosen added an intriguing and entertaining dimension to their writing, revealing the messenger as well as the midrashic message. Yet there is a significant difference in the conception of and purpose to which each person employed midrash, and this article will attempt to explore that difference and determine the weight it gave to their respective work.

Rashi's utilization of midrash has been well studied in the academy, and the work of such scholars as Isaac Avineri,[2] Sarah Kamin,[3] Avraham Grossman[4] and others, have added greatly to our appreciation of his work.

In contrast, relatively little scholarship has been devoted to Maimonides' use of Midrash, though the impressive studies of

---

1. Dedicated to the loving memory of my grandfather, Israel Isaac Ivri, z"l. He introduced me as a child to Rashi's use of midrash, and quoted Rashi often in עברי ילקוט (Shulsinger Bros., New York, 1938), his own commentary of biblical and Talmudic passages. I also wish to thank Ephraim Kanarfogel, Eric Lawee and Shai Cherry for sharing their knowledge of this subject with me.
2. Cf. his היכל רש"י, Mosad Harav Kook, Jerusalem, 1979.
3. Cf. her רש"י – פשוטו של מקרא ומדרשו של מקרא, Magnes Publishing, Jerusalem, 1986.
4. Cf. Grossman's survey of the critical literature on Rashi and evaluation of Rashi's work, in "The School of Literal Jewish Exegesis in Northern France," in *Hebrew Bible/ Old Testament: the History of Its Interpretation*, ed. Magne Sæbø (Vandenhoeck & Ruprecht, Göttingen, 1996), pp. 321–22, 332–346.

Sara Klein-Braslavy and James Diamond have done much to repair that omission.[5]

Of course, both men, and Rashi in particular, do not belong to scholars only. Rashi's Torah commentary, which is steeped in Midrash, continues, in traditional circles, to be consulted avidly when studying the weekly reading. Through Rashi, midrash has shaped the Jewish understanding of that most sacred text. Indeed, the "Pentateuch" may be distinguished from the *ḥumash* precisely by Rashi's general absence in the former, and presence — whether explicit or implicit — in the latter.

So widely revered is Rashi that legends have arisen testifying to his greatness. We learn, for example, that Abraham was reluctant to remove Isaac from the Akedah altar until God promised him that Rashi would come along one day. This is hinted at, it is suggested, in the promise to Abraham that "your descendents will inherit the gate of their enemies," (וירש זרעך את שער אויביו), where the letters of וירש are metastatically equated with ורשׁי.[6]

Another story has it that Rashi sat as a penitent (ישב בתענית) 613 days to purify himself for the task of commenting on the Torah. When he completed his work, Moses appeared and congratulated him, saying כי דברי התורה את להבין זכית אתה שרק ,בני אשריך הגבורה מפי קיבלתי כך בבאורך: "Joy to you, my son, for you only have been privileged to understand the words of Torah, for your commentary is just as I received it from the mouth of the Almighty."

This last story captures the traditional sentiment among Jews referred to above, that the five books of Moses are somehow incomplete without Rashi, that the real *ḥumash* is a *ḥumash* with Rashi, the two forever twinned. This, of course, is an extension of

---

5. Cf. Diamond's *Maimonides and the Hermeutics of Concealment: Deciphering Scripture and Midrash in* The Guide of the Perplexed, SUNY Press, Albany, 2002. See now Klein-Braslavy's survey of Maimonides' use of midrash, in her entry on "Bible commentary" in *The Cambridge Companion to Maimonides*, ed. Kenneth Seeskin (Cambridge University Press, New York, 2005), pp. 259–68. Cf. also the midrashically attuned philosophical analyses of Josef Stern, *Problems and Parables of Law*, SUNY Press, Albany, 1998.

6. Avineri, I:22.

the traditional Jewish coupling of the Oral with the Written Law, for so much of Rashi is a repository of the earlier rabbinic legacy.

Yet, for all the admiration, and even adulation of Rashi, there is much in his work that teases scholars.[7] He claims frequently that he wishes to promote the plain, literal sense of Scripture, פשוטו של מקרא, but often he transmits midrashim that are the opposite of that, more in keeping with what we understand as *derash*, homiletical expansions of the text. It is these *derushim*, mostly taken from the midrashic corpus, that expand the imaginative parameters of the text and unlock possible moral and theological entailments.

Rashi often offers multiple, alternative midrashic explanations of a passage. He will, on occasion, reject all the midrashim to a given verse, and suggest that one is "most fitting." His criterion for that, however, is not always clear. Take, for example, the first time he explains his supposed, or rather desired methodology, in his comment on Genesis 3:8, where Adam and Eve are said to hear the voice of the Lord walking in the garden, וישמעו את קול ה' אלקים מתהלך בגן.

To this, Rashi first comments that "there are many midrashei aggadah which the rabbis have arranged in their place in Bereshit Rabbah and in other midrashim,[8] and I have come only to champion the plain meaning of the Scriptures and the aggadah that resolves biblical passages in a fitting manner": ואני לא באתי אלא לפשוטו של מקרא ולאגדה המישבת דברי המקרא, דבר דבור על אפניו.

As scholars have noted,[9] the phrase דבר דבור על אפניו, rendered as "in a fitting manner," is used elsewhere by Rashi in reference to grammar and syntax, issues of linguistics, the area in which Rashi exhibits the greatest originality in his commentary on the Ḥumash. This appears to be the case in our passage, for the

---

7. Grossman, p. 335.
8. Cf. Moshe Aryeh Mirkin's edition of Bere'shit Rabbah, published in his multi-volume *Midrash Rabbah*, Yavneh Publishing, Tel Aviv, third edition, 1977. Mirkin cites Rashi's use of particular midrashim as they appear within the totality of sources on a given passage, affording an appreciation of the choices which Rashi faced.
9. Grossman, p. 335.

next comment Rashi offers is an explanation of the apparent awkwardness of the sentence, in which the subject that is heard walking in the Garden would seem to be God's voice: וישמעו את קול ה' אלוקים מתהלך בגן.

Rashi clarifies this by simply adding one word (two in English), making it clear that it was God walking in the garden, not merely his disembodied voice: מה שמעו? שמעו את קול הקדוש ברוך הוא שהיה מתהלך בגן. "What did they hear? They heard the voice of the Holy One, blessed be He, *who was* walking in the garden."[10]

Interestingly, Rashi is not troubled by the anthropomorphism involved in the notion of a divine walk, though presumably his theological sensibilities are offended by the thought of a *voice* walking. If Rashi has a clear conception of the limits of possible construals of God's being (beyond the axiom of divine oneness, however understood), he does not spell it out.

Another place where Rashi explains his methodology is in his introduction to Canticles. He begins by quoting Psalm 62:12, "One thing God has spoken, two things have I heard" (אחת דבר אלוהים שתים זו שמעתי); and proceeds to endorse two Talmudic principles of biblical hermeneutics: (a) that a single verse can yield many meanings; and (b) that the exegesis of a Scriptural passage must not deviate from its plain meaning.[11]

Despite the excellence of the midrashic corpus, it needs organizing, he claims. He will seize the meaning of Scripture, משמעות המקרא, and order the midrashim accordingly. It is clear, however, that he does not have linguistic criteria in mind here. As we read, Canticles is for him, as for the Rabbis, a love song and lament between God and the people of Israel.

So, too, his commentary to Canticles 2:7, in which, following the program he outlines in the introduction to his commentary,

---

10. The additional (masculine) verb שהיה, literally "who" or "that was," would have been understood by Rashi's readers to refer to God, though the noun קול, voice, is also masculine. Thus, the emendation may affect the desired emphasis upon the true subject of the sentence, but does not change matters gramatically.

11. מקרא אחד יוצא לכמה טעמים וסוף דבר אין לך מקרא יוצא מידי פשוטו ומשמעו. Cf. Nahum Sarna, "Rashi the Commentator," *Studies in Biblical Interpretation* (Jewish Publication Society, 2000), p. 133.

he relates the verse to not awaken love until it so wishes[12] to Jewish history, from the exodus to the destruction of the second temple.

Here and elsewhere, Rashi is far from being a plain and straightforward exegete of Scripture, or a grammarian. As has been argued by Elazar Touitou, it is likely that portions of his commentary relate, albeit elliptically, to the socio-political and historical situation of European Jewry in his day. Towards the end of the eleventh century, historians tell us, a new Europe began to emerge in Christendom, with greater vitality and ambitions of both a political and intellectual/religious sort.[13] An energized church expressed itself in both the Crusades and in works of theology and biblical commentary, which tended towards literal interpretations. Rashi may well be responding to these developments, his commentary informed to a degree by the historical and theological challenges posed by Christianity.

Touitou identifies in Rashi's commentary on Genesis chapters 1–6 a number of then contemporary issues, including the conquest of Jerusalem by the Crusaders; an argument opposing the identification of the "spirit of God that hovered over the waters" with the Third Person of the Trinity; and the rejection of the doctrine of Original Sin.[14]

Rashi's commentary on Genesis 1:1 is indeed patently political. He explains that the Torah begins with the creation of the world, rather than with the first commandment that God issued to Israel, found in Exodus 12:2, because God wished to make the point that the whole world belongs to Him, and if He chose to give the land of Canaan to the people of Israel, He — and therefore they — had a right to it.

This explanation of the opening verse of Genesis is but one of many in the midrash,[15] and Rashi's choice may well be motivated by political as well as theological challenges to the legitimacy of

---

12. ‫אם תעירו ואם תעוררו את האהבה עד שתחפץ‬.

13. Elazar Touitou, "Rashi's Commentary on Genesis 1–6 in the Context of Judeo-Christian Controversy," *HUCA* 61, 1990, p. 160.

14. Touitou, pp.171–183.

15. Cf. *Bereshit Rabbah* I, ed. Mirkin, p. 4, paragraph 2.

Judaism's claims upon the Holy Land (a subject not foreign to us today as well). It is interesting to note, however, that Rashi interrogates the midrash by saying also that the Torah ought to have begun with the laws of Exodus, and not with the creation epic. Apparently, for him creation is not a Jewish issue, at least not uniquely so, and thus ideally it ought not be the initial concern of Torah.

This position brings us sharply to Maimonides, who would have objected strongly to it. He thought the subject of the creation of the world was not only one that should concern Jews, it was crucial for their faith. The topic forms the centerpiece of his arguments against the doctrine of the eternity of the world, as formulated by philosophers.[16] Moreover, he links the belief in creation to the belief in revelation, so that the belief in Torah is dependent upon belief in creation, or so it would seem (*Guide* II:25–31).

Maimonides refers to the opening chapter of Genesis in various places in the *Guide*, adapting it to the cosmological premises of Aristotelian physics and metaphysics[17]; for after the first moment of creation, and especially after the first six days of creation (*Guide* II:29), the world goes its essentially Aristotelian course for all eternity. It is critical for Maimonides that his readers realize that this is part of God's will, making the study of metaphysics truly a divine science.

Rashi's faith is not confronted with these complex challenges, for all his awareness of contemporary issues and themes in the larger Christian culture. Yet, he does not have to answer to perplexed students or sophisticated *mutukallimûn* and *falâsifa*, his responses to Christianity are reaffirmations in their own terms of classical rabbinic beliefs, not translated into the terms of a systematic theology. He remains conceptually within the world of Bible and Talmud, with full access to both מדרשי הלכה and מדרשי

16. Cf. Moses Maimonides, *The Guide of the Perplexed*, trans. Shlomo Pines (The University of Chicago Press, Chicago, 1963), II:13–24, pp. 281–327. Page citations of the *Guide* will be to Pines' translation.

17. *Guide* II:17, II:30, and *passim*.

אגדה. His commentaries come to affirm that world, to enhance and vivify it. Aggadot are taken at what appears to be face value, unquestioned and uninterpreted, once selected; his interrogation of them lay in the choices he made. Rashi's world is still a place of unlimited possibilities and miracles. The Torah, in its written and oral tradition, is God's gift to His people, to be studied in reverence and, with the aid of midrash, delight.

Maimonides is equally reverential towards the Torah and classical rabbinic tradition, though lacking the gentle and playful spirit of Rashi. He has a developed theory of language and epistemology however, which Rashi lacks; a theory in which midrash is contextualized according to Maimonides' philosophical guidelines.

In the very beginning of his introduction to the first part of the *Guide of the Perplexed*, Maimonides sets out to disabuse his readers of what he regards as a simplistic literal reading of Scripture. Generally speaking, he says that linguistic terms have various meanings, some equivocal, others derivative or amphibolous. Going beyond individual words, however, lie complete parables the internal or esoteric meaning of which must be appreciated, lest a person becomes confused or perplexed.

Disabusing persons of their customary understanding of Scripture is a thankless task, Maimonides comments, exposing the would-be benefactor of his people to rebuke (and harm, possibly).[18] It is therefore incumbent upon the wise teacher to offer his interpretations of Scripture discreetly, not in a comprehensive, explicit manner. This practical consideration is buttressed by the authority of religious tradition itself, that forbids one from divulging the secrets of מעשה בראשית and מעשה מרכבה, which Maimonides understands as physics and metaphysics, to all but a very select few.[19]

---

18. A version of portions of this article, referring to Maimonides' use of Midrash, has appeared in a Festschrift to Haggai Ben Shammai, *A Word Fitly Spoken*, (Hebrew), ed. Meir M. Bar-Asher, et al (Ben-Zvi Institute, Jerusalem, 2007), pp. 7–17.
19. *Guide*, Introduction, Pines trans., pp.5–7. This position amounts to a retreat from Maimonides' earlier intention, as stated in his Mishnah Commentary, to collect and

While this statement, in BT Hagigah (11b, 13a), is of rabbinic provenance, Maimonides sees it as the prophets' own guiding principle, leading them to disguise their metaphysical teachings in parables and riddles, establishing thereby a precedent that was then followed by the rabbis. These necessarily secret truths are amenable to parables also because of their intrinsic difficulty, which makes discursive analysis difficult if not impossible. This causes the parables themselves to be obscure often, their composition varied in nature. Yet this is the only way to convey these truths, Maimonides affirms, saying that "the situation is such that the exposition of one who wishes to teach without recourse to parables and riddles is so obscure and brief as to make obscurity and brevity serve in place of parables and riddles."[20]

Maimonides submits the biblical account of creation as a first and prime example of the method of parabolic and enigmatic speech. He brings a midrashic prooftext, his first in the *Guide*, to bear on this: להגיד כח מעשה בראשית לבשר ודם אי אפשר. לפיכך סתם לך הכתוב בראשית ברא אלהים וכו'.[21] As Shlomo Pines translates, "As the sages, may their memory be blessed, have said: It is impossible to tell mortals of the power of the Account of the Beginning. For this reason Scripture tells you obscurely (סתם לך הכתוב): In the beginning God created, and so on."

Maimonides is consumed in the *Guide* with explaining what he views as the parabolic, allegorical nature of prophetic speech and the equivocal, multiple meaning of Scriptural terms. The purported statement of King Solomon in Proverbs 1:6 is quoted,

---

explain the meanings of talmudic derashot, i.e., reveal their esoteric dimensions. Cf. משנה עם פירוש רבנו משה בן מימון, סדר נזיקין, ed. and trans. Joseph Kafah (Jerusalem, 1964), p. 209.

20. *Guide*, p. 8. Pines regularly renders as "parable" that which Maimonides presents as תמויל (Hebrew משל, though Shmuel Ibn Tibbon prefers המשל). Cf. for the Arabic here and elsewhere, Salomon Munk, ed. דלאלה' אלחאירין (in the further edition of I. Joel, Jerusalem, 1929), 4:27 (citing page and line). This term is generally translated by Munk himself as allegory (I:13). Cf. Munk's translation, *Le guide des égarés* (1856–66, translation reprint, 1960), vol. I, p. 13.

21. *Batei Midrashoth, Midrash Shenei Ketubim*, as given by Pines, p. 9, n. 19; Michael Schwarz, trans. מורה נבוכים (Tel Aviv, 2002) I:14, n. 41, offers full bibliography and statement in full.

that his work is intended להבין משל ומליצה, דברי חכמים וחידותם, "to understand משל and מליצה (Maimonides probably taking this as parable and rhetorical figure), the words of the wise and their riddles."[22]

Maimonides follows this with his second citation from midrashic literature, that of the midrash on Canticles 1:1, in which King Solomon is praised for his skill in creating parables, facilitating thereby understanding of the Torah. This is itself worded parabolically, Solomon fashioning a rope (of parables) by which to draw the water of Torah from a deep well. The water Maimonides drinks, however, is scientifically filtered.

Maimonides is clearly taken with the style of midrashic commentary. He introduces the reader to two kinds of prophetic parables (or allegories), one in which each word has meaning, another in which the parable has to be taken as a whole, without demanding interpretation of each word. For most parables, he says, the latter is the case. "In some matters it will suffice you to gather from my remarks that a given story is a parable, even if we explain nothing more; for once you know it is a parable, it will immediately become clear to you what it is a parable of. My remarking that it is a parable will be like someone's removing a screen from between the eye and a visible thing."[23]

Rashi, too, intended each midrash he brought to have a meaning, but he mostly kept its meaning or meanings to himself. A brief look at his opening comments on Genesis should give us some sense of his midrashically enhanced world. At Genesis 1:5, he comments on the anomalous usage, at the completion of the first day of creation, of the term יום אחד instead of יום ראשון, "one day" rather than "the first day." He says that this is to attest to God as the one and only agent of creation on the first day, since angels, as *Bereshit Rabbah* (1:5, 3) tells us, were not created until the second day.

---

22. Pines, p. 11, "To understand a proverb and a figure; the words of the wise and their dark sayings."

23. *Guide*, p. 14. Pines' "screen" is a translation of אלשי אלחאיל (Munk, 9:25), given more literally by Munk (I:22) as "ce qui s'interposait" and by Schwartz (I:19) as דבר החוצץ.

We are left to ponder the significance of this remark and whether or not it is part of a deliberate strategy of Rashi to minimize the role of angels,[24] given that the midrashic tradition offered alternate scenarios of their creation. It is clear, however, that Rashi accepts the existence of angels without question, as he does with whatever the Bible presents.

Angels appear again to Rashi in Genesis 1:26 as the presumed co-subject of the verb נעשה, in the sentence נעשה אדם בצלמנו כדמותנו, "let us make man in our image after our own likeness." Following the midrash, Rashi says that this is to teach modesty, that the mighty should consult with and ask permission from the lowly.[25]

Rashi comments very briefly on the second half of this verse. He says בצלמנו, "in our image," is "in our imprint," בדפוס שלנו, without further elaboration; and כדמותנו, "after our likeness," refers to our ability to understand and think, להבין ולהשכיל; again, without further elaboration.

The moralizing and charming quality of Rashi's commentary is evident in his remark on Genesis 2:18, in which God decides to give Adam a companion, or as the text has it, עזר כנגדו, usually translated as a "helpmeet for him." Following the midrash, Rashi translates more literally, saying זכה עזר, לא זכה כנגדו להלחם; "if (man) is worthy, (she will be) a helpmeet; if he is not worthy, (she will be) against him, to fight."[26]

Marital relations, and sexual relations in general, are a major concern of the Bible and therefore of Rashi as well. The serpent in the Garden of Eden is said by Rashi, following the midrash, to have coveted Eve after seeing her and Adam copulate. Eve is innocent and gullible, no match for the wily snake.[27] The fall of Adam and Eve is also the downfall of the snake, whom Rashi treats literally, for all his mythic powers.

A final example of Rashi's style and priorities is taken from

---

24. Cf. Touitou, p.174.
25. CF. Bereshit Rabbah (henceforth BR), 1:54, 8.
26. BR 1:122, 3. להלחם, "to fight," is added by Rashi.
27. BR 1:133, 6. Rashi says this twice, first in his comment to Gen. 3:1, and again at Gen. 3:20.

Genesis 28:12, where we read of Jacob's dream of a ladder "set on the earth, with its top reaching to the heavens, and angels ascending and descending on it." Rashi adopts the midrash's explanation (BR 3:88, 12) that the ascending angels are those who preside only over the land of Israel, the descending ones coming to accompany him abroad.

The importance of Jerusalem is also stressed in Rashi's comment on the ladder itself. Adapting a midrashic source (BR 3:96, 17), Rashi comments in Gen. 28:17 that the ladder reached from Beersheva to Jerusalem. The particular reason for this apparently is that Jacob calls the place of his dream בית אלקים, the house of God, and the ladder links him to the primary site of that house, or temple, which is Jerusalem.

These various themes all have their counterparts and striking differences in the *Guide*, beginning in Chapter One with Maimonides' interpretation of the equivocal meanings of צלם and דמות, image and likeness, and the consequent identification of God with intellect, and of man's conjunction through his intellect with God. This is shortly followed with a broad attack upon all biblical terms that describe God as possessing physical organs and faculties. The justification that Maimonides finally cites, in *Guide* 1:26, for the misleading image of a corporeal God that these anthropomorphic terms convey, is the Talmudic statement that "the Torah speaks in (literally as) the language of man," דברה תורה כלשון בני אדם.[28]

Maimonides bases his entire radical interpretation of the biblical text upon this rabbinic dictum. And it is a radical interpretation, for Maimonides proceeds to divest God not only of physicality, but also of any attribute that would entail multiplicity, and hence corporeality, in the Divine being. Maimonides is left, as we know, with a God of whom nothing, or nearly nothing, can be known, and nothing positive said.

It is worth noting that Maimonides barely utilizes midrashic sources in making his case for the allegedly metaphorical language

---

28. *Guide*, p. 56 and elsewhere, cited from BT Yebamoth 71a, Baba Metsi 'a 31b.

of Scripture, or for his analysis of appropriate attribution.[29] Nor does he engage in midrashic prooftexts to supplement his discussions of Kalam and philosophy, including his philosophical interpretation of Job. Parable though it is, Job is given Maimonides' own non-allegorical interpretation, one in keeping with his understanding of Divine Providence.

Maimonides would seem to create very few parables of his own. The most impressive one is his treatment of Adam and Eve in the Garden of Eden, in the *Guide* 1:2, as an allegory with an essentially political message, that the fall of man is his descent into politics and society.[30] As such, it is obvious why Maimonides does not adduce midrashic sources for this view, contrary as it is to rabbinic beliefs.

We must wait until *Guide* II:30 (p. 355) for Maimonides to revisit Adam and Eve in Paradise, as part of his exegesis for the creation epic. This time Maimonides explicitly refers to midrashim that he says were unambiguously understood as allegories. In keeping with he general attitude towards not divulging secret teachings, Maimonides simply recounts a few of these midrashim, leaving it to the reader to get the point.

We are told, in one midrash that he brings, that the serpent in the Garden had a rider who was Sammael, a.k.a. Satan, and that this was the devil who deceived Eve.[31] Maimonides interprets the biblical text with the help of this midrash, pointing out that the serpent had no direct relations with Adam, but only with Eve, and it was through Eve that the serpent destroyed Adam.

While, again, Maimonides does not spell out the moral of his teaching, we know that in the introduction to the *Guide* (p. 13)

---

29. As Mordechai Z. Cohen has shown, Maimonides distinguishes between the denotative and circumscribed language of those terms he regards as metaphors (somewhat ironically called "equivocal" terms), and the connotative and more open-ended meanings of allegorical passages in midrash. Cf. Cohen's *Three Approaches to Biblical Metaphor* (Brill, Leiden, 2003), pp. 112–126, 179–226.

30. Cf. Lawrence V. Berman, "Maimonides on the Fall of Man," *AJSReview* (5, 1980), 1–15. See the full analysis of this chapter in Sarah Klein-Braslavy, *Maimonides' Interpretation of the Adam Stories in Genesis* (Hebrew, Jerusalem, 1986), pp. 39–168.

31. Chapters of Rabbi Eliezer, XIII.

and in *Guide* III:8 (p. 431) he identifies woman, and therefore Eve, with matter, and matter with evil, personified here as Satan. The midrash is thus taken to support Maimonides' view that man's fall was due to his involvement in material existence, a key argument in Maimonides' theodicy and theory of Providence.

Maimonides explains the lack of midrashic support for his thesis against anthropomorphisms in *Guide* I:46 (p. 102). He believes the rabbis never entertained the notion of God's corporeality, not "even for a single day." This was so clear to them that they could indulge in anthropomorphic language with no worry of being misunderstood; using, e.g., the allegory of a king, with all that entails in terms of rewards and punishments.

Maimonides believes there is one "comprehensive dictum" (קולה׳ ג׳מיעה, Munk 69:8) that governs the rabbinic attitude, and he cites Bereshit Rabbah (27) by name to bring it: גדול כחן של נביאים שהם מדמים את הצורה ליוצרה, שנאמר ועל דמות הכסא דמות כמראה אדם; "Great is the power of the prophets; for they liken a form to its creator. For it is said: and upon the likeness of a throne was a likeness as the appearance of a man" (Ezek. 1:26, *Guide*, p.103).

This statement would appear to mean that the rabbis understood the prophets to depict God in human terms. Maimonides takes it as a statement emphasizing the imagination of the prophets, however divinely inspired it may be. "All the forms apprehended by all the prophets in the vision of prophecy are created forms of which God is the creator. And this is correct, for every imagined form is created," כל צורה מתכילה פהי מכלוקה (Munk 69:24).

Maimonides insists upon the significance of this midrash, saying that, "(the rabbis) have thus made clear and manifest, as far as they themselves are concerned, that they were innocent of the belief in the corporeality of God; and furthermore, that all the shapes and figures that are seen in the vision of prophecy are created things."

Maimonides concludes the chapter on an aggressive note that reveals the contentiousness of his interpretation: "If, however, after these things have been said, someone out of malice (עלי ג׳הה׳ אלשראה) wishes to think ill of (the rabbis), depreciating men whom he has not see and whose worth he does not know, no harm will come to them, may their memory be blessed."[32]

In this manner, Maimonides makes it clear that it is wicked, futile and disrespectful of the early sages to disagree with him on this issue, one that goes to the heart of his understanding of revelation. For Maimonides is making the claim that the rabbis of the Talmudic period understood, as he does, that all prophecy is a function of the prophet's divinely inspired imagination. Every appearance of God and His surrogates in Scripture is to be understood as an imaginative construction, not to be taken literally. The events depicted did not occur other than in the prophet's imagination.[33]

This is a claim which with few rabbis of Maimonides' day, or of days past and present, would agree, as his barely suppressed polemic intimates. It puts into question Maimonides' attitude towards the historicity of the Bible, and particularly the Torah, which historicity he appears to take as a given fact. Yet the Torah is the legacy of Moses' prophecy.

We know, however, that Maimonides distinguishes the nature of Mosaic prophecy from all other forms of prophecy, viewing it as solely an intellectual experience, without involving Moses' imaginative faculty whatsoever. This is an article of faith for him, so expressed in his rabbinic writings and confirmed in the *Guide*.[34] As such, it serves many purposes, one of which is to foreclose questions of the sort just raised. (Whether it does is another subject entirely.)

However, barring Mosaic philosophy, Maimonides insists upon the mediation of the imagination in all prophetic

---

32. Following Schwartz's translation (p. 106) more than Pines, p. 103, and cf. Munk, 70:4–6.

33. See A. Reines, "Maimonides' Concept of Mosaic Prophecy," *HUCA* 40–41 (1969–70), 351–55; Kalman Bland, "Moses and the Law According to Maimonides," in *Mystics, Philosophers and Politicians*, ed. Jehuda Reinharz, Daniel Swetschinski (Durham, 1982), pp. 62–64; Alfred Ivry, "Ismâ'îlî Theology and Maimonides' Philosophy," in *The Jews of Medieval Islam*, ed. Daniel Frank (Leiden, 1995), pp. 294–96.

34. *Guide* II:37, p. 373; II:45, p. 403; cf. *Mishnah Commentary*, Sanhedrin 10 (Heleq), introduction, seventh principle; *Mishneh Torah*, יסודי התורה VII, 6.

experiences, be they in dreams or visions. Even where prophets say they saw God, which Maimonides in *Guide* II:45 counts as the seventh degree of prophecy, they just imagined it, he believes (p. 403).

As worded in that chapter, Maimonides seems to be conceding that in such cases the imagination functioned on its own, without the appearance of an angel. He has, however, already in *Guide* II:6 (p. 264), identified angels with the imagination, building upon the statement in Midrash Kohelet (10:20), which he names, that "when man sleeps, his soul speaks to the angel, and the angel to the cherub," בשעה שאדם ישן נפשו אומרת למלאך ומלאך לכרוב.

For Maimonides, this is clear evidence for "one who understands and cognizes intellectually (למן יפהם ויעקל, Munk 184:17) that the imaginative faculty is likewise called an angel and that the intellect is called a cherub." Hence, the distinction he draws for the seventh degree of prophecy, as for all the others, is more phenomenological than substantive.

Guide II:6, however, does much more for angels than relegating them to the imagination. Maimonides begins the chapter with the confident assertion that no proofs need be brought from the Torah for the existence of angels, since the Torah explicitly records their presence a number of times (*Guide*, p. 261). The real meaning of "angel," however, is messenger, Maimonides explains, and anyone who may be seen as carrying out God's intentions is an angel, or is affected by one. Thus it is natural that Balaam's she-ass (Numbers 22:23) is said to encounter an angel.

As Maimonides warms to the subject, angels multiply. He says he shall deal only with those angels which are separate intellects, a definition he proposed already in *Guide* I:49 (p. 108). He cannot restrain himself, however, from making the claim now that "all forces (i.e., all natural forces) are angels," אלקוי כלהא מלאיכה' (Munk, 183:15); even the building blocks of nature, the four elements, are angels, he says (p. 262), basing himself on Psalm 104:4.

Again we find Maimonides going on the offensive to chastise those who would differ with him, who prefer in their ignorance to believe in angels as supernatural beings rather than as expressions of the natural order designed by God. Yet true greatness and power is "the bringing into existence of forces active in a thing," Maimonides says: איג'אד אלקוי אלפאעלה' פי אלשי.[35] This is likely an allusion to God's role as the Necessary Existent, אלואג'ב אלוג'וד (*Guide* II:1, p. 247), He who necessitates the existence of everything else, but through the utilization of the natural forces that are deemed messengers, or angels.

Thus the Agent Intellect, that last of the separate intellects of the heavens from which, Maimonides says, all the forms on earth derive, is the very angel and prince of the world, שרו של עולם, "constantly mentioned by the Sages... (They) have stated explicitly for the benefit of him who is a Sage that every force appertaining to the bodily forces is an angel — all the more, the forces distributed in the world — and that every force has only one particular activity proper to it and not two activities."[36]

This last statement, puzzling as it seems, is apparently necessitated by the midrash that Maimonides brings to support his thesis, taken, as are many of his prooftexts, from Bereshit Rabbah תני אין מלאך עושה שתי שליחות ואין שני מלאכים עושין שליחות אחת (50): "It has been learnt: one angel does not perform two missions, nor do two angels perform one mission."

Maimonides is aware, however, of other midrashim that attest to the permanent status of angels, a position that he is in total agreement with as well, particularly as regards the angelic intellects of the spheres. He resolves the apparent contradiction by distinguishing between those forces/angels that inform mortal individuals, and those that represent the permanent species of the world.

As does Rashi, Maimonides devotes considerable treatment to Jacob's ladder and dream, it being an exegetical treasure for his teachings of metaphysics.[37] In *Guide* II:10, Maimonides integrates the ladder into his description of the activities of the heavenly

35. *Guide* p. 264, Munk 183:24.
36. *Guide* II:6, p. 264.
37. Cf. Diamond, pp. 85–130.

bodies that govern this world. They are they efficient causes of the motion of the four elements, in combinations of which everything on earth is composed.

The number four attracts Maimonides, and he offers a "possible" arrangement of the universe in sets of four. All of nature is comprehensible in broad terms through this scheme, which Maimonides then connects, with the assistance allegedly of Midrash Tanhuma,[38] to Jacob's ladder, now said to have four steps. The angels are then arranged in four camps, following midrashic precedent,[39] and Maimonides (claiming midrashic unanimity) places what must be a representative of each one on the ladder, all four on the same step.

Following the dictum of Bereshit Rabbah 10 that the angel is the third part of the world (המלאך שלישו של עולם), Maimonides then reckons that the breadth of the ladder was one third greater than that of the world. This is more than enough to make his point, namely, that the dream of the ladder encompasses allegorically the essential teachings of metaphysics and physics. A second point, no less important for Maimonides, is that the midrashic — and hence rabbinic — tradition supports these teachings, and corroborates them.

It is clear that Maimonides understands these allegories for what they are: coded and discreet messages that are wonderfully helpful to the wise, but misunderstood by the bulk of his coreligionists and their leaders. Maimonides has brought a philosophical depth and daring to a literature that was largely innocent of it.

There are legends that have Rashi visiting Rambam, and showing him some of his commentaries. Maimonides is then said to have written that he had intended to write additional commentaries, לולי שקדמני הצרפתי, "had not the Frenchman preceded me."[40] Maimonides would indeed have been impressed with

---

38. Pines, p. 272, as Munk in *Mélanges*, does not find it there and refers instead to *Yalqut Reubeni, Mal'akh* 99, which Schwartz, p. 288, n. 27 cites in full.

39. במדבר רבה IV, פרקי רבי אליעזר.

40. Avineri, p. 25.

Rashi's mastery of the midrashic corpus, and would no doubt have admired his occasional defense of the Jewish people and his interpretation of halakha; but he would not have been intimidated by Rashi's treatment of midrash.

12.

Maimonides vs. Rashi: Philosophical and Philological-Ethical Approaches to Job

Mordechai Z. Cohen

The popularity of Job among the great medieval Jewish commentators rivals that of the Torah. Nahmanides, for example, wrote commentaries only on the Torah and Job.[1] In the French school, commentaries were penned by Rashi, Joseph Qara, Rashbam, and Rabbenu Tam among others.[2] Maimonides devotes two full chapters of his *Guide of the Perplexed* to Job in which he offers a philosophical reading following a template pioneered by Saadia Gaon and adopted by Abraham Ibn Ezra.[3]

---

1. Nahmanides' commentary on Job appears in כתבי רבינו משה בן נחמן, ed. Hayyim Dov Chavel (Jerusalem 1964), I:9–128. On Nahmanides' choice to write a commentary on Job, see ibid., 9–10.
2. See Moshe Ahrend (ed.), *Rabbi Joseph Kara's Commentary on Job* (Hebrew; Jerusalem 1988); Sara Japhet (ed.), *The Commentary of Rabbi Samuel Ben Meir (Rashbam) on the Book of Job* (Hebrew; Jerusalem 2000); Avraham Shoshana (ed.), *The Book of Job with the Commentaries of Rashi, Rabbenu Jacob b. Meir Tam, and a Disciple of Rashi* (Hebrew; Jerusalem 2000). Some scholars question the attribution of the Qara and Rashbam commentaries; see Sara Japhet, "The Nature and Distribution of Medieval Compilatory Commentaries in Light of Rabbi Joseph Kara's Commentary on the Book of Job," *The Midrashic Imagination*, ed. Michael Fishbane (New York 1993), 98–130; Martin Lockshin, "'Rashbam' on Job: A Reconsideration," *Jewish Studies Quarterly* 8 (2001): 80–104. On the commentary by Rabbenu Tam, see also Benjamin Richler, "Rabbeinu Tam's 'Lost' Commentary on Job," *The Frank Talmage Memorial Volume*, ed. Barry Walfish (Haifa 1993), 191–202.
3. See Moses Maimonides, *The Guide of the Perplexed*, trans. Shlomo Pines (Chicago 1963), III:22–23;486–497. Subsequent references to the *Guide* will be from this translation (cited according to section, chapter and page), though at times I make minor changes according to the original Judeo-Arabic text, *Dalālat al-Ḥāʾirīn*, ed. S. Munk and I. Joel (Jerusalem, 1930/31). A number of studies have been devoted to Maimonides' reading of Job; see Robert Eisen, *The Book of Job in Medieval Jewish*

In light of the subject of this conference volume, I would like to compare Maimonides with Rashi and his students on Job in order to shed light on the exegetical methods of the northern French *peshat* school by comparison with the philosophically oriented Babylonian-Iberian tradition.

1. The Commentaries

We begin with Rashi, who evidently inspired his greatest followers to write commentaries on this book. This concentration of exegetical activity in twelfth century northern France is curious: Why Job of all biblical books? The first thought that comes to mind is its subject matter, the perennial dilemma of evil befalling the righteous, צדיק ורע לו in rabbinic parlance, a matter that undoubtedly would have been of special interest during the troubled Crusader Era. In the opening chapters of this biblical book, Satan is granted God's permission to afflict Job, the perfectly righteous man, with terrible calamities: the loss of his wealth and his children, and ultimately a deforming disease. His three friends, Eliphaz, Bildad and Zophar, come to console Job and engage him in dialogues that comprise the bulk of the book. While Job insists that his suffering is unjust, the friends endeavor to reconcile his predicament with divine justice and providence. Once their discussion dies down, a fifth interlocutor, Elihu, enters the fray, criticizing

---

Philosophy (New York 2004), 43–77; Hannah Kasher, "Job's Image and Opinions in *Moreh Nevukhim*" [Hebrew], *Da'at* 15 (1985), 81–87; Moshe Greenberg, "*Iyyov Hayah o Lo' Hayah: Sugyah be-Parshanut Yemei ha-Beinayim*," *Sha'arei Talmon: Studies in the Bible, Qumran, and the Ancient Near East Presented to Shemaryahu Talmon*, ed. Michael Fishbane and Emanuel Tov (Winnona Lake, IN 1992), 3*–11*; Leonard Kravitz, "Maimonides and Job: An Inquiry as to the Method of the *Moreh*," *HUCA* 38 (1967): 149–158; Joel Laks, "The Enigma of Job: Maimonides and the Moderns," *Journal of Biblical Literature* 82 (1964): 345–364; Jacob Levinger, "Maimonides' Exegesis of the Book of Job," *Creative Biblical Exegesis*, ed. Benjamin Uffenheimer and Henning G. Reventlow (Sheffield 1988), 81–88; Shalom Rosenberg, "*Iyyov Mashal Hayah*," *Mehqarim ba-Miqra' u-ve-Hinnukh Muggashim li-Professor Moshe Ahrend*, ed. D. Rappel (Jerusalem 1996), 146–158. The discussion of Maimonides' reading of Job in this paper is based, in part, on my study, "A Philosopher's *Peshat* Exegesis: Maimonides' Literary Approach to the Book of Job and its Place in the History of Biblical Interpretation" [Hebrew], *Shnaton: An Annual for Biblical and Ancient Near Eastern Studies* XV (2005): 213–264.

the others for failing to arrive at the truth, which he proceeds to expound. Finally, Job receives two divine visions that prompt his contrite response to God, after which the story closes with the restoration of Job's health, wealth and new children.[4] For the sake of comparison, it is helpful to consider that Saadia, in his introduction to Job, enumerated what he considered to be the chief difficulties facing those who wish to unlock the secrets of this book:

> Thus says the one who undertakes its interpretation: Indeed I have found that many of our nation look upon this Book of Job as an enigma, difficult to interpret and construe in several respects.... [including] the suffering of the prophet Job, despite the book's testimony that he was a "blameless, upright and God-fearing man" (Job 1:1)... [Furthermore] what is the course of the argument between him and his companions and Elihu: what did each of them claim? How did they answer one another and where did they object to one another? ...[This endeavor is especially difficult because] the sentences which contain the point of each speech... are obscured... by the plethora of arguments and profusion of discourse. The counterpoint of statement and rejoinder, rhapsodic embellishment, padding and flourishes often smothers the argument which is the point intended.[5]

For Saadia, developing a theodicy is an integral part of the interpretation of this biblical book, which therefore requires extracting from the dialogues the analytic views expressed by Job and his

---

4. Perhaps we may wonder how this makes up for the loss of his original children. It would seem that this question prompted Nahmanides (comm. on Job 42:10, Chavel ed., 127–128) to posit that Job's children never really died but were merely taken captive by Satan and returned unharmed.

5. Lenn Goodman, trans., *The Book of Theodicy: Translation and Commentary on the Book of Job by Saadiah ben Joseph al-Fayyūmī* (New Haven 1988), 130, with slight changes, according to the Arabic original appearing in: Joseph Kafih (ed. and trans. into Hebrew), איוב עם תרגום ופירוש הגאון רבנו סעדיה בן יוסף פיומי ז"ל (Jerusalem 1973), 19–20.

companions. Doing so requires more than merely interpreting the language of the text; it also requires isolating the conceptual point in each speech, which is often obscured by the prolix rhetoric of the interlocutors. It is in this spirit that Abraham Ibn Ezra wrote a double commentary on Job: first a running commentary on the language, *perush ha-millot* (lit. interpretation of the words), followed by an analytic interpretation *perush ha-ṭeʿamim* (lit. interpretation of the meanings), where he outlines the philosophical views that emerge therein.[6]

I mentioned Saadia and Ibn Ezra for the sake of contrast, since when we actually explore the northern French commentaries, we find that they lack any comparable analytic discussions of theodicy, as Moshe Sokolow has observed.[7] Instead, their focus is almost exclusively textual, with a strong emphasis on philological and grammatical issues, and occasional analysis of structural features of the arguments and the narrative frame. Particularly noteworthy in this respect is Rashbam, who also manifests a keen sense of biblical poetics in analyzing the literary features of the text.[8] None of this should be surprising, since a linguistic-literary focus would seem to fulfill Rashi's stated goal of explicating *peshuto shel miqra*, as he writes, e.g., in his commentary on Gen 3:8, "There are many aggadic *midrashim*, and the Rabbis have already arranged them in their place in *Bereshit Rabbah* and other *midrashim*, but as for me, I have come only for *peshuto shel miqra*."[9] Here is not the place to address the thorny issue of Rashi's heavy reliance on Midrash in his Torah commentary notwithstanding that programmatic statement.[10] However, Rashi scholars have noted that elsewhere in Scripture,

---

6. See Mariano Gómez Aranda, *El Commentario de Abraham Ibn Ezra al Libro de Job: Edició crítica, traducción y estudia introductorio*, Madrid 2004, 6*, 90*-94*.

7. Moshe Sokolow, "A Job Well Done," *The Torah u-Madda Journal* 11 (2002–03): 273–280.

8. See Japhet, *Rashbam on Job*, 160–208.

9. For a detailed analysis of this methodological statement in light of Rashi's actual commentaries, see Sarah Kamin, *Rashi's Exegetical Categorization in Respect to the Distinction Between Pesha and Derash* [Hebrew] (Jerusalem, 1986), 62–110.

10. For a recent survey of views on this question, see Avraham Grossman, *The Early Sages of France* [Hebrew] (Jerusalem 1995), 193–201.

i.e., in *Nevi'im* and *Ketuvim*, he adheres more consistently to his *peshat* agenda, i.e., contextual linguistic analysis.[11] Rashi's Job commentary is thus restricted to an interpretation of the language of the text, and it was this project that his students refined in their subsequent commentaries. The French commentaries, as a rule, do not step back from the text and ask: in the final analysis, what did Job believe? What conceptual positions do his three friends advance? What does Elihu add in this respect?[12] Which of the interlocutors comes closest to the truth? Since these questions, by and large, are not associated with pressing textual exegetical difficulties, they fall outside the parameters of *peshat* exegesis in the northern French sense.

The importance of this textual criterion in the French school becomes clear when we explore the discussions of the following questions that may arise in the course of studying this biblical book: *When* did Job live? Was he even a real character? This very question is the subject of an involved talmudic discussion and is raised consistently within the Babylonian-Iberian tradition by Saadia, Abraham Ibn Ezra, Joseph Kimhi, Moses Kimhi, Maimonides and Nahmanides.[13] Yet neither Rashi nor his students discuss it,[14] evidently because it is not a direct textual

---

11. See Grossman, *Sages of France*, 194. Elazar Touitou argues that many midrashic comments appearing in the printed text of Rashi's Torah commentary actually are the result of additions by his students and other copyists; see Elazar Touitou, "Concerning the Presumed Original Version of Rashi's Commentary on the Pentateuch" [Hebrew], *Tarbiz* 56 (1987): 211–242. If so, the original text of Rashi's Torah commentary resembled his more philologically focused commentaries on *Nevi'im* and *Ketuvim*.

12. Japhet (*Rashbam on Job*, 125–127) pieces together a theory that, in her view, reflects Rashbam's analysis of Elihu's solution to the theodicy, which Rashbam regarded as correct. However, Rashbam never explicitly states that Elihu uttered the correct philosophy (on his interpretation of 42:7, see below), as Saadia and his followers did. It would seem, rather, that Rashbam simply intended to explain the language of Elihu, but not necessarily to create a coherent philosophic position out of his speeches; see Cohen, "Maimonides' Literary Approach," 256n.

13. See: Saadia, comm. on 1:1 (Kafih ed., 24); Ibn Ezra, comm. on 1:1; Joseph Qimhi, comm. on 1:1, in: *Tiqwat Enosh*, ed. Israel Schwartz (Berlin 1868), p. 149; Moses Kimhi, introduction to Job, in: *Moses Kimhi: Commentary on the Book of Job*, ed. Herbert Basser and Barry D. Walfish (Atlanta 1992), 1; Maimonides, *Guide*, III:22;486; Nahmanides, comm. on 1:1 (Chavel ed., 27).

14. See the following commentaries on Job 1:1: Rashi, Rabbenu Tam and Rashi's

concern. On the other hand, they do discuss *where* Job lived in connection with the first verse of the book, "There was a man in the Land of Uz," which raises the interpretive question: Where is Uz?[15] But the non-textual, or we might say meta-textual issue of Job's time period is ignored by the northern French exegetes. It is important to stress that they did not have to know Saadia or Ibn Ezra to be interested in this matter, which is discussed in the Talmud (b. *Baba Batra* 15a), as a great rabbinic scholar like Rashi, and his grandsons, the great tosafists Rashbam and Rabbenu Tam, were certainly well aware. Yet they deemed this talmudic discussion — like many others — to fall outside of the parameters of their *peshat* exegesis.

What, then, motivated the northern French interest in Job? This question, of course, does not apply to Rashi, who in any event commented on almost all of Scripture. But what would have drawn the attention of more selective exegetes such as Rashbam and Qara, and certainly Rabbenu Tam,[16] if not the theoretical subject matter of Job? It is, of course, conceivable that the story of Job itself simply spoke to them in their own difficult situation in Christian Europe in the aftermath of the First Crusade. In other words, even if the book — as analyzed by Rashi and his students — did not yield a philosophical solution to the problem of evil, they may have found solace in identifying with the righteous sufferer Job.[17]

---

anonymous student (Shoshana ed., 1–2); Qara (Ahrend ed., 3); Rashbam (Japhet ed., 349); for analysis of the views of Rashi and Rashbam, see Japhet, *Rashbam on Job*, 120–122.

15. See references in the preceding note.

16. As far as we know, Job is the only biblical book for which Rabbenu Tam wrote a commentary. Of Rashbam's commentaries only those on the Torah, Job, Qohelet and Song of Songs are extant; although he may have also written commentaries on a few other biblical books (see Japhet, *Rashbam on Job*, 10). Qara's commentaries were more extensive, covering a large part of prophetic literature, Psalms, Job and perhaps Song of Songs and the Torah; see Grossman, *Sages of France*, 290–316.

17. Chavel (*Kitvei Ramban* I:9) attributes such a motive to Nahmanides. None of the commentators in Rashi's school, however, states this openly, and none identifies Job as a symbol for the nation of Israel, an approach attested in rabbinic literature and the fourteenth century Provençal commentator Gersonides; see Hananel Mack, *Ela' Mashal Hayah: Job and the Book of Job in Rabbinic Literature* (Hebrew; Ramat Gan 2004), 46–47; Eisen, *Job in Medieval Philosophy*, 163–165.

Yet it is also interesting to consider another possible motive, one directly associated with the focused linguistic exegetical concerns of the northern French *peshat* school. Perhaps part of the appeal of interpreting this biblical book was its difficult language, which posed a challenge that such brilliant interpreters as Qara, Rashbam and Jacob Tam would have found hard to resist. During the so-called twelfth century renaissance, a bold wave of intellectual innovation swept through northern France, where the winds of new Latin scholarship seem to have made a significant impact on Jewish scholars there, spurring them to devise new methods of interpreting the traditional texts of Hebrew learning, i.e., Bible and Talmud.[18] Qara, Rashbam and Rabbenu Tam were celebrated — and prided themselves — for their ability to pioneer new approaches and offer innovative solutions to previously intractable difficulties.[19] It is thus not hard to imagine that such personalities would be eager to prove that the nascent *peshat* method devised in northern France could decipher the seemingly incomprehensible Hebrew text of the book of Job.

2. Maimonides

We now turn to Maimonides, whose depiction as a biblical exegete may require some explanation, since he is normally viewed exclusively as a talmudist and philosopher. Although he did not compose actual biblical commentaries, recent scholarship has shown that Maimonides' reading of Scripture in the

---

18. See Elazar Touitou, *Exegesis in Perpetual Motion: Studies in the Pentateuchal Commentary of Rabbi Samuel ben Meir* (Hebrew; Ramat Gan 2003), 102–104; Israel Meir Ta-Shma, *Talmudic Commentary in Europe and North Africa: Literary History, Part One: 1000–1200* (Hebrew; Jerusalem 1999), 61–63, 67–82; Grossman, *Sages of France*, 473–475.

19. See Grossman, *Sages of France*, 261–263; Touitou, *Perpetual Motion*, 69–70, 75–76; Ezra Ziyyon Melammed, *Bible Commentators* (Jerusalem 1978), 488–489; Ephraim Kanarfogel, "Progress and Tradition in Medieval Ashkenaz," *Jewish History* 14 (2000): 295–302. The self-reliant attitude of this school, which to some observers bordered on arrogance (especially among students of these great luminaries), sparked sharp criticism; see Haym Soloveitchik, "Three Themes in *Sefer Hasidim,*" *AJS Review* 1 (1976): 339–345.

Guide reflects the thinking of the Babylonian-Iberian exegetical tradition represented by authors such as Saadia and Ibn Ezra. [20] To be sure, exegetical concerns in the *Guide* are subordinated to philosophical ones; and indeed, it is against the backdrop of Maimonides' own philosophical analysis of divine providence in *Guide* III:17–18 that he turns to Job. Yet we should note that this is the only biblical book he interprets in its entirety; other parts of Scripture are addressed piecemeal, according to topic (creation, prophecy, anthropomorphism) in chapters scattered throughout the *Guide*.[21] In sharp contrast, the book of Job is treated as a complete literary unit in *Guide* III:22–23, to which we now turn.

Maimonides did not comment on Job verse-by-verse, but rather analyzed and summarized the major themes of the book, citing and interpreting the critical passages he considered decisive. In this respect, we can compare his analysis with the "introduction" genre in modern biblical scholarship.[22] True to his philosophic interest, Maimonides opens his analysis of Job by stating that his story was recounted in Scripture "to set forth the opinions of people concerning providence" (III:22;486). The first matter he addresses is the question of when Job lived, as well as the literary nature of this biblical tale, for which he cites the relevant talmudic discussion in b. *Baba Batra* 15a. Among the various talmudic opinions about Job's time period, which range from the

---

20. See Cohen, "Maimonides' Literary Approach," 217–220.
21. See Sara Klein-Braslavy, *Maimonides' Interpretation of the Story of Creation* (Hebrew; Jerusalem 1987²); idem, *Maimonides' Interpretation of the Adam Stories in Genesis* (Hebrew; Jerusalem 1986). On Maimonides' exegetical approach to anthropomorphism, see Simon Rawidowicz, *Hebrew Studies in Jewish Thought* (Hebrew; Jerusalem 1969), 237–264; Mordechai Z. Cohen, *Three Approaches to Biblical Metaphor* (Leiden 2003), 201–216; on Maimonides' approach to prophecy, see Alvin J. Reines, *Maimonides and Abarbanel on Prophecy* (Cincinnati 1970). On the exegetical nature of the *Guide* in general, see Hillel Fradkin, "Philosophy or Exegesis: Perennial Problems in the Study of Some Judaeo-Arabic Authors," *Judaeo-Arabic Studies*, ed. Norman Golb (Amsterdam 1997), 103–122; Josef Stern, "Philosophy or Exegesis: Some Critical Comments," *Judaeo-Arabic Studies*, 213–228.
22. Allowing for differences between modern critical scholarship and medieval exegesis, Maimonides' analysis can be compared with the treatment of Job, e.g., in Samuel R. Driver, *An Introduction to the Literature of the Old Testament* (New York 1913), 408–435; Otto Eissfeldt, *The Old Testament: An Introduction*, trans. Peter Ackroyd (New York 1965), 454–470.

time of the forefathers to the Babylonian exile, Maimonides favors the view that "Job never was and was never created, but was only a *mashal*," i.e., a parable or fictional didactic tale.[23] But in the spirit of Aristotle's notion that "poetry is more philosophical than history" because it expresses universals rather than particulars,[24] he goes on to say that "with regard to cases like his, which always exist, all reflecting people become perplexed" (*Guide*, ibid.). In other words, even if the story of Job is fictional, it addresses a distressing and recurring reality that calls into question the fundamental notion of divine justice and providence, namely "that a righteous and perfect man... [is] stricken — without having committed a sin warranting this — with great and consecutive calamities with respect to his fortune, his children and his body" (ibid.).

Much as Saadia had done in his introduction to Job, Maimonides outlines his exegetical program of selecting key verses from the dialogues to assign a distinct philosophical view to each of the interlocutors:

> I want... to explain to you the opinion ascribed to Job and the opinion ascribed to each of his friends, using proofs that I gleaned from the discourse of each of them. You should not, however, pay attention to the dicta rendered necessary by the order of the discourse, as I explained to you in the beginning of this treatise. (*Guide* III:22;490)

Saadia had alerted his readers to the rhetorical aspects of the dialogues that obscure the line of argument; in a similar vein, Maimonides here invokes his principle — articulated in his introduction to the *Guide* — that as a rule a *mashal* must be interpreted as a whole rather than piecemeal, since many details of this biblical genre are typically employed merely for literary purposes,

---

23. In the talmudic discussion, this view was rejected, and it was likewise marginalized in the post-talmudic tradition. On Maimonides' choice to revive it, see Greenberg, "*Iyyov*"; Cohen, "Maimonides' Literary Approach," 230–253.

24. *Poetics*, chap. 9, 1451b, trans. Ingram Bywater, in: *The Basic Works of Aristotle*, ed., Richard M. McKeon (New York 1941), 1464.

either to enhance its elegance or to create a coherent narrative tale.[25] Accordingly, many details in the book of Job, which in his view are required merely for the sake of "the order of the discourse" — i.e., to enhance the storyline — must be ignored, since they do not contribute to the book's primary purpose, namely clarifying the views on providence.

Maimonides goes on to delineate the four philosophies expressed by Job and his three friends. Without going into all of the details here,[26] we can observe that the great philosopher manifests a decisive mastery of this difficult biblical book when selecting the verses in the dialogues that articulate clear conceptual positions. This is not a haphazard assortment of suggestive biblical locutions, but rather a cogent, systematic selection informed by a methodical, comprehensive reading of the entire text, in the spirit of the Babylonian-Iberian philological-contextual interpretive school. For example, to epitomize the opinion of Job himself, Maimonides immediately identifies the harshest words uttered by this unfortunate sufferer:

> Job's opinion… is that this happening [i.e., his suffering] proves that the righteous man and the wicked are regarded as equal by Him, may He be exalted, because of His contempt for the human species and abandonment of it. This is what he says in all his speeches: "It is all one — therefore I say: He destroyeth the innocent and the wicked. If the flood slay suddenly, He will mock at the calamity of the guiltless" (Job 9:22–23). He says thus that if a torrent comes suddenly killing all those it meets and sweeping them away, He laughs at the calamity of the innocent. (*Guide* III:23;491)

---

25. On this principle and its application in the *Guide*, see Cohen, *Three Approaches*, 180–201. On the difference between the *literary* nature of Maimonides' principle, and the *rhetorical* account given by Saadia, see Cohen, "Maimonides' Literary Approach," 245–253.

26. Detailed analysis of the views Maimonides attributes to the interlocutors can be found in the studies cited above, n. 3.

These verses — perhaps more than any other in Job's speeches — express his conclusion that God ignores human affairs, allowing the righteous to suffer the same fate as sinners.

Unlike their unfortunate companion, the three friends who initially came to console Job, Eliphaz, Bildad and Zophar, attempt to justify the ways of God in the face of the seeming injustice. In his reading of Eliphaz, the first friend to speak, Maimonides once again zeroes in on the most decisive verse in all of his speeches:

> The opinion of Eliphaz... is... that everything that befell Job was deserved by him, for he had committed sins because of which he deserved these misfortunes. This is what he says to Job: "Is not thy wickedness great? Are not thine iniquities without end?" (Job 22:5). (*Guide* III:23;493).

It is worth noting that Maimonides did not simply turn to Eliphaz's first speech (Job 4–5), which is actually conciliatory, but instead turns to his third speech, which more sharply presents his solution to the dilemma of Job's suffering, namely that Job was not, in fact, blameless. The first speech, however, is cited in order to reconcile this argument with Job's manifest righteousness, as Maimonides continues:

> He began to tell Job: the righteousness of your actions and your excellent way of life upon which you relied do not entail your being perfect before God so that you should not be punished: "Behold, He putteth no trust in His servants, and His angels He chargeth with folly; how much less in them that dwell in houses of clay, whose foundation is in the dust" (Job 4:18–19). Eliphaz does not cease turning around this point, I mean to say that he believes that everything that befalls a man is deserved, but the deficiencies for which we deserve punishment... are hidden from our perception. (*Guide*, ibid.)

According to Maimonides, Eliphaz in chapter 4 argues that man, by his very nature, is mired in sin and can thus never be truly blameless. In this way the great philosopher reconciles the two seemingly incongruent Eliphaz speeches: the mitigation of the first speech and unequivocal assertion of Job's guilt in the third.[27]

After analyzing the views of Bildad and Zophar similarly, Maimonides summarizes what he has demonstrated, namely that the book of Job "sets forth the opinions of people concerning providence," by which he means the opinions known to him from Greco-Arabic philosophy:

> The opinion attributed to Job is in keeping with the opinion of Aristotle; the opinion of Eliphaz is in keeping with the opinion of our Law (i.e., the Torah[28]); the opinion of Bildad is in keeping with the doctrine of the Mu'tazila, the opinion of Zophar is in keeping with the opinion of the Ash'ariyya. (*Guide* III:23;494)

And, indeed, these views correspond to those Maimonides had outlined in *Guide* III:17.

---

27. One might argue, of course, that Eliphaz's thinking developed over the course of the dialogues, an assumption made by Nahmanides (see his preface to chapters 4, 15 and 22 [Chavel ed., 36–37, 59–60, 76]). If so, it is possible that originally Eliphaz did not wish to assert Job's guilt, a thought that only came to him as Job began to criticize God more openly. Perhaps Maimonides did not consider this possibility because he viewed Eliphaz as a fictional character devised by the author of Job merely to represent a philosophical position, a view that precluded delving into his changes of heart. Nahmanides, on the other hand, manifests a psychological approach to this book (which he assumed to be historical) and regularly posits that the interlocutors' views changed because of the debates; see Mordechai Z. Cohen, "Great Searchings of the Heart: Psychological Sensitivity in Nahmanides' Commentaries on the Torah and Job" [Hebrew], *Teshura Le-Amos: Collected Studies in Biblical Exegesis Presented to 'Amos Hakham*, ed. Moshe Bar-Asher, Noah Hacham and Yosef Ofer (Alon Shevut 2007), 218–233.

28. The Arabic term *sharī'ah* that Maimonides uses here refers to Islamic religious law; "our *sharī'ah*" thus means Jewish religious law, rooted in the Torah; see Joel L. Kraemer, "Naturalism and Universalism in Maimonides' Thought," *Me'ah She'arim: Studies in Medieval Jewish Spiritual Life in Memory of Isadore Twersky*, ed. Ezra Fleischer et al (Jerusalem 2001), 49–51. Notwithstanding this seeming endorsement, Maimonides does not, in the end, accept Eliphaz's solution to the dilemma posed by Job. What he means, evidently, is that a simplistic — but ultimately imprecise — reading of the Torah leads to such a solution. On this matter, see Leo Strauss, *Persecution and the Art of Writing* (Glencoe, IL 1952), 83; see also Mordechai Z. Cohen, "Maimonides' Disagreement with 'The Torah' in His Interpretation of Job," *Zutot: Perspectives on Jewish Culture* 4 (2004): 66–78.

Naturally, Scripture's intent in presenting these views was to clarify which is correct, and to this end Maimonides goes on to evaluate them. With respect to Job's theory, he could easily draw upon the Talmud to label Job's doctrine as heretical — and incorrect:

> You know the dictum of the Sages that this opinion of Job's is most unsound.... They say (BT *Baba Batra* 16a): "Job denied the resurrection of the dead." They also say of him: "He began to blaspheme." (*Guide* III:23;492)

To assess the views of the three friends, something the Rabbis did not do quite as clearly,[29] Maimonides turns to the concluding chapter of Job. After receiving the two divine visions, Job utters a contrite response, at which point the Lord turns to Eliphaz in 42:7 saying: "I am incensed at you and your two friends, for you have not spoken of Me what is right (נכונה) as [did] my servant Job." God Himself thus confirms Elihu's criticism and repudiates the views of Eliphaz, Bildad and Zophar. In the end, then, Elihu alone expresses the truth endorsed by God Himself, a conclusion drawn by Saadia, and echoed by Ibn Ezra.[30] Following in their footsteps, Maimonides (*Guide* III:23;494–496) praises him as the wisest of the interlocutors, after which he defines Elihu's correct view on providence, which not coincidentally appears to be equivalent to his own.

Maimonides' doctrine of providence and reading of Elihu are complex subjects — analyzed at length by Charles Raffel — that we need not dwell on here.[31] Instead, we focus on an exegetical crux Maimonides addresses in connection with Job 42:7, where God seems to imply that "my servant Job," in contrast to Eliphaz, Bildad and Zophar, "spoke... what is right" (דבר נכונה). But this

---

29. Some brief, scattered comments in rabbinic literature are gathered by Mack, *Ela' Mashal Hayah*, 103–105.
30. See Saadia on Job, introduction, Kafih ed., 18–19; and Ibn Ezra, introduction to Job, Gómez Aranda ed., 6*.
31. "Providence as Consequent Upon the Intellect: Maimonides' Theory of Providence," *AJS Review* 12 (1987): 25–72. See also Rosenberg, "*Iyyov*," 153–154; for an opposing view, see Kasher, "Job's Image," 81–87.

blatantly contradicts the assessment that Job's opinion is absolutely incorrect. Reflecting his immersion in rabbinic literature, Maimonides first records a solution found in the Talmud:

> the Sages... say, "A man is not to be blamed for [what he does when] suffering," meaning that he was excused because of his great suffering (BT *Baba Batra* 16a; *Guide* III:23;492).

But the great philosopher rejects this solution, saying that "it has nothing to do with this parable" (*Guide*, ibid.).[32] Instead, he argues that Job is credited for "speaking what is right" because he renounced his erroneous view in his contrite response to God in the immediately preceding verse, "now my eye seeth... wherefore I... repent of dust and ashes" (Job 42:6; *Guide*, ibid.). It is possible that Maimonides arrived at this explanation independently; yet it is worth noting that this interpretation can also be found in Abraham Ibn Ezra's commentary on Job 42:7.

3. Maimonides' Exegetical Sources

At this point we should comment on Maimonides' exegetical sources. The passages we have seen so far reflect a dual tendency in the *Guide*. On the one hand, practically the only source Maimonides acknowledges explicitly is rabbinic literature, i.e., Talmud and Midrash. In fact, at the outset of his analysis of Job, he credits the Rabbis alone as the source of his understanding of this book: "I shall mention to you the words of the Sages (*kalām al-ḥakhamim*) that have drawn my attention to everything that I understand of this great parable" (*Guide* III:22;486; Munk-Joel ed., 352). Yet on the other hand, there are numerous indications throughout the *Guide* and elsewhere that Maimonides read Scripture not merely as a talmudist, but as an interpreter familiar

---

32. והד'א אלנחו מן אלכלאם ליס מן קביל הד'א אלמתֿל (Munk-Joel ed., 357); i.e., this solution is incorrect. I have diverged here from Pines' translation ("this kind of speech does not accord with the parable"); for further discussion of this point, see Cohen, "Maimonides' Literary Approach," 229.

with the Babylonian-Iberian tradition.[33] For example, Ibn Janah's linguistic influence is evident throughout the lexicographic chapters in part one of the *Guide*.[34] Maimonides' sporadic (and at times oblique) references to Saadia, Moses Ibn Chiquitilla, Moses Ibn Ezra and other authors in the Babylonian-Iberian tradition suggest their decisive influence on his exegetical thinking as well.[35] Indeed, the philosophical template Maimonides' applies to Job follows a precedent established by Saadia and embraced by Abraham Ibn Ezra.[36] The question of Ibn Ezra's influence on Maimonides — a matter of controversy in recent scholarship — was addressed at length in a dedicated study by Isadore Twersky;[37] the only thing I would add here is that we must consider each of Ibn Ezra's works according to its date of completion. Much of the scholarly debate has focused on the possible influence of Ibn Ezra's *Yesod Mora'*, written in London in 1158, on Maimonides' *Sefer ha-Mitswot*, completed in Egypt around 1168.[38] For Maimonides to have used Ibn Ezra's work as his model, it would have had to have traveled from the northwestern corner of Christian Europe to Egypt in less than a decade — lightening speed in the twelfth century. On the other hand, Ibn Ezra's Job commentary — among his first — was

---

33. It is intriguing to consider if Maimonides knew anything of Rashi and his *peshat* school of biblical interpretation or even the northern French Tosafist school. The scholarly consensus is that he was unaware of these developments; see Herbert A. Davidson, *Moses Maimonides: The Man and His Works* (New York 2005), 141. A generation later, however, we do find contacts between Abraham ben Maimonides and Tosafist scholars; see Ephraim Kanarfogel, "Rashi and Maimonides Meet in a Geniza Fragment: A Reference to *Mishneh Torah* in a Letter from a Tosafist" [Hebrew], *Tarbiz* 67 (1997–1998): 411–416.
34. See Cohen, *Three Approaches*, 104–108.
35. See Wilhelm Bacher, *Die Bibelexegese Moses Maimûni's* (Budapest 1896), vi–vii, 168, 171–174; Isadore Twersky, *Introduction to the Code of Maimonides* (New Haven 1980) 58, 449 n. 227; Davidson, *Maimonides*, 117–118; Cohen, *Three Approaches*, 14, 98n; idem, "A Poet's Biblical Exegesis," *JQR* 93 (2003): 538–539.
36. See Cohen, "Maimonides' Disagreement," 75–78; idem, "Great Searchings of the Heart," 224–226 and references to Saadia and Ibn Ezra above.
37. "Did R. Abraham Ibn Ezra Influence Maimonides?" [Hebrew], *Rabbi Abraham Ibn Ezra: Studies in the Writings of a Twelfth Century Jewish Polymath*, ed. Isadore Twersky and Jay Harris (Cambridge, MA 1993) 21–48 [Hebrew Section].
38. See Abraham Ibn Ezra, *Yesod Mora ve-Sod Torah (The Foundation of Piety and the Secret of the Torah)*, ed. Joseph Cohen and Uriel Simon (Ramat Gan 2002), 21, 29–30; Davidson, *Maimonides*, 174–175.

written in Rome, around 1140,[39] and therefore could have made its way back to Muslim Spain even before Maimonides emigrated to Fez around 1159.[40] Or he may have seen it later on, either in North Africa or Egypt, still giving him enough time to absorb the great exegete's commentary before Maimonides turned to Job himself when writing the *Guide* in the 1180's.[41]

In any event, it is in the spirit of the medieval philosophical approach to Job, coupled with the generally liberal attitude of the Babylonian-Iberian attitude toward rabbinic exegesis,[42] that Maimonides felt free to reject the rabbinic solution אין אדם נתפס בשעת צערו. Like Saadia and Ibn Ezra before him, Maimonides assumed that the purpose of the book of Job is to clarify the theological issue of divine providence. If so, the standard for evaluating the interlocutors must be an analytic one: how close did they come to the truth? The fact that Job's suffering led him to err is thus irrelevant: even if his blasphemy is excusable from a psychological and religious perspective, that does not make it correct and he therefore cannot be said to have spoken נכונה.

4. Northern French Exegetical Approaches

Returning to the northern French exegetical school, we note that Maimonides' comprehensive approach highlights the very issues that fall outside the narrow linguistic *peshat* agenda of Rashi and his students. It is important to note that none of these exegetes wrote an introduction in which he discussed his methods or

---

39. See Gómez Aranda, *Commentario*, xxxix; see also Shlomo Sela, *Astrology and Biblical Exegesis in Abraham Ibn Ezra's Thought* (Hebrew; Ramat-Gan 1999), 16.

40. See Davidson, *Maimonides*, 28.

41. We know that Maimonides' son, Abraham, used Ibn Ezra's commentaries in Egypt, since he cites them copiously in his own Torah commentary; see פירוש התורה לרבנו אברהם בן הרמב"ם ז"ל על בראשית ושמות, ed. and trans., Yosef ben Saliḥ Duri and Efraim Yehuda Wiesenburg (London 1959), 539. In the ethical will attributed to Maimonides addressed to his son we find an admonition to study the works of Abraham Ibn Ezra diligently; but this document has proven to be a forgery; see Twersky, "Influence," 22–23.

42. See Jacob Elbaum, *Medieval Perspectives on Aggadah and Midrash* (Hebrew; Jerusalem 2000), 47–94.

goals, let alone the concepts he derived from the book of Job.[43] And yet, the "pressure points" in Job identified by Maimonides may help us extrapolate an overarching approach to the book attested in Rashi's school. The clearest indication I have found of some comprehensive approach to the book within this school is in a commentary penned by Rashbam on Job 42:7 (which appears in the printed text of Rashi's commentary, in a section at the end of Job that Rashi himself never completed[44]):

> For you have not spoken of Me what is right as My servant Job — for you did not utter for me a correct (or: appropriate) argument, as did my servant Job, for he did not sin toward Me, except for what he said "He destroyeth the innocent and the wicked" (9:22), by means of the Satan who prosecutes throughout the world, as it says "If the one who roams (i.e., Satan[45]) slays suddenly, He will mock at the calamity of the guiltless" (9:23). And even if he continued to speak, he only spoke [in that vein] because of the sufferings that weighed upon him heavily and overpowered him.[46]

---

43. Such comprehensive introductions, while common in the Babylonian-Iberian tradition of biblical commentary, were all but unknown in Rashi's school, in which practically all programmatic and methodological statements are buried in glosses on individual verses, e.g., Rashi on Gen 3:8, Qara on I Sam 1:17, Rashbam on Gen 37:2; see Avraham Grossman, "The School of Literal Jewish Exegesis in Northern France," *Hebrew Bible / Old Testament: The History of its Interpretation*, ed. Magne Sæbø et al (Göttingen, 2000), I/2:335,351; and below, n. 59. The exception that proves the rule is Rashi's introduction to the Song of Songs, which includes a clear expression of interpretive theory and a comprehensive overview of the book; see Kamin, *Categorization*, 77–86, 123–124; idem, "Rashi's Commentary on the Song of Songs and Jewish-Christian Polemic" (Hebrew), *Jews and Christians Interpret the Bible*, ed. Y. Zakovitch (Jerusalem 1991), 32–34.

44. See Japhet, *Rashbam on Job*, 16–19. There are only small variations between the text of Rashi in the *Miqra'ot Gedolot* on 42:7 and Rashbam ad loc. (Japhet ed. 445).

45. This reading of Job 9:22 (which diverges, e.g., from that of Maimonides cited above) is consistent with Rashbam's commentary on that verse: אם שוט ימית פתאום וגו' – פירוש שׁל אחת היא. שׁוט – לשׁון 'משׁוט בארץ' (איוב א ז). למסת נקיים ילעג – על שׁהוא ממיס את הנקיים, הוא לועג, השׂטן (Japhet ed., 364).

46. The same interpretation appears in Qara's commentary on 42:7 (Ahrend ed., 130); according to Japhet (*Rashbam on Job*, 36–48), this is simply an interpolation on the basis of Rashbam's commentary. The commentary of R. Tam on this verse reads: לא דברתם בעדי נכונה כאשר עבדי איוב נכון, אשר הרשׁעתם אותו והוא צדיק וישׁר (Shoshana ed.,

To be sure, Rashbam here addresses a direct exegetical difficulty: How could God imply that Job spoke properly in light of his earlier blasphemy? As evidence of that blasphemy, Rashbam cites the very same two verses Maimonides had selected in the *Guide* to demonstrate Job's heretical view. As it turns out, then, this difficult, lengthy biblical book yielded the same result to both careful readers of Scripture seeking to identify Job's most pointed utterances. Furthermore, the mitigation that Rashbam finds for Job can be traced to the talmudic view rejected by Maimonides: the patient sufferer's heretical outbursts are understandable — and excused by God — because they were uttered out of his pain and anguish.

Reflecting no small measure of creativity, Rashbam expands upon the reasoning he found in the Talmud to apply a similar standard to the other interlocutors:

> But you (i.e., Eliphaz and his two friends) sinned toward me by declaring him wicked… whereas you should have comforted him as Elihu did. Was it not enough for Job with his trouble and suffering, that you had to heap iniquity upon your sin by insulting him?![47]

Rashbam does not adopt Maimonides' philosophical analytic standard, but rather an ethical-religious one. Just as Job is excused notwithstanding his heretical utterances, the three friends are blameworthy not because of doctrinal error, but rather because they spoke harshly to Job, failing to empathize with the righteous

---

275). It would seem that he does not construe the verse to mean that Job *spoke* נכונה (rightly, properly), but rather that he *is* נכון (right, righteous). A similar approach can be found in Saadia's Arabic translation of this verse (Kafih ed., 206–207), which reads: אד' לם תקולון בחצ'רתי אלצואב פי עבדי איוב ("for you have not spoken regarding me that which is correct about my servant Job"), evidently based on the *Vorlage* בעבדי איוב, rather than כעבדי איוב. On the textual basis for such a reading, see Samuel R. Driver and George B. Gray, *A Critical and Exegetical Commentary on the Book of Job*, The International Critical Commentary (New York 1921), 348.

47. Rashbam on Job 42:7 (Japhet ed., 445); this interpretation is also found in the printed edition of Rashi's commentary on Job as well as Qara (Ahrend ed., 130) on this verse. It is possible that R. Tam's commentary here (see previous note) is based on this criticism of the friends for impugning Job's righteousness. In that commentary, however, there is no analogous commendation of Elihu's behavior.

sufferer. Elihu's merit emerges by contrast, and he is spared from divine wrath because of the sensitivity he manifested in consoling Job, not necessarily because he arrived at the correct conception of providence. In his reading of Job 42:7, Rashbam evidently did not take נכונה to mean true or correct, but rather *ethically and religiously appropriate*, a view adopted in the twentieth century, for example, by Moshe Zvi Segal.[48]

Rashbam's gloss on 42:7 seems to reflect the view of his grandfather Rashi, who offers — in his commentary on Job 36:8–9 — an overall assessment of Elihu's tone:

> "If they are bound in shackles [and caught in trammels of affliction]" — And if you see righteous people bound in the shackles of sufferings... it is only because they sinned to Him and He comes to collect from them, for their benefit, to cleanse them and to caution them to repent (lit. return to Him).
>
> "He declares to them what they have done" — With these sufferings he informs them that they have sinned to Him. All of the words of Elihu were complete consolation, not abuse. That is to say: "If you are righteous, do not worry about the sufferings, for they are for your benefit."[49]

This gloss goes beyond a local exegetical difficulty and addresses the larger question of what Elihu adds to the debate. To be sure, Rashi here is probably anticipating the difficulty that will emerge in 42:7: Why is Elihu spared from the divine wrath visited upon the other three friends? And yet, in the course of addressing that issue he arrives at an overall assessment of Elihu's new approach, in contrast to the other three friends.

---

48. 'איב', Tarbiz 13 (1942) 75. For support, Segal cites verses such as Ps 5:10; Exod 8:22.
49. Shoshana ed., 220–221. As far as I could tell, the concluding remark has no precise parallel in any of the other commentators in the French school. Partial echoes of Rashi's words, however, can be discerned in his students' commentaries. Rashbam on Job 36:12 (Japhet ed., 425; see also ibid., 125) identifies a conciliatory tone in the words of Elihu, including the notion that all men are bound to sin. Joseph Qara makes a similar remark in his comm. on 36:9 (Ahrend ed., 103).

Nahmanides, however, notes the weakness in Rashi's assessment that Elihu has truly found a new approach, since the very same ideas can be found in the words of the other three friends. If so, he concludes:

> I do not know what makes these words of consolation, and why he considered the words of the friends abuse. Perhaps Elihu spoke them (i.e., his words) gently, and in a quiet voice, whereas the friends spoke them with shouting and a loud voice?[50]

Nahmanides — a product of the Andalusian exegetical school — clearly worked with the analytic standard of Ibn Ezra and Maimonides.[51] But Rashi implicitly applies another standard, one of ethical propriety. While Nahmanides seems to offer his suggestion ironically, he may be onto something: Rashi seems to say that even if Elihu adds nothing new conceptually, it is conceivable that his tone was different, that he encouraged Job rather than berating him as the three friends had done. And indeed, this gloss by Rashi can be seen as the source of Rashbam's words on 42:7, "you should have comforted him as Elihu did." [52]

We might say, then, that Rashi and Rashbam adopt a decidedly non-philosophical approach to Job and derive a very different message that does not clarify the doctrine of providence at

---

50. Comm. on 36:9 (Chavel ed., 109).
51. To be sure, Nahmanides sharply criticizes these Andalusian predecessors, and at times even seems to embrace views of the talmudically-oriented northern French school; yet his point of origin can generally be found within his Andalusian exegetical heritage. On the complex nature of Nahmanides' exegetical allegiances, see Bernard Septimus, "Open Rebuke and Concealed Love: Nahmanides and the Andalusian Tradition," *Rabbi Moses Nahmanides (Ramban): Explorations in His Religious and Literary Virtuosity*, ed. Isadore Twersky (Cambridge 1983), 11–34. In his commentary on Job, likewise, Nahmanides follows in the footsteps of Saadia, Ibn Ezra and Maimonides in seeking to extrapolate analytic positions from the dialogues. Indeed, adhering to their template, he reaches the conclusion that אליהוא תירץ קושייותיו של איוב יפה וכהוגן (comm. on 36:9 [Chavel ed., 109]), although he invokes a kabbalistic notion to support this assessment; see comm. on 33:16–30 (Chavel ed., 99–101) with Chavel's notes ad loc.; see also Yaakov Hocherman, הטענה המכרעת בטענות אליהו בן־ברכאל הבוזי לפי שיטת הרמב"ן, *Beit Mikra* 37 (1992): 339–347.
52. An echo of Rashi's formulation appears in Rashbam on Job 39:13 (Japhet ed., 425): וכן היה מוכיחו ומנחמו אליהוא.

all. Instead, they learn from Job that a righteous sufferer must be treated with sensitivity and understanding — even if he utters heretical remarks, as Job had done. The three friends who criticized Job to defend God's honor were in the end scolded by God Himself, whereas Elihu who spoke gently to Job was spared from divine wrath.

5. Conculsion

Based on the preceding survey of the tradition of Jewish exegesis of the book of Job, we can make the following general observations. Maimonides' goal of biblical analysis is to extrapolate fundamental principles, to see the "big picture." He therefore adopts a meta-textual approach that abstracts a clear analytic message from the book of Job as a whole, as he states rather triumphantly at the end of his analysis:

> If you meditate upon everything I have told you… and if
> you consider this book of Job, its meaning will become
> clear to you; and you will find that I have summed up
> all its notions (or: the totality of its ideas — *jumlat*
> *ma'āniha*), nothing being left aside except such matters as
> figure there because of the arrangement of the discourse
> and the continuation of the parables, according to what
> I have explained to you several times in this Treatise.
> (*Guide* III:23;497; Munk-Joel ed., 361)

This, of course, is another reference to his rule of global rather than piecemeal *mashal* analysis.[53]

While Maimonides' reading of Job follows a path paved by Saadia and Ibn Ezra, it bears his unique imprint, reflecting his distinct capacity to organize disparate data, to generalize, classify and conceptualize. The great philosopher-talmudist displays this talent eminently in his monumental code of Jewish law, *Mishneh*

---

53. Above, at n. 25.

Torah.[54] An analogous challenge of interpretive classification also underlies the next major topic Maimonides addresses in the *Guide* in his highly detailed and comprehensive analysis of *ṭaʿamei ha-mitswot*. In *Guide* III:27–28, he establishes that all of the biblical commandments serve one of three basic goals: (a) establishment of a civilized society by prohibiting injustice; (b) development of the ethical personality through attainment of moral virtues; (c) intellectual perfection by acquiring "correct opinions" that lead to a true knowledge of God.[55] After establishing some further principles of classification in III:29–34, he proceeds, in III:35–49, to explain how those three goals illuminate the rationale of all Torah commandments within fourteen categories that he devises for this purpose.[56] Upon completion of that discussion Maimonides remarks:

> I have now dealt one by one with all the commandments included in these [fourteen] classes and we have drawn attention to the reasons for them. There are only a few and some slight details for which I have not given reasons, even though in truth we have virtually given reasons also for these to him who is attentive and comprehending. (*Guide* III:49;613)

Once again, Maimonides expresses his aim to ascertain the overarching meaning of Scripture by discerning its theological and philosophical messages.[57] In this endeavor, he would not be distracted by the details of the biblical text (which, as he explains,

---

54. See Twersky, *Introduction*, 238–311.
55. See Twersky, *Introduction*, 387–388.
56. On the correspondence between these and the fourteen books of *Mishneh Torah*, see Twersky, *Introduction*, 300–301, 321–323, 389–391, 430–439; see also Lenn E. Goodman, "Maimonides' Philosophy of Law," *Jewish Law Annual* 1 (1978): 98–99.
57. It is instructive to note that even Abraham Ibn Ezra — otherwise well known for his linguistic interests — likewise deems the attainment of theological and philosophical wisdom to be the ultimate goal of biblical study, which must therefore be supplemented by expertise in various secular disciplines; see Uriel Simon, *Four Approaches to the Book of Psalms*, tran. Lenn J. Schramm (New York, 1991), 200–216.

were necessary primarily for literary purposes), nor a single-minded focus on its linguistic dimension.[58]

A very different concept of interpretation emerges in the northern French *peshat* school, which was inspired by a desire to re-establish the centrality of the text in the face of midrashic exegesis, which had sacrificed philological-contextual analysis of Scripture in pursuit of an ideological (or: homiletical) reading.[59] Accordingly, Rashi and his students produced commentaries on Job that enabled readers to experience the story of Job, to listen attentively to the dialogues with his friends and God's voice from the whirlwind. Deeper philosophical messages that one might extrapolate from the book of Job, it would seem, were beyond the scope of their *peshat* interests. Indeed, Rashbam in his commentary on Qohelet disavows speculation about what he refers to as "deep wisdom" (חכמה עמוקה) the subjects of *Sefer Yetsirah* and *Ma'aseh Merkavah*, which include the workings of

---

58. To be sure, Maimonides at times seems to project his philosophical views onto the biblical text rather than seek its original meaning, a critique articulated forcefully by Spinoza, and repeated in modern times by M.Z. Segal, who referred to Maimonides' exegesis as mere "philosophical *derash*"; see Benedict de Spinoza, *Theologico-Political Treatise* (trans. R.H.M. Elwes; New York 1951), 114–118; Moshe Zvi Segal, פרשנות המקרא (2d ed.; Jerusalem, 1971), 51–52. For a rejoinder to these critiques, see Shalom Rosenberg, "על פרשנות המקרא בספר מורה נבוכים", *Jerusalem Studies in Jewish Thought* 1 (1981): 85–157.

59. This thinking is especially apparent in the methodological statement by Rashbam in his commentary on Gen 37:2, where he writes:

ישכילו ויבינו אוהבי שכל מה שלימדונו רבותינו כי אין מקרא יוצא מידי פשוטו, אף כי
עיקרה של תורה באת ללמדנו ולהודיענו ברמיזת הפשט ההגדות וההלכות והדינין...
והראשונים מתוך חסידותם נתעסקו לנטות אחרי הדרשות שהן עיקר, ומתוך כך לא
הורגלו בעומק פשוטו של מקרא.

These words suggest that Rashbam acknowledges the importance of Midrash for defining the essential (עיקר) ideological message of Scripture, though for his part, Rashbam seeks to establish an alternative, methodologically sound, linguistic-contextual reading of the biblical text (פשוטו של מקרא). On Rashbam's attitude toward the relationship between *peshat* and *derash*, especially as manifest in this and similar methodological comments of his, see Touitou, *Perpetual Motion*, 51–74; Sarah Kamin, "Affinities Between Jewish and Christian Exegesis in Twelfth Century Northern France," *Jews and Christians*, 12*-17*; Sara Japhet, "The Tension Between Rabbinic Legal Midrash and the 'Plain Meaning' (Peshat) of the Biblical Text — an Unresolved Problem? In the Wake of Rashbam's Commentary on the Pentateuch," *Sefer Moshe: The Moshe Weinfeld Jubilee Volume*, ed. Chaim Cohen, Avi Hurvitz and Shalom M. Paul (Winona Lake, IN, 2004), 419–422; Mordechai Z. Cohen, "Rashbam Scholarship in Perpetual Motion," *The Jewish Quarterly Review* 98 (2008): 389–408.

divine providence.[60] (By contrast, *Ma'aseh Bereshit* and *Ma'aseh Merkavah* were the very matters that interested Maimonides most in his investigation of Scripture, as he states in his introduction to the *Guide* [Pines trans., 6].) It is in this spirit that we can understand why neither Rashi nor his successors present an overarching meta-textual objective in their commentaries on Job. Instead, they focus exclusively on the language and the exegetical difficulties it presents, such as the obvious dilemma posed by 42:7 in comparison with Job's denial of divine justice. And yet, their very lack of an analytic agenda enables them to let the biblical text speak for itself, without conforming to a strict philosophical template.[61] Consequently, they could view the book of Job as a guide to proper ethical behavior rather than correct philosophical doctrine, a view favored in modern biblical scholarship.[62]

---

60. See Sarah Kamin, "Rashbam's Conception of the Creation," *Jews and Christians*, 55*-57*, 68*. The references are to Rashbam's commentary on Qoh 7:23–24. Sara Japhet has found a similar anti-mystical strain in his commentary on Job, in response to Rashi, who occasionally drew upon mystical teachings to illuminate the text of Job; see Japhet, *Rashbam on Job*, 153–159. (See, however, the cautionary, seemingly anti-mystical stance Rashi expresses in his commentary on Prov 25:2.) On Rashbam's anti-mystical attitude, which was echoed by Rabbenu Tam, see Ephraim Kanarfogel, *Peering Through the Lattices* (Detroit 2000), 158–175. On this basis, Professor Kanarfogel (personal communication) has suggested that the very choice of Rashbam and Rabbenu Tam to pen commentaries on Job in particular may have been motivated by a desire to demonstrate that this book — which would seem to deal with an esoteric topic — can be interpreted without recourse to mystical teachings.

61. This, of course, does not exclude the possibility that even the northern French *peshat* exegetes — much as any reader of Scripture — were at times influenced by their own preconceived notions — whether ideological or rational — when interpreting the biblical text. On this aspect of Rashbam's exegesis, e.g., see Japhet, *Rashbam on Job*, 127–146, 158–159.

62. See, e.g., Marvin Pope, *Job: A New Translation with Introduction and Commentary: The Anchor Bible* (New York 1965), lxxiii–lxxxiv; Segal, "איוב", 73–91; Alan Cooper, "The Sense of the Book of Job," *Prooftexts* 17 (1997): 227–244; Yair Hoffman, דמותו של המאמין בספר איוב, *Hagut ba-Miqra* 3 (1980): 84–94.

13

ואע"פ שרז"ל קבלו: Peshat and Halakhah in Radak's Exegesis

Naomi Grunhaus

Challenging rabbinic *aggadot* and the suggestion of *peshat* interpretations that contradict them was much more prevalent in the medieval Jewish world than the questioning of rabbinic halakhic interpretations. As other exegetes, Radak regularly disputes rabbinic *aggadot*, usually on the grounds of either flawed reasoning or deviation from the biblical record of events.

This paper analyzes the much less frequent phenomenon of Radak's challenges to rabbinic halakhic interpretations, which has not been studied extensively. Owing to the powerful influence of the rabbis as those who set the standards of normative religious practices and due to the importance of those standards for the devout Jewish community, rejection of rabbinic legal decisions was always considered more complicated and awkward than rejection of *aggadot*.[1] Radak's reasoning in this area is important because of the scarceness of medieval exegetes who present *peshat* interpretations that contradict rabbinic halakhah.

From the point of view of intellectual history, the existence of *peshat* explanations that contradict rabbinic halakhah is a vital

---

1. See, e.g., M. Lockshin, "Tradition or Context: Two Exegetes Struggle with Peshat," in *From Ancient Israel to Modern Judaism: Intellect in Quest of Understanding. Essays in Honor of Marvin Fox*, J. Neusner, E. S. Frerichs, and N. M. Sarna, eds. (Atlanta: Scholars Press, 1989), Vol. 2: 175 n. 9. I thank Sara Japhet and Marty Lockshin for reading and commenting on a fuller version of this paper, which will appear in my forthcoming *The Challenge of Received Tradition in Medieval Exegesis: Dilemmas of Interpretation in David Kimhi's Biblical Commentary*, and for helping me clarify a number of issues.

aspect of Radak's approach. However, it must be emphasized that this is still a very limited phenomenon in his works.

In contrast to Radak's explicit methodological statements that *aggadot* sometimes contain illogical material,[2] no broad programmatic statement about rabbinic halakhic traditions appears to exist in his writings. There are also no extant commentaries written by Radak on the legal books of Exodus through Deuteronomy.[3] Therefore, his approach to rabbinic halakhic material can only be derived from his comments on specific biblical narrative and legal texts.

In discussing interpretations that contradict halakhah, scholars distinguish between non-halakhic and anti-halakhic comments. It is feasible to abide by both the *peshat* and rabbinic interpretations presented in non-halakhic comments. On the other hand, since there is direct opposition between the *peshat* and rabbinic interpretations presented in anti-halakhic comments, one could not possibly act upon both simultaneously. For example, Rashbam's metaphorical interpretation of the sign in Exod. 13:9 (והיה לך לאות על ידך "This shall serve you as a sign on your hand") does not negate the rabbis' halakhic interpretation of the verse as a source for the law of phylacteries. But if the Atonement Scapegoat is set free as Rashbam explains at Lev. 16:10, it can not also be killed as the rabbis required.

Anti-halakhic statements appear to be more revolutionary than non-halakhic ones because, even though both may oppose rabbinic halakhic decisions, only anti-halakhic statements directly cancel and preclude the rabbis' halakhic interpretations of verses. Radak's commentaries include bold, blatantly non-halakhic comments, but no explicit anti-halakhic comments.

---

2. One can point to Radak's comments on 1 Sam. 28:25, in which he quotes and appears to agree with Samuel ben Hofni's assertion that rabbinic interpretations need not be accepted when they contradict reason. At 1 Kings 18:26, Radak prefaces his quotation of an aggadah by saying that *aggadot* sometimes contain material that is remote from reason.

3. In a private conversation, S. Japhet suggested that Radak avoided writing on the legal biblical books because he realized the gravity of contradicting rabbinic halakhic traditions.

Taken together, the examples analyzed in this paper demonstrate that Radak did not differentiate between narrative and legal
biblical sections when using the *peshat* technique. Furthermore,
and perhaps even more significant, Radak was willing to question
rabbinic halakhic statements based on his *peshat* exegesis. While
Radak may have learned elements of this method from others, he
moved beyond his predecessors in a number of ways.

1. Precedents

Even though they did not hesitate to challenge rabbinic *aggadot*, many of Radak's recognized predecessors who came from
the Babylonian and Spanish traditions deliberately avoided anti-
halakhic and non-halakhic *peshat* interpretations. The *geonim*
"unquestionably retained their complete allegiance with regard
to matters of law in the broadest possible sense."[4] Philological
exegetes are generally characterized as not arguing against
accepted halakhah.[5]

A known precedent for offering *peshat* explanations that conflict with halakhah can be found in the northern French school,
in the pioneering work of Rashbam (ca. 1080–1160) and other
twelfth century exegetes.[6] Rashi usually does not offer *peshat*
explanations that conflict with halakhah. In some exceptional
cases, he does this without mentioning the fact that a contradiction is inherent in his explanation.[7]

Even though Rashbam viewed rabbinic interpretations as the

---

4. R. Brody, "The Geonim of Babylonia as Biblical Exegetes," in *Hebrew Bible/Old Testament*, M. Saebo, ed. (Göttingen: Vandenhoeck und Ruprecht, 2000), Vol. 1 Part 2, 86.
5. See, e.g., S. Abramson, מפי בעלי לשונות (Jerusalem: Mosad Harav Kook, 1988), 199, and A. Maman, "Peshat and Derash in Medieval Hebrew Lexicons," *Israel Oriental Studies* 19 (1999): 349, 353. See also M. Perez, "פרשנותו הפילולוגית של ר' יהודה אבן בלעם", PhD dissertation (Bar Ilan University, 1978), 326. For an analysis of Radak's Spanish and Babylonian predecessors' views, see my *Challenge of Received Tradition*.
6. M. Kasher cites numerous examples of medieval *peshat* explanations that conflict with rabbinic halakhah in תורה שלמה (New York: American Biblical Encyclopedia Society, 1955/6), Vol. 17: 298–301.
7. See B. Gelles, *Pashat and Drash in the Exegesis of Rashi*, (Leiden: E. J. Brill, 1985), 34–41.

main meaning of the text, as he states explicitly in his comments on Exod. 21:1, he insisted on writing an almost exclusively non-rabbinic commentary that offered *peshat* alternatives to both halakhic and aggadic rabbinic interpretations.[8] Rashbam conceptually divorced his *peshat* exegesis of legal verses from the rabbinic exegesis of those verses, remaining steadfast in his commitment to offer the former, while accepting the latter as religiously binding.

In Rashbam's famous programmatic statement in his comments on Gen. 37:2, he mentions both rabbinic halakhah and aggadah in the same breath, treating them similarly.[9] Rashbam's work represents the high point of *peshat* exegesis in northern France.[10]

Because of the innovation in Rashbam's approach and because Radak moved significantly beyond his Babylonian and Spanish predecessors with his forthright contradictions of rabbinic halakhah, the influence of Rashbam's boldness on Radak cannot be ignored.[11] Radak appears to build on Rashbam's work, even if

---

8. See E. Touitou, "על שיטתו של רשב"ם בפירושו לתורה", *Tarbiz* 48 (1978/9): 253, and idem, "The Method in Rashbam's Commentary on the Halakhic Parts of the Torah," *Milet: Everyman's University Studies in Jewish History and Culture* 2 (1985): 275–88.

9. Even though Rashbam believed that *peshat* interpretations were valid in both legal and narrative biblical sections, he differentiated between the two types of biblical texts. His commentary on the legal sections is shorter than his commentary on the narrative sections, because halakhah often left little room for "speculative" *peshat* interpretations, which would not be binding on a practical level.

10. According to Y. Nevo, פירושי רבי יוסף בכור שור על התורה (Jerusalem: Mosad Harav Kook, 1994), 5, Rashbam's method shaped the approach of others in the northern French school. Nevo quotes a number of cases in which Rabbi Joseph Bekhor Shor presents *peshat* interpretations that contradict halakhah (6–8). In at least some of these cases, Nevo shows how Bekhor Shor relied on dissenting opinions already found in rabbinic literature. On Rashbam's influence on his contemporaries and later thinkers, see also M. Sabbato, "פירוש רשב"ם על התורה", *Mahanayim* 3 (1992): 122–4; D. Rosin, *R. Samuel b. Meir als Schrifterklärer* (Breslau: F. W. Jungfer, 1880), 52–54; and S. Japhet, "The Tension between Rabbinic Legal Midrash and the 'Plain Meaning' (*Peshat*) of the Biblical Text — An Unresolved Problem?: In the Wake of Rashbam's Commentary on the Pentateuch, in *Sefer Moshe: The Moshe Weinfeld Jubilee Volume*, C. Cohen, A. Hurvitz, and S. M. Paul, eds. (Indiana: Eisenbrauns, 2004), 422–425.

11. After exploring possible rabbinic and medieval precedents for Rashbam's approach to legal verses, M. B. Berger, "The Torah Commentary of Rabbi Samuel ben Meir," PhD dissertation (Harvard University, 1982), 290–313, concludes "As an exegetical

none of his comments directly cancels or precludes the rabbis' halakhic interpretation of a verse.

Although Radak almost never quotes Rashbam,[12] he was probably aware of the approaches of the *peshat* school in northern France. Evidence exists of other northern French ideas having been disseminated in southern France.[13] Even if Radak did not know Rashbam's work directly, it may have influenced the Provencal environment sufficiently to promote greater readiness to accept non-halakhic interpretations, which in turn led Radak to offer them.

If Rashbam and others in his school did not pave the way for Radak's license to explain biblical texts contrary to halakhah, then Radak must have arrived at the same conclusions as Rashbam did independently, building on the basic tools he had learned from his Babylonian and Spanish predecessors. In any case, Radak's approach when he contradicts rabbinic halakhah points to an affinity between himself and the exegetes of northern France.[14]

Radak's challenges to rabbinic halakhic traditions are evident when he comments on both legal and narrative texts. His inter-

---

endeavor, however, Rashbam's work is without precedent in rabbinic Jewish history — both ancient or medieval...Important for us to remember is that Rashbam himself was well aware of the newness of his endeavor and readily admits to it." (313)

12. Of the northern French school, Radak mentions Rashbam and Joseph Bekhor Shor by name in his comments on Gen. 45:24 and Joseph Kara by name in his comments on Gen. 19:31. According to H. Cohen, ed., *The Commentary of Rabbi David Kimhi on Hosea* (New York: Columbia University Press, 1929), xxxv n. 1, the references in Gen. 45:24 are a later addition into Radak's commentary.

13. See I. Twersky, *Rabad of Posquieres* (Cambridge: Harvard University Press, 1962), 35, 232–236. According to I. M. Ta-Shema, רבי זרחיה הלוי בעל המאור ובני חוגו (Jerusalem: Mosad Harav Kook, 1992), 104–112, the halakhic works of the northern French Tosafists were known in southern France in the twelfth century. R. Abraham b. Nathan ha-Yarhi of Lunel travelled extensively all over France and incorporated material from northern France into his *Sefer ha-Manhig*. See E. Kanarfogel, *Peering through the Lattices: Mysical, Magical and Pietistic Dimensions in the Tosafist Period* (Detroit: Wayne State University Press, 2000), 51 n. 50, and 56 n. 65.

14. Certainly, the early Babylonian and Spanish precedents may themselves have influenced Rashbam and others in northern France. On this possibility, see A. Grossman, חכמי צרפת הראשונים (Jerusalem: Magnes Press, 1995), 471–3, 554–64 and M. Cohen, "מקור ספרדי אפשרי למושג פשוטו של מקרא אצל רש"י", *Rashi: His Image, His Work and His Influence for Generations*, S. Japhet and A. Grossman (Jerusalem: Zalman Shazar, 2008), 353–79.

pretation of legal texts will be analyzed first, since his method is closest to Rashbam's in that area.

2. Radak's Interpretations of Biblical Legal Texts

The following two cases are the ideal point at which to compare Radak's method to Rashbam's, since both cases deal with interpretation of explicitly legal verses in Deuteronomy. Radak even takes Rashbam's method one small step forward by making the *peshat* interpretations more essential than the rabbinic ones.

In commenting on 2 Kings 3:19, Radak acknowledges that his *peshat* explanation is non-halakhic. In that verse, Elisha tells the kings of Israel, Judah and Edom that they will emerge victorious against the Moabites and וכל עץ טוב תפילו "You shall fell every good tree." A rabbinic interpretation (*Tanhuma Buber* Phinehas 5) points out the apparent inconsistency between Elisha's prophecy and Deut. 20:19, which commands one not to destroy fruit trees. Radak observes:

> כי הכתוב לא אמר, "לא תשחית את עצה" (דב' כ:יט) אלא כשיצורו
> על עיר כמ"ש הטעם, "כי ממנו תאכל", ואע"פ שרז"ל קבלו כי בכל
> מקום ובכל זמן אסור להשחית עץ מאכל, פשט הכתוב הוא שלא
> אמר אלא בעת המצור.

> Because the text did not say, "You must not destroy its trees" (Deut. 20:19) except when they would besiege a city as the reason is written, "You may eat of them", and even though our rabbis of blessed memory received [a tradition] that in every place and at every time it is forbidden to destroy fruit trees, the *peshat* of the text is that it was commanded only at the time of a siege.

While rabbinic halakhah dictates that one may never destroy fruit trees,[15] Radak limits the biblical prohibition in Deut. 20:19 to

---

15. See, e.g., Kiddushin 32a, where Deut. 20:19 is understood to forbid destruction even of objects other than trees.

the specific context of a siege.[16] He reasons that since the three kings were not engaged in a siege and were thereby permitted to fell fruit trees, Elisha did not violate the law when he commanded them to do it.

By restricting his non-halakhic comment to the *peshat* sphere, Radak's analysis demonstrates a complete severance between the *peshat* and halakhic realms, which is a well-known feature of Rashbam's work. On the other hand, whereas Rashbam insists that rabbinic interpretation is more primary than *peshat*, Radak specifically states the opposite, and has Elisha expecting his audience to obey the simple meaning of a legal verse rather than the rabbinic one.[17]

The following example is slightly less radical than the previous case, because Radak's *peshat* interpretation can easily coexist with the rabbinic one, even though Radak himself does not view them as coexistent. 2 Kings 14:6 justifies Amaẓiah's actions in not killing the sons of those who had killed his father by a reference to Deut. 24:16, which states "nor shall children be put to death for parents." In commenting on the verse in 2 Kings, Radak negates the significance of the rabbinic approach to the verse in Deuteronomy when he says:

כי משמעות הכתוב כן הוא כמו שאמר "איש בחטאו יומתו" (דב'
כד:טז) אלא שרבותינו ז"ל קבלו, כי בכלל לאו זה עדות קרובים, כמו
שתרגם אונקלוס...אבל עיקר האזהרה היא כי לא יומתו אבות בעון
הבנים, ולא בנים בעון האבות, כמו שהביא ראיה הנה הנה מן הפסוק.

Because the meaning of the verse is just this as it states [later in the same verse] "A person shall be put to death

---

16. Rashbam interprets Deut. 20:19 in the context of a siege, but his explanation does not negate the rabbinic inclusion of other cases besides a siege. By introducing the reason behind the commandment in Deut. 20:19, Radak highlights his resemblance to Maimonides, whose most radical anti-halakhic statements are found in his discussions of the reasons for the commandments.

17. Berger, "Torah Commentary," 273, cites several examples in which Rashbam offers reasons for the *peshat* laws "as if they [the anti-halakhic interpretations] and not the halakhic traditions were actually practiced." At 2 Kings 3:19, Radak is more direct about the practical implementation of his anti-halakhic interpretation than Rashbam is in the examples Berger quotes.

only for his own crime" (Deut. 24:16) but our rabbis of blessed memory received [a tradition] that included in this prohibition is the testimony of relatives, as Onkelos translated…but the essence of the prohibition is that parents should not be put to death for the sin of their sons, and not sons for the sin of their parents, as he brought proof in this case from the verse.

As Radak understood them, when the rabbis (B. Sanhedrin 27b) explained the first half of the verse as excluding the testimony of relatives, they meant to overshadow the plain interpretation that sons should not be killed for their fathers' sins. Radak's wording of "but" shows that his *peshat* explanation and the rabbinic view of the verse do not concur. Radak's comment in this case again demonstrates a complete separation between the *peshat* and halakhic realms. Radak asserts that the rabbinic explanation should be viewed as only a secondary interpretation of the verse, leaving the primary intent of the verse intact.

The wording Radak uses when discussing this case is as important as his choice of interpretation. Labeling the simple meaning of the verse "the essence of the prohibition" establishes that it is the more important one. While Radak's explanation of Deut. 24:16 is not original,[18] his characterization of the *peshat* as primary is innovative.

Radak provides two pieces of evidence that the plain meaning is the primary intent of the verse, one from the second half of the verse from Deuteronomy, and the other from the biblical quotation in 2 Kings of the verse from Deuteronomy. These proofs show that Radak found biblical evidence convincing justification and sufficient motivation to counter the rabbinic view.

Rashbam regularly, but not always, quotes the rabbinic halakhic interpretations he contradicts by his *peshat* explanations of legal verses, even though he hardly does this when his *peshat* interpretations conflict with rabbinic *aggadot*. Scholars explain

---

18. See, e.g., Judah Ibn Balaam's interpretation on Deut. 24:16.

these quotations as an attempt to prove his respect for rabbinic halakhah or to counteract the uneasiness his audience might experience when reading anti-halakhic or non-halakhic *peshat* explanations. E. Touitou sees these quotations of rabbinic halakhic traditions as proof that Rashbam was aware of the tension between his *peshat* interpretations and rabbinic halakhic traditions, something that others have questioned. Rashbam also often acknowledges the anti-halakhic or non-halakhic character of his interpretations, for the same reasons.[19]

In the two cases discussed above, Radak quotes the rabbinic halakhic interpretations of the verses and concedes the non-halakhic aspect of his interpretations. However, in a number of cases (where the number is of statistical significance) Radak does not explicitly recognize that his views contradict rabbinic halakhah. In these cases, Radak also does not quote the halakhic opinions he is rejecting. These cases validate Radak's connection to Rashbam, by showing that both exegetes offer explicit as well as undeclared *peshat* interpretations that contradict rabbinic halakhah.

Cases in which Radak does not identify an interpretation's anti-halakhic or non-halakhic character or the rabbinic halakhic opinion he is rejecting are not relatively more frequent in Radak's work than in Rashbam's. However, Rashbam usually does not quote rabbinic traditions, which makes his quotation and reference to them specifically in halakhic contexts noteworthy. Radak, on the other hand, quotes rabbinic traditions constantly in both halakhic and aggadic contexts. Therefore, his **lack of** reference to, or quotation of, these rabbinic halakhic traditions is especially noteworthy. Following Touitou's logic regarding Rashbam, when Radak fails to note the rabbinic sources he contradicts, he

---

19. For a discussion of this phenomenon in Rashbam's work, see Berger, "Torah Commentary," 275–279 and E. Touitou, *Exegesis in Perpetual Motion: Studies in the Pentateuchal Commentary of Rabbi Samuel ben Meir* (Ramat Gan: Bar-Ilan University Press, 2003), 178. Rashbam's comments on Exod. 22:1–2 and 29:37 are typical cases in which Rashbam does not state that his interpretations contradict rabbinic halakhah.

demonstrates a greater ease and lack of hesitation than Rashbam concerning non-halakhic interpretation of legal verses.

Another way in which Rashbam deflects criticism is by placing programmatic statements favoring rabbinic interpretations near his more radical anti-halakhic and non-halakhic interpretations. Radak does not appear to make any such programmatic statements that stress the supremacy of rabbinic halakhic traditions, which further proves his lack of hesitation to contradict rabbinic halakhic traditions.

Lev. 19:26 states: לא תאכלו על הדם. לא תנחשו ולא תעוננו "You shall not eat anything with its blood. You shall not practice divination or soothsaying."[20] The rabbis (B. Sanhedrin 63a) offered multiple explanations of the first prohibition by itself, while a number of exegetes base their *peshat* interpretations of "You shall not eat anything with its blood" on the imitation of sorcerers or magicians. For example, Rashbam explains that the sorcerers ate at the grave of a murdered man to prevent his being avenged or for some other magic. Naḥmanides explains that the sorcerers collected blood in vessels so that demons would come eat the blood and tell them the future. Rashbam and Naḥmanides acknowledge that the *peshat* and rabbinic interpretations of "You shall not eat anything with its blood" diverge, since the rabbinic interpretations are not connected to magic or sorcery.

1 Sam. 14:32 asserts, "The troops ate on the blood." Many exegetes understand the people's sin to be a violation of Lev. 19:26.[21] Typical of exegetes who do not connect the verse in 1 Samuel to the verse in Leviticus is Radak, who (in 1 Sam.) says:

ואין זה פירוש "לא תאכלו על הדם," רק פירושו כמו שהוא חק
הזובחים לשדים, שאוכלים סביב הדם אחר שזבחו להם, וזה הדבר

---

20. I thank my colleague Mordechai Cohen for bringing this example to my attention and for discussing it and other aspects of this paper with me.
21. Of commentators on the Pentateuch at Lev 19:26, ibn Ezra and Naḥmanides are representative of those who connect 1 Sam 14:33 to Lev 19:26. Ibn Ezra says: "והעד הנאמן דברי שאול... כי כן כתוב הנה אוכלים 'על הדם'". "The proof [of my interpretation of Lev 19:26] is the words of Saul...and so is it written behold they are 'eating on the blood.'" See also Ibn Ezra's יסוד מורא וסוד תורה, ed. J. Cohen with U. Simon (Ramat Gan: Bar Ilan University Press, 2002), 72.

למד מעניינו "לא תנחשו ולא תעוננו." ורז"ל פירשו כי היו מקדישים
שלמים ואוכלים לפני זריקת הדם.

This is not the meaning of "You shall not eat anything
with its blood," only its meaning is like the rite of the
sacrificers to the demons, that they eat around the blood
after sacrificing to them, and this matter is learned from
its context "You shall not practice divination or soothsaying." And our rabbis of blessed memory explained that
they were dedicating peace offerings and eating before
applying the blood. [22]

Radak's interpretation of Lev. 19:26 does not match any rabbinic
interpretation of the verse from B. Sanhedrin 63a. In fact, it is
almost the same as Rashbam's and Naḥmanides' *peshat* interpretations. Yet Radak does not identify his interpretation as *peshat*, nor
does he mention that it does not fit the rabbis' halakhic interpretations of the verse from Leviticus.[23]

In his comments on Ezek. 33:25, Radak explains, "You shall
not eat anything with its blood" as he did in 1 Samuel, saying:

"על הדם תאכלו": ואני צויתי לכם "לא תאכלו על הדם" כי היא
עבודת עכו"ם, שהיתה חק מן הזובחים לשדים שאוכלים סביב הדם
אחר שזבחו להם, וזהו דבר הלמד מעניינו "לא תאכלו על הדם לא
תנחשו ולא תעוננו."

"You eat with its blood": And I commanded you "You
shall not eat anything with its blood" because this is idol

---

22. The rabbinic interpretation in this case assumes a connection between the verse in
Samuel and the verse in Leviticus, even though Radak in his *peshat* interpretation
does not. Rabbi Isaiah of Trani is another commentator on the Prophets who does
not connect the verse from 1 Samuel to the verse from Leviticus.

23. Later in the same passage, Radak states: זה פירשו רבותינו ז"ל כי על השלמים אמר שהיו
אוכלים בלא זריקת דם. אבל אין משמעות פשטי הפסוקים אלא כמו שפירשנו כי החטא היה מפני הדם
נבלע בבשר ולא היה מתמצה היה... "This is the way the rabbis of blessed memory interpreted that it is about the peace offering that it says that they were eating without
applying the blood. But the significance of the peshat of the verses is none other
than as we explained that the sin was because the blood was ingrained in the meat
and it was not extracted...". Here, Radak's insistence on his peshat interpretation
relates to the historical question of the people's sin and not to the halakhic meaning
of Lev 19:26.

worship, as there was a rite from the sacrificers to the demons that they eat around the blood after they sacrifice to them, and this is a matter learned from its context "You shall not eat anything with its blood. You shall not practice divination or soothsaying."

In this passage, Radak repeats his non-rabbinic explanation of Lev 19:26, without identifying this interpretation as *peshat*; neither does he quote rabbinic interpretations of that verse. This case demonstrates the incongruity of Radak's failing to note a well-known, rabbinic tradition, while Rashbam mentions it.[24]

In discussing Deut. 21:23, Radak again fails to note his interpretation's apparent conflict with rabbinic interpretations of that verse. The verse forbids leaving a corpse hanging overnight and connects this act to desecration of the Land of Israel. The rabbis (B. Sanhedrin 46b) understood the verse's prohibition to include all corpses, not just those that were hanged, and in any land, not just the Land of Israel. In his comments on Josh. 8:29, Josh. 10:27, and Ezek. 39:12, Radak appears to limit the prohibition to corpses that were hanged and to corpses in the Land of Israel, which follows a strictly straightforward interpretation of Deut. 21:23. Radak's interpretation, which is similar to Rashbam's explanation of the verse in Deuteronomy, is non-halakhic.

In another example, Maimonides recognizes "eye for eye, tooth for tooth" (Lev. 24:20) as a paradigmatic case of rabbinic halakhic interpretation conflicting with the plain sense of Scripture. In discussing the verse, Maimonides states:

---

24. Radak might have been specifically inclined to explain Lev. 19:26 non-halakhically because the verse is known as a לאו שבכללות "a prohibition that includes multiple, unrelated proscriptions." The manifold rabbinic explanations of the verse may have signalled its potential to include other valid interpretations. In his *Sefer ha-Riqmah* (Jerusalem: The Academy of the Hebrew Language, 1964), 363, and his *Book of Roots* (Jerusalem: The Academy of the Hebrew Language, 1966), 74, Ibn Janah appeals to the multiple, rabbinic interpretations of Lev. 19:26 to justify non-halakhic interpretation, which may further have influenced Radak. Naḥmanides later uses similar reasoning to support a novel interpretation of the injunction כל חרם אשר יחרם מן האדם לא יפדה "No human being who has been proscribed can be ransomed" at Lev 27:29, arguing that the verse may include multiple, unrelated proscriptions, including his own.

The punishment meted out to anyone who has done wrong to somebody else consists, in general, in his being given exactly the same treatment that he has given to somebody else. If he has injured the latter's body, he shall be injured in his body, and if he has injured him in his property, he shall be injured in his property... and he who has deprived someone of a member shall be deprived of a similar member, "The injury he inflicted on another shall be inflicted on him" (Lev. 24:20). You should not engage in cogitation...[25]

In his comments on Judg. 15:11, Radak uses the same straightforward, anti-halakhic explanation of Lev. 24:20 as Maimonides, in order to justify Samson's revenge against the Philistines. Radak appears to be explaining Lev. 24:20 as referring to bodily harm, since that is exactly what Samson did to the Philistines, despite the well-known rabbinic explanation (B. Baba Kamma 83b) that the verse demands monetary and not bodily retribution. While his interpretation of Lev. 24:20 directly contradicts and precludes the rabbinic halakhic interpretation of that verse, Radak makes no mention of this fact when he says:

רע עשו לי, ורע עשיתי להם. וכן "כאשר יתן מום באדם כן ינתן בו"
(וי' כד:כ).

They (the Philistines) did evil to me (Samson), so I did evil to them. So too "The injury he inflicted on another shall be inflicted on him" (Lev. 24:20).[26]

---

25. *Guide* 3:41. Translation follows S. Pines, *The Guide of the Perplexed* (Chicago: University of Chicago Press, 1963), 3:558, with minor adaptations.
26. Ibn Ezra might have served as Radak's source for this interpretation. See his short and long commentaries on Exod. 21:24, short and long commentaries on Exod. 21:29, and his commentary on Lev. 24:19. See also Lockshin, "Tradition or Context," 185 and n. 70.

3. Radak's Interpretations of Biblical Narrative Texts

When interpreting legal texts, Radak's method is similar to Rashbam's method, although there are some differences between them. However, Radak boldly challenges rabbinic halakhic traditions even based on his reading of biblical narrative texts, although Rashbam and other twelfth century northern French exegetes rarely do this.[27]

It is understandable that Radak is more innovative when interpreting narrative rather than legal texts. Evidently, since he primarily interpreted narrative texts, Radak thought his exegesis in that area was most secure. Nevertheless, the northern French boldness in legal contexts, which allowed for biblical exegesis that contradicted rabbinic halakhic traditions, probably paved the way for Radak's non-halakhic interpretation of narrative texts.

In grappling with the question of whether King Solomon was permitted to marry Pharaoh's daughter or not, Radak analyzes two rabbinic views from B. Yevamot 77b, although the talmudic passage does not mention King Solomon specifically. Rabbi Judah's view, which rabbinic decisors accept as binding, is that both male and female Egyptian converts may not marry into the Israelite congregation for three generations. According to this position, King Solomon would have been forbidden to marry Pharaoh's daughter, even if she converted to Judaism. Rabbi Simeon's view is that only male Egyptian converts are prohibited. Radak reasons that since the biblical text does not fault him for doing it, King Solomon must have been permitted to marry Pharaoh's daughter,

---

27. Gen. 1:5 is one famous case in which Rashbam's explanation of a narrative was understood as having halakhic ramifications. However, his comments on Gen. 1:14, s.v. ולימים, apparently temper the anti-halakhic implications of Rashbam's remarks on Gen. 1:5. For a discussion of Rashbam's interpretation of Gen. 1:5 and reactions to it, see M. Lockshin, *Rabbi Samuel ben Meir's Commentary on Genesis* (Lewiston: Edwin Mellen Press, 1989), 38–9. Another example in which Rashbam's interpretation of a narrative opposes rabbinic halakhah is at Num 25:4. Rashbam explains the root יקע to mean killing by hanging, while rabbinic halakhah (B. Sanhedrin 45b) assumes that hanging is only done after the sinner is killed. Radak at 2 Sam. 21:6 appears to follow Rashbam's non-halakhic interpretation.

which supports Rabbi Simeon's opinion.[28] At 1 Kings 3:3 Radak says:

...היתה אסורה לו לפי שהיתה מצרית ראשונה. ומרבותינו ז"ל
שאמרו (יבמות עז:) כי מותרת היתה לו, כי מה שאמר "בנים אשר
יולדו להם דור שלישי" (דב' כג:ט) בנים ולא בנות. ואף על פי שלא
נקבעה ההלכה כדברי זה החכם, אף על פי שאמר כי קבלה היתה בידו,
נראין דבריו. כי לא ראינו בכתוב שחטא שלמה על שלקח בת פרעה...

...She was forbidden to him because she was a first generation Egyptian convert. And [one] of our rabbis of blessed memory said (B. Yevamot 77b) she was permitted to him, because when the verse says "Children born to them in the third generation" (Deut. 23:9) this means sons and not daughters. Now even though the halakhah was not decided in accordance with the words of this sage, even though he said that he had a received tradition in his hand, his words appear to be correct. Because we do not see in the text that Solomon sinned by taking the daughter of Pharoah...

Radak accepts the rabbis' decision against Rabbi Simeon's opinion, even while making a strong case for it. This acceptance is seen in his initial statement that "she was forbidden to him because she was a first generation Egyptian convert," as per Rabbi Judah's opinion.

Radak's acquiescence to the rabbinic decision renders his seemingly non-halakhic backing of Rabbi Simeon's opinion as purely theoretical and seems to illustrate that he understood the gravity of making anti-halakhic suggestions. Radak hesitates because Rabbi Simeon's stance was not accepted as binding, but he buttresses Rabbi Simeon's opinion by labeling it a received tradition and registers puzzlement that the rabbis rejected it.

For an exegete, using his textual analysis to scrutinize rabbinic

---

28. The biblical text censures Solomon only for marrying many women, for allowing them to turn his heart astray, for permitting them to worship idols, and for worshipping on the forbidden shrines (1 Kings 11:1–5).

law is more complicated than simply disagreeing with rabbinic interpretation of a legal text, because such scrutiny goes against the normal flow of information. Rabbinic literature usually informs exegetes' reading of the biblical text, but their reading of the biblical text does not usually inform their understanding of rabbinic literature. Radak is acting more like a rabbi in the Talmud, whose reading of the biblical text informs his understanding of halakhic questions. In fact, his reasoned endorsement of Rabbi Simeon's viewpoint is comparable to Rabbi Simeon's own justifications in the Talmud.

In his comments on Judg. 18:5, Radak again tries to use his biblical analysis to change a halakhic ruling, but stops short of doing it decisively. The rabbis in B. Shevuot 35b state that all divine names in the narratives about Micah are references to idols, except for the one in Judg. 18:31. Because these names do not refer to God, they have no special sanctity and one is permitted to erase them.

Radak challenges the rabbinic assertion that all divine names in the Micah narratives refer to idols. He further rules that one who abides by Jewish law is not permitted to erase these divine names, as they may have special sanctity based on his interpretation. Radak's analysis renders much of the legal discussion in B. Shevuot 35b meaningless. He says:

...אם כן, "באלקים" זה אינו נמחק כי קדוש הוא. ולדברי רבותינו ז"ל שאמרו (שבועות לה:) כל "אלהים" האמור במיכה חול חוץ מאחד שהוא קדש "כל ימי היות בית אלהים בשילה" (שו' יח:לא). אם כן, "באלהים" זה חול הוא ונמחק. והנה הדבר אצלינו ספק ומספיקא אני אומר שאינו נמחק. ואני תמיה על "כי נתנה אלהים בידכם" (שו' יח:י), איך אמרו עליו שהוא חול? ואף רבי אליעזר ש... והנה לא הסכים עמו יונתן בן עוזיאל. ואם זה "באלהים" הוא חול ...

...If so, this [instance of the word] "God" is not erasable because it is holy. According to our rabbis of blessed memory who said (B. Shevuot 35b) every [instance of the word] "God" in the Micah narratives is unholy [refers to idols] besides one that is holy "throughout the time that the house of God stood at Shiloh" (Judg. 18:31). If so, this [instance of the word] "God" is unholy and erasable. Now the matter is in doubt by us and in doubt I say that it may not be erased. I am amazed at "For God has delivered it into your hand" (Judg. 18:10), how could they say that it is unholy? Even Rabbi Eliezer who [did not completely agree with the other rabbis, agreed with them in this instance]...But Jonathan did not agree with him [that the word "God" in Judg. 18:10 is unholy]. And if this [instance of the word] "God" is unholy [the verse is understood as follows]...

In contrast to the case of 1 Kings 3:3, Radak's interpretation does not concur with any of the various talmudic opinions. Moreover, and quite significantly, Radak's interpretation at Judg. 18:5 is limited to exegesis of the narrative. Radak only questions the rabbis' reading of the biblical narrative, not their halakhic premise that divine references to God may not be erased. Nevertheless, Radak specifically states that his disagreement with the rabbis has practical halakhic ramifications. According to the rabbis, one may erase the divine name in Judg. 18:5, but following Radak, he may not.

Certainly, Radak is not the only exegete who disagrees with the rabbis about what biblical names are or are not divine.[29] The novelty in Radak's comment on Judg. 18:5 lies in his advocating a change in the practical Jewish approach to the text and in his unabashed tone when doing that.

In spite of Radak's innovative claim, he is deferential to the rabbinic view. To begin with, he registers hesitation in his phraseology והנה הדבר אצלנו בספק, ומספיקא אני אומר אינו נמחק "Now the matter is in doubt by us and in doubt I say it may not be erased." By saying that "the matter is in doubt," Radak means that he is not so certain that his interpretation is correct that he is willing

---

29. See, e.g., Rashbam's comment on Deut. 21:23, where his interpretation of "God" in the verse to mean judges differs from the midrashic traditions and Rashi's interpretation. Rashbam interprets the tetragrammaton at Gen. 18:13 as a reference to one of the angels.

to decisively cancel the rabbinic view. Nevertheless, he finds his explanation sufficiently convincing to cast aspersions on the rabbinic explanation and force a change in the practical law regarding the sanctity of the verse, even if it is only because "the matter is in doubt." Radak's uncertainty mitigates the significance of his comment, but it does not necessarily derive from the halakhic implications of his view, as he often compares his views to those of others and evaluates the relative merits of each.

Radak's challenging at Judg. 18:5 of the rabbinic interpretation of Judg. 18:10 is essentially the same as his regular critiques of rabbinic aggadic interpretation, except for its halakhic outcome. His tone and rationale are similar to the tone and rationales he uses when questioning rabbinic *aggadot*. Similarly, when Radak challenges rabbinic *aggadot*, he does not always decide against them conclusively, just as in this case.[30] Overall, his attitude towards rabbinic halakhot and *aggadot* is equivalent, which is one of the hallmarks of Rashbam's method.

In the following case, Radak's comprehension of a biblical narrative weakens a rabbinic ruling. His sole interest appears to be interpretation of the biblical events, and Radak seems ready to promote his explanation of the narrative regardless of its halakhic consequences.

In contrast to his comments on 1 Kings 3:3 and Judg. 18:5, Radak does not acknowledge that his explanation undermines the basis of a halakhic ruling, although he asserts that his explanation contradicts the rabbinic understanding of the narrative. Just as in the case of legal texts, Radak does not always acknowledge that his interpretations of narrative texts contradict rabbinic halakhah. This failure to publicize his approach demonstrates that Radak was quite comfortable with his potential undermining of rabbinic halakhah.

The rabbis (B. Nazir 4b) were of the opinion that Samson was different from other nazirites in that he was permitted to come

---

30. See, e.g., Radak's comments on Josh. 4:11 and 2 Chron. 5:9, in which he ends complex challenges to rabbinic traditions by saying "their insight is broader than our own."

into contact with corpses. Even though Radak acknowledges the rabbinic view, in commenting on Judg. 13:4 he assumes that Samson was forbidden to come into contact with a corpse, just like any other nazirite. Radak also bases his explanations of Judg. 14:19 on the assumption that Samson was just like any nazirite.

Radak's rejection of the rabbinic view of Samson carries halakhic significance. The Mishnah in Nazir 1:2 defines a category of נזיר שמשון "Samson-like nazirite," determining differences between a regular nazirite and a Samson-like nazirite. The rabbis in B. Nazir 4b debate whether a "Samson-like nazirite" may be exposed to dead bodies, just as Samson was. By Radak's reasoning that Samson was forbidden to be defiled by corpses just like any other nazirite, the rabbinic discussion in B. Nazir 4b and the category of a Samson-like nazirite lose much of their significance.

In his comments on Judg. 13:4 and 14:19, Radak categorizes the rabbis' view of Samson's status as a received tradition. This classification makes Radak's rejection of the rabbinic view all the more fundamental. Not only does he question rabbinic reasoning, he is even willing to argue with rabbinic received traditions, "*Kabbalah*."

In another case at 2 Kings 15:1, Radak's comprehension of biblical chronology again potentially weakens a rabbinic ruling. Radak concedes that the rabbis learned a halakhic ruling from their understanding of the narrative, but he stands by his interpretation of the biblical narrative nonetheless. This he does despite his recognition that his interpretation might weaken the rabbinic halakhic ruling.

4. Radak's Explicit Comparison of Biblical Legal and Narrative Texts

The following examples confirm that Radak did not treat legal verses differently from narrative ones. In both examples, Radak quotes legal verses to support his explanation of narrative texts.[31]

---

31. For a thorough discussion of Radak's attitudes towards biblical repetition, including

The rabbis sometimes read halakhic meaning into redundancy in halakhic contexts. For instance, the rabbis explained the repetitive command זכור...לא תשכח "Remember...do not forget [Amalek's deeds]" (Deut. 25:17–19) as two separate injunctions — one not to forget with one's heart, and one to recollect verbally. Radak at 1 Sam. 1:11, on the other hand, explains that the repetition at Deut. 25:17–19 strengthens the commandment, even though this non-halakhic explanation is akin to his customary והכפל לחזק "and the doubling is to strengthen" in narrative contexts. Radak equates the verses in Deuteronomy with the narrative verse in Samuel, saying:

"וזכרתני ולא תשכח את אמתך" – הכפל לחזק התפלה והבקשה, וכן "זכור את אשר עשה לך עמלק...לא תשכח" (דב' כה:יז-יט) לחזק המצוה, ודרשו רז"ל ...

"And will remember me and not forget Your maidservant" — The doubling is to strengthen the prayer and the pleading, and so too "Remember what Amalek did to you on your journey...Do not forget" (Deut. 25:17–19) to strengthen the commandment, and our rabbis of blessed memory interpreted...

Another case in which Radak equates legal verses with narrative ones is at Gen. 24:39, where he analyzes Eliezer's description of his encounter with Rebecca. Radak says:

ובשנות הדברים האלה, יש בהם שנוי מלות, אבל הטעם אחד. כי גם בעשרת הדברים, שהוא עקר התורה, בשנותו אותם במשנה תורה (ראה דב' ה:ו-יח), שנה בהם במקומות המלים, אבל הטעם אחד.

And when repeating these words, there are changes in the words, but the meaning is one. Since also in the Ten Commandments, which is the essence of the Torah, when

a brief analysis of these two examples, see A. Seidler, "דרכו הפרשנית של רבי דוד קמחי", PhD dissertation (Bar Ilan University, 2003), 63–108 and idem, "הכפל לחזק כשאין לו טעם אחר – 'טעמו האחר' של הכפל בפירוש רד"ק", Tarbiz 77: 3–4 (2009): 555–571.

he repeated them in Deuteronomy (5:6–18), he changed
the words in some places, but the meaning is one.[32]

Certainly, Radak sometimes accepts rabbinic interpretations of
biblical repetition in legal contexts.[33] Nevertheless, these examples show that he also did not hesitate to equate legal verses with
narrative ones.

5. Conclusion

Taken together, the examples analyzed in this paper demonstrate
that Radak did not differentiate between narrative and legal biblical texts when using the *peshat* technique. He also believed that
the biblical text could be understood concurrently by a number
of different methods. Radak sometimes concedes that his interpretations are non-halakhic, but sometimes he does not recognize
the non-halakhic aspect of his interpretations. At least one of his
interpretations is anti-halakhic, although he does not explicitly
state this fact.

While a general framework and isolated examples of anti-halakhic and non-halakhic interpretations existed in the Spanish and
Babylonian traditions that influenced Radak, both the innovative
boldness in Radak's approach and the similarity of his presentation to Rashbam's, suggest that Rashbam's work influenced Radak
or his audience. Radak's connection with twelfth century northern French exegesis was always disputed, but it is confirmed by
his method in halakhic contexts.

Rashbam's ideas are usually understood as having limited

---

32. Radak here appears to follow Ibn Ezra, who read little meaning into discrepancies
between the two sets of the Ten Commandments. See Ibn Ezra's long commentary
on Exod. 20:1. Ibn Ezra and Radak appear to ignore various halakhic interpretations
of discrepancies between the two versions of the Ten Commandments. Among
these is the rabbinic explanation (Berakhot 20b) that זכור "Remember [the Sabbath
day]" (Exod. 20:8) applies to positive commandments, while שמור "Observe" (Deut.
5:12) applies to negative commandments. The rabbis (Mekhilta of Rabbi Simon Bar
Yohai ad loc) also explained that לא תחמוד "You shall not covet" (Exod. 20:14) applies
to actions, while לא תתאוה "You shall not crave" (Deut. 5:18) applies to thoughts.
33. See, e.g., Radak's comments on Jer 36:27 and a short list in Seidler, "לדרכו", 99 n. 145.

influence on exegetes outside of northern France.[34] Radak's method in halakhic contexts demonstrates that Rashbam's ideas spread south to Provence and were accepted to some extent in that environment.

The significant impact of Rashbam's ideas is seen in Radak's wanting to carry them even a bit further than Rashbam did in a number of ways. In the first place, Radak designates *peshat* interpretations as more primary than rabbinic, halakhic interpretations. He also bases contradictions of rabbinic, halakhic interpretations on his interpretations of narrative texts, and appears to suggest overturning those rabbinic, halakhic rulings. Radak's slight extensions of Rashbam's method do not signify any great innovation, but rather attest to the ease with which Radak accepted Rashbam's revolutionary approach.

Radak differs significantly from Rashbam and other twelfth century, northern French, radical *peshat* exegetes who followed his lead. While Rashbam was not fond of rabbinic quotation in his commentaries, Radak quotes rabbinic traditions constantly and they are necessary in his view. Therefore, Radak's readiness to question rabbinic halakhic traditions shows that he, and most likely others of his contemporaries, did not view this questioning as contradictory to the necessity and authority of rabbinic traditions.

---

34. Berger, "Torah Commentary," 332–351, explores various reasons that Rashbam's method was not more popular among readers in later generations. M. Lockshin, "Rabbi Samuel ben Meir's Commentary on Genesis," PhD dissertation (Brandeis University, 1983), 428, claims that Rashbam's commentary was not well-liked because it disregarded the tension between *peshat* and homiletical interpretation. Touitou, "על שיטתו", 253 n. 26, maintains that already in the generation after Rashbam lived, *peshat* commentators warned of the dangers inherent in his exegetical freedom. Touitou also lists numerous later religious commentators who preferred IbnEzra's approach to Rashbam's. See also M. Lockshin, "Truth or *Peshat*: Issues in Law and Exegesis," in *Law, Politics and Society in the Ancient Mediterranean World*, B. Halpern and D. W. Hobson, eds. (Sheffield: Sheffield Academic Press, 1993), 271.

14

Nahmanides on The Dynamics of Biblical Dialogue in the Book of Genesis

Michelle J. Levine

Introduction

In his quest to discover the message and meaning of the Genesis narratives, Rabbi Moses ben Nahman (Ramban), a leading exegete of thirteenth century Spain, demonstrates his literary acumen in discerning the role of dialogue as a compelling strategy of characterization in the Bible.

The dialogue scene affords the reader a firsthand glimpse into the dynamic forces shaping the biblical personalities.[1] By portraying these lively encounters as they unfold, rather than describing them in a dry summary report, Scripture allows the reader to experience these scenes directly, as though he were actually present.[2] While Scripture mediates what the reader hears and

---

1. An expanded version of this article appears as part of my recent book, *Genesis: The Art of Biblical Portraiture*, (Brown Judaic Studies, 350, Providence, 2009). My thanks to Brown University Press for allowing this material to appear in the present article.

   Shimon Bar-Efrat, *Narrative Art in the Bible*, trans. Dorothea Shefer-Vanson (Almond Press, Sheffield, 1989 reprint from the 1979 Hebrew edition), p. 96, observes that biblical conversations are usually restricted to "duologues," with only two participants at a time. Conversations involving groups are also regarded as duologues since the groups are related to as a unit.

2. In this manner, direct discourse contributes to the scenic nature of biblical narrative; the reader is made to feel as though he is hearing their words directly and seeing the events in the sequence that the characters experience them. For a discussion of the scenic mode of biblical narrative, see Jacob Licht, *Storytelling in the Bible* (Magnes Press, The Hebrew Univ., Jerusalem, 1978), pp. 29–31; Bar-Efrat, *ibid.*, pp. 34–35, 149–50; and Adele Berlin, *Poetics and Interpretation of Biblical Narrative* (Almond Press, Sheffield, 1983), pp. 44–46, 64.

observes,[3] in these scenes its presence is generally muted in order to allow the biblical figures to hold center stage. Accordingly, the astute reader must play an active role in order to sketch a character profile from the verbal exchanges between the biblical characters. By paying close attention to what is said, to whom it is said, how it is said, and in what context the speech transpires, the perceptive reader may learn much about the traits, attitudes, and points of view of the biblical personages.[4] The predominance of dialogue within the context of biblical narrative, as compared to the mode of narration,[5] highlights the significance of this literary technique for characterizing the biblical figures.[6]

In his commentary on the Book of Genesis, Ramban illustrates how the dialogue scene provides important clues to creating portraiture of the biblical personalities.[7] By applying literary cat-

---

3. Cf. Bar-Efrat's observations, *Narrative Art*, pp. 41–44. Compare his comment, p. 148, "Conversations in biblical narrative are never precise and naturalistic imitations of real-life conversations. They are highly concentrated and stylized, are devoid of idle chatter, and all the details they contain are carefully calculated to fulfil a clear function."

4. On the direct and indirect ways in which biblical speech contributes to characterization of the biblical figures, cf. Bar-Efrat, *ibid.*, pp. 53–77, 89–90. See as well Berlin, *Poetics and Interpretation*, pp. 38–39, 64. Compare the broad observations of Meir Sternberg, *The Poetics of Biblical Narrative: Ideological Literature and the Drama of Reading* (Indiana Univ. Press, Bloomington, 1985), pp. 253–54, on the active role of the reader of biblical narrative in creating a portrait of the biblical figures, since, as Sternberg notes, p. 253, "... each biblical character is *sui generis*, a unique combination of universals and idiosyncrasies. His behavior is therefore referrable to no psychological (and with the exception of a few villains, no moral) character-type." Accordingly, Sternberg, p. 254, concludes that "the portraiture involves such art... It calls for distinctive and complex operations of reading." Compare his observations, *ibid.*, pp. 315, 323–24, 326.

5. Compare Robert Alter's observations, *The Art of Biblical Narrative* (Basic Books, New York, 1981), p. 65. Cf. Bar-Efrat, *Narrative Art*, pp. 147, 149–50.

6. Biblical dialogue is also an important vehicle for plot development, as will become apparent in the course of this study. Cf. Bar-Efrat, *ibid.*, pp. 95, 147, and Berlin, *Poetics and Interpretation*, p. 38. This paper will focus predominantly on the role that dialogue plays in illuminating character. Furthermore, this study will not focus on monologue speeches, in which characters speak to themselves. On this, see my study, "The Inner World of Biblical Character Explored in Naḥmanides' Commentary on Genesis," *Journal of Jewish Studies*, 56/2 (Autumn, 2005), pp. 309–15.

7. While the literary term, "character," will be employed throughout this study, it is important to note that Ramban maintains the historical authenticity of the biblical figures and their speeches.

egories to a critical analysis of Ramban's commentary, this study will demonstrate Ramban's perception of the poetics of biblical dialogue. Throughout his investigation of the Genesis narratives, Ramban classifies the tone of the biblical speech, exposes the purposeful way in which the characters express themselves, and highlights ambiguities which result in more than one reading of the style and tone of the dialogue encounter. By exploring *how* the Bible depicts the biblical personages through the mode of dialogue, Ramban determines *what* the Bible intends for its readers to learn about them. In his introduction to his biblical commentary, Ramban declares that the stories of Genesis are intended to "educate the people [concerning] the path [they should follow] about the subject of faith."[8] Through his study of the dialogue scenes in Genesis, Ramban illuminates how the literary dimension of the Bible plays an integral role in promoting its pedagogic and theological messages.

I. The Literary Strategy of Naming in Biblical Dialogue

Ramban observes how the biblical speaker characterizes various individuals directly by descriptive titles or designations in order to convey an attitude and point of view toward those who are the focus of interest of the speech.[9]

---

8. See Ramban, Introduction to his commentary on the Pentateuch, in *Mikra'ot Gedolot 'Haketer': A revised and augmented scientific edition of 'Mikra'ot Gedolot' Based on the Aleppo Codex and early Medieval MSS*, ed. by Menachem Cohen, 2d. printing (Bar-Ilan University Press, Ramat Gan, 2001), Vol. I on Genesis, Introduction, p. 35, who notes that the stories of Genesis "*moreh ha-ʾanashim ba-derekh be-ʿinyan ha-ʾemunah*." All subsequent citations from Ramban's commentary on Genesis derive from this edition, 2 volumes (2001, 2004). Citations from Ramban's commentary on other books of the Pentateuch derive from *Ma'agar Haketer*, ed. by Menachem Cohen, 2d. ed., CD ROM, University of Bar Ilan, 1998–2005. Translations of biblical verses and Ramban's commentary are my own.
9. The literary technique of "naming," which also includes titles and designations presented in the voice of the narrator that reflect the perspective of a particular character, has been discussed by Boris Uspensky, *A Poetics of Composition: The Structure of the Artistic Text and Typology of a Compositional Form*, trans. Valentina Zavarin and Susan Wittig (Univ. of Calif. Press, Berkeley, 1973), pp. 20–32. The strategy of naming has been identified in biblical narrative by Meir Weiss, "*Melekhet*

In his commentary on Genesis 21, Ramban reveals how Sarah employs the strategy of naming effectively in order to express her viewpoint regarding the position of Hagar and Yishmael within Avraham's household in relation to her son, Yiẓḥaq.[10]

Ramban interprets that when Sarah observes Yishmael "*mezaḥeq*" in 21:9, she detects that his mockery of Yiẓḥaq and the feast in his honor has foreboding implications for the future destiny of her beloved son.[11] Accordingly, she commands Avraham, "Drive out this slave woman (*ha-ʾamah ha-zot*) and her son (*benah*), for the slave woman's son (*ben ha-ʾamah ha-zot*) shall not inherit with my son (*beni*), with Yiẓḥaq" (21:10). By characterizing Yishmael and Hagar with descriptive epithets, Sarah lays bare her stark opinion of the inferior status of these individuals within Avraham's household. Yishmael's mocking signifies a slave's challenge to his subordinated status, which Sarah will not tolerate for she does not want this lowly servant to claim Avraham's estate

---

ha-Sippur ba-Miqraʾ: Ḥeqer ha-Sippur ha-Miqraʾi le-'Or Shittot ʾAḥaronot be-Viqqoret ha-Sifrut," *Molad* 20/2 (1962), pp. 403–4; Bar-Efrat, *Narrative Art*, pp. 36–40; and Berlin, *Poetics and Interpretation*, pp. 59–61.

10. The strategy of naming in this context has been noted by modern biblical scholars like Neḥama Leibowitz, "*Qeiẓad Likroʾ Pereq be-Tanakh*," in *Nefesh va-Shir: In Memory of A.L. Strauss. ʿIyyunim la-Madrikh ve-la-Moreh*, no. 19/20 (Dept. of Youth Immigration, Jerusalem, 1954), pp. 100–101; Weiss, *ibid.*, p. 403–4; and Bar-Efrat, *ibid.*, pp. 36–37, 73.

11. Ramban, 21:9, renders *mezaḥeq* as mockery and scorn (*mal'ig*), in contrast to Rashi, 21:9, who presumes that Yishmael's behavior of *mezaḥeq* reflects other heinous acts, such as the committing of the three cardinal sins (idolatry, sexual immorality, murder) or the challenging of Yiẓḥaq's inheritance. All citations from medieval Jewish exegetes derive from *Mikraʾot Gedolot Haketer*, 2 volumes on Genesis (2001, 2004), unless noted otherwise. Ramban, 21:9, quotes Rabbi Shimon ben Elazar's opinion (*Tosefta Sotah* 6:6) that contests the plausibility of such criminal acts taking place in the house of a righteous person like Avraham. He also disagrees that Yiẓḥaq and Yishmael were arguing over their legacy, for this argument could only transpire when they were older, and based on the context, Yishmael's reaction takes place at the feast celebrating Yiẓḥaq's weaning. Contrast Ramban's approach with Ibn Ezra, 21:9, who interprets *mezaḥek* merely as a sign of child playfulness, and reveals that Sarah was jealous because Yishmael was the eldest child and Yiẓḥaq could not keep up with him. Ramban also does not apply Radak, 21:9, who explains that Yishmael was "as if mocking Yiẓḥaq because he was born to elderly people." Cf. the interpretation of Sforno, 21:9, based on *b. Baba Meẓʿia* 87a, in which he maintains that Yishmael was scoffing because he claimed that Sarah had conceived from Avimelekh.

as his own.[12] While Yishmael's scornful attitude deserves harsh punishment for overstepping the bounds of his servile status, Sarah only demands his expulsion so that he will not wrestle the inheritance from the lawful successor, the son of the mistress of the household. As Ramban interprets,

> "Meẓaḥeq" (21:9): And the correct opinion in my eyes is that this occurred on the day that Yiẓḥaq was weaned, and she saw him mocking Yizḥaq or the great feast.... And therefore she said, "'Drive out this slave woman and her son" (21:10). For she said, "The slave who derides his master is obligated to die or to be lashed; but I want only that you should expel him from before me, so that he should not inherit your possessions with my son at all, who is the son of the mistress (ben gevirah)." And she said to drive out his mother also, for the young lad (naʿar) cannot leave his mother; if he leaves his mother, he shall die.[13]

Ramban also suggests how Scripture narrates this scene from Sarah's perspective by designating Yishmael in 21:9 as "the son of Hagar the Egyptian (ben Hagar ha-miẓrit)." This description promotes Sarah's impression of Yishmael as the son of the foreign slave woman whose other-status confirms that he is worthy of being shunned from Avraham's legacy.[14]

---

12. Ramban does not concur with Rashi, 21:9 [based on GenR. 53:11, in Midrash Bereshit Rabba, eds. Ch. Albeck and J. Theodor, 2nd ed. (Shalem Books, Jerusalem, 1996), pp. 567–68], ## and Radak, 21:10, that Yishmael is the one to initiate the challenge to Yiẓḥaq's inheritance. Ramban indicates that it is Sarah who perceives how Yishmael's mocking behavior suggests that he will challenge his subservient status and portends that in the future he will lay claim to Avraham's inheritance. Cf. parallel to Ramban, Rashbam's comment, 21:9.

13. Ramban, 21:9. Cf. Isaac Abarbanel, 21:10, in Perush ha-Torah le-Rabbenu Yiẓḥaq Abarbanel, ed. by Yehudah Shaviv, Vol. I, Genesis (Chorev Pub. House, Jerusalem, 2007), pp. 461–62, who challenges Ramban's explanation of Sarah's demand to drive out Hagar. Abarbanel claims that in line with Ramban's analysis, it was imperative that Hagar be expelled from the household as well in order to nullify Yishmael's rights to Avraham's inheritance.

14. Cf. Ramban, 21:9. Compare Abarbanel, 21:9 [Shaviv, 461], who also observes how this epithet intends to demean Yishmael. Contrast this approach with that of Phyllis Trible, "Hagar: The Desolation of Rejection," in idem, Texts of Terror:

Avraham's reaction is not recorded in dialogue mode, but through Scripture's mediation. "The matter was very perturbing in the eyes of Avraham *concerning his son (beno)*" (21:11). Ramban suggests that Scripture's relational naming of Yishmael as "his son" underscores Avraham's deep attachment to his flesh and blood and his unwillingness to succumb to Sarah's demands concerning him.[15] Furthermore, in order to grasp the intensity of Avraham's emotions, Ramban presumes that the epithet, "his son," sets up a dichotomy between Yishmael and Hagar. This approach also establishes a direct correlation between Avraham's response and Sarah's multiple demands not only to drive out Yishmael but also to cast out Hagar. By omitting any mention of Hagar, Scripture accentuates Avraham's praiseworthy concession to detach himself from Hagar, whom he already regards as a concubine, and not as the "wife" Sarah had intended her to be.[16] Nevertheless, Avraham draws the line when asked to drive out *his* son. He may be able to quell his desire for Hagar, but he will not willingly betray his relationship to his child.

> The correct [interpretation] appears to me that Scripture spoke in honor of Avraham (*ha-Katuv sipper bikhvod Avraham*), saying that the matter was not very upsetting in his eyes because of his desire for his concubine and his craving for her. For if [Sarah] had said to him to drive out only the slave woman, he would have fulfilled Sarah's

---

Literary-Feminist Readings of Biblical Narratives (Fortress Press, Minn. and Phila., 1984), p. 20, who notes, "The description 'the son of Hagar the Egyptian' highlights mother, not child." This insight leads Trible to view the designation of 21:9 as reflective of Sarah's negative relationship with Hagar more than Yishmael. Ramban, on the other hand, regards this character epithet as Scripture's mirroring of Sarah's point of view toward Yishmael, as the son of a foreign mother and therefore one who has a lowly status in Avraham's household. For Ramban, Hagar plays a minor role in this episode.

15. Ramban, 21:11.

16. Compare Ramban, 16:11 and 25:6, who observes that Avraham did not regard Hagar as a full wife but assigned her the status of a concubine (*pilegesh*), despite Sarah's initial intent to offer Hagar as a second wife in the household (on this, see Ramban, 16:2–3.)

wish. Because of his "son," however, he was very angered
and he did not want to obey her.[17]

Responding to Sarah's demand and Avraham's reaction, God
declares,

> Let it not be upsetting in your eyes concerning the
> lad (naʿar) and on account of your slave woman
> (ʾamatekha). Whatever Sarah says to you, listen to her
> voice, for through Yiẓḥaq your progeny will be called
> by your [name]. And also the slave woman's son (ben
> ha-ʾamah), I will make a nation of him, for he is your
> progeny. (21:12–13)

Ramban exposes how God employs the strategy of naming in
order to highlight His acknowledgment of Avraham's disparate
relationships toward Yishmael and Hagar.

> But God said to him that it should not seem troubling
> in his eyes about the lad or about the slave woman at
> all (she-loʾ yeraʿ be-ʿeinav ʿal ha-naʿar ve-loʾ ʿal ha-
> ʾamah klal), but he should listen to the voice of Sarah,
> for through Yiẓḥaq alone his name will be carried on
> (21:12), and Yishmael will not be called his seed (zeraʿ).
> But because Avraham feared for him [Yishmael] that an
> accident should not happen to him (she-loʾ yiqraʾenu
> ʾason) when he sent him away from him, [God] said
> that He will make him into a nation and He will bless
> him because he [Yishmael] is indeed his [Avraham's] son
> (21:13).[18]

---

17. Ramban, 21:11–13. In this comment, Ramban contests Rashi's presumption, 21:11, that
"ʿal ʾodot beno" refers to something extrinsic which he learns about his son or to the
demand of expulsion itself. Ramban claims that this phrase focuses on Avraham's
emotional reaction to abandoning his beloved son, in contrast to his ambivalence
toward driving out Hagar. Cf. Radak, 21:10, who parallels Ramban's interpretation
of Avraham's reaction concerning "his son;" Ramban, however, elicits the profound
implications of this epithet by exposing Avraham's unspoken but implied indiffer-
ence toward Hagar as well.
18. Ramban, 21:11.

God designates Hagar as the "slave woman" that she is, concurring with Sarah's perspective and recognizing that Avraham is willing to dissociate from Hagar. On the other hand, God's designation of Yishmael as a young lad (*na'ar*) reflects His acknowledgment of Avraham's attachment to his son and his concern for the child who is being driven away from the comforts of Avraham's household.[19]

Ramban's deductions appear to be based on his correlation of the *na'ar* designation here with a similar labeling of Binyamin in the Yosef narrative. In that context, Ya'aqov is concerned for Binyamin's wellbeing, fearing that if he would descend to Egypt, a tragedy might occur to him on the way (*u-qera'ahu 'ason*) [42:38; 44:29]. Yehudah acknowledges Binyamin's status as a young lad by remarking to Yosef (the Egyptian vizier), "And we said to my lord, 'The *na'ar* cannot leave his father. Should he leave his father, he would die'" (44:22).[20] Similarly, using the language of Gen. 44:22, Ramban notes that Sarah commands Hagar to be driven out with Yishmael, for without his mother he will die. Accordingly, Avraham fears for the life of his young son when he is sent away from his home, "lest an accident should happen to him (*she-lo' yiqra'enu 'ason*)." Taking Avraham's perspective into consideration, God promises Avraham that while Yizḥaq is the designated heir to Avraham's legacy, Yishmael, being the offspring of Avraham, will also be blessed and protected, developing into a great nation of his own.[21]

Ramban also perceives that the genealogical designations which characters employ to refer to themselves or to others underscore the mindset of the speaker or the audience. Identifying

---

19. Contrast Weiss, "*Melekhet ha-Sippur ba-Miqra'*," p. 403; Bar-Efrat, *Narrative Art*, p. 37; and Trible, "Hagar," p. 21, who maintain that this epithet intends to minimize Avraham's relationship to his son.

20. In his commentary on 44:22, Ramban identifies the subject of "he will die" as the youthful Binyamin. See also the *na'ar* designation of Binyamin in Gen. 44:32–33.

21. For another example of Ramban's literary insights into the strategy of naming in biblical dialogue, cf. his comments on Gen. 32:5, 33:8. In that context, Ramban points out how Ya'aqov deliberately refers to his brother, Esav, as "*'adoni* (my master)," in order to give the impression that the sale of the birthright was void and Esav still deserved the honor of the firstborn. In doing so, Ya'aqov aimed to quell the hatred which Esav harbored against his younger brother.

herself to Avraham's servant in their encounter at the well, Rivkah declares, "I am the daughter of Bethuel, the son of *Milkah*, whom she bore to *Nahor*" (24:24). According to Ramban, Rivkah's mention of her father's maternal side first, reflects the propensity of young females. As he observes, Rivkah speaks "in the manner of young women (*derekh ha-ne'arot*)."[22]

The way in which Rivkah arranges her genealogical referents aligns with Scripture's initial description of her lineage in 24:15. Immediately following the servant's prayer to find Yizhaq a suitable wife, Scripture relates, "He had barely finished speaking when, look, Rivkah was coming out, who was born to Bethuel, son of *Milkah*, the wife of *Nahor*, Avraham's brother." While Rivkah's elaborate identification is unknown to the servant,[23] the all-knowing voice of Scripture privileges the reader with this information, relating it from Rivkah's point of view by assigning precedence to her female relations. As Ramban explains,

> Since the young woman mentioned the mother of her father first, "I am the daughter of Bethuel, the son of Milkah" (24:24), for this is the way of young women ... therefore, *Scripture mentions thus (lakhen yazkirenu ha-Katuv ken)* that he [Bethuel] is the "son of Milkah, the wife of Nahor" (24:15).[24]

On the other hand, Ramban perceives that in 24:47, the servant transposes the sequence of Rivkah's genealogy in his speech to

---

22. Ramban, 24:15. Ramban supports his presumption by observing that Rivkah chooses the "house of her mother" (24:28) to communicate her experiences. Thus her actions and the sequence of her words reflect her feminine persona. On this, compare Ramban, 29:12. He does not comment, however, about Rivkah's omission of her mother's name. Apparently, her identification has no significant bearing on the advancement of the plot.

23. Additionally, Avraham's servant is not aware of Rivkah's name nor that she was a virgin, as revealed in 24:16. See Meir Sternberg, "Lashon 'Olam u-Ferspectivah be-'Omanut ha-Miqra': ha-Maba' he-'Aqif ha-Hofshi ve-'Ofanei ha-Hadirah ha-Semuyah," ha-Sifrut 32 (1982), p. 111, who notes the multiple perspectives in this verse, wherein the servant's subjective point of view is placed alongside the biblical narrator's privileged perspective.

24. Ramban, 24:15. Ramban is apparently unique among medieval exegetes in his analysis of 24:15, 24.

her family, describing her genealogy as "the daughter of Bethuel, son of Naḥor, whom Milkah bore to him." In order to cater to the social expectations of his male audience, especially Lavan and Bethuel (24:50), the servant consciously assigns priority to Rivkah's father's paternal side. As Ramban explains, "He rectified the matter by way of etiquette (tikken ha-davar be-derekh musar)."[25] With these observations, Ramban underscores how alternating female and male viewpoints influence the various strategies of characterization employed in biblical speech and in Scripture's parallel narration of the episode.[26]

II. The Tone of Biblical Dialogue

In his analysis of a dialogue scene, Ramban classifies the tone of a biblical speech in order to illuminate the speaker's outlook toward his audience and his attitude toward the subject which he addresses.[27]

Following His rejection of Kayin's offering in Genesis 4:5, God attempts to channel Kayin's angry feelings toward positive ends by adopting a pedagogical tone. As Ramban observes, "[God]

---

25. Ramban, 24:15. Ramban comments further that perhaps in order to appeal fully to his male audience, the servant should have omitted reference to Milkah as well. He concludes that she is mentioned in order to accentuate Bethuel's worthiness as the progenitor of Avraham's legacy; for Bethuel is the son of a full ranking wife of Naḥor (22:23), and not the son of Naḥor's concubine, Reʾumah (22:24). For this latter insight, compare Ḥezeqiah bar Manoaḥ (Ḥizzequni), 24:24, in Perush ha-Torah le-Rabbenu Ḥezeqiah bar Manoaḥ, ed. by Ḥayyim Chavel (Mosad Harav Kook, Jerusalem, 1981). Compare Abarbanel, 24:24, 47 [Shaviv, 511–12], whose commentary demonstrates the influence of Ramban's analysis in this context.

26. See as well Ramban, 29:5, who demonstrates his literary sensitivities to Laban's incongruous reference to himself as the son of Naḥor, his grandfather, omitting his father, Bethuel.

27. On the definition of the "tone" of a speech in a literary work, see M.H. Abrams, A Glossary of Literary Terms (Holt, Rinehart, and Winston, Inc., New York, 6th edn., 1981), p. 156, who, quoting I. A. Richards' work, Practical Criticism, explains tone "as the expression of a literary speaker's 'attitude to his listener' ... The tone of his utterance reflects ... his sense of how he stands toward those he is addressing." Further defining the tone of a speech, Abrams explains, "The way we speak reveals, by subtle clues, our conception of, and attitude to, the things we are talking about, our personal relation to our auditor, as well as our assumptions about the social level, intelligence, and sensitivity of that auditor."

instructed him concerning repentance (*horehu ʿal ha-teshuvah*), that it is in his power to return at any time that he desires, and God will forgive him."[28] Perceiving that Kayin's reaction stems from his embarrassment at having been outdone by his rival brother in the sacrificial ritual,[29] God offers Kayin an attractive solution which will result in his eventual domination over his sibling.[30] As God exhorts in 4:7, following Ramban's rendition,

> "*Ha-loʾ ʾim teitiv, seʾet*"- If you will correct your ways, you will achieve abundant pre-eminence over your brother, for you are the firstborn (*yihyeh lekha yeter seʾet ʿal ʾahikha ki ʾatah ha-bekhor*).[31]

---

28. Ramban, 4:7. Compare Radak 4:6, for a parallel analysis of the tone of God's speech.
29. Ramban, 4:7, maintains that Kayin's anger is not caused by God's repudiation of his sacrifice as much as by his ignominious defeat before his younger brother. Observing the correlation between Scripture's narrated description of Kayin's reaction in 4:5 and God's reflection of Kayin's feelings in 4:6, Ramban notes Kayin's double reaction of embarrassment and jealousy because of his brother's achieved superiority in this instance. "And this is the meaning of 'Why are you incensed,' for because of his embarrassment from his brother his face fell, and because of his jealousy of him, he killed him. And behold, God said to him, 'Why are you incensed-concerning your brother [and your jealousy of him]- and why has your face fallen- on account of him [because of your embarrassment]?'" Compare Hugh White, *Narration and Discourse in the Book of Genesis* (Cambridge Univ. Press, Cambridge, 1991), p. 160, who notes that Kayin "sees his problem not as an inner spiritual struggle with the power of sin, but as a contest on the material level with his rival double." Cf. Sternberg's observations on the parallels between 4:5, 6 in *Poetics*, pp. 92, 389.
30. Notably, however, God does not reveal the reason for His rejection of Kayin's offering, but focuses His speech on teaching Kayin how to come to terms with his circumstance and recover from it with success. While many of Ramban's exegetical predecessors put forth various theses why God preferred Hevel's sacrifice [cf., for example, Rashi, Bekhor Shor, Ibn Ezra, and Radak, 4:3–5], Ramban is silent. Ramban demonstrates that the focus of the narrative is on the aftermath of God's relation to Kayin, and not on the underlying causes behind God's decision. For a similar approach, compare White, *Narration and Discourse*, p. 156.
31. Interestingly, Ramban, 4:1, interprets Kayin's name to mean that his mother blessed him to be "an acquisition for God" to carry on his parents' worship of God after their deaths. Furthermore, Ramban, 4:3–4, does not paint Kayin's initiative to sacrifice in a negative light. Just the opposite. He notes how both Kayin and Hevel "understood the great secret" of sacrifice offerings before God. Based on this analysis, one may deduce that God attempts to assuage Kayin's angry feelings in order to help Kayin realize his potential and carry on the spiritual legacy bestowed upon him by his parents.

But, if you do not improve your ways (*"ve'im lo' teitiv"*)

Evil will come upon you not only because of him [Hevel].

For at the door of your house, your sin lurks to cause you to falter in all of your ways (*"la-petaḥ ḥatat rovez"*).

For your sin will desire to cleave to you all of the days (*"ve-'elekha teshuqato"*)

But you will be able to conquer it if you so desire

For you can improve your ways and detach [the desire to sin] from you (*"ve-'atah timshal bo"*).[32]

While Kayin does not heed God's prudent advice and murders Hevel,[33] Ramban maintains that Kayin becomes remorseful and penitent when faced with God's forceful retribution. Kayin is cursed that the land will not bring forth sustenance from the ground,[34] and he is condemned to an eternal state of wandering

---

32. Ramban, 4:7. Ramban's interpretation of God's response in relation to the competition between the two brothers finds its parallel in Ḥizzequni's rendering of *"ve-'atah timshal bo,"* 4:7, which identifies *"bo"* as a reference to Hevel. Ḥizzequni, however, does not interpret *"se'et"* as Kayin's superiority over Hevel, as does Ramban. Furthermore, Ramban extends the concept of "sin lurking by the door" to Kayin's specific grievance against Hevel as the catalyst for these future temptations. Contrast Rashi, 4:7, based on Onqelos, and Radak, 4:7, who render *"se'et"* as forgiveness, parallel to Exod. 34:7, *"nose' 'avon."* Ibn Ezra, 4:7, finds a parallel between Kayin's fallen face and God's promise that if he improves his ways, then he will have *"se'et,"* an uplifting. Umberto Cassuto, *A Commentary on the Book of Genesis*, trans. Israel Abrahams (Magnes Press, Hebrew Univ., Jerusalem, 1961), 1:209–10, has a parallel reading to that of Ibn Ezra. While Ramban quotes his predecessors' interpretations, he opts for an alternative that illustrates how God attempts to dispel the direct cause of Kayin's anger. Cf. Neḥama Leibowitz's discussion of these readings, *'Iyyunim be-Sefer Bereshit* (World Zionist Federation, 1968, Jerusalem, 2nd edn.), p. 31, as well as her clarifications of the linguistic basis for the various exegetical interpretations of *"se'et,"* idem, *Limmud Parshanei ha-Torah u-Derakhim le-Hora'atam- Sefer Bereshit* (Jerusalem, 1975), pp. 3–4.

33. Ramban, 4:7, observes, "Because of his jealousy of him, he killed him." Cf. Ramban, 4:8, who diagnoses the intensity of Kayin's jealous feelings and speculates that Kayin envisioned himself as the sole progenitor of the world's future generations, without the taint of his brother's presence.

34. With this interpretation of 4:11–12, Ramban concurs with Ibn Ezra, 4:11–12, but disagrees with Rashi, 4:11–12, who claims that the land was cursed because of Kayin's sin, similar to the consequences of Adam's sin. Compare White, *Narration and Discourse*, p. 163, who has an approach similar to that of Ramban. Ramban elaborates further that not only will Kayin's cultivation of the land fail to yield sustenance,

and exile, which has the psychological consequence that "his heart will not rest and he will not have peace of mind to stand in one place on it [the earth]."³⁵ Classifying the tone of Kayin's response in 4:13–14, Ramban declares, "And the correct interpretation according to its apparent contextual meaning (ve-ha-nakhon bif-shuto) is that [Kayin's speech] is a confession (vidduy)."³⁶ In order to highlight his analysis, Ramban amplifies Kayin's reaction and renders "Gadol ᶜavoni mi-nesoᵓ" in 4:13: "It is true (ᵓemet) that my sin is too great to be forgiven."³⁷ Ramban elaborates how Kayin spotlights his repentant demeanor by acknowledging "that You, God, are righteous, and Your judgments are just, even though You have punished me very greatly."³⁸ Kayin reiterates the magnitude of his punishment by focusing particularly on the grievous consequence of his wandering (ve-hayyiti naᶜ va-nad ba-ᵓareẓ- 4:14c),

---

but the land will not grow naturally for him either, resulting in two curses in relation to Kayin's agricultural occupation. Additionally, Ramban explains that the punishment of the land not yielding produce is typical for one who murders, "for the blood [of the slain] pollutes the earth" (Num. 35:33). On this point, compare White, ibid., p. 164.

35. Contrary to Ḥizzequni, 4:11 and Radak, 4:12, who contend that the punishment of wandering relates to Kayin's compulsion to search endlessly for physical sustenance, Ramban, 4:11, maintains that this aspect of Kayin's curse is one of psychological proportions. Compare Avivah Gottlieb Zornberg's analysis of Ramban's commentary, Genesis: The Beginning of Desire (The Jewish Publication Society, Phila. and Jerusalem, 1995), p. 21. Cf. as well Leibowitz's observations, Limmud Parshanei ha-Torah, 7. Compare Ramban, 4:16, who notes the incongruity between this curse and the subsequent narration that "Kayin settled in the land of Nod" (4:16), and deduces that Kayin's wandering was confined to this particular land. For a different approach, see Radak, 4:16. Based on his analysis, Ramban, 4:17, views Kayin's building activity as symptomatic of the curse of having a restless existence. Sensitive to the unusual syntax of this verse, Ramban observes that "Va-yehi boneh ᶜir," as opposed to va-yivven ᶜir, signifies that Kayin built the city throughout his lifetime, constantly delaying its completion because of his wandering and restless spirit. Contrast Cassuto, A Commentary on Genesis, 1:229–30, who maintains that the ambiguity in 4:17 allows for the possibility that Kayin's son, Ḥanokh, built the city as a long term project because Kayin was doomed. On the different exegetical approaches to 4:16, cf. Leibowitz, Limmud Parshanei ha-Torah, 14–15.

36. Ramban, 4:13. Compare Abarbanel, 4:13 [Shaviv, 226], who cites Ramban's interpretation as the correct reading of the tone of Kayin's speech.

37. Ramban, 4:13. Note that Ramban interprets this phrase in concurrence with its parallel meaning in Exod. 34:7, "noseᵓ ᶜavon," rendering it to mean forgiveness from sin. Cassuto, A Commentary on the Book of Genesis, 1:222, cites Ramban as giving the "correct interpretation" for this verse.

38. Ramban, 4:13.

which has resulted in God banishing him from the face of the earth (4:14a- *hen gerashta ʾoti ha-yom meʿal penei ha-ʾadamah*).[39]

Cursed with the inability to stand in one place on the earth, Kayin banishes himself from standing before God through spiritual communication and ritual. As Ramban explains, Kayin's declaration in 4:14b should be interpreted, "And I must hide from your presence (*u-mipanekha ʾesater*), for I will not be able to stand before you to pray or bring a sacrifice or meal-offering, 'for I was ashamed, and humiliated (*boshti ve-nikhlamti*), for I have borne the disgrace of my sin.'"[40]

Kayin's acceptance of the full weight of divine justice explains the motivation behind his plea for protection from those who seek to murder him. Amplifying Kayin's speech in 4:14 in order to accentuate the tone of the dialogue, Ramban explains,

> But what shall I do, for "whoever finds me will kill me" (4:14d), and You in Your great kindness did not condemn me to death. And the intent of what he said before Him, may He be exalted, is: "Behold, my sins are great and You have heaped upon me much punishment. But, protect me so that I should not be punished more than You have obligated me, for because I will be a wanderer ... the

---

39. Ramban, 4:14, rearranges the structure of Kayin's speech in order to highlight its primary theme. Contrast this reading of "You have banished me today from the face of the earth," with that of Radak, 4:14, who interprets that Kayin refers to his specific banishment from the "land of Eden which was near the garden of Eden for there were his father and mother." Hizzequni, 4:14, analyzes that Kayin's words refer to the curse of the land which will not bear produce for him.

40. Ramban, 4:13; the last phrase derives from Jer. 31:18. Ramban does not render "*u-mipanekha ʾesater*" (4:14) as another aspect of Kayin's punishment, but he regards this statement as Kayin's acknowledgment that his sinful actions preclude him from keeping company with God. Compare Zornberg's analysis of Ramban on this context, *Genesis*, p. 21. Ramban, 4:16, observes that Kayin's "departure from God" represents his spiritual disengagement from God. Cf. Leibowitz's analysis of Naḥmanides' comment, *Limmud Parshanei ha-Torah*, p. 13. For a similar analysis, see the Tosafist commentary in the ms Oxford 268, cited in *Sefer Tosafot ha-Shalem*, ed. by Jacob Gelis (Hoẓaʾat Mifʿal Tosafot ha-Shalem, Jerusalem, 1982), 1:163–64, paragraph 2, on 4:14. Contrast the approaches of Bekhor Shor; Ibn Ezra; and Radak, 4:14, who interpret *u-mipanekha ʾesater* to refer to God's concealment of His manifest Divine presence and providence from Kayin.

wild beasts will kill me, for Your shade of protection has departed from me (*sar ẓilkha meʿalai*)."[41]

Approaching God in a tone of sincere contrition and humility, Kayin does not ask God to alleviate his punishment but to help him survive his torment. Kayin presumes that his fate as a wanderer condemns him to a life where God's providence has departed from him. While God did not decree his death, he fears that he might suffer an unnatural fate if he is left without divine protection. Apparently, Ramban assigns a double meaning to the phrase, "*u-mipanekha ʾesater*" (4:14). Not only will Kayin hide himself from God, refraining from establishing a connection through prayer and sacrifice, but Kayin perceives that God hides Himself and His providence from him as a result of the curse that He imposes upon him.[42]

Through his reading of the tone conveyed in Kayin's speech, Ramban reveals how Kayin's plea also entails a form of repentance, in which he demonstrates his understanding of God's relationship to man. "[Kayin] *confessed* (*hodah*) that man is powerless to save himself [from harm] by his own strength, but [he can do so] only with the protection of the Most High upon him."[43]

Kayin's acknowledgment of God's providence coupled with his confession of the greatness of his sin and the justice of his fate prompt God to act on his behalf. God places a permanent sign with Kayin to protect him (4:15).[44] Furthermore God promises,

---

41. Ramban, 4:14. The latter phrase derives from Num. 14:9. In that context, Ramban explains that the departure of God's protection spells a fate of death for the nations living in Canaan, ensuring the success of the Israelites' military campaign in their conquest of the land.

42. Perhaps in this regard Ramban was influenced by the interpretations of his predecessors, such as Radak and Bekhor Shor, 4:14, on the meaning of "*u-mipanekha ʾesater*." Radak also indicates that Kayin fears his wandering will make him fodder for the wild animals to kill him because of the lack of divine providence. On the other hand, one might conclude that Ramban infers that Kayin's hiding from God results in God being hidden from Kayin.

43. Ramban, 4:14.

44. Ramban, 4:15, observes Scripture's deliberate description that God "set" a sign upon Kayin (not "gave" or "made"), as an indication that this sign accompanied Kayin at all times.

according to Ramban's understanding, "Therefore whoever kills Kayin, sevenfold will he be punished (*shiv ͨatayim yuqqam*)" [4:15].[45] Ramban observes that this apparently extreme response reflects God's acknowledgment of Kayin's sincere repentance and recognition of his dependency on God's providence. Elaborating on God's speech, Ramban interprets, "For I will punish whoever kills him, sevenfold for his sin, for I assured Kayin that he would not be killed because of his fear of Me and his confession before Me."[46]

As noted by Neḥama Leibowitz, Ramban's reading of the tone of Kayin's speech illustrates the influences of his predecessors in their attempt to understand the portrayal of Kayin which emerges from this episode.[47] Midrashic tradition offers divergent characterizations of Kayin, ranging from the unrepentant, stubborn offender to the repentant sinner.[48] Following one midrashic approach, Rashi interprets that Kayin remains unrepentant and

---

45. Ramban's rendition, 4:23–24, of "*shiv ͨatayim yuqqam*" in 4:15, concurs with Bekhor Shor and Radak, 4:15.

46. Ramban, 4:23–24. Ramban presents his commentary of 4:15 within the context of the lament of Lemekh's wives, who fear that Lemekh will be killed because of the sin of his ancestor, Kayin. While God had said he would not kill Kayin, He did not absolve Kayin from his sin, and it was possible that He would exact retribution from his descendants. This did happen. As Ramban notes in his commentary on 4:17, Scripture delineates Kayin's genealogy in order to highlight how God postponed his retribution of Kayin for many generations, but in the end, his descendants perished in the flood. Rashi and Ibn Ezra, 4:15, based on Onqelos, relate the concept of delayed retribution to God's reaction of 4:15, rendering "*shiv ͨatayim yuqqam*" to mean that Kayin's lineage will be decimated in the seventh generation with the sons of Lemekh. On the comparison between Rashi, Radak, and Naḥmanides' interpretations to 4:15, cf. Leibowitz, *Limmud Parshanei ha-Torah*, pp. 11–13, where she notes how Naḥmanides' interpretation of this context coheres with his overall portrayal of Kayin as being repentant.

47. Compare Leibowitz's analysis of the comparisons between the different exegetical approaches of Rashi, Ibn Ezra, and Naḥmanides, to 4:13 in particular, *ibid.*, pp. 8–10; 12–13.

48. Compare the discussion in *GenR.* 22:11–13 [Theodor-Albeck, pp. 217–220] and *LevR.* 10:5, in *Midrash Va-Yiqraʾ Rabbah*, ed. Mordechai Margaliyot (Hoẓaʾat Misrad ha-Ḥinukh ve-ha-Tarbut, Jerusalem, 1953), pp. 204–06, on 4:13, 16. See also *b. San.* 101b, where Kayin is branded as one of the biblical personalities who challenged God inappropriately. On the other hand, see *Pesiqta Rabbati*, ed. Meʾir ʾIsh Shalom, with notes by M. Gideman (rpt. Israel, 1962), *Hosafah 1, Parashah 3*, p. 199b, on Hosea 14:2, where Kayin's repentance is cited as a role model for the Israelites to repent in the time of Hosea.

audaciously confronts God to forgive him in 4:13, challenging, "You bear the worlds above and below, and my sin you cannot bear?"[49] Rendering "ʿavoni" in 4:13 as punishment and not sin, Ibn Ezra interprets that Kayin laments the grievous repercussions of his actions: "My punishment is too great to bear." Whereas Kayin appears chastened by the weight of his curse, he seems to be more concerned with his punishment than with repenting for the crime itself.[50] Although Radak interprets 4:13 like Ibn Ezra, he infers that with this declaration, Kayin repents and expresses regret for his sin. Nevertheless, Radak acknowledges that Kayin aims to ask God to soften his punishment. Radak intimates that while Kayin may have embarked on the road to repentance, he is not wholly focused on making amends for his sin but on attempting to avoid the consequences of his actions.[51]

Ramban is apparently influenced by the exegetical tradition, which portrays Kayin as a sincere penitent who acknowledges the greatness of his sin and the justice of God's punishment. With this approach, he resolves the contextual difficulty as to why God heeds this sinner's request.[52] Perhaps Ramban also chooses this

---

49. See Rashi, 4:13. Compare Rashi's analysis in 4:16 (parallel to his interpretation of 4:9), in which he perpetuates Kayin's portraiture as the recalcitrant offender.

50. Ibn Ezra, 4:13, mentions "the opinion of all the commentators" who read Kayin's statement as a confession of his sin, but he prefers a different reading. Ibn Ezra observes that in accordance with his rendition, Kayin reiterates the parameters of his punishment, harping on its harsh consequences. Kayin especially focuses on the realization that "he will be hidden from God's presence (u-mipanekha ʾesater)" (4:14), because his wandering will cause him to be distanced from God's manifest presence in the areas closest to the Garden of Eden. Compare Bekhor Shor, 4:13. White, Narration and Discourse, p. 164, renders 4:13 in this manner, classifying his speech as a "lament," in which he still appears to be "shameless."

51. See Radak, 4:13.

52. Significantly, in this regard, Ramban qualifies the midrashic portrayal of Kayin as a sincere repentant as a peshat interpretation. On the other hand, Ramban does not agree with the midrash's contention in LevR. 10:5 that Kayin's confession had the effect of mitigating his fate as an eternal wanderer, as one might conclude from the fact that he is allowed to settle in the land of Nod (4:16). Ramban maintains that Kayin's repentance only guaranteed that he would be protected from a fate that was harsher than his punishment. White, Narration and Discourse, p. 164, who has taken the position that Kayin has not repented, is perplexed why God listens to his demands. As he notes, p. 165, "His plea proves surprisingly [my emphasis] effective." Perhaps this is why Radak, while accepting Ibn Ezra's rendition of 4:13 and acknowledging that Kayin seeks to alleviate the burden of his punishment,

approach to the tone of Kayin's speech based on his global reading of this entire narrative and its purpose within the Genesis narratives. From his perspective, the overriding message of this episode is not only the power of sin and its consequences but even more, the power of repentance and its ability to reach God.[53]

Indeed, Ramban's analysis of the narrative episodes at the beginning of Genesis forms a thematic continuum. Ramban analyzes how the episode of eating from the Tree of Knowledge teaches the power of sin to transform one's spectrum of "choice" and the type of choice with which one is faced.[54] The Kayin episode teaches the power of repentance in the face of horrific sin, and it further relates God's patience and forbearance, since Kayin's lineage was only decimated during the Flood.[55] Finally, the Flood narrative focuses on the power of the righteous to save themselves from the perils of the wicked. As Ramban emphasizes, Noaḥ was an absolutely innocent person who prevailed against the wicked individuals of his generation.[56]

Ramban displays further his finely honed ability to detect the tone of biblical speech and its ramifications in his analysis of Yaʿaqov's interactions with his family members.

Initially, Ramban detects a tone of excuse and defensiveness (hitnaẓẓelut) in Yaʿaqov's unexpected justification of the circumstances of Raḥel's burial in the midst of blessing Yosef's two sons.[57] Although Yaʿaqov's motivation for burying Raḥel at the place of her death was not revealed in the narrative describing her burial (35:19–20), he discloses to Yosef in 48:7, "But, as for me,

---

nevertheless claims that his lament incorporates a measure of repentance and regret.

53. The power of repentance is an important theme throughout Ramban's biblical commentary. See in particular Ramban, Deut. 30:11, in which he classifies repentance as a commandment in its own right. For a discussion of the subject of repentance in Ramban's biblical commentary and its relation to the episode of Kayin, see Uzi Kalkhayyim, "Teshuvah ve-Shavim ve-Tikkun ha-ʿOlam be-Mishnat ha-Ramban," in Teshuvah ve-Shavim (Misrad ha-Ḥinukh ve-ha-Tarbut, Jerusalem, 1979), pp. 69–80.

54. See Ramban, 2:9.

55. On this latter point, see Ramban, 4:17.

56. Cf. Ramban, 6:9, 7:1, who does not accept the midrashic tradition cited by Rashi, 6:9, which debates the relative righteousness of Noaḥ in comparison to other righteous individuals, such as Avraham.

57. Ramban, 48:7.

when I was coming from Paddan, Raḥel died on me (*metah ʿalai Raḥel*) in the land of Canaan on the way, still some distance from Ephrath, and I buried her there on the road to Ephrath, which is, Bethlehem." Clarifying Yaʿaqov's intent, Ramban explains that Yaʿaqov's responsibility to his family (*ʿalai*)[58] compelled him to bury Raḥel at the place of her death. He could not leave his family and cattle in order to bury her in the cave of Makhpelah in Ḥevron. Furthermore, had he taken all of his entourage with him, it would have been days before her body was laid to rest, and there were neither doctors nor medicines to embalm her body to preserve it. Because it is especially dishonorable to delay a woman's burial, Yaʿaqov buried Raḥel on the road to Ephrath.[59]

Perplexed by the timing of Yaʿaqov's revelation, Ramban interprets that Yaʿaqov's recollection is linked to his earlier command to Yosef to bury him in Canaan (47:29–31).

> And by way of the *peshat* ... Yaʿaqov said this [matter] to him *as one who is making excuses* (*ke-mitnazzel*) so that Yosef would not be angry when he realizes his [Yaʿaqov's] desire for burial in the cave [of Makhpelah], that he [Ya'aqov] did not bury his mother [Raḥel] there, as he had buried Leah there.[60]

By vindicating his actions, Yaʿaqov hopes to avert any grudge that Yosef might hold against his father for not burying Raḥel together with the other matriarchs. His justification sets the stage for reiterating to Yosef the importance of carrying out his deathbed wish

---

58. See Ramban, 48:7, for this understanding of ʿalai. Compare Radak, 48:7; see as well Rashi and Ibn Ezra, Gen. 33:13.

59. See Ramban, 48:7, who cites *b. Moʿed Qattan* 27a–28a, concerning the laws of a woman's burial. Cf. Rashbam, Ibn Ezra, and Radak, 48:7, for parallels to Ramban's approach. Compare Ḥizzequni, 35:19, and Rashbam, 48:7. For an explanation of why Yaʿaqov chooses to bury Raḥel on the road to Ephrath rather than in the city proper, see Ramban, 35:16; compare Rashi, 48:7, based on *GenR.* 82:10 [Theodor-Albeck, p. 988]. On this midrash, which interprets that Yaʿaqov perceives through divine inspiration how Raḥel 's burial on the road would be a source of consolation for her descendants going into exile, see Ramban, 48:7, who attempts to find a textual basis for this exposition. Cf. as well Zornberg's discussion of this midrash, *Genesis*, pp. 213–14 and 374–78.

60. Ramban, 48:7.

to be buried in Canaan, despite Pharaoh's possible objections. Ya'aqov underscores to Yosef that Raḥel received an honorable burial inside the land of Canaan, a situation which would not ensue were he to be buried in Egypt.[61]

Although Ramban's reading of Ya'aqov 's defensive tone has precedent among his exegetical predecessors,[62] he questions if there is more to Ya'aqov's declaration, which seems to be unnecessary in light of Yosef's presumed awareness that his father provided his mother with an honorable burial in Canaan.[63] Accordingly, Ramban detects a strategy of "double talk" in Ya'aqov's speech. Ya'aqov deliberately formulates his reasoning for not burying Raḥel in the cave of Makhpelah as an excuse in order to divert his son from discerning his premeditated motivation, which has no bearing on the geographic location and suddenness of her death. What may have appeared to be a sincere attempt to vindicate his actions is actually meant to suppress Ya'aqov's true reasons for his actions.

> And I am of the opinion that these are only words of excuse (*Va-ʾani savur she-hayu ʾelu divrei hitnazzelut*) ... But, Ya'aqov's [genuine] intent (*ʾaval ha-kavvanah le-Ya'aqov*) for not carrying her to the cave was in order that he should not bury two sisters there, for he would be ashamed before his ancestors [who are buried there]. Now, Leah was the one whom he married first [and thus her marriage was] permissible, while he married Raḥel out of his love for her and because of the pledge he had made to her.[64]

---

61. See Ramban, 48:7, who elucidates the motives behind Ya'aqov's defensive words. On Ya'aqov's fears of Pharaoh's objections to his burial in Canaan and the necessity to swear Yosef to commit to fulfill his father's wishes, see Ramban, 47:31, 49:29.

62. See especially Radak, 48:7, from whom Ramban probably derives the description of *hitnazzelut* with regard to classifying the tone of Ya'aqov's speech.

63. Ramban, 48:7.

64. Ramban, 48:7. Cf. Rabbi Yiẓḥaq Abuhab, *Beʾur ʿal Perush ha-Ramban la-Torah* (rpt. Jerusalem, 1973), on 48:7, who paraphrases Ramban's statement, "And I am of the opinion that these are only words of excuse," as, "And I am of the opinion that this is not a sincere excuse (*hitnazzelut ʾamiti*), but an excuse of deception

Yaʿaqov's marriage to two sisters concurrently transgresses a biblical prohibition (Lev. 18:18). Adopting the rabbinic premise that the patriarchs fulfilled the Torah's commandments before they were formally given to the Israelites, which, Ramban claims, were in effect only while they resided in the land of Canaan, Ramban explains that while Yaʿaqov married the two sisters outside of Canaan, where it was not prohibited, he would be mortified if he were buried together with both of them in Ḥevron.[65] The manner of his burial would appear to attest to his violation of a biblical commandment while he lived in Canaan. Since his marriage to Raḥel after his marriage to Leah actuated the prohibition of being married to two sisters, Yaʿaqov determined that Leah would be the wife buried next to him in the cave of Makhpelah.[66]

(*hitnaẓẓelut kozev*)." Perhaps Ramban alludes to his second approach already in his first interpretation by stating, "Yaʿaqov said to him thus *as one* who is making excuses *ke-mitnaẓẓel* so that Yosef would not be angered," instead of declaring outright that Yaʿaqov was speaking defensively (*mitnaẓẓel*).

65. See Ramban, 26:5, who interprets the rabbinic statements that the patriarchs fulfilled the Torah's commandments [see, for example, *m.Qiddushin*, 4:14; *b. Yoma*, 28b; *GenR*. 95:3 (Theodor-Albeck, pp. 1188–90)], with the intent that the patriarchs did so only when they resided in the holy land of Canaan, but not outside of it. See also Ramban, Lev. 18:25, who discusses that "in his [Yaʿaqov's] merit, he did not reside in the land [of Canaan] with two sisters [in his lifetime]," since Raḥel died when they reached Canaan. On Ramban's approach and the influence of Ibn Ezra (Gen. 26:5; Lev. 18:26) on his analysis, see Uriel Simon, "*ha-Parshanut ha-Pashtit shel ha-Historiyah ha-Miqra'it- Bein Historiyyut, Dugmatiyyut, u-Beinyyamiyyut*," in Mordechai Cogan, Barry L. Eichler, and Jeffrey H. Tigay, eds. *Tehillah le-Moshe: Biblical and Judaic Studies in Honor of Moshe Greenberg* (Eisenbrauns, Winona Lake, Indiana, 1997), pp. 183*-194*. Simon, however, does not refer to Ramban's commentary on Gen. 48:7. In this latter context, Ramban adopts the midrashic presumption (and not his *peshat* analysis of Gen. 26:5) as the basis for his interpretation of the tone and dynamic of this dialogue scene.

66. Interestingly, the later medieval commentator, Samuel David Luzzatto, 48:7, in *Perush Shadal ʿal Ḥamishah Ḥumeshei Torah*, ed. by Phil Schlesinger (Dvir Pub., Tel Aviv, 1965), connects Yaʿaqov's statement about Raḥel's death with the blessings of Yosef's sons in 48:5–6, 12–20. He interprets that while Yaʿaqov cannot demonstrate his love for Raḥel by being buried next to her, since his commitment to the honor of his forefathers takes precedence, he exhibits his love for Raḥel's descendants by assigning Yosef's two children the status of Israelite tribes. Compare Robert Alter, *Genesis: Translation and Commentary* (W.W. Norton and Co., New York/London, 1996), p. 288, who, translating 48:7, "Raḥel died to my grief," does not read a tone of excuse into Yaʿaqov 's words, but regards them as an expression of Yaʿaqov's preoccupation with the loss of his beloved wife. Alter concludes, "... his impulse to adopt Rachel 's two grandsons by her firstborn expresses a desire to compensate, symbolically and legally, for the additional sons she did not live to bear."

Ramban does not elaborate why Ya'aqov feels that he cannot reveal his true motivations to Yosef. Nevertheless, it is apparent from his commentary that Ya'aqov intends to portray his actions in a more positive light, focusing his son on the honor that he bestowed on Raḥel at the time of her death, while concealing the more complex reasons from view. Through his defensive speech, Ya'aqov molds his son's point of view in his evaluation of his father's initiatives, swaying him to do his bidding and bury him in Canaan.[67]

III. The Interrelationship Between Style and Tone in Biblical Dialogue

Ramban explores the interrelationship between the style and tone of biblical speech in his analysis of the dialogue scenes in the Yosef narrative, illustrating how the speaker tailors his words to convey a particular outlook to his audience.[68]

In order to rescue Yosef from his brothers who plot to murder him (37:20), Re'uven presents his siblings with an alternative plan. "We must not take a life (lo nakkenu nafesh)! .... Do not spill blood (’al tishpekhu dam)! Throw him into this pit in the wilderness (ha-bor ’asher ba-midbar) but do not raise a hand against him" (37:21–22). Whereas the brothers plan to discard Yosef's dead body in a pit, Re'uven tries to sway them to throw Yosef into the pit alive, presumably so that he should die through abandonment. Attempting to minimize culpability, Re'uven argues, as Ramban clarifies, "The punishment of one who causes [death] indirectly

---

67. Ya'aqov's relationship with Raḥel is also revealed through Ramban's analysis of the tone of the dialogue between these biblical figures in 30:1–2; see Ramban's analysis of these verses. For other examples of Ramban's classification of a biblical speech as "hitnazzelut" which has direct bearing on his analysis of the dialogue scene, cf. Ramban, 20:12; 26:29; 31:35; and especially 49:5, in which he illustrates an additional instance of defensive speech in Ya'aqov's deathbed declarations.

68. For an elaborate discussion of various aspects of the style of biblical narrative, see Bar-Efrat, *Narrative Art*, pp. 197–237. These examples will illustrate Ramban's sensitivity to style in the dialogue scenes of Genesis.

(*ha-gorem*) is not like the punishment for one who spills blood with his own hands."[69]

While Scripture reveals to the reader that Re'uven plans to save Yosef from the pit and bring him back to his father (37:22),[70] Ramban suggests that Re'uven manipulates the style of his speech in order to promote his pretense that he is acting as a co-conspirator before his brothers. As Ramban observes,

> He [Re'uven] said to them... Do not spill "blood (*dam*)" with your own hands, but he did not say "*his* blood (*damo*)," for he made himself appear (*her'ah 'azmo*) that he is not saying thus [his alternative plan] because of his love [for Yosef] but only that they should not shed blood.[71]

Describing the ramifications of the brothers' plot from an objective standpoint, Re'uven adopts the demeanor of one who is anxious only to wash his hands and those of his brothers of the guilt associated with the murder of another human being. With this deliberate style, Re'uven precludes his brothers from thinking that he has a personal stake in Yosef's welfare.[72]

---

69. Ramban, 37:22. Ramban, 37:26, however, observes that Yehudah convinces his brothers to sell Yosef to traveling merchants by clarifying that their guilt would not be minimized even if they murdered Yosef indirectly through abandonment. Better to sell him and dispose of him alive.

70. Scripture does not clarify why Re'uven dissociates himself from his brothers, and Ramban does not speculate in this context. R. Bahya, 37:21, in *Rabbenu Bahya- Be'ur 'al ha-Torah*, ed. by Hayyim Chavel (Mosad Harav Kook, Jerusalem, 1966), posits that Re'uven was disturbed by his brothers' plot. On the other hand, Luzzatto, 37:21, observes that Re'uven's motives are not wholly altruistic, as is evident from his self-centered reaction upon discovering Yosef's disappearance, "The boy is gone and *I*, where can *I* turn?" (37:30). Rashi, 37:22, based on *GenR*. 84:15 [Theodor-Albeck, p. 1018], and Bekhor Shor, 37:21, suggest that Re'uven fears Ya'aqov will hold him the most accountable because of his firstborn status. Compare Hugh White, "The Joseph Story: A Narrative Which 'Consumes' Its Content," *Semeia* 31 (1985), p. 63, who has a similar observation. Luzzatto, 37:21, also conjectures that Re'uven is attempting to correct the ill will his father exhibits toward him as a result of his interference with Ya'aqov's relations with Bilhah (35:22), or at the very least, he does not want to add to his transgressions.

71. Ramban, 37:22.

72. Bekhor Shor, 37:21, also observes that Re'uven speaks in the first person plural form, "*We* must not take a life," as opposed to the second person plural, "*You* should not

In order to further this mode of dissemblance, Reʾuven emphasizes that the pit into which they will throw Yosef is not any pit, but a particular one (*"this* pit"), and he reiterates an obvious fact -the pit into which they will throw Yosef is a "pit in the wilderness." Analyzing the literary significance of this emphatic style, Ramban observes, "And the meaning of *into this pit in the wilderness* is to indicate that behold, 'this pit' is deep, and he will not be able to escape from it and it is 'in the wilderness,' and if he will cry out, there will be no one to save him, for there is no passerby."[73] By highlighting the advantage of using the deep pit as a means of killing Yosef indirectly, Reʾuven strengthens his persuasive argument before his brothers.[74]

Ramban suggests further how Reʾuven draws attention to his seeming concurrence with the plot to eliminate Yosef by reminding his brothers of his participation in the initial stages of planning Yosef's demise.[75] Significantly, Ramban claims that

---

take a life," in order to demonstrate that he is one of them. R. Baḥya, 37:21, supplements that Reʾuven did not say merely, "Let us not kill him," but he added "a life (*nefesh*)," to mitigate any personal concern for Yosef and to highlight his attempt to avoid the brothers' guilt in murdering another human being.

73. Ramban, 37:22. Compare Rashbam, 37:22. For other examples of Ramban's literary awareness of redundancies in a character's speech which are reiterated to highlight a particular message, see his commentary on Gen. 47:5 and 48:9.

74. Compare Neḥama Leibowitz's analysis of Ramban's insights into this aspect of Reʾuven 's speech, *Limmud Parshanei ha-Torah*, p. 173. Ramban's interpretation of the implications of Reʾuven's redundant reference to the pit in the wilderness parallels the brothers' guilty declaration in 42:21, in which they reveal that Yosef had indeed cried out, and they had ignored his pleas. In that context (42:22), Reʾuven endeavors to dissociate himself from his brothers, reminding them of his other attempts, which Scripture had not recorded previously, to stymie their ill-conceived schemes against Yosef; on Reʾuven's earlier attempts, see Ramban, 37:22 and compare his analysis of 42:21–22. Based on Ramban's interpretation of Reʾuven's speech in 37:22, an unsettling irony emerges. In order to rescue Yosef, Reʾuven persuades his brothers to throw Yosef into the pit from which his cries would not be heard. This very suggestion and its subsequent realization form the core of the brothers' guilt, and it is from this guilt that Reʾuven now tries to distance himself by emphasizing that in actuality he never wanted to harm Yosef.

75. Ramban observes that the brothers' original plot against Yosef undergoes numerous modifications until they finally resolve to sell him to traveling merchants. See Ramban, 37:25, who concludes that the brothers did sell him to the merchants; Ramban agrees with Bekhor Shor, 37:28. His opinion diverges from the approach of other commentators, such as Rashbam and Ḥizzequni, 37:28, as well as R. Baḥya, 42:21, who claim that the merchants removed Yosef from the pit without

the brothers attempt to kill Yosef even before he reaches them at Dothan. As Scripture relates, "And they saw him *from afar* and *before he came close to them*, they conspired against him to kill him (*va-yitnakkelu ʾoto le-hamito)*" [37:18]. Puzzled by Scripture's reiteration of Yosef's relative geographic distance to his brothers, Ramban posits that this text relates the brothers' scheme to kill Yosef from afar through crafty means (*nekhalim*), without laying a hand directly on him. When their undertaking fails to come to fruition or is unsuccessful, and Yosef, "that dreamer," approaches (37:19), they renew their efforts, declaring, "*And now* [having failed to kill Yosef indirectly], let us go and kill him [with our hands]" (37:20).[76] Having participated in the brothers' initial plot to kill Yosef,[77] Reʾuven bolsters his guise as co-conspirator by reminding them of his loyalty to their ruthless plan from the very beginning, while attempting to convince them for their own good not to kill Yosef directly. As Ramban explains,

> He said to them, "Behold, I was tolerant of you (*hayyiti sovel lakhem*) when you proposed to kill him with your crafty means (*le-hamit ʾoto be-nikhleikhem*). For, I, too, hated him and I wanted him to be put to death by others. But, you, do not spill blood with your hands. Far be it

---

the brothers' knowledge.

76. For this analysis, see Ramban, 37:18. Compare *Perush ha-Ramban ʿal ha-Torah*, ed. by Menaḥem Ẓvi Eisenstadt (Cong. Zikhron Joseph, New York, 1959–62), p. 288 n. 81. Compare *GenR.* 84:14 [Theodor-Albeck, p. 1017], which indicates that the brothers planned to send out the dogs against Yosef, and Jacob ben Asher, *Perush ha-Tur he-ʾArukh ʿal ha-Torah* (rpt. Yiẓḥaq Stern, Jerusalem, 1961), p. 81, on Ramban, 37:18, who maintains that the murder was to be accomplished possibly by means of arrows. Note that Ramban differs from the approaches of Rashi, Ibn Ezra, and Radak, 37:18, who claim that this verse refers only to the brothers' wily thoughts to kill him deceitfully, which is followed through in their statement of 37:19–20.

77. Compare Eisenstadt's analysis of Ramban, 37:22, *ibid.*, p. 288 n. 81. Ramban, however, does not clarify why Reʾuven went along with this initial scheme only to change his mind later on. Perhaps his hatred for Yosef impels him to go along with their plan to eliminate Yosef indirectly, without tracing the murder to them. When Reʾuven realizes, however, that the brothers intend to kill Yosef even if it means having blood on their hands, he hatches a plot to try to save Yosef from an untimely death.

from you!" And Reʾuven 's intent in all of this was to save him, to return him to his father.[78]

Fleshing out Reʾuven 's speech which was reported in compact form, Ramban points out how Reʾuven formulates his argument in a manner that deflects attention from his intent to save Yosef's life.

Ramban's analysis of the stolen goblet incident in Genesis 44 also illustrates his literary sensitivities to the ways in which biblical characters formulate their speeches in order to present a particular posture to their audience.

According to Ramban, Yosef plants his silver goblet deliberately in Binyamin's sack in order to test his brothers' loyalty to their younger brother. By alleging that Binyamin stole his silver goblet, Yosef compels Binyamin to remain with him while determining whether his siblings retain the same jealous or hateful feelings toward their younger brother, which they had demonstrated to Yosef.[79] Immediately after the brothers depart from the city, Yosef sends his house steward to pursue them, commanding him to pronounce, according to Ramban's rendition:

> "Why have you repaid evil for good?
> Indeed, this is *the* one from which my lord drinks
> (ha-lo zeh ʾasher yishteh ʾadoni bo)
> and because of which he has sought out his diviners [to tell him who stole it]
> (ve-hu naḥesh yenaḥesh bo)[80]

---

78. Ramban, 37:22.

79. Ramban, 42:9, indicates that Yosef "suspected" his brothers' hatred of Binyamin as a consequence of their jealousy of Yaʿaqov's love for Yosef. Furthermore, he was concerned that perhaps Binyamin sensed they had harmed Yosef, and hatred had erupted between the brothers. Before Yosef sends Binyamin home, he wants to test his siblings' attitude toward his younger brother, lest they harm him on the way. Compare Sternberg, *Poetics*, p. 302, who observes that this is "the brothers' decisive test" of "fraternal solidarity"; cf. his discussion of this episode, pp. 302–6. Contrast Radak, 44:1, who asserts that Yosef intended to vex his brothers through the goblet incident, without causing them physical or financial harm, as retribution for having sold him to Egypt.

80. This translation follows Ramban, 44:5, who renders 44:15 in this manner as well. Compare Bekhor Shor, Ibn Ezra (quoting Ibn Janaḥ), (and Radak's first opinion,

You have inflicted evil in what you did!" (44:4–5)

Ramban deciphers how Yosef manipulates the style of his speech and the structure of his argument in order to frame his brothers for stealing the goblet while ensuring that they do not suspect foul play. First, Yosef shrewdly omits any explicit reference to his goblet, referring to it merely by a demonstrative pronoun, "the one from which." This stylistic anomaly betrays Yosef's ulterior strategy to shock his brothers into thinking that he is convinced they are the guilty party. Paraphrasing Yosef's accusation, Ramban explains,

> He did not mention the goblet to them, but he spoke with them *as if it were known* (*keʾilu be-yaduʿa*) that they had taken the goblet, and therefore he said, "Indeed, this one (*zeh*) which you took, is the one from which my master drinks!"[81]

To intensify the psychological effect of his allegation, Yosef specifies that the goblet is special to him because he drinks from it. As Ramban elucidates, this elaboration on the goblet's purpose was designed to set up "a pretext in order to exaggerate their guilt (*ʿalilah le-hagdil ʿaleihem ha-ʾasham*)."[82] By stealing the lord's treasured possession, the guilty party "disgraces the royalty (*bozeh ʾet ha-malkhut*) and even if he were to pay an abundant bribe or ransom, it would be of no avail."[83] Finally, to impress upon

---

44:5. Contrast Rashbam, 44:5, who interprets *"naḥesh yenaḥesh bo"* as "in which he always divines," implying that Yosef used his goblet for predicting the future. Alter's translation, *Genesis*, p. 260, follows this rendition; see also his notes, p. 260.

81. Ramban, 44:5. Alter, *Genesis*, p. 260, notes on 44:5, observes, "The fact that the goblet is referred to only by a demonstrative pronoun … may reflect a flaunting of the assumption that, as all concerned should recognize, the only thing at issue here is the goblet."

82. Ramban, 44:5.

83. Ramban, 44:5. Ramban, 44:1, also perceives how Yosef precludes his brothers from finding a way out of the goblet allegation by making sure that they know of the other silver placed in their sacks, reported in 44:1. Although they were unaware the first time Yosef returned their money (42:25, 28) [even though they were aware of the provisions provided in their sacks- cf. Ramban, 42:25], this time they knew that Yosef put the silver in their bags. "For if he had done like the first time, without their knowledge, they would have had an excuse in the matter of the goblet, that the same

his siblings the gravity of their crime, Yosef stresses that once he realizes the cup is gone, he immediately asks his diviners to identify the perpetrators. That is why he knows to pursue them more than any other visitors to his palace.[84] By pointedly phrasing his allegation, Yosef maintains his charade, declaring that it is apparent they stole his goblet but feigning ignorance that it is in Binyamin's sack. As Ramban indicates, "And all of this was for the sake of setting up a pretense (le-hitnakker ba-ʿinyan)."[85]

In order to contest Yosef's accusation, the brothers consciously phrase their rejoinder in a way that directly counteracts his charges against them. While they had apparently seen that the goblet was silver when they ate and drank with Yosef (43:34),[86] the brothers deflect attention from the goblet by declaring in 44:8 that they did not steal *anything* from the lord's house, "*silver or gold.*" Ramban indicates that the accuser blames them "*as if* it were known (keʾilu be-yaduʿa) that they took the goblet," and the accused retort "*as if* they do not know (keʾilu ʾeinam yodeʿim) [about] what he is asking."[87]

Confident that they are in the clear, the brothers declare that if anything of the lord's possessions is found among them, the

---

thing happened to it as had happened to the money." Ramban, 44:1, also considers that the second placing of the silver in the brothers' sacks was done without their knowledge. In that case, Ramban exclaims with political insight that the ruler has a right to accuse them anyway of wrongdoing, despite the inconsistencies in his allegations; for "who can challenge one more powerful than himself?"

84. Ramban, 44:5. Since Yosef reveals that the cup has meaning to him because he drinks from it, Ramban concludes that "ve-hu naḥesh yenaḥesh bo" does not speak of a second function for this cup. This statement refers to the diviners whom Yosef allegedly sought in his quest to identify the guilty party.

85. Ramban, 44:5. This charade began, as Ramban, 42:7, observes, when Yosef changed his appearance in order to act as a stranger to them. Ramban, 42:9, notes further that this deception is maintained throughout his accusation that his brothers are spies, describing this allegation as an ʿalilah, a pretense, and attempting to find the grounds for Yosef being able to get away with his false charges. It continues here with the goblet incident. Yosef perpetuates this guise by conducting his search of the sacks from the eldest to the youngest brother, as noted by Ramban, 44:5.

86. See the comment of Eisenstadt, Perush ha-Ramban, p. 344 n. 6. Compare Alter, Genesis, p. 260, notes on 44:5.

87. Ramban, 44:5. This analysis demonstrates how Ramban links his interpretations of various aspects of a narrative episode through internal repetition of his own key phrases.

guilty one will be put to death, and the remaining brothers will indenture themselves to the lord as his servants. As Ramban paraphrases 44:9, "He of your servants with whom shall be found, *any stolen silver or gold*, shall die."[88] The brothers' purposeful evasion of any reference to the goblet underscores their ulterior strategy to convince Yosef of their innocence of the charges leveled against them.[89]

IV. Ambiguities in Biblical Dialogue

Ramban displays an acute sensitivity to the apparent ambiguities within a character's speech, which allow for more than one interpretation of the style and tone of the dialogue.[90] A case in point is Ramban's keen analysis of Avraham's negotiations with the Hittites for a burial plot for Sarah in Genesis 23.[91] According to Ramban, Avraham does not approach the Hittites asking for favors or pleading for their good graces but demands his legal

---

88. See Ramban, 44:5. Compare Ramban, 44:10, who analyzes how the brothers assume an innocent posture, and their offer that the guilty one should die and all the others would become slaves was considered by them to be extravagant. The house steward, on the other hand, contends they are all guilty by association, but he will be extravagant in his good will gesture that only the one who actually stole the goblet will become his slave. Compare Alter, *The Art of Biblical Narrative*, pp. 172–73, who develops the theme of ignorance versus knowledge in this narrative unit. Cf. *idem*, *Genesis*, p. 261, notes on 44:9, on his observations concerning the brothers' excessive proposal which reflects their certainty of their innocence.

89. Compare Abarbanel, 44:5, 10 [Shaviv, 723], in which Ramban's influence on his commentary is apparent.

90. Compare William Empson, *Seven Types of Ambiguities* (Oxford Univ. Press, London and Toronto, 1930), p. 1, who defines, "An ambiguity... [applies to] any verbal nuance, however slight, which gives room for alternative reactions to the same piece of language." See also his observations, *ibid.*, pp. 5–6, "Ambiguity itself can mean an indecision as to what you mean, an intention to mean several things, a probability that one or other or both of two things has been meant, and the fact that a statement has several meanings."

91. Meir Sternberg has analyzed this episode in depth from a literary perspective in "Double Cave, Double Talk: The Indirections of Biblical Dialogue," in *Not In Heaven: Coherence and Complexity in Biblical Narrative*, eds. by Jason P. Rosenblatt and Joseph C. Sitterson, Jr. (Indiana Univ. Press, Bloomington and Indianapolis, 1991), pp. 28–57, 227–31. In the following notes, I will show how Ramban parallels and differs from Sternberg's poetic approach to this episode. Sternberg does not refer to Ramban's commentary on this episode.

rights as a lawful resident. "*Ger ve-toshav ꞏanokhi ꞋImakhem. Tenu li aḥuzzat qever ꞋImakhem ve-ꞏeqberah meti mi-lefanai*" (23:4). While Avraham is a stranger (*ger*) from another land who did not inherit a family burial place, he is now living among them (*ꞋImakhem*) as a resident citizen (*toshav*). This legal status confers upon him the right to demand that the Hittites "give" him a plot of land (*tenu li*) for an everlasting possession (*aḥuzzah*) so that he may bury his dead. [92]

Ramban detects how the Hittites misread Avraham's ambiguous demand to "give" him the possession of a burial plot as a request for the bestowal of a gift.[93] Regardless of how Avraham describes himself, the Hittites conclude that Avraham demands a gift because he is a king, who has the right to take whatever he chooses from the sojourners of the land, who are his subjects. As they respond, "Hear us my lord. You are a *nesiꞏ ꞏElohim* among us! In the most select our graves, bury your dead. No one among us will withhold his burial site from you for burying your dead" (23:6). Ramban does not render *nesiꞏ ꞏElohim* as an honorific designation of pre-eminence, but interprets that the Hittites attribute

---

92. See Ramban, 23:4–6, for this reading. Ramban's rendition presumes that *ger* and *toshav* have two distinct meanings; compare Rashi, his first opinion; Rashbam; and Radak, on 23:4, as well as Bekhor Shor, 23:4, 6. On the other hand, Sternberg, "Double Cave," p. 33, renders 23:4, "Although I am an alien and a resident, give me a holding." Accordingly, Sternberg, *ibid.*, interprets that Avraham's status as a "foreign settler" precludes him from having the "citizen's right" to acquire land, and he concludes that Avraham's opening statement has "the force of a concessive, because it is precisely a concession that he seeks." Cf. Alter, *Genesis*, p. 109, and notes to 23:4. Differentiating between *ger* and *toshav*, Ramban maintains that Avraham presents himself to the Hittites as a permanent resident who demands his citizen's rights.

93. The printed editions diverge slightly in their rendition of Ramban's commentary on this point. Cohen, *Miqraꞏot Gedolot Haketer,* Vol. I on Genesis, 210, has the version, "They *thought (ḥashvu)* that he asked for it as a gift from them." Ḥayyim Chavel, ed., *Perush ha-Ramban Ꞌal ha-Torah*, (Mosad Harav Kook, Jerusalem, 1959), 1:129, has the version, "They [the Hittites] suspected (*ḥashdu*)" that Avraham was asking for a present from them, which has a more negative nuance, even though both readings convey the same perception on the part of the Hittites. Cf. Sternberg, *ibid.*, p. 34, who also observes that the Hittites compel Avraham to qualify his intent when he demanded that they "give" him what he wants, even though Avraham, who had rejected riches from the king of Sodom in Genesis 14, would never contemplate a free gift.

to Avraham the veritable stature of royalty among the Canaanite nations.[94] This distinguished rank gives Avraham the right to take any one of the Hittites' existing burial plots, and by virtue of the fact that he buries his wife there, the land becomes his everlasting possession for burying his dead as he has requested.[95]

Capitalizing on the Hittites' open-ended offer to select a burial ground of his choosing and at the same time, responding to their misguided interpretation of his intent, Avraham rejoins,

> "If you desire to bury my dead from before me, hear me, and entreat for me Efron son of Zohar, and let him give (*ve-yitten*) me the cave of Makhpelah that belongs to him which is at the edge of his field. At the full price let him give it to me in your midst as a possession for a burial site. (23:8–9)

---

94. Ramban, 23:4–6. While Ramban does not cite a midrashic source, perhaps he is influenced by *GenR.* 42:5; 43:5; 58:6 [Theodor-Albeck, pp. 410, 419, 624, respectively], in which Avraham is designated as a "king" over the Canaanite nations as a result of his military victory in Genesis 14. Throughout his commentary on Genesis, Ramban reiterates the patriarchs' royal status, especially noting that this privilege is a fulfillment of God's promises to Avraham regarding his position among the Canaanite nations. Cf. Ramban, 13:17; 23:19; 25:34; and 33:18. Contrast Radak, 23:6, who views *nesiʾ ʾElohim* as an honorific designation of exaltation, and Ibn Ezra, 23:6, who maintains that Avraham's prophetic status earns him this title. Sternberg, "Double Cave," p. 55, also maintains that this title is not to be understood literally. See as well Alter, *Genesis*, p. 109, notes on 23:6.

95. See Ramban, 23:4–6. While Ramban does not clarify, based on his interpretation, it is apparent that the Hittites have essentially disqualified Avraham from attaining the status of a resident citizen, separating him from them by virtue of his royal stature. Although they have provided Avraham with a burial plot, they have not given him the legal rights to purchase property as accorded a lawful citizen of their society. Compare Radak's analysis of the Hittite proposal, 23:6. Sternberg, "Double Cave," pp. 31–32, highlights the tone of the Hittite response, observing that the "plural form given to the declarations," "the extravagant offer of 'our choicest burial grounds,'" and "the double negative, 'No man of us will deny thee,'" all add up to a response that is "indefinite and inoperative … A plurality or community of non-deniers does not yet make a single giver." While Sternberg, *ibid.*, p. 32, characterizes the Hittites as "double-talkers," who aim "to preserve their façade of goodwill," Ramban does not necessarily read an undertone of cunning into the Hittites' counter-proposal. Based on his literal application of the title, *nesiʾ ʾElohim*, Ramban appears to maintain that the Hittites give Avraham what they think he wants, a "gift" befitting a ruler of their land. Nevertheless, their selective interpretation of "give" and their rejection of Avraham's classification of his status as a "stranger and now a resident among them," does indicate that they have reinterpreted Avraham's demand.

Clarifying Avraham's reply, Ramban explains that Avraham demands to be treated like a resident citizen, who has the legal entitlement to purchase a previously undesignated plot of land for a family burial place. Since the Hittites have offered Avraham to choose a burial holding, he tells them to entreat Efron[96] for the cave at the end of his property, which does not serve as an ancestral burial ground, but "is a field to them (le-sadeh hi' lahem)."[97] Avraham also informs the Hittites to tell Efron to "give" him the land by means of a sale for its full purchase price. His reiterated usage of the term, "give," is intended to make the offer more palatable, implying that he would consider the transaction as though a gift were being bestowed upon him, or it is considered to be standard verbiage in a transaction, even though the Hittites had initially interpreted otherwise.[98]

Efron, however, changes the parameters of Avraham's offer. "No, my lord, hear me. The field I have given to you and the cave that is in it I have given to you. In the presence of the sons of my people, I have given it to you. Bury your dead" (23:11). Questioning Efron's ulterior motive, Ramban suggests that the tone of Efron's speech is ambiguous, and the speaker may be purposely infusing his words with more than one tone.

> And behold Avraham only asked to sell him the cave,
> for it was at the edge of the land, and the [remaining]
> field would remain with Efron, but he [Efron] said to

---

96. Ramban, 23:8, notes that Avraham is aware Efron might reject the offer on the grounds that it would be dishonorable for him to sell his inheritance; he therefore enlists the help of the Hittites to ensure that the transaction is carried out. It appears that the reading of this verse in *Moshav Zekeinim*, ms Paris 260, on 23:8, cited in Gelis, *Tosafot ha-Shalem*, 2:236, paragraph 1, is adopted from Ramban's analysis. Compare Sternberg's analysis, "Double Cave," p. 38.

97. See Ramban, 23:8. Compare Sternberg, *ibid.*, pp. 38–39.

98. See Ramban, 23:9. For Ramban's first approach, compare the Tosafist comment noted in Gelis, *Tosafot ha-Shalem*, 2:238, paragraph 6, on 23:9. Sternberg, "Double Cave," p. 34, also observes, "… his 'Give' must be a shorthand for 'Give me permission to acquire or to proceed.'" See his comments, *ibid.*, p. 40, "Instead of changing the operative verb, Avraham repeats it with a gloss designed to correct a possible (or probable) misapprehension: 'When I said *give*, I hope you did not understand me to have in mind a present or even a token payment. At the full price, it would still remain a gift from a kind donor to a grateful recipient.'"

him *by way of proper etiquette (derekh musar) or by way of cunning (mirmah)* that he would give him (*she-yitten lo*) the field and the cave in it, for it is not possible for an honorable man like himself to own the cave as a possession for burial and the field should belong to another. And Avraham was *happy* about it, and he bought the whole [plot of land] for the price which he [Efron] cited to him.[99]

On the surface, Efron assumes the veneer of an ethical individual, expressing his concern for Avraham's honor.[100] Yet, Ramban also discerns that underlying this sincere impression lurks a cunning businessman who aims to capitalize on this opportunity. Although his offer appears to be generous, in actuality, Efron means to drive up the price of the sale by expanding the transaction to include both the cave and its nearby field. By considering both upstanding and cunningly deceptive tones for Efron's rejoinder simultaneously, separating his alternative readings by the simple qualifier, "or," Ramban discloses how a character can manipulate his speech to present himself in one guise, while masking the true character that lurks underneath.[101]

Although Efron also adopts the terminology of "give" for this transaction, Ramban presumes that Efron employs a shorthand

---

99. This analysis of 23:11 is found in Ramban, 23:9.
100. While Ramban does not comment, the irony of Efron's proposal is apparent in relation to the Hittites' initial response. The same honorable status which the Hittites had invoked in order to avoid selling their property to Avraham is now applied by Efron not only to sell property but to expand its borders beyond Avraham's original demand.
101. For a parallel analysis of Ramban's comment, see Yehudah Meir Devir, *Perush ha-Ramban 'al ha-Torah 'Im Be'ur Beit ha-Yayin* (Makhon Megillat Sefer, Jerusalem, 2000), Vol. I on Genesis, 300–1 n. 7, on 23:9. On the other hand, R. Baḥya, 23:9, who is apparently influenced by Ramban, only cites the tone of Efron's speech as courteous, not deceptive. Cf. Sternberg, "Double Cave," p. 41, who reveals that "he [Efron] means to drive a hard bargain by raising the sale from a cave to the field that encloses it... the facade of piety and courtesy lifts to reveal the politician with a vested interest." See also his analysis, *ibid.,* pp. 43, 46. While Ramban also reads into Efron's words an undertone of cunning, he does not view Avraham's response ultimately as a forced concession to a threatening ultimatum. See further on in my discussion.

term for the purchase of the land.[102] This approach contrasts with that of Rashi and Radak who claim that Efron presents himself as magnanimous by offering Avraham the land as a gift.[103] Ramban portrays Efron as the quintessential businessman who would never dream of giving up his land without payment. Not only does he intend to be paid for his land, but he raises the price of the sale by including the surrounding field with the purchase of the cave.

When Avraham hears Efron's counter-offer, he is delighted and immediately pays Efron the stipulated price of four hundred silver shekels (23:16). From Ramban's perspective, Avraham's response does not reflect his coerced surrender to Efron's ultimatum.[104] Avraham reacts with joy that Efron has expanded the boundaries of his burial plot, and he pays the worth of the property.[105]

Ramban observes, however, that Avraham does not trust

---

102. Ramban, 23:9, emphasizes that "Avraham only asked *to sell him* the cave," and when Efron extended the offer and said "he *will give* him the field and the cave in it.... Avraham was happy with this, and he *bought* it all for the price that he [Efron] cited to him." From this formulation, it is apparent that Ramban means that Avraham understood Efron's offer to be that of a sales transaction, not as an outright gift. Had Ramban understood otherwise, he probably would have stipulated the two aspects of Efron's seeming magnanimity more clearly, as did his predecessors, Rashi and Radak, 23:11 (see next note). Compare Sternberg, *ibid.*, pp. 41, 43, who does not view Efron's "give" as having the intent of a gift.

103. See Rashi, 23:11, 13, 16, and Radak, 23:11. Rashi, 23:15–16, maintains that Efron's cunning personality comes through when he not only accepts Avraham's refusal of his "gift," but asks an exorbitant price for the land. Compare Rashbam, 23:11.

104. As Sternberg, "Double Cave," pp. 45–46, interprets. Ramban does not portray Avraham as a vulnerable individual who must cower to the coercion of Efron and his people, but views Avraham's acceptance of the deal as one of joy and delight. From this reading, one may conclude that Ramban felt Avraham was in agreement with the changed terms of the deal, perhaps because Avraham was getting what he really wanted in the first place, but had not dared to ask.

105. With regard to the price of four hundred silver shekels stipulated by Efron (23:15), Ramban, 23:15, concludes that Efron does not betray ulterior motives. Although he is aware of the midrashic approach that contends Efron asked for an exorbitant price [cf. *GenR.* 58:7 (Theodor-Albeck, pp. 626–27)], Ramban maintains that this was the price originally paid for the land by Efron or his ancestors. Contrast Sternberg, "Double Cave," p. 47, who correlates the prices for land noted elsewhere in the Bible (as in 2 Sam. 24:24; Jer. 32:9), and concludes that the price for the cave is rather steep, proving how Efron's apparent largesse betrays his greed.

Efron's apparent sincerity.[106] While Efron offers in a magnanimous gesture that Avraham may bury his dead even before the deal is concluded, citing his people as witnesses to the irrevocable nature of the transaction (23:11), Avraham takes no chances. He pays the full price for the cave and surrounding field and takes legal possession of his property before all the people of the city; only then does he bury his beloved wife on his newly acquired burial ground (23:16–20).[107]

Conclusion

Ramban's investigation of the dialogue scenes in the Book of Genesis exposes the complex portraiture of the biblical personalities. Through his analysis of the characters' spoken words, Ramban reveals their attributes, feelings, attitudes, concerns, and relationships with others. Although Ramban does not aim to provide a systematic discussion of the poetics of biblical narrative, this study has applied literary classifications in order to demonstrate that his exegetical insights hinge upon a poetic approach to biblical dialogue. Ramban's focused investigation of the point of view, tone, style, and ambiguities in biblical dialogue illustrates his discriminating perception of the compositional elements which form the cornerstone of biblical speech. Through his exploration of the mode of dialogue, Ramban divulges the ways in which Scripture presents the biblical personalities and their relationships as a means of promoting the ultimate message and meaning of the biblical stories.

---

106. For this analysis, see Ramban, 23:11, on 23:17–20.
107. For another example of ambiguities in dialogue, see Ramban's analysis of the confrontation between Ya'aqov and Lavan in Gen. 29:15. In this example, the gapping of narrative information regarding the impetus for Ya'aqov's employment for Lavan leads Ramban to contemplate two divergent readings of the tone of Lavan's speech, conjecturing that either Lavan is speaking sincerely or deceptively. In this case, the ambiguity is present from the reader's perspective, not necessarily in the character's intent in the context of the story. In his interpretation of Lavan's subsequent speech of 29:27, however, Ramban exposes the deceptive tone of Lavan's words.

15

Words Unfitly Spoken: Two Critics of the Role of Midrash in Rashi's *Commentary on the Torah*[1]

Eric Lawee

Though assured, by early modern times, of its standing as the most authoritative and widely studied of Jewish biblical commentaries, Rashi's *Commentary on the Torah* elicited, in centuries closer to its inception, highly variegated responses, from reverent admiration to stiff resistance. Restricting consideration to the later Middle Ages, there stands at one extreme the anonymous mid-fifteenth-century author of the Spanish kabbalistic work, *Sefer ha-meshiv*, who admonished his reader never to entertain the notion that Rashi "composed his ... plain-sense interpretations of scripture on the basis of his own understanding (*me-rosho*)." Rather, Rashi explained holy writ (and the text of the Babylonian Talmud) under the mystically inspired aegis of the "secret of the garment" (*sod ha-malbush*). Standing at the other extreme were critics of Rashi familiar to Moses Ibn Gabbai, a Sefardic refugee scholar who took asylum in North Africa after the anti-Jewish riots that decimated Spanish Jewry in 1391. While himself venerating Rashi as a "master, eminence, father of Israel," Ibn Gabbai reproved naysayers who denigrated Rashi's biblical scholarship for, among other things, being "utterly rife with *derashot* and *'aggadot*." Here, then, are starkly divergent evaluations of Rashi's

1. I wish to express my gratitude to the Social Sciences and Humanities Research Council of Canada for its generous support of the larger project of which this study forms a part.

exegesis on a broad spectrum of opinion: mystically inspired interpretation on one reckoning and scandalously over-midrashic interpretation on the other.[2]

If the *Commentary* could be viewed with reserve for various reasons, most of its late medieval detractors focused on the rabbinic dicta that Rashi so often invoked in explicating and expounding on the divine word. While forgoing any systematic account of his overarching exegetical methods and goals, Rashi espoused, and in large measure executed, a mode of Torah commentary that was largely novel, at least by the standards of biblical scholarship carried out in the Franco-German sphere. He would relay scripture's "plain" or "literal" or "contextual" sense (*peshuṭo shel miqra'*, to use the term he minted, which quickly became a common usage under his influence) while also adducing such rabbinic dicta as "conformed to (*miyashevet*) the words of scripture, in the manner of 'a word fitly spoken'" [Prov. 25:11].[3] Left unexplained were the details of just how this "method" was to be implemented and here Rashi's practice proved enigmatic. At times, Rashi recorded contextual and homiletical-midrashic interpretations alongside one another and at other times not.

2. For the passage in *Sefer ha-meshiv* and analysis of it, see Moshe Idel, "'Iyyunim be-shiṭato shel ba'al 'sefer ha-meshiv': pereq be-toldot ha-qabbalah ha-sefardit," *Sefunot* 17 (1983): 240–41; idem, "'Nocturnal Kabbalists," *Archævs* 4 (2000): 63–67; Abraham Gross, "Rashi u-mesoret limmud ha-torah she-bi-khetav bi-sefarad," in *Rashi: 'Iyyunim bi-yeṣirato*, ed. Zevi Aryeh Steinfeld (Ramat-Gan: Bar Ilan University Press, 1993), 52. For the metamorphosis of Rashi "into a mystic who learned everything from supernal sources," see Moshe Idel, *Kabbalah: New Perspectives* (New Haven: Yale University Press, 1988), 238–39. On the "secret of the garment," see Elliott Wolfson, "The Secret of the Garment in Naḥmanides," *Daat* 24 (1990): xxv–xlix. The fifteenth and sixteenth centuries saw a general proliferation of claims to knowledge, and the composition of books, under the auspices of pneumatic inspiration. See Lawrence Fine, *Physician of the Soul, Healer of the Cosmos: Isaac Luria and His Kabbalistic Fellowship* (Stanford: Stanford University Press, 2003), 113–15. For Ibn Gabbai's report, see his *'Eved shelomo*, ed. Moshe Filip (Petah Tikvah, 2006), 43. For discussion, see Gross, "Rashi," 41–43.
3. For statements of exegetical intent by Rashi and their meaning, see Benjamin Gelles, *Peshat and Derash in the Exegesis of Rashi* (Leiden: Brill, 1981), 9–27; Sarah Kamin, *Rashi: peshuṭo shel miqra' u-midrasho shel miqra'* (Jerusalem: Magnes, 1986). For "*miyashevet*" as "conforming to" rather than "settling a difficulty in [scripture]," see Yonah Fraenkel, "Ha-piyyut ve-ha-perush: le-meqorot ha-'aggadah be-ferushav shel rashi la-torah," *'Iyyunei miqra' u-farshanut* 7 (2005): 475 n. 1.

At times, he offered a single midrashic interpretation and on other occasions several. Occasionally, he noted an interpretation's midrashic provenance but far more frequently, he adduced rabbinic expositions without identifying them as such. On rare occasion, he explicitly flagged a textual trigger to his exposition. Usually, however, he left readers to discern such spurs for themselves (and modern scholars to debate whether a prompt in the text should be sought, and could be found, in all cases).[4] However all this may be, Rashi's combination of contextual and midrashic interpretations proved appealing, leading a modern scholar to propose that it was just this "pleasing combination" and the "attractive fleshing out of the terse biblical text by rabbinic interpretation" that, along with Rashi's "concise, lucid language," explains the *Commentary*'s "tremendous popularity" over the ages.[5] As Moses Ibn Gabbai's report indicates, however, not everybody was pleased. Some lamented — and others maligned — the *Commentary*'s regular recourse to midrash, however selective it might be and whether or not the midrashim in question in some way "conformed to scripture's words."

The following essay provides preliminary orientation in two especially forthright critiques of the role of midrash in Rashi's *Commentary*. The first, in point of chronology though not comprehensiveness, takes the form of a series of "animadversions" directed against "Rabbi Solomon the Frenchman in his interpretation of the Torah." This tract, likely of eastern Mediterranean provenance, may have been composed around the turn of the

---

4. In modern times, Nehama Leibowitz has argued the existence of a textual warrant for more or less all of Rashi's glosses but the pendulum seems currently to be swinging towards a view of Rashi as one who at times expounded scripture by way of midrash even where textual moorings were lacking. See Fraenkel, "Ha-piyyut ve-ha-perush"; Avraham Grossman, "Pulmus dati u-megamah ḥinukhit be-ferush Rashi la-torah," in *Pirke Neḥamah: sefer zikaron le-Neḥamah Lebovits*, ed. Moshe Ahrend and Ruth Ben-Meir ([Jerusalem]: Ha-sokhnut ha-yehudit le-ereṣ yisraʾel, 2001), 187–205 (which also summarizes Leibowitz's contrary view).

5. Avraham Grossman, "The School of Literal Jewish Exegesis in Northern France," in *Hebrew Bible / Old Testament: The History of Its Interpretation*, vol. 1, pt. 2, *From the Beginnings to the Middle Ages: The Middle Ages*, ed. Magne Sæbo, in co-operation with Chris Brekelmans and Menahem Haran (Göttingen: Vanderhoeck and Ruprecht, 2000), 344.

fifteenth century. It was copied, in the sole version that has come down, on the island of Crete in 1410. The second critique appears in a work of combined Torah commentary and supercommentary on Rashi's *Commentary* written around mid-fifteenth century by Aaron Aboulrabi, a Sicilian-born exegete familiar with the earlier critical work. That two works wholly or largely devoted to a fiercely independent critical audit of what was fast becoming medieval Judaism's most influential work of biblical scholarship emerged in close temporal proximity to one another draws attention to questions of larger context. In the essay's penultimate section, some of these are addressed on the basis of another late medieval broadside against Rashi's biblical exegesis. The emergence of critiques of the *Commentary* should, it is proposed, be largely understood as a response to the special standing that Rashi's work was coming to enjoy as it moved towards its eventual destination as the closest thing Jews have ever seen to a canonical commentary on holy writ.[6]

---

6. The term "canonical" is used here in awareness that, as applied to a work such as Rashi's *Commentary*, it raises larger questions of appropriateness and definition. I attempt to address these in a monograph in progress. In the meantime, note the title of a recent article by Yitzhak S. Penkower that (as best one can tell) casually ascribes canonical status to the *Commentary*: "Tahalikh ha-qanonizaṣiyah shel perush rashi la-torah," in *Limmud ve-daʿat be-maḥashavah yehudit*, ed. Haim Kreisel (Beer Sheva: Ben Gurion University Press of the Negev, 2006), 123–46. Cp. Mayer I. Gruber, *Rashi's Commentary on Psalms*, 1st paperback ed. (Philadelphia: Jewish Publication Society, 2007), 53 n. 84, which speaks of the "canonical status" that, in many Jewish circles, Rashi's *Commentary* "retains to this day." There is, it would seem, a growing trend to understand some developments in post-rabbinic Judaism in terms of the hermeneutics of canonicity. See, e.g., Moshe Halbertal, *People of the Book: Canon, Meaning, and Authority* (Cambridge, Mass.: Harvard University Press, 1997). The trend seems pronounced in Kabbalah studies. See Boaz Huss, *Ke-zohar ha-raqiaʿ: peraqim be-hitqablut ha-zohar u-ve-havnayat ʿerko ha-simli* (Jerusalem: Mosad Byalik, 2008); idem, "*Sefer Ha-Zohar* as a Canonical, Sacred and Holy Text: Changing Perspectives on the Book of Splendor Between the Thirteenth and Eighteenth Centuries," *Journal of Jewish Thought and Philosophy* 7 (1998): 257–307; Moshe Idel, "The Vicissitudes of Kabbalah in Catalonia," in *The Jews of Spain and the Expulsion of 1492*, ed. Moshe Lazar and Stephen Haliczer (Lancaster, CA: Labyrinthos, 1997), 29, 38 n. 33; idem, "Kabbalah in Spain: Some Cultural Observations," in *Encuentros and desencuentros: Spanish Jewish Cultural Interaction Throughout History*, ed. Carlos Carrete Parrondo, et. al. (Tel Aviv: University Publishing Projects, 2000), 66–68, 71; Moshe Halbertal, "From Oral Tradition to Literary Canon: Shem Tov Ibn Gaon and the Critique of Kabbalistic Learning," in *Homer, the Bible, and Beyond: Literary and Religious Canons in the*

I

Before describing the two aforementioned adversarial reactions to the *Commentary*'s midrashic hermeneutic, it will be helpful to capture, if only fleetingly, some rejoinders to Rashi's approach registered by better known Jewish exegetes of the high and late Middle Ages.

For an early stratum in Rashi's *Commentary*'s reception-history, one thinks of Samuel ben Meir (Rashbam), who, while endorsing Rashi's aspiration to explicate the Torah's contextual meaning, often doubted Rashi's success on this score. In a celebrated passage, this grandson of Rashi related the manner in which he wrested an admission from his grandfather about the need to produce "other" commentaries based on "the new contextual interpretations revealing themselves each day." It was towards this end that Rashbam composed his own commentaries in which he freed the biblical text "even more than Rashi had, from the confines of traditional [midrashic] exegesis."[7] Still, Rashbam "had no desire to supplant Rashi's commentary"[8] and at times recommended it while generally eschewing demonstrative displays of disdain for Rash's interpretations, midrashic or otherwise.[9]

Ancient World, ed. Margalit Finkelberg and Guy G. Stroumsa, Jerusalem Studies in Religion and Culture 2 (Leiden: Brill, 2003), 253–66. Notions of canon adapted only slowly or guardedly in the study of medieval and early modern Jewish intellectual history have apparently become almost de rigueur in studies of modern Hebrew literature. See, e.g., Hannan Hever, *Producing the Modern Hebrew Canon: Nation Building and Minority Discourse (New York: New York University Press, 2002)*; Michael Gluzman, *The Politics of Canonicity: Lines of Resistance in Modernist Hebrew Poetry* (Stanford: Stanford University Press, 2003).

7. Martin I. Lockshin, *Rabbi Samuel Ben Meir's Commentary on Genesis* (Lewiston, NY: Edwin Mellan Press, 1989), 21. Lockshin argues (18) that opposing Rashi's exegesis was Rashbam's "primary goal" in his own commentary. For Rashbam's account of his exchange with Rashi, see his gloss on Gen. 37:1 (ed. David Rosin [Breslau, 1881], 49).

8. Lockshin, *Rabbi Samuel*, 21. Note further Sara Japhet's observation ("Major Trends in the Study of Medieval Jewish Exegesis in Northern France," *Trumah* 9 [2000]: 43) that Rashbam's commentary "was probably consulted only as a supplement to that of Rashi."

9. Rashbam recommends study of Rashi's *Commentary* at the end of his commentary on Exodus and beginning of his commentary on Leviticus, even as his "appraisal of

The Spanish exegetical tradition first encountered Rashi when Rashbam's contemporary, the twelfth-century Andalusian polymath Abraham Ibn Ezra, fled the "animosity of harassers" and inaugurated his life of itinerant scholarship in Christian Europe.[10] Along the way, he cultivated his principal métier, biblical interpretation, using a method grounded in the achievements of such Andalusian predecessors as Moses Ibn Gikatilla and the grammatical insights of the two giants in the field, Judah Hayyuj and Jonah Ibn Janach. The method's warp was linguistic accuracy, or "the bonds of grammar," as Ibn Ezra poetically put it in his Torah Commentary's introduction. Its woof was principles of reasonability, or "the eyes of knowledge," as he called these in the same preface.[11] In one of his grammatical tomes, Ibn Ezra affirmed the ancient sages' keen awareness of the distinction between *peshaṭ* and *derash* and implied their preference for the former (their preoccupation with the latter notwithstanding). He then lamented the abandonment of scripture's contextual sense

---

his grandfather's works is more nuanced and more conflicted than these comments imply" (Martin I. Lockshin, *Rashbam's Commentary on Leviticus and Numbers* [Providence: Brown Judaic Studies, 2001], 11). For evidence of conflictedness, and a rare sample of Rashbam's openly disdainful comments of Rashi's exegesis, see Moshe Sokolow, "'He-peshaṭot ha-mitḥadshim' — qeṭaʿim ḥadashim mi-perush ha-torah le-rashbam — k[etav] y[ad]," *ʿAlei sefer* 11 (1988): 73–80. Indicative of the indirectness of Rashbam's "attacks" is the need to adduce statistical evidence (Lockshin, *Rabbi Samuel Ben Meir's Commentary on Genesis*, 17–18) to demonstrate a trend that might otherwise be missed.

10. For the vexation that spurred his departure, see the rhymed introduction to his commentary on Lamentations. For facets of his diverse intellectual creativity, see *Rabbi Abraham Ibn Ezra: Studies in the Writings of a Twelfth-Century Polymath*, ed. Isadore Twersky and Jay M. Harris (Cambridge, Mass.: Harvard University Center for Jewish Studies, 1993). Arriving in Rome in 1140, Ibn Ezra would, in decades following, alight in numerous Italian and French centers and roam as far north as England, where he apparently died in 1164. For his itinerary, see Norman Golb, *The Jews in Medieval Normandy* (Cambridge: Cambridge University Press, 1998), 253–96.

11. *Perushei ha-torah le-rabbenu 'Avraham Ibn 'Ezra*, ed. Asher Weiser (Jerusalem: Mosad ha-rav Kuk, 1976), 1:1. For discussion, see Uriel Simon, "Shnei 'eqronot-yesod shel perush ha-torah le-Raʾbaʿ: ba-ʿavotot ha-diqduq niqshar uve-ʿenei ha-daʿat yikhshar," in *Meḥqarim be-miqra' uve-ḥinukh*, ed. Dov Rappel (Jerusalem: Touro College, 1996), 109–13. For Ibn Ezra's need to accommodate Jewish audiences not privy to Judeo-Arabic learning, see idem, "R. 'Avraham Ibn 'Ezra — ben ha-mefaresh le-qoreʾav," in *Divrei ha-qongres ha-ʿolami ha-teshiʿi le-madaʿei ha-yahadut* (Jerusalem: World Union of Jewish Studies, 1985), 23–42.

by "subsequent generations" who made "each *derash* primary and paramount." Nowhere was this regrettable trend more obvious than in the figure of "R. Solomon [Rashi], who explained the Torah, Prophets, and Writings by way of *derash*, though he thought it was *peshaṭ*." Weighing Rashi's explanations against his twin standards of accuracy, grammatical precision and reasonability, Ibn Ezra determined that, aim notwithstanding, Rashi had successfully grasped and imparted the contextual sense "but one time in a thousand." [12] Yet he ruefully conceded that "scholars of our generation" (and ordinary Jews all the more, one presumes) "sing the praises of these [midrashically oriented] books." Even allowing for exaggeration,[13] here was an evidently acute critique.[14]

Though more evenhanded in their evaluation of Rashi's *Commentary* than Ibn Ezra, later exegetes of the Spanish school and its offshoots continued to dissent, at times strongly, from elements of Rashi's midrashic approach. The thirteenth century saw Rashi's *Commentary* attain new levels of Sefardic prominence due to frequent engagement by Moses ben Nahman (Ramban), the first great Jewish scholar "belonging totally to the cultural environment of Christian Spain" who, as a thinker and writer, in many stood "between Ashkenaz and Andalusia."[15] Though Ramban famously described Rashi as the "first-born" among biblical

12. *Safah berurah*, in *Devir* 2, ed. M. Wilensky (1924): 288.
13. Aharon Mondschein, "'Ve-'en bi-sefarav peshaṭ raq 'ehad meni 'elef': le-derekh ha-hityaḥasut shel ra'ba' le-ferush rashi la-torah," *'Iyyunei miqra' u-farshanut* 5 (2000): 226.
14. Ibn Ezra was, in his biblical commentaries as elsewhere, not only presenting the "outstanding achievements of Judeo-Arabic culture to his readers" but also challenging and preaching against "the values of the local culture he encountered" in Christian Europe. See Joseph Yahalom, "Aesthetic Models in Conflict: Classicist Versus Ornamental in Jewish Poetics," in *Renewing the Past, Reconfiguring Jewish Culture*, ed. Ross Brann and Adam Sutcliffe (Philadelphia: University of Pennsylvania Press, 2004), 22.
15. See, respectively, Bernard Septimus, "'Open Rebuke and Concealed Love': Nahmanides and the Andalusian Tradition," in *Rabbi Moses Naḥmanides (Ramban): Explorations in His Religious and Literary Virtuosity*, ed. Isadore Twersky (Cambridge, Mass.: Harvard University Press1983), 11 and the title of the concluding chapter of Moshe Halbertal, *'Al derekh ha-'emet: ha-ramban vi-yeṣiratah shel masoret* (Jerusalem: Shalom Hartman Institute, 2006). For Ramban as one who did much to enshrine Rashi's work as a pivot of later Jewish Bible study, see the comment of Isadore Twersky in his introduction to *Rabbi Moses Naḥmanides (Ramban)*, 4.

commentators,[16] and though he was certainly more rhetorically deferent before Rashi than Ibn Ezra, he nevertheless offered a far more "sustained" critique of Rashi's midrashic interpretations in his *Commentary on the Torah* than Ibn Ezra,[17] even on the view that Ibn Ezra related to Rashi more than has been suspected.[18] In addition to disputing what he considered linguistically untenable or theologically unreasonable rabbinic expositions advanced by Rashi, Ramban faulted Rashi's citation of enigmatic or ostensibly esoteric midrashim without any clarification. While all for economy of style, he worried that unadorned citations of such rabbinic dicta could obfuscate rather than enlighten.[19]

More muted than its role in Ramban's exegesis was the place of Rashi's exegesis in the commentaries of David Kimhi (Radak), the most influential of southern French biblicists. Though Kimhi hewed to the *peshaṭ*-oriented method pioneered by the likes of

---

16. *Perushei ha-torah le-rabbenu Moshe ben Naḥman (Ramban)*, ed. C.D. Chavel, 2 vols. (Jerusalem: Mosad ha-rav Kuk, 1959), 1:16. For a rather labored (intertextual) ironic reading of this epithet, see James Diamond, "Nahmanides and Rashi on the One Flesh of Conjugal Union: Lovemaking vs. Duty," *Harvard Theological Review* 102 (2009): 95.

17. Septimus, "Open Rebuke," 16 n. 21. For case studies, see Yosef Morgenstern, "Hityaḥasuto shel ha-ramban le-ferush rashi be-ferusho la-torah," MA diss., Bar Ilan University, 2000.

18. On the surface, Ibn Ezra related to Rashi hardly at all. Weiser supplies fourteen references (*Perushei ha-torah*, 1:68) to which an additional one from the unfinished long commentary on Genesis can be added (Mondschein, "Ve-'en bi-sefarav," 226 n. 16). Such "sporadic" engagement with Rashi (if it rises even to that level) has been explained as a function of Ibn Ezra's thoroughly condescending attitude towards Rashi who, on this view, as one lacking what Ibn Ezra considered the most basic tool of sound exegesis, failed to rise to the level of a worthy adversary (Simon, "R. 'Avraham Ibn 'Ezra," 40–42; Gross, "Rashi," 28–29). Given, however, Ibn Ezra's clear animus against Rashi and evident awareness of Rashi's appeal to the *derash*-addicts of Christian Europe, this account becomes hard to accept. The alternative explanation would be that Ibn Ezra remonstrated against Rashi "often" but almost always in oblique fashion, this being the burden of Mondschein's argument in "Ve-'en bi-sefarav."

19. For a sampling, see Miriam (Hoffman) Sklertz, "Yaḥas ramban le-midrash ha-'aggadah 'al-pi perusho la-torah li-vereshit peraqim 12–36," Ph. D. diss., Bar-Ilan University, 1998, 76–96. For an example from the halakhic realm, see Ramban's commentary on Deuteronomy 17:11, concerning the gnomic statement of (ostensibly) rabbinic origin cited by Rashi that one must heed the high court even if it "tells you right is left or left is right." After citing it, Nahmanides begins to expound it ("its explanation"; *ve-'inyano*) in such a way as to suggest that Rashi had no business adducing this idea without clarification.

Abraham Ibn Ezra (and his father Joseph Kimhi), he more readily accepted midrashim into his commentaries than these mentors, now for their valid interpretations of scriptural plain sense and now for the added dimension of meaning that they conveyed.[20] Rashi's commentaries served as a valuable storehouse of midrashic lore upon which Radak drew.[21] At the same time, Radak's works foreshadow a trend that figures in the works sampled below: the felt need to refute particular midrashim on the assumption that they were familiar, and viewed as authoritative, in consequence of Rashi's evocation of them.[22]

Turning to the later Middle Ages, the period that is the focus of this study, one finds that leading Sefardic exegetes rued Rashi's overemphasis on midrash. Though Ramban's disciple, Bahya ben Asher, cast Rashi's *Commentary* as an exemplification of the "contextual method" (*derekh ha-peshat*) at its best,[23] Isaac ben Moses (known also as Profet Duran or "Efodi"), writing at the turn of the fifteenth century, was less kind. While granting Rashi's "pleasing commentaries" and even defending Rashi's grammar, he nevertheless complained that "most" of Rashi's interpretations derived from "expositions of the rabbinic sages [said] in the manner of *derash*," leaving little behind by way of *peshat*.[24] Isaac Abarbanel concurred, in one place offering the surprisingly incisive observation that "it is an evil and bitter thing to me that the great rabbi Rashi contented himself in his commentaries on holy scripture

---

20. Frank Ephraim Talmage, *David Kimhi: The Man and the Commentaries* (Cambridge, Mass.: Harvard University Press, 1975), 54–134 (especially 133). See further Yitzhak Berger, "*Peshat* and the Authority of *Ḥazal* in the Commentaries of Radak," *AJS Review* 31 (2007): 41–49.

21. Naomi Grunhaus, "The Dependence of Rabbi David Kimhi (Radak) on Rashi in His Quotation of Midrashic Traditions," *The Jewish Quarterly Review* 93 (2003): 415–30.

22. Ibid., 417. I have documented, though only in the most fledging way, this barely studied "major trend" in the history of Jewish thought; namely, Rashi's untold influence on the specific midrashic ideas that later Jewish scholars chose to — or were impelled to — address. See, e.g., "From Sefarad to Ashkenaz: A Case Study in the Rashi Supercommentary Tradition," *AJS Review* 30 (2006): 393–425; "Sins of the Fauna: Midrashic Motifs, Rashi, and Their Medieval Interlocutors," *Jewish Studies Quarterly*. 17 (2010): 56–98.

23. *Be'ur 'al ha-torah*, ed. H. D. Chavel, 3 vols. (Jerusalem: Mosad ha-rav Kuk, 1966), 1:5.

24. *Ma'aseh 'efod*, ed. John Friedländer and Jakob Kohn (Vienna, 1865), 17, 41. See further Gross, "Rashi," 43–45.

in most matters with that which the rabbinic sages expounded."[25] Abarbanel often articulated his own aspiration in terms of Rashi's proclamation that he had come "only to present scripture's *peshaṭ*" while tellingly omitting the second half of Rashi's statement, which spoke of the inclusion of rabbinic dicta that conformed to scripture in the manner of "a word fitly spoken."[26] While the *Commentary's* dearth of *peshaṭ*, as Abarbanel understood it, undoubtedly rankled, other considerations governed his disapprobation of Rashi's midrashically top-heavy approach. One, characteristically Sefardic, was a concern with rabbinic interpretations that, even by Abarbanel's in some ways moderately antirationalist lights, failed the test of empiricism or scientific tenability. Another, more peculiar to Abarbanel, was an insistence on exegesis that expounded the polysemous divine word on levels beyond the contextual and midrashic.[27]

As the above inventory of attitudes towards the *Commentary* shows, many of Rashi's successors rejected the thrust of Rashi's exegetical practice and subjected his midrashic interpretations to critical appraisal — and this, not only in centers at a far remove from the Ashkenazic religious-intellectual milieu in which his biblical scholarship originated but also, though more for exegetical than theological reasons, in his native northern Europe. Doubts about Rashi's dominantly midrashic approach were registered by generally less influential exegetes writing in Byzantine lands as well.[28] Yet among his critics, none would match either for their forthrightness or for their tone of superiority with respect to Rashi the two writers to whose critiques of the role of midrash in the *Commentary* we now turn.

---

25. *Perush 'al nevi'im rishonim* (Jerusalem: Torah Ve-Da'at, 1955), 13. See my *Isaac Abarbanel's Stance Toward Tradition: Defense, Dissent, and Dialogue* (Albany: SUNY Press, 2001), 37–38.
26. Lawee, *Isaac Abarbanel's Stance*, 94.
27. Ibid., 94–95, 97–100.
28. See my "Maimonides in the Eastern Mediterranean: The Case of Rashi's Resisting Readers," in *Maimonides after 800 Years: Essays on Maimonides and His Influence*, ed. Jay Harris (Cambridge, Mass.: Harvard University Center for Jewish Studies, 2007), 183–206.

II

In his sole surviving work, a hybrid commentary on the Torah and supercommentary on Rashi's *Commentary*, Aaron Aboulrabi, a mid-fifteenth-century Sicilian-born peripatetic theologian and exegete, explained that since Rashi's biblical exegesis was "mostly hewn from the eminent oaks of old" — that is, the rabbinic sages — he would focus on it rather than on the interpretations of commentators "whose words reflect individual opinion" alone.[29] In other words, the dominantly midrashic side of Rashi's exegesis set it apart from that of others, lending it an aura of authority and thence its claim on Aboulrabi's attention. Turning to the reception that Aboulrabi accords the dicta of these eminent sages, what immediately leaps off his pages are the many sharp renunciations of midrashim found there, many of them cited by Rashi, including midrashim with halakhic import. Little wonder that the nineteenth-century eastern European champion of Haskalah, Joshua Heschel Schorr, eulogized Aboulrabi as "one of those rare individuals" whose love of justice begets a refusal to "cover up transgression among the ancients." In particular, Schorr lauded Aboulrabi's willingness to "express his teaching publicly ... even when it contradicted the teaching transmitted from our rabbinic sages."[30]

Aboulrabi's formulations of criticisms of Rashi's midrashic

---

29. *Perushim le-rashi* (Constantinople, [1525?]), 13v. For one of several bibliographic problems appertaining to this volume, see Yitzhak Yudlov, "Kamah she'arim le-sefer *perushim le-rashi* defus qushta?" *'Alei sefer* 17 (1992): 137–38. For more on Aboulrabi and his work, see my "Graven Images, Astromagical Cherubs, Mosaic Miracles: A Fifteenth-Century Curial-Rabbinic Exchange," *Speculum* 81 (2006): 754–95 and the bibliography cited there.

30. "R. 'Aharon Al-Rabi," *Ṣiyyon* 1 (1840): 167–68. Schorr's attraction to Aboulrabi's criticism of midrash is readily understood. For one thing, in tumultuous discussions of Judaism's need to adapt to the modern world, nineteenth-century Jewish savants debated the nature and authority of the midrashim on which traditional Jewish life was based (Jay M. Harris, *How Do We Know This? Midrash and the Fragmentation of Modern Judaism* [Albany: SUNY Press, 1995], 137–250). For another, as part of their effort to remold time-honored practices and beliefs, radical Maskilim like Schorr took "special delight in pointing to historical antecedents which reflected unorthodox views" (Ezra Spicehandler, "Joshua Heschel Schorr: Maskil and Eastern European Reformist," *Hebrew Union College Annual* 31 [1960]: 213).

interpretations can be withering. The claim that the two yods of *vayyiṣer* (Gen. 2:7) reflect the human being's "two formations," one for this world and one for the next: a "*derash* of barbarians (*barbarim*)."[31] Esau as the Amorite from whom Jacob wrested land with sword and bow (Gen. 48:22): "a worthless *derash*."[32] Pharaoh going to the water (Exod. 7:15) "to relieve himself" — "the *derash* of a dolt (*hedyot*); for had he no way to relieve himself in a concealed place such that he had to go down to the river?"[33] The idea that the tabernacle erected itself with only the appearance of involvement from Moses — so much hot air (*divrei ru'aḥ*); *huqam* (Exod. 40:17) invariably implies agency by another.[34] Some of Rashi's midrashic readings are said to be as awry as figments of the overwrought female imagination. The interpretation that Jacob moved spasmodically whenever Rebecca passed a place of Torah study while Esau did the same when she passed a house of idol-worship is "all yarns of [mentally unstable?] menstruating women."[35]

There is more to Aboulrabi's evaluation of midrashim cited by Rashi than his fiery rhetoric with respect to them.[36] Some main features of his critique are best glimpsed in the presence of concrete examples. Though hardly comprehensive, the following samples suffice to illustrate a few of the angles of collision, exegetical and otherwise, that yield Aboulrabi's objections to a range of midrashim and their foremost medieval broadcaster.

In the first instance, Aboulrabi evaluates midrashim in terms of their moorings within the biblical text. Where these are deemed wanting or wholly absent, or where countervailing evidence exists, midrashim can meet with a stout rebuff. An example is the identification of Melchizedek with Shem that Rashi weaved into his *Commentary* on two occasions. Accounting for

---

31. *Perushim le-rashi*, 16v.
32. Ibid., 58v.
33. Ibid., 70v.
34. Ibid., 98v.
35. Ibid., 30r-v.
36. A fuller discussion will be forthcoming in a monograph in progress that focuses in large part on Aboulrabi.

the temporal particle of Genesis 12:6, "And the Canaanite was then in the land," Rashi stated that when Abraham arrived in the land, the Canaanites were "then" gradually conquering it from Shem's descendants "for it had fallen to the portion of Shem ... as it is said, 'And Melchizedek king of Salem' (Gen 14:18)." Unpacking this latter verse, Rashi affirmed the "*midrash 'aggadah, that he is identical with Shem son of Noah.*" The identification of Melchizedek and Shem (and Salem with Jerusalem) was engendered, among other things, by the rabbinic reflex to bring "focus" to biblical narratives by identifying obscure figures mentioned therein with scriptural personages known from elsewhere,[37] yet it was also of potentially far-reaching theological consequences. For one thing, it suggested the Jewish people's aboriginal connection with the holy land. After all, it was to Shem that "all of the descendants of Eber" (Gen. 10:21), including the father of the Hebrew nation, Abraham, traced their origins. Seen thus, the identification helped to turn what might seem like a later Israelite war of conquest against an indigenous population into the Jewish people's return to the land bequeathed to its most ancient postdiluvian ancestor.

What of Aboulrabi? He was disinclined to accept the rabbinic identifications of biblical figures that Rashi propounded.[38] In the case at hand, he finds a number of points pulling in the opposite direction:

> "And the Canaanite was then in the land." The Straight One [Rashi] explained that "[the Canaanite nation] was gradually conquering [the land of Israel] for it had fallen to the portion of Shem, etc." I do not know whence the rabbis saw fit to say that the land [of Israel] fell to Shem's

---

37. Isaac Heinemann, *Darkei ha-'aggadah*, 3rd. ed. (Jerusalem: Magnes, 1974), 29. For Melchizedek as a figure who "suddenly emerges from the shadows and as suddenly retreats into oblivion," see Nahum Sarna's comment on Gen. 14:18–20 in *The JPS Torah Commentary: Genesis* (Philadelphia: Jewish Publication Society, 1989), 109. By way of a specific rationale for this identification, Heinemann notes that it procures a chronological linkage between the generation of the flood and the generation of Abraham. For the identification itself, see, e.g., *Nedarim* 32b.
38. See, e.g., his commentary on Gen. 46:10 (*Perushim le-rashi*, 55v).

portion. On the contrary, it is more correct to say that it fell within Canaan's lot as it states, 'And the border of the Canaanite [was from Zidon ...] unto Gaza as you go toward Sodom' (Gen. 10:19), and so forth."

To support his contention, Aboulrabi summons the fact that "these lands are all close to Jerusalem." (He estimates a "two-day distance" in a way that suggests first-hand familiarity with the regional geography, a fact that occasions no great surprise given his travels in Jerusalem.)[39] He further observes that "we find always that the land is associated with the name of Canaan and his progeny." Aboulrabi concludes with an admonishment of those who would still acquiesce in the midrash undergirding Rashi's ill-conceived reconstruction, asking his reader what warrants the assumption of Melchizedek's identification with Shem or Salem's with Jerusalem "but for much *derash*."[40]

Aboulrabi's strictures on Rashi at times reflect his inability to see, or refusal to countenance, conventional modes of rabbinic discourse at play in Rashi's *Commentary*. An example is Rashi's reading of the dramatic scene depicting Jacob's and Joseph's reunification after many years of separation. Explaining the Torah's ambiguous description of one of the two crying on the other's neck, Rashi, on midrashic authority, proposed that Joseph had wept on his father's neck while his father's thoughts were directed elsewhere, as Jacob was just then in the middle of reciting the *Shema*. Ramban, by contrast, finding this reconstruction psychologically implausible, asked who was more likely to burst into tears in such a situation, "the aged parent who finds his son alive after despairing of his return and mourning him or the young son now ruling [the whole of Egypt]"? For his part, Aboulrabi asserts the "spuriousness" of Rashi's explanation, wondering how

---

39. In his commentary on Deut. 25:4 (*Perushim le-rashi*, 165v), he relates how he verbally "kicked in the teeth" of Karaites who buttressed their proof for an injunction against Sabbath use of fire lit even before the Sabbath by citing the scriptural analogy of the prohibition on muzzling an ox while threshing (Deut. 25:4).

40. *Perushim le-rashi*, 19v-20r (understanding "*derash rabbot*" as an erroneous version of some phrase like "*midrashot rabbot*").

Jacob could have been reciting the Shema when that prayer's main components ("Hear, O Israel ..."; "Blessed be the Name ...") "originated" only later with Jacob on his deathbed — as, he pointedly notes, astutely pitting the ancient rabbis against themselves and against Rashi, "the sages have said."[41] Studiedly ignored in such barbed rejoinders is the "trans-temporal" character of so many midrashim concerning Israel's patriarchs and matriarchs[42] and the manner in which anachronistic expositions found in the midrashic literature might yet prove religiously edifying.

An allied example is Aboulrabi's sally against Rashi's midrashic view that Jacob sought to exit the womb when Rebecca passed a house of Torah-study and Esau the same when she passed a house of idol-worship. To upend this interpretation, which he takes to imply the boys' predestined character, Aboulrabi pits against it the biblical report that "when the lads grew up, Esau became a skillful hunter ... but Jacob was a mild man" (Gen. 25:27), finding proof therein that the boys' characters developed only long after their birth.[43] That the midrash might speak to the relationship between Jews and gentiles and the "gulf" separating their world-views either escapes Aboulrabi[44] or is an interpretation of Rashi's reading from which he prescinds. Minimally, Aboulrabi prefers to blame the midrash rather than interpret it in a way that could yield inspiration or insight.

Though Aboulrabi does not limit his consideration of midrashim to ones cited by Rashi, he mainly considers rabbinic dicta that bear Rashi's stamp of approval. In rejecting these, Aboulrabi typically ascribes such sayings to Rashi rather than the rabbinic expositors who originated these misguided interpretations.[45] In some places, individual midrashim are spared criticism

---

41. See Rashi's comment on Gen. 46:29 and *Perushim le-rashi*, 56r. For Rashi's rabbinic sources, see *Ḥamishah ḥumshei torah: rashi ha-shalem*, 7 vols. (Jerusalem, 1986 —), *Bereshit*, 3:129. For Ramban, see *Perushei ha-torah*, 1:255–56.

42. Heinemann, *Darkei ha-'aggadah*, 36–37.

43. *Perushim le-rashi*, 30r.

44. So the opinion of Nehama Leibowitz in *Limmud parshanei ha-torah u-derakhim lehorotam: sefer bereshit* (Jerusalem: World Zionist Organization, 1975), 103.

45. See, e.g., at Gen. 1:11, where Aboulrabi rejects Rashi's idea that the earth engaged in

but some aspect of Rashi's handling of them is faulted. In others, the midrashim are deemed problematic, with Rashi's deployment of them in some way compounding the problem. Rashi may be charged for his presentation of contradictory midrashic opinions alongside one another in a way that yields exegetical incoherence or for his mishandling of rabbinic dicta bearing esoteric purport or for his inappropriate inclusion of esoteric rabbinic sayings in his *Commentary* when they should have been omitted, either due to Rashi's inability to handle such dicta responsibly or the need to withhold them from Rashi's general readership.

Consider Aboulrabi on Genesis 1:4–5. Rashi glossed these verses as follows:

> "God saw that the light was good and God separated ..." — for [a proper understanding of] this we require words of 'aggadah': He saw that the wicked were unworthy of using it [the light] and [therefore] separated it for the righteous in the world to come. But according to its contextual meaning, explain it thus [in accordance with another midrashic interpretation]: He saw that it was good, and that it was not seemly for it [the light] and the darkness to function together in a confused manner....[46]

Here as elsewhere, despite Rashi's explicit recourse to rabbinic teachings, Aboulrabi ascribes the ideas in question to Rashi and castigates their deficiencies accordingly:

> "God saw the light ..." **The Straight One** interpreted that 'the wicked were unworthy of using it, etc.' I fail to grasp this utterance's rationale since if it [the light] is something sensate how can it be concealed and if it is

---

an act of prelapsarian insubordination in failing to yield a tree tasting like its fruit (ibid., 15r: "he interpreted ..."; for Rashi's rabbinic sources, see *Rashi ha-shalem* 1:8). Also at Exod. 15:21, where Aboulrabi rejects Rashi's midrashic understanding that Miriam's "song" was directed towards the women in particular (ibid., 81r: "the Straight One explained that Miriam chanted a song to the women...."; for rabbinic sources see *Rashi ha-shalem*, *Shemot*, 2:73).

46. For Rashi's glosses and their rabbinic sources, see *Rashi ha-shalem*, *Bereshit*, 1:4–5.

something spiritual how can the wicked use it? **He also said**: "He saw that it was good, and that it was not seemly for light and darkness to function together in a confused manner." But this [admixture of light and darkness] is an impossibility so there is no need to state it [i.e., that the two should be segregated].[47]

Going beyond the inherent difficulties present in Rashi's midrashic interpretations, Aboulrabi adds that "if you will scrutinize [these interpretations] carefully [in tandem] you will find that the second interpretation contradicts the first since how should it [the light] admix [with the darkness] inasmuch as He had already concealed it." Having now criticized these interpretations and Rashi's deployment of them from a number of angles, Aboulrabi enters a further critique of Rashi that points towards the redemption of his midrashic materials by way of a non-literal interpretation of them, without justifying Rashi thereby: "even though these things were not intended to be understood literally, still he [Rashi] should have refrained from expressing them, let alone writing them."[48]

Aboulrabi's disapprobation of Rashi's midrashic exposition of Genesis 1:5 (whose rabbinic origins Rashi also stressed) is, if by no means wholly luminous, more damning yet. Regarding Genesis 1:5, Rashi had asked why scripture had written "*yom eḥad*," which could be read as "the day of [the] one [Being]," rather than, on the pattern of the other days, "the first day." On the authority of the midrash, he answered that it was "because the Holy One blessed be He, was one alone in His universe [on that day] since the angels were not created until the second day. Thus it is explained in Bereshit Rabbah." Rashi's explicitly identified rabbinic source notwithstanding, Aboulrabi makes Rashi the object of his emphatic, if substantively somewhat elliptical, condemnation:

Rashi said: "Because the Holy One blessed be He, was

---

47. *Perushim le-rashi*, 14r.
48. Ibid.

one alone in His universe." This *derash* has no purchase
[*'en lo damim*] [since] He is always not alone (*ve-tamid
'eno yaḥid*).⁴⁹ In addition, he [Rashi] stated [here] the
opposite of his words [as found elsewhere, such as] where
he explained [in accordance with a midrashic view], "And
God made the expanse" [Gen. 1:6] [to mean that] "even
though the heavens had already been created on the first
day [they were still liquid, this being an indication that
the heavens existed even on day one and hence that God
was never alone]. He [Rashi] also said that the light was
created before the heavens. If so, He was [not] alone in
His world....⁵⁰

[Indeed] he [Rashi] said [that the Holy One blessed
be He was alone] in His world," whence it may be inferred
that the world existed [and hence that God was not alone
even on day one].⁵¹

Aboulrabi's scathing final verdict is that the midrash adduced by
Rashi, properly understood, may have merit but that this fact
neither pardons Rashi's failure to grasp its meaning nor excuses
Rashi's contamination of a midrash through his admixture of
misguided views, some of his own invention: "The Straight One
admixed the words of [Bereshit] Rabbah with surmises (*sevarot*)
that no wise men have ever conceived and with his own understanding (*da'ato*). 'How great is wickedness of the person' (Gen.
6:5) who says things devoid of insight."⁵²

---

49. Assuming the text should not simply be emended to read that God **is** always alone
(e.g., reading *ve-tamid hu' yaḥid* or *ve-tamid heno yaḥid*), Aboulrabi could be saying
that God is "always not alone" because God co-existed with primordial matter prior
to its division into particulars — a view that comports with his larger understanding
of the processes of creation (see Dov Schwartz, "Divine Immanence in Medieval
Jewish Philosophy," *Journal of Jewish Thought and Philosophy* 3 [1994]: 275–77). On
this view, the midrash cited by Rashi would be wrong in asserting that God was
alone at any point. This reading seems to fit best with the continuation of Aboulrabi's
comments, suitably emended (see next note).
50. Reading "*lo' hayah yaḥid be-'olamo*" since as the text currently reads — "if so, He
was alone in His world" — the flow of ideas is much harder to sustain.
51. *Perushim le-rashi*, 14v.
52. Ibid.

Having dismissed Rashi's handling of Genesis 1:5, Aboulrabi announces his plan to explain the rabbinic dicta that Rashi mentioned, albeit in an independent manner that shows "no regard for the elder' [i.e., Rashi; cf. Deut. 28:50] 'for I shall not acquit the wrongdoer'" [Exod. 23:7]).[53] His own exposition forms part of a complex cosmogony that, though syncretistic in its critical vocabulary (especially in its conflation of kabbalistic and philosophic terminology), leaves no doubt as to Aboulrabi's essentially rationalist approach.[54]

In light of his evident aptitude as a talmudist and travels in locales where Karaism lived (e.g., Jerusalem, Kaffa in the Crimea),[55] Aboulrabi's handling of the *midrashei halakhah* adduced by Rashi invites attention. While more inclined to defer to these midrashim than their non-legal counterparts, Aboulrabi by no means suppresses his critical instincts when considering legal midrash. As Rashi reported, in the first half of Lev. 11:8 — "You shall not eat of their [forbidden animals'] flesh" — the rabbis found an enactment applicable to all Jews. By contrast, in the verse's second half — "or touch their carcasses" — they found a prohibition applicable only to priests. Aboulrabi comments that while "the rabbinic sages explained it as they fancied (*pereshu rabotenu mah she-rasu*)," according to the *peshat* it is clear that both prohibitions apply to all Jews.[56] Similarly, "according to the *peshat*," the prohibition on castration ("you shall have no such

53. Ibid. Here as elsewhere, Aboulrabi adopts the position that Rashi's citation of esoteric midrash was a mistake but that once done, Aboulrabi might as well speak to the issues at stake. See also *Perushim le-rashi*, 16r: "I say that even though their [the rabbinic sages'] words are true and allude to profound wisdom ... they ought not to have been recorded at any rate, lest the words reach one who is not full of wisdom with the result that the idea will be sabotaged. In any event, since it has fallen into our hands, I will say my piece...."
54. See, e.g., the reference to "*sifrei ha-filosofim*" in *Perushim le-rashi*, 15r. Cf. Schwartz, "Divine Immanence in Medieval Jewish Philosophy," 275–77.
55. For these locales and other visited by Aboulrabi, see his commentaries to Gen. 25:23 and 49:10 (30v, 59r), Num. 13:22 (130r), and Deut. 25:4 (166r). For Kaffa as a home to both Karaite and Rabbanite communities in the fifteenth century, see the entry on "Feodosiya" (modern-day Kaffa) in *Encyclopedia Judaica*, 1st ed., vol. 6, col. 1224.
56. *Perushim le-rashi*, 105r. In a legal context such as this, Aboulrabi is more prone to ascribe the midrashic interpretation in question to the rabbis, bearers and conveyors of the "oral law," rather than Rashi.

practices in your land"; Lev. 22:24) is restricted to the land of Israel. Though he does not specifically note the rabbinic finding propounded by Rashi that the verse yields a ban in all locations, Aboulrabi does observe that scripture should have written "you shall not do such" without adding a geographic qualifier were a blanket prohibition on gelding intended.[57]

Like his subversions of non-legal midrashim, so Aboulrabi's criticism of legal midrash requires multidimensional study. As a Rabbanite, Aboulrabi ultimately grants that in cases of legal interpretation, "we cannot determine against the rabbinic sages who are stronger (*taqifin*) than us."[58] An open question is the extent to which his approach to the midrashic segment of Rashi's *Commentary* reflects the impact of oral interchanges with Karaites or his reading in Karaite literature. Minimally, it at times seems to reflect this Rabbanite's deep frustration as he seeks to defend the barely defensible. However this may be, as in the case of countless non-legal midrashim, so in the case of legal midrash it was often Rashi's "codification" of certain views of the "eminent oaks of old" that provoked Aboulrabi's negative response.

III

In his stance towards Rashi, Aboulrabi at times follows in the path of an earlier author who composed a pseudonymous work under the name of the twelfth-century talmudist Abraham ben David preserved in a manuscript created by Shabbatai Hakohen Balbo in Crete in 1410. The hefty manuscript includes a very wide variety of works copied by Balbo interspersed with studies composed by Balbo himself.[59] The very first entry in the manuscript bears the bulky title: *Book of Animadversions in which Rabbi Abraham ben David Censured Our Teacher Solomon the Frenchman in His Regarding his Commentary on the Torah (Sefer hassagot she-hissig*

---

57. Ibid., 114v.
58. Ibid., 113r.
59. See S. M. Schiller-Szinessy, *Catalogue of the Hebrew Manuscripts Preserved in the University Library, Cambridge* (Cambridge, 1876), no. 35 (pp. 51–52).

ha-rav 'Avraham ben David zal 'al rabbenu Shelomo ha-ṣarfati zal be-ferush ha-torah).[60] The only later writer whose awareness of this series of strictures is documented is Aaron Aboulrabi.[61]

Putting aside unanswered questions surrounding *Sefer hassagot's* authorship, which some ascribe to Balbo himself,[62] one notes that the unidentified author immediately spotlights Rashi's disabilities as an exegete by stressing, in a caustic preamble to the adversarial glosses on selected interpretations of Rashi to follow, the role of midrash in Rashi's exegetical program:

> In the Torah Commentary designated as belonging to "Rashi the Frenchman" I have seen rabbinic homilies (*haggadot*) and interpretations (*perushim*) that deviate from the way of the Torah's intention in many places, in some being the very opposite of the correct intention and correct contextual meaning and the grammar and that which accords with reason (*sekhel*). I thought to record some of the places wherein he erred with *haggadot* and *peshaṭim* as my limited understanding allows.[63]

---

60. Cambridge, MS Add. 377.3 (= film no. 15872 at the Institute for Microfilmed Hebrew Manuscripts in Jerusalem), 1v-11r. This work receives some attention in my "Maimonides in the Eastern Mediterranean: The Case of Rashi's Resisting Readers," 183–206.

61. Ephraim E. Urbach, "Hassagot ha-rabad 'al perush rashi la-torah?" *Qiryat sefer* 34 (1958–59): 101–8.

62. Zevi Malachi, *Be-no'am si'aḥ: peraqim mi-toldot sifrutenu* (N.p.: Habermann Institute for Literary Research, 1983), 255; Shalom Rosenberg, "Mifgash filosofi birushalayim be-sof ha-me'ah ha-'arba' 'esrei," *Shalem* 4 (1988): 422. That Abraham ben David of Posquières was not the work's author is a fact that its originator makes little effort to conceal. Already Urbach showed that the stances towards Rashi and midrash adopted by *Sefer hassagot's* author do not comport with the views of Rabad. Certainly the author's reference to Maimonides' "precious book" (i.e., the *Guide*) puts him at a far remove from the twelfth-century Rabad ("Hassagot," 101–2), and not only because "it is impossible to maintain that Rabad knew the *Moreh* at first hand.... The most that can be said is that Rabad had ... received some oral reports." (Isadore Twersky, *Rabad of Posquières: A Twelfth-Century Talmudist* [Cambridge, Mass.: Harvard University Press, 1962], 181.) On medieval Jewish pseudepigraphy — a genre still in search of systematic students — see Joseph Dan, *The 'Unique Cherub' Circle: A School of Mystics and Esoterics in Medieval Germany*, (Tübingen: Mohr Siebeck, 1999), 6–15.

63. *Sefer hassagot*, 1v.

Having announced Rashi's exegetical lapses due in large part to his midrashic missteps, the author now turns to a different dimension of the problem. Prefacing his remarks with the jibe that Rashi was "devoid of all wisdom save for [facility in his] navigation of the Talmudic discussion (*sugyah*) alone," he observes that Rashi's *Commentary*'s omits the vast majority of rabbinic dicta regarding "the Work of the Beginning, metaphysical wisdom (*hokhmat ha-'elohut*), prophecy, or other branches of wisdom." To be sure, all this is little wonder as Rashi's comprehension of such esoterica was "next to nil." And if, in some places, Rashi did reproduce weighty midrashic dicta, he did so as one who has been taught to utter words in a foreign language that he repeats "without understanding them, whereas another person understands those words coming out of his mouth."[64] Aboulrabi would imply that Rashi ought to have left such esoteric midrashic materials out of his *Commentary*. For his part, pseudo-Rabad seems pleased at their inclusion even as he denies Rashi any credit for it.

With the preface behind him, pseudo-Rabad sets forth his forceful refutations of what he deems egregious examples of Rashi's exegesis, focusing mostly on the midrashic glosses. Though the animadversions await systematic study, some patterns that they evince are discernible. One is to demonstrate the falsity of a midrash that Rashi cites by undermining the textual irregularity on which it supposedly hinges. One tool in his arsenal is the *reductio ad absurdum*, whereby the author establishes the outlandish consequences that ensue when a midrashic principle is applied elsewhere. Regarding "When Abram entered Egypt, the Egyptians saw how very beautiful the woman was" (Gen. 12:14), Rashi suggested that Scripture should have said "when *they* [i.e., Abram and Sarai] entered Egypt." He then transmits the rabbinic inference that Abram must have kept Sarai hidden in a chest such that it was only after they entered Egypt that the Egyptians appreciated how beautiful she was. For pseudo-Rabad, however, the ostensibly problematic combination of plural subject and singular

---

64. Ibid.

masculine verb is a commonplace — a point he reinforces by asking: when it later states that "Jacob arrived safe in the city of Shechem," does it mean that his entire household arrived in chests?[65]

In another line of criticism, pseudo-Rabad rejects midrashic expansions that supply background details or incidents not openly stated in scripture on the grounds that since the divine word recorded details more trivial than those relayed by Rashi in his *Commentary*, it surely should have recorded these expansions were they accurate. To illustrate, if Nimrod had really cast Abram into an open fire whence he was miraculously saved, scripture would have said so. After all, it records lesser miraculous happenings in Abraham's and Sarah's lives for the purpose of "publicizing the miracles and good things that the Creator did for those righteous ones."[66]

Though he occupies himself more with biblical narrative than law, pseudo-Rabad anticipates Aboulrabi in debunking some *midrashei halakhah* cited by Rashi. On rabbinic authority, Rashi read "*min*" in the phrase "*min ha-baqar*" found at the outset of Leviticus as a pleonasm that imparted additional meaning; namely, that a *terefah* should not be brought for sacrifice. Pseudo-Rabad rejoins that "from '*min*' he [i.e., Rashi] wrote words of futility" (*divrei havai*), nay "words of falsehood" (*divrei sheqer*) suggestive of the sort of thing condemned by God through Jeremiah when this prophet spoke of things "I never commanded, which never came to My mind [Jer. 7:31]."[67] One assumes that the dispute is methodological rather than substantive, as it seems unlikely that pseudo-Rabad was arguing a *terefah*'s permissibility for sacrifice. Be that as it may, pseudo-Rabad, like Aboulrabi

---

65. Ibid., 2v-3r. For subversion along similar lines of another midrash cited by Rashi at Genesis 23:1 to the effect that Sarah was as free of sin at age one hundred as at age twenty (or, in pseudo-Rabad's rendering of Rashi, age seven), see ibid., 3v.

66. Ibid., 2v. For another case involving Moses' scripturally unrecorded miraculous recovery of Joseph's bones, see ibid., 7v.

67. Ibid., 7v. (Cf. See Rashi's gloss on Lev. 1:2.)

subsequently, directs his protest more at "Rashi the Frenchman" than the ancient sages upon whom Rashi relies.

Of course, pseudo-Rabad's (and Aboulrabi's) indictment of the rabbinic sages who provisioned Rashi with the majority of his interpretations cannot be gainsaid. Sometimes it is harshly direct. Witness this response to the midrash cited by Rashi concerning the magical manner in which Moses raised Joseph's coffin from the depths of the Nile. Pseudo-Rabad insists that the sages upon whom Rashi draws "hewed down the tree and cut it branches; for all this is false, concocted from the hearts of worthless men who cause Israel to be in error and who transpose the words of the living God, this being the written Torah, into words of foolishness and futility which they concocted from their heart."[68] Still and all, despite such periodic direct assaults on the ancient sages, pseudo-Rabad, in even more direct and concentrated fashion than Aboulrabi, reserves the brunt of his criticism for Rashi, as the reference to "Solomon the Frenchman" in his title indicates.

IV

Having limned two largely unprecedented critiques of the place of midrash in Rashi's *Commentary on the Torah*, it remains to explain something of the larger intellectual-religious setting in which these unusual specimens of late medieval Hebrew literature ought to be placed.[69] Like Aboulrabi, pseudo-Rabad most often excoriates Rashi for his midrashic ideas. At the same time, like Aboulrabi, he alludes to the view of Jewish rationalists that some midrashim preserve the most profound elements of rabbinic teaching, then blames Rashi for its failure to reflect this side of the rabbinic legacy in his *Commentary*. This apparently schizophrenic attitude towards midrash appears in yet another pseudonymous

---

68. Ibid. (Cf. Rashi's comment to Exod. 32:4.)
69. "Largely unprecedented," because Eleazar Ashkenazi ben Natan Ha-bavli, a fourteenth-century Maimonidean, served as a forerunner. See Avraham Epstein, "Ma'amar 'al ḥibbur ṣafenat pa'neaḥ," in *Kitvei R. 'Avraham 'Epshtein*, ed. A. M. Haberman, 2 vols. (Jerusalem: Mosad ha-rav Kuk, 1949), 1:116–29.

work ascribed to "Palmon ben Pelet of the Nameless" (or perhaps "of the Fameless"), a work that also contains a broadside against Rashi's biblical exegesis. For current purposes, it matters not whether 'Alilot devarim is a fourteenth-century production by the Spanish-born Joseph ben Eliezer, as Reuven Bonfil argued,[70] or the fifteenth-century work of a Jew of Ashkenazic stock composed in Italy, as urged by Israel M. Ta-Shma.[71] What matters is that 'Alilot devarim condemns Rashi's scriptural scholarship in terms familiar from Aboulrabi and pseudo-Rabad while, it would seem, providing a key to the emergence of harsh Rashi criticism in later medieval times.

'Alilot devarim's consideration of Rashi arises out of an attempt to explain the interminability of Jewish exile, which the author traces mainly to a steep decline in post-rabbinic religious and intellectual life, especially among Ashkenazic Jews.[72] While conceding Rashi's significant, if not wholly salutary, accomplishments as a talmudic exegete, the author insists that Rashi's parallel efforts to "open the eyes of the blind" in the area of the "written Torah" were central to the spiritual decline that he laments — this, since most of Rashi's explanations comprise not actual interpretations (perushim) but "talmudic expositions." True, some midrashim cited by Rashi are "sweet" but the author also contends, in the manner of Aboulrabi and pseudo-Rabad, that these esoteric dicta require enlightened (read: rationalist) clarifications beyond Rashi's ken. He also deems it crucial to understand that such esoteric rabbinic utterances were never intended as "explanations of

---

70. "Sefer 'Alilot devarim': pereq be-toldot ha-hagut ha-yehudit be-me'ah ha-yud-dalet," Eshel beer-sheva' 2 (1980): 229–64.
71. "Hekhan nithabber sefer 'Alilot devarim," 'Alei sefer 3 (1977): 44–53.
72. Oṣar neḥmad 4 (1854): 181–95. The work's publisher, who also wrote under a pseudonym ("Michael ben Reuven"), detected Aaron Aboulrabi's hand in this remarkable specimen of late medieval Jewish rationalism (178). More remains to be said about its historiographic outlook and theory of divine providence, especially as it appears in the work's closing segment, about which Bonfil and Ta-Shma had little to say. For some of the author's daring ideas in this sphere, see Benzion Netanyahu, The Marranos of Spain from the Late 14th to the Early 16th Century according to Contemporary Hebrew Sources (New York: American Academy for Jewish Research, 1966), 227–37.

the verses." Like pseudo-Rabad and Aaron Aboulrabi, then, 'Alilot devarim's author implies that Rashi cited many a midrash the true purport and profundity of which eluded him. Like pseudo-Rabad, he indicates that Rashi's attempt to explain scripture using rabbinic sayings that had no exegetical intent to begin with traced to Rashi's ignorance of "wisdom," and especially logic. This ignorance, a *pars pro toto* for the falling away from rationality by which Judaism has too long been afflicted, explains many of the corrupt features of Jewish life that the author assails.[73]

Like Aboulrabi and pseudo-Rabad, 'Alilot devarim counterposes Rashi's midrashic approach to the quest for contextual sense. In so doing, he echoes, perhaps wittingly, Ibn Ezra's aforementioned critique of Rashi's failure to achieve his exegetical goal.[74] In our author's version of this argument, though Rashi often averred that "scripture does not depart from its contextual sense" and though he often claimed that his interpretations embodied this plane of meaning, most of his explanations amounted to midrashic homily pure and simple *(raq derush)*.[75]

Now here is the point. Such deficiencies as 'Alilot devarim's author found in Rashi's exegesis might have gone unremarked

---

73. 'Alilot devarim, 182. Palmon's own "conversion" from superstition to rationality has its germ in his growing appreciation of "the wisdom of logic" (ibid., 191). The central role of logic in later medieval Jewish hermeneutics, in Iberia especially, has increasingly come into view. See Daniel Boyarin, *Ha-'iyyun ha-sefardi: le-farshanut ha-talmud le-megoreshei sefarad* (Jerusalem: Ben-Zvi Institute, 1989); Aviram Ravitsky, "Talmudic Methodology and Aristotelian Logic: David ibn Bilia's Commentary on the Thirteenth Hermeneutic Principles," *The Jewish Quarterly Review* 99 (2009): 184–99.

74. Above, n. 12.

75. More remains to be said about criticism of Rashi in the eastern Mediterranean sphere in particular, such as is exemplified by pseudo-Rabad and Aboulrabi, and possibly by the author of 'Alilot devarim, in light of ibn Ezra's unsurpassed esteem as a biblical exegete in this region. Nicholas De Lange observes ("Abraham Ibn Ezra and Byzantium," in *Abraham Ibn Ezra y su Tiempo*, ed. Fernando Díaz Esteban [Madrid: Asociación Española de Orientalistas, 1990], 188) that far more manuscripts of Ibn Ezra's writings have come down from Byzantium than of works of Rashi, David Kimhi, or even Maimonides. Ibn Ezra proved popular among Karaite exegetes of the region as well, some of whom came to regard him as a closet Karaite, Ibn Ezra's trenchant critiques of Karaism notwithstanding (Daniel Frank, "Ibn Ezra and the Karaite Exegetes Aaron Ben Joseph and Aaron Ben Elijah," in *Abraham Ibn Ezra y su Tiempo*, 99–107).

were it not for a new development that he highlights: the spread of Rashi's exegesis far and wide within the Jewish world and it growing authority in large numbers of Jewish communities. When lamenting this trend, the author begins to talk about Rashi's "commentary" in the singular as opposed to his exegesis in general, presumably referring to the increasingly widespread popularity of the *Commentary on the Torah* in particular. "This commentary of his has reached everywhere that his [Rashi's] name is invoked," says the author somewhat mysteriously.[76] The work's self-proclaimed "explicator" (*mefaresh*), who is almost certainly identical with its author, renders the idea only slightly less ambiguous in commenting that the reference is to places where Jews are "accustomed to [studying] his commentary." Here, too, the singular noun ("*she-nohagim perusho*") suggests that the *Commentary on the Torah* in particular is intended.[77]

Of the deleterious impact of the *Commentary*'s growing ubiquity, 'Alilot devarim's author has no doubt. It has left Jews

> denuded of the Torah's and scripture's contextual meanings such that if a person were to cite before them clarifications of one who explained the verses' words according to their contextual meaning, having removed any strangeness (*zarut*),[78] they will deride him and pronounce his words remote from the scripture's contextual sense. This is a cause of blindness and confusion (*bilbbul*) in the quest for spiritual perfection (*shelemut ha-nefashot*).[79]

In sum, designed to "open the eyes of the blind" to the true meaning of the "written Torah," Rashi's midrashic rendering instead impaired Jewish appreciation of its "contextual sense." In

---

76. Ibid., 182.
77. Ibid., 199.
78. In rationalist works this term often signifies "remoteness from rationality." See Isadore Twersky, *Introduction to the Code of Maimonides* (Mishneh Torah) (New Haven: Yale University Press, 1980), 387.
79. 'Alilot devarim, 182.

combination with Rashi's mishandling of esoteric midrashim, this development had much wider implications, deflecting attention from Judaism's highest theological-philosophic insights and thereby diverting Jews from their national-redemptive and individual-soteriological quests.

By stating the effect of Rashi's ever-increasing influence on Torah study in such terms, 'Alilot devarim's author seemingly illumines the issue raised at the outset: why, in close temporal proximity, did writers like pseudo-Rabad and Aaron Aboulrabi invest so much intellectual energy in an effort to discredit Rashi's midrashic interpretations? This effort apparently had much to do with their awareness of the creeping canonization of Rashi's *Commentary* in ever wider segments of the Jewish world to which their rough contemporary, the author of 'Alilot devarim, gives striking testimony.

V

Whether their concerns were methodological, exegetical, or theological or, as was usually the case, some combination of these (whatever the precise interlacings), Rashi's successors had good reason to scrutinize the dominantly midrashic side of his *Commentary on the Torah.* Some who rued the results of such scrutiny were linguistically oriented scholars who found many of Rashi's ungrammatical or philologically fanciful midrashic expositions untenable. Others were savants steeped in Greco-Arabic philosophy who found some of Rashi's midrashic readings bizarre, unscientific, or even morally repellent.[80] For thinkers who viewed segments of the midrashic inheritance as a repository of one or another type of esoteric lore, Rashi's deployment of

---

80. For a case study of the appropriation of a midrashic interpretation of Rashi deemed religiously intolerable and morally repugnant by many later writers, see my "From Sefarad to Ashkenaz" 393–425; "The Reception of Rashi's *Commentary on the Torah* in Spain: The Case of Adam's Mating with the Animals." *Jewish Quarterly Review* 97 (2007): 33–66. For a midrashic interpretation of Rashi that presented philosophical problems, and responses to it, see my "Sins of the Fauna."

midrash could raise additional questions. Did Rashi incorporate esoteric midrashim into his *Commentary*? If so, did he grasp their meaning, despite the seemingly thoroughgoing exoteric character of his exegesis? Were there times when Rashi, wittingly or otherwise, broadcast bits of rabbinic esoteric lore that ought to have remained the preserve of a sophisticated few? As has been seen, pseudo-Rabad and Aaron Aboulrabi could adjudge Rashi's midrashic explanations "unfitly spoken" on all of these scores and more.

In taking issue with Rashi, pseudo-Rabad and Aaron Aboulrabi were hardly innovators; yet their approach to the *Commentary* betokens something new. Unlike other thinkers who expressed dissatisfaction with Rashi's midrashic hermeneutic, like Isaac Abarbanel, these authors centered exegetical activities on *Rashi's Commentary*, targeting its midrashic elements directly and systematically. The reason, it has been urged, is suggested by *'Alilot devarim* as well as, of course, other data emanating from the later Jewish Middle Ages, such as the rise of a vast supercommentarial literature on the *Commentary* (in, of all places, Spain)[81] and the fact that among works churned out by the newly invented Hebrew printing press at the end of the Middle Ages, only the Bible was more oft reproduced than Rashi's *Commentary* during the incunable period (1470–1500).[82] These data fill out the picture sketched by the author of *'Alilot devarim*, who makes clear the very high degree to which the "singing of praises" of Rashi's *Commentary* had gotten louder since Ibn Ezra's day. With Rashi's anthology of rabbinic interpretations fast becoming entrenched as a classic of Jewish literature, some who were disturbed by Rashi's midrashic

---

81. Lawee, "The Reception of Rashi's *Commentary*" (as cited in the previous note).
82. The medium of printing produced, in three short decades, some three thousand printed copies of the *Commentary* where only a few hundred had circulated in manuscript in the four centuries before. See A.K. Offenberg, *A Choice of Corals: Facets of Fifteenth-Century Hebrew Printing* (Nieuwkoop: De Graaf Publishers, 1992), 147. The first eight works ever to roll off a Hebrew press, sometime between 1469–1472 in Rome, included the *Commentary* and the *Commentary* was the first dated Hebrew book ever printed, on 17 February 1475, at the press of Abraham Garton in the southern Italian town of Reggio de Calabria (ibid., 133–37).

readings, like Abarbanel or his Iberian colleagues Isaac Arama or Isaac Caro, chose to dispute or reorient them episodically.[83] Others, however, perceiving that world Jewry were becoming uniquely "accustomed" to Rashi's interpretation of holy writ, complete with its aura of rabbinic authority, invested time and energy in the production of overt, systematic refutations of the *Commentary*. Their efforts remain of considerable interest, even if they did nothing to halt this commentary's march towards its ultimate destination as the closest thing Judaism has ever known to a canonical interpretation of holy writ.

---

83. Lawee, "From Sefarad to Ashkenaz" (n. 22).

Contributors

J. David Bleich, Yeshiva University
Robert Chazan, New York University
Mordechai Cohen, Yeshiva University
Naomi Grunhaus, Yeshiva University
Scott J. Goldberg, Yeshiva University
Moshe Idel, Hebrew University of Jerusalem
Alfred Ivry, New York University
Ephraim Kanarfogel, Yeshiva University
Menachem Kellner, Haifa University
Daniel Lasker, Ben-Gurion University of the Negev
Eric Lawee, York University
Michelle J. Levine, Yeshiva University
Nahum Rakover, Bar-Ilan University
Aviezer Ravitzky, Hebrew University of Jerusalem
Dov Schwartz, Bar-Ilan University
Moshe Sokolow, Yeshiva University